THE ROAD TO XANADU

A STUDY IN THE WAYS OF THE IMAGINATION

BY

JOHN LIVINGSTON LOWES

British Library Cataloguing-in-Publication Data
A catalogue record for this book is available from the
British Library

CONTENTS

John Livingston Lowes

John Livingston Lowes was born on 20th December 1867, at Decatur, Indiana, USA. He was a highly respected scholar and critic of English literature, especially interested in the works of Samuel Taylor Coleridge and Geoffrey Chaucer.

Lowes achieved his first degree from *Washington and Jefferson College* in 1888, before embarking on postgraduate work in Germany, and also at *Harvard University*. He spent his early career teaching mathematics at *Washington and Jefferson College*, until 1891, when he received his M.A. degree. In 1909, Lowes made the considerable jump from mathematics to English literature, and worked as an English professor at *Washington University* in St. Louis, remaining in the post for nine years. He also became the Dean of Arts and Sciences; a position bridging Lowes' considerable knowledge base. From 1918 however, he was appointed as a professor of English at Harvard, where he stayed until 1939. It was here that he wrote *Conventions and Revolt in Poetry* (1919) which included a major critique on free verse (a form of poetry which does not use consistent meter patterns, rhyme, or any other musical pattern, generally following the rhythms of natural speech). Lowes' time at Harvard was the most prolific academically, and he followed up on this publication with an edited edition of the *Poems of Amy Lowell* (1928) and *Of Reading Books – Four Essays* (1929). Perhaps his most famous and well received publication is *The Road to Xanadu: A Study in the Ways of the Imagination* (1927). The book deals with Coleridge's poems *The Ancient Mariner* and *Kubla Kahn*, and Lowes critically analyses Coleridge's spectacularly wide breadth of reading (particularly sixteenth and seventeenth century travel books). Lowes discusses the process by which Coleridge dredges up multitudinous snippets of information to create the nightmare sea voyage of the *Mariner* and the fantastical architecture of *Kubla Kahn.* He managed to recreate the imaginative process so crucial, and so unique to great literature, and for this, has remained an important figure in literary analysis to this day. Lowes died in 1945, in Boston, Massachusetts, aged seventy-seven.

TO

MARY CORNETT LOWES

WHO

LIKE THE WEDDING-GUEST

COULD NOT CHOOSE

BUT HEAR

THE CORPOSANTS

From Erasmus Francisci, *Der Wunder-reiche Ueberzug unserer Nider-Welt*, Nürnberg 1680

Faust. Wohin der Weg?

Mephistopheles. Kein Weg! Ins Unbetretene.

Eight chapters of this book and parts of six other chapters were read in 1926 as lectures on two Foundations—an endowed lectureship in the University College of Wales, and the Norman Wait Harris Foundation in Northwestern University—each of which stipulates the publication of its lectures as a book. The Harris Lectures of 1926 and the corresponding lectures at the University College of Wales consist, accordingly, of Chapters I (*in part*); *II and III; VII and parts of IX, X, and XI; XIII and XIV; XV* (*in part*) *and XVI; XIX* (*in part*), *XX, and XXII. And I wish to acknowledge the generosity of the Trustees of both Foundations in their willingness to accept, as fulfilling their requirement, a book of which the lectures constitute but a part.*

PREFACE

THE story which this book essays to tell was not of the teller's choosing. It simply came, with supreme indifference to other plans, and autocratically demanded right of way. A glittering eye and a skinny hand and a long gray beard could not have done more summary execution, nor, for that matter, could the Wedding-Guest himself (who also had other fish to fry) have been, at the outset, a more reluctant auditor. But the reluctance swiftly passed into absorbing interest, as the meaning of the chance glimpse which did the business was disclosed. For the agency which cast the spell was not, as it happened, a pair of marvellous fairy-tales at all, nor even the provocative and baffling personality of their creator. It was the imaginative energy itself, surprised (as it seemed to me) at work behind these fabrics of its weaving. If I was right, and if I could make clear to others what I thought I saw myself, I had no alternative. That the *aperçu*, such as it was, should come through 'The Ancient Mariner,' when I was intent at the moment upon Chaucer's rich humanity, was, to be sure, more than a little disconcerting. It was so, however, that it chose to come, and Wyrd goeth as she will.

Once started on, however, the story has been written in

its present form (I fear I must confess) quite frankly for the writer's own enjoyment—in part for the sheer pleasure of following into unfamiliar regions an almost untrodden path; not a little for that fearful joy one snatches from the effort to exhibit, with something that approaches clarity, the order which gives meaning to a chaos of details. It would have been easy in comparison to communicate, for the edification of a narrow circle only, a mass of observations to the pages of some learned journal, and let it go at that. But the subject in itself was far too interesting, and the light it seemed to throw upon a wider field far too significant, to warrant any but the broadest treatment I could give it. I am not sure, indeed, that one of the chief services which literary scholarship can render is not precisely the attempt, at least, to make its findings available (and interesting, if that may be) beyond the precincts of its own solemn troops and sweet societies. At all events, that is the adventurous enterprise of this volume. Its facts I think I can safely vouch for. As for the interpretation thereof, that is the core of the book. And nothing which I might say here has not already been said there.

A good deal, perhaps most, of the material of the study is what, in academic circles, we somewhat humorously call 'new.' Since the term may be applied with equal relevance to exhumed treasure redolent of the dust of centuries and to facts still sparkling with their pristine dew, the adjective, to the uninitiated, is apt to be ambiguous. In so far as most of the facts which I have here attempted to interpret have either not been previously observed in this connection, or, if observed, have not been put upon their inferences, the term, in its faintly Pickwickian sense, is not impertinent. But this 'newness' is a quality of little moment, except as it renders possible a fresh synthesis. That I believe it does, and so the use of hitherto unused evidence becomes a factor of some importance in the reckoning.

There are, however, two matters about which I want to be quite clear. In the first place, this is not a study of Coleridge's theory of the imagination. It is an attempt to get at the workings of the faculty itself. Coleridge wrote a great deal about the imagination, and (I am very sure) talked more. And in the course of his wanderings through what he once pleasantly called 'the holy jungle of transcendental metaphysics' he evolved the nebulous theory propounded in the twelfth and thirteenth chapters of the *Biographia Literaria*. With that I have just now nothing to do. It belongs to the history of critical opinion; our interest is in a study of the imaginative processes themselves. And I am deliberately excluding the one in favour of the other. For I cannot but think that Coleridge's most precious contribution to our understanding of the imagination lies, not in his metaphysical lucubrations on it after it was lost, but in the implications of his practice while he yet possessed the power.

In the second place, there are considerations, in themselves of obvious importance, which, with reference to my purpose, are beside the point. How far 'The Rime of the Ancient Mariner,' for example, is 'romantic'; how far it has or has not the Aristotelian σπουδαιότης; where it stands in this or that hierarchy of eternal values—questions such as these are not, for the moment my affair. I am attempting to do this only—to discover how, in two great poems, out of chaos the imagination frames a thing of beauty. The implications of the facts, I believe, have value far beyond that single poem. But I know, too, that the imagination operates in many ways, and before conclusions of universal application can be reached, other studies of other works must check and supplement the results of this.

Even these results have been subject to remorseless limitations. 'I have read almost everything,' said Coleridge, not without warrant, a year before he wrote 'The Ancient Mariner,' and he who sets out to track him through his reading leaves unread at his peril anything readable whatsoever that was extant in Coleridge's day. Nothing short of the *omne scibile* will do. That, in a world of exacting duties, is a bliss to die with, rather than a goal attained. And I am sadly certain that there is much which I have overlooked—a regret which has its compensation in the fact that there is left for others a chance at the joy of the chase which I have had. It is far too much to hope, moreover, that in weighing particulars like the sand for multitude, every appraisal of details has been correct.

There will be without question specific inferences which may challenge doubt or dissent. But making all allowances for tracts still unexplored and human fallibility, the mass of cumulative evidence, I think, is overwhelming, and it is as a whole—a whole of which the parts are mutually corroborative—that I could wish this essay at interpretation to be judged. More than that no mortal can in reason ask.

Since the date on the title-page is 1927, it is proper to state that the substance of the book, though not in its present form, was given as lectures at the Brooklyn Institute of Arts and Sciences in March and April, 1920. And much of it had already found place in courses at Harvard and Radcliffe as early as 1919. A number of chapters as they now stand have since been read at the Universities of California and Texas, in 1922 and 1924. The acknowledgement to the two Foundations which stipulate publication of their lectures has been made elsewhere. But I could not there acknowledge the charming courtesy which, both at Aberystwyth and Evanston, as at Austin and Berkeley, made my term as lecturer delightful.

Welcome confirmation of a few details has come while the book has been in preparation, through independent observations which have at intervals been printed here and there. But all such matters will be found, where they belong, in the notes. Mr. Hugh d'Anson Fausset's *Samuel Taylor Coleridge* was published after this volume was completed and in the printer's hands. I have referred in the notes to two or three of

Mr. Fausset's statements. Beyond these brief references it has been impossible, under the circumstances, to go.

There are those who find the notes in a book more interesting than the text. I often do myself. But for the sake of others otherwise inclined the notes in this book are, for the most part, securely kennelled in the rear. There they will molest no incurious reader who is circumspect enough to let them lie. Their objects, for those who care to turn to them, are two: to make possible the verification of all statements which rest in any way upon authority; and to sketch in, through details which would have violated the unity of an ordered treatment, the complex and often vividly human background of the poems. But the text may be read, by those who will, as if the notes did not exist.

Debts such as mine are pleasant to acknowledge, even though they can never be repaid. Grateful homage first of all is due to the memory of the two great recent editors of Coleridge, James Dykes Campbell and Ernest Hartley Coleridge, whose unwearied investigation of everything which bears upon the text has laid the only foundation on which a study such as this may safely build. And since I have had to make constant use of early editions, my debt to the monumental bibliography of Thomas Wise—whose personal kindness I, with many others, know—is scarcely less. With these three must be named for special thanks Professor Alois Brandl of Berlin. For he it was who printed, just thirty years ago, the manuscript in which lie the clues to much that follows. His edition of the so-called 'Gutch Memorandum Book' is not always accurate (as I shall now and then in these pages find it necessary to point out), and his notes, which are often of the utmost value, leave many important entries unidentified. A new edition is needed, and I hope before too long to publish one—with full knowledge that I too shall leave many riddles still unsolved. But to Professor Brandl belongs the honour of first recognizing the potential value of a priceless document—a recognition, one must add, in which few scholars since have followed him.

To colleagues and students and other friends I owe kindnesses far too many to enumerate. Most of them are, I hope, acknowledged in the notes. A few are too special to pass over here. Professor A. E. Longueil, Dr. George M. Vogt, Professors Stanley P. Chase, Paul F. Kaufman and Harold Golder, Bertram R. Davis, Esq., of Bristol, and Mr. Hale Moore have from time to time looked up for me various matters of detail at the British Museum, the Bristol Library, and elsewhere, and Mr. Kaufman sent me in manuscript, before it was printed, his record of the borrowings of Coleridge and Southey from the Bristol Library. Professor Garland Greever also sent me in manuscript the pages of his book, *A Wiltshire Parson and his Friends*, which deal with his discovery of Coleridge's hitherto unrecognized reviews. Permission to print a letter from Joseph Conrad, which I had hoped to ask of Mr. Conrad himself, has been given me since his death by his literary executor, Mr. Richard Curie, and also by his publisher, Mr. F. N. Doubleday. To Dr. John L. Haney (over and above his bibliography) I am indebted for valuable help in tracing a number of volumes containing Coleridge's annotations; nor may I omit the courtesy of many booksellers in London and New York who have given aid in the same quest. Mr. B. H. Blackwell and Mr. H. S. Rowles of Oxford have been especially kind. Particular acknowledgement is due to the Reverend Gerard H. B. Coleridge, great-grandson of the poet, for permission to print unpublished letters; and to Mrs. Lucy Gillman Watson, granddaughter of Dr. James Gillman, the late Miss Amy Lowell, H. T. Butler, Esq., Dr. James B. Clemens, W. van R. Whitall, Esq., Professor Chauncey Brewster Tinker, J. A. Spoor, Esq., Professor George McLean Harper (former custodian of the collection of the late Mrs. Henry A. St. John), and Professor Phillip Ogden (owner of the collection of the late Miss Frances Bennett) for generous permission to use important and unpublished notes in Coleridge's hand in books which they owned or controlled.

To Norton Perkins, Esq. (and I leave the words as they stood before his death), I owe pleasure as great as the debt which goes with it. For his gift to the Harvard College Library of his collection of Coleridge editions, manuscripts, and marginalia came at a strategic moment in these investigations, and his continued generosity contributed, like the support of a friend, to the later stages of this study, and has particularly enriched the notes. And the additions to the collection made in his memory by Mrs. Norton Perkins and by his classmate, the late C. C. Stillman, Esq., have enhanced my debt.

At the British Museum I owe many courtesies to Mr. J. A. Herbert and the officials of the Manuscript Department. And without the wealth of documents and the large freedom of the Harvard College Library—with which must always be associated the cordial and unstinted cooperation of its officers (very specially Mr. Walter B. Briggs) and its attendants—there could really have been no book at all.

The deepest debt of all, however, must remain, save for the dedication, unexpressed.

J. L. L.

CAMBRIDGE, MASSACHUSETTS
10 *January*, 1927

PREFACE TO REVISED EDITION

THE chief, indeed the sole function of this second Preface is the pleasant one of recording renewed indebtedness. The book grew out of a thousand questions, and in the happiest fashion for its writer it has provoked a response in kind. For from scores of readers has come a stream of suggestions, queries, and corrections, far too numerous for individual acknowledgment, except as that has been already made, or as quite special assistance calls for special note. The sheaf of Addenda and Corrigenda which follows the original Notes is largely made up of such contributions, and others would have been included had the exigencies of space allowed. Save for a few minor corrections, the body of the book remains unchanged.

I owe to Bertram R. Davis, Esq., of Bristol, the solution of the riddle of the (mythical!) 'Erastus Galer's hat'; and it was only through Professor Alice D. Snyder's earlier researches that it became possible at last, with the aid of Edgar H. Wells, Esq., to trace the whereabouts of the long-lost manuscript in Coleridge's hand, which contains, among other things, 'that drama in which Got-fader performs.' And my particular thanks are due to Dr. Max Farrand, Director of Research of the Henry E. Huntington Library, and to Captain R. B. Haselden, Curator of Manuscripts, for permission to use the document, and for invaluable information about it. Commander (Retired) I. V. Gillis, U.S.N., of Peking, has put me again and again in his debt, through the light which his knowledge of the Orient has thrown on this and that detail. Owen D. Young, Esq., and Frank Brewer Bemis, Esq., have generously allowed me the use of letters and marginalia in their collections. Still other obligations, incurred with no less gratitude, are recorded in the Addenda. And my Research Assistant, Miss Keith Glenn, has rendered invaluable aid.

J. L. L.

19 *March*, 1930

THE ROAD TO XANADU

THE ROAD TO XANADU

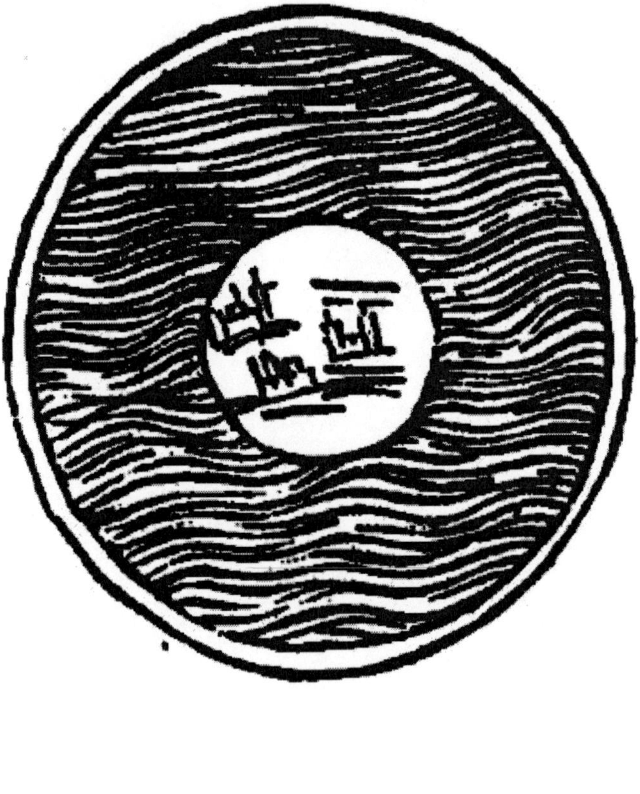

BOOK I

The deep well knows it certainly.
HUGO VON HOFFMANSTHAL

CHAPTER I

CHAOS

THE title of this volume is less cryptic than it seems. I propose to tell the story, so far as I have charted its course, of the genesis of two of the most remarkable poems in English, 'The Rime of the Ancient Mariner,' and 'Kubla Khan.' If that should appear a meagre theme on which to lavish all these pages, I can only crave of the judicial reader a suspended sentence. For a quest which began with a strange footprint caught sight of accidentally just off the beaten track became in the end an absorbing adventure along the ways which the imagination follows in dealing with its multifarious materials—an adventure like a passage through the mazes of a labyrinth, to come out at last upon a wide and open sky. Those ways are the theme of the book. 'The Road to Xanadu' is but a symbol of something which, when all is said, remains intangible.

But the road, as we shall actually travel it, leads through half the lands and all the seven seas of the globe. For we shall meet on the way with as strange a concourse as ever haunted the slopes of Parnassus—with alligators and albatrosses and auroras and Antichthones; with biscuit-worms, bubbles of ice, bassoons, and breezes; with candles, and Cain, and the Corpo Santo; Dioclesian, king of Syria, and the dæmons of the elements; earthquakes, and the Euphrates; frost-needles, and fog-smoke, and phosphorescent light; gooseberries, and the Gordonia lasianthus; haloes and hurricanes; lightnings and Laplanders; meteors, and the Old Man of the Mountain, and stars behind the moon; nightmares, and the sources of the Nile; footless birds of Paradise, and the observatory at Pekin; swoons, and spectres, and slimy seas; wefts, and water-snakes, and the Wandering Jew. Beside that compendious cross-section of chaos, nightmares are methodical. Yet of such is the kingdom of poetry. And in that paradox lies the warrant of our pilgrimage.

For out of the heart of the chaos sprang the poems. And our attempt to grasp the implications of that fact will bring us ultimately to the workings of the imaginative energy itself. No such outcome was foreseen or even suspected when, for the zest of the game, this tracking of a poet through heaven and earth was begun. It was only when facts pursued farther kept ramifying into other facts, and unforeseen links between them began by degrees to disclose themselves, that certain inferences became (as it seemed) inevitable, and certain tentative conclusions assumed gradually clearer form. Those conclusions are offered with reasonable confidence in their broad validity. But in any case this at least is true: they rest, every one of them, not upon preconceived notions, but on concrete facts. If the conclusions are faulty, the facts are there by which they may be tested, and (at need) amended. And therein lies, I think, such value as this study may possess.

Our first business, then, will be with the incongruous, chaotic, and variegated jumble out of which emerged the two unique poems which I have named.* The goal of our passage through chaos, however, lies, not in the phantasmagoria itself, but in the operations of that shaping spirit of imagination which, likewise moving through the welter, fashions its elements into lucid and ordered unity. That the moulding imagination in this instance happens to be Coleridge's and not another's, is the accident of a chance page of Purchas, which one day flew a signal and beckoned down a trail which turned out to lead through the uncharted regions tributary to 'The Ancient Mariner' and 'Kubla Khan.' Coleridge as Coleridge, be it said at once, is of secondary moment to our purpose; it is the significant process, not the man, which constitutes our theme. But the amazing *modus operandi* of his genius, in the fresh light which I hope I have to offer, becomes the very abstract and brief chronicle of the procedure of the creative faculty itself. I am not so rash, I trust, as to essay to pluck out the heart of the mystery. But the game of coming to close quarters with the riddle is more than worth the candle.

We shall be occupied first, accordingly, with the raw stuff of poetry. The finished product will concern us later. With that positive assurance to support us, we may strike at once into the thick of a farrago which will triumphantly justify, I think, the title of this chapter.

I

In the British Museum is a small manuscript volume of ninety leaves, which is, in my judgment, one of the most illuminating human documents even in that vast treasure-house.[1] It is a note book kept by Samuel Taylor Coleridge, partly in pencil, partly in ink, and always with most admired disorder. There are just two dates from cover to cover, but internal evidence makes clear that it embraces a period of about three years, from the spring of 1795 to the spring or summer of 1798,[2] the years which lead up to and include the magnificent flowering of Coleridge's genius on which his renown as a poet rests. It was printed thirty years ago by Professor Brandl of Berlin,[3] but it lies so effectively buried in a German philological periodical that the latest English edition of Coleridge refers to it as vaguely as if it had been published in the moon.[4] Yet its value is incalculable, not only for the understanding of Coleridge, but also as a document in the psychology of genius, and as a key to the secrets of art in the making. And its service is inestimable to our present enterprise.

It is, on the whole, the strangest medley that I know. Milton's Commonplace Book is a severely ordered collectanea of extracts culled from his reading, docketed alphabetically, and methodical as a ledger.[5] Shelley's note books, written upside down, sidewise, and even right side up, with their scribbled marginal sketches of boats and trees and human faces—these battered and stained and happy-go-lucky little volumes are a priceless record of the birth-throes of poetry.[6] But it is chiefly poetry, beating its wings against the bars of words, which they contain. There are few notes of Shelley's reading. The Coleridge Note Book* is like neither. It is a catch-all for suggestions jotted down chaotically from Coleridge's absorbing adventures among books. It is a repository of waifs and strays of verse, some destined to find a lodgement later in the poems, others yet lying abandoned where they fell, like drifted leaves. It is a mirror of the fitful and kaleidoscopic moods and a record of the germinal ideas of one of the most supremely gifted and utterly incalculable spirits ever let loose upon the planet. And it is like nothing else in the world so much as a jungle, illuminated eerily with patches of phosphorescent light, and peopled with uncanny life and strange exotic flowers. But it is teeming and fecund soil, and out of it later rose, like exhalations, gleaming and aerial shapes.

How those shining shapes arose from chaos it will be our ultimate task to see. But our way at the moment lies through a veritable tohu-bohu, which is 'neither Sea, nor Shore, nor Air, nor Fire, But all these in their pregnant causes mix'd Confusedly.' And as expositor and guide I am at once confronted by the horns of a dilemma. On the one hand is a natural leaning toward all achievable lucidity of outline and arrangement. The document, on the other hand, of which above all things I wish to give a true impression, is almost everything else under Heaven, but lucid it emphatically is not. It is singularly like a collection of the flashing, fleeting, random, and disjointed thoughts and fancies which dart, with the happy inconsequence of aquatic insects, across the surface of the stream of consciousness—all jotted down impartially by an interested, and sometimes amazed, Recording Angel. A shower of meteors is not more erratic, and you cannot impose upon a shower of meteors the luminous sequence of the wheeling constellations without its forthwith ceasing to be the thing it is. And it is precisely the incredible *olla-podrida* as it is which I am anxious, before going farther, to set forth: confusion at its worst confounded, as the elemental stuff of poetry—its '*materies . . . et corpora prima*'—waiting only for the informing spirit which broods over chaos to draw it (in Milton's rendering of the magnificent Lucretian phrase) into 'the precincts of light.' In order, then, to exhibit at the outset the formlessness out of which eventually form was wrought, I must forego for the moment the aid of orderly arrangement, and can only ask those readers who may quite intelligibly object to being hurled unceasingly from alligators to maniacs and from birds of Paradise to rainbows in the spray to believe that the disorder of this opening chapter is itself an essential factor in an ordered plan.

Without more ado, then, let us plunge into the wilderness which the strange document before us exhibits. And I shall first excerpt a dozen consecutive pages,[8] and shall then, without regard to sequence, pick from the remainder such characteristic jottings as may serve our later ends.

Let us begin with the most dramatic moment in the Note Book. Coleridge has been tinkering at some pretty verses, touched here and there with his own elfin magic, about 'Moths in the Moonlight.'[9] Then, without break, he has set down, as if oblivious of the implications of the contrast, one of the most profound and haunting phrases ever penned—

the prophetic soul
Of the wide world dreaming on things to come—

and has followed it with a second excerpt from the Sonnets, more poignantly personal than the first:

Most true it is, that I have look'd on truth
Askance and strangely.[10]

Next on the page appears a jotting later to find its way, transformed, into the magical opening of 'Christabel':

Behind the thin
Grey cloud that cover'd but not hid the sky
The round full moon look'd small.—[11]

And then, on the heels of a bit of poetized observation of snow curling in the breeze,[12] comes without warning 'the alligators' terrible roar,' and the captivating entry thus proceeds:[13]

> The alligators' terrible roar, like heavy distant thunder, not only shaking the air and waters, but causing the earth to tremble—and when hundreds and thousands are roaring at the same time, you can scarcely be persuaded but that the whole globe is dangerously agitated—[14]
>
> The eggs are layed in layers between a compost of ~~earth~~, mud, grass, and herbage.—The female watches them—when born, she leads them about the shores, as a hen her chickens[15]—and when she is basking on the warm banks, with her brood around, you may hear the young ones whining and barking, like young Puppies.[16]
>
> 20 feet long—lizard-shaped, plated—head vulnerable—tusked—eyes small and sunk—[17]
>
> —Hartley fell down and hurt himself—I caught him up crying and screaming—and ran out of doors with him.—The Moon caught his eye—he ceased crying immediately—and his eyes and the tears in them, how they glittered in the Moonlight![18]
>
> —Some wilderness-plot, green and fountainous and unviolated by Man.[19]
>
> An old Champion who is perhaps absolute sovereign of

a little Lake or Lagoon (when 50 less than himself are obliged to content themselves with roaring and swelling in little coves round about) darts forth from the reedy coverts all at once on the surface of the water, in a right line; at first, seemingly as rapid as lightning, but gradually more slowly until he arrives at the center of the lake, when he stops; he now swells himself by drawing in wind and water thro' his mouth, which causes a loud sonorous rattling in the throat for near a minute; but it is immediately forced out again thro' his mouth and nostrils with a loud noise, brandishing his tail in the air, and the vapor ascending from his nostrils like smoke. At other times when swollen to an extent ready to burst, his head and tail lifted up, he twirls round on the surface of the water. He retires—and others, who dare, continue the exhibition—all to gain the attention of the favorite Female—[20]

The distant thunder sounds heavily—the crocodiles answer it like an echo—[21]

Now Coleridge got his alligators from one of the most delightful books which he or anybody ever read, William Bartram's *Travels through North and South Carolina, Georgia, East and West Florida* (the amplitude of the title is prophetic of the book's own leisured pace), *the Cherokee Country, the Extensive Territories of the Muscogulges, or Creek Confederacy, and the Country of the Chactaws*. There is more of the title,[22] but just now the crocodiles and not Bartram hold the stage. Coleridge wanted his alligators badly, but even his genius found them a trifle intractable as boon companions for moths in the moonlight, and in the strange and demon-haunted setting to which he finally transferred them they stubbornly declined to stay.[23] Poor little hapless Hartley, sandwiched weeping between their layered egg-heaps and their thunder-echoing roars, he extricated later in the closing lines of 'The Nightingale.'[24] And the green and fountainous wilderness-plot belongs in the complicated history of 'Kubla Khan.'[25]

From the exciting domestic life of alligators Coleridge now passes to exotic plants:

> Describe—
>
> —the never-bloomless Furze—
>
> and then transi to the Gordonia Lasianthus. Its thick foliage of a dark green colour is flowered over with large milkwhite fragrant blossoms on long slender elastic peduncles at the extremities of the numerous branches—from the bosom of the leaves, and renewed every morning—and that in such incredible profusion that the Tree appears silvered over with them and the ground beneath covered with the fallen flowers. It at the same time continually pushes forth new twigs, with young buds on them; and in the winter and spring the

> third year's leaves, now partly concealed by the new and perfect ones, are gradually changing colour from green to a golden yellow, from that to a scarlet; from scarlet to crimson; and lastly to a brownish purple, and then fall to the ground. So that the Gordonia Lasianthus may be said to change and renew its garments every morning thro'out the year. And moreover after the general flowering is past, there is a thin succession of scattering blossoms to be seen, on some parts of the tree, almost every day thro'out the remaining months until the floral season returns again.—It grows by ponds and the edges of rivers – – –[26]

The never-bloomless furze later found a modest place in 'a green and silent spot, amid the hills' where 'Fears in Solitude' was written.[27] The Gordonia lasianthus wasted its sweetness on the desert air, so far as Coleridge is concerned, for he never used it—though Wordsworth, in a poem fairly steeped in Bartram, did.[28] That, however, is another story, and sticking to Coleridge we pass, still under Bartram's conduct, from alligators and never-fading trees to birds:[29]

> Perhaps—the Snake bird with slender longest neck, long, strait and slender bill, glossy black, like fish-scales except on the breast which is cream-coloured—the tail is very long of a deep black *tipped** with a silvery white; and when spread, represent an unfurled fan. They delight to

> sit in little peaceable communities on the dry limbs of trees, hanging over the still waters, with their wings and tails expanded—I suppose to cool themselves, when at the same time they behold their images below—when approached, they drop off as if dead—invisible for a minute or two—then at a vast distance their long slender head and neck only appear, much like a snake—no other part to be seen except sometimes the silvery tip of their Tail.

Bartram hazards the guess that 'if this bird had been an inhabitant of the Tiber in Ovid's days, it would have furnished him with a subject, for some beautiful and entertaining metamorphoses.'[30] And with a dubious 'perhaps,' which is, I think, unique in the annals of his projects, Coleridge files the old traveller's hint away for future reference.

The next entry is somewhat startling, even for the Note Book:[31]

> A dunghill at a distance sometimes smells like musk, and a dead dog like elder-flowers.—

Whether that amazing dictum is to be regarded merely as a symptom of olfactory perversion, or as a truth hitherto hidden from the wise and prudent, I can only guess. All I know is that one half of the apothegm turns up again in *Omniana*, where the musk of the dunghill has played puss-in-the-corner with the dead dog's elder flowers: 'We here in England received a very high character of Lord———during his stay abroad. "Not unlikely, sir," replied the traveller; "a dead dog at a distance is said to smell like musk." '[32] Brandl, in his edition of the Note Book, still further enriches the potpourri by misreading 'musk' as 'mush.'[33] The theme is tempting, but we may not linger.† And so, passing over four brief memoranda on plagiarists, abrupt beginnings, an infant playing with its mother's shadow, and a flat pink-coloured stone adorned with lichens,[35] we return to the green savannahs of Florida:[36]

> The Life of the Siminole playful from infancy to Death compared to the Snow, which in a calm day falling scarce seems to fall and plays and dances in and out, to the very moment that it reaches the ground—

The 'Siminole' (misread by Brandl as 'Simioli,' a vocable which calls up distracting images of little apes), together with the wilderness-plot, the Gordonia lasianthus, and the snake-birds were all, like the alligators, drawn from Bartram. And I shall only add that in *Omniana* this last entry, slightly changed, has shifted its application from the Seminoles to Sophocles![37] The next four entries will round out the dozen pages I have chosen.

> The Sun-shine lies on the cottage-wall
> Ashining thro' the snow—[38]

A maniac in the woods—
She *crosses* (heedlessly) the *woodman's* path—
Scourg'd by rebunding [*sic*] boughs—/[39]

—The merry nightingale
That crowds and hurries and precipitates
With fast thick warble his delicious notes;
As he were fearful, that an April night
Would be too short for him to utter forth
His love-chant, and disburthen his full soul
Of all its music!—[40]

That last is a fragment of the poem which was the destined setting for Hartley's tranquillizing visit to the glimpses of the moon. 'Written in April, 1798,' says the title as it stood in the *Lyrical Ballads;* and the reading of Bartram's fascinating pages, interrupted only long enough to pick up Hartley, belongs, it is clear, to those same vernal hours. But for the moment alligators and Indians and maniacs in the woods have passed away, and it is the exceeding loveliness of spring in Somerset—the spring which this year had come slowly up that way—seen and poignantly felt on moonlit walks with Dorothy and William Wordsworth, which now filled Coleridge's mlind. 'A rainy morning—very pleasant in the evening,' wrote Dorothy in her *Journal* on May sixth. 'Met Coleridge as we were walking out. Went with him to Stowey; heard the nightingale; saw a glow-worm.'[41] There is record in the *Journal* of similar evening strolls in April too, and in nothing that Coleridge ever wrote is the comradeship between the 'three persons, one soul' so interpenetrated with the beauty in the midst of which they lived as in the poem which grew from the hurried scrawl about Hartley's tumble and the magic of the moon, and from the rapturous lines which I have just quoted from the Note Book. And then Coleridge's wayward fancy veered sharply back to an alien world:

> A country fellow in a village Inn, winter night—tells a long story—all attentive etc. except one fellow who is toying with the Maid—/ The Countryman introduces some circumstance absolutely incompatible with a prior one—/The *Amoroso* detects it/—/etc.—The philosophy of this.—Yes! I do'nt tell it for a true story—you would not have found it out if you had [not been?] smooring with *Mall*—[42]

And since 'smoor' is good Somerset dialect,[43] it is a safe guess that the quaint psychological problem which Coleridge propounded for Heaven knows what excogitation later, had its birth in some alehouse tale, native, like the nightingale, to the environs of that 'dear gutter of Stowey' which he once so feelingly apostrophized.

The next two pages of the book are blank.

II

Chaos precedes cosmos, and it is into chaos without form and void that we have plunged. But a spirit was moving upon the face of the waters. Latent in that circumscribed tract of the bewildering gallimaufry which we have just traversed lay germs that were to come to their development, by devious ways, in 'Christabel,' 'The Wanderings of Cain,' 'The Nightingale,' 'Kubla Khan,' 'Lewti,' 'Fears in Solitude,' 'Love,' Wordsworth's 'Ruth,' and indirectly in 'The Rime of the Ancient Mariner.'

I am not sure, indeed, that the greatest value of the Note Book does not lie in this: that it gives us some inkling of the vast, diffused, and amorphous nebula out of which, like asteroids, the poems leaped. It makes possible, in other words, at least a divination of that thronging and shadowy mid-region of consciousness which is the womb of the creative energy. For it is the total content of a poet's mind, which never gets itself completely expressed, and never can, that suffuses and colours everything which flashes or struggles into utterance. Every expression of an artist is merely a focal point of the surging chaos of the unexpressed. And it is that surging and potent chaos which a document like the Note Book re-creates.

III

It is worth while, then, to penetrate the jungle a little farther. This time, however, we shall turn the pages of the Note Book rapidly, and cull here and there. And in order to preserve unimpaired the distinctive flavour of the document itself, I shall, so far as possible, refrain from comment. But complete abstention, in the face of some of the entries, is a virtue too high for human frailty to attain to.

The first seven memoranda in the list are also the first seven in the manuscript.[44] And the mocking spirit which presides over the fall of the cards in the Note Book is from the outset dealing true to form. For the dance of the Epicurean atoms is no more capricious than the piquant juxtapositions of these seven notes.

The Vernal Hours.
Leg. Thomson

Moon at present uninhabited owing to it's little or no atmosphere but may in Time—An atheistic Romance might be formed—a Theistic one too.—Mem!—

I mix in life and labor to seem free,
With common persons pleas'd and common things—
While every Thought and action tends to thee
And every impulse from thy Influence springs,[45]

Sometimes to a gibbet, sometimes to a Throne—always to Hell.

The flames of two Candles joined give a much stronger light than both of them separate—evid. by a person holding the two Candles near his Face, first separate, and then joined in one.

Picture of Hymen—

The lowest part of the flame [of a] Candle is always blue—w[hen] the flame is sufficiently el[ongated] so as to be just ready to [smoke] the Tip is always red.—*

Little Daisy—very late Spring. March—Quid si vivat?—Do all things in Faith. Never pluck a flower again!—Mem.—[46]

And so, with the queerest jumble ever conceived—a fleeting hint of spring, freakish fantasy run wild, tender sentiment, sardonic humour, keen observations of ocular phenomena, and pious resolve—a record begins which seldom belies the manifest tokens of its opening. We are by no means done with some of these seven notes; but their purpose for the moment is fulfilled.†

*

Jonas—a monodrama—
Vide Hunter's Anatomy of a Whale—[47]

That speaks for itself, but its implications are too exquisite to let pass without a word. For Coleridge cannily proposed to make sure of the structural equipment of the whale before committing himself to a dramatization of Jonah's great adventure. And his reference is to a ponderous Memoir of seventy-five pages in the *Philosophical Transactions of the Royal Society*.[48] The monodrama ('I detest monodramas,' he wrote Southey in 1794)[49] got no farther than its title.

*

Upas Tree—a poem—or article.
Mem.[50]

A Ruffian flesh'd in murthers[51]

Dioclesian King of Syria
fifty Daughters in a ship unmann'd
same as Danaides—land in England—commit‡
with Devils.[52]

It is a little disconcerting to identify behind this none too edifying memorandum the grave features of John Milton, but there is no mistaking them. Milton, however, like Spenser, washes his hands of the unseemly gossip of the chroniclers. 'But too absurd and too unconscionably gross,' he writes severely in the *History of Britain*, 'is that fond invention that wafted hither the fifty daughters of a strange Dioclesian king of Syria . . . turned out to sea *in a ship unmanned*'—and so on through the rest of the episode, Danaus, devils, and all.[53] Whether or not Coleridge saw in the uncanny legend fit stuff for his loom I do not know; but the fact remains that this belated echo of a notorious antediluvian scandal was apparently the only thing which he jotted down from his reading of the *History*. The antechamber of consciousness was rapidly being peopled with strange shapes.

Protoplast—[54]

*

Wandering Jew, a romance

A Robber concealed over a room and hearing the noise of Mirth and dancing—his Reflections/—

Strait Waistcoat Madhouse etc.—a stratagem—[55]

The key to this sinister seeming project is happily extant, with little doubt, in a *chef d'œuvre* of undergraduate humour, preserved, through an act of prescient piety, in the University Library at Cambridge. The record of the diverting episode, which takes us back to Coleridge's college days, will be found in the Notes.[56]

*

Light cargoes waft of modulated Sound
From viewless Hybla brought, when Melodies
Like Birds of Paradise on wings, that aye
Disport in wild variety of hues
Murmur around the honey-dropping flowers.[57]

*

Clock
My ~~guts~~ here (patting his guts) chime twelve—

TheSisterofHaroun—belovedbytheCaliph—Giafar
Her verses to Giafar—Giafar's answer—good subjects.[58]

The memories which rose to the surface in this entry had lain deep. Three times Coleridge's vivid recollection of the spell worked upon his early childhood by the *Arabian Nights' Entertainments* found words—that 'anxious and fearful eagerness' ('a strange mixture of obscure dread and intense desire,' he calls it again), 'with which I used to watch the window in which the books lay, and whenever the sun lay upon them, I would seize it, carry it by the wall, and bask and read.' And with the 'one volume of these tales' he read, in the Vicarage at Ottery St. Mary, other 'romances, and relations of giants and magicians and genii'—'Tom Hickathrift,' and 'Jack the Giant-Killer,' and *Belisarius*, and *Robinson Crusoe*, and *The Seven Champions of Christendom*, and that now long forgotten tale of a mysterious island, *The Hermit* of Philip Quarll.[59] 'My whole being was,' he wrote of his boyhood again, 'with eyes closed to every object of present sense, to crumple myself up in a sunny corner, and read, read, read.'[60] And the passionate intensity with which the boy read books remained a characteristic of the man, and is the key to much that lies before us.

The next entry but one, however, brings us to a later love:

*

Burnet's theoria telluris translated into Blank Verse, the original at the bottom of the page.[61]

The prose of Burnet's 'grand Miltonic romance,' which Pepys once lent to Evelyn to reread,[62] and which Coleridge himself names in the same breath with Plato,[63] appears again, still challenging to versification, a little later in the Note Book:

Burnet/de montibus in English Blank Verse.[64]

No one who knows Burnet's blending of imaginative splendours with a daringly impossible cosmogony (and the *Telluris Theoria Sacra* is well worth knowing) will wonder that Coleridge was stirred. Even Lucretius might have been, I think, could Burnet's grandiose cosmic drama have reached him beyond the *flammantia mœnia mundi*. But Coleridge's reach had a trick of exceeding his grasp, and his visions of the *Theoria Sacra* in epic verse smack, I fear, of those vanished pipe-dreams which in the early 'nineties glorified the 'Salutation and Cat.' We are by no means done, however, with *The Sacred Theory*. Its 'Tartarean fury and turbulence' (as Coleridge once put it)[65] will cross our path again.

*

> Dumb Waiter—Bed—Little Tommy—Cerberus—and D[u]pp[e]—[66]

This cryptic utterance, beside which the abracadabra is lucid as waters stilled at even, awaits its Œdipus. I think I know what 'Cerberus' stands for, and for whom 'Little Tommy.' The mysterious final word, which ends exasperatingly in a curlicue instead of in a letter, may be 'Duppe,' or 'Dappe,' or 'Dupper,' or 'Dapper,' but scarcely (as, scenting a bit of West Indian folk-lore, I once hopefully surmised) 'Duppies.' A 'dumb Waiter' then was a portable affair with revolving shelves, and might readily be associated with a bed.[67] I strongly suspect that the entry stands in close relation to a letter of November, 1796, written under the influence of 'twenty-five drops of laudanum every five hours,'[68] and one is at liberty under the circumstances to choose between a Freudian complex and a mute, inglorious 'Kubla Khan.'

*

By an accurate computation 90 millions of Mites' Eggs make one Pigeon's Egg!—Encyclo—[69]

*

And the two mighty Bears walk round and round the Pole—in spite of Mr. Gunston—Watts.[70]

The point (for it has one) of this once tantalizing entry has been lost in the printed text through Brandl's misreading of the last three words as 'Mr. Grinston-Watt'—'wohl ein unbedeutender Mensch aus Coleridge's Bekanntschaft.' There never was a Mr. Grinston-Watt. But what, one still inquires (the name once rightly read), had Mr. *Gunston* done—or tried to do—to stay the two Bears in their march? The answer is as simple as it is beguilingly complete. Thomas Gunston was a friend of Isaac Watts, and Isaac Watts had written a long Funeral Poem upon his death. And in it occurs this somewhat magniloquent assertion of an incontrovertible fact:

Yet nature's wheels will on without control,
The sun will rise, and tuneful spheres will roll,
And the two nightly bears walk round and watch the pole.[71]

Coleridge's sense of humour had been tickled by the implications of the passage, and incidentally we gain another glimpse into his reading at this period.

*

an horrible phiz that would castrate a cantharadized Satyr—[72]

*

Some hundred years ago, when the Devil was a little boy and my grandmother had teeth in her head—[73]

as difficult

as to separate two dew-drops blended together on a bosom of a new-blown Rose.[74]

A belly of most majestic periphery![75]

her eyes sparkled, as if they had been cut out of a diamond quarry in some Golconda of Faery land—and cast such meaning glances, as would have vitrified the Flint in a Murderer's blunderbuss—[76]

*

Describe a Tartarean Forest all of Upas Trees—[77]

The Recording Angel would have smiled a little disdainfully at that, celestially aware, as Coleridge was not, that the tale of the Upas Tree of Java was a howling myth. It had turned up in England ten or a dozen years before this entry, for the hoax had found a place in the *London Magazine* as early as 1783.* Coleridge, however, owed his acquaintance with the yarn to irreproachable scientific authority, for he undoubtedly got it from Erasmus Darwin, who, in 'The Loves of the Plants,' not only expatiates with gusto on the subject in his text and notes, but also clinches the matter by solemnly including among his Additional Notes two highly circumstantial accounts—one Dutch, one Swedish—of the 'Hydra-Tree of death.'[78] Now it so happens that Coleridge quotes verbatim, in a curious and hitherto unidentified note of his own on 'Light from Plants, practically the whole of Darwin's long Additional Note which immediately precedes the sensational tidings of the tree.[80] And Coleridge was certainly not the man to skip that toothsome morsel when the gods and Dr. Darwin threw it in his way. A single paragraph from Darwin is enough to give an inkling of what was stirring in his brain behind the entry in the Note Book:

> This, however, is certain, though it may appear incredible, that from fifteen to eighteen miles round this tree, not only no human creature can exist, but that, in that space of ground, no living animal of any kind has ever been discovered. I have also been assured by several persons of veracity, that there are no fish in the waters, nor has any rat, mouse, or any other vermin, been seen there; and when any birds fly so near this tree that the effluvia reaches them, they fall a sacrifice to the effects of the poison.[81]

For what Gothic tale of terror Coleridge's baleful setting

was designed it is, alas! impossible to say. But of one ironical pleasure we are not deprived. For the sinister conception of 'A Tartarean Forest all of Upas Trees' (which Poe, had he known it, might have envied) was born of a perusal of that amiable and innocuous performance 'The Loves of the Plants'! The four things too wonderful for Agur the son of Jakeh should be supplemented by a fifth: the way of a genius with a book. As for the Upas trees, they were no fleeting impression only. For earlier in the Note Book, in the harmonious context of 'A Ruffian fleshed in murthers,' and the monstrous legend of Dioclesian's fifty daughters, stands, as we have seen, this memorandum: 'Upas Tree—a poem—or article. Mem.'[82]

*

Mars rising over a gibbet—

Two Lover's [*sic*] privileged by a faery to know each other's Lives and Health in Absence by olfaction of[83]

What object it was, the odour of which was to play the courier between the lovers, we shall probably never know. For in the place where the revealing word should be is a row of faint loops and spirals, as if Coleridge's hand had been idly moving while he cudgelled his brain for an object to fit his fantastic theme.[84] The one thing of importance which the entry does disclose is another nook of the bizarre and visionary regions through which his mind was roving.

The next nine pages of the Note Book are packed with matter of uncommon interest. The first of them is headed

My Works[85]

Here they are:[86]

Imitations of the Modern Latin Poets with an Essay Biog. and Crit. on the Rest. of Lit.—2 Vol. Octavo.

Answer to the System of Nature–

~~1 Vol~~. Oct.

The Origin of Evil, an Epic Poem.

Essay on Bowles

Strictures on Godwin, Paley etc. etc.—

Pantisocracy, or a practical Essay on the abolition of Indiv[id]ual Property.

Carthon an Opera

Poems.

Edition of Collins and Gray with a preliminary Dissertation

A Liturgy	On the different Sects of Religion and Infidelity—philosophical analyisis [*sic*] of their Effects on mind and manners—.
A Tragedy	

What (it is worth while to ask) became of these portentous plans? The 'Imitations' lived for a year or so in that vast limbo of unrealized dreams which was Coleridge's brain. They were in his mind even before the discharge of the quondam Silas Tomkyn Comberbacke from the dragoons, when, with only one shirt to his back that was not 'worn to rags,' and 'so sick at stomach that it is with difficulty I can write,' he asked his brother George to buy back for him the books he meant to translate, but which he had, unfortunately, been obliged to sell.[87] That was in March, 1794, and in June of the same year the 'intended translation' was advertised in the *Cambridge Intelligencer*.[88] The following October, torn between his love for Mary Evans and his pledge to Sarah Fricker, and between his growing doubts of pantisocracy and his loyalty to his associates, he writes Southey in a long and distracted letter: 'When a man is unhappy he writes damned bad poetry, I find.

My Imitations too depress my spirits—the task is arduous, and grows upon me. Instead of two octavo volumes, to do all I hoped to do two quartos would hardly be sufficient.'[89] In December he proposes to 'accept of the reporter's place to the "Telegraph," live upon a guinea a week . . . finishing in the same time my "Imitations." '[90] The next October, four days after his marriage, the 'Imitations,' still unfinished, already divided his thoughts with Sara: 'In the course of half a year I mean to return to Cambridge . . . and taking lodgings there for myself and wife, finish my great work of "Imitations," in two volumes. My former works may, I hope, prove somewhat of genius and of erudition. This will be better; it will show great industry and manly consistency.'[91] One is in a strait betwixt tears such as angels shed, and inextinguishable laughter. The painful truth is that 'there is a good deal of *omne meus oculus*' (as Coleridge once elegantly phrased the proverbial 'All my eye and Betty Martin')[92] in this high asseveration of the last quality on earth which he possessed. For the only list of Coleridge's works in which the *magnum opus* will be found is that on the manuscript page before us.

As for the Epic on the Origin of Evil: 'I have a dim recollection,' wrote Lamb to Coleridge in February, 1797, 'that, when in town, you were talking of the Origin of Evil as a most prolific subject for a long poem. Why not adopt it, Coleridge? there would be room for imagination.'[93] But the Epic, like the 'Imitations,' never saw the light.

The Opera faintly glimmers through a letter too. Ten days after the queasily written note about buying back the books he needed for the 'Imitations,' Coleridge blithely wrote his brother George again: 'Clagget has set four songs of mine most divinely, for two violins and a pianoforte. . . . He wishes me to write a serious opera. . . . It is to be a joint work. I think of it.'[94] The Opera lived long enough to reach the Note Book, and then vanished into oblivion with the rest.

What of 'Pantisocracy'? 'In the book of pantisocracy,' writes Coleridge in October, 1794, 'I hope to have comprised all that is good in Godwin.'[95] The book of pantisocracy, then, as Coleridge saw it, was written. In a later letter, however, that same autumn, he again writes Southey: 'But must our system be thus necessarily imperfect? I ask the question that I may know whether or not I should write the Book of Pantisocracy.'[96] The book of pantisocracy, accordingly, was *not* yet written. But to Coleridge the thing thought was always as the thing which is; and that eager and vivid realization of thoughts as things, which incorrigibly kept seeing in ambitious projects accomplished actualities, gave to its world of dreams, *when that became the theme of poetry*, the clear and palpable verity of the world of corporeal fact. The quality of mind which dictated the proud caption '*My* Works' for a list of unwritten octavos was but the obverse of the very quality which, given its true direction, created 'The Rime of the Ancient Mariner,' and 'Christabel,' and 'Kubla Khan.'*

The rest of 'My Works' need not detain us. 'You spawn plans like a herring,' Southey wrote Coleridge in 1802.[97] The only phantom in the galaxy, besides the Poems, which materialized was 'A Tragedy.'

And now, as if Coleridge, like the Psalmist, were weary of exercising himself in things too high for him, the next entry comes down from the clouds with a leap:[98]

> Six Gallons of Water—
> Twelve
> ~~Eighteen~~ pounds of Sugar.
> Half a pound of Ginger
> Eighteen Lemons

> Ginger to be sliced—Lemons to be peeled—The Sugar and Water to be boiled together, and the Scum—viz—the Monarchica[l] part must go to Pot—and out of the Pot—*Then* put in the Ginger with the Peels of the Lemons, and let the whole be boiled together gently for half an hour—When cold, put in the Lemon juice strained etc—then let the Sum total be put in the Barrel with three Spoonfuls of Yeast—let it work three Days (Sundays excepted—) and then put in a Gallon of Barrel [*sic*]—Close up the Barrel—Nota bene: you may do it legally the habeas corpus act being suspended,[100]—let it remain a fortnight—then bottle it.—The Wine not to be used even in warm weather till three Weeks after

Bottling—in Winter not till after a month.—*

It is to creatures not too bright and good for human nature's daily food that the next entry also confines itself:

> Very fond of Vegetables, particularly Bacon and Peas.—Bacon and Broad Beans.—[101]

Brandl, mistaking a cancelled opening of the note for 'P,' surmises that the reference is to Thomas Poole. But Coleridge had his own autobiography in mind. 'I am remarkably fond of beans and bacon,' he wrote in the memoranda of his life; 'and this fondness I attribute to my father having given me a penny for having eat a large quantity of beans on Saturday. For the other boys did not like them, and as it was an economic food, my father thought that my attachment and penchant for it ought to be encouraged.'[102] And since 'manly consistency' has been in question, it is pleasant to observe that in the matter of broad beans Coleridge obeyed the voice at eve obeyed at prime. 'Shall I trouble you,' he wrote the long-suffering Cottle in 1795 '(I being over the mouth and nose, in doing something of importance . . .) to send your servant into the market and buy a pound of bacon and two quarts of broad beans; and when he carries it down to College Street, to desire the maid to dress it for dinner, and tell her I shall be home by three o'clock?'[103]

I am inclined to think that few documents in the world afford so veracious a register of those discrepancies between high and low which are the stuff of consciousness, as the microcosm of this Note Book. The vision of an Epic on the Origin of Evil rubbing elbows with the admission of a hankering for beans is irresistibly symbolic. 'You would smile,' wrote Coleridge to Thelwall, a little later, 'to see my eye rolling up to the ceiling in a lyric fury, and on my knee a diaper pinned to warm.'[104] 'I should much wish, like the Indian Vishnu,' he confided to Thelwall yet again, 'to float about along an infinite ocean cradled in the flower of the Lotus, and wake once in a million years for a few minutes just to know that I was going to sleep a million years more.'[105] That was the insubstantial, faëry world where flitted the ghosts of Epics and Operas; in the corporeal world of Bacon and Broad Beans, it was no lotus flower which cradled him: 'The second day after Wordsworth came to me, dear Sara accidentally emptied a skillet of boiling milk on my foot, which confined me during the whole time of C. Lamb's stay.'[106] One lingers fascinated over the unutterable volumes in 'dear Sara'*—and then remembers that the skillet of boiling milk gave being to a completed poem, 'This Lime-Tree Bower my Prison,' six lines of which stand, in rough draft, in ironical juxtaposition to 'My Works,'[107] which lacked, alas! Sara's casual aid to composition.

And so, in view of life's (and the Note Book's) queer concatenations, the variegated weft of the next four entries[108] needs no further comment.

Receipt for brewing Wine—
Get two strong faithful men by proper Instruments—
Vide Thieves' Calendar—break into a Wine merchant's
Cellar—carry off a hogshead of best Claret or other ad
arbitrium—given me by Mrs. Danvers—expertæ crede†

Mem. To ~~write in~~ **reduce to** a regular form the Swedenborgian's Reveries—/

Mem. To remember to examine into the Laws upon Wrecks as at present existing

Mem. I asserted that Cato was a drunkard—denied by S.—to examine it—.

The next entry (after a pair of addresses) introduces us to a fresh batch of 'Works':

Poem in ~~three~~ **one** Books is the manner of Dante on the excursion of Thor.[109]

Joseph Cottle's brother Amos (who now chiefly lives in Byron's malicious line, 'O Amos Cottle! Phœbus, what a name!') printed in 1797 a translation of the 'Edda of Saemund,' which Coleridge read,[110] and to which Southey prefixed a long poetical epistle, beginning: 'Amos! I did not leave without regret The pleasant home of Burton.' The translation is equally uninebriating. Amos's masterpiece, however, may quite possibly have done for Coleridge what Mallet's *Northern Antiquities* had earlier done for Gray—except, indeed, for one important difference, that Gray's eggs hatched.

And now, almost overlapping another modest proposal (this time to write '2 Satires in the manner of Donne')[111] follows this agitated memorandum:[112]

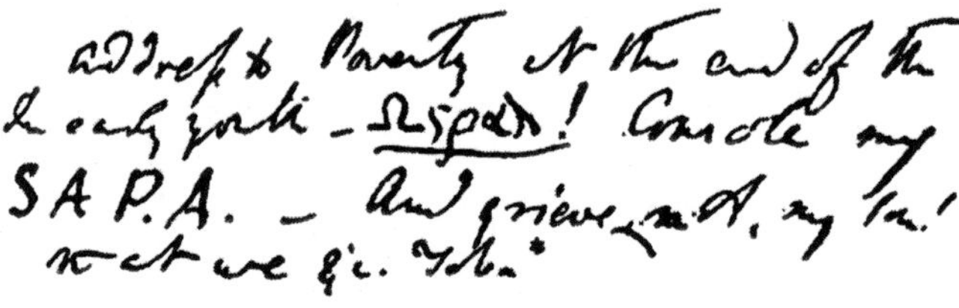

There needs the ghost of Coleridge himself come from the grave to unriddle that! A glimmer of light is shed, to be sure, by a letter of October, 1796, in which Coleridge links the theme of poverty in early youth with this same twenty-first verse of the fourth chapter of *Tobit.*[113] But 'Ōstral' remains inscrutable. It is, I suspect, in one of the cryptograms which Coleridge invented for his own private use,[114] but the cipher is employed too little in the Note Book to afford the key, nor does a set of Coleridge's cryptographs which Mr. Gerard Coleridge was kind enough to send me seem to lend aid. 'My Sara'[115] stood in pretty constant need of consolation, but the possible skeleton that lurks in the mysterious symbols is effectually concealed. However, such emotional tension as may be divined beneath the incoherence of this enigmatic entry is reassuringly relaxed in the next:

> Take a pound of Beef, Mutton, or Pork; cut it into small pieces; a pint of Peas; four Turnips sliced—

and so on through a full-page recipe for an Irish stew![116]

At the head of the next page Coleridge takes a fresh start on his register of topics destined never to put on immortality in prose or rhyme, and sets down in succession twenty-eight.[117] They are nothing if not catholic in their inclusiveness, ranging from 'An Essay on Tobit' and a 'Life of David' to a 'Hymn to Dr. Darwin—in the manner of the Orphics,' an 'Ode to a Looking Glass,' and an 'Ode to a Moth—against accumulation.' But four of the twenty-eight can scarcely be dismissed so cavalierly.

The first is this:[118]

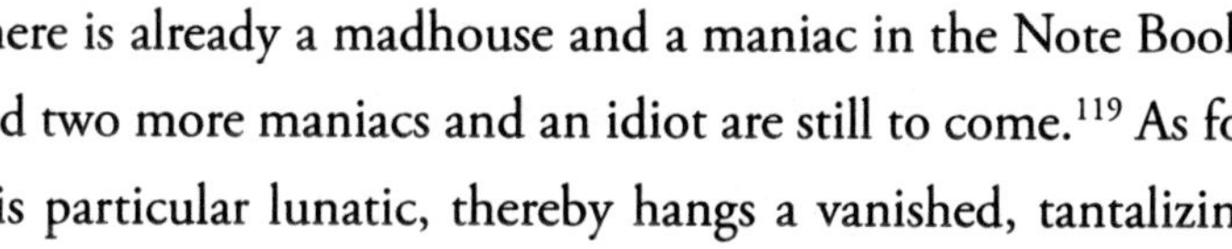

There is already a madhouse and a maniac in the Note Book, and two more maniacs and an idiot are still to come.[119] As for this particular lunatic, thereby hangs a vanished, tantalizing tale. For the cryptic addendum in Greek characters, after long puzzling, one day (thanks to the aid of Professor Manly's eye) suddenly flashed into sense. Transliterated, it reads thus:

'Erastou Galēros hat.' Turn the two good Greek genitives into English, and plain as a pikestaff there stands: 'Erastus Galer's hat.' Who Erastus Galer was, and what the tale about his hat, I would gladly give my own to know. I do know that Galer is a not uncommon English surname (incidentally, it turns up in Somerset),[120] and Erastus himself may survive in some dusty civic record of Bristol or Nether Stowey. But the riddle of his hat, I fear, is a question above antiquarism, not to be resolved by man, and he himself as shadowy as Henry Pimpernel, and Peter Turph, and old John Naps of Greece.

The entry which comes next is also 'wild,' and mad enough to boot, as anyone will recognize who recalls the ravings of Edgar on the heath in *Lear*. It is:[121]

12. Ode on St. Withold.

The letters once more piece out the Note Book. 'Would not this,' wrote Coleridge to Southey in December, 1794, 'be a fine subject for a wild ode?[122]

St. Withold footed thrice the Oulds,
He met the nightmare and her nine foals;*
He bade her alight and her troth plight,
And, "Aroynt thee, Witch!" he said.

I shall set about one [he continues], when I am in a humour to abandon myself to all the diableries that ever met the eye of a Fuseli!'[123] And now in the limbo of unborn poems, the demon Asmodeus from the Book of Tobit, and the nightmare and her apocryphal brood from *Lear*, and Erastus Galer who has something to do with a hat, all hover together, as in a Walpurgis Night's Dream, over a single phantasmagoric page of the Note Book.

The twenty-second topic, however, sets its sails for the unknown seas. It has to do with an event of surpassing contemporary interest, the thrilling story of the mutiny on H.M.S. *Bounty*, off the Friendly Islands in 1789:

22. Adventures of CHRISTIAN,† the mutineer. – – –[124]

Fletcher Christian, the leader of the mutineers, after setting the commander, Lieutenant Bligh, and eighteen officers and men adrift in an open boat, sailed off the map in the *Bounty*. The rest, save for Lieutenant Bligh's report, was silence. And Christian's actual adventures remained utterly unknown, except for a rumour in 1809, until, twenty-five years after the mutiny, a colony of the descendants of the mutineers was discovered on an island in the remote South Seas.[125] Then Byron, with his hawk's eye for romance, seized on the tale, and wrote 'The Island.' But Coleridge, like his contemporaries, could only guess. And we, in turn, can only wonder what part his inspired surmises may later have played in the adventures of the ancient Mariner in these same seas. At all events, there was at least one sentence in Bligh's matter-of-fact narrative which must have leaped from the page as Coleridge read—a sentence opposite which in the margin we can almost see him noting (as he noted once before): 'The philosophy of this.' 'When they were forcing me out of the ship,' wrote Bligh, 'I asked him [Christian], if this treatment was a proper return for the many instances he had received of my friendship? he appeared disturbed at my question, and answered with much emotion, "That,—captain Bligh,—that is the thing;—I am in hell—I am in hell." '[127] The adventures of Christian the mutineer, as Coleridge conceived them, may well have been, like those of the guilt-haunted Mariner himself, the adventures of 'a soul in agony.'

The sixteenth topic—

> Hymns to the Sun, the Moon, and the Elements—six hymns—[128]

is so closely interwoven with the genesis of 'The Ancient Mariner' that I shall reserve it till we reach that chapter of our story.[129]

The remainder of the Note Book we may barely touch. The essential characteristics of the document are by now sufficiently clear, and it only remains to fix the impression through a few more entries, and pass on.

> An ideot whose whole amusement consisted in looking at, and talking to a clock—which he supposed to be alive—/the Clock was removed—/

> he supposed that it had walked off—and he went away to seek it—was absent nine days—at last, they found [him], almost famished in a field—He asked where it was buried—for he was sure it was dead—/he was brought home and the clock in its place—his joy—etc. He used to put part of every thing, he liked, into the clock case.[130]

Coleridge's 'Idiot Boy' happily remained unwritten, but the escape seems to have been a narrow one. For, half a dozen years after the magic of 'The Ancient Mariner' might be supposed to have exorcised the spell of imbeciles forever, the idiot and his clock were still hanging fire. This time they appear in a note book of 1803: 'The sopha of sods. Lack-wit and the clock—find him at last in the Yorkshire cave, where the waterfall is.'[131] In some now inexplicable fashion the outlandish theme had got itself tied up with the idiot son of Betty Foy, and with Dorothy Wordsworth's haunts on Windy Brow, and with the portentous letter to Christopher North (eight printed pages long)[132] which William and Dorothy spent three June days composing in 1802.[133] Apart, however, from the curious human interest of its history, the entry discloses once more the strange fascination which abnormal psychology always exercised on Coleridge—a fascination without which, after all, 'The Rime of the Ancient Mariner' had never been.

But all this tells by no means the whole story. Between the

Wild Poem on a Maniac and the idiot and his clock, stand, among other entries, excerpts from the Greek text of the *Phædo* and the *Republic:* a phrase which contains the core of the Platonic doctrine of pre-existence, and the beginning of the great Parable of the Cave.[134] And the passage from the *Republic* is slipped in between a reference to Aristotle's *Metaphysics* and a direct quotation from it. And the citation from the *Phædo* and the reference to the *Metaphysics* are separated by a sentence from Plotinus.[135] The ancient landmarks still look out across the shifting tangle of strange ways.

A dozen more specimens, and I have done.

Hymns Moon

In a cave in the mountains of Cashmere an Image of Ice, which makes its appearance thus—two days before the new *moon* there appears a bubble of Ice which increases in size every day till the 15th day, at which it is an ell or more in height: then as the moon decreases, the Image does also till it vanishes.[136]

*

Air etc—Five Mathem. spend every night in the lofty tower—one directs his eye to the Zenith—2nd to the E. 3rd. to the W. 4. S. 5th. N. They take notice of the Wind and rain and stars—Grand Observatory in Pekin.—[137]

*

Vide Description of a Glory, by John Haygarth, Manchester Trans. Vol. 3. p. 463.*
the beautiful colors of the hoarfrost on snow in sunshine—red, green, and blue—in various angles.[139]

*

Mrs. Estlin's Story of the Maniac who walked round and round.

Epistle to Mrs. Wolstoncraft urging her to Religion. Read her Travels.

Sun paints rainbows on the vast waves during snowstorms in the Cape.[140]

a dusky light—a purple *flash*
crystalline splendor—light blue—
Green lightnings—[141]

*

Ham—lustful rogue—Vide Bayle under the Article *Ham*.

Nimrod, the first king, taught Idolatry, and persecuted for Religion's sake. He was the first who wore a crown (according to the Persian writers) having seen one in the Heavens—made war for conquest.—[142]

*

> Secret Journal of a self observer or Confessions and Letters from the German by J. C. Lavater.[143]
>
> Avalonian Isle[144]

And finally, among the very last entries in the book is this:

> With skill that never Alchemist yet told
> Made drossy Lead as ductile as pure Gold.[145]

And it is drossy lead with a vengeance that lies in heaps along the path which we have travelled. The alchemist and his alchemy we have yet to reckon with.

IV

I have left two-thirds of the mass of entries in the Note Book completely untouched. But the whole could not make clearer one fact of profound significance for us. For there, in those bizarre pages, we catch glimpses of the strange and fantastic shapes which haunted the hinterland of Coleridge's brain. Most of them never escaped from their confines into the light of day. Some did, trailing clouds of glory as they came. But those which did not, like the stars of the old astrology, rained none the less their secret influence on nearly everything that Coleridge wrote in his creative prime. 'The Rime of the Ancient Mariner,' 'Christabel,' 'Kubla Khan,' 'The Wanderings of Cain,' are what they are because they are all subdued to the hues of that heaving and phosphorescent sea below the verge of consciousness from which they have emerged. No single fragment of concrete reality in the array before us is in itself of such far-reaching import as is the sense of that hovering cloud of shadowy presences. For what the teeming chaos of the Note Book gives us is the charged and electrical atmospheric background of a poet's mind.[146]

---

*I have not included 'Christabel,' for the reason that 'Christabel' has failed completely to include itself. Wherever the mysterious tracts from which it rose may lie, they are off the road which leads to 'The Ancient Mariner' and 'Kubla Khan.' And we are following only where known facts lead. I wish I did know in what distant deeps or skies the secret lurks; but the elusive clue is yet to capture.

*It is commonly (and properly) referred to as the 'Gutch Memorandum Book.' But since it will be mentioned many scores of times in the course of the following pages, I shall call it, for convenience, simply the 'Note Book.' When others of the more than fifty extant 'pocket-books, notebooks, copy-books of all shapes, sizes, and bindings'[7] are referred to, they will be so designated that there will be no confusion.

*The italics are Coleridge's. But hereafter, whenever the italics in a quotation are found in the original, I shall state that fact in the Notes. Otherwise, the italics in quotations are always mine.

†Except to marvel anew at coincidence and the mocking ironies of Time. For Carlyle (who could not have seen the Note Book) wrote, in his fullest flavoured vein, in a letter of January 22, 1825: 'Coleridge is a mass of richest spices putrefied into a dunghill.'[34]

*The bracketed letters are missing in the Note Book, since the upper corner of the leaf has been torn off. Brandl, who had not the clue, guessed wrong. The entry will meet us later.

†An asterisk between two entries indicates that they are not consecutive Between consecutive entries the asterisk is omitted.

‡For this absolute use of the verb compare *Lear*, III, iv, 83-84: 'Commit not with man's sworn spouse'; and add the quotation in *N.E.D.* under *commit*, 6. c.

*'This account, we must allow,' remark the editors of the *London Magazine*, 'appears so *marvellous*, that even the Credulous might be staggered. . . . But this narrative certainly merits attention and belief. The degree of credibility which is due to the several circumstances rests with Mr. Foersch. With regard to the principal parts of the relation, there can be no doubt. The evidence of the tree, and the noxious powers of its gums and vapours, are certain. For the story of the *thirteen*

concubines, however, we should not choose to be responsible.' The italics, I hasten to add, are the editors', and whether the scruples were mathematical or ethical, I do not know. For further references, and for the credibility of the plausible Mr. Foersch, the interested reader is referred to the Notes[79]—or better still, to the *London Magazine*

*Months after this was written (but, I now add, long before Mr. Fausset's closing page was published!) I read with pleasure what Coleridge said of Lord Nelson: 'To the same enthusiastic sensibilities which made a fool of him with regard to his Emma, his country owed the victories of the Nile, Copenhagen, and Trafalger.'[99]

*I hope that Professor Saintsbury, whose *Notes on a Cellar Book* have crowned the long record of a happy life, has never seen this pathetic formula. I fear it would well nigh break his heart.

*There is something irresistibly alluring in the inverted imprecations of the great and good. 'At Vauxhall I took a boat for Somerset House,' wrote Coleridge to Matilda Betham in a letter of later date. 'Two mere children were my Charons; however . . . we sailed safely to the landing-place, when, as I was getting out, *one of the little ones* (*God bless him!*) moved the boat. On turning half-way round to reprove him, he moved it again, and I fell back on . . . a large stone which I struck against just under my crown' (*House of Letters*, pp. 107–08). The italics I am guilty of myself.

†Is this Mrs. Danvers's righteous protest against the thin potations of the earlier entry, in favour of addiction, at any cost, to sack?

*Address to Poverty at the end of the In early youth—*Ōstral!* Console my SAP. A.—And grieve not, my son! that we etc. Tob—

*Shakespeare, to be sure, wrote 'The nightmare, and her ninefold' (*Lear* 3.4. 125–29), but Coleridge's nightmares were fruitful and multiplied.[126] His memory played him false elsewhere in the lines.

†The word 'Christian' is doubly underlined.

*This highly characteristic memorandum will be found in full in the Notes.[138]

CHAPTER II

THE FALCON'S EYE

BUT that is only half the story. For anything which has so far appeared, the concourse of atoms in the chaos we have just traversed might be wholly fortuitous. But with the salient features of the strange jumble now before us, we are in a position to observe another set of facts, which will at once clarify and define our larger problem. For the import of the Note Book reaches far beyond its contribution to our knowledge of the man who kept it. Obviously the mass of incongruous, and exotic, and even monstrous facts and fancies which interested Coleridge throw into sharp relief the idiosyncrasies of Coleridge himself. That needs no argument. But the paramount importance of the document lies in the fact that it points the way to conclusions of general validity—conclusions which, in turn, owe their illuminating quality to the vivid concreteness of the details on which they rest. I am not forgetting that we have to do with genius. But after making all allowance for those elements which are unique in Coleridge, as the incommunicable essence of every genius is unique, there remains a precious residuum which is peculiar to no individual, but which inheres in the nature of the imaginative faculty itself.

I

Now the bewildering inconsequence of the Note Book is not always what it seems. The figure of a charged and electrical atmosphere flashing into desultory brilliance holds good, but behind the seeming fitfulness of the flashes an intense and consecutive energy was at work. And half the meaning of the subliminal aspect of the phenomena we have just been scanning is dependent upon recognition of the conscious activities which we have now to see. Let us, accordingly, approach the Note Book from another angle. *How did Coleridge actually read books?* Few more significant questions can be asked about any man, and about Coleridge probably none. The answer of the Note Book is the more conclusive in that it must be read between the lines. Three typical extracts will suffice.

On the 45th leaf of the volume is the entry which we have already read, about the cave in the mountains of Cashmere in which was the image of ice.[1] Upon this follows at once the memorandum:

> Read the whole 107th page of Maurice's Indostan.[2]

Maurice's 107th page starts out with the bubble of ice which had captured Coleridge's fancy, and which was to reappear in the strangest dream, perhaps, that ever mortal dreamed. Why Coleridge meant to re-read the page *in toto* we can only guess.[3] But the record of his intention is at least eloquent of the way in which impressions from his reading came to stamp themselves ineffaceably upon his memory. The next entry is as illuminating as to all appearance it is dull:[4]

> Sun
> Hymns—Remember to look at Quintius [*sic*] Curtius—lib. 3. Cap. 3 and 4.

What sent Coleridge to Quintus Curtius? Turn the preceding leaf of Maurice's *Hindostan*, and the answer is revealed. For on the 105th page stands this footnote:

> See Quinti Curtii, lib. 3. cap. 3. Ibid. lib. 3. cap. 4.

Coleridge, then, was verifying Maurice's references. And the reason why he made the note is also clear enough. Quintus Curtius, in the passage referred to, gives a vivid description of an image of the *sun* in *gold*,[5] which offered a striking counterpart to Maurice's image of *ice* that waxed and waned with the *moon*. And the two unwritten hymns to the sun and moon—which, with the Hymns to the Elements, were to have been (as we shall see) a *magnum opus*—were clearly to centre about the two contrasting images. Coleridge, that is to say, was reading with a falcon's eye for details in which lurked the spark of poetry. It is no wonder that, seen with such intensity of vision, they stuck like limpets in his memory.

The next entry is at first blush singularly unrewarding. It is a solitary name: 'Major Rennell.'[6] But the brevity of the jotting is no index of its significance. Major James Rennell was one of the most distinguished geographers of his day.[7] Why, however, should Coleridge set down his name in just this context? The answer is again not far to seek. Maurice has referred to Major Rennell in terms of the highest praise, as the author of a weighty memoir on the geography of Hindostan and as one of his own chief authorities.[8] Coleridge, that is, was reading Maurice, but he was doing more: *he was also going back at first hand to the sources of Maurice's information*. He made, accordingly, a memorandum of another book to read. And when he did read it, he came upon at least one particular which haunted his recollection, and entered into the complex out of which 'Kubla Khan' mysteriously appeared.[9] One hundred and seventy pages farther on in Maurice,[10] Coleridge, this time with his Hymn to the *Air* in his head and the Note Book still at his elbow, pounced, hawk-like again, upon the picturesque detail of the five vigilant mathematicians on the lofty tower of the Grand Observatory in Pekin, taking solemn notice of the wind, rain, and stars. And with that, apparently, he laid Maurice aside.

II

It is difficult to emphasize too strongly the importance of the inferences we have just drawn. If we can run down the references and quotations in the Note Book, we can thereby identify books which Coleridge certainly read. And in those books are matters which never got into the Note Book at all, but which none the less stuck in Coleridge's memory and germinated there. And to track a poet like Coleridge through his reading is to lay bare still further what touched the springs of his imagination. For the unique value of the Note Book lies in the insight which it affords us into the polarizing quality of a poet's reading—a reading in which the mind moved, like the passing of a magnet, over pages to all seeming as bare of poetic implications as a parallelogram, and drew and held fixed whatever was susceptible of imaginative transmutation. And two more brief entries will throw into still clearer light one element of our problem which it is essential that we should understand.

The second entry in the Note Book is a curious yet enlightening case in point. It is this: 'Moon at present uninhabited owing to its little or no atmosphere but may in Time—An atheistic Romance might be formed—a Theistic one too.—Mem.!'[11] What fantastic rivalry with Cyrano de Bergerac Coleridge had in contemplation I do not know.[12] But I do know what it was that he beheld when his heart leaped up at the conception of an atheistical romance staged in the moon. He was reading his way (as I, reading after him, know to my sorrow) through that portentous sediment of scientific notes precipitated from the metallic couplets of Erasmus Darwin's *Botanic Garden*,[13] when, after some sixty pages of the conglomerate, he came on this:[14]

> *Hence it is not probable that the moon is at present inhabited*, but . . . a sufficient quantity of air *may in process of time* be generated to produce an atmosphere . . . and thence become fit for the production of vegetables and animals.
>
> *That the moon possesses little or no atmosphere* is deduced from the undiminished lustre of the stars, at the instant when they emerge from behind her disk.*

The mass of equally encyclopædic information (for I have humanely omitted the bulk of the note) with which in the preceding pages Darwin, like a competent mechanic, had been shoring up his poem seems to have left Coleridge unmoved. All at once, for some inscrutable reason, this particular item gave a fillip to his imagination. And questionable as the resulting inspiration was, it serves to demonstrate how at any moment a page which Coleridge was reading might become electrical, and set free the currents of creative energy.

III

I am not sure, however, that the first entry in the Note Book is not even more illuminating for our purpose than the second. It is the most unpromising looking scrap imaginable: 'The Vernal Hours. Leg. Thomson.'[15] Since the second entry was inspired by the *Botanic Garden*, it seemed worth while to act on the surmise that the first had been noted from the same sitting. A glance back over the earlier pages of the *Garden* confirmed the guess. In the first canto of 'The Economy of Vegetation' occur the following lines, the capitals, after Darwin's wont, falling with the fine impartiality of the rain:

> Unite, ILLUSTRIOUS NYMPHS! your radiant powers,
> Call from their long repose the VERNAL HOURS.
> Wake with soft touch, with rosy hands unbind
> The struggling pinions of the WESTERN WIND.[17]

On the last line Darwin has Notes and Additional Notes which foot up sixteen closely printed quarto pages.[18] I suppose Coleridge read them; if he did, they left him mute. But the lines on the Vernal Hours naturally enough suggested Thomson's 'Spring,' and Coleridge made memorandum to read (or re-read) the *Seasons*.[19] In Thomson's 'Winter,' as he read, he found a long account of Lapland, a country which held for him a singular fascination.[20] And in a footnote to Thomson's reference to the Lapland lake Niemi were and are two most alluring extracts from 'M. de Maupertuis, in his book on the Figure of the Earth.'[21] Now Maupertuis's book on the Figure of the Earth is an account—equipped, as it should be, with a formidable apparatus of mathematical tables and calculations—of a scientific expedition sent to Finland by the king of France to measure an arc of the meridian which cuts the polar circle.[22] It is not precisely the sort of book one expects to find feeding the springs of Helicon. But Coleridge, upon reading Thomson's footnotes (which happened to deal not with angles and parallels but with roses and fairies),[23] proceeded to hunt up Maupertuis. Of that fact there can be no doubt, for Maupertuis forthwith blossomed into poetry—once in the sonnet to Godwin; again and again, interwoven with lore extracted from Leemius's treatise *De Lapponibus*, in 'The Destiny of Nations'; and later, in 'The Ancient Mariner.'[24] Darwin, that is to say, sent Coleridge to Thomson; Thomson sent him to Maupertuis; and once more an incorrigible habit of verifying footnotes led the imagination upon fresh adventures.

Now thanks to a somewhat searching interrogation of half a dozen entries in the Note Book, we have assured ourselves on two points of extreme significance. In the first place, Coleridge (at least during the years of the Note Book) read with an eye which habitually pierced to the secret spring of poetry beneath the crust of fact.[25] And this means that items or details the most unlikely might, through some poetic potentiality discovered or divined, find lodgement in his memory. In the second place, Coleridge not only read books with minute attention, *but he also habitually passed from any given book he read to the books to which that book referred.*[26] And that, in turn, makes it possible to follow him into the most remote and unsuspected fields. And his gleanings from those fields, transformed but recognizable, will meet us again and again as we proceed. For to follow Coleridge through his reading is to retrace the obliterated vestiges of creation.

---

*It is characteristic of Coleridge, who, like Chaucer, had the trick of recollecting a number of things at a time (which forthwith proceeded to combine), that he should also have remembered the wording of the abridgement of all this in Darwin's elaborate table of 'Contents of Notes': 'Moon has little or no atmosphere. Its ocean is frozen. It is not yet inhabited, *but may be in time.*'[16]

CHAPTER III

THE DEEP WELL

THE statement which I have just ventured is not one to be lightly made. Let us, then, summon the Note Book again to the witness-stand in its corroboration. This time, however, we shall be led far beyond the pages of the book itself into untrodden ways.

I

Coleridge, as we know, was a profound admirer of Joseph Priestley, 'Patriot, and Saint, and Sage,'[1] and I cherished a stubborn suspicion (why, need not now concern us) that he had read Priestley's *Opticks*, or, to be more exact, his *History and Present State of Discoveries relating to Vision, Light, and Colours.*[2] But I wanted to prove it, for the reason that in Priestley's curious chapter on 'Light from Putrescent Substances' occurred a tantalizing account of the phosphorescent sea, and of fishes which, 'in swimming, left so luminous a track behind them, that both their size and species might be distinguished by it.'[3] That was so like the water-snakes in 'The Ancient Mariner,' which 'moved in tracks of shining white,'[4] that it seemed a reasonable guess that Coleridge, who had not yet been at sea, might have got his suggestion there. But had he read Priestley's *Opticks?* The book is a ponderous quarto of eight hundred and twelve pages.[5] With the Note Book pretty definitely in my head, I began on the *Opticks*, and plodded doggedly through eight hundred and six obsolete pages of the heroic dimensions of those unhurried days, still nursing the unconquerable hope that a jewel might at any moment turn up in the dust-heap. But the eight hundred and six pages were as bare of a clue as the palm of my hand. The eight hundred and seventh completed the text. I turned the page before it with a sigh of relief; that job, at least, was done! And there, on the very last page of the text, before my weary but not yet quite disillusioned eyes, stood this:

> Dr. Franklin shewed me that the flames of two candles joined give a much stronger light than both of them separate; as is made very evident by a person holding the two candles near his face, first separate, and then joined in one.[6]

I was not at all sure that the statement was correct. I do not know now, for I have never put it to the test. But what I did know was this—that on the very first page of the Note Book were rather illegibly scribbled these words:

> The flames of two Candles joined give a much stronger light than both of them separate—evid. by a person

> holding the two Candles near his Face, first separate, and then joined in one.[7]

And immediately below, in a line to itself, and evidently written at a different time, were the words: 'Picture of Hymen.'[8]

Coleridge, then, had read the *Opticks*—at least the 807th page! He had also (probably because he was thinking at the moment of Mary Evans whom he wanted to marry, or Sarah Fricker whom he married) seen in Franklin's two candles which gave more light together than when separate what certainly, on the occasion of a pair of candles, never entered the heart of Benjamin Franklin to conceive—to wit, the emblem of a happy marriage. But the touch of sentiment is incidental. As if to make double sure the assurance of Coleridge's knowledge of the *Opticks*, another observation of Franklin's from the same 807th page of Priestley appears on the next page of the Note Book:[9] 'The lowest part of the flame of a candle is always blue; and when the flame is sufficiently elongated, so as to be just ready to smoke, the tip is always red.'*

Coleridge, then, had read in the *Opticks*, as the Note Book proves. But can we be sure that he had read the particular page about the phosphorescent fishes? It is notorious, as Petrarch wrote Boccaccio in a famous letter, that the beginning and end of a book are often read, and the remainder skipped. May Coleridge, perhaps, not being spurred on by an obstinate quest like mine, have turned idly to see how the *Opticks* ended, and left its ample bulk unread? That, to be sure, would be unlike Coleridge; nor does the treatise exactly leave us on tenterhooks to know how it turns out. But with the Note Book we have more than likelihood to lead us.

To the passage in the *Opticks* about the shining fishes Priestley, as it happens, has appended a footnote.[11] It is a reference to the *Philosophical Transactions of the Royal Society* (*Abridged*), Vol. V, p. 213.[12] Now Coleridge was not only an omnivorous reader; he was also an extremely thoroughgoing one. And he had, as we have seen, the habit of verifying references. If the luminous fishes did impress him, there is at least the possibility that he had looked up Priestley's reference to find out more. Let us turn, then, to Volume Five of the *Abridgement*, on the chance that Coleridge did so too. The account of the fishes in the *Transactions*, to which Priestley had referred, turns out to be taken from certain observations of Father Bourzes on 'Luminous Appearances in the Wakes of Ships in the Sea,' extracted from that vast repository of universal information, the *Letters of the Missionary Jesuits*.[13] The pertinent sentences are these:

> Not only the Wake of a Ship produces this Light, but Fishes also in swimming leave behind em *a luminous Track;* which is so bright that one may distinguish the Largeness of the Fish, and know of what Species it is. *I have sometimes seen a great many Fishes playing in the Sea, which have made a kind of artificial Fire in the Water, that*

> *was very pleasant to look on.*[14]

That is what Coleridge read, *if* he looked up Priestley's reference. And when one recalls his vivid phrase: 'They coiled and swam; and every track Was a flash of golden fire,'[15] the question becomes an interesting one.

But did he look up Priestley's reference? The Note Book once more affords the clue. As the *Transactions* lie open at the passage about the shining fishes, the following sentences stand on the opposite page of Father Bourzes's letter:

> I shall add one Observation more concerning *Marine Rain-bows*, which I observed after a great Tempest *off of the Cape* of Good Hope. The Sea was then very much tossed, and the Wind carrying off the Tops of the *Waves* made a kind of Rain, in which the Rays of the *Sun painted the Colours of a Rain-bow.*[16]

On leaf 76 of the Note Book stands this:

> *Sun paints rainbows* on the vast *waves* during snow-storms *in the Cape.*[17]

How the snow-storms got into the picture we shall later see; but meantime the source of the jotting is unmistakable.

Coleridge, then, *had* verified Priestley's reference, had read Father Bourzes's letter, with its fuller description of the phosphorescent sea, and had actually made note of a detail on the next page which, for some reason, had struck him. And Father Bourzes's vivid account of the shining fishes with their luminous tracks was there in his memory, with a host of impressions which it carried in its train, when he came to write 'The Ancient Mariner.'

But that is not all. When Coleridge once started on a book, he was apt to devour it whole. We know now, by the aid of the Note Book, that he got hold of the Fifth Volume of the *Philosophical Transactions*. It is a safe guess that he would not let it out of his hands till he had looked it through. Let us see what else would meet his eye. Some fifty-odd pages earlier than Father Bourzes's story, at the very top of the page, where it leaps to catch the attention of the most careless reader, is this: 'He says, there is a Tradition among them, that in November 1668, *a Star appear'd below the Body of the Moon within the Horns of it.*'[18] Now turn to 'The Rime of the Ancient Mariner':

> Till clomb above the eastern bar
> *The hornèd Moon, with one bright star*
> *Within the nether tip.*[19]

There, in the *Philosophical Transactions of the Royal Society*, is obviously what Coleridge remembered when he wrote the famous lines which have caused the spilling of so much good ink.

But the interest of the passage does not stop with that. The page at the top of which the star within the horns of the moon appears is headed: 'Remarkables in New-England.' Turn back two pages, arid the author is divulged. It is Cotton Mather, in a communication to Mr. Waller of the Royal Society, 'dated at *Boston*, Nov. 24, 1712.'[20] The 'star within the nether tip' harks back to Beacon Hill! And we have reached it by way of experiments in light which Benjamin Franklin performed in London; luminous fishes observed on a voyage to the Indies; and rainbows at sea off the Cape of Good Hope. And that is but the prologue to the play.

II

The curious fragments, then, about the flame of two candles and a bow in the sprindrift have pointed the way to unexpected treasure-trove. The Note Book has already served us well. But before we go farther, now that the facts which have just been rehearsed are fresh in mind, I mean to turn them to immediate account. For the entries now before us, together with their implications, epitomize the processes which underlie the poem as a whole. Let us pause at this point, accordingly, and put our present findings on their inferences. The hornèd moon and its one bright star must be reserved to occupy us later.[21] But the water-snakes have light to throw at once upon the path ahead of us. Here, then, in their immediate context, are the stanzas which describe them, as they played by the ship in the rays of the moon:

Her beams bemocked the sultry main,
Like April hoar-frost spread;
But where the ship's huge shadow lay,
The charmèd water burnt always
A still and awful red.

Beyond the shadow of the ship,
I watched the water-snakes:
They moved in tracks of shining white,
And when they reared, the elfish light
Fell off in hoary flakes.

Within the shadow of the ship
I watched their rich attire:
Blue, glossy green, and velvet black,
They coiled and swam; and every track
Was a flash of golden fire.[22]

Two preliminary considerations will lend us aid and comfort on the adventurous enterprise into which we are about to plunge. The first is in one of Coleridge's letters. 'My memory,' he wrote to his brother George in 1794, apropos of a chance acquaintance whom he met 'smoking in . . . a chimney corner of a pot-house,' and who 'kept [him] awake till three in the morning with his ontological disquisitions'—'my memory, *tenacious and systematizing*, would enable [me] to write an octavo from his conversation.'[23] There is abundant evidence that Coleridge was not drawing the long bow in this off-hand appraisal of his capabilities, and the phrase 'tenacious and systematizing' is as accurate as it is exact. The testimony, too, of one of his fellow Cantabrigians is much to the point. Apropos of Coleridge's rooms at Jesus, C. V. Le Grice long after wrote:

> What evenings have I spent in those rooms! What little suppers, or *sizings*, as they were called, have I enjoyed; when Æschylus, and Plato, and Thucydides were pushed aside . . . to discuss the pamphlets of the day. Ever and anon, a pamphlet issued from the pen of Burke. There was no need of having the book before us. Coleridge had read it in the morning, and in the evening he would repeat whole pages verbatim. Frend's trial was then in progress. Pamphlets swarmed from the press. Coleridge had read them all; and in the evening, with our negus, we had them *viva voce* gloriously.[24]

We have to do, in a word, with one of the most extraordinary memories of which there is record, stored with the spoils of an omnivorous reading, and endowed into the bargain with an almost uncanny power of association. And that it will be well to keep in mind.

The second *vade mecum* has to do with a familiar trick of memory and association. Even you and I, at vivid moments, know the sudden leap of widely sundered recollections, through some flash of association, into a new and sometimes startling unity. And that, assuredly in no less degree, is also the experience of poets. Here, to be concrete, is a case in point. Chaucer (than whose mental processes there are none more normal) is imitating, in the 'Parlement of Fowles,' a stanza of Boccaccio which contains a list of famous lovers of antiquity. They are Semiramis, Pyramus and Thisbe, Hercules, and Biblis. And Semiramis is referred to, not by name, but by a phrase: 'the spouse of Ninus' ('sposa di Nin'). But Dante, in the great fifth canto of the *Inferno*, has a list of lovers too, which likewise begins with Semiramis, and runs through Dido, Cleopatra, Achilles, and Paris, to Tristan. And Dante also refers to Semiramis by a phrase: she is one of whom we read that she succeeded Ninus, and was his spouse ('che succedette a Nino, e fu sua sposa'). In Boccaccio's list, then, which Chaucer was translating, occurs the phrase '*sposa di Nin.*' In Dante's list appear almost identically the same words: '*Nino, e fu sua sposa.*' Now Chaucer knew his Dante thoroughly.[25] What happened? Boccaccio's phrase, as he read it, called up Dante's, and Dante's phrase, once recollected, *carried along with it its accompanying list.* And as a result Chaucer's bead-roll of ladies dead and lovely knights included not only every lover in Boccaccio's list, but every one of Dante's lovers too![26] Through a flash of association by way of a common phrase, two objects have telescoped into a third. And at moments of high imaginative tension associations, not merely in pairs but in battalions, are apt in similar fashion to stream together and coalesce.

And now we may come at last to the scattered elements of poetry towards which we have been heading. Can we recover impressions which we know must have lain in Coleridge's mind—images of which we can say with assurance that at some time or other they had flashed before his inner eye? And if we can, are there among them impressions which, like Chaucer's, are fitted with links which might catch them together, and render some sort of coalescence possible? Coleridge speaks, in *The Friend*, of what he calls 'the *hooks-and-eyes* of the memory.'[27] And the enterprise now before us is to follow (for the moment holding conclusions in abeyance) a singular series of impressions, its members equipped with open and palpable hooks and eyes, from books which we know Coleridge to have read. And since, if I am right, they will lead us to the very alembic of the creative energy, I shall ask indulgence, in this next section, for what may seem to be a somewhat pedantic insistence on details. We shall come to broad inferences soon enough.

III

Our initial certainty (and on this point the evidence of the Note Book is irrefragable) is this: Coleridge read both Priestley's chapter in the *Opticks* on 'Light from Putrescent Substances,' and Father Bourzes's letter in the *Philosophical Transactions* on 'Luminous Appearances in the Wakes of Ships.' Moreover, his reading of the letter was due to his interest in those portions of it which he had already seen in Priestley—an interest which was keen enough to send him directly to Priestley's source of information. He came to the letter, then, not casually, but with an alert and receptive mind. And he read, for the second time, the statements which had stirred his curiosity. This time, however, they were detailed in a remarkably interesting record (touched with an engaging personal charm) of first-hand observations in distant seas. And here are a few of the sentences which Coleridge read—repeated, in part, for us as for him:

> In my Voyage to the Indies . . . when the Ship ran apace, we often observed a great Light in the Wake of the Ship. . . . The Wake seemed then like a River of Milk. . . . Particularly, on the 12th of June, the Wake of the Vessel was full of large Vortices of Light. . . . When our Ship sailed slowly, the Vortices appeared and disappeared again immediately *like Flashes of Lightning*. Not only the Wake of a Ship produces this Light, but Fishes also in swimming leave behind 'em *a luminous Track*. . . . I have sometimes seen a great many Fishes *playing in the Sea*, which have made *a kind of artificial Fire in the Water*, that was very pleasant to look on.[28]

Then follows, on the next page, the account of the marine rainbow, which Coleridge set down in his Note Book.

Now even a passing glance at the stanzas, though it catch no more than 'flash,' 'track,' 'fire,' and the play of shining creatures, suggests that Coleridge turned his pursuit of Priestley's reference to good account. But it also needs but a glance to show that the playing fishes thus lighted on have somehow struck up relations with something else. For the creatures of the great calm in the poem are no longer fishes; they are snakes. They are not merely luminous; they have vivid hues. Remember, too, that the ship is under the Line and becalmed; and that, a few stanzas before, the Mariner has spoken of 'the *rotting* sea,' where 'slimy things did crawl with legs Upon the *slimy* sea.' Now let us follow Coleridge a little further in his reading.

Few books were more widely and eagerly read at the close of the eighteenth century than the accounts of Captain James Cook's voyages to the Pacific Ocean. Coleridge, with his passion for narratives of exploration, could not have overlooked them, and a remark which he made to John Sterling affords clear evidence that he did not.[29] Here, then, is part of the 257th page of the second volume of the narrative of Cook's last voyage. The 'Resolution' is off Sir Francis Drake's 'New Albion,' out a little distance from what is now the coast of Oregon:

> *During a calm*, on the morning of the 2d, some parts of the sea seemed *covered with a kind of slime;* and some small sea animals were *swimming about*. The most

> conspicuous of which, were of the gelatinous . . . kind, almost globular; and another sort smaller, *that had a white, or shining appearance*, and were very numerous. Some of these last were taken up, and put into a glass cup, with some salt water. . . . When they began to swim about, which they did, with equal ease, upon their back, sides, or belly, they emitted the brightest colours of the most precious gems. . . . Sometimes they . . . assume[ed] various tints of *blue* . . . which were frequently mixed with a ruby, or opaline *redness;* and glowed with a strength sufficient to illuminate the vessel and water. . . . But, with candle light, the colour was, chiefly, a beautiful, pale *green*, tinged with *a burnished gloss;* and, in the dark, it had a faint appearance of *glowing fire*. They proved to be . . . probably, an animal which has a share in producing some sorts of *that lucid appearance, often observed near ships at sea, in the night.*[30]

There, then, is another account of luminous creatures swimming about, like Father Bourzes's fishes, beside a ship, and like them producing the effect of fire in the waters of a slimy sea. It needs no elaborate reasoning to show that the two accounts are peculiarly adapted to recall each other. But this time there is a significant increment. Captain Cook's animalculæ are described as '*shining*' white, and blue, and '*glossy*' green. And those are precisely the colours which in the poem are associated with the water-snakes.[31] Cook's *Voyage*, then, along with the *Transactions*, must be taken account of in the reckoning.

But neither Father Bourzes's fishes nor Cook's protozoa are 'velvet black' or, for that matter, black at all. Where did the rich array of the water-snakes acquire its shadowed livery? Probably none of the books which Coleridge was reading during the gestation of 'The Ancient Mariner' left more lively images in his memory than Bartram's *Travels*. The fascinating fifth chapter of Part Two in particular had awakened him to all manner of poetic possibilities, and prompted copious transcriptions in the Note Book. And these transcripts form, as it happens, a significant cluster. The alligators (punctuated by Hartley's moonlit tears) were set down from pages 127–30 of the *Travels;* the 'little peaceable community' of snake-birds, from pages 132–33; the antiphonal roarings of the crocodiles and the thunder, from page 140; the wilderness plot, green, fountainous, and unviolated, from page 157; and the Gordonia lasianthus, from pages 161–62. Coleridge's memory, it is clear, had been greedily absorbing impressions from these thirty-odd pages, as Gideon's fleece drank up the dew. Now on pages 153–54 of the *Travels*, at the very heart of the cluster, flanked on both sides by passages which Coleridge actually transcribed, appears a long and vivid description of 'the yellow bream or sun fish.' 'What a most beautiful creature is this fish before me!' exclaims Bartram, 'gliding to and fro, and figuring in the still clear waters, with his orient attendants and associates.' 'The whole fish,' he goes on, 'is of a pale gold (or *burnished* brass) colour . . . the scales are . . . powdered with *red*, russet, silver, *blue* and *green* specks,' while at the gills is 'a little spatula . . . encircled with silver, and *velvet black*.'[32]

Once more, then, Coleridge read of creatures (this time, as in the *Philosophical Transactions*, fishes) endowed with the red, blue, and green of the animalculæ, and also with an appearance of 'burnished brass' which was the counterpart of the protozoa's 'burnished gloss.' The associative links between Cook and Bartram are patent at a glance, and Coleridge's faculty of association was preternaturally acute. If Cook's protozoa and Bartram's sun fish did not recall each other and amalgamate, it was not because they lacked facilities for combination. But again there was an increment. For the bream rejoiced in the velvet black which completes the water-snakes' rich attire. If, then, Coleridge's reminiscences did coalesce (and by this time we may fairly adopt that assumption as our working hypothesis) the water-snakes have so far levied tribute on a voyage to the Indies; on the waters of what Purchas terms 'the backside of America';[33] and on a camp (as Bartram describes it) 'at a charming Orange grove bluff, on the East side of [a] little lake . . . in the wilderness of Florida.'[34] And the Azores and Lapland and the South Pacific are immediately in the offing.

But before going farther, I want to be very explicit on a point of some importance. This study (to state it categorically once for all) is concerned with what in professional lingo we call 'sources' only in so far as they give us the crude substance which has undergone imaginative transformation. In everything that I shall say, accordingly, the emphasis lies on the raw materials solely in their relation to the new whole which has been wrought from them. For that ultimate unity is not, like Melchisedek, King of Salem, without descent. And the recognition of its possibly dubious lineage simply heightens the glory of its latter state. In movement direction is everything, and the amazing fact is not that there was once a time (as Meredith has it) 'when mind was mud,' but rather that mud in due course mounts to mind, and alligators and idiots and slimy seas become the stuff that dreams are made on. That, I suspect, is one of the most momentous functions of the imagination—its sublimation of brute fact. Yet without a knowledge of the crass materials, the profoundly significant process is unintelligible. And if at the moment we are assiduously accumulating raw materials, it is in order to a clearer understanding of the ways in which, through the operations of the shaping spirit, they are transmuted into elements of beauty.

With that clear as our guiding principle, we may return to our waiting water-snakes. For at once the question arises, why are the creatures snakes at all, instead of the fishes or animalculæ which were their prototypes? The answer to that will be found with the rest, I suspect, in that storehouse of multifarious impressions acquired through a cormorant's avidity for reading, the 'tenacious and systematizing' memory of Coleridge himself. At all events, one of Coleridge's 'midnight darlings,' as Elia would say, was the 1617 folio of *Purchas his Pilgrimage*, which will swing within our orbit more than once. In a chapter with the beguiling title: 'Of the Caniball-Ilands; the Whale, Thresher, Sword-fish, Sharke, and other Fishes and Observations of those Seas,' Purchas quotes from the *Observations of Sir Richard Hawkins, Knight, in his Voyage into the South Sea.* And this is what he says:

> . . . an instance whereof he [Hawkins] sheweth in the Queenes Nauie, in the yeere of our Lord 1590, at the Asores many moneths becalmed, the Sea thereby being replenished with seuerall sorts of gellies and formes of Serpents, Adders, and *Snakes, Greene*, Yellow, *Blacke, White*, and some partie-coloured, *whereof many had life*, being a yard and a halfe, or two yards long. *And they could hardly draw a Bucket of Water, cleare of some corruption withall.*[35]

Once again, accordingly, Coleridge read of a ship becalmed in a rotting sea, with creatures that were green, and black, and white about it. Such details might well become hoops of steel to grapple Sir Richard Hawkins, if occasion should arise, to Father Bourzes, and Captain Cook, and William Bartram.[36] But this time too there is an increment. The 'living things' observed from the Queen's Navy just two years after the Armada were neither fish nor animalculæ, but *snakes*. And incidentally, in view of the 'silly buckets' on the Mariner's rotting deck, the reference to buckets in a context electrical with associations is not without a passing interest.

But the exact term '*water-snakes*' does not occur in Purchas's account of Hawkins's observations. It does, however, in the narrative of another great mariner whom Coleridge read with admiration, the *New Voyage round the World* of Captain William Dampier. It was from Dampier that he drew the unlucky suggestion about the turtle-shell boat which replaced the no less unhappy household tub in Wordsworth's 'Blind Highland Boy';[37] it was Dampier whom he would have the naval and military writers of his own day read and imitate[38]—'old Dampier, a rough sailor, but a man of exquisite mind';[39] and he refers to his book by volume and page.[40] Even more to the point is a scrap of MS. in Coleridge's hand, now in the British Museum,[41] in which are jotted down, from 'Dampier's Voyages and Adventures,' a curious collection of observations upon snakes. And water-snakes, explicitly so called, play freely (and even 'rear') through Dampier's narrative: 'In the Sea we saw . . . Abundance of Water Snakes of several Sorts and Sizes'; 'This Day we saw two Water Snakes'; 'The Snake swam away . . . very fast, keeping his Head above Water.'[42] There is, moreover, another absorbing book which I cannot say with certainty that Coleridge read: *The History of the Bucaniers of America*. It would at least be very strange indeed, had it escaped him. However that may be, it is worthy of note that in Basil Ringrose's famous narration, in the *History*, of 'The dangerous Voyage, and bold Attempts of Capt. Bartholomew Sharp, and others, in the South Sea,'[43] the water-snakes, like Coleridge's, are many-coloured: 'As we sailed we saw Multitudes of Grampusses every Day; as also Water-Snakes of divers Colours'; 'We saw likewise multitudes of Fish . . . Also Water-Snakes of divers Colours.'[44]

Here, then, is a series of passages which might have been devised by an ingenious psychologist expressly to illustrate the association of ideas—that, and the resultant interlocking of originally quite distinct impressions into one. Far, however, from being a *tour de force* of expert fabrication, it contains on the contrary, I think, the key to the genesis not only of the two remarkable stanzas before us, but also of the poem as a whole. And it may be that its reach is wider still. But that is to run ahead of the story, and meantime our miscellany of marine fauna is even yet not quite complete.

For there was another curious volume over which Coleridge diligently pored. It did not get into the Note Book, but it furnished 'The Destiny of Nations' with a formidable *chevaux de frise* of notes. Leemius *De Lapponibus*—Norwegian and Latin in parallel columns—was precisely the sort of book in which Coleridge revelled, and both footnotes and text of 'The Destiny of Nations' demonstrate the thoroughgoing application with which its contents were absorbed. Now Leemius has two passages, flanked on both sides, like Bartram's sunfish, by pages to which Coleridge specifically refers, which bear upon our stanzas. The first is a description of the dolphin, which, '*playing in the sea (in mari ludens)*, moves curvingly in manifold circles and *coils* (in varios se vertat *gyros et spiras*), part of it being hidden by the waves, part of it *rearing* (*exserta*) above the surface of the water.'[45] A few pages later the *serpens marinus* (sea-serpent or water-snake, as one prefers) also rears from the deep: 'In the dog-days, when the sea lies unruffled by the winds, the sea-serpent is wont to emerge, *arched into all sorts of coils* (*in varias spiras sinuatus*), of which some project from the water, while the rest are hidden under it.'[46]

Now if ever two phrases (to revert to Coleridge's figure) were fitted to slide one into the other, as hook slips into eye, and grip together their respective contexts in the memory, they were Father Bourzes's phrase about his fishes '*playing in the sea*,' and Leemius's identical '*in mari lndens*.' Even Boccaccio's 'sposa di Nin,' which hooked into Dante's 'Nino, e fu sua sposa' in Chaucer's memory, and drew along with it Dante's context too, was not so apt a link. And in the context which Leemius's phrase would carry with it into Coleridge's storehouse was the increment of the *coiling* movement through the sea. And so, in a word (to paraphrase Saint Peter), to the luminousness of

Father Bourzes's fishes have been added, on our hypothesis, the colours of Cook's animalculæ and Bartram's bream; and to the shape which they had in Hawkins the name which they bore in Dampier; and to all these, the coiling and rearing which were the special trick of the dolphins and the *serpens marinus* in the edifying treatise *De Lapponibus*. And our already alarmingly crescent aquarium must admit, I fear, one pair of inmates more.

Coleridge, who was deeply versed in eighteenth-century poetry, must have known Falconer's 'Shipwreck.'[47] And two of the glaringly purple patches of 'The Shipwreck' are its accounts of certain dolphins and porpoises which disport themselves in a wild riot of eighteenth-century poetic diction, one hundred and forty lines apart:[48]

> But now, beneath the lofty vessel's stern,
> A shoal of sportive dolphins they discern,
> Beaming from *burnish'd* scales refulgent rays,
> Till all the *glowing* ocean seems to blaze:
> *In curling wreaths* they wanton on the tide,
> Now bound aloft, now downward swiftly glide;
> Awhile beneath the waves their *tracks* remain,
> And burn in silver streams along the liquid plain . . .
>
> Now to the north, from Afric's burning shore,
> A troop of porpoises their course explore;
> In curling wreaths they gambol on the tide,

> Now bound aloft, now down the billows glide:
> Their tracks awhile the *hoary* waves retain,
> That *burn* in sparkling trails along the main.

What place, if any, do Falconer's dolphins and porpoises hold among the spoils of the multitudinous seas which Coleridge's net has dragged?

The links, at least, are once more plainly there. Falconer and Father Bourzes agree in their reference to the playing fishes' phosphorescent wake as 'tracks'; Falconer and Leemius have in common the theme of playing dolphins; Falconer and Captain Cook both mention 'burnished' objects in a 'glowing' sea. Moreover, Falconer's 'curling wreaths' is good eighteenth-century jargon for 'gyros et spiras' in Leemius. The hooks and eyes between Falconer on the one hand, and Father Bourzes and Captain Cook and Leemius on the other, are clear and definite. Cross-reminiscences of some sort, once given Coleridge's memory and his known acquaintance with the books, are at least a safe hypothesis, and once again, over and above the common elements, there is in 'The Shipwreck' an increment of large significance.

For beneath the preposterous verbal toggery of the lines is a crude and mechanical symmetry, which, through its very obtrusiveness, links the two pictures powerfully together:

In curling wreaths they wanton *on the tide,*
Now bound aloft, now downward swiftly *glide;*
Awhile beneath the waves *their tracks* remain,
And burn in silver streams *along* the liquid plain . . .

In curling wreaths they gambol *on the tide,*
Now bound aloft, now down the billows *glide:*
Their tracks awhile the hoary waves retain,
That burn in sparkling trails *along* the main.

There, without much question, Coleridge found one of the hints on which he wrought the exquisitely balanced structure of the pair of stanzas which are now our theme—that lovely mould into which he poured his wealth of metamorphosed images:

Beyond the shadow of the ship,
I watched the water-snakes:
They moved in tracks of shining white,
And when they reared, the elfish light
Fell off in hoary* flakes.

Within the shadow of the ship
I watched their rich attire:
Blue, glossy green, and velvet black,
They coiled and swam; and every track
Was a flash of golden fire.[49]

But more than a recollection of 'The Shipwreck' entered into that poised symmetry. For in the strange genesis of the huge shadow of the ship a subtler alchemy than Falconer's was at work. But that is a story to be later told.

Those, then, at last, are the raw materials. The result is all of them and none of them—it is a new creation. The fishes which Father Bourzes saw in tropical seas and Bartram in a little lake in Florida, and the luminous blue and green protozoa which Captain Cook observed in the Pacific, and the many-hued, ribbon-like creatures that Sir Richard Hawkins marvelled at off the Azores, and Dampier's water-snakes in the South Seas, and Leemius's coiling, rearing marine serpents of the North, and Falconer's gambolling porpoises and dolphins—all of them or some of them—have leaped together like scattered dust at the trumpet of the resurrection, and been fused by a flash of imaginative vision into the elfin creatures of a hoary deep that never was and that will always be. The shaping spirit of imagination must have materials on which to work, and a memory steeped in travel-lore was this time the reservoir on which it drew.

IV

But something had obviously been happening beneath the surface of the reservoir. And so—waiving for the moment, but only for the moment, the exquisite and finished art which gives to the picture as a whole its balanced unity, and holding rigidly to the conception of the creatures which move playing through it—I am going to pursue a little farther what Conan Doyle would call 'The Adventure of the Water-Snakes.' In what fashion did their heterogeneous elements merge into organic unity? How, in a word, did the creatures get, through recollections of scattered bits from possibly seven books, into that immortal sea in which their shining simulacra coiled and swam? Did Coleridge have the seven books before him, or even definitely in his mind, when the stanzas were composed? Did he 'get up' his facts, and then deftly or laboriously dovetail them together? Or were there subtler processes involved?

The simple and obvious answer seems, at first blush, to be this: Coleridge, with that 'tenacious and systematizing memory' of his, consciously recalled, through their strong associative links, the various details which he had read, and no less consciously combined them. Some one of them, that is—the luminous fishes, the multicoloured animalculæ, the dolphins (who can say which?)—touched off the train of associations, and simultaneously or in succession the crowd of images rose as separate and distinct impressions consciously before him, this to be stripped of its colour, that of its shape, the other of its phosphorescent light, for incorporation in the new conception of the water-snakes. Now without much question we may at once assume, I think, that conscious recollection and recombination played their part in the complex operations which brought the diverse elements together. But the assumption that conscious reconstruction was *all* that was involved leaves us with a deeper mystery than ever on our hands. The explanation is more baffling than the fact explained. The discrepancy between the most consummate craftsmanship in joinery and the magical blending of sheer light and colour into moving forms remains, on the hypothesis of conscious combinings alone, inexplicable. For the creatures of the calm are not fishes + snakes + animalculæ, as the chimæra was lion + dragon + goat. No mere combination of entities themselves unchanged explains the facts. Whatever else x may be, the thing it is *not* is $a + b + c$. On the contrary, the unity that has somehow come about is as integral as the union of the seven colours which blend in a beam of white light. You may break up the beam into its spectrum, as we have resolved our shapes of light into their elements. The result in either case is the same: the enhancement of the miracle of their unity. I do not believe that any conscious piecing together, however dexterous, of remembered fragments could conceivably have *alone* wrought the radiant forms which the Mariner saw. The question still persists: How were the latent images raised up? And with what body did they come? That is the question which I mean to try to answer.

It is a venturesome quest on which we are embarking, as I know full well, for we shall have to sound our dim and perilous way through chartless tracts. And if I seem to trench with some temerity on ground which is not my own, I can only plead, in extenuation of a rashness regarding which I cherish no illusions, that my facts leave me no alternative. There they are, and they cry out for a synthesis. And no synthesis based on mere mnemonic joiners-work will, in my judgment, serve. The strange blendings and fusings which have taken place all point towards one conclusion, and that conclusion involves operations which are still obscure. I am not a trained psychologist, and I am fully aware that in using, as I shall sometimes have to use it, the term 'unconscious,' I am playing with fire. But I cannot ignore the testimony of Coleridge himself and (as we shall see) of Dryden and Goethe and Henry James and Henri Poincaré—all practised and acute observers of their mental processes. The term, then, as I shall employ it, assumes the existence of what Coleridge called 'the twilight realms of consciousness';[50] it assumes that 'in that shadowy half-being' (as he once put it), 'that state of nascent existence in the twilight of imagination and just on the vestibule of consciousness,' ideas and images exist;[51] it assumes (and again I am quoting Coleridge) a 'confluence of our recollections,' through which 'we establish a centre, as it were, a sort of nucleus in [this] reservoir of the soul.'[52] All that, I take it, however phrased, is reasonably sure ground. For the rest, I am simply putting tentatively on their inferences observed phenomena. My essay, then, at the interpretation of a group of facts which have never before been reckoned with must be regarded for the moment frankly as a working hypothesis, in support of which, I hope, evidence will accumulate as we go on. We are confronted, in fine, by a problem in which two fields meet. Regarding the facts themselves I can speak with some assurance; their interpretation involves, in part, the provisional conclusions of a layman. But that once freely granted, I must nevertheless insist that only on some such grounds as I shall indicate are the facts as they stand susceptible of any but the most crassly mechanical explanation.

Above all (to get the lumber of provisos out of the way at once), it may not be forgotten that we are disengaging the strands of an extremely complex web. It is, however, one of the limitations of our finite minds that we are compelled to consider in succession things which in reality are simultaneous. That renders inevitable at any given stage of a discussion the projection into sharp relief of a single aspect of the subject, to the seeming exclusion of others no less significant. It is not a gratuitous precaution, therefore, to repeat that in the paragraphs which follow the whole story is not being told at once.

'This,' as the Friar remarked with justice to the Wife of Bath, 'is a long preamble of a tale.' And so, without more ado, I shall proceed to state what seems to me to be the probable *modus operandi* through which a clutter of remembered details got themselves metamorphosed into the sheerest poetry.

It is in a notable discussion of nightmares that Coleridge makes an observation which concerns us nearly. He is explaining how a limb deadened by some interruption in the circulation 'transmits double touch as single touch, to which,' he goes on, '*the imagination . . . the true inward creatrix, instantly out of the chaos of elements or shattered fragments of memory, puts together some form to fit it.*'[53] That comment bares, as it happens, the secret springs of 'Kubla Khan.' Waiving for the moment its dream psychology, it is no less relevant to those workings of the imagination which underlie 'The Ancient Mariner.' And it might have been written as a pregnant comment on the genesis of the stanzas now before us. The Note Book gave us the clue to the facts; the observation which I have just quoted offers the key, I think, to their interpretation. 'The chaos of elements or shattered fragments of memory' is sufficiently exhibited in the farrago of marine phenomena dispersed through the seven books. How, under the impulse of the inward creatrix, the imagination, have they taken form? Let us set out, at least, from what is measurably familiar ground.

Most of us have had the experience of looking up what we recalled as a vivid, even radiant passage which we have sometime read, and of finding instead a commonplace, colourless thing. What has happened? Something, I think, which bears in an odd fashion on the processes which, through a permissible analogy, we call creative. One of the most significant phrases which I know is that in which Henry James rather casually tells how he took the original suggestion for the plot of *The American*, and, as he says, 'dropped it for the time into the deep well of unconscious cerebration.'[54] Now that procedure,

I take it, is what has done the business in the matter of the dull original of our glorified recollection. Into that same deep well has dropped, without an inkling of its disappearance, the thing which we once read, and it has undergone strange transformation there. It has merged insensibly, in hues and outline, with others of the myriad denizens of that mysterious deep, and what we think we have remembered we have actually, in large degree, unconsciously created. Let me make clearer what I mean.

Few of us nowadays, I fear, smile over the lively pages of the *Autocrat of the Breakfast Table*. Once everybody did, and here is one of the Autocrat's remarks: 'Put an idea into your intelligence and leave it there an hour, a day, a year, without ever having occasion to refer to it. When, at last, you return to it, you do not find it as it was when acquired. It has domiciliated itself, so to speak,—become at home,—entered into relations with your other thoughts, and integrated itself with the whole fabric of the mind.'[55] I have quoted that not particularly memorable dictum for an ulterior end, for it so happens that this very passage offers a curious and suggestive case in point. It is now, as I write, just thirty years, to judge from the date on the flyleaf of my copy of the *Autocrat*, since I first read the remark in question, and I have not, I am sure, come back to it since. It flashed on my memory, none the less, as I was trying to put this difficult business into words. But it came back to me in so striking a configuration that when I looked it up I could barely believe my eyes. For what I thought I had remembered was no matter-of-fact statement such as stood unmistakably on the printed page in the words I have just quoted. What I recalled (or thought I had recalled) had been cast in a vividly figurative form—the figure of something germinating and expanding, dimly and occultly, with white and spreading tentacles, like the plant life which sprouts beneath a stone, or burgeons in the obscure depths of a pool. And that was not on the page before my eyes at all; it was, so to speak, a creature of the well. But it was a creature, as I soon discovered on reading farther, which had had associations in the well. For in another passage, elsewhere in the book, in an entirely different context, the Autocrat *had* used the figure of the uncanny life which breeds beneath a stone,[56] and far below the surface of my consciousness the two had undergone amalgamation. And the result was neither the Autocrat's nor mine. It was, despite its utter triviality, a veritable birth of the subliminal deep.

Now that, to compare small things with great, is a process which, it would seem, goes on with peculiar intensity in a poet's mind, and which in Coleridge's case apparently went on incessantly. One after another vivid bits from what *he* read dropped into that deep well. And there, below the level of conscious mental processes, they set up their obscure and powerful reactions. Up above, on the stream of consciousness (which is all that we commonly take into account) they had floated separate and remote; here in the well they lived a strangely intimate and simultaneous life. I am speaking in parables, I know, for there seems to be no other way; but the thing itself, however phrased, is, I believe, in its essentials, true. Facts which sank at intervals out of conscious recollection drew together beneath the surface through almost chemical affinities of common elements, as my trivial fragments from *The Autocrat* swam together and coalesced. And there in Coleridge's unconscious mind, while his consciousness was busy with the toothache, or Hartley's infant ills, or pleasant strollings with the Wordsworths between Nether Stowey and Alfoxden, or what is dreamt in this or that philosophy—there in the dark moved the phantasms of the fishes and animalculæ and serpentine forms of his vicarious voyagings, thrusting out tentacles of association, and interweaving beyond disengagement. Father Bourzes's playing fishes 'made a kind of artificial Fire in the Water'; Captain Cook's protozoa 'in the dark . . . had a faint appearance of glowing fire.' And about the common element of fire the other traits of fish and animalculæ alike converged, and blended into a *tertium quid* endowed with the qualities of both. But just as inevitably another something gravitated into the curious complex of associations which was dimly assuming form. Light that simulated fire had drawn the phosphorescent fishes and the shining animalculæ together. But the animalculæ, as Captain Cook (and Coleridge through his eyes) had seen them in the Pacific calm, were white, and blue, and green with a burnished gloss in a slimy sea. And now, denizened through a page of Purchas in the same glimmering tract, were Hawkins's snake-like creatures of the calm, with their rich attire of green, yellow, black, and white, in the waters of a rotting sea. Colour and calm and a corrupted sea were affinities far too potent to resist, and the fragment from Purchas melted into those from Father Bourzes and Captain Cook, and (through the blue, and green, and velvet black) from William Bartram too. Leemius had links with Father Bourzes, as we have seen, and Falconer with both. And as a result of the confluence (I dare not say of all, but certainly of some) the shining, playing, many-hued Something which was vaguely taking shape received a definite snake-like form and coiling movement, and through the further and inevitable link with Dampier's water-snakes acquired a name. The creatures of the great deep had become the new creation of a yet deeper deep. And when the flash of inspiration at last came—that leap of association which, like the angel in the Gospel, stirred to momentary potency the waters of the pool—it was neither fish, nor animalculæ, nor snake-like things, nor veritable water-snakes, but these radiant creatures of the subliminal abyss that sported on the face of a sea lit by a moon which had risen from the same abyss.

> They moved in tracks of shining white,
> And when they reared, the elfish light
> Fell off in hoary flakes. . . .
>
> Blue, glossy green, and velvet black,
> They coil'd and swam; and every track
> Was a flash of golden fire.

No mortal eye had ever seen them actually coil and swim—certainly neither Father Bourzes, nor Cook, nor Hawkins, nor Bartram, nor Dampier—in the waters of any earthly sea. They were the birth of that creative deep, which is peculiar to the poet only in degree.

Now I suspect that precisely in that difference in degree lies one of the specific differentiæ of genius. The 'deep well of unconscious cerebration' underlies your consciousness and mine, but in the case of genius its waters are possessed of a peculiar potency. Images and impressions converge and blend even in the sleepy drench of our forgetful pools. But the inscrutable energy of genius which we call creative owes its secret virtue at least in part to the enhanced and almost incredible facility with which in the wonder-working depths of the unconscious the fragments which sink incessantly below the surface fuse and assimilate and coalesce. The depths are peopled to start out with (and this is fundamental) by conscious intellectual activity, keyed, it may be, as in Coleridge's intense and exigent reading, to the highest pitch. Moreover (and this crucially important consideration will occupy us in due time), it is again conscious energy, now of another and loftier type, which later drags the deeps for their submerged treasure, and moulds the bewildering chaos into unity. But interposed between consciousness and consciousness is the well. And therein resides the peculiar significance of such a phantasmagoria as lies before us in the Note Book, the seemingly meaningless jumble of which we have tried to grasp.

For the more multifarious, even the more incongruous and chaotic the welter, the freer play it offers to those darting and prehensile filaments of association which reach out in all directions through the mass. The more kaleidoscopic the chaos of shattered fragments of memory, the more innumerable the reflections and refractions between the shifting elements. And in Coleridge's case there was assuredly God's plenty! Nightingales, and snake-birds, and footless birds of Paradise; the fauna of polar and of tropic seas, and of strange inland pools and subterranean streams; the dæmons of the elements, stars and their angel guardians; maniacs and murderers and mutineers; shipwrecks and gibbets; dew-drops and dunghills and diamonds and lichened stones; haloes over frosty meadows, and rainbows in the spray, and the ice-blink, and the luminous wake of ships; Jonah, and Tobit, and Nimrod, and Ham, and the uncanny legends of the antediluvian world—all these and a thousand others, one after one, sank below the level of

Coleridge's conscious mental processes, and disappeared. But in that nebulous tract into which they slipped they caught from each other hues unborrowed from the sun, and like the two serpent-forms which Dante saw in the *Inferno* their very shapes transfused. How indeed could it possibly be otherwise? Propinquity does business merrily in the unconscious world, as well as up in the realms of light, and in both strange couples mate. Dew-drops blended together on the bosom of a new-blown rose, and Mars rising over a gibbet; diamond quarries in some Golconda of faëryland, and Tartarean forests of Upas trees—such conceptions could not coexist in a region charged with secret currents, and remain unmodified. 'That synthetic and magical power . . . the imagination' (it is Coleridge's own words that I am using) must perforce 'blend and (as it were) *fuse* them, each into each.'[57] Mars willy-nilly must shed a baleful light upon the dew-drop, and the diamonds of faëryland blink dull in the shade of Upas trees. Or else the Tartarean forests must glimmer with faint rays from faëry Golcondas, and Mars be reflected, mild and luminous, in a drop of dew. Or else both processes at once and all together must go on, until, as in 'The Ancient Mariner,' and 'Christabel,' and 'Kubla Khan,' beauty insensibly takes on something elfin and uncanny, and the fantastic and the sinister an unearthly radiance. The elfish light—to return once more to our water-snakes—the elfish light which as they reared fell off in hoary flakes was borrowed from neither Father Bourzes, nor Captain Cook, nor Falconer, nor any single record of actuality on land or sea. In a sense which the disclosures of the Note Book help to make intelligible, it was caught from that 'swimming phantom light,' born of the commingled phantasms of strange moons, and phosphorescent seas, and the ghostly shine of polar skies, which was the very atmosphere of those secret tracts in which Coleridge's creative energy wrought. And in that phantom light 'The Ancient Mariner,' and 'Christable,' and 'Kubla Khan' are steeped.

If all that should wear, as it may, the aspect of a fabric woven of cobwebs from a Romantic poet's brain, let me summon two witnesses whose intellectual stability and poise admits no such impeachment. The first is a man who was, by common consent, the most eminent scientist of his generation, Henri Poincaré. In that remarkable chapter on 'Mathematical Discovery' ('L' invention mathématique') in *Science et Méthode*[58] Poincaré is dealing, on the basis of personal experience, with the part which the subliminal ego (the 'moi inconscient') plays in mathematical discovery, and with the relation of that unconscious element to conscious intellectual activities before and after. That, it is clear, is precisely the problem, *mutatis mutandis*, which has just confronted us. It so happens that I first read Poincaré's chapter fifteen months after the preceding paragraphs were written as they stand, and the mutual corroboration of his analysis and mine has the added weight which attaches to independent observations. The illuminating records of Poincaré's actual experience—his attempt to show 'what happens in the very soul of a mathematician'—must be passed over here. *Science and Method* is happily not an inaccessible book. There is space for a cento of excerpts only, disclosing the bare drift of a lucid and cogently reasoned argument—an argument which for us has double force for the very reason that the 'combinations' of which it treats belong not to poetry but to mathematics. Poincaré is discussing 'these appearances of sudden illumination, [which are] obvious indications of a long course of previous unconscious work.' And he proceeds:

> This unconscious work . . . is not possible, or in any case not fruitful, *unless it is first preceded and then followed by a period of conscious work.*[59] . . .
>
> It is certain that the combinations which present themselves to the mind in a kind of sudden illumination after a somewhat prolonged period of unconscious work are generally useful and fruitful combinations, which appear to be the result of a preliminary sifting. . . . This, too, is most mysterious. How can we explain the fact that, of the thousand products of our unconscious activity, some are invited to cross the threshold, while others remain outside? Is it mere chance that gives them this privilege? Evidently not. . . . [60]
>
> Perhaps we must look for the explanation in that period of preliminary conscious work which always precedes

all fruitful unconscious work. If I may be permitted a crude comparison, let us represent the future elements of our combinations as *something resembling Epicurus's hooked atoms* (*atomes crochus*). When the mind is in complete repose these atoms are immovable; they are, so to speak, attached to the wall. This complete repose may continue indefinitely without the atoms meeting, and, consequently, without the possibility of the formation of any combination.

On the other hand, during a period of apparent repose, but of unconscious work, some of them are detached from the wall and set in motion. *They plough through space in all directions, like a swarm of gnats, for instance, or, if we prefer a more learned comparison, like the gaseous molecules in the kinetic theory of gases. Their mutual collisions may then produce new combinations. . . .* [61]

All that we can hope from these inspirations, which are the fruits of unconscious work, is to obtain points of departure for [our] calculations. As for the calculations themselves, *they must be made in the second period of conscious work which follows the inspiration. . . . They demand discipline, attention, will, and consequently consciousness.* In the subliminal ego, on the contrary, there reigns what I would call liberty, if one could give this name to the mere absence of discipline and to disorder born of chance. *Only, this very disorder permits of unexpected couplings.*[62]

There once more, between consciousness and consciousness, is the Well. And there in the Well goes on the same incessant activity of combination and amalgamation which, on other evidence, we have postulated for the poet's mind. The bearing of Poincaré's observations and conclusions on our essay at the solution of a kindred problem needs no comment.

The other witness I shall summon is one of the sanest intellects that ever exercised itself in verse. And the testimony which I shall quote, itself a superbly imaginative conception, is, like the mathematician's, a document of first-hand experience. 'This worthless Present,' wrote John Dryden of *The Rival Ladies* to the Earl of Orrery, 'was design'd you, long before it was a Play; *when it only was a confus'd Mass of Thoughts, tumbling over one another in the Dark:* When the Fancy was yet in its first Work, *moving the Sleeping Images of things towards the Light,* there to be distinguish'd, and then either chosen or rejected by the Judgment.'[63] That is an incomparable picture in little of the creative process, and John Dryden was no sentimentalist.

Our concern so far, accordingly, has been with that process at its inception—with poems long before they were poems at all; with the confused and chaotic welter of their elements tumbling over one another in the dark, before the imagination entered on its initial task of moving the sleeping images towards the light, or achieved its final triumph in their lucid ordering. Coleridge has a formulation of the process too. The imagination 'dissolves, diffuses, dissipates, in order to re-create'—as we have watched the tangible realities of known and charted seas waver, and disintegrate, and dissolve, like the evolutions of the mist, to reassemble into the luminous apparitions of insubstantial deeps. But there was moving among the reassembling images a conscious power whose operations we have yet to see.

---

*It did not rob this modest *dénouement* of a pleasant thrill of interest to observe that the copy of the *Opticks* which I was reading had been presented to the Harvard College Library by Benjamin Franklin himself. For some hint of the peculiar fascination which lighted candles always exercised on Coleridge, I must refer the reader to the Notes.[10]

*Out of Falconer's stilted phraseology Coleridge seized upon one felicitous word.

CHAPTER IV

THE SHAPING SPIRIT

ON a moonlit sea, spread white and glistening like frost, lies printed the huge shadow of a ship. The picture is as sharply etched as its beauty is strangely and powerfully suggestive:

> Her beams bemocked the sultry main,
> Like April hoar-frost spread;
> *But where the ship's huge shadow lay,*
> The charmèd water burnt always
> A still and awful red.[1]

Within the black shadow, and without it in the white expanse, move the creatures of the great calm. And their hueless coruscation in the moonlight is set off against their rich and particoloured radiance in the shadow through the exquisite structural balance of two stanzas which answer to each other, phrase upon phrase, like an antiphon:

Beyond the shadow of the ship,
I watched the water-snakes:
They moved in tracks of shining white,
And when they reared, the elfish light
Fell off in hoary flakes.

Within the shadow of the ship
I watched their rich attire:
Blue, glossy green, and velvet black,
They coiled and swam; and every track
Was a flash of golden fire.[2]

The magical symmetry of the pair of stanzas unfolds from the initial concept of the ship's huge shadow with the inevitableness of a leaf expanding from a bud. Somehow, upon the chaos of images which thronged up from their sleep, a luminous unity has been imposed. And a new element enters into our synthesis.

For the subliminal world in which we have been moving is not, in the highest sense, architectonic at all. In it impressions disintegrate, and move together, and coalesce, as we have seen, in endless flux.

That which is firme doth flit and fall away,
And that is flitting doth abide and stay.[3]

But that is only half the story. For precisely that flux, in its dissipations and dissolvings, constitutes the stuff upon which the imagination exerts its integrating power. And to that supreme creative exercise the unconscious processes, creative in their own way though they be, are, once for all, subordinate.

But even that is not quite the whole story. The subliminal blendings hold a subordinate place, it is true, but they stand none the less in vital and indivisible union with the more exalted power. The web of creation, like the skein of life, is of a mingled yarn, conscious and unconscious inextricably inter-twined. We are bound to *distinguish* (if we are ever to understand) between the constituents of any state or process worthy to be called a whole. We *divide* at the cost of our saving hold on integrality. The caution is Coleridge's,[4] not mine; and imaginative creation, if we have learned anything at all from the strange phantasmagoria which we are studying, is one process, and not two—an infinitely complex process, in which conscious and unconscious jointly operate. There is beyond gainsaying the deep Well, with its chaos of fortuitously blending images; but there is likewise the Vision which sees shining in and through the chaos the potential lines of Form, and with the Vision the controlling Will, which gives to that potential beauty actuality. And the triad of stanzas now before us, in which the shaping spirit has imposed upon the swirling dance of reminiscences a limpid clarity of form, is an epitome of all which this implies. For in that strange confluence of plastic visual impressions already lay, with little doubt, the germs of the design.

I

That the crude yet telling parallelism of Falconer's stilted lines about his porpoises and dolphins lent to the balanced loveliness of Coleridge's stanzas at least some fleeting hint of form, I think there is a good reason to suppose. But to grant that leaves a far more interesting question quite unanswered. How did it come about, in the stanza of the moon-mocked sea, that the charmèd water burnt 'where *the ship's huge shadow* lay'—that monstrous cantle of night flung down upon the April hoarfrost of the sea in such fashion that shining white, and still and awful red, and golden fire all fall into place, as in some magical canvas, about its blackness? Whence came, in a word, the three-fold, spell-like iteration of 'the shadow of the ship'? That it came through a visual image in Coleridge's mind we may be reasonably sure. And that brings us face to face with a paradox.

For two things must never be lost sight of as we proceed. It was six months after 'The Ancient Mariner' was finished that Coleridge for the first time went down to the sea in a ship, and then only to sail from Yarmouth to Cuxhaven.[5] He is describing things which he could have known from books or tales of the sea alone. *He had seen none of them.* That is the first fact to hold steadily in mind. The second is that *he had seen them all.* And in that paradox lies the clue to more than one of our enigmas.

For when Coleridge's imagination was working at high

tension, actual pictures seem to have passed before it with the preternatural vividness of those after-images which the eighteenth century loved to call 'ocular spectra'—not spectra as we to-day understand the term, but impressions retained on the retina of the eye with an independent luminousness and precision after the passing of some flash of vision, as a window which has leaped at night into dazzling configuration in a blaze of lightning hangs printed for an instant in sharp definition upon the dark. In the act of metrical composition (so Coleridge wrote Sir Humphry Davy) 'voluntary ideas were every minute passing, *more or less transformed into vivid spectra*.' 'While I wrote that last sentence,' he declares in a letter to Southey, 'I had a vivid recollection, *indeed an ocular spectrum* of our room in College Street, a curious instance of association.' 'I bent down to pick something from the ground,' he wrote Godwin in 1801, '[and]. . . as I bent my head there came a *distinct, vivid spectrum* upon my eyes; it was one little picture—a rock, with birches and ferns on it, a cottage backed by it, and a small stream. Were I a painter I would give an outward existence to this, but it will always live in my memory.'[6] Ben Jonson, in those racy conversations with Drummond of Hawthornden, told his host that 'he heth consumed a whole night in lying looking to his great toe, about which he hath seen Tartars and Turks, Romans and Carthaginians feight in his imagination.'[7] We of the workaday brains are apt to forget that there is for the poet (to use a modern painter's phrase) 'a tense state of concentration, when the brain becomes luminous.'[8] And in that intense luminousness of Coleridge's brain scraps of remembered fact or lines on the printed page flashed, as he says, 'into vivid spectra,' and words sprang into pictures as he read or wrote. Now let us return to our stanzas. What apposite images, once seen to live always in his memory, can we trace?

The answer to that question is best come at by going round Robin Hood's barn and asking another. What pictures do we know to have been, through his reading, in Coleridge's mind, and to have been there in conjunction with the sleeping images which underlie these very stanzas? Let us go back once more to the Note Book. Coleridge's jotting from Father Bourzes's letter in the *Philosophical Transactions* reads as follows:

> Sun paints rainbows on the *vast* waves *during snow storms* in the Cape.[9]

And I shall set down once more for comparison Father Bourzes's text, italicizing for a reason which will soon appear:

> I shall add one Observation more concerning *Marine Rainbows*, which I observed after a great Tempest off of the Cape of Good Hope. The Sea was then very much tossed, and *the Wind carrying off the Tops of the Waves made a kind of Rain*, in which *the Rays of the Sun* painted the Colours of a Rain-bow. . . . In the Marine Iris we could distinguish only *two Colours, viz. a dark Yellow on that side next the Sun*, and a *pale* Green on the opposite

side.[10]

Now there is still another question which I asked in the last chapter and for the moment left unanswered, but which it is essential that we answer now. Where did Coleridge get the *snow* storms in the Note Book? There is not a trace of snow in Father Bourzes's letter to account for it. Let us, however, look for a moment at another sea-bow.

It is in a delightful book which Coleridge, as we shall see, quite certainly knew,[11] Frederick Martens's *Voyage into Spitzbergen and Greenland:*

> I must not forget, that we see in these falling Needles *a Bow like a Rain-bow* of *two colours*, white and *a pale yellow, like the Sun*, reflected by the dark Shadows of the Clouds.
>
> After this I proceed to the Description of an other Bow, which I call a *Sea-bow*. This is seen when the Sun shines clear and bright, not in *the great Waves, but in the Atmosphere of the Sea-water, which the Wind blows up, and which looks like a Fog.*[12]

One might search long and patiently, and search in vain, for two passages more opulently furnished forth with 'hooks and eyes of the memory' than the accounts of those two sea-bows, Frederick Martens's and Father Bourzes's. The striking similarity of the descriptions of the spindrift; the identical detail of the 'two colours'; the recurrence of 'pale' and of 'yellow,' in each case in association with the sun—the correspondences are little less than startling. Our adventurings among the 'hooked atoms' of the water-snakes have given us some inkling of the bent towards conjunction latent in passages of high visualizing power which are equipped with just such links. Did these two visual images actually blend in Coleridge's memory, as Boccaccio's stanza and Dante's line blended in Chaucer's list?[13] And now we come back to the riddle of the interpolated snow.

For the lines in Martens about the 'falling Needles,' out of which the description of the sea-bow springs, are actually a charmingly characteristic picture of the needles of the *snow:*

> Concerning the Meteors generated in the Air, I observed that the *Rime* fell down in the shape of *small Needles of Snow* into the Sea, and covered it as if it was sprinkled all over with Dust: *these small Needles* increased more and more, and lay as they fell cross one over the other, and looked very like a Cobweb. . . [so] that the Sea seemed covered by them, as with a Skin, or a tender Ice. . . . This hapneth in clear Sun-shine and intense cold weather, and it falleth down as the Dew doth with us at Night invisibly, in dull weather . . . but you see it plainly, if you look when the Sun shines towards a shady place; for then it sparkles as bright as Diamonds; shews like the Atoms in Sun-shine. . . . Sometimes we see in our

> Country, something a little like *these small Needles, which is what we call Rime*, and falleth from the Trees in Atoms like Dust. *This is small Snow. . . . These Needles* are not the Exhalation of Vapour that uses in cold Weather, *to stick to the Hair of Men* and Beasts. I must not forget, that we see in these falling Needles a Bow, etc.[14]

There is, moreover, evidence that Coleridge had had quite recently these very needles of the frost (which is also snow) in mind. For in the fourth act of *Osorio*, finished just the month before 'The Ancient Mariner' was begun, occur these two striking lines:

> *Or if it drizzled needle-points of frost*
> Upon a feverish head made suddenly bald.[15]

That is pretty clearly Frederick Martens's picture, fleetingly recalled as Coleridge wrote.

Martens's bow in the falling needles, then, is a bow in 'Needles of *Snow*' ('This is small *Snow*,' he goes on a moment later), and the waves from which the wind blows up the spindrift are '*great* Waves.' And with only a page between there follows a graphic account, enhanced by a full page of pictured crystals, of the treasures of the snow—flakes 'like unto small Roses, Needles and small Corns,' or again, 'like Stars, with many points like the Leaves of Ferne,' or yet again, 'all sorts of Snow, both starry and of other shapes.'[16] Moreover, a few pages earlier are 'Waves. . . *as bigg as Mountains*,' and from them '*in a hard storm* the froth of the Sea drives like dust, and looketh as when the wind driveth the *Snow* along upon the Ice.'[17] Snow and waves like mountains are the setting of Martens's bow. And the evidence makes clear beyond reasonable doubt what happened. When Coleridge scrawled (I suspect from memory) his jotting in the Note Book, there coalesced with the picture called up by Father Bourzes the powerfully linked imagery from Frederick Martens already in his mind, and the '*vast* waves during *snow* storms' slipped into the one reminiscence from the other. The brief entry in the Note Book is an epitome of Coleridge's imaginative processes, and it embodies once more that inveterately amalgamating bent of his mind which was a prime factor of his genius.

There is a curious dream of Coleridge's—he got up instantly at ten minutes past five in the morning to write it down!—which is relevant here. 'Dozing, dreamt of Hartley as at his christening,—how, as he was asked who redeemed him, and was to say "God the Son," he went on humming and hawing in one hum and haw (like a boy who knows a thing and will not make the effort to recollect) so as to irritate me greatly. Awakening gradually, I was able completely to detect that it was the ticking of my watch, which lay in the pen-place in my desk, on the round table close by my ear, and which . . . had fretted on my ears. I caught the fact while Hartley's face and moving lips were yet before my eyes, *and his hum and haw and the ticking of the watch were each the other*.'[18] In some such dream-fashion as that, it would seem, the sea-bow off Spitzbergen and the bow in the waves off the Cape of Good Hope, beyond reasonable question, telescoped in Coleridge's memory.

II

Martens's sea-bow, then, which was linked with the frost-needles got itself interfused in Coleridge's brain with Father Bourzes's marine rainbow, which in turn was linked with the phosphorescent fishes. There *was* a picture in Coleridge's memory in close conjunction with the sleeping images which underlay these very stanzas. So much, if we accept the evidence, is clear. And no less clear is thereupon something else. The two bows, with all that appertained to them, had sunk into the deep Well. But the image of Martens's sea-bow had carried with it more than snow. For the bow was only part of a picture of singular vividness—a ship, and a shadow, and a flashing, many-hued wonder in the shadow. For Martens's description of the sea-bow continues without pause:

> Commonly we see this [Bow] before the Ship, and sometimes also behind to the Lee-ward . . . over-against the Sun, where *the Shadow of the Sail* falleth. It is not *the Shadow of the Sail*, but a Bow sheweth itself *in the Shadow of the Sail*. We see this pleasant reflexion, in the small drops of the Salt-water of several colours, like the

Rainbows in the Skies.[19]

And that is part of a picture one detail of which had already coalesced in Coleridge's memory with the 'spectrum' of another marine rainbow upon which it had exerted a curious modifying influence; while the frost-needles which were the setting of this very bow had been recalled, it seems clear, not long before to give a figure to *Osorio*. We have to do, in a word, with a cluster of images which were markedly susceptible of active recombination in Coleridge's brain.

Here, then, are the conclusions to which, link by link, our chain of inferences has led us. Father Bourzes's 'luminous Tracks [which] Fishes in swimming leave behind 'em,' together with flashing vortices of light, coexisted in the complex which was taking shape in Coleridge's mind with the marine rainbow just across the page. The marine rainbow had blended in Coleridge's memory with Martens's sea-bow. And in Martens that flying, iridescent apparition in the spindrift 'sheweth itself *in the Shadow of the Sail*.' 'It is not *the Shadow of the Sail*'—this 'pleasant reflexion' in the wind-tossed spray—but it is '*where the Shadow of the Sail falleth*.' The picture, trebly fixed by the quaint iteration, once caught is unforgettable. Now read, in light which falls from a fresh angle, the familiar lines:

But *where the ship's huge shadow lay,*
The charmèd water burnt alway
A still and awful red.

Beyond the shadow of the ship.
I watched the water-snakes:
They moved in tracks of shining white,
And when they reared, the elfish light
Fell off in hoary flakes.

Within the shadow of the ship
I watched their rich attire:
Blue, glossy green, and velvet black,
They coiled and swam; and every track
Was a flash of golden fire.

Unless all our inferences are wrong, in a chaos of teeming reminiscences the shaping spirit saw and seized upon a hint of Form, and, through a miracle of conscious art, out of chaos itself has been moulded a radiant and ordered whole.

III

Goethe is speaking in the *Gespräche*, as he so often spoke, of the dæmonic—that inscrutable power through which, without our will, our winged thoughts, our aperçus, stand unannounced before us, like veritable children of God ('reine Kinder Gottes'),[20] and cry out, 'Here we are!'[21] Call the *Dämonisches*, if you will, the Spirit of the Well, and we shall not be far, I think, from the reality. But, Goethe insists, the dæmonic is not the only factor in creation. 'In such matters,' he goes on, 'it is much as in the game the French call Codille, in which the fall of the dice is to a large degree decisive, but in which it is left to the skill of the player to meet the situation thus created.'[22] That is strangely like Epictetus's answer to the question how one is to deal with the same two elements of chance and volition in *life*. 'If he take example,' says Epictetus, 'of dice players. The numbers are indifferent, the dice are indifferent. How can I tell what may be thrown up? *But carefully and skilfully to make use of what is thrown*, that is where my proper business begins.'[23]

Well, the subliminal ego doubtless deals the cards, as the throng of sleeping images, at this call or that, move toward the light. But the fall of the cards accepted, the shaping spirit of imagination conceives and masterfully carries out the strategy of the game. Grant all you will to the involuntary and automatic operations of the Well—its blendings and fusings, each into each, of animalculæ, and rainbows, and luminous tracks across the sea, and all the other elements of chaos. There still remains the architectonic imagination, moving, *sua sponte*, among the scattered fragments, and discerning, latent in their confusion, the pattern of a whole. And the shadow of a sail in an old travel-book and the rude parallelism of a pair of sketches of porpoises and dolphins—themselves among the recollections tumbling over one another in the dark—may through an act of imaginative vision gather up the whole chaos into consciousness as a poised and symmetrical shape of light.

There is little need of further comment. But anyone in quest of a compendious symbol of the shaping office of the imagination may find it within the compass of those dozen lines, in their disengagement of limpid clarity and untroubled beauty from such labyrinthic and bewildering confusion as we have just been threading. And this analysis, which, if it were to be taken as a dissection of poetry for the mere sake of laying bare its 'sources,' might fitly be regarded as a mournful exhibition of misdirected ingenuity, reveals, I hope, matter of worth. For the facts which it discloses provide a commentary, than which I know none more enlightening, upon that fundamental fact of mind on which we have already dwelt. Coleridge himself has once for all put it in ten pregnant words: '*the streamy nature of association, which thinking curbs and rudders.*'[24] And that 'streamy nature of the associative faculty,'[25] curbed and ruddered by the disposing imagination, is the prime instrument in the hands of genius, and its implications lie at the very roots of art.

Heaven forbid that anybody should suppose that I suppose that in all this I am 'explaining' poetry! But the incalculable power which we call Imagination, whose goal is the unfathomable something we name Beauty, is no alien visitant, but an agency which operates through faculties of universal exercise upon that streaming chaos of impressions through which we hourly move. The time for a final appraisal of results has not yet come. But we have at least seen enough to recognize that one office of the imagination is to curb and rudder the clustering associations which throng up from the nether depths of consciousness, until out of the thick of the huddle springs beauty.

CHAPTER V

THE MAGICAL SYNTHESIS

BUT beauty often springs from most unlovely origins. And the primal stuff of poetry may be as utterly remote in nature from its metamorphosed state as the constituents of Helen's flesh and blood are unlike Helen's loveliness. 'Doubtless this could not be'—and now I am following Coleridge, as he applies to the imagination words which Sir John Davies once used of the soul—

> Doubtless this could not be, but that she turns
> Bodies to spirit by sublimation strange,
> As fire converts to fire the things it burns. . . .
>
> From their gross matter she abstracts their forms,
> *And draws a kind of quintessence from things.*[1]

And that amazing discrepancy between the stuff of poetry and poetry itself, an incongruity which we shall meet a hundred times, will never meet us more impressively than now. For if ever beauty's ingredients were more effectively disguised, or if ever stranger alchemy 'glorified,' as Donne would say, 'the pregnant pot,' than in the eight lines now to come, I know not where to turn for instances.

For there are two other stanzas, with the elements of which in the Well the elements of the three which we have just been dwelling on were intimately joined. And out of one bewildering complex there arose two distinct yet closely correlated unities. One was the pellucid vision of the charmed waters across which lay the shadow of the ship; the other was a veritable *danse macabre* on the face of this same enchanted sea. And the story of the last rivals in interest the tale of the first. It stands, however, in curious relation to a grandiose but abortive project of Coleridge's earlier poetical career. And that must have a moment now.

I

'The Rime of the Ancient Mariner' is to a remarkable degree a poem of the elements. Its real protagonists are Earth, Air, Fire, and Water, in their multiform balefulness and beauty—these, and the dæmons who are their invisible inhabitants. Now Coleridge's long-pondered masterpiece, which was still *in petto* in the year which saw 'The Ancient Mariner' begun, was to have been the sequence of 'Hymns to the Sun, the Moon, and *the Elements*—six hymns,' queer adumbrations of which are scattered through the Note Book.[2] One can follow their prenatal history (which is all they ever had) in Charles Lamb's amiable solicitude during the period of their gestation.

In a letter to Coleridge of June, 1796, they are 'your embryo "hymns." ' 'When they are mature of birth,' he adds '(were I you), I should print 'em in one separate volume.'[3] In October he anxiously inquires: 'What progress do you make in your hymns?'[4] By the following February, Coleridge had apparently resolved on drastic measures, for Lamb writes: 'As you leave off writing poetry till you finish your Hymns, I suppose you print now all you have got by you.'[5] But Coleridge did not leave off writing poetry, and the Hymns remained as infants which never saw light.

They would have been, it is sadly safe to say, a monstrous birth, in spite of the happy auspices of the bubble of ice in the cave of Cashmere, and the five picturesque mathematicians in Pekin. For Coleridge, alas! jots down what I suppose we must call a few seed thoughts: 'In one of them [the Hymns] to introduce a dissection of Atheism—particularly the Godwinian System of Pride—Proud of what? an outcast of blind nature ruled by a fatal Necessity—Slave of an ideot nature! . . . In the last Hymn a sublime enumeration of all the charms or Tremendities of nature—then a bold avowal of Berkeley's System!!!!!'[6] The saving grace of humour lurking in the serried exclamation points might in the end have exorcised Coleridge's evil genius, but we cannot greatly grieve that the Hymns to the Elements remained, in his own mournful words, 'a mere dream.'[7]

I have disquieted their tenuous shades to bring them up,

because, through the ways of genius, 'The Ancient Mariner' is of their lineage. 'Your proposed Hymns,' wrote Lamb again, 'will be a fit preparatory study wherewith "to discipline your young noviciate soul." '[8] And in a sense of which Lamb was unaware, they constituted for Coleridge a preparatory study of immense significance. 'I had present to my mind the *materials*, as well as the scheme, of the Hymns,' he wrote, twenty-five years later, of 'the proud time when [he] planned them.'[9] And the intent vigilance of his reading, during that masterful period when Sun, Moon, and the Elements were still to furnish forth his *magnum opus*, was directed, as we have seen, upon every accident of light and shade, every trick of line and colour, through which the very expression on the face of sea, sky, earth, and their fiery exhalations might be seized and held. The six Hymns into which the mass of impressions was meant to crystallize joined the innumerable company of Coleridge's unexecuted projects; but the dream itself found unforeseen fulfilment, and the host of sleeping images their access to the light, in the play of elemental forces in 'The Ancient Mariner.' For Sun, Moon, Air, Fire, and Water—no longer hid in a mist of Godwinian and Berkeleyian speculations, but in visible, tangible, trenchantly concrete reality—weave the very fabric of the poem. And they weave it in visual imagery as vivid as when—Fire, Air, and Water blended into one—the sun paints rainbows in the spindrift.

Coleridge never wrote his Hymn to Water. But water—the

charmèd water that burns a still and awful red, white foam, the western wave all aflame, the hidden brook that sings all night, the dripping of dew from sagging sails, water that burns like a witch's oils, rain pouring from the cleft of a thick, black cloud, the harbour white with silent light—'water, water everywhere' is present or implied in almost every stanza of 'The Ancient Mariner.' Above all, during those tragically brief months which rise like a glorious islet of pure poetry out of the haze of the years before and after, there poured into the radiant lines which describe the water-snakes, and into the uncanny pair of stanzas towards which we are advancing, a throng of impressions which might have enriched, had not the capricious gods willed otherwise, this particular one of the six Hymns. What form (one is tempted to ask) would all this wealth of imagery have taken, had the Hymn and not 'The Ancient Mariner' been born? The question is not an idle one. For even the barest glance at a specimen or two of Coleridge's performance during the period when the Hymns were stirring in his brain will point an illuminating contrast.

To ask what the Hymn to Water would actually have been is as bootless as to inquire what song the Sirens sang. But it is not hard to guess at the influences which would have had a hand in it. For flanking in the Note Book the five Chinese mathematicians who were to play some mysterious part in the Hymn to Air, are two brief anticipatory jottings for this other Hymn. The first reads simply: 'Water—Thales—'; the second, under the heading 'Waters,' consists of two scraps of Greek (one of them from Aristotle's *Metaphysics*), which rehearse the mythological genealogy of Ocean.[10] Not only Berkeley and Godwin, then, but Thales and Aristotle too were to preside at the birth of the Hymn to Water. Coleridge the poet was still struggling, like a limed bird, in the clutches of Coleridge the metaphysician.[11] The sure flight of his imagination when no abstract speculations clogged its wings was yet to come.* And here is a passage, in which Nature and Metaphysics are strange bedfellows, from that unhappy fragment of Southey's and Coleridge's *Joan of Arc* which afterwards became 'The Destiny of Nations,' and which is contemporary with 'the proud time' of the Hymns.[12] The lines are still worse in the version which I do not quote,[13] if that is any comfort.

> But Properties are God: the naked mass
> Acts only by its inactivity.
> Here we pause humbly. Others boldlier think
> That as one body is the aggregate
> Of atoms numberless, each organiz'd;
> So by a strange and dim similitude,
> Infinite myriads of self-conscious minds
> Form one all-conscious Spirit, who directs
> With absolute ubiquity of thought
> All his component monads, that yet seem
> With various province and apt agency
> Each to pursue its own self-centering end.

Some nurse the infant diamond in the mine;
Some roll the genial juices thro' the oak;
Some drive the mutinous clouds to clash in air—[14]

and so on to the meteor-lighted Lapland skies.

Coleridge himself, when he was twenty years sadder and wiser, came back to his own and Southey's joint performance, and read it with larger, other eyes—but not, like Tennyson's happy dead, to make allowance.[16] He gave Joan herself short shrift as 'a Tom Paine in Petticoats.' He commented caustically on 'the schoolboy wretched Allegoric Machinery.' And he was 'really astonished' at 'the absence of all Bone, Muscle, and Sinew in the single Lines.' The astonishment was warranted, but the trouble was not with single lines. There is no 'blood, bone, marrow, passion, feeling' whatsoever in the metaphysical maunderings themselves. Poetry is 'swamped near to drowning,' as Carlyle said of the listener to Coleridge's talk, 'in [a] tide of ingenious vocables, spreading out boundless as if to submerge the world.' The shaping spirit of imagination is floundering in the fog, intent on pure abstractions, instead of cleaving to the penetralia of fact, and finding beauty. And since 'The Destiny of Nations' belongs to the period of the Hymns to the Elements, I strongly suspect that the engulfing abstractions of the Hymn to Water would have been no less devastating. At all events, it will be worth, I think, the light affliction of a moment to move one short step nearer to the charmèd waters of 'The Ancient Mariner.'

Tropical calms had early made a deep impression upon Coleridge's mind, and they will meet us in a moment in 'The Rime.' And here are the tropical calms as, once more in 'The Destiny of Nations,' an affable familiar ghost exhibits them to a Tom Paine in petticoats:

> 'Maid beloved of Heaven!
> (To her the tutelary Power exclaimed)
> Of Chaos the adventurous progeny
> Thou seest; foul missionaries of foul sire,
> Fierce to regain the losses of that hour
> When Love rose glittering, and his gorgeous wings
> Over the abyss fluttered with such glad noise,
> *As what time after long and pestful calms*
> *With slimy shapes and miscreated life*
> *Poisoning the vast Pacific*, the fresh breeze
> Wakens the merchant-sail uprising. Night
> An heavy unimaginable moan
> Sent forth, when she the Protoplast beheld
> Stand beauteous on Confusion's charmèd wave.
> Moaning she fled, and entered the Profound
> That leads—[17]

whither we happily need not follow her. Opposite this passage, on the margin of a copy of the quarto edition of *Joan of Arc*, Coleridge later wrote with engaging frankness the following note:[18] 'These are very fine lines, tho' I say it that should not: but, hang me, if I know or ever did know the meaning of them.' With which pithy and eloquent comment we may leave the fogs behind.

II

It is clear air, stained by no shadow of ambiguity, when—all this fumbling with Properties and Monads and Protoplasts and the Profound cut short by the sharp impact of reality—Coleridge's imagination in 'The Ancient Mariner' drives straight as an arrow to the central substance of these same 'pestful calms':

> The very deep did rot: O Christ!
> That ever this should be!
> Yea, slimy things did crawl with legs
> Upon the slimy sea.
>
> About, about, in reel and rout
> The death-fires danced at night;
> The water, like a witch's oils,
> Burnt green, and blue, and white.[19]

In the earlier poems, turgid and nebulous as they were, Coleridge, in Hazlitt's magnificent phrase, was 'like an eagle dallying with the wind';[20] here is the swift and unerring flight. And for the stark directness of that *tour de force* of concrete imagery neither Bishop Berkeley nor William Godwin nor

Thales nor Aristotle stood sponsor. The elements which fused in the conception may still be found where Coleridge found them—in Captain Cook, and Priestley's *Opticks*, and the *Philosophical Transactions*, and Frederick Martens, and Shakespeare. In large degree they are the very elements which merged, by another trick of the Spirit of the Well, in the flashing shapes of the 'creatures of the great calm.' And both pair and trio of stanzas, sharply contrasted as boot and bale, sprang from the stirring of the same subliminal tract.

Here, then, are the constituent elements of the imaginative conception embodied in the two stanzas now before us: water that burns; that burns green, and blue, and white; that burns not merely like oils, but like a witch's oils; fires which are ominous of death, and which dance 'about, about'; a rotting sea; and slimy creatures that actually crawl on it with legs. What, in the first place, do we know of the huddle of images which were tumbling over one another in the glimmering dark of Coleridge's brain at the moment when these details were compacted into a triptych of creeping things on a nightmare sea, and dancing fires, and water that glowed with uncanny light?

We know, as it happens, a good deal. For, thanks to the accident of an entry in the Note Book, we have already seen the confluence of reminiscences from Coleridge's reading which enters into that other group of stanzas which picture this same sea—the stanzas through which the water-snakes move in the light of the moon. And among the books which we therefore know to have left their luminous tracks in his memory were Captain Cook's *Voyage*, through its paragraph about the multi-coloured animalculæ, and Priestley's *Opticks*, through its chapter on 'Light from Putrescent Substances,' and the fifth volume of the *Philosophical Transactions*, through Father Bourzes's account of the shining appearances in the wakes of ships. These, then, we have again to reckon with. They had been stirring, no doubt, in their subliminal sleep as the voyage which was taking form in Coleridge's brain approached the Line. But when the directing imagination brought the ship at last into tropical seas, the images they had flashed—those vivid 'eye-spectra' of Coleridge's recurring mention[21]—sprang to the level of consciousness, for the shaping spirit to deal with as it would. And its dealings were remarkable enough. 'Hath not the potter,' wrote Saint Paul, 'power over the clay, of the same lump to make one vessel unto honour, and another unto dishonour?' That hoary rhetorical question is answered here, for out of the same shapeless mass of reminiscences Coleridge fashioned both the shining sea of creatures which coil and swim in water that falls off like flakes of light, and also its sharp antithesis in the rotting deep of slimy things which crawl on water lurid as a witch's oils. The one wonder we have seen; the other is before us.

It will be simplest to reverse the order of the two stanzas and work backwards. The last two lines of the second stanza, then, are these:

> The water, like a witch's oils,
> Burnt green, and blue, and white.[22]

Let us set beside these lines enough of Captain Cook's description of the protozoa of the phosphorescent sea to save turning back:

> *During a calm* . . . some parts of the sea seemed *covered with a kind of slime;* and some small sea animals were swimming about . . . that had a *white*, or shining appearance. . . . When they began to swim about, which they did, with equal ease, upon their back, sides, or belly, they emitted the brightest colours of the most precious gems. . . . Sometimes they . . . assume[ed] various tints of *blue*. . . . But . . . the colour was, chiefly, a beautiful, pale *green*, tinged with a burnished gloss; and, in the dark, it had a faint appearance of *glowing fire*. They proved to be . . . probably, an animal which has a share in producing. . . *that lucid appearance, often observed near ships at sea, in the night.*[23]

Now Cook is describing the phenomena of phosphorescence under two aspects, which are closely connected, and yet distinct. The water glowed with the colours of the protozoa; that is one. The protozoa, as they moved, gave off the colours; that is the other. And it is not surprising that an eye to which words habitually called up images saw both—saw the sea by the side of the ship in the night glowing like particoloured fire; saw also the sea-animals themselves, 'emitting the brightest colours' as they swam. Both pictures apparently flashed from the page; both sank below the surface and there merged with other images; and both reappeared. The picture called up by the gyrations of the many-hued protozoa suffered a subliminal sea-change into the 'rich attire' of the coiling water-snakes—their 'blue, glossy green,' and their tracks that were 'shining white' and 'golden fire.' The picture which was its counterpart—water with the colours of Joseph's coat, that had in the dark the appearance of glowing fire—kept, when it reappeared, the same green, blue, and white, but they had turned into baleful portents in a slimy sea which burnt with ill-omened fires. It is simply the phantasmagoria of dreams, save that here the dreamer is consciously curbing and moulding the stuff of the dream.[24]

What Coleridge saw, then, as the background of his picture—a sea lit ominously with three lurid hues—bears all the marks of one of his 'ocular spectra,' evoked by the powerfully visualized paragraph in Captain Cook. But other spectra of the sea had been called up by other pages which we know that he had read. Did some of these flash into the panorama too? We know, for one thing, on the evidence of the water-snakes, that Priestley's chapter and Father Bourzes's letter, inextricably interwoven with Cook's paragraph, were also in his memory.

What images had they this time called up? Why, for example, did the picture in the stanza paint its unearthly colours upon a slimy sea that burnt like *oils*? Coleridge had undoubtedly so seen it with his inner eye. But where?

There is one page in Priestley's account of the luminous fishes which the Note Book proves beyond doubt that Coleridge had read.[25] There is also a page of Father Bourzes from which a sentence got into the Note Book itself.[26] And on that page of Priestley, and again not two score lines from the account, on Father Bourzes's page, of the marine rainbow which printed itself so vividly on Coleridge's retina, stood two curious observations: 'I may assert . . . that the Light is largest *when the Water is fattest*'; 'And I have often observed, that when the Wake of the Ship was brightest, the *Water was more fat* and glutinous.'[27] Clearly that fat water, 'full of Vortices of Light,' in which the fishes 'made a kind of artificial Fire' (fishes of which 'the Mouth of [one] appeared in the Night like a burning Coal')—that glutinous water, shot with fiery light, might well have called up the picture of a sea that burnt like oils. But in this same prolific cluster-point of images from a scant score of pages in Cook and Priestley and the *Philosophical Transactions* was another and much more salient hint.

The article in the *Transactions* immediately preceding Father Bourzes's letter is a tremendously vivid and realistic account by Father Gorée, also from the *Lettres édifiantes et curieuses*, 'Of a New Island raised out of the Sea near Santerini.'[28] It must be read entire to get the impression which it conveys of titanic and cataclysmic force. Father Gorée's account of the volcanic island ends, and Father Bourzes's tale of the phosphorescent fishes and the rainbow in the spray begins, on the same page of the *Transactions;* and nobody (least of all Coleridge) who read the one would be likely to forego the other. And in the startling description 'of central fires through nether seas up-thundering'[29] at Santerini, Coleridge had read how 'the Sea was seen to emit Smoak at two several Places,' and how 'in these two Places, both of which were perfectly round, *the Water of the Sea looked like Oil*, and seemed to rise up and bubble'[30]—a pair of veritable witch's cauldrons in a deep that boiled like a pot.[31] Moreover, three pages on from that page in Priestley's *Opticks* which had actually sent Coleridge on his quest of Father Bourzes, the suggestion of oiliness in connection with the 'artificial Fire' of fishes reappears in another guise. Priestley is rehearsing M. Anton Martin's 'experiments on the light of fishes'[32] ('visible light . . . in sundry rotten mackerel and other *smashy* matters,' as Coleridge tersely put it when, some six years later, the chapter which had so impressed him rose up to consciousness again),[33] and he sets down Martin's observation of '*an oiliness*' about them, 'which . . . would *burn in the fire*.'[34] There was no lack of visualizing suggestion in those few crowded pages which Coleridge had read!

This at least, then, is clear. At the period of the Note Book images of a smoking, bubbling sea that looked like oil had beyond peradventure coexisted in Coleridge's mind with images of shining creatures in water that had the appearance of glowing fire. Now read the lines again:

> *The water, like* a witch's *oils*,
> *Burnt* green, and blue, and white.

It is, I think, an unforced conclusion that scraps of the *Opticks* and of the *Transactions* and of the *Voyage* had had commerce, conscious or unconscious, in Coleridge's brain one hundred and fifty lines before the water-snakes emerged from another confluence of the same elements.

As for 'burnt,' that, as Coleridge knew, is the exact and inevitable word. 'At night, when the Sea dasheth very much, it shines like fire, the Sea-men call it *burning:* This shining is a very bright glance, like unto the lustre of a Diamond. But when the Sea shines vehemently in a dark night, and *burns;* a South or West-wind followeth after it.'[35] That is from a book which Coleridge, as we have seen, knew well—the fascinating *Voyage* of Frederick Martens. Nor was he likely to have read without the instant flashing of a picture this graphic bit of Purchas, from the account of 'the second Voyage of John Davis . . . into the East-Indies, in the Tigre,' in 1604: 'In which place [seven degrees south of the Line] at night, I thinke I saw the strangest Sea, that ever was seene: which was, That the *burning* or glittering light of the Sea did shew to us, *as though all the Sea over had beene burning flames of fire*, and all the night long, the Moone being downe, you might see to read in any booke by the light thereof.'[36] 'Burn' in this association was proverbial. 'Whence that Proverb,' says old Daniel Pell, writing in his Πελαγος of the 'ignifluous lustre' of the sea, '*As true as the Sea burns.*'[37]

But why 'like *a witch's* oils'? The opening words of the first line, 'About, about,' are (as the commentators with one accord observe) the words of the witches in *Macbeth:*

> The weird sisters, hand in hand,
> Posters of the sea and land,
> Thus do go *about, about.*[38]

Nor is it difficult to see what put the witches into Coleridge's head. The First Witch has just been setting her tongue to a lusty curse which recites, apropos of another shipman, the Mariner's very plight:

> I'll drain him dry as hay.
> Sleep shall neither night nor day
> Hang upon his pent-house lid;
> He shall live a man forbid.
> Weary sevennights nine times nine
> Shall he dwintlle, peak, and pine.
> Though his bark cannot be lost,
> Yet it shall be tempest-tost.[39]

The witches from *Macbeth*, then, were hovering in the

background of the picture when the stanza began to take form. And, once there, just two lines later they exert their spell again. For the 'witch's oils' are theirs—that 'fat and glutinous' water of a slimy sea, which 'looked like Oil, and seemed to rise up and bubble,' now lambent to Coleridge's inner eye with the light from beneath the witches' charmèd pot, where likewise fire burned and cauldron bubbled. And the detail which does most to intensify the horror that lurks in the phosphorescent tropical sea, entered the picture through a flash of association which saw in the dance of the death-fires the winding of the weird sisters' charm.

But what of the dancing fires themselves? Whatever they are, they seem to betray a singular slip. If they are 'death-fires,' they have no place about a ship, and if their theatre of operations is a ship, they are something else than 'death-fires.' The thing which they *ought* to be is the corpo santo, or Saint Elmo's fire. And the antics of the corpo santo had met Coleridge in half the voyages he had read.[40] He could scarcely have missed in his Purchas, for instance, the passage which (read elsewhere) had given a speech to Ariel in the *Tempest*—that pleasing picture, in the account of Sir George Somers's shipwreck in the Bermudas, of 'an apparition of a little round light, like a faint Starre, trembling, and streaming along with a sparkeling blaze, halfe the height upon the Maine Mast, and shooting sometimes from Shroud to Shroud . . . halfe the night.'[41] And that was but one of the innumerable reports of the corpo santo which Coleridge must have run across. The thing, on the other hand, which the dancing fires *purport* to be is another matter—those 'flaming meteors [which] fly about the church-yards' (as they are described, for instance, in the great *Collection of Voyages and Travels* which Wordsworth owned),[42] and which had already flickered ominously in Coleridge's verse:

> Mighty armies of the dead
> *Dance, like death-fires,* round her tomb![43]

How did the curious confusion come about?

Confusion and all, the wild dance of the death-fires goes back, it seems clear, to the staid pages of Priestley's *Opticks*. For in that obsolete but still highly entertaining chapter on 'Light from Putrescent Substances,' Priestley is knitting together, in workmanlike fashion, three seemingly divergent things. Let us for the moment be pedantically explicit. The account of the experiments[44] with 'sundry rotten mackerel' (just two pages beyond that extract from Father Bourzes which Coleridge looked up) passes at once into a discussion of the light emitted by putrefying human bodies, with the remark that 'the lights which are *said to be seen in burying grounds*'[45] may be due to this cause. There are the death-fires. A couple of pages later another light, likewise '*said to be very often seen in burying grounds,*'[46] appears—this time the *ignis fatuus;* and one lively *ignis fatuus* in particular 'kept *skipping about a dead thistle,* till a slight motion of the air . . . made it jump to another place.'[47] The death-fires and the marsh-fires, then, through their predilection for graveyards, have strong associative links. But the marsh-fires *skip*. And now the skipping *ignis fatuus*, linked already with the death-fires, is brought into immediate conjunction with the corpo santo, which likewise skips. For Priestley's account of an uncommonly ubiquitous Will o' the Wisp observed in Palestine concludes as follows: 'In the same kind of weather he . . . has observed those luminous appearances, which, at sea, *skip about the masts and yards of ships*, and which the sailors call Corpusanse.'[48] Even the elements of the water-snakes could boast no more efficient hooks and eyes! In a word, through his theory of their common origin in putrescent matter, Priestley has brought together within the compass of a dozen pages three things closely linked: the phosphorescence of the sea, the wandering fires which hover above graveyards, and the corpo santo. And precisely these dozen pages Coleridge read with an interest so alert that he hunted up at least one of the authorities referred to. And when he came to write 'The Ancient Mariner,' the death-fires telescoped by way of the marsh-fires with the corpo santo, and, so merged, fell into their old juxtaposition with the fat and oily sea, within the compass of four telling lines:

About, about, in reel and rout
The death-fires danced at night;
The water, like a witch's oils,
Burnt green, and blue, and white.[49]

In the *Biographia Literaria* Coleridge rehearses the famous case which occurred in a town in Germany a year or so before his arrival there, of the illiterate young woman who, in the delirium of fever, recited incessantly passages in Latin, Greek, and Hebrew—passages which (it turned out) she had heard repeated years before by an old scholar in whose house she had lived as a servant.[50] And Coleridge strikes to the heart of the matter in one of those illuminating remarks which reveal, in passing, his own mental processes: 'Reliques of sensation may exist for an indefinite time in a latent state, *in the very same order in which they were originally impressed.*'[51] Facts, then, from his own reading were slipping, as we have seen, continually below the level of his conscious memory, and resting latent there. And among them the images from the *Opticks* sank together into the deep well. Then, when his brain was busy with 'The Ancient Mariner,' some flash of association set them free. And when transfigured fragments of them floated up to consciousness, like whorls of bubbles through still water, they came not singly, but one after one in their old sequence.[52] The assumption imposes no strain whatever upon credulity. Precisely so do your associations and mine behave—except that with us for the most part the bubbles break, and melt into thin air. Which is only to say, in other words, that few of us are poets, save potentially.

III

The same strangely assorted trio of strange sowers of the seeds of poetry—sailor, scientist, and priest—meet again in the other stanza of the pair:

> *The very deep did rot:* O Christ!
> That ever this should be!
> *Yea, slimy things did crawl with legs*
> *Upon the slimy sea.*[53]

The downright Saxon of 'the very deep did *rot*' finds ample warrant in fact, if not in trenchancy, without going farther (as we readily might go) than the 'viscous and glutinous' water, thick with 'slimy and other putrescent matter,' which Priestley and Father Bourzes describe,[54] and the water of which Sir Richard Hawkins's sailors could hardly draw a bucket 'cleare of some corruption withall.'[55] And it is Captain Cook's 'sea that seemed covered with a kind of slime'[56] on which, in place of shapes of light which coiled and swam, countless unspeakable creatures crawled. But the slimy things that crawled with legs had been seen through other eyes.

One of the most delightful books which Coleridge read was Frederick Martens's *Voyage into Spitzbergen and Greenland.* We have met with it already, and we shall encounter it more than once as we go on, but never more engagingly than now. For with that calm indifference to locality which was a distinctive trait of Coleridge's imaginative syntheses, the slimy things that crawled on slime had been swept down into the Tropics from Martens's fascinating pages, where they disport themselves at large in Arctic seas. Coleridge found in Martens, in a word, a whole Alice-in-Wonderland chapter devoted to '*Rotz-fish* (or *Slime-fishes*) . . . that in themselves are nothing else but Slime.'[57] And the chapter is divided into alluring sections: '*Of the Snail Slime-fish*';[58] '*Of the Hat Slime-fish,*' which 'hath a blew Button or Knob, that . . . may also be compared unto such a Straw Hat as our Women wear';[59] '*Of the Rose-like-shaped Slime-fish,*' which has 'round about his Belly . . . seven brown small Threads, like spun Silk, or like unto the Threads that flye in the Air about Autumn,' and which, like the other two, 'are numerous in the North Sea as Atomes in the Air";[60] '*Of the Slime-fish like a Cap,*' the body of which 'is divided like unto a Pumpkin into six Ribs,' and is 'as white as Milk';[61] '*Of the Slime-fish like a Fountain,*' which last 'is a very notable Fish,' to picture which Martens levies tribute on the Quill of a Goose, a Funnel, a Straw, the Back bones of a Snake, a Rainbow, a Fountain, Milk, and a Cloud.[62] As for the Snail Slime-fish, 'it is very remarkable, that out of the utmost part of him come two Stalks, like unto the Beam of a pair of Scales. . . . With these Stalks he moves himself up and down. . . . The Seamen take these small Fish for Spiders. . . . They swim in great numbers in the Sea, as numerous as the Dust in the Sun.'[63] No need to look farther for the Mariner's 'million million slimy things'![64] More-over, in a description of the star-fish, in another chapter, we learn that 'where *the Legs* come out of the Body, they spread themselves double into Twigs, and . . . are . . . like unto the Feet of a Spider. . . . When they swim in the Water *they hold their Legs together, and so they row along*.'[65] And from that amazing carnival of miniature monsters Coleridge, with an artistic restraint which must none the less have cast a longing look behind, seized upon the one touch which for sheer uncanny realism is unsurpassed: 'Yea, slimy things did crawl *with legs* upon a slimy sea.' One more grotesque for good measure—this time from Purchas—and I have done: 'In the tenth of March in fortie two degrees, the Sea was all red as if it had beene mixed with bloud, being full of red Wormes, which taken up leaped like Fleas.'[66]

I suppose that small red water-worms which leap like fleas, and fantastic shapes of slime which look like hats and roses and pumpkins and fountains, and skipping exhalations from putrescent matter in graveyards and at sea, would not be regarded by most of us as promising material for poetry. But when they and their like are subjected to the potent alchemy of what Coleridge himself has called 'that synthetic and magical power,' which 'blends and (as it were) *fuses*, each into each,'[67] then the miracle may happen.

It happened again a few stanzas later, and now the road winds back to the shadow of the ship. Cook's animalculæ burnt not only green and blue and white, but also *red*. 'The various tints of blue,' Coleridge read, 'were frequently mixed with a ruby, or opaline *redness;* and *glowed with a strength sufficient to illuminate the vessel and water*.'[68] Would that strong suggestion of a windless sea glowing red in the night be likely to leave his imagination quite unstirred? Or would the 'synthetic and magical power' rather act on the hint with uncommon intensity? One is not left to guesswork for the answer. In the great stanza which leads from the soft ascent of 'the moving Moon' to the luminous shapes whose blue and glossy green derived from those same animalculæ, the redness of the protozoa burns ominous in the very sea which before had burnt with their green, and blue, and white:

Her beams bemocked the sultry main,
Like April hoar-frost spread;
Eut where the ship's huge shadow lay,
The charmèd water burnt alway
A still and awful red.[69]

There is, I suspect, no magic in the poem more potent than this blending of images through which the glowing redness of animalculæ once seen in the Pacific has imbued with sombre mystery that still and boding sea and the image which lies across it with utter distinctness in a hush of brooding light.

IV

And so, from the alembic of the creative energy, slime and animalculæ and oily seas and flickering grave-lights have some-how come forth poetry—*de forti egressa est dulcedo*. And now is it possible to reach some unifying conception, however tentative it be, of the bewildering and elusive phenomena which we have been tracing?

It is essential to remember, first of all, that the dozen or so pages from Cook and Priestley and the *Transactions* with which in this chapter we have had most to do were read when Coleridge was eagerly seeking grist for his mill, and was assiduously compiling memoranda in the Note Book for his Hymns, the Hymn to Water explicitly among the rest. The entries in the Note Book offer ample evidence of the vigilance with which some of these very passages were read, and of the corresponding permanence, presumably, of the impressions which they stamped on Coleridge's visual memory. There is no question of fortuitous parallels. 'I had present in my mind,' said Coleridge categorically, 'the materials . . . of the Hymns'; and ocular images seen when the Hymn to Water was lending keenness to his inner eye lay ready to flash back to consciousness when at last upon the abyss the shaping spirit actually moved.

Few passages, indeed, which Coleridge ever read seem to have fecundated his imagination so amazingly as that 257th page of Cook's second volume, which described the 'small sea animals swimming about' in 'a kind of slime,' with 'a faint appearance of glowing fire'—unless, indeed, it be the page in the *Opticks* which sent him to a no less prolific leaf or two of Father Bourzes. And the images evoked by these scant dozen pages sank into the deeps which we have called the Well.

The pages from Priestley carried in with them the shooting exhalations about graveyards and the masts of ships. The very texture of the page from Captain Cook was woven of its four lustrous colours, and the four colours went in too. The page from Father Bourzes, as Coleridge read it, lay open opposite the marine rainbow painted in the spray, and the rainbow would slip in with the rest. Will o' the Wisps, accordingly, and the corpo santo, water glowing faintly with the light from phosphorescent protozoa, the shining wake of ships and fishes playing in its 'artificial Fire,' the iridescence of the wind-tossed spray and the shadow of a sail—all these luminous images of sea and air unconsciously ramified and dovetailed and interpenetrated so inextricably that when any one detail of any one of them flashed up to consciousness it seems to have carried with it the implications of the complex as a whole. 'Seeing a mackerel,' says Coleridge in an attempt to elucidate the association of ideas, 'it may happen, that I immediately think of gooseberries, because I at the same time ate mackerel with gooseberries as the sauce. The first syllable of the latter word, being that which had coexisted with the image of the bird so called, I may then think of a goose. In the next moment the image of a swan may arise before me, though I had never seen the two birds together.'[70] And if the imagination happened to be actively awake when mackerel and gooseberries and geese and swans (like fishes and sea-slime and graveyards and rainbows) were in conjunction, it is conceivable that they might so coexist thereafter in the brain that no one of them could emerge without trailing with it the blended phantasms of the rest. Something like that, I suspect, was the case with the strange congeries of shining simulacra which had streamed together and modified each other, and set up a sort of subconscious communal existence of their own. The Well had exercised its magic potently.

But the Well was not the artificer of the powerfully conceived and executed lines before us. Nowhere, indeed, in the poem more than in the two intimately related groups of stanzas which sprang from remembered images of the multitudinous creatures of the sea is it so necessary to keep not only the subliminal blendings but also the controlling will in mind. And there are no apter words for the strange medley before us (with its still stranger outcome) than those of Coleridge's own brief and penetrating phrases, to which I must persistently recur. In these stanzas, then, it is again Coleridge's own 'chaos of elements or shattered fragments of memory' through which the 'inward creatrix,' the imagination, moves.[71] We, on our part, have once more had to pick our way, step by step, through the pages of books. For him, the pages of books had dissolved into a streaming interplay of images. And the central core of this study lies in the implications of that fact. For that aimless flow of association from 'the twilight realms of consciousness'[72] is, when uncurbed, the bane of all those who, like Coleridge himself, are what he called 'reverie-ish and streamy.'[73] Yet it is also that very flux of interweaving phantasms of association which, when the creative energy imposes its will upon it, becomes the plastic stuff both of life and of art. And we are doggedly making our way 'through strait, rough, dense, and rare, With head, hands, wings, or feet,' because it is worth infinite pains to see that the difference between art, in whatever sphere, and the chaotic welter of the stream of consciousness lies not in their constituents, but in the presence or absence of imaginative control. Baudelaire put the gist of the matter in a dozen scornful words, when he referred to Musset's 'total inability to comprehend *the labour by which a reverie becomes a work of art*'—'son impuissance totale à comprendre le travail par lequel une rêverie devient un objet d'art.'[74] And if this study so far has had any value, that value lies in the concrete exemplification of the way in which the floating images of reverie, through the interposition of the compelling power of the imagination—'lo fren dell' arte'—are marshalled into shapes of ordered beauty.

---

*Nobody ever hit off his own failings in more vivid and telling phrase than Coleridge himself. And what he wrote of another attempt applies with exquisite aptness to the lucubrations of the 'Destiny': 'Instead of a covey of poetic partridges with whirring wings of music . . . up came a metaphysical bustard, urging its slow, heavy, laborious, earth-skimming flight over dreary and level wastes.'[15]

CHAPTER VI

JOINER'S WORK: AN INTERLUDE

'THERE are diversities of operations, but the same Spirit,' wrote Saint Paul. And Saint Paul, who himself possessed the poet's imagination if ever mortal did, might have been formulating, instead of a universal truth, a very special aspect of our problem. For the myriads of impressions which poured into Coleridge's mind from books were dealt with by the Spirit with which we have to do in three strikingly diverse ways. They were blended, as we have already begun to see, by the controlling power of the imagination into organic entities which bore no marks of the fusing fire upon them. But precisely similar, and even identical impressions, garnered from his reading, had already been the subject of quite different operations, and they were soon to undergo yet more remarkable transmutation. And each stage of the richly rewarding history throws light upon the others. 'The Rime of the Ancient Mariner,' in a word, stands, with respect to the imaginative processes which underlie it, between the mechanical dovetailings of 'The Destiny of Nations' and the dream-wrought fabric of 'Kubla Khan.' And before we enter upon the splendid synthesis, in 'The Ancient Mariner,' of masses of disparate reminiscences into the large and sustained unity of a coherent plan; and before we approach the swift, half-intermitted burst of images flung up from the subliminal depths, in 'Kubla Khan,' we shall gain a truer perspective and a surer grasp if we turn back for a moment to Coleridge's highly illuminating period of handicraft. And I shall choose for the purpose his tentative essays at a theme which recurs in 'The Ancient Mariner' itself—'strange sights and commotions in the sky and the element' above 'the land of ice.'

I

The sides of the North had for years drawn Coleridge's fancy, as the needle is set towards the pole. The great stanzas in 'The Rime of the Ancient Mariner' which depict the terrors of the polar ice were not put together from material got up for the occasion. There had been, on the contrary, a long, slow charging of the cells before the final release of creative energy. And that gradual storing of Coleridge's mind with images, and those tentative feelings after adequate expression, throw curious and interesting light upon the genesis of the masterpiece itself, and on the operations of the, power which begot it. For that reason, a batch of earlier essays at poetry merit release from oblivion, to live in this discussion one day more.

If ever in the world a 'confus'd Mass of Thoughts [were] tumbling over one another in the Dark,' it was when Coleridge made his first naïve attempts to turn the polar regions into poetry. None of his embryo efforts attained the proportions of an independent whole; they were all woven into other fabrics on the somewhat crazy loom of a group of four poems. Just about the time, in 1794, when Coleridge began the Note Book, he was collaborating with Southey in *Joan of Arc* and *The Fall of Robespierre.* His fragment of *Joan of Arc*, after a chequered career, became our old friend 'The Destiny of Nations'; his contribution to *The Fall of Robespierre* ended with Act I.[1] As early as December, 1794, he began the sonnet 'To William Godwin' with eight lines, 'the mediocrity of [which],' he cheerfully and emphatically confided to Southey before he printed it, was '*most miserably magazinish!*'[2]—a damnatory judgment in which we may unreservedly concur. Between March and October, 1797 ('The Ancient Mariner,' when he finished, being but a month ahead in the seeds of time) he wrote *Osorio.*[3] And into them all—'The Destiny of Nations,' *The Fall of Robespierre*, the sonnet to Godwin, and *Osorio*—the hoardings of his already notable reading about polar seas and skies were already entering, and taking on configurations of their own.

The only books of that reading which we need to know just now are also four. Leemius's *De Lapponibus* and Crantz's *History of Greenland* are frankly quoted, as sources of such dubious inspiration as they have evoked, in the footnotes to 'The Destiny of Nations.'[4] The first two entries in the Note Book, as we have seen,[5] disclose the fact that Coleridge, when he made them, was reading, footnotes and all, the preposterous pages of Darwin's *Botanic Garden*. And in the sea of footnotes in which we are swimming, hopeful of poetry somewhere in the offing, we shall perhaps remember that the first of these same two entries led us to the inference that it was one of Thomson's footnotes to his 'Winter' which served as bait to lure Coleridge on to Maupertuis's *Figure of the Earth*.[6] And now, galvanized into life by his amazing memory, Leemius, Crantz, Maupertuis, and Darwin played fantastic tricks in Coleridge's brain.

We may profitably set out from the brief episode of the blameless fisher. Coleridge found him, coasting unconcernedly among impending perils, in a dully informative paragraph of Crantz's chapter 'Of the Sea and Ice':

> This [snow] by degrees waxes to a body of ice, *that can no more be overmastered by the sun*. . . . Such a body of ice is often prominent far over the rocks; it . . . cracks into many larger or smaller clefts, from whence *the thawed water* trickles out; by which it becomes at last so weak, that . . . it breaks loose, and . . . plunges into the bays in such *huge pieces* . . . and with such an agitation of the water, as will overset a boat a good way off; *and many a poor Greenlander, coasting without concern along the shore,*

has lost his life by it.[7]

On this hint Coleridge completed as follows, in *Joan of Arc*, a sentence which Southey had begun:

. . . yet its *fragments many and huge*
Astounded ocean with the dreadful dance
Of *whirlpools* numberless, *absorbing* oft
The blameless fisher at his perilous toil.[8]

To go farther and fare worse were impossible; and so, in *Osorio*, Coleridge tackled his luckless fisherman again:

. . . Ye too split

The ice-mount, and with *fragments many and huge*,
Tempest *the new-thaw'd* sea, whose sudden gulphs
Suck in, perchance, some Lapland wizard's skiff.
Then round and round the *whirlpool's* marge ye dance,
etc.[9]

Minerva was still undeniably reluctant, and was also leaning hard on the remembered diction of her earlier attempt. Even the 'Lapland wizard' of *Osorio*, who supplants the fisher *sans peur et sans reproche*, owes his being to a '*Greenland* wizard' who turns up in the immediate context in *Joan of Arc*.[10] But the '*Lapland* wizard' hails from the territory of Leemius, whereas the 'Greenland wizard' is at home in Crantz. Lapland

and Greenland, accordingly, after the familiar fashion of the sleeping images, have already begun to merge horizons in Coleridge's visionary landscape. And having gained this modicum of information from the blameless fisher, we may leave him to his fate.

The aurora borealis will prove more enlightening. But we shall have to reach it through two passages which nobody, I am certain, save the most deep-dyed Coleridgian ever reads. The first is again from 'The Destiny of Nations'; the second is the opening quatrain of that 'miserably magazinish' octave of the Godwin sonnet; and the momentary penance exacted by their reading will, I hope, find its reward.

And what if some rebellious, o'er dark realms
Arrogate power? yet these train up to God,
And on the rude eye, unconfirmed for day,
Flash meteor-lights better than total gloom.
As ere from Lieule-Oaive's vapoury head
The Laplander beholds the far-off Sun
Dart his slant beam on unobeying snows,
While yet *the stern and solitary Night*
Brooks no alternate sway, *the Boreal Morn*
With *mimic lustre* substitutes its gleam,
Guiding his course or by Niemi lake
Or Balda Zhiok, or the mossy stone
Of Solfar-kapper, while the snowy blast
Drifts arrowy by, or eddies round his sledge,

Making the poor babe at its mother's back
Scream in its scanty cradle: he the while
Wins gentle solace as with upward eye
He marks the streamy banners of the North,
Thinking himself those happy spirits shall join
Who there in floating robes of *rosy light*
Dance sportively.[11]

Lamb wrote Coleridge: 'Your simile of the Laplander "by Niemi's lake Or Balda Zhiok or the mossy stone Of Solfar Kapper"—will bear comparison with any in Milton for fullness of circumstance and lofty-pacedness of Versification.'[12] But Lamb, I fear, was writing (as he would say) 'by punch-light.' So much for 'The Destiny of Nations.'

Now for the sonnet, which, since it belongs with those on Bowles, Priestley, and Burke, was probably like them written (as Lamb in reminiscent mood reminded Coleridge two years later) 'in that nice little smoky room at the Salutation [and Cat], which is even now continually presenting itself to my recollection, with all its associated train of pipes, tobacco, Egghot, welch Rabbits, metaphysics and Poetry.' And if the effusion bears (as Lamb lovingly puts it of another 'Salutation poem') 'the mark of the beast "Tobacco" upon it,'[13] strange visions were surely hovering over the welsh-rabbit in the smoke:[14]

O form'd t'illume a sunless world forlorn,

As o'er *the chill and dusky brow of Night*,
In Finland's wintry skies *the Mimic Morn**
Electric pours a stream of *rosy light*. . . .

There, then, are the two specimens. What of their ingredients? The only ostensible begetter of the lines just quoted from 'The Destiny of Nations' is Leemius. For the outlandish Lieule-Oaive, and Balda Zhiok, and Solfar-kapper, together with the Lapland mother and her babe, are drawn (as copious footnotes from the Latin version of Leem apprise us) from the treatise *De Lapponibus*.[15] But the two passages, taken in conjunction, are in reality a mass of dovetailing, and interweaving, and sometimes merging reminiscences of the three other books already named. And to make the dance the merrier, Coleridge is again reverting unabashedly, as my telltale italics show, to his own recollected phraseology.[16] Let us see what the *mélange* has to offer.

The first thing which sharply challenges attention is the fact that our touchingly edifying Laplander pierced by the arrowy blast still manages, as he drags his sledge, to find 'gentle solace' in 'the streamy banners of the North, Thinking himself *those happy spirits* shall join *Who there* in floating robes of rosy light *Dance sportively*.' Now that last is not the voice of Leemius at all, but of Crantz, who tells us, not without charm, how the good dead Greenlander's soul 'rests the very same evening in the mansion of the Moon, who was a Greenlander, and there it can dance and play at ball with the rest of the souls; *for they interpret the Northern Lights to be the dance of sportive souls.*'[17] Crantz, then, together with Leemius, was bubbling in the cauldron from which the lines we are considering emerged.

But Maupertuis and Darwin were also in the brew. For there were northern lights in each of them, and that 'tenacious and systematizing memory' was curiously responsive to auroras. And first Maupertuis. In the course of a strikingly vivid description of the northern lights in *The Figure of the Earth*, we read that 'their Motion is most commonly *like that of a pair of Colours waved in the Air*, and the different Tints of their Light give them the appearance of so many *vast Streamers* of that sort of Taffetas which we call changeable. Sometimes they line a part of the Sky with Scarlet.'[18] There, then, are 'the streamy banners of the North,' and so much, at the moment, for *The Figure of the Earth*.

But what of 'the Mimic Morn Electric,' and *its* stream? There is, in the first place, a curious entry in the Note Book, which has interest for us here. It is on folio 16[a]:

> Motives from Religion like the light from the Sun—*the earth principally heated* from *within itself—the Sun the cause of winter and summer by a very small quantity of heat in addition to that residing in the earth.*[19]

I first took it to be a reminiscence of Burnet's *Sacred Theory*, certain parts of which it strikingly parallels.[20] But some time after I had come to this conclusion, on turning for (I suppose) the twentieth time the pages of the *Botanic Garden*, my now 'armed eye'[21] caught this:

> M. De Mairan . . . has endeavoured to shew that *the earth* receives but a small part of the heat which it possesses, from the sun's rays, but is *principally heated* by fires *within itself*. He thinks *the sun* is *the cause of* the vicissitudes of our seasons of *summer and winter by a very small quantity of heat in addition to that* already *residing in the earth*.[22]

That is the beginning of an Additional Note (entitled 'Central Fires') on 'The Economy of Vegetation,' Canto I, l. 139—a line which touches on the fires at the 'still centre' of the earth. Now the central fires *are* a conspicuous theme in Coleridge's beloved Burnet, and it is obvious that he was reading Burnet at the time. For on the next page but one of the Note Book is an entry ('And cauldrons the scoop'd earth a boiling sea!') which is unmistakably inspired by the *Sacred Theory*.[23] And the fact that Coleridge was deep in Burnet accounts, with little doubt, for his interest in Darwin's Note. But he had obviously turned to the Note from the line which it elucidates. He had, accordingly, been reading with his characteristic attention* that section of the first canto of 'The Economy of Vegetation' in which the 139th line occurs. And in lines 129–30, in the same paragraph, Darwin refers to certain meteors (duly identified in the Argument with the aurora borealis) which

Dart from the North on pale *electric streams*,
Fringing Night's sable robe with transient beams.

And in another of those Additional Notes in which he revelled, uncurbed by metrical restrictions, he expatiates for almost five pages more upon Meteors, including among the rest 'the *electric streams*, which constitute these northern lights.'[24] That Note, moreover, is separated by but four pages from the passage which Coleridge transcribed. And so in the sonnet to Godwin 'the Mimic Morn *Electric* pours a *stream* of rosy light.' The *Botanic Garden*, accordingly, has a finger in the pie—or, to adopt its author's more urbane phraseology, has helped 'deck with lambent flames the shrine of Night.'[25]

Now let us take stock, and count our jewels. Leemius's Laplander, who sees Crantz's souls dance sportively, sees them dancing in Maupertuis's 'streamy banners of the North.' That is sufficiently involved, but there is more to come. For when, in the Godwin sonnet, the Mimic Morn 'Electric pours a stream of rosy light,' it is fed by a current generated in the laboratory of the *Botanic Garden;* while 'Finland's wintry skies' in which it plays are the skies, not of the *Botanic Garden* at all, but of *The Figure of the Earth!* And (to cap the climax) the 'rosy light' in which the Finnish heavens are suffused is reflected from the Greenland spirits' floating robes.

The mountains are labouring, if you please, and their litter is ridiculous enough. Yet the exquisitely subtle blending of reminiscences from which picture after picture in the 'Mariner' later took shape, derives from precisely the same complex mental processes (there interplaying with sovereign and unconscious ease) which here still halt and jar laboriously as they move. For I am not in the least concerned with the intrinsic value of the notoriously feeble verse we are considering. On the contrary, the very fact that Coleridge's craftsmanship is as yet crassly mechanical and rudimentary makes it easier to observe his incipient powers at work. And that, for the moment, is our object.

What Coleridge did with Maupertuis's *Figure of the Earth* (to return for a moment to our medley) is so absolutely characteristic, despite the immaturity of the results, that I shall relentlessly squeeze the paragraph in 'The Destiny of Nations' a little dryer. For Coleridge, like Chaucer (whose earlier imaginative processes I am illustrating in this chapter on every page), could gather grapes of thorns and figs of thistles. And in his browsings among Maupertuis's astronomical computations he cropped about every flower which grew in that seemingly arid soil. And since he was everlastingly extracting poetry—elsewhere of supernal beauty—from the most unlikely sources, it is not a work of supererogation to set down, with the minimum of comment, the further gleanings which adorn our paragraph.

Just before the account of the aurora, then, Maupertuis writes as follows:

> In this Season the Sun but just showed himself above the Horizon towards Noon. But the long Twilights, the whiteness of the Snow, and *the Meteors that are continually blazing in this Sky*, furnished us light enough to work four or five hours every day.[34]

In the account of the aurora itself he remarks that 'this Light, which was fixt at first, soon moved, and changing into other colours, Violet and Blue, *settled into a Dome*.[35] Coleridge's eye rested approvingly upon Maupertuis's phraseology. And so, in 'The Destiny of Nations,' there '*Flash meteor-lights* better than total gloom,'[36] while later in the poem we meet 'the icepil'd mount And *meteor-lighted dome*.'[37] The last paragraph but one of the First Part of *The Figure of the Earth* (to turn to another instance) reads as follows:

> It was curious enough to see [the Sun] enlighten for so long a time, a whole Horizon of Ice, and to see Summer in the Heavens, while Winter still kept possession of the Earth. We were now in the Morning of that long Day of several Months; *yet the Sun, with all his assiduity, had wrought no change either upon the Ice or Snows*.[38]

That, together with Crantz's ice 'that can no more be overmastered by the Sun,'[39] sank deep. For in the first act of *The Fall of Robespierre* occur the lines:

> And love and friendship on his coward heart

> Shine like the powerless sun on polar ice;[40]

while our ardent Laplander, 'prompt and watchful more than ordinary men,'*

> beholds the far-off Sun
>
> Dart his slant beam on *unobeying snows.*[41]

Finally, in the list of barbarous names which, so far as anything that Coleridge tells us is concerned, call Leemius father, stands 'Niemi lake.'[42] But Niemi lake is not in Leemius. One of the purple patches, however, with which Maupertuis relieved his angles and elevations was a charming account of Mount Niemi, with its beautiful surrounding lakes which 'gave it the Air of an enchanted Island in a Romance.' 'We had been frighted with Stories of Bears that haunted this place,' the account goes on, 'but saw none. It seemed rather a place of resort for Fairies and Genii than for Bears.' It was this passage which Thomson seized on in his footnotes, together with Maupertuis's remark that 'as we sailed along I was surprized to see, upon the banks of this River, Roses of as lively a red as any that are in our Gardens.'[44] And it is no great wonder that these dainty vignettes of fairies and roses sent Coleridge to see what manner of book a treatise must be, which, beneath the forbidding title of *The Figure of the Earth determined from Observation at the Polar Circle*, harboured such inmates.[45]

One other passage will serve to round out this brief survey

of Coleridge's earlier poetic interest in the North. In five lines which now form the concluding fragment of 'The Destiny of Nations,' scattered recollections (it would seem) of perhaps the most splendid of all the old narratives of unflinching courage under the terrors of the long polar night—the account of William Barents's voyages as found in Purchas[46]—have crystallized into an unforgettable picture of stark desolation:

> And first a landscape rose
> More wild and waste and desolate than where
> The white bear, drifting on a field of ice,
> Howls to her sundered cubs with piteous rage
> And savage agony.[47]

II

Here, then, are precisely such fragments of remembered reading as we found dissolved, diffused, and then re-created, in the elfish beauty and creeping horror of the equatorial seas. The nature of the shattered fragments is identical; the complexity of their interweavings is the same. But there the likeness ends. The meteorological reminiscences before us dovetail into each other trimly, but they remain essentially themselves. They have not melted into one another and transfused their several identities into a new and integrated whole. The skies of 'The Destiny of Nations' are exactly what the water-snakes are not: they are combinations of entities themselves substantially unmodified—Leemius, and Crantz, and Maupertuis, and Darwin adroitly pieced together, as if by some deft cabinet-maker's craft. Instead of a miracle, we get marquetry.

Now I suppose that both Coleridge and Wordsworth would insist that we are confronted, in these diverse products, with the operations of two different powers: Fancy in the lines from the 'Destiny,' Imagination in the stanzas from the 'Mariner'—Fancy, which 'has no other counters to play with, but fixities and definites'; Imagination, which 'dissolves, diffuses, dissipates, in order to re-create';[48] Fancy, which 'does not require that the materials which she makes use of should be susceptible of change in their constitution from her touch'; Imagination, which 'recoils from everything but the plastic, the pliant, and the indefinite.'[49] But I have long had the feeling, which this study has matured to a conviction, that Fancy and Imagination are not two powers at all, but one. The valid distinction which exists between them lies, not in the materials with which they operate, but in the degree of intensity of the operant power itself.[50] Working at high tension, the imaginative energy assimilates and transmutes; keyed low, the same energy aggregates and yokes together those images which, at its highest pitch, it merges indissolubly into one. The utter discordance and intractability of the elements which coalesced, with the ease of blending dew-drops, in the dancing death-fires and the water-snakes and the charmèd water where the ship's huge shadow lay, have established, if anything can, the fact that there is nothing under Heaven which is not plastic as potter's clay to the touch of the shaping spirit, when it moves over chaos with plenary power. Once let that sovereign energy relax, and even the tractable glories of auroral skies may yield no more than materials for a mosaic. The raw stuff with which the imagination works is of secondary moment in determining the character of its achievement. That achievement owes its quality, as miracle or mosaic, to the measure of the synthesizing control which the creative faculty itself exerts.

To that—and to the potency of the Well. For there it is, in the unconscious depths, that the 'synthetic and magical power' which blends and fuses finds free play for its *magic*. And one reason why our Arctic landscape under a meteor-lighted dome shows dexterous joinery instead of the authentic alchemy is pretty certainly the fact that Solfar-kapper, and Balda Zhiok, and Niemi, and the unhappy Lapland babe were not dipped deep enough or long enough in the subliminal pools. Unless Coleridge's footnotes are misleading witnesses, the bits of Crantz and Leemius, at least, spent little time in transit between the printed and the written page. There is wanting the descent into the flux and reflux of the twilight realms of consciousness, and the melting into one another of the elements, and the flash, and the rising of new shapes from the abyss—new shapes which never could have been without the old ones, and yet which are not they. In 'The Destiny of

Nations,' for the most part, consciousness is playing a lone hand.

Now we have yet to see, in 'Kubla Khan,' the unconscious playing *its* game alone—as it happens, with conspicuous and perhaps unique success. But at the zenith of its power the creative energy is both conscious and unconscious in one and the same exercise—controlling consciously the throng of images which in the reservoir have undergone unconscious metamorphosis. And that loftiest exercise is our chief concern. But in Coleridge, as in no other poet whom I know, great masses of the same materials are dealt with by the imagination in all three ways. And the meaning of the puissant blending of the conscious and the unconscious in the supreme creative process is most clearly realized when it is set sharply off against either agency at work, at least in large degree, without the other's aid. And so the lines in 'The Destiny of Nations' attain for our purpose an importance beyond their own intrinsic worth. With that purpose, then, never lost sight of, I mean to draw on the 'Destiny' for one more specimen of sheer joinery. It is both admirable as a foil and curiously interesting as a human document, and I do not think that its brief story has been told before.

III

The first number of *The Watchman* was published on March 1, 1796. It had been heralded by the 'memorable tour' in quest of subscribers, which was later to give to the world, in the *Biographia Literaria*, the Calvinist tallow-chandler of Birmingham and the poet's ill-starred adventure with a pipe.[51] 'In the second number,' in Coleridge's own words, 'an essay against fast days, with a most censurable application of a text from Isaiah for its motto, lost me near five hundred of my subscribers at one blow.'[52] The text—'Wherefore my Bowels shall sound like an Harp'—*was* perhaps a trifle open to question as the motto of an 'Essay on Fasts'! And any charitable suspicion which we might harbour that the five hundred subscribers were scandalized under a misapprehension is set at rest, I fear, by the deplorable fact that Coleridge used the same text of little Hartley, when he was, as 'sometimes, inspired by the God Æolus.'[53] At all events, that was not the way to win the hearts of Calvinist tallow-chandlers and 'stately and opulent wholesale dealers in cottons'; and after a precarious existence of eight more weeks, the tenth and last number of *The Watchman* ended with another excerpt from Isaiah: 'O Watchman! thou hast watched in vain'!

At some time not far from the close of this same year, Coleridge, having broken with Southey, began revamping his own contribution to *Joan of Arc*, in order to print it as an independent poem.[54] And in the resultant 'Destiny of Nations' Joan was retained as the heroine. Obviously, however, she could no longer be Southey's Joan. What new twist, then, should she receive? Just about this time Coleridge, it is clear, was reading

Voltaire, for in the third act of *Osorio*, written between June and September, 1797, he paraphrases half a dozen lines from the *Désastre de Lisbonne*.[55] But nobody who read Voltaire at all could conceivably write about Joan of Arc without having at least begun the scandalous *Pucelle*.[56] And Joan sets out on her career in *La Pucelle* as a pretty bar-maid in a rustic inn. Now Coleridge sent the draft of his new lines to Lamb (and apparently to Wordsworth) for their opinion,[57] and we have, under date of February, 1797, Lamb's reply. And from that we gather unmistakably that Coleridge's Joan has turned bar-maid too. 'You cannot surely mean to degrade the Joan of Arc,' wrote Lamb, 'into a pot-girl. You are not going, I hope, to annex to that most splendid ornament of Southey's poem all this cock-and-a-bull story of Joan the publican's daughter of Neufchatel, with the lamentable episode of a waggoner, his wife, and six children.'[58] Whereupon he proceeds without mercy to 'enumerate some woeful blemishes,' with comments which, racy though they be, are not now our affair. Coleridge, however, deeply discouraged by Lamb's pungent strictures, 'had not heart to finish the poem,'[59] and the fragment lay *perdu* until its appearance twenty years later, as 'The Destiny of Nations,' in *Sibylline Leaves*.

Now Joan, as we have her in the extant 'Destiny,' is no longer a 'pot-girl,' though she still

. . . minister[s] refreshment to the tired
Way-wanderer, when along the rough-hewn bench
The sweltry man had stretched him, and aloft
Vacantly watched the rudely-pictured board
Which on the Mulberry-bough with welcome creak
Swung to the pleasant breeze.[60]

And my guess that Voltaire had a hand, or at least a main finger, in Coleridge's original conception of the *ci-devant* 'Tom Paine in petticoats' need not detain us, except as it adds one more ingredient to our witch's cauldron. But the 'lamentable episode of a waggoner, his wife, and six children' touches us more nearly. For, in a modified form, that still survives.

The 'healthful Maid' has set out alone before dawn of a frosty winter morning:

. . . when, behold . . .
An unattended team! The foremost horse
Lay with stretched limbs; the others, yet *alive*
But stiff and cold, stood motionless, *their manes*
Hoar with the frozen night-dews. Dismally
The dark-red dawn now glimmered; but its gleams
Disclosed no face of man. The maiden paused,
Then hailed who might be near. No voice replied.
From the thwart wain *at length there reached her ear*
A sound so feeble that it almost seemed
Distant: and feebly, *with slow effort pushed,*

A miserable man crept forth: his limbs
The silent frost had eat, scathing like fire.
Faint on the shafts he rested. She, meantime,
Saw crowded close beneath the coverture
A mother and her children— *lifeless all,*
Yet lovely! *not a lineament was marred—*
Death had put on so slumber-like a form!
It was a piteous sight; and one, a babe,
The crisp milk frozen on its innocent lips,
Lay on the woman's arm, its little hand
Stretched on her bosom.[61]

Lamb, who recanted handsomely on February 13 most of the derogatory opinions which he had expressed on February 5, is still unable to reconcile this particular episode (in its earlier form) with 'the solemn openings' of the poem. 'After all this' (to wit, these 'deep preluding strains'), he insists again, 'cometh Joan, a *publican's* daughter, sitting on an ale-house *bench*, and marking the *swingings* of the *signboard*,* finding a poor man, his wife and six children,† starved to death with cold, and thence roused into a state of mind proper to receive visions emblematical of equality; which what the devil Joan had to do with, I don't know.'[62] Lamb's critical acumen was not at fault. You can lift the episode out of its context intact, like a bit of enamel from a pattern in cloisonné. And the reason is not far to seek. The thing is a fragment, retrieved and carried over bodily, undipped and unassimilated, from the miscellaneous wreckage of *The Watchman!*

In the issue of April 19, 1796, Coleridge prints, 'with the deepest regret,' a series of State Papers which disclose the failure of the negotiations 'to re-establish General Tranquillity, on conditions just, honourable and permanent.' 'The horrors of war,' he at once continues, 'must therefore be recommenced.—Let those who sit by the fire-side, and heár of them at safe distance attentively peruse the following

> *Interesting Narration relative to the Campaign of 1794 and 1795.*'[63]

The narrative begins on a familiar note—'Abuses unheard of in any former war existed in almost every department'[64]—and then, since it is the Medical Staff which is at the moment under fire, plunges at once into a circumstantial account of the 'poignant sufferings [of the sick] during the retreat to Deventer.' And in the light of our sifting of Joan's adventure, the paragraphs which follow make interesting reading:

> On the morning of the 17th Jan. 1795, I was sent upon a particular duty, to trace out a road over the common, by which the army and artillery might safely proceed to Looners. When the party marched, it was scarcely light, and as the day broke in upon us, the horrible scenes which it revealed, afforded a shocking proof of the miseries of a winter's campaign.—On the common, about half a mile

> off the high road, we discovered a baggage cart, with a team of five horses, apparently in distress; I galloped towards the spot, and found the poor animals were *stiff, but not dead; the hoar frost on their manes*, plainly shewing they had been there the whole night. Not perceiving any driver with them, I struck my sword repeatedly on the canvass tilt, *enquiring at the same time if there was any person in the cart; at length, a very feeble voice answered me, and someone underneath the canvass appeared to be making an effort to rise. A pair of naked frost-nipt legs were then advanced, and the most miserable object I ever beheld, sunk heavily upon the ground;* the whole of his clothing so ragged and worn, that I can scarcely say he was covered.[66]

The account of the horrors of the day's march proceeds, and after a score of lines we read this:

> One scene made an impression upon my memory, which time will never be able to efface. Near another cart, a little further on the common, we perceived a stout looking man, and a beautiful young woman with an infant, about seven months old, at the breast; *all three frozen and dead.* The mother had most certainly expired in the act of suckling her child, as with one breast exposed, she lay upon the drifted snow, *the milk to all appearance, in a stream, drawn from the nipple by the babe, and instantly*

> *congealed.* The infant seemed as if its lips had but just then been disengaged, *and it reposed its little head upon the mother's bosom, with an overflow of milk, frozen as it trickled from the mouth; their countenances were perfectly composed and fresh, resembling those of persons in a sound and tranquil slumber.*[67]

What Coleridge has done is patent at a glance. He has deftly fitted the incidents of the two carts together, neatly tongued and grooved into one another, and then, with the same adroitness, has set the resulting combination into his design. Nothing is dissolved, nothing diffused; no inward creatrix has exercised its re-incorporating spell. It is a strange paradox. Are not the dead mother and her babe, with their moving human appeal, of more value as stuff for the poet's loom than all the gyrations of varicoloured animalculæ and all the shining tracks of fishes in all the seven seas? Yet the shapes of light that play within the shadow of the ship are sheer, quintessential poetry; the tragic figures in the snow are untouched by the finger of that plastic spirit which on occasion sweeps through chaos with imperial sway. For faith without works is not more dead than the loftiest themes of poetry may, *as poetry*, be dead, if they have not been drenched in the creative deeps, and fashioned afresh by that architectonic energy which is the effluence of the creative will. I hold no brief for luminous protozoa and the light from rotten mackerel as matter which, *sua sponte*, sparkles still the right Promethean fire. 'I am dying, Egypt, dying' stirs depths that the Mariner's plummet never sounded, and touches heights beyond the zenith of the moving moon. But it does so, because in the tragic and glorious conception of which it is an integral portion, the same synthetic and magical power which swept the multitudinous pageantry of the four elements within the frame of 'The Ancient Mariner' has there been exercised upon facts of nobler, import and a larger mould. Yet facts of the same nobility of import, immobile and unmetamorphosed, form the matter of poems by the thousand which lie beneath the stratified sands of the marching centuries, extinct as pterodactyls. The appeal from Coleridge the artisan to Coleridge the supreme creative artist demonstrates beyond cavil one truth of cardinal importance. The essential virtue of poetry is resident, not in its matter, but in the power that moulds brute matter into form. And Coleridge's procedure in 'The Destiny of Nations,' which I have touched no further than sufficed my purpose, is of incalculable value, because against it there stands out, with a clearness which nothing else, I think, could give, the ways of the shaping spirit when it moves in plenitude of power.

IV

Our object gained, then, we may abandon the by-path for the main highway, and return to 'The Ancient Mariner.' And we must now enter upon a new stage of our journey.

The controlling power of the imagination, so far as we have yet observed its workings, has fashioned its materials into constituent units of small compass. It is only stanzas, or pairs or triads of stanzas at most, with which we have had to do. The large design of the poem as a whole is still before us. And that design is as rich in the complexity of its elements as any of the component parts themselves. For into the seeming simplicity of the structure of 'The Ancient Mariner' there have entered at least three great strands, which have been interwoven with the same consummate art that gave lucid outline to the huddle of images which coalesced into beauty at the touch of the shadow of a sail. And it is these three structural elements, first alone and then in their interpenetration, to which we must now come.

There is, in the first place, the background of the voyage itself, with its own enthralling and memorable history. There is what Wordsworth called 'the spectral persecution,'[68] which has its roots in 'all the strange phantasms that ever possessed "your philosophy" . . . from Thoth the Egyptian to Taylor the English pagan.'[69] And finally there is the theme—not this time rooted in the phantasmal, but deep in experience itself—of the act which makes the actor forever after 'the deed's creature.' And in the blending of these diverse elements the architectonic power of the controlling imagination is revealed in its full exercise.

The grand sweep of the voyage comes first.

*A footnote prudently identifies 'the Mimic Morn' with the aurora borealis.

*The first two entries in the Note Book were drawn from the first two cantos of the *Botanic Garden;*[26] a long note from 'The Loves of the Plants' were copied verbatim in the *Poems* of 1796;[27] and we shall later find still another jotting from this same nest of Notes.[28] The entry in the Note Book now before us is followed on the next page by a none too laudatory comment on Darwin's verse, which begins: 'Dr. Darwin's Poetry, a succession of Landscapes or Paintings—*it arrests the attention too often.*'[29] It undoubtedly arrested Coleridge's! And the fact is not surprising. He was, as we know on his own authority,[30] garnering supplies for a galaxy of poems on Sun, Moon, Earth, Air, Fire, and Water. And a list like the following *would*, in the circumstances, be alluring: 'Shooting Stars. Lightning. Rainbow. Colours of the Morning and Evening Skies. Exterior Atmosphere of Inflammable Air. Twilight. Fire-balls. Aurora Borealis. Planets. Comets. Fixed Stars. Sun's Orb.' That modest prospectus is the Argument for the verse-paragraph of twenty-two lines (115–36) which is now engaging our attention. And the first item in the next section is 'Fires at the Earth's Centre.' All that was little short of Heaven to an earnest seeker after 'all the charms or

Tremendities of nature'![31] A glance over Darwin's 'Argument to the First Canto' explains much. 'I absolutely nauseate Darwin's poems,' Coleridge wrote Thelwall in 1796.[32] But they had an uncanny fascination for him nevertheless. And these fantastic pages of the Note Book, with their hodge-podge of Darwin and Burnet,[33] reveal strange fecundating influences which were obscurely but powerfully at work. And that is the warrant for our preoccupation here with seeming trivialities.

*Coleridge (I cannot forbear remarking) at one time contemplated investing the wind-beaten babe who screamed at its mother's back, with the paternal receptiveness to gentle solace from the Arctic skies. For in a delectable list of subjects having to do with infants and infancy, between No. 7 ('Kissing itself in the looking-glass') and No. 9 ('An infant's prayer on its mother's lap'), stands No. 8: 'The Lapland infant seeing the sun.'[43] But we were mercifully spared that.

*Either Lamb had read carelessly the lines as they now stand, or it was Joan, and not the tired way-wanderer, who originally sat on the rough-hewn bench.

† 'By the way,—why not nine children?' he had written in

January. 'It would have been just half as pathetic again.' The number, it will be observed, is now left to the imagination.[65]

BOOK II

My purpose is now to lead you into the Pallace, where you shall have a clear and delightful view of all those various objects, and scattered excellencies, that lye up and down upon the face of the creation, which are onely seen by those that go down into the Seas, and by no other.

DANIEL PELL, *Πελαγος*

For here, millions of mixed shades and shadows, drowned dreams, somnam-bulisms, reveries; all that we call lives and souls, lie dreaming, dreaming, still.

HERMAN MELVILLE, *Moby-Dick*, 'The Pacific'

There go the ships:
there is that leviathan, whom
thou hast made to play therein.

THE BOOK OF PSALMS

CHAPTER VII

THE LOOM

COLERIDGE'S imagination, at the period we are concerned with, was playing, like heat-lightning, about the remote horizons of the world. I know that for some this fact will forthwith damn him as a poet. His vagrant fancy should, we shall be told, have kept at home, within the bounds of Bristol or of Nether Stowey, looked into the heart of Amos Cottle, or of 'dear brother Jem,' or of the Calvinist tallow-chandler of Birmingham, and found its Northwest Passage and its Indies there. Poetry, in a word, should be centripetal, not centrifugal, and its serious business is not with caverns in Cashmere, or upas trees in Java, or alligator-holes in Florida, but with what is common to our kind. That is sound doctrine, to which I heartily subscribe. But it is doctrine which is sometimes pushed so far as to exclude its essential complement. What seas washed the insubstantial shores that harboured Circe and Calypso, and on what chart is Prospero's island found? The imagination which may and does strike to the centre of what is universally valid in experience without passing across the threshold of the straitest hut, may also draw no less triumphantly within the compass of that same experience, for incorporation with it, the multifarious riches of the four corners of the earth. And one of the touchstones of supreme imaginative vision lies in its unerring recognition of what is universal in the remote and strange. To set such metes and bounds to the scope of the shaping spirit as will exclude from its operations either centre or periphery—either antres vast and deserts idle, or familiar matter of to-day—is to contravene that very power of assimilation in which the faculty essentially consists.[1] We shall do well, accordingly, to get clear at once the sovereign dealings of the imagination with the near and far. And the attempt will bring us in the end to the vast and grandly human background of 'The Rime of the Ancient Mariner' itself.

I

The long, slow process, old as the race, through which the frontiers of the known have steadily encroached upon the territory of the unexplored, has been a progressive conquest of new worlds for the imagination. For the imagination has always had two focal points: one fixed, the other perpetually advancing; one deep in the nature of men themselves, the other in 'that untravell'd world whose margin fades Forever and forever when [we] move.' In the great fictions of wayfaring and adventure, like the *Odyssey*, the two foci draw together. The imagination strikes to what is universal—the unquenchable spirit of adventure and the insatiable desire to know—in the experience of men to whom new suns bring daily new horizons. And it also exercises its assimilating power upon whatever the quest has swept from the unknown within the widening circle of the known. Ulysses himself, and 'straunge strondes' at the outposts of the world—the voyager, and the lore of lands beyond familiar sea-marks—furnish alike materials for the creative energy.

It is small wonder, then, that voyages into unknown seas and travels along uncharted roads have always profoundly stirred imaginative minds. On the one hand, the human qualities called into play in the face of the unexplored have evoked a vicarious response in kind. Daring and the ardour to gain experience of the world ('l'ardore . . . a divenir del mondo esperto'); a will of steel, the icebrook's temper; and an insouciant and even gay contempt of fortune—traits such as these the imagination has always seized on as its own, from Homer down. That is one reason why 'it is observable,' as Sir Arthur Quiller-Couch remarks, 'how many of the great books of the world—the *Odyssey*, the *Æneid, The Canterbury Tales, Don Quixote, The Pilgrim's Progress, Gil Blas, Pickwick*, and *The Cloister and the Hearth*—are books of wayfaring.'[2] The bead-roll might be made far longer, from Lucian's splendidly false *True History*, through *Sindbad the Sailor*, and *Pantagruel*, and *Gulliver*, and *Robinson Crusoe*, to 'The Rime of the Ancient Mariner.' Fortunes by land and sea have always been treasure-trove for the imagination, because they reveal the universal human traits, not static, but in their protean presentation of new fronts to the imperious summons of emergency.

But voyages and travels have most powerfully engaged imagination in another way. For they are part and parcel of an almost cosmic process. Above all things else, we must recall, the imagination is an assimilating energy. It pierces through dissimilarity to some underlying oneness in which qualities the most remote cohere. Now the perpetual adventurings of humanity along the perilous edges of the world have been steadily shifting the boundaries of the unknown and the known, and drawing what lies across the line within the circle. But fresh conquests from the unknown arrive as aliens, invested with strangeness, and mystery, and romance. Not only on the fascinating fringes of early maps, but universally, the advancing territory of the known is rimmed and bounded by a dubious borderland in which the unfamiliar and the strange hold momentary sway. And that zone of the marvellous (which is merely the unknown in its transition to the wonted) draws like a loadstone the incorporating energy of the imagination, which penetrates to the core of the familiar behind the outward semblance of the strange, and completes the conquest which discovery began. And so the borderland between the unknown and the known keeps merging on its hither edge with the familiar, at the same time that its outer verge is pushing on into the unexplored. The centripetal force of the imagination which assimilates, serves as a check to the centrifugal sweep of the spirit which adventures, and the balance which is thus set up between the two is one of the cardinal facts in human progress.

Voyages and travels, then, play no minor part in the vast and continuous operation through which the unknown is incorporated with the known. Above all the appearance of new visitants from beyond the confines of the familiar challenges the creative impulse of the poet to exert its power, and domiciliate the stranger. And the imagination has always leaped to seize, from the vivid and chaotic welter of fresh impressions which crowd the pages of the adventurers, matter which it may transmute into elements of whatever fabric it is shaping. Flotsam and jetsam from seafaring and shipwreck along the coasts of the New World quickened Shakespeare's imagination to the intensity of vision through which *The Tempest* was conceived.[3] And then in turn, under the spell of that very power which they had themselves evoked, the fragments picked up from books of travel were metamorphosed into immortal shapes compact of the universal truth of poetry. Prospero's island—the integration into the everlastingly valid frame of things of unaccommodated waifs from alien shores—is the compendium and symbol of a process of immense significance.

Now that process finds, in the work of Coleridge's tragically brief creative period, as remarkable an embodiment as I know in the whole range of poetry. And in these wider implications of his procedure lies our warrant for following a trail which seems at first to lead as far away from poetry as possible. But even the ancient Mariner returned in the end to the kirk and the hill and the lighthouse top, and however remotely we may for the moment range afield, the ways of the poetic faculty which are our starting-point will also be the upshot of our travel's history.

II

For almost two thousand years a vast and mysterious austral continent beckoned through the mists of terrible and haunted seas. Its shifting outlines hover along the southern rim of the world in those fantastic old cosmographies and mappemondes which record with such vivid fidelity the indomitable struggle of the imagination to overleap the barriers which it could not yet pierce. Nothing, I think, is harder to translate into terms of our own blasé experience than the pregnant fact that the little pre-Columbian world was literally islanded in the unknown—an unknown, none the less, across which came drifting signs and rumours of some kindred knowable beyond, as if to us, whose surfeited generation has set foot on both the poles, strange signal lights should flash from Mars. For centuries across the horizons thronged 'calling shapes, and beckoning shadows dire, And airy tongues, that syllable men's names On sands, and shores, and desert wildernesses.' I am not invoking the spell of Milton's lines for the sake of any adventitious beauty they may lend. They were themselves born of actual impressions recorded in a mediæval travel-book,[4] and their haunting voices are echoes of what for generations men soberly believed they heard. East, West, North, and South were all electrical with premonitions of continents to be, whose looming shapes were the stuff of dreams, till dreams daringly followed where they led became more amazing actuality. And the South, like that West beyond which was thought to lie the Orient, held with particular tenacity the imagination which strove to grasp and comprehend the world—a world which, as it happened, demanded to complete it an *alter orbis*, its counterpart and complement, at the Antipodes. And the Antipodes lay, enveloped in mystery, in the oceans about the austral pole.

But between were fire and ice and the terrors of impenetrable mists. No documents in the world are more eloquent than the laconic legends of the early maps. One word and only one stretches in dim capitals across the whole southern hemisphere on a fifteenth-century chart. It is BRUMÆ:[5] fogs—the dense and chilling mists, which, like the flesh of the spectre-woman on the skeleton-ship, 'thick man's blood with cold.' 'Frigida' and 'Perusta':[6] 'frozen' and 'burned'—the icy breath of polar seas and the fiery noon of equatorial calms—front each other across the huge trough of the ocean (alveus Oceani);[7] that ocean which under the heat of the sun (as the *Imago Mundi* states) boils like a pot (magnus Oceanus qui solis calore dicitur fervere ut cacabus).[8] As the 'ocean unknown to the sons of Adam' (Oceanus filiis Ade incognitus)[9] of a score of maps, it repels access of mortals (accessus repellit hominum)[10] to the South. 'Humanus oculus non videt':[11] no human eye beholds it, declares the legend on a twelfth-century map, and a contemporary mappemonde tells us why: it is the ocean which no mortal sees by reason of that zone in which the elements melt with fervent heat (Oceanus quem nemo vidit hominum propter zonam torridam).[12] And like sea, like land. 'Dixerto dexa-bitado per caldo'[13] (a desert uninhabited on account of heat) stands in red along the sides of the South on a fifteenth-century planosphere. But beyond the ocean lies another barrier: circulus australis que est ex frigore inhabitabilis,[14] as a map of the twelfth century has it—the austral zone where nobody can live by reason of the cold. It is a grim vocabulary, that of the mappemondes. To dare the South was literally, in the mediæval mind, 'to bathe in fiery floods, or to reside In thrilling regions of thick-ribbed ice.' And so, between the three known continents of the North and the mysterious antipodal world of the Antich-thones there was a great gulf fixed—a gulf like that between the living and the dead. Nullus nostrum ad illos, neque illorum ad nos pervenire potest: none of us can go to them, and none of them come to us, Guillaume de Conches declares of the Antipodes, in words that have the finality of doom.[15] Fire, and ice, and mist keep us from them; and as for them, Albertus Magnus hazards the guess that perhaps some magnetic agency holds them fixed, as the magnet holds the iron.[16] But there were perils enough without magnetic intervention to daunt those who go down to the sea in ships.

For the seas were haunted. Glacial moons and blazing suns, the blackness of darkness of the Mare Tenebrosum and the whiteness of engulfing mists, winds meeting winds from the four corners of the world and the sinister collision of the seas (that *maris utriusque collisio* of the mappemondes)[17]—these were blind forces, the endless jar of the elements that clip us round about. But the great deep was alive as well with baleful and sentient things. Any one who turns to the 1560 edition of the *Nomenclator aquatilium animantium*[18] of Conrad Gessner (the same Gessner from whose larger work was drawn Topsell's engaging volume *Of Four-footed Beasts*) will find in the section 'Concerning Sea-monsters' (De Cetis) the stuff that nightmares are made on.[19] The Physeter, which in English (we are told) is called the Whirlpool;* the ill-omened creature with human face and a monkish cowl, whose German name is Wasserman; the delicate monster seen off Poland in 1531, whose scaly skin assumed the likeness of a bishop's garb; the bat-winged demon worthily named the Satyr of the Sea; the grisly Ziphius; the Rosmarus, an elephant in size, which lumberingly scales the mountains bordering on the sea; the Scolopendra, with face of flame, and eyes which measure twenty feet around; the formidable Monoceros[20]—all these and more are graphically pictured, in habit and office as they lived, within the compass of eleven pages. Spenser transferred them bodily to that strange Odyssey of Sir Guyon and the Palmer to the Bower of Bliss.[21] They are the creatures of the 'monstrous world,' under the whelming tide, of 'Lycidas.' And like the magnetic rock, and the *mer betée* (that thick and viscous *Lebermeer* from which no ship can move), and the Gulf of Dragons, and a host of other perils of the abyss,[22] they might wander all the seven seas. But the South had its own forbidding shapes and sorceries. And this time a single map will give us ample store.

It is a mappemonde of the fourteenth century in a manuscript of Higden's *Polychronicon* in the British Museum, and it may be seen in Santarem's great *Atlas*.[23] Like the famous mappemonde of Hereford Cathedral,[24] it is a teeming chart of that *pays des chimères* which before the great age of discovery bounded the mediæval world. Along the southern extremity of the map is strung a line of cramped and obscure legends, which pithily set forth the nature of the denizens of the remoter South. I shall here and there insert the crabbed Latin, for the sake of those who love to savour uncanny phrases with the wicked dew still on them, and freely paraphrase. There are first the Androphagi (Androphagi humanas edunt carnes)[25]—Othello's 'cannibals that each other eat, The Anthropophagi.' Then come the Garamantes, dwelling in a land whose waters boil by day and freeze by night.[26] Next adjoining are the

Farici who eat raw flesh—by preference gobbets of panthers arid lions, as we are elsewhere told.[27] Their neighbours are the Monoculi (Monocollus caput cum pede tegit), a race of cheerful vagabonds with one leg (able none the less to run with marvellous celerity) who sit in the sun and hold their single foot as a parasol above their head. They are depicted in this pleasing posture on the Hereford map, and, like most of the others, their family tree is rooted in the fertile soil of Pliny and Solinus.[28] Beyond the Virgogici, who live on insects, and the Troglodytes, whose voices are melodious, and whose pabulum is serpents,[29] dwell the Antipodes, who dance in ecstasy and have sixteen fingers (Antipodes extasi saltantes octenos habent digitos).[30] The terrors of the deep were surely well worth braving if one could thereby see them 'tossing their heads in sprightly dance,' like a host of Antichthonic daffodils, and could share the secret of their multidigital raptures. Their next-door neighbours are a folk, delineated as well as labelled on the Hereford map, who have their heads and their mouths in their breasts (gens ista habet caput et os in pectore)[31]—those 'men whose heads do grow beneath their shoulders,' to hear of whom Desdemona once did seriously incline. Farther East live a people whose lips, like the solitary foot of the Mono-culus, perform the office of an umbrella against the sun (gens ista obumbrat faciem cum labro [pendente] contra solis ardorem).[32] The Hereford map assuages our curiosity by graphically showing how they do it. Next come the Presumbani, who have no ears;[33] an anonymous people without tongues; a third whose faces are innocent of noses; while between the tongueless and the noseless dwells a race whose mouths are so minute that they are reduced to liquid nourishment imbibed through a straw (hic gentes habent ora conserta et cum avenarum calamis liquidum cibum potant).[34] Beyond them are Gorgons and the Gulf of Dragons,[35] and sea-monsters (bellua), and the Fortunate Isles;[36] and in the same seas on the Hereford map lies an island with the seductive legend: hic sirene habundant—here Sirens are plentiful![37]

That is the phantasmagoria of the early maps.[38] The unknown South was a wild chaos of fantastic marvels, awaiting incorporation within the slowly advancing borders of a known and ordered world. But tropic heat, and polar ice, and mists, and monsters were first to be reckoned with.

III

Reckoned with they were, and what happened not only typifies the universal process through which the strange is assimilated with the familiar, the unknown with the known, but it also leads us straight to 'The Ancient Mariner,' whose weft runs inextricably through the warp of this vaster loom. And the attempt to follow a little farther the weaving of a pattern which took shape through centuries will disclose, I think, the intimate interlacing of the very structure and substance of the poem with a great constructive movement of the imagination across the uncharted spaces of the world.

The monsters were the first to fade into the light of common day. They had been, in the main, grotesque refractions of those persistent rumours which for ages obscurely travelled from the brooding depths of equatorial Africa, or from involuntary temptings, through the caprice of winds and currents, of forbidden seas—rumours of apes, and of bestial and uncanny races, and of formidable shapes half seen across mysterious waters. Even the voyages of Sindbad the Sailor, we now know, were distorted transcripts of reality. But chimeras at close quarters merge into the tangible forms of which they were projections, and as the ends of the earth came together, the fictions of the maps resolved themselves into more amazing facts. And by the opening of that tremendous era of discovery which burst through all the barriers of the mediaeval world, it was only shuddering reminiscences of half-forgotten monsters that now and then still haunted wayfarers by sea, and lent a piquant flavour to the pages of their narratives.[39] But the palpable terrors of polar ice and a vertical sun, instead of dissolving, like the spectres, before the advancing sails, are wrought, with the mists, into the very fabric of the epic record of discovery. And now we touch reality.[40]

Behind the mists, far down beneath the Southern Cross, instead of a continent woven of dreams, two great and formidable capes thrust their beaked promontories into warring seas. And their stern actuality, conjoined with the unquenchable vitality of the ancient dreams, was to determine for centuries the ways of the ships in the midst of the sea. And the course of the Mariner's voyage was charted long before Coleridge's century dawned.

Africa, on the mediæval maps, swept in a vast, blunt, wavering semicircle from the eastern horn of the continent which juts into the Gulf of Aden, to the Pillars of Hercules in the West. Beyond that unstable semicircle lay, to the south, the menacing, and beckoning unknown—repelling through the ominous figment of that impassable zone where the furnace of the sun was insupportable; alluring with visions of an expeditious route by sea around the shallow projection of the continent to the Indies and Cathay. Three quarters of a century before Columbus sailed west to find the east, Prince Henry the Navigator sent expedition after expedition down the west coast of Africa in the attempt to sail around it eastward to the same goal. But the farther south his intrepid mariners pushed, the farther stretched beyond them the interminable coast. At last, in 1487 or 1488, Bartholomew Diaz, driven by storms beyond his predecessors' farthest south, turned east—and lo! there was no land. The terrible cape, 'The Lion of the Seas,' behind which darkness was to hover for four more centuries, had been rounded, and the flaming barriers of the sun had been safely passed. Ten years later Vasco da Gama circumnavigated Africa, and dropped anchor in Calicut. A new and tremendous outline had been added to the map, and the austral continent receded still farther into the mists.

Meantime, within half a dozen years of Diaz's triumph, Columbus, with no supporting line of coast to lead him, daringly followed his star to the sentinel islands of the western world. And at once the prows turned south again. The Spaniard Pinzon touched Brazil in 1500, and later coasted as far south as the Argentine. Almost in his wake came the Portuguese Cabral, who, setting out to follow Vasco da Gama's course, was storm-driven westward, and instead of rounding Africa reached Brazil. And once more, into the unknown south, stretched an interminable, beckoning coast. At last, in 1520, Magellan, braving Patagonian giants and their head-devil Setebos, turned west, and, sailing through the strait which bears his name, was the first that ever burst into that silent sea, which his ship was also the first to cross in the completed circumnavigation of the globe. But south of the straits, desolate and forbidding and still unattempted, rose Terra del Fuego, the Land of Fire. Whither did that extend? Were Magellan's giants and their crew of devils the outposts of the monstrous world—that *mundus alter et idem*—which lay, encircled by ice and fire, about the Antarctic pole? Fifty-eight years later, Sir Francis Drake, after sailing, like Magellan, through the straits, was caught and driven, like the ancient Mariner, towards the pole, and having reached a point south of the Horn, found open sea. The second of the giant capes—unseen and unnamed for a third of a century longer—had been passed; a new and tremendous outline had again been added to the map; and the austral continent still lurked behind its mists.

Then, with the vast continental masses of Africa and the two Americas slowly assuming definite contours, as ship followed ship along their shores, the invincible quest of the old chimera began anew. And for two centuries that quest pivoted upon Cape Horn. For around the grim promontory, as about the turning-post of some huge cosmic race-course under the wheeling stars, all through the seventeenth and eighteenth centuries, French, Dutch, and English sails, wind-swept and battered, fought their way into the Pacific, where, below those illimitable horizons, the unknown still securely waited.

But the frozen silence below the rim of the Antarctic Circle gave no sign, and voyager after voyager turned north into the trackless immensity of the Pacific. And the land of wonders which they failed to find below the Circle they discovered in yet more marvellous archipelagoes beneath the Line. Even the phantom continent itself slipped its moorings and flitted north, to materialize for a moment in the huge bulk of Australia. But it was left to the greatest of all the voyagers in southern seas to lay the ghost of the Antipodes forever. In 1772 Captain James Cook sailed on his second voyage with the definite end of settling the problem of the *alter orbis* once for all. And when he returned, the elusive phantom of the dreams of centuries had vanished beyond recall. But before it faded, and in large part through the irrepressible pursuit of it, the shores of the world had been at last marked out.

IV

What has all this to do with 'The Rime of the Ancient Mariner'? Well, here was a route from sea to sea, to which repeated use had given the familiarity of an established type. Ship after ship sailed south into the Atlantic, past the great skull-shaped westward rondure of Africa, across the Line, and down around the jutting shoulder of Brazil toward the Horn. They were driven (unless luck was with them) past the tempestuous headland into fields of floating ice. Once round the cape, they ran before the trade winds toward the Line again, to lie becalmed for days or weeks, under a heaven that was burning brass above them, in a tranced and breathless sea. Beyond which sea to their several havens we need not follow them. But that vast, sweeping curve, cutting the Equator, with its apex toward the pole, and bending up again from the white terrors of the austral ice to the long nightmare of equatorial calms—that mighty loop thrown round a continent from flaming heat to pitiless cold and back to heat again—not merely translates into living fact the fabulous barriers of the antique maps, but is also the graphic symbol of the track of a host of ships, the absorbing tales of which by the end of the eighteenth century, had been set down in books.

Now read the Mariner's log, as Coleridge gives it baldly in the Argument:

> How a Ship having passed the Line was driven by storms to the cold Country towards the South Pole; and how from thence she made her course to the tropical Latitude of the Great Pacific Ocean; and of the strange things that befell; and in what manner the Ancyent Marinere came back to his own Country.

That might have been a ship of Drake, or Le Maire, or Roggeveen, or Cook, or Bligh. So also might have been the ship of the more explicit gloss:

> The Mariner tells how the ship sailed southward with a good wind and fair weather, till it reached the line. . . . The ship driven by a storm toward the south pole. The land of ice, and of fearful sounds where no living thing was to be seen. . . . The ship . . . return[s] northward through fog and floating ice. . . . The fair breeze continues; the ship enters the Pacific Ocean, and sails northward, even till it reaches the Line. The ship hath been suddenly becalmed.

The basic structure of the voyage regarded as a voyage is as austerely true to fact as an Admiralty report. Yet that stark outline, as we have seen, is itself a compendium of the premonitory dreams, and the imaginative vision, and the intrepid daring of two-score generations. And now on this frame, as upon a loom, the imagination was to weave another, and this time a magic pattern. But the magic plays, like strange light over a familiar landscape, upon a groundwork of fact deep-rooted as the continents themselves, and permeated with the elemental experience of humanity.

---

*The Physeter may be seen on p. 111 above.

CHAPTER VIII

THE PATTERN

LET us follow, then, for a moment this fixed warp through which the weaving shuttle of the shaping spirit moved. The grand structural line of the voyage is the first determining factor of the poem. How has Coleridge plotted its course?

He does it in a way that is his own. In few other poems in the language, I suspect, is Lessing's injunction never to clip the wings of the imagination followed with more finished art.

> 'God save thee, ancient Mariner!
> From the fiends, that plague thee thus!—
> Why look'st thou so?'—With my cross-bow
> I shot the ALBATROSS.[1]

No circumstantial delineation of horror in a human countenance could touch in telling effect the powerful suggestion of that horrified interruption.[2] And in similar fashion Coleridge, with the scheme of the voyage charted as lucidly in his mind as on a map, bends his own imagination to the end of stirring ours to reconstruct it. And he first sets us framing the basic loop of the voyage through the agency of another trenchant interruption.

I

The ship is at the Equator twice. It crosses it in the Atlantic sailing south, and the equatorial calms of the Pacific are the stage for half the action of the story. To hold the ship in the tropics going south would be to blunt the keen edge of anticipation when the great stanzas are reached in which the imaginative splendour of the poem culminates. Yet the southward passage of the tropics is the first range of that vast arch on which the narrative is built. How is it to fulfil its structural office in the poem, and still be left to the imagination? Here are the stanzas in which the trick is done:

> 'The Sun came up upon the left,
> Out of the sea came he!
> And he shone bright, and on the right
> Went down into the sea.
> Higher and higher every day,
> *Till over the mast at noon—*'
> The Wedding-Guest here beat his breast,
> For he heard the loud bassoon.[3]

And red as a rose, before the merry minstrelsy, the bride has paced into the hall, and when the tale is taken up again, the ship is driving before the storm-blast toward the pole.[4] It is all as expeditious as a magic carpet. The vertical sun stands over the mast for an instant at noon, to mark the crossing of the Line. Then the dramatic incursion of the wedding revelry, like the knocking in *Macbeth*, snaps for a moment the spell of the tale, and, with the fine economy of practised art, blots the superfluous first passage of the tropics completely from the poem. And then the vertical sun itself, its temporary function as a seamark briefly served, is snuffed from the sky like a candle, to reappear at its appointed hour as a disastrous portent in the element above a rotting sea. That is the most superb *tour de force* in the poem—but it is not the only one.

II

We have had to construct the first lap of the voyage on the pregnant hint of the sun above a mast. What, now, of the perilous circuit of the Cape? The Horn was a shape of terror to all the navigators whom Coleridge knew—and one looks in vain for note or mention of it in the poem. Has the keystone dropped out of the arch? The Cape, on the contrary, is securely there, but it looms by implication behind a consummately adroit expedient through which the doubling of it is suggested—a manœuvre more dexterous, if less dramatic, than the obliteration of a troublesome stretch of the voyage by the sound of a bassoon. And it is perfectly in keeping with the bewildering genesis of the poem that the hint for this device should have come to Coleridge from the traditional rounding of the Cape of Good Hope by Phœnician sailors six hundred years before Christ, and two thousand before Bartholomew Diaz; and that it should have reached him from Herodotus by way of the West Indies.

Nowhere in the poem are we told directly that the formidable spur of the continent has been securely passed. As the ship drives south,

> The Sun came up *upon the left*,
> Out of the sea came he!
> And he shone bright, and *on the right*
> Went down into the sea.

Then follow the terrors of the polar ice; the albatross is shot; and the next we know,

> The Sun now rose *upon the right:*
> Out of the sea came he,
> Still hid in mist, and *on the left*
> Went down into the sea.[5]

Now one of the books which we know, on Coleridge's own testimony, that he had been reading at just about this time[6] was Bryan Edwards's *History, Civil and Commercial, of the British Colonies in the West Indies*. And he read it with a receptive mind. For it was 'Bryan Edwards's account of the effects of the *Oby* witchcraft on the Negroes in the West Indies' which (together with 'Hearne's deeply interesting anecdotes of . . . the Copper Indians') was the immediate inspiration of 'The Three Graves.'[7] But there was another passage in the volume which could not have escaped Coleridge's eye. Edwards is discussing the perennial question of the possibility of pre-Columbian voyages to the western world, and he quotes a paragraph from Herodotus: 'The Phenicians therefore sailing from the Red Sea navigated the Southern Ocean. . . . Thus two years having elapsed, they returned to Egypt, passing by the Pillars of Hercules; and they reported a circumstance which I can scarcely credit, but other people may, *that sailing round Lybia the sun rose on the right hand*.'[8] The italics are there in the *History*, to catch even the dullest eye, and Edwards proceeds at once to drive home their import. The phrase they have thrown into saliency is, he points out, conclusive evidence that the Cape of Good Hope had been rounded. 'The circumstance,' he continues, 'that the sun rose on the right, is decisive of the main fact;—for it demonstrates that they had then actually doubled the southern promontory, and were steering in a northerly direction.' That is as plain as a pikestaff, and the singular circumstance which had so impressed Herodotus lay fallow in Coleridge's brain.[9] And when he found himself faced by the problem of getting his Mariner expeditiously around the sister cape, Herodotus and the tell-tale shift of the sun to the right flashed up to memory, and the Phœnicians contributed two stanzas to 'The Ancient Mariner.'

III

The pivotal point of the Cape once turned, the next stage of the voyage was the long, northwesterly run before the trade winds toward the Line. Has Coleridge, in laying down his curve with rigorous exactness, overlooked the trades?* Again, like the Cape and the equator, the trades are punctually there. The curious vicissitudes incident to words have for us effectively disguised them, but here, unmistakably, they are:

> *The fair breeze blew*, the white foam flew,
> The furrow followed free.[10]

Nobody can read the old voyages into the southern hemisphere without meeting at every turn 'the Brises.' I shall not cumber the page with the cloud of witnesses who might be summoned. Purchas alone will amply serve our turn. 'At the Indies, and in all the burning Zone,' writes the 'learned Jesuit, Josephus Acosta,' 'the Easterne winde which they call Brise is . . . very healthfull and pleasant.'[11] And on Acosta's phrase, 'the *Brise*, or Easterly windes,' we are edified by the margent to this effect: 'The Brize (or motion of the aire with the heavens) is a winde.'[12] With Purchas's marginal gloss once more—'What thing the Brises are'—Herrera, in his *Description of the West Indies*, writes more explicitly:

> The Brises are windes which comprehend all the Easterne windes with all their quarters, and are so ordinarie and firme, because the swift motion of the First Moover, doth carry after him the Element of the

> Aire . . . and so the Aire followeth alwaies the motion of the Day, going from East to West, never varying . . . and therefore the Brise winde which runneth from the East, is so continuall in those parts.[13]

The Brises, accordingly, now familiar to every school-boy as the trade winds, were of absorbing interest to the early voyagers, and cut a significant figure in their narratives.[14]

Now Coleridge first wrote (and for us it is a pity that he changed it) 'the breezes':

> *The breezes* blew, the white foam flew,
> The furrow follow'd free.[15]

That is not, as most of us take it, the whispering breeze which rhymes conveniently with 'trees' in poetry. The Mariner's ship, like the 'Golden Hind' or the 'Endeavour,' has rounded the Cape, and has come into the region of the trades, which sweep, 'following alwaies the motion of the Day,' from the southeast towards the Equator. To the first readers of the poem the line could have no other meaning. Even 'the fair breeze'—the 'Brise' of the voyagers*—in the later version was open, I think, to little or no contemporary misunderstanding. For us, unluckily, the loss to common usage of the old nautical sense of the term has robbed the passage of an essential part of its significance. Coleridge, to be sure, was incidentally composing a stanza which was to be among the most memorable in English poetry. But beyond that, at the moment, he was building up, step by step, the great basic structure of the poem. And in the large economy of his design the Breezes constituted an essential factor. The lost point of the line is worth retrieving, not merely as another index of the poem's underlying fidelity to fact, but because it keeps us, in salutary fashion, from forgetting that through the chaos of impressions which were pouring into 'The Ancient Mariner,' moved all the while a plan.

IV

Then, all at once, its adhesion to fact no whit relaxed, the plan in its unfolding is transfigured before us, and the thrill of the supreme experience of all the discoverers who ever sailed the seas is caught from its fleeting moment into permanence in two unforgettable lines:

> The fair breeze blew, the white foam flew,
> The furrow followed free;
> *We were the first that ever burst*
> *Into that silent sea.*[17]

Coleridge must have read, in the Introduction to that auspicious little octavo which gave him Frederick Martens, how Magellan and his men 'found out a great Streight leading into the South Sea, called afterwards, by the Inventor's Name, the Magellan Streight; through which *he was the first that passed from the Atlantick into the Pacifick Ocean*, and so round the Globe home again';[18] and so another phrase from the voyagers wrought its spell. Moreover, he had read in Purchas how, when Magellan 'was past the Strait, and saw the way open to the other maine Sea, hee was so glad thereof that for joy the teares fell from his eyes.'[19] And Coleridge would not have been himself—or a poet—had he not (as Keats was now Achilles shouting in the trenches, now the sparrow picking about the gravel before his window)[20]—had he not *been* Magellan, at that thrilling entrance into a vast and unknown sea. 'For,' as he wrote years later (and the very essence of the poetic faculty finds expression in his words), 'from my very childhood, I have been accustomed to abstract, and as it were, unrealize whatever of more than common interest my eyes dwelt on, *and then by a sort of transfusion and transmission of my consciousness to identify myself with the object.*' Then, with a strange harking back to what had moved him long before, he declares that if he ever 'should feel once again the genial warmth and stir of the poetic impulse,' he would transfuse himself into 'a rock, with its summit just raised above the surface of some bay or strait in the Arctic Sea . . . all around me fixed and firm . . . as my own substance, and near me lofty masses . . . in such wild play with meteoric lights, or with the quiet shine from above . . . that it was . . . a place of healing to lie.'[21] That is the child (the father of the man, if ever this was true) who used to 'read through all the gilt-cover little books that could be had . . . and likewise all the uncovered tales of Tom Hickathrift, Jack the Giant-killer, etc., etc., etc., etc. And I used to lie by the wall and *mope*, and my spirits used to come upon me suddenly; and in a flood of them I was accustomed to race up and down the churchyard, and act over all I had been reading, on the docks, the nettles, and the rank grass.'[22] So does every child. But the poet is he in whom the Vision does not die away, and in 'The Ancient Mariner' the child grown man was still 'acting over all he had been reading,' but now the docks and nettles and rank grass had given place to the elements which clothe the sea with mystery and terror. And even as Coleridge transfused himself into Magellan, so and no otherwise John Keats *was* Cortez, when, stirred by a similar reminiscence of high adventure[23] (magnificently true to the spirit of fact, even if a little shaky in the letter) he wrote:

> Then felt I like some watcher of the skies
> When a new planet swims into his ken;
> Or like stout Cortez when with eagle eyes
> He star'd at the Pacific—and all his men
> Look'd at each other with a wild surmise—
> Silent, upon a peak in Darien.

And those two metamorphoses of fact into imaginative vision may stand as an epitome of the power whose ways we are seeking to understand.

V

And now, with an abruptness like that of the fall of the shot bird off the Cape, the ship is at the Line:

> Down dropt the breeze, the sails dropt down.[24]

Unheralded, save by that descending stroke of one laconic line, the horror of tropical seas to men becalmed is all at once about us.

And beneath the Line the voyage, as an architectonic factor in the poem, ends. For at the close of Part Five the ship is still at the Equator. And there, facing Coleridge with his task five-sevenths completed, stretched still the interminable sail, around the Cape of Good Hope, home. Something must be done, if the poem is to put a girdle round about the earth in forty minutes. And Ali Baba himself could not have managed better. 'The air is cut away before, And closes from behind'[25]—and the ship drifts over the harbour-bar, while the same moonlight which had just bemocked the sultry main now steeps in silentness the steady weathercock. Captain James (from whose log-book Coleridge took more than one leaf, and perhaps this hint among them) writes scornfully of 'what hath beene long agoe fabled by some Portingales, that should haue comne this way out of the South Sea . . . who neuer speake of any difficulties, as shoald water, ice, nor sight of land, but [write] as if they had beene brought home *in a dreame or engine.*'[26] Even so, the supernatural motion of the ship casts the Mariner into a serviceable trance, and when he awakes, it is his native country he beholds. But such sovereign devices belong in the sphere of another of the great unifying influences which shape the poem, and not here. When the calms at the Line are left behind, the office of the course from Equator to Equator round the Horn has been fulfilled.

VI

Now just as the shadow of the ship imposed pellucid unity upon the throng of images which poured up into the hoar-frost of the moon, so the bold outline of the voyage exercised its incorporating power upon the chaos of reminiscences which underlie the poem as a whole. Or rather, into the magnetic field of that formative conception were drawn, from the broad range of Coleridge's reading, the myriad fragments of memory which had rested, dormant and unmustered, in the Well. But there were two cluster-points of the sleeping images which were stirred to peculiarly intense activity, as the plastic agency of the design exerted its attraction. For the two stretches of the actual voyage which inevitably stamped on the mind the most powerful impressions were the 'Frigida' and the 'Perusta' of the ancient maps—the tract of calms at the Equator, and the fields of ice about the pole. And nowhere else in the poem is there such an incredible flocking together and coalescence of scattered recollections as at these two points—when the ship is passing through the ice-packs, and when it is lying becalmed at the Line.

But there were tributary streams of recollections flowing in. Quite apart from their connection with the voyages around the Horn, precisely these same two regions—the purlieus of the Equator and the poles—had long held for Coleridge an independent fascination of their own. Greenland and Lapland and Spitzbergen, as we have seen, had been fermenting oddly in his brain three years and more before 'The Ancient Mariner' was written. The enthralling accounts in Purchas of moving accidents and disastrous chances in the Arctic ice had been read and vividly remembered. That stubborn and pious old Bristol seaman, Captain Thomas James, had provided in his *Strange and Dangerous Voyage*, with a certain grim satisfaction in his hardships, the raw materials for a new *Inferno*, all ice; and Coleridge could no more have escaped in Bristol the shade of his ancient fellow-townsman than the Wedding-Guest could have given the ancient Mariner the slip.[27] Other books too there were, but these were enough. There was no lack of ice afloat on the seas of that capacious memory.

As for Coleridge's addiction to the tropics, that had two quite special focal points. As early as his salad days at Cambridge his Prize Greek Ode on the Slave Trade had turned his eyes to the West Indies,[28] and the residence of his Bristol friends the Pinneys on the island of St. Nevis later gave birth to one of his wildest flights of fancy—the scheme of emigrating there himself, with Southey and Wordsworth, and of 'makling] the Island more illustrious than Cos or Lesbos!'[29] Books on the

West Indies, then, he had eagerly read for years, and books on the West Indies are full of the calms and the tempests, the dews and the twilights, of tropical latitudes. But there was a further centre for tropical imagery in his memory. Scarcely second, in its perennial interest, to the quest of the austral continent itself, was the attempt to penetrate to the mysterious sources of the Nile. And there was one book of the day which everybody who read at all was reading—Bruce's *Travels to Discover the Source of the Nile*. It had been the topic of discussion in April, 1794, in Coleridge's circle at Cambridge.[30] On Christmas Eve, 1794, Coleridge quoted one of its purple patches in a note to his 'Religious Musings,'[31] and thirteen years later we find Dorothy Wordsworth writing to Lady Beaumont: 'Coleridge says that the last edition of Bruce's "Travels" is a book that you ought by all means to have.'[32] And so tropical Africa joined forces with the West Indies to store the deep Well with images. And the grand curve of the voyage struck with its magnetic compulsion through these tracts with the rest.

For the Well knows neither time nor place. The poles converge and the Line shrinks to a point. The ice of the North and the ice of the South are one, and the vertical sun above the mast is blood in a copper sky alike in the East and the West. And into the warp of the voyage—the great historic route of discovery and adventure from Magellan to Captain Cook—was woven a woof the threads of which were caught up from the four quarters of the globe. For our purpose it is sufficient to trace their interweavings where the pattern is richest and most intricate—in the fields of ice, and the courts of the Sun. And blended with the rest we shall find a strain which is redolent of the fields and combes of Somerset.

---

*It is here, at last, that I can count with absolute assurance on some exasperated reader who will say: 'But, in the name of all the unities and the proprieties at once, isn't this a fairy-tale? And what under the vertical sun and the hornèd moon has rigorous exactitude to do with the charting of seas beneath which polar dæmons lurk, and on which spectre-barks appear and vanish?' Such seas, we may own, they undoubtedly are. But mystery is then tenfold mysterious when it comes upon us out of the fixed and definite, and unfolds against the background of the surely known. And Coleridge's art is nowhere more supreme than in his scrupulous adherence to tangible fact in his universe of sheer imagination. And anyway, who of us dare lay a magisterial finger on the evanescent point at which the sea's tangible realities melt into its eternal, impalpable, brooding mystery? As for Coleridge, he, at least, was aware that haunted seas have trade winds—or that the seas swept by the trades are haunted, as you please.

*And of Burton, who, like Coleridge, followed them. In that most delightful of all the divagations in the *Anatomy*, the 'Digression of the Air,' Burton writes of the torrid zone, once held to be uninhabitable, 'but by our modern travellers found to be most temperate, bedewed with frequent rains, and moistening showers, *the brise* and cooling blasts in some parts . . . most pleasant and fertile.'[16]

CHAPTER IX

THE FIELDS OF ICE

COLERIDGE, when he wrote 'The Ancient Mariner' (to reiterate what cannot be too constantly recalled), had never even crossed the Channel, much less sailed, like Emerson's lone seaman or his own, 'all night, astonished, among stars.' Yet here in the poem are the authentic splendours and terrors of the polar ice. A romantic Laplander suffused in rosy light and mimic lustre is one thing; this sinister world of menacing shapes and fearful sounds is quite another. Neither shapes nor sounds were to be seen or heard at Bristol or Nether Stowey. 'Out of whose womb came the ice?' That incisive question, which the Lord once asked out of the whirlwind—and would not stay for an answer!—is curiously pertinent here.

Let us hark back for a moment to a theme already touched on—those ocular images which flashed from the printed word as Coleridge read. What shifting procession of vivid spectra passed before his inner eye, to live beyond the moment in his memory, as he bent his head over the pages of his voyages in frozen seas? In the answer to that second question lies, I think, the answer to the first.

I

We have seen how 'The Ancient Mariner' fell heir to the garnerings, conscious and unconscious, for the unwritten Hymns to the Elements. There were two other abortive projects (not to mention 'The Destiny of Nations') which kept Coleridge's eye alert, as he read, for telling accounts of the pageantry of ice and snow on the frontiers of the poles. It was not by accident that his memory, when he came to write the 'Mariner,' was crowded with impressions of the terrible beauty of desolate and icy seas. Before the plan of the poem was hit upon, he had meditated—if De Quincey is to be trusted—'a poem on delirium, confounding its own dream scenery with external things, *and connected with the imagery of high latitudes*.'[1] That rings so true to Coleridge that, despite De Quincey's notorious frailties as a witness, it carries its own conviction. But the other abandoned scheme needs no reservation on the score of evidence.

In January, 1798, while 'The Ancient Mariner' was under way, Coleridge wrote a long letter to Wordsworth from Shrewsbury, chiefly about 'Monk' Lewis's *Castle Spectre*.[2] He had just met, as it happened, a young Cambridge undergraduate. 'Talking of plays, etc., he told me that an acquaintance of his was printing a translation of one of Kotzebue's tragedies, entitled "Benyowski." The name startled me, and upon examination I found that the story of my "Siberian Exiles" has been already dramatized.' Coleridge, then, had meant to write a play on 'Benyowski,' but had been forestalled by Kotzebue. What, however, has that irrefragable fact to do with 'The Ancient Mariner' and polar ice?

The *Memoirs and Travels of Mauritius Augustus, Count de Benyowsky*, translated from the French in 1790, constitute one of the most thrilling and dramatic narratives of the period. They contain, among other things (to draw on the succinct epitome of the title-page), 'His Exile into Kamschatka, [and] his Escape and Voyage from that Peninsula through the Northern Pacific Ocean, touching at Japan and Formosa, to Canton in China.' And Coleridge drew the book from the Bristol Library December 1, 1797 (just seventeen days after 'The Ancient Mariner' was begun), and he retained it until December 15.[3] He was reading, that is, for his 'Siberian Exiles' while the poem was getting under way—not far (in all probability) from the very time when the Mariner's ship was passing, like Benyowski's,[4] through the ice. The forgotten story, of absorbing interest still, we need not rehearse; the pertinent matter is the setting which its dramatization required. And it is curious to observe what actually happened when Kotzebue's play was staged in Boston in 1799.[5] The paramount place in the announcements in the current prints is given (as if it were to-day!) to the scenery: 'A Snow Scene, and Mountains of Ice at a distance . . . Winter Landscape by Moon Light, covered with Snow and Ice . . . Half Moon descending'—with the huts of the exiles, and the harbour of Bolcheretsk. And it is a polar setting which Coleridge's intended treatment of the subject constrained him to provide. Projects hovering in his fertile brain, in a word, although they never reached fruition, served none the less as magnetic fields for imagery; and as he read, 'spectra' of ice mast-high and snowy clifts and fog-smoke white, set, as infallibly as the ocean currents, towards these cluster-points.

And when at last he actually saw the ice, precisely the things which had struck home to his imagination in the tales which he had read of the regions about the poles exercised a similar fascination on his bodily eye and ear. One of the most vivid letters which he ever wrote he sent back from Germany to Mrs. Coleridge, just one year after he had written Wordsworth about his 'Siberian Exiles.' The whole Lake of Ratzeburg, as he saw it, was 'one mass of thick transparent ice.' One morning, 'the moment the Sun peeped over the Hill, the mist broke in the middle, and in a few seconds stood divided, leaving a broad road all across the Lake; and between these two Walls of mist the sunlight *burnt* upon the ice, forming a road of golden fire' (he had not forgotten his water-snakes!) 'intolerably bright. . . . About a month ago . . . there was a storm of wind; during the whole night, such were the thunders and howlings of the breaking ice' ('the images of memory' were still 'flowing in on the impulses of immediate perception'[6]) 'that they have left a conviction on my mind, that there are Sounds more sublime than any Sight *can* be. . . . On the evening of the next day, at sun-set, the shattered ice . . . appeared of a deep blue, and in shape like an agitated sea; beyond this, the water, that ran up between the great Islands of ice . . . shone of a yellow green; but all these scattered Ice-islands, themselves, were of an intensely bright blood colour—they seemed blood and light in union.'[7] The rest of the letter is sheer magic of subtle imaginative observation,[8] but the part which we have read is sufficient to make clear the peculiar sensitization of Coleridge's visualizing faculty to the imagery of ice. And as late as twenty years after 'The Ancient Mariner' was written the spell still held. For what is that haunting picture of the meteor-lighted rock in the Arctic sea, with which Coleridge longed in imagination to identify himself, but a stirring, in their ashes, of the wonted fires? There came, it is clear, to the creation of the great stanzas which depict the austral ice, not merely masses of assembled images, but a powerful bent.

And the images themselves were compelling to the last degree. Let me give a single picture which certainly met Coleridge's eye. One of the most absorbing narratives in Purchas is Gerrit de Veer's account of William Barents's last voyage 'Northward to the Kingdomes of Cathaia and China, in Anno 1596.' Coleridge, as we shall see, read it with a connoisseur's eye for its artless felicities of phrase, no less than for its profoundly human interest. Just at the beginning of the narrative occurs this sentence: 'And when the Sunne was about South South-east, *wee saw a strange sight in the Element.*'[9] What it was that they saw, de Veer tells at once: 'On each side of the Sunne there was another Sunne, and two Raine-bowes, that past cleane thorow the three Sunnes, and then two Raine-bowes more, the one compassing round about the Sunnes, and the other crosse thorow the great rundle.' Now the man who entered in his Note Book the marine rainbow off the Cape of Good Hope and John Haygarth's 'Description of a Glory' above the Vale of Clwyd would never let an optical wonder like that escape him.[10] Nor did he. For in the gloss to Part Five of 'The Ancient Mariner' he wrote: 'He . . . *seeth strange sights* and commotions *in* the sky and *the element.*' And two paragraphs later in de Veer he came upon the sudden and dramatic advent of the ice, set down with the vivid simplicity which gives to the whole narrative its unrivalled charm:

> The fifth, wee saw the first Ice, which we wondered at, at the first, thinking that it had beene white Swannes, for one of our men walking in the Fore-decke, on a sudden began to cry out with a loud voyce, and said; that hee saw white Swannes: which wee that were under Hatches hearing, presently came up, and perceived that it was Ice that came driving from the great heape, showing like Swannes, it being then about Eevening.[11]

And from that first sight of the ghostly ice-shapes in the

evening light to the end of the unforgettable story, 'the ice is here, the ice is there, the ice is all around,' as it is in a score of other brave accounts. And pouring in, now from this, now from that narrative among them, impressions of the coming of the ice had permeated Coleridge's memory.

Now I have read a fair share of the voyages which Coleridge read. And I have read none of them which deal with polar ice and equatorial seas without incessant recognition of the fact that when one reads the voyages one finds at every turn 'The Ancient Mariner,' and finds no less, when one reads the 'Mariner,' the very essence of the voyages. It is as if the separate images from Coleridge's reading had carried with them into their new environment a shadowy penumbra of other images with which they had once been joined, or as if each focussed in itself subtle potentialities of suggestion caught from associations which it had before the poem was. And some sense of that, at least, I think it may be possible to give.

That, and I hope something else. 'The Ancient Mariner,' as Wordsworth said of it, 'grew and grew.'[12] It grew from 'half-past four in the afternoon'[13] of November 13, 1797, when the fateful walk among the Quantock Hills began, until the evening of March 23, 1798, when Coleridge went to dine with the Wordsworths at Alfoxden, and 'brought his ballad finished.'[14] And there were moments during those four months when Coleridge's powers were operating with magical precision and intensity, until words ceased to be mere symbols of things, and became (as he said of Pascal's style) 'a robe of pure light.'[15] That we have seen, and shall see again. The same verbal magic, to be sure, is present, in a measure, in the pictures of the polar ice, but I mean to turn these graphic stanzas to another purpose. 'Longinquitie,' wrote shrewd old Purchas apropos of a particularly far-fetched yarn—'longinquitie cannot easily be confuted.'[16] The longinquity of the polar seas is obvious enough, and under cover of that unassailable remoteness Coleridge was free to smuggle into his stanzas fiction upon fiction, had he pleased. Yet in place of that, the most striking trait they actually show (utterly paradoxical as it may seem) is an astonishing fidelity to fact. That is one thing.

Moreover, in these same half-dozen stanzas, recollections of what Coleridge had read were crowding up to consciousness *en masse*, as iron-filings cluster to the magnet. Yet (as James Russell Lowell, writing of Coleridge's finished art, felicitously puts it) 'he gives us the very quintessence of perception, the clearly crystallized precipitation of all that is most precious in the ferment of impression after the impertinent and obtrusive particulars have evaporated from the memory. It is the pure visual ecstasy disengaged from the confused and confusing material that gave it birth.'[17] That is in part sheer divination, for Lowell could not have dreamed the whole amazing truth—could not have known, for instance, that before 'the confused and confusing material' fell into ordered sequence there were fermenting beneath this single group of stanzas Arctic and Antarctic seas, Greenland and Spitzbergen and the Horn, the sixteenth, seventeenth, and eighteenth centuries, Hakluyt and Purchas and Harris, Magellan and Captain James, Barents and Dithmar Blefkins, to say nothing of Frederick Martens and David Crantz. Yet there they are, and were they absent, the crystalline stanzas had not been, and were they *recognizable* as there, the crystals had been things of flaws and blemishes. And that is the second consideration.

Nowhere more clearly, then, than in the recital of the passage through the ice is it possible to see these two conspicuous characteristics of the poem: its close adherence to actuality; and its power of striking through confused masses of recollections to the luminous point upon which they all converge. And so, leaving other matters for exemplification by other groups of stanzas, I shall try to exhibit for these not only the ferment of impression, but also the crystallized precipitation: to reconstruct, in a word, so far as possible, the chaos which Coleridge was carrying about with him, and to set beside it the succinct and lucid entities to which the hodge-podge was reduced.

II

It will be necessary to strip of the setting which gives them half their fascination the passages which we shall use. And I wish it were possible instead to display them as they lie, broadcast and alluring, like the jewels in Sindbad's valley, in the pages of the voyagers. They lie there still, however, unrifled and intact, for those happy adventurers who care to seek them. And we may first turn once more to Frederick Martens.

'On the 2d of June . . . in the night we saw the Moon very pale, as it used to look in the day time in our Country, with clear Sun-shine, whereupon followed *mist and snow.*'[18] Six pages later, '*the Ice came a floating* down apace . . . *and it was very cold.*'[19] And Coleridge wrote:

> Listen, Stranger! *Mist and Snow,*
> *And it grew wond' rous cauld:*
> *And Ice* mast-high *came floating* by
> As green as Emerauld.[20]

That seems to leave us 'mast-high' and 'green as Emerauld' as Coleridge's own! But have we even those? In the *Strange and Dangerous Voyage*, Captain James, with the iteration inseparable from a log-book, records the height of the ice: 'We had Ice not farre off about us, and some pieces, *as high as our Top-mast-head*'; 'In this course, we were much tormented, pestered and beaten with the Ice: many pieces being *higher then our Top-mast-head*'; 'We continued on our course, blinded with foggie and durtie weather; and that, intermixt with snow, and frost; amongst disperst pieces of Ice: many of them *higher then our Top-mast head*'—'mountainous Ice; farre *higher then our Top-mast head*,' we read on the same page. And elsewhere the ice is 'full halfe *mast high*.'[21] As for the emerald-green, the colours of the ice profoundly impressed the voyagers. Now it is blue (of such bright and various hues that the old navigators are put to delightful shifts to describe them),[22] and now 'white as alabaster.'[23] But it is also green. It 'is of a pale green colour like vitriol,' says Crantz,[24] and it is seen in water which de Veer declares to be 'as greene as Grasse,'[25] and Martens '*as green as an Emerald*.'[26] And finally, in Harris, after an account of the 'many odd and strange Figures' of the ice, follows the statement: 'Nor do their Figures and Shape alone surprize, but also their Diversity of Colours pleases the Sight; for some are like white Chrystal, others as blue as Saphires, and others again *green as Emeralds*.'[27]

We have, then, a remarkable and at first blush disconcerting fact to reckon with. The very words of the stanza are the words of Martens and Harris and James. Even the 'wondrous' rings true to James. 'The sixteenth,' the dogged old captain noted in his log, 'was *wondrous* hot.'[28] And the dream-like suddenness with which in the poem the ice is all at once about us merely repeats the ominous absence of warning with which in the voyages the looming shapes appear: 'About twelve of the clocke this night it being still calme, wee found our selves *suddenly* compast round about with great Ilands of Ice'[29] 'When *on a sudden* a Mountain of Ice began to appear out of the Fog'[30]— and so on, *ad libitum*. Has our confidence in the supreme originality of a work of genius been after all misplaced?

Well, there is the stanza! Hunt till doomsday through Martens and Harris and Captain James, and you will not find it. The words are severally the words of the voyagers; the shining constellation of images—simple as kirk or hill, and clear as air—which rose out of their confluence, was the birth of a shaping brain that was not the travellers'. And the stanza bears Coleridge's image and superscription stamped on every line. 'Origins prove nothing,'[31] William James bluntly declared with reference to a very different problem; nor do they prove anything here. All they do is to afford a welcome answer to the question: *What has creative genius framed from its inert stuff?* The raw materials and the manner of their framing possess for most human beings, as they should, perennial interest; but both matter and process are subsidiary to the fabric which crowns the work—a fabric which nevertheless reveals to the full the artificer's triumph only when they too come into the reckoning. And in the lines before us the case is clear. Coleridge's memory has struck straight as a homing pigeon through its chaos of hovering impressions.of the polar ice to the exact, concretely visualizing phrase. The ice is 'mast-high'; it is 'green as emerald'; it 'comes floating by.' Every word, with the instant intelligibility of speech daily on the lips, calls up its picture, and the thing which is Coleridge's is the marshalling of a shapeless confusion of scattered recollections into clarity, order, and form. The originality of 'The Rime of the Ancient Mariner' is the originality of every great work of art, and any shock which our preconceptions may now and then experience will find, I hope, reasonable compensation in a possibly fresh conception of the way in which the imagination operates. At all events, we may safely maintain our composure until the facts are all before us.

III

One of the most salient phenomena of the polar skies was the strange sheen or lustre sent off by the ice. Crantz gives a long and detailed description of 'the famous Ice-glance, or shining ice, in the charts named the Eis-blink, or *de witte Blink*. It is a great high field of ice, whose glance in the air may be seen for many leagues at sea, resembling the Aurora Borealis.'[32] Captain Cook tells of 'a brightness in the Northern horizon, like that reflected from ice, commonly called the blink.'[33] But in Martens snow takes the place of ice: 'the snow was marbel'd, and . . . gave as bright and glorious a shining or gloss to the Air or Skies, as if the Sun had shin'd.'[34] 'The true Rocks,' he goes on, 'look't fiery, and the Sun shin'd pale upon them, the Snow giving the Air a bright reflection.'[35] And in his chapter 'Of the Ice' he adds: 'where the Ice is fixed upon the Sea, you see a snow-white brightness in the Skies, as if the Sun shined, for the Snow is reflected by the Air, just as a Fire by Night is; but . . . where there is many small Ice-fields, that are as the Meadows for the Seales, you see no lustre or brightness of the Skies.'[36] And by way of the faithful Crantz, or Captain

Cook, or Frederick Martens, the aërial sheen of the snow was predestined to find lodgement in Coleridge's memory.

But it is 'snowy *clifts*' which in the stanza send their dismal sheen. And there are 'clifts' a-plenty in the voyagers. The hinder part of Barents's ship 'lay in a *clift* of Ice,'[37] and they buried the ship's carpenter 'under the sedges, in the *clift* of a hill.'[38] During one of those almost daily encounters with the fierce polar bears that beleaguered their makeshift house, 'one of [our men] fell into a *Clift* of Ice, which,' de Veer goes on, 'grieved us much: for we thought verily that the Beares would have ranne unto him, to devoure him, but God defended him: for the Beares still made towardes the ship after the men that ranne thither to save themselves. Meane time, wee and the man that fell into the *Clift* of Ice, tooke our advantage.'[39] Again, 'about the South Sunne we saw a *Clift* that was full of birds.' But this last was no 'cleft,' but a 'cliff.' For de Veer proceeds to tell how easy it was to take the birds from their nests, because 'they feared no bodie . . . that could not climbe up the high *Clifts*'; and how the men were in danger of breaking their arms and legs as they came down, 'because the. *Clift* was so high and so steepe'; and how, finally, the nests 'lay upon the bare *Clift* without any straw or other thing under them.'[40] Untorn to bits, as I am tearing it, it is all (as Coleridge read it) vivid with life and racy with human interest, and the word sticks in the reader's memory as firmly as the unlucky seaman stuck in the clift itself. Coleridge was undoubtedly familiar with the term in both its senses.[41] But, as it happens, the pages which gave it to 'The Ancient Mariner' were not in Purchas, but in the well-thumbed volume containing Sir John Nar-borough, and Captain Wood, and Frederick Martens.

Both Martens and Wood lay stress on 'cliffs' or 'clifts' of *snow*. 'Below, at the feet of the Mountains,' says Martens, 'stand the Hills of Ice very high . . . *the Cliffs are filled up with Snow*.'[42] And Martens's 'cliffs' are beyond question clefts. Not only is there mention a little later of the melting of the snow, so that '*in the Cliffs between the great Rocks* was no more Snow to be seen, although the holes were very deep';[43] but, to make assurance double sure, the inserted plate two pages before the earlier passage shows two great headlands flanking a fiord, the black mass of each cleft vertically by gigantic, snow-filled 'cliffs,' which constitute the most salient feature of the landscape. Moreover, these snow-packed fissures give off a 'sheen.' For it is of these same high and creviced rocks depicted in the plate that the text declares: 'the Sun shin'd pale upon them, *the Snow giving the Air a bright reflection*.'[44] So Martens; and now, only a score of pages earlier in the volume, Captain Wood: 'the Snow being in high *Clifts* on Shore was unaccessible';[45] and again: 'in all other Climates the Snow melteth soonest away near the Sea side, but here the Sea beateth against *the snowy Clifts*.'[46] And once more Coleridge wrote:

> And through the drifts *the snowy clifts*
> *Did send a* dismal *sheen*.[47]

'What nedeth,' as Chaucer was wont to observe—'What nedeth wordes mo?'

And the 'drifts,' which have often been a stumbling-block to readers, now fall into place in a picture as clear as it is accurate. There is no question of their meaning. 'Drifts,' in the sense of 'floating ice,' were fresh in Coleridge's memory as he wrote. He was reading for one thing, actually during the days just after the plan of 'The Ancient Mariner' was conceived,[48] Benyowsky's *Memoirs*. And in one passage of thirteen pages in the *Memoirs*, the compound 'ice-drifts' occurs ten times, and once the simple 'drifts': 'ice-drifts of enormous magnitude'; 'the sea covered with ice-drifts'; 'few drifts'—and so on.[49] That precise passage, moreover, Coleridge would certainly have read, for one crucial act of the strange drama of his 'Siberian Exiles' was coming to its climax at the moment when their ship was passing through the ice. And in any case, through his predilection for Arctic and Antarctic voyages, 'drifts' had long been known to him. Crantz speaks of 'these frightful drifts of ice';[50] and 'drift-ice' met him constantly.[51] The scene as Coleridge saw it is unmistakable. Land is in the offing, as the gloss makes clear, and between it and the ship are the 'drifts' of floating ice, mast-high and emerald-green. And through them strikes, from the snow in the great crevasses of barren hills, that 'glance in the air' which 'may be seen for many leagues at sea.' Every particular is flawlessly correct.

But the stanza is not yet ended:

Nor shapes of men nor beasts we ken—
The ice was all between.[52]

That lifeless desolation of the landscape, too, is a commonplace of the voyages—'that wilde Desart, irkesome, fearefull, and cold Countrey,' de Veer breaks out, as he thinks of the 'desolate and fearefull place' where they wintered.[53] But in this instance we are taken back, I think, to the very genesis of the poem. For within three sentences of the shooting of the albatross in Shelvocke's *Voyage* we read: 'The heavens were perpetually hid from us by gloomy, *dismal* clouds. . . . One would think it impossible that *any thing living* could subsist in so rigid a climate; and, indeed, *we . . . had not had the sight of one fish of any kind . . . nor one sea bird*, except a disconsolate black Albitross.'[54] 'The land of ice,' says the gloss ('this Land of Ice,' says Captain Weymouth in the *Pilgrimes*)[55] '. . . *where no living thing was to be seen*.' And still another stanza, in every detail, is minutely faithful to distinctive fact. But through the potency of a single word it has become something more. For the 'bright reflection' of the snow-filled cliffs, as Martens saw and pictured them, is now, on the hint of Shelvocke,'a *dismal* sheen,' and the picture is tinged with the sombre light of the Mariner's own haunted memories.

IV

Even more terrifying to the Arctic voyagers than the ominous lustre of icy cliffs were the noises of what 'The True

State of Iceland' in Hakluyt calls 'this hell of ice.'[56] Coleridge's own gloss reads: 'The land of ice, *and of fearful sounds*,' and the mariners concur. 'There was such a frightful rumbling, and *cracking* of the ice,' says Crantz, 'as if many cannons had been fired at once, and then ensued a violent noise, like the *roaring* of a cascade.'[57] So, too, the 'mighty great *roaring*' of the ice in the thick fog alarmed the 'hardy seamen' of Davis's expedition.[58] 'At some times,' we read again in 'The True State of Iceland,' 'by shuffling together [the ice] maketh monstrous soundings and *cracklings*, and againe at some times with the beating of the water, it sendeth forth an hoarse kind of murmuring.'[59] Dithmar Blefkins, in Purchas, writes: 'I sayled not without great feare unto this Ice, and I observed, that this Ice was violently cast against the Rockes by force of the winds, and so made a mournfull sound afarre off, as if miserable *howlings* were heard there. Hereupon the Islanders thinke the soules of the damned are tormented in this Ice.'[60] Captain Weymouth tells in Purchas how 'as wee were breaking off some of this Ice [to make us fresh water] . . . the great Iland of Ice gave a mightie *cracke* two or three times, *as though it had bin a thunder-clappe*';[61] and in Barents's last voyage, while they were trying to save the ship, '*the ship burst out of the Ice* with such a noise, and so great a *cracke*, that they thought verily that they were all cast away.'[62] Finally, in Commodore Phipps's *Voyage to the North-East*, in a passage which for its simple piety I wish I might quote in full, we are told how 'the men were worn out with fatigue in defending the ships with their ice-poles from being engulphed; and now nothing but scenes of horror and perdition appeared before their eyes. But the Omnipotent . . . caused . . . the ice to part in an astonishing manner, rending and *cracking* with a tremendous noise, *surpassing that of the loudest thunder*. At this very instant the whole continent of ice . . . moved together in various directions, *splitting* and dividing into vast bodies'—and with sails all spread the ships came through.[63]

But there is one account of the noises of the ice which has a peculiar significance. And it, too, is in de Veer's engrossing narrative. As Barents's men, in the winter of their terrible third voyage, lay in their cabins, with heated stones to warm their feet ('for that both the cold and the smoake were unsupportable,' and 'wee lookt pittifully one upon the other'), 'wee might heare,' writes de Veer, 'the Ice *cracke* in the Sea . . . which made a huge noyse.' And as they thus lay, with the doors and the chimney stopped to keep in the heat of an eagerly anticipated but disastrous sea-coal fire, 'at last we were taken,' the tale proceeds, 'with a great *swounding* and dazeling in our heads.' Then they opened the door, 'but he that opened the doore fell downe *in a swound* upon the Snow.' However, de Veer goes on, 'when the doores were open, we all recovered our healths againe, by reason of the cold Ayre . . . otherwise without doubt, we had dyed *in a sudden swound*, after that the Master . . . gave every one of us a little Wine to comfort our hearts.'[64]

Here, then, is a mass of absorbingly realistic detail, scattered broadcast through narratives most (if not all) of which Coleridge knew. There is ice which cracks, and roars, and howls; there are ships released from ice which splits, with a crack like thunder, for their deliverance; and there are, in an episode of arresting vividness, men in a swound, the 'huge noyse' of cracking icebergs sounding in their ears. And once more that tenacious and systematizing memory has lent its stores to the power whose supreme gift it is to 'see all things in one,' and so

> The ice was here, the ice was there,
>   The ice was all around:
> *It cracked and growled, and roared and howled,*
>   *Like noises in a swound!* . . .
>
> *The ice did split with a thunder-fit;*
>   *The helmsman steered us through!*[65]

For two years, as Goethe relates in *Dichtung und Wahrheit*, the stuff of *Werther* occupied his mind without taking form. Then he tells us what happened. He received one day the startling news of his friend Jerusalem's suicide, and, as he says, 'at that instant the plan of *Werther* was found; *the whole shot together from all directions, and became a solid mass, as the water in a vase, which is just at the freezing point, is changed by the slightest concussion into ice*.'[66] So, through a flash of inspiration from a paragraph of Purchas, the scattered noises of the ice have shot from all sides together, to be submerged, through the power of one compelling line, in that limbo of alien terror and unearthly detachment from reality where goblin sounds beat at the gates of consciousness as one emerges from a swoon.[67] And to grasp the imaginative synthesis embodied in 'Like noises in a swound' is worth a passage—not unlike Satan's!—'nigh foundered,' through 'a universal hubbub wild Of stunning sounds, and [noises] all confused.'

V

All these noises of the ice, and all its sheen and colour were heard and seen, by the men with whom Coleridge vicariously sailed, beneath the *Arctic* Circle. But the Mariner's ship is in *Antarctic* seas. Coleridge, in other words, throwing space relations to the dogs, has imperturbably reversed the poles. Ice is ice, be it austral or boreal waters in which it floats and howls—and anyway, none of his readers has ever been the wiser! With perfect consistency, then, from the ship off the Horn, Coleridge's memory flies north again, and reminiscences of the sailors' shouts in an Arctic voyage, and impressions of frosty fog that drifted and hung like smoke about Greenland and Spitzbergen, and the seaman's phrase 'the good south wind,' are tacitly transferred to the southern seas. Crantz notes the fact that '*luminous circles round the moon* are oftener seen [in Greenland] than anywhere, *which are formed by the frost-smoke.*'[68] Martens tells of a hill in Spitzbergen, 'commonly covered with *a fogg*, and if the wind bloweth over it, it darkneth the Haven, and *seemeth as if it smoaked*,'[69] and he describes elsewhere 'a Rain-bow, figured by the Sun, which Bow are the Drops that by the Heat of the Sun are changed into a Vapour or *Fog*, and this Vapour *shews like smoak in the Air*.'[70] 'We saw daily,' he writes again, near the beginning of his narrative, 'many Ships, sailing about the Ice. I observed that as they passed by one another, they haled one another, crying *Holla*.'[71] And finally, in de Veer's narrative we read: 'The fourteenth, it was faire weather, with *a good South Wind*, and then the Ice began to drive from the Land, whereby wee were in good hope to have an open water.'[72]

And now 'The Ancient Mariner' once more:

> And *a good south wind* sprung up behind;
> The Albatross did follow,
> And every day, for food or play,
> Came to the *mariner's hollo!*
>
> In mist or cloud, on mast or shroud,
> It perched for vespers nine;
> Whiles all the night, *through fog-smoke white*,
> Glimmered the white Moon-shine.[73]

Scattered images of memory flash like sudden stars and coalesce, and Crantz and Martens and de Veer dissolve, to reëmerge sheer Coleridge.

VI

Meantime the albatross has come, like the icebergs, through the fog, and the stanza which ends with the helmsman steering through the splitting ice began, in 1798, with this historic line:

> The Marineres gave it *biscuit-worms*.[74]

The biscuit-worms (not unlike the 'toothless mastiff *bitch*' in 'Christabel,' discreetly cloaked for many years, to satisfy the scruples of 'an honoured friend,' as the 'toothless mastiff, *which*'!)[75] were somewhat squeamishly expunged,* and the offending line became (and remains) as tame as a villatic fowl:

> It ate the food it ne'er had eat.

But the biscuit-worms have a more than passing interest.

Coleridge clearly remembered them from a famous passage which curiously links *The Tempest* with 'The Ancient Mariner.' For he had evidently been reading in Purchas the same account of Magellan's voyage around the world which Shakespeare had probably read in Eden's *History of Travayle*, and which he remembered when Caliban was conceived. Moreover, in the setting of the incident, Purchas exactly parallels 'The Ancient Mariner,' and a few sentences from the fine old story of the voyage will serve not only to bring Shakespeare and Coleridge together, but also to throw the 'Rime' itself once more against its broad background of the circumnavigation of the globe. Magellan's ship, like the ancient Mariner's, has passed the Line, and come under the Antarctic pole—in this case, to a land of giants. By stratagem some of them are captured. And now I shall quote just enough of the account to give the *mise en scène:*

> When they [the Giants] saw how they were deceived, they roared like Bulls, and cryed upon their great Devill Setebos. . . . They say, that when any of them die, there appeare ten or twelve Devils . . . and that among other, there is one seene bigger then the residue, who maketh great mirth and rejoycing. This great Devill they call Setebos. . . . Approching to the two and fiftie degrees, they found the Strait now called the Strait of Magellanus. . . . On both the sides of this Strait, are great and high Mountaines covered with Snow, beyond the which, is the entrance into the Sea of Sur. This entrance the Captaine named Mare Pacificum. . . . When the Captaine Magalianes was past the Strait, and saw the way open to the other maine Sea, hee was so glad thereof, that for joy the teares fell from his eyes [for he was in very truth 'the first that ever burst into that silent sea'] and named the point of the Land from whence he first saw that Sea, Capo Desiderato. . . . Departing out of this Strait into the Sea called Mare Pacificum, the eight and twentieth day of November, in the yeere 1520. they

> sayled three moneths and twentie dayes before they saw any Land: and having in this time consumed all their *Bisket* and other Victuals, they fell into such necessitie, that they were inforced to eate the powder that remayned thereof, *being now full of Wormes.*[76]

The biscuit-worms have gone, but their brief sojourn is illuminating none the less. For it enables us to grasp once more the broad and sweeping outline of the spectre-haunted voyages around the southern Cape into which Coleridge's thronging memory was pouring its reminiscences of the terrors of the northern ice—the same vast background of the quest of the Antipodes which looms behind the stanzas we have just left. For 'the land of ice, and of fearful sounds, where no living thing was to be seen' is our old southern circle of the mappemondes which is uninhabitable by reason of the cold (circulus australis que est ex frigore inhabitabilis); and the warders of the austral seas in 'The Ancient Mariner' are still the grim 'Brumæ' and 'Frigida'—'Mist and Snow'—of the ancient maps.

For years, then, the wonders of the ice, as Coleridge read and read, had been printing their sharp-cut, vivid imagery upon the sensitive retina of that amazing inner eye, to be transmitted to the crowded tracts below the levels of conscious mental processes. What the structural conception of the voyage did was first to wake and summon up to consciousness the dormant reminiscences, and then to marshal the chaotic dance of recollected 'spectra' into patterns as clean of definition as the trenchant outlines of the ice itself. But the curve of the voyage swept out of frozen into burning seas, and other images were stirred to life, to fall, in turn, into quite different shapes.

---

*I suspect, however, that there was more than squeamishness behind the change. If an honoured friend this time reminded Coleridge of the *dimensions* of the albatross—but that is getting ahead of the story!

CHAPTER X

THE COURTS OF THE SUN

THE Mariner's ice-fields swim in Antarctic seas, as the scheme of the poem requires. But the ice itself is good Arctic ice, seen, heard, and felt in the 'infernall bitter cold' of Barents's Sea, and in the 'stinking fogge' of Hudson's Bay, and off the 'snowy Clifts' of Greenland and Spitzbergen.[1] Coleridge has poured into that sector of his voyage which lay through austral seas the winnowed, spoils of his singularly happy excursions into the literature of the other pole. South is North, where the albatross is shot. But that is only half the story. The sails of the spectre-bark glance in the sun of an East that is also West—and sometimes North and South to boot! For into the courts of the Sun, beneath the Line in the Pacific, Coleridge's teeming recollections flocked from the four corners of the world—from the West Indies, and the Nile, and Boston, and Florida, and even (once more) from the icy seas and meteor-lighted skies of Finland, Spitzbergen, and Canada. The creative imagination is as magnificently eclectic as Isaiah's spirit of the Lord: 'I will bring thy seed from the east, and gather them from the west. I will say to the north, Give up; and to the south, Keep not back: bring my sons from far, and my daughters from the ends of the earth.'[2] And something very like that spirit was brooding above the chaos which by now should need no laboured demonstration. Then the poetic impulse came, and out of the myriad chambers of Coleridge's brain an amazing throng of latent images flew up to consciousness[3] when his will turned from its essays at polar cold to try its powers on equatorial heat.

How those thronging images blended in the Well, and how, at the touch of the shaping spirit they fell into the likeness of ominous seas which glowed with unearthly fires and were tenanted by slimy things that crawled with legs, and things of light that were comely in going—all that we have already seen. For, thanks to the Note Book, our journey began in the courts of the Sun. And there, indeed, is like to be our journey's end, unless from the wealth with which this section of the poem is crowded, we somewhat rigorously select. And in the courts of the Sun no choice could be more fitting than the metamorphoses of the sun itself.

I

The reappearance of the vanished sun heralds the dramatic entrance of the ship into that silent sea at the heart of which were waiting the charmèd waters that burnt their still and awful red. And its auspicious rising, ushering in the flying foam before the good south wind, was also the mocking prelude to the moment when the sun was a goblin in the sky above the trance of the sea. And so, as prologue to the omen coming on, the place of the description of the sunrise off the Cape is here.

There is, I think, no passage in the poem which so desperately needs to be read in the light of the setting which it had in Coleridge's mind. A poet's words mean more at times than the poet knew they meant. But oftener, as even Marlowe's soaring spirit understood, after the poets have distilled from words their quintessential potency, 'Yet should there hover in their restless heads One thought, one grace, one wonder, at the least, Which into words no virtue can digest.'[4] Sometimes, however, it befalls a poet simply to fumble, like the rest of us, round about a meaning that is luminous to him, and by maladroit expression to obscure it. And that, I suspect, is what has happened in the two unlucky lines which, through a grotesque grammatical ambiguity that lies in wait for the unwary reader, have given the sons and daughters of the Philistines occasion for rejoicing:

> Nor dim nor red, like God's own head,
> The glorious Sun uprist.[5]

That fails to suggest, I believe, to most readers, the picture which Coleridge saw. But the lines acquire new meaning when they are read in conjunction with the records of poignantly human experience which, with little doubt, suggested them—records which so nobly typify the spirit of the early voyagers that I shall serve more purposes than one by quoting freely.

In that perennial fountain-head of inspiration, de Veer's account of the last voyage of William Barents, is an episode which Coleridge certainly knew.[6] It is in the chapter to which Purchas has contributed the compendious heading: 'Their cold, comfortlesse, darke and dreadfull Winter:* the Sunnes absence, Moones light, *Sunnes unexpected returne with miraculous speed.* Of Beares, Foxes, and many many Wonders.'[7] On the page next after the account of the 'swounding' in the fumes of the sea-coal fire, stands this bit of simple and moving prose:

> The nineteenth, it was faire weather, the winde being South: then we put each other in good comfort, that the Sunne was then almost halfe over, and ready to come to us againe, which wee sore longed for, it being *a weary time* for us to bee without the Sunne, and to want the greatest comfort that God sendeth unto man heere upon the earth, and that which rejoyceth every living thing.[8]

On that (and no wonder!) Coleridge paused, and one of its phrases struck deep. For the 'weary time' of the long Arctic night is transferred to the mariners becalmed at the Equator, and by dint of judicious iteration ekes out a stanza:

> There passed *a weary time*. Each throat

Was parched, and glazed eacheye.
A weary time! A weary time!
How glazed each weary eye,
When looking westward, I beheld
A something in the sky.[9]

Two pages later de Veer goes on: 'About noone time wee saw *a certaine rednesse in the skie* [the significant italics are in Purchas], as a shew or messenger of the Sunne that began to come towards us,' and so '. . . [we] comforted each other, giving God thankes that the hardest time of the Winter was past, *being in good hope that we should live to talke of those things at home in our owne Countrey*'[10]—surely as touching a 'forsan et hæc olim meminisse juvabit' as was ever uttered. That Coleridge was moved by its brave and unaffected pathos is evident enough, for the wonder of the impossible come true which pervades those last six words—'*at home in our owne Countrey*'—is the very wonder which first dazes, then floods with its incredible meaning, the Mariner home from sea:

Oh! dream of joy! is this indeed
The light-house top I see?
Is this the hill? is this the kirk?
Is this mine own countree?. . .

And now, *all in my own countree,*
I stood on the firm land![12]

The Virgilian *lacrimœ rerum* are in 'a weary time' and 'at home in our owne Countree,' and it would not be strange if the moving tale the phraseology of which twice set the chords of memory vibrating should touch them once again. And it seems clear that it did.

For the 'certaine rednesse in the skie' (which Purchas archly glosses: 'Aurora blusheth to lie so long in bed,' and in which Coleridge saw, I think, his 'dim' and 'red') was indeed the messenger of the hidden sun. Six days later de Veer writes: 'The foure and twentieth [of January] . . . I, and Jacob Heemskerke, and another with us went to the Sea-side . . . where . . . I first saw the edge of the Sunne, wherewith wee went speedily home againe, to tell William Barents, and the rest of our companions that joyfull newes: but William Barents being a wise and well experienced Pilot, would not beleeve it, esteeming it to be about fourteene dayes too soone for the Sunne to shine in that part of the World; but we earnestly affirmed the contrarie, and said, that we had seene the Sunne.'[13] So for three days there was 'striving and contending about it' among them, and then, at midnight on the twenty-sixth, one of their little company died. The next day they went out to dig the grave, and now I shall let the fine old narrative draw its own unforgettable picture.

> And so wee digged by turnes, every man a little while, and then went to the fire, and another went and supplied his place, till at last wee digged seven foot depth where

> wee went to burie the dead man, after that when we had read certaine Chapters, and sung some Psalmes, wee all went out and buried the man, which done we went in and brake our fasts, and while we were at meate, and discoursed amongst our selves, touching the great quantitie of snow that continually fell in that place, wee said that if it fell out, that our house should bee closed up againe with snow, wee would finde the meanes to climbe out at the chimney, whereupon our Master went to trie if hee could climbe up through the chimney, and so get out, and while hee was climbing one of our men went forth of the doore, to see if the Master were out or not, who standing upon the snow, *saw the Sunne*, and called us all out, wherewith we all went forth, and saw the Sun *in his full roundnesse*, a little above the Horizon, and then it was without all doubt, that wee had seene the Sunne upon the four and twentieth of January, which made us all glad, and *we gave God heartie thankes*, for his grace shewed unto us, *that that glorious light appeared unto us againe.*[14]

Even so, after a weary time of snow-fog and floating ice, 'wanting the greatest comfort that God sendeth unto man,'

> *Nor dim nor red*, like God's own head,*
> *The glorious Sun uprist.*

But I suspect that more than the vicissitudes of Barents and his men came back to memory as the stanza assumed form. There is another heroic tale of hardship and courage and resource which is worthy to stand beside de Veer's great narrative. It is fitly entitled: '*God's Power and Providence; Shewed, In the Miraculous Preservation and Deliverance of eight Englishmen, left by mischance in Green-land, Anno 1630, nine moneths and twelve dayes. . . . Faithfully reported by Edward Pellham, one of the eight men aforesaid.*[15] I cannot be sure that Coleridge had read it, but it is probable that he did. For it was reprinted in Churchill's *Collection of Voyages*, and that he certainly knew.[16] And here are two passages from Pellham's narrative.

> But, as if it were not enough for us to want meate, we now began to want light also: all our meales proved suppers now, for little light could we see; even *the glorious Sunne* (as if unwilling to behold our miseries) masking his lovely face from us, under the sable vaile of cole-blacke night. Thus, from the fourteenth of October till the third of February, we never saw the Sunne. . . .
>
> But our recourse was in this, as in other our extremities, unto Almighty God, who had helps, we knew, though we saw no hopes. And thus spent wee our time untill the third of Februarie. This proved a marvellous cold day; yet a faire and cleare one; about the middle whereof all

> cloudes now quite dispersed, and nights sable curtaine drawne; Aurora, with her golden face, smiled once againe upon us, at her rising out of her bed;[17] for now *the glorious Sunne*, with his glittering beames, began to guild the highest tops of the loftie mountaines. The brightnesse of the Sunne, and the whitenesse of the snow, both together was such, as that it was able to have revived even a dying spirit.[18]

And Coleridge wrote:

> Nor dim nor red, like God's own head,
> *The glorious sun* uprist.

Thrown against the affecting background which they had in Coleridge's mind (whether that owed its being to de Veer or Pellham, or to both) the lines lose their faint touch of the grotesque, and become eloquent.

II

But that eloquence is after all dependent on our knowledge of something hovering in Coleridge's mind which failed of full liberation in his words. It is as much Gerrit de Veer or Edward Pellham as Coleridge. There is another stanza of that potential Hymn to the Sun which lies imbedded in 'The Ancient Mariner,' in which expression as far transcends suggestion as in the earlier lines it fell short of it. And we have again to do with that gift of the imagination in which it owns peculiarly its kinship with the wizardry of dreams—the gift through which, on the most arid hint, vivid ocular images spring, as in sleep, into magical clearness. For the ways of the imagination are manifold and strange, and it sometimes comes about that when weighty matter clogs its wings, the bare shred of an intimation will stir it to powerful flight.

The Mariner's ship has reached the Line, and lies, without breath or motion, in the silent courts of the Sun.

> All in a hot and copper sky,
> *The* bloody *Sun, at noon,*
> *Right up above the mast did stand,*
> No bigger than the Moon.[19]

It had stood there, in the poem, it will be remembered, for an instant once before, to mark the crossing of the Line as the ship sailed south. Then it had been brushed from the narrative with a magnificent sweep of the hand that had set it there, to await its appointed reappearance here.[20]

Now Coleridge, like everybody else who read voyages at all, had met with the vertical sun at the Line a score of times.[21] But unless all signs fail, the phrase which struck home to his imagination was once more in his never-failing Purchas: 'On the eighteenth, *the Sunne was right over them at noone* . . . and a calme continued tenne dayes.'[22] It is an utterly bald and matter-of-fact statement, but it flashed or germinated (who can say which?) into the intensely visualized masterpiece of succinct description of which it remains, still almost verbally intact, the core. How much that absolute visualization of a sun straight up in the sky of a tropic noon may have owed to Coleridge's reading of the face of the only sky he knew, it is impossible to say with certainty. Things actually, seen and things only read undoubtedly coalesced during their strange sleep in his brain. What I do feel that I know is that his imagination sprang habitually to creative activity on the spur of words—those 'words that' (in his own repeated phrase) 'flash images.'[23] But this time things both seen and read may have merged in the image of the sun above the mast.

The sixty-fifth chapter of White's *Natural History of Selborne* begins as follows:

> The summer of the year 1783 was an amazing and portentous one, and full of horrible phænomena; for, besides the alarming meteors and tremendous thunder-storms that affrighted and distressed the different counties of this kingdom, the peculiar haze, or smokey fog, that prevailed for many weeks in this island, and in every part of Europe, and even beyond it's limits, was a most extraordinary appearance, unlike anything known within the memory of man. . . . *The sun, at noon, looked as blank as a clouded moon*, and shed *a rust-coloured ferruginous light* on the ground, and floors of rooms; but was particularly lurid and *blood-coloured* at rising and setting. All the time *the heat was . . . intense*. . . . The

> country people began to look with a superstitious awe at the red, louring aspect of the sun; and indeed there was reason for the most enlightened person to be apprehensive; for, all the while, Calabria and part of the isle of Sicily, were torn and convulsed with earthquakes; and about that juncture a volcano sprang out of the sea on the coast of Norway.[24]

That lies, like some dark pool, across the tranquil flow of what Coleridge once called 'this sweet, delightful book.'[25] By contrast it is the most salient passage in the *History*.[26]

Now Coleridge read White's *Selborne* at Keswick in 1810, and left in its margins a peculiarly happy sheaf of notes.[27] I do not know whether he had read it earlier or not; it is highly probable that he had. And if he did, the link with Purchas in the words 'the sun, at noon' was there to draw the two together, and to suggest the telling reference to the moon. But whether he did or not, as a boy of eleven in London he had himself experienced that 'amazing and portentous' summer, and the memory of the sun at noon, lurid and blood-coloured, looking as blank as a clouded moon, may have lain waiting among the sleeping images.

But there is another strong probability. A writer whom one couples with Plato and dreams of turning from prose into verse is a personage whose occupancy of the mind leaves footprints. And in the Note Book, between the two jottings which betray the wild project of a versified translation of Thomas Burnet's *Telluris Theoria Sacra*, stand certain entries unmistakably inspired by Burnet's richly freighted and eloquent prose. I shall leave the demonstration of this statement to the notes.[28] The fact which is pertinent here is this: the passages which the Note Book proves Coleridge to have been reading with a quickened impulse to create are in the terrific Third Book 'Concerning the CONFLAGRATION.' And just that portion of the Third Book which had stirred him to expression is ominous with the bloody sun: 'the sun . . . of a *bloody* or pale countenance'; 'the darkness or *bloody* colour of the sun and moon'; 'the sun often hides his head, or appears with a discoloured face, pale, or dusky, or *bloody*'; 'and in some foggy days, *the sun hangs in the firmament as a lump of blood*.'[29] That such phrases should carry in their train the sombre glories of the Biblical imagery is probable enough: 'the sun shall be turned into darkness, and the moon into blood';[30] 'and thy heaven that is over thy head shall be brass.'[31] But no one who studies the Note Book can doubt, I think, that the bloody sun which hung in the firmament above the ship had stood, murky and sinister, not only over England in 1783, but also, a sign of doom, above a troubled sea in Burnet's graphic pages.[32] And though the *Theoria Sacra* never got itself rendered into verse, it lent, at least, its powerful aid to the leap of Coleridge's imagination from the bare hint of 'the Sunne right over them at noone' to the intense realization of a picture unsurpassed for vivid clarity in English verse.

And what has happened is, without hyperbole, amazing enough. Here is the way in which Falconer, in 'The Shipwreck,' says approximately the same thing:

> Thro' the wide atmosphere condensed with haze,
> *His glaring orb emits a sanguine blaze.*[33]

Set, without mercy, Coleridge beside that:

> All in a hot and copper sky,
> The bloody Sun, at noon,
> Right up above the mast did stand,
> No bigger than the Moon.

In the one, the image, if there ever was an image, is lost in an engulfing, verbal haze; in the other every word, nakedly simple, prints on the brain with the pure and pellucid definition of a landscape reflected in a pool. Coleridge read: 'the Sunne was right *over them*'; the sun he saw was 'right *up above the mast*'—a rayless lump of blood, 'no bigger than the moon.' It is the same trenchant simplicity of phrase which brought, with lucid exactness, the appearance of the polar ice before our eyes—'mast-high,' 'as green as emerald,' 'came floating by.' Every image is cut clean, shorn as by magic of whatever blurs its powerful directness of impression. Mere trafficking with the voyagers will never account for that. Purchas may plant, and Burnet water, but Coleridge gives the increase!

I hope it is clear that I do not care a rap for the question of so-called literary borrowing *per se*. The most supremely original performances I know (and 'The Rime of the Ancient Mariner' is among them) have sprung into being through some electric contact of one mind with another, and that for the moment is our sole concern. We have dealt with a sun that rose, and another that reached its highest noon, in Purchas. There is a third, which set in a spectral sky that embraced 'the varying shore o' the world.'

III

With the splendidly imaginative gloss: 'No twilight within the courts of the Sun,' Coleridge commented on an even more superb stanza:

> The Sun's rim dips; the stars rush out:
> At one stride comes the dark;
> With far-heard whisper, o'er the sea,
> Off shot the spectre-bark.[34]

Did there once lie, beneath that entire and perfect crysolite, 'shattered fragments of memory' which 'flashed images,' and coalesced?

In April, 1797, Southey wrote his brother Tom: 'Have you ever met with Mary Wollstonscroft's [*sic*] letters from Sweden and Norway? She has made me in love with a cold climate, and frost and snow, with a northern moonlight.'[35] In Coleridge's

Note Book, scrawled in pencil between 'Mrs. Estlin's Story of the Maniac who walked round and round,' and the entry about the sun painting rainbows on the vast waves at the Cape, stands the following: 'Epistle to Mrs. Wolstoncraft urging her to Religion. Read her travels.'[36] Whether Coleridge carried out his pious purpose with reference to the future mother of Mary Shelley, I do not know. He afterwards thought Godwin 'in heart and manner . . . all the better for having been [her] husband,' and, 'thinking' (as he says) 'of Mary Wollstonecraft,' he was oppressed one day he dined there after her death, by 'the cadaverous silence of Godwin's children [which] is . . . quite catacombish';[37] so I suppose his interest in her soul was friendly. His interest in her travels—whether friendly too, or sheer omnivorousness, or both—bore fruit in something more definite than falling in love with a cold climate and a northern moonlight. For he read, in the *Letters written during a Short Residence in Sweden, Norway, and Denmark*, this sentence: 'Getting amongst the rocks and islands as the moon rose, and *the stars darted forward* out of the clear expanse, I forgot that the night stole on.'[38] And one of those 'vivid spectra,' which were incessantly leaving their imprint on his memory, flashed as he read.

The absence of twilight in the tropics he knew from his keen and long-standing interest in the West Indies and the Nile, and the ocular impressions from his reading seem to have carried scraps of phrases with them into their subliminal half-way house. 'In the afternoons, *the sun is no sooner dipped*, than a sensible change in the air . . . is immediately felt.'[39] That is Long, from a page devoted to the crepuscular phenomena of the West Indies, which so took Bryan Edwards's fancy that, after the happy practice of the travel-Books, he appropriated part of it intact. 'I regret the want of twilight here,' says the author of a gossipy little volume on the West Indies, printed in 1790, 'for *the dark comes on very suddenly*, a few minutes after the sun is beneath the horizon.'[40] 'In these Parts,' Rochefort writes in his *History of the Carriby-Islands*, 'there is in a manner *no Crepusculum or Twilight*.'[41] And Bruce, in a context of unusual interest to Coleridge, agrees for the regions of the Nile: 'In countries such as . . . Hanno was then sailing by . . . there is *no twilight*.'[42] And later in Bruce's great narrative Coleridge would read: 'The twilight . . . is very short, almost imperceptible. . . . As soon as the sun falls below the horizon, night comes on, and all the stars appear.'[43]

There was, moreover, a strange, crack-brained book, with flashes of imaginative splendour playing through its incoherence, written by a young barrister, himself a native of Antigua, whom Coleridge knew in his Bristol days.[44] It is *The Hurricane: A Theosophical and Western Eclogue*, 'grounded,' the Preface tells us, 'on a THEOSOPHICAL view of the relation between AMERICA and EUROPE but concatenated . . . with the two old Quarters of the Globe,' and its copious Notes are as mad as a hatter. It was, however, a noble mind that was here o'erthrown, and both Wordsworth and Southey have paid tribute to its powers.[45] Coleridge, Cottle tells us, 'once objected to the metre of some of Gilbert's lines,' and Gilbert's Advertisement is an answer to these strictures.[46] There is evidence elsewhere, as we shall see, that snatches from *The Hurricane*, the scene of which is laid in the West Indies, stuck in Coleridge's memory, and two lines are pertinent here:

> *No* lingering *twilight* in the proud-robed WEST
> Shews indecision in the Paths of Day![47]

This, then, is roughly what we have in the travel books: 'the sun is no sooner *dipped*'; 'the stars *darted forward*'; '*the dark comes on very suddenly*'; 'there is *no twilight*.' And Coleridge wrote:

> The Sun's rim *dips;* the stars *rush out:*
> *At one stride comes the dark—*

with the gloss: '*No twilight* within the courts of the Sun.'

There, it would seem, are both the shattered fragments of memory, and the surpassing form with which the 'inward creatrix' fitted them. I am not, indeed, so rash as to assert categorically that the identical phrases which I have quoted, and only those, were the star-dust of the stanza. Some, if not all, without doubt had stamped impressions on a brain which 'had the impression of individual images very strong,'[48] and on a memory of extraordinary tenacity. Coleridge had read

The Hurricane not only with a friend's, but with a critic's eye. How effectively Bruce had seeded the crannies of his memory we shall later have to see.[49] Mrs. Wollstonecraft, as the Note Book shows, would certainly fall neither by the wayside, nor on stony ground. Long's three volumes were among the standard works on the West Indies, and Coleridge's ardent interest in the islands dates as far back as the halcyon days of the Greek Ode at Cambridge. About the *Short Journey to the West Indies* one cannot feel so sure, in spite of another phrase which Coleridge may have remembered from it.[50] But whether facts and phrases reached him from these books or from others, the point of capital significance is this. The magnificent conception of the fall of the tropical night is once more the result of a fusing flash of imaginative energy through chaos—that very 'chaos of elements and shattered fragments of memory' of which Coleridge himself was so keenly cognizant. Every shattered fragment has been new-minted—sharp, and clear, and salient as the sun that stood above the mast, or the emerald ice. 'The sun's *rim*[51] dips. . . . *At one stride* comes the dark.' Reread, for a fresh commentary on the intensely visualizing quality of Coleridge's imagination, the phrases from the books: *The sun* was no sooner dipped's; 'The dark comes on *very suddenly*.' Yet that vivid concreteness must yield first place to something else—to a synthesis of disparate elements which even for Coleridge is remarkable.

For the large, general impression of a sudden shift from day to night diffused through the various accounts which he had read, all at once gathers and concentrates into a downward leap of night like that of lightning, while on the instant,

> With far-heard whisper o'er the sea,
> Off shot the spectre-bark.

I doubt whether even Dante has surpassed, for sheer trenchancy and compression, the art with which Coleridge has made, through the agency of his scraps of recollection, the sense of an appalling swiftness palpable. And the unification of a clutter of details from Norway, the West Indies, and the Nile into one breathless instant between sky and sea epitomizes once again the ways of that shaping spirit of imagination which is our theme.

IV

If the genesis of the stanza is thus illuminating, what of the evolution of its gloss? I am not sure that this, in quite different fashion, is not of equal interest. For, thanks to a chapter of its history which until now has never seen the light, it becomes possible to watch Coleridge's imagination as it tentatively felt its way, until at last the inevitable image, invested with its felicitous phrase, was reached. For the terse scholium 'No twilight within the courts of the Sun' did not (to borrow Goethe's phrase once more) stand suddenly before Coleridge, and cry out 'Here I am!'

The marginal gloss to the poem was first printed in *Sibylline Leaves* in 1817. When it was first written, no one knows. Wordsworth told Miss Fen wick, forty-five years after the date of the *Lyrical Ballads*, that 'the gloss with which [the poem] was subsequently accompanied was not thought of by either of us at the time, at least not a hint of it was given to me, and I have no doubt it was a gratuitous after-thought.'[52] But that is purely negative evidence, and the gloss may have been composed a good deal earlier than the year which saw it printed.[53] Be that as it may, the pertinent fact for us is this. In *Sibylline Leaves* the margin opposite the stanza in which the sun's rim dips and the dark comes at one stride, is blank. The telling paraphrase: 'No twilight within the courts of the Sun' was accordingly an afterthought to an afterthought. But neither the striking image nor its succinctness of expression was achieved at once. The addition did not appear in the printed gloss until 1828, but what happened eleven years before is both curious and enlightening.

There is now in the collection of Mr. H. T. Butler (it was formerly in the possession of Sir Stuart Montagu Samuel) 'a proof copy of *Sibylline Leaves*, corrected by Coleridge himself shortly after publication.'[54] And in this copy Coleridge has made the following annotation:

> Between the Tropics there is no Twilight. As the Sun's last segment dips down, and the evening-gun is fired, the constellations appear arrayed.[55]

No one can question the clarity of that expository comment, and the reference to the sunset gun strongly suggests that Coleridge was directly recalling some specific account which he had read. But his critical eye (as the sequel shows) observed a flaw. For the second sentence is a feeble echo of the powerful suggestion of the text, and it is only the first phrase that counts: 'Between the Tropics there is no Twilight.' That is a sound geographical and meteorological observation, sententiously expressed, and it might have stood—had Coleridge not been a poet!

But he was; and we can actually see the sleeping image moving toward the light. In looking over a copy of *Sibylline Leaves* which was then in the possession of Miss Amy Lowell,[56] and which is inscribed by Coleridge to 'Miss Fricker, in mark of high regard from her affectionate Brother, S. T. Coleridge. Aug. 1817,' I was startled to find in the margin opposite the 'Sun's rim' stanza, in Coleridge's hand, this unrecorded version of the gloss:

> No Twilight where
> there is no Latitude
> nor yet on either
> side within the Park
> and Race-course of the
> Sun.—

That this attempt postdates the sketch in the proof copy is

clear,[57] and we have before us a second essay at the formulation of the elusive will o' the wisp of an idea which was behaving much like a forgotten word that hovers teasingly just outside the rim of recollection. The redundant paraphrase of the stanza has disappeared, and the imagination is now feeling after the potential poetry in the bald fact which, in the first version, underlay the words 'Between the Tropics.' But the new phrase, 'where there is no Latitude nor yet on either side,' still projects the terrestrial map obtrusively upon the splendid pathway of the sun. And Coleridge's trump card was to *suggest*. When he reaches the final words, to be sure, 'within the Park and Race-course of the Sun,' he plays it. But though the nineteenth Psalm, with its 'sun, which . . . rejoiceth as a strong man to run a race,' was pretty surely stirring in his memory, the intrusion of 'the *Park*,' in immediate conjunction with the noble figure of the Race-course of the Sun, brings us, not unlike the unhappy Phaeton, abruptly back to earth again. But it was 'Park,' I suspect, in its ancient and still living sense of an enclosed domain, which really pointed the way to the goal, and the goal was at last in sight.

If we strike out the superfluous paraphernalia from these two early ventures, we have left two pithy affirmations: 'Between the Tropics there is no Twilight'; 'No Twilight . . . within *the Park and Race-course* of the Sun.' One stroke of inspiration and the goal is won: 'No twilight within the *courts* of the Sun'! And these are the words which just one month later Coleridge wrote in the margin opposite the stanza in a copy of *Sibylline Leaves* which now belongs to Dr. James B. Clemens, and which is inscribed, with the date 'Sept^{r}., 1817,' to 'W. Hood, Esqre from the obliged Author.'[58] The striking alternative which had lain within Coleridge's grasp—'No Twilight within the *Race-course* of the Sun'—would have disconcertingly imposed upon the wide and breathless stillness of the Mariner's seas the hurtling movement of the sun along his pathway through the stars. 'The *courts* of the Sun' left that boding stillness between the tropics uninfringed. And the concord is now absolute between the stanza, and the comment, and the pervading spirit of the poem. The little Odyssey of the wayfaring imagination was over; and if ever a phrase might seem, in its sheer inevitability, to have leaped spontaneously into being, it is that pellucidly simple gloss.

But Coleridge would not have been Coleridge, I suppose, had he not dallied further with the more elaborate version of his gloss. At all events, we find him, apparently three years later,[59] reverting to his earlier attempts. There is now in the Norton Perkins collection in the Harvard College Library[60] a copy of *Sibylline Leaves* inscribed, in Coleridge's hand, 'Miss Ford in testimony of respect and regard from S. T. Coleridge. Highgate, 29 July 1820.' And in the margin opposite the 'Sun's rim' stanza Coleridge has written:

Within the Tropics
there is no Twilight.
At the moment, the
second, that the Sun
sinks, the Stars appear
all at once as if at
the word of command
announced by the
evening Gun, in
our W. India Islands.

That, with its specific and (for us) illuminating reference to 'our W. India Islands,' was obviously not meant for permanence as a comment on the Mariner's haunted seas. And at least two other copies of *Sibylline Leaves* contain in Coleridge's hand, undated, the final form,[61] while yet another has, undated, the initial sentence of the 1820 gloss: 'Within the Tropics there is no Twilight.'[62] That still other drafts are extant I have little doubt.

Once more, the ways of the shaping spirit are manifold and strange. A flash of vision may leap, unheralded, out of the blue, to carry in its train the gradually unfolding glories of a great imaginative design. And there may be no initial flash at all, but only the persistent groping of the imagination towards a point where, through the agency of its own abortive essays, 'with a fine suddenness,' the magical synthesis is reached. The unimaginable vastness of the sun will lie reflected in a cup of water, and though an eight-word gloss is neither *Hamlet*, nor even the 'Rime of the Ancient Mariner' itself, one aspect of the workings of the same faculty which gave them being finds its epitome in the evolution of a phrase.

V

But the ancient Mariner's eyes had been fixed on the sun before the swift submerging of its rim. And the moment is the most dramatic in the poem. The spectre-bark is nearing; the Mariner, who sees it first, has bitten his arm and sucked the blood to enable his baked lips to articulate: 'A sail! a sail'; and the others, called by the cry, are staring at the 'sign in the element':

> The western wave was all a-flame.
> The day was well nigh done!
> Almost upon the western wave
> Rested *the broad* bright *Sun;*
> When that strange shape *drove suddenly*
> *Betwixt us and the Sun.*[63]

The identical rhyme—'the . . . Sun . . . the Sun'—falls dully on the ear, as if the Mariner were still clutching at the familiar word to reassure himself that it really was the blessed sun of heaven which, as he looked, peered suddenly through the nameless horror of a shape that was 'A bare Anatomy, a plankless spectre' of a ship.[64] What the incomparable vividness of the picture owes to the irretrievably lost 'strange dream' of John Cruikshank, we shall never know. But the dream of his friend, we may be sure, was merged, like everything else, with the mass of other images in Coleridge's memory.[65] And one or two of these seem still to be faintly traceable.

We have been treading hitherto on reasonably firm ground; our footing here is not so sure. But a tentative step or two will at least not take us far afield. It would be absurd to assume that Coleridge needed the aid of any but his own two eyes to write of the sun hanging broad and bright above a flaming sea. He must have watched scores of times, from the Bristol coast and the coombes of Somerset, the sun go down into the sea—as Dorothy Wordsworth, walking home with him from Stowey one bright moonlight February night, saw 'Venus almost like another moon,' and made note in her *Journal* of the fact that she was 'lost to [them] at Alfoxden long before she goes down the large white sea.'[66] But Coleridge, when he wrote 'The Rime of the Ancient Mariner,' was living in a visionary world tenanted by the shapes which had startled the eyes of living voyagers. And nobody (least of all Coleridge) who had ever read Captain Thomas James could well forget the entry (next before the note made 'when the Easterne edge of the Moone did touch the Planet Mars') in which James declares that 'the one and twentieth, I obserued the Sunne to rise *like an Ouall alongst the Horizon. I cald three or foure to see it*, the better to confirme my Iudgement, and we all agreed that it was twice as long as it was broad.'[67] Long is broad, and broad is long, when the thing is round, according as one looks at it, and sunset and sunrise are one in a world of blending forms. The picture which actually met an old Mariner's astonished gaze was not likely to escape a keen-eyed observer foraging for six hymns to the Sun, Moon and the Elements. But whether or not the oval sun swam up to consciousness, it formed, at least, part of the vast and shadowy concourse of images out of which the poem sprang, and as such aids us to reconstitute its background. And one cannot help wondering, as one reads the last line of the stanza, whether Coleridge did not after all succeed in getting another phrase of his beloved Burnet into English verse. For in that same Third Book of the *Sacred Theory* 'Concerning the CONFLAGRATION,' which is so often murkily lighted by the bloody sun, he had read how 'the moon, when eclipsed, may think herself affronted by the earth *interposing rudely betwixt her and the sun*.'[68] The image is powerful and vivid enough (even apart from its setting in a cosmic panorama which fired Coleridge to emulation) to stamp itself on anybody's memory, and it is hard to believe that the book which left so deep an impress upon Coleridge's mind should not have found some echoes in his poetry. But however in keeping with his mental processes the reminiscences would be, the parallels in this instance are such as might easily be accidental, and I present them only as possibilities.

Into the plan of the voyage, then, moved at the summons of the power that wrought the plan, reminiscences—weighty and trivial, simple and interfused—of books which Coleridge had read about polar ice, and the fiery demesnes of the vertical sun. But suns rose and set and the moving moon went softly up the sky at Nether Stowey. And as the ship lay at the Line, the very moon that hung above the airy ridge of Quantock wandered, 'like one that had been led astray,' among alien stars, a strange sign in the element; and the brook at Alfoxden sang its quiet tune to sleeping tropical seas; and like a dream within a dream, Somerset melted into the Equator.

---

*Coleridge knew more about that by experience later. 'In Germany, in the excessive, cold, vile winter of 1799,' is a note of his in a copy of White's *Natural History of Selborne*.[11]

*It was only when I found, after all this had been written, the delightful print of the 'strange sight in the element' in the early editions of de Veer's narrative, that the probable suggestion of the phrase 'like God's own head' occurred to me. The engraving is reproduced opposite page 138 above. And there, in sober sadness, is a sun 'like God's own head'—with the other two persons of the Trinity as supporters (if one will) to make assurance treble sure! I know no positive evidence that Coleridge saw the translation of de Veer's narrative in the 1609 edition (which has the plates), as well as in Purchas (which has not); but if one will turn to Chapter XIII, Note 31, below, the probability that he knew it will be seen, I think, to be anything but remote.

CHAPTER XI

THE JOURNEYING MOON

IN 'those wonderful descriptions of the skyscape,' as Thomas Hutchinson calls them, 'written down during the *nuits blanches* of 1802–3,'[1] there is singularly impressive evidence of Coleridge's exact yet imaginative observation of the moon. And no one who reads the entries (for example) recorded in *Anima Poetœ* under the telltale rubrics of 'Nov. 2, 1803, Wednesday morning, 20 minutes past 2 o'clock' (that log of the voyaging moon through the rack, set down in the watches of the night, while 'the voice [of Greta] seemed to grow like a flower on or about the water beyond the bridge'),[2] and of 'Nov. 10, 1/2 past 2 o'clock, morning,' and of 'Sunday morning, Nov. 13, 1/2 past 2,' and of 'Friday, Nov. 25, 1803, morning, 45 minutes past 2'[3]—no one who reads these strange, almost clairvoyant transcripts of immediate impression can cherish doubts that the same intensity of regard which stored Coleridge's memory with images from books was also exercised upon the aspects of the sky. The white nights in which these notes were written followed the black days of the melancholy period of residence at Keswick. But during the halcyon time when 'The Ancient Mariner' and 'Christabel' were taking shape at Nether Stowey, Coleridge shared the harvest of another pair of eyes.

I

Dorothy Wordsworth, of whom William wrote: 'She gave me eyes, she gave me ears,'[4] was more closely akin, through the exquisite delicacy of her perception, and through something aërial and spiritlike in its property, to Coleridge than to her brother. The central stanzas of 'Three years she grew in sun and shower,' whether they were written with her in mind or not, disclose the secret of the rare loveliness of the Alfoxden and Grasmere *Journals;* and the *Journals*, in turn, reveal the springheads of her quickening influence on Coleridge's genius. She saw, one 'grave evening,' the moonlight fall on the island-house in Rydal Water, when all else was in shadow. 'When I saw this lowly Building in the waters,' she wrote, 'among the dark and lofty hills, with that bright, soft light upon it, it made me more than half a poet.'[5] And more than half a poet in truth she was,* if an eye sensitive to subtlest beauties and an instinctive feeling for apt words are any evidence.[6]

There is her favourite birch-tree: 'The sun shone upon it, and it glanced in the wind like a flying sunshiny shower. It was a tree in shape, with stem and branches, but it was like a spirit of water.'[7] There are the daffodils, that 'tossed and reeled and danced, and seemed as if they verily laughed with the wind';[8]

there are the crows, that became 'white as silver as they flew in the sunshine, and when they went still further . . . looked like shapes of water passing over the green fields';[9] there is the deep stream which, as you hang over the wall in the evening and look at it, is 'a ghostly white serpent line.'[10] The waves, one evening, 'round about the little Island seemed like a dance of spirits that rose out of the water';†[11] another evening 'there were two stars beside [the distant moon], that twinkled in and out, and seemed almost like butterflies in motion and lightness';[12] on still another night 'the fog overhead became thin, and I saw the shapes of the Central Stars.'[13] Those are half a dozen pure, perspicuous impressions out of hundreds. But there is one in which she unconsciously reveals the inward vision which added such a precious seeing to her eye. 'As I lay down on the grass,' she writes, 'I observed the glittering silver line on the ridge of the backs of the sheep, owing to their situation respecting the sun, which made them look beautiful, but with something of strangeness, like animals of another kind, as if belonging to a more splendid world.'[14] Precisely that beauty 'with something of strangeness' in it, which touches the familiar with a transforming radiance until it seems 'as if belonging to a more splendid world,' is the peculiar gift of Coleridge's own genius, and by some secret divination Dorothy, in kindred fashion, read her world. What that divining eye meant to Coleridge in the intimate years of their association may be dimly guessed as one ponders over the excerpts from the Alfoxden *Journal* which Ernest Hartley Coleridge has set beside the text of 'Christabel' in his great edition of the poem.[15] And in ways which are more difficult, if not impossible, to trace, the same influence that manifests itself in 'Christabel' pervades, we may be sure, 'The Ancient Mariner.'

It is possible, thanks to the *Journals*, to gain at least some intimation of what this influence was—the influence of that fugitive thing, the spoken word, so often more deeply penetrating than the printed page. And we reckon ill, if, in our study of blending impressions of every provenance, we leave it out. I shall not, however, go to 'Christabel' for the indications which give countenance to my surmise, but to another poem, which has never, I believe, been brought into this connection.

On May 4, 1802, after the happy record of a day among the Westmoreland hills, when 'William and Coleridge repeated and read verses,'* occurs this entry in the *Journal*: 'We had the crescent moon with the "auld moon in her arms." '[16] The next day, 'the moon had the old moon in her arms, but not so plain to be seen as the night before.'[17] Had the afternoon's reading awakened some train of associations in that exquisitely responsive mind?

On April 4, 1802, exactly a month before, Coleridge wrote at Keswick 'Dejection: An Ode,' which in its first form was addressed to Wordsworth.[18] And prefixed to the Ode as its motto is a stanza from 'The grand old ballad of Sir Patrick Spence':

> Late, late yestreen I saw the new Moon,
> With the old Moon in her arms;
> And I fear, I fear, my Master dear!
> We shall have a deadly storm.

On that same April 4, as the *Journal* shows, William and Dorothy Wordsworth were at Keswick, and Dorothy, at least, 'walked down to Coleridge's.'[19] May we venture a guess at one thing which they talked about?

Early in the month before, Dorothy Wordsworth had set down this entry in her *Journal*:

> On Friday evening the moon hung over the northern side of the highest point of Silver How, like a gold ring snapped in two, and shaven off at the ends. *Within this ring lay the circle of the round moon, as distinctly to be seen as ever the enlightened moon is*. William had observed the same appearance at Keswick, perhaps at the very same moment, hanging over the Newland Fells. Sent off a letter to Mary H., *also to Coleridge*, and Sara.[20]

That was written on a Monday, which (it is clear from other entries) was the eighth of the month. And if we turn back to the record of the Friday just referred to, which was the fourth of March, we read this:

> *No letters. I was sadly mortified. I expected one fully from Coleridge.* Wrote to William, read the L.B., got into sad thoughts, tried at German, but could not go on. Read L.B. Blessings on that brother of mine! *Beautiful new moon over Silver How.*[21]

There is no mistaking the drift of that. When Dorothy Wordsworth saw the March moon within its ring of light, her troubled mood was pervaded with thoughts of Coleridge. So much for her; now let us turn to him. Four weeks later, in 'Dejection,' he composed the most magical lines he ever wrote about the moon:

> For lo! the New Moon, winter-bright!
> And overspread with phantom light
> (With swimming phantom light o'erspread,
> But rimmed and circled with a silver thread)
> I see the Old Moon in her lap foretelling
> The coming on of rain and squally blast![22]

On a Friday in March, then, Dorothy Wordsworth saw the new moon with Coleridge poignantly in mind. On the following Sunday William came home, and she talked over with him her light-encircled moon, which he also had seen, at Keswick—as Coleridge, 'perhaps at the very same moment,' pretty surely saw it with him too. On Monday evening, when she made her detailed note of the circumstance, she sent off a letter to Coleridge. And on the very day in the evening of which the poem was written, she had talked with him. Is it possible to believe that that rimmed circle of the moon (to which only Coleridge in all the world could have given its 'swimming phantom light')[23] was in neither the letter nor the conversation?

However that may be, of this at least we may be sure. When the next new moon came with the old moon in its arms, on the evening of a day when Coleridge (now on his way back to Keswick) had been reading and repeating verses, it was through the eyes of the poem that Dorothy Wordsworth saw it, as she and William walked home. 'We had the crescent moon with the "auld moon in her arms." '[24] And the next night too (when she wrote to Coleridge again) she saw it through the poem—but doubly now: 'The moon had the old moon in her arms, but not so plain to be seen as the night before. When we went to bed *it was a boat without the circle.*'[25] What did she mean? The answer is clear. For in the verses which Coleridge (who can doubt?) had read aloud the day before stood this:[26]

> Yon crescent moon, as fix'd as if it grew
> In its own cloudless, starless lake of blue,
> *A boat becalm'd!* thy own sweet sky-canoe!*

And the next night (when a letter from Coleridge did come) she wrote once more: 'The moon was a perfect boat, a silver boat.'[27] If Coleridge, perchance, borrowed from her eyes, she was amply recompensed through his.

The facts, as they stand, speak for themselves, with their involuntary witness to an intimate community of observation and expression,[28] the influence of which may often be divined, where the fleeting give-and-take of daily intercourse has left no trace. So far as 'The Ancient Mariner' is concerned, there is nothing which is susceptible of proof, nor have I the slightest desire to make a case. But the presence of Dorothy Wordsworth, felt, though not seen ('her voice,' wrote her brother, 'was like a *hidden* Bird that sang'),[30] lingers like a gracious and somewhat wistful shade—*tendens manus ripæ ulterioris amore*—behind some of the loveliest portions of the poem. And that is all we need to know—or care.

II

Just before the three stanzas across which falls, like a cincture, the shadow of the ship, stand four lines of limpid simplicity and beauty:

> The moving Moon went up the sky,
> And no where did abide:
> Softly she was going up,
> And a star or two beside.[31]

That is no moon of the books, I think we may be sure. It is the moon which shone quietly down on Stowey and Alfoxden, and the trodden ways between. Yet it is no transcript of immediate perception either, like most of those vigilant records of the panorama of the sky as the dawn came slowly up in Cumberland. Something has intervened between the ocular impression and this profoundly imaginative rendering of 'the moon's beauty and the moon's soft pace,' as something had intervened between the data of books and the lucent shapes that played in the light of this very moon. Is it possible to gain some inkling of what that influence was?

In one of those strange night-pieces written at Keswick, Coleridge has been watching from his window the great half moon as it slowly sunk behind the mountain ridge, till its last segment, no longer distinguishable from a tiny star, went out. 'And now where is it?' he asks. 'Unseen—but a little *fleecy cloud* hangs above the mountain ridge, and is *rich in amber light*.'[32] And that little cloud has more to offer than a casual glance suggests.

For it was tinged with the light, not of one moon, but of two: one which had slipped that instant behind the Cumberland hills; the other which more than a century and a half before had soared above Milton's head as he walked at Horton,

> To behold the wandering Moon,
> Riding near her highest noon,
> Like one that had been led astray
> Through the heaven's wide pathless way,
> And oft, as if her head she bowed,
> Stooping through *a fleecy cloud*.[33]

And the 'amber light' had borrowed a portion of its radiance from still another moon, and also from the remembrance of a long-vanished sun. For Coleridge, as he jotted down his question at the window, was thinking of his own moonlit cloud in 'Lewti':

> I saw a cloud of palest hue,
>   Onward to the moon it passed;
> Still brighter and more bright it grew,
> With floating colours not a few,
>   Till it reached the moon at last:
> Then the cloud was wholly bright,
> With *a rich and amber light!*[34]

But that amber light of the moon was in turn reflected doubly from the sun, for Milton had seen it

> Right against the eastern gate,
> Where the great Sun begins his state,
> Robed in flames and *amber light.*[35]

What was it that Coleridge really saw, as he looked out of the window?

If ever the thing was done, he was most assuredly writing 'with his eye upon the object.' But the picture printed on the retina 'was supported' (to use again the words of another early morning reverie at that same magic casement) 'by *the images of memory flowing in on the impulses of immediate impression.*'[36]

And as the image of a floccule of shining vapour hung on the sensitive curtain of his eye, behind it gathered, like trooping ghosts, shadowy images that were akin to it, until the visual impression was, as it were, rimmed and circled by a luminous atmosphere of its own. Behind even Milton's 'wandering moon' hovered the wraith of Virgil's—and Shakespeare's.*

For the eyes of the great dead yet look through ours, and our past eyes still see. The flake of cloud above the sunken moon is a symbol of that convergence of the wealth of the inward eye upon the witness of the outer which is the rich gift of imaginative minds. And the imagination is never more authentically creative than when it suffuses an object of present or bygone vision, in its integrity, with this inner light which is the effluence of past impressions—that cloud of witnesses below the threshold of consciousness, whose eyes may be the eyes of Virgil, or Milton, or Dorothy Wordsworth, or ourselves. The moving moon with its soft ascent (to come back to our starting point) is sheer, familiar, unaltered and undisturbed reality, imbued, like the wisp of cloud at Keswick, with the influences of remembered moons that still tenanted the chambers of the brain.

And one of those moons had originally moved through remote and occult skies. Coleridge later wrote a gloss which has captured 'one wonder, at the least' that floated in the stanza's pellucid depths:

In his loneliness and fixedness he yearneth toward the

> journeying Moon, and the stars that still sojourn, yet still move onward; and every where the blue sky belongs to them, and is their appointed rest, and their native country and their own natural homes, which they enter unannounced, as lords that are certainly expected and yet there is a silent joy at their arrival.[38]

The stateliness of that soft-paced prose sets off the moving simplicity of the diction of the stanza—a simplicity that achieves all which, in these same *Lyrical Ballads*, Wordsworth strove for and missed—and one of its phrases serves, in its implications, as an epitome of all we have been saying.

The Mariner 'yearneth toward the journeying Moon, and the stars *that still sojourn, yet still move onward.*' That was the vision of one of those dreamers who were Coleridge's 'darling studies,' the Neoplatonic mystic Iamblichus. And Iamblichus in his treatise on the Mysteries of the Egyptians (*De Mysteriis Ægyptiorum*), written fifteen hundred years before, tells how the celestial bodies hold the even tenor of a way which, like that of the gods, is ever fixed, yet ever moving: 'imitatur ergo corpus cæleste deorum tenorem ilium, *qui semper eodem modo permanet, currit enim motu sempiterno.*'[40] The passage of the journeying moon through the sojourning yet ever onward moving stars owed the most deeply spiritual element of its beauty to the influence of remembered imagery present only to Coleridge's inward eye.[41] Like a hundred other impressions which had flashed from the page as he read, it had come, and gone, and now from its occultation comes anew. That mystical utterance of Brahma is no less the voice of the Spirit of the Loom:

> They know not well the subtle ways
> I keep, and pass, and turn again.

Nor did the stanza itself have long to wait before *its* words, in turn, flowed in on the impulse of immediate impression. At the close of the entry in her *Journal* for 8th February, 1802, Dorothy Wordsworth wrote: 'N.B.—The moon came out suddenly when we were at John's Grove, *and a star or two besides.*'[42] Associations are strange and potent things. Dorothy and her brother had set out that evening towards Rydale for letters; had met the postman on the way; and had received from him a letter from Coleridge. 'I put it in my pocket,' Dorothy continues. 'At the top of the White Moss I took it to my bosom—a safer place for it.'[43] And when, a few minutes later, the moon came out, it was Coleridge's moon that she saw.

III

And now, with the phenomenon of the new moon in the old moon's arms fresh in mind, we may come back at last to the hornèd moon which we have left so long suspended above the eastern bar. For this time, where the old moon's opaque, rimmed body lies, within the crescent, is a star. And that is not a usual spectacle.

The sun's rim has dipped, and the spectre-bark with its far-heard whisper, has vanished over the sea:

> We listened and looked sideways up!
> Fear at my heart, as at a cup,
> My life-blood seemed to sip!
> The stars were dim, and thick the night,
> The steersman's face by his lamp gleamed white;
> From the sails the dew did drip—[44]
> Till clomb above the eastern bar
> *The hornèd Moon, with one bright star*
> *Within the nether tip.*[45]

The extract from Cotton Mather's letter which Coleridge had read in the *Philosophical Transactions* gives, as we have already seen, the tradition that at Boston, 'in November, 1668, *a Star appear'd below the Body of the Moon within the Horns of it.*'* And there we are!

Now whether the star was 'within the nether tip' of the crescent, as Coleridge finally left it, or 'almost atween the tips,' as apparently he first placed it, there was pretty clearly, as in the case of the water-snakes, a confluence of reminiscences. The tradition of the star observed within the horns at Boston, to which the Note Book led us, was undoubtedly in his mind. But so, with little doubt, were other things which he had read, and which, like Cotton Mather's letter, have never been taken account of since. Coleridge, as we have more than once already had to note, was an ardent reader of the *Philosophical Transactions of the Royal Society*, the most distinguished scientific publication of his day. Now in the *Transactions* for 1794, three years before 'The Ancient Mariner' was written, appeared two remarkable sets of observations, communicated this time by the distinguished Astronomer Royal, Nevil Maskelyne, himself, each with the barely less than sensational heading: 'An Account of an Appearance of Light, like a Star, seen in the dark Part of the Moon, on Friday the 7th of March, 1794.'[46] The repetition of the title makes it (though it would be so anyway) the most striking entry in the volume, and the communications fill eleven pages. Moreover, these two articles in the *Philosophical Transactions* were reviewed, with their arresting titles given in full, and with substantial extracts, in the *British Critic* of June, 1795. And Coleridge at just this time was an attentive reader of the *British Critic*.[48] Not merely once, then, but possibly (I should say probably) twice, or even thrice, the one bright star within the tip of the horned moon had flashed upon Coleridge's inner eye in such a startling fashion as to leave an indelible impression. I confess to a thrill myself as I turned the yellowed leaves and came upon the wonder. And I suspect that our interpretation of the baffling lines in 'The Ancient Mariner' must admit a fresh alternative. For the idea of strange lights, not impossibly of stars, observed within the illuminated crescent of the moon, was clearly one with which even the scientific thought of the day was dallying. Whether Coleridge read them or not, at least two other notices of such lights are recorded, on eminent scientific authority, in learned publications of which Coleridge certainly knew.[49] Instead, then, of stupidly blundering on the one hand, or of saying, on the other, ambiguously or obscurely what he meant—or even of assuming (as has been suggested)[50] that the laws of nature are abrogated on a spectral sea—instead of doing any of these, Coleridge may have felt free, with the *Philosophical Transactions* as ample backing, to turn to his own imaginative ends, as an appearance admitted on high authority to be within the range of possibility, the startling image of the crescent moon with 'a Star . . . within the Horns of it.' With the Royal Society behind him, in fine, it is undeniable that he had warrant for counting on 'a semblance of truth' in his picture 'sufficient to procure for these shadows of imagination that willing suspension of disbelief for the moment, which constitutes poetic faith.'[51]

But what of a hornèd moon which climbed 'above the eastern bar' at a time when both it and the stars were visible? That, we are told, no crescent moon (unless it were over the valley of Ajalon!) was ever known to do. It is broad daylight, as everybody knows who stops to think, when the new moon rises, and both it and the stars are then invisible to mortal eyes. So be it. I have long been inclined, however, to suspect that

Coleridge at times knew more than his critics. And I have to thank the Director of the Harvard Astronomical Observatory, my colleague Professor Harlow Shapley, for corroborating a suggestion which clears Coleridge, I think, of the charge of ignorance or inadvertence which the commentators, sadly or cheerfully after their kind, have brought against him. 'It is curious,' writes (for instance) Mr. W. Hale White,[52] 'that . . . [Coleridge] did not detect the mistake of a rising, horned moon at sunset'—a stricture to which Hutchinson refers as 'irrefragable.' But *is* it at sunset? And is the *crescent* moon (etymologically speaking) the only *hornèd* moon? I fear the charge of ignorance or inadvertence lies against the critics rather than the poet. The *waning* moon each month is hornèd too—that is (to be exact), 'for the three days before its conjunction with the sun at the time of new moon.' And (to remain exact) 'for those three days (or four or five) it would rise between two A.M. and sunrise, depending on the lunar age.'[53] In other words, if, in the poem, it was early morning when the doomed mariners eyed the east, the hornèd moon, which they saw rising was as regular a visitant as the crescent moon which sets, at a more convenient season, in the west. And early morning, not sunset, it assuredly is. Between the swift fall of the tropical night and the rising of the moon an indefinite time has elapsed.

The stars were dim, and thick the night,
The steersman's face by his lamp gleamed white,
From the sails the dew did drip—
Till clomb above the eastern bar
The hornèd Moon.

It would be hard to suggest more powerfully than by that slow, dull beat of falling drops the passage of time for white-faced men—while fear sucked, like a vampire, the blood from their hearts—between the cast of the spectre dice and the inexorable nearing of the unknown but appointed signal, when 'One after one, *by the star-dogged Moon* . . . his shipmates drop down dead.' The sun's rim has dipt haunted hours before, and it is the *dying* moon (hugged close by the star of ill omen at sea)* whose rising releases the spectral curse.

And there is one thing more. The man who later jotted down at '20 minutes past 2 o'clock,' '1/2 past two o'clock, morning,' '1/2 past 2,' '45 minutes past 2' his exact and vivid observations of the changing aspects of the moon before his eyes—that watcher of the morning skies was not the person to be guilty of the slip with which he has been charged. With no thought whatever of the *new* moon in his mind, he was writing (I think we may be certain) of the rising of the waning moon, as he, like the Mariner, had doubtless seen it during sleepless nights. There *is* no blunder. It is we who have been stupid, and not he.[55]

As for the reading 'almost atween the tips' (to return for a moment to the position of the star) moons seen over remote and perilous seas and dogged by a solitary star met Coleridge at every turn. In the *Strange and Dangerous Voyage of Captain Thomas James* he had read: 'The sixe and twentieth, I obserued, *when the Easterne edge of the Moone did touch the Planet Mars*, the Lions heart was then in the East quarter'[56]—a statement, penned in the ultimate climes of the Pole, which needs but Poe's magic touch to give us 'Ulalume.' In Captain Cook he had met with 'an immersion of [a star] behind the moon's dark limb.'[57] In one of the great Halley's voyages toward the Antarctic pole, 'the Moon did exactly touch this star [in Virgo] with her Southern limb,' and five minutes later, 'the Southern horn was just 2 minutes past the Star.'[58] In Bruce's *Travels to Discover the Source of the Nile* Coleridge had read how in Abyssinia 'a star passing near the horns of the moon denotes the coming of an enemy.'[59] And in Sir Richard Hawkins's *Voyage to the South Seas* he may have come upon this curious fragment of sailor's lore: 'Some I have heard say, and others write, that there is a starre which never seperateth it self from the moone, but a small distance.'[60]

In a word, like almost everything else in 'The Ancient Mariner,' the star-dogged moon sprang from a mind that had voyaged by proxy through strange seas, and was ever after haunted by their marvels, until they achieved expression in a poem the very secret of whose unique illusion lies in its imaginative rendering of fact, as fact takes form to the eyes of men alone in a wide, wide sea.

There is again, however, a charming human touch, which no one seems to have observed,* that brings the horned moon of Coleridge's vision from its silent seas to the pleasant paths between Nether Stowey and Alfoxden. On March 21, 1798, Dorothy Wordsworth wrote in her *Journal:* 'We drank tea at Coleridge's. . . . At our return the sky partially shaded with clouds. The *horned moon was set.* Startled two night birds from the great elm tree.' Two days later, on the 23d, she wrote: 'Coleridge dined with us. *He brought his ballad finished.* We walked with him to the Miner's house. A beautiful evening, very starry, *the horned moon.*'[61] The ballad which Coleridge brought finished was 'The Rime of the Ancient Mariner.' Now elsewhere in the Alfoxden *Journal* Dorothy always speaks of the '*crescent* moon' (January 23: 'The crescent moon, Jupiter, and Venus'; February 18: 'first observed the crescent moon, a silvery line, a thready bow'; April 20: 'The moon crescent. "Peter Bell" begun').[62] What, however, had she heard read, we may be sure, on one or both of those memorable March evenings in Coleridge's company? This:

> With never a whisper in the Sea
> Off darts the Spectre-ship;
> While clombe above the Eastern bar
> *The horned Moon*, with one bright Star
> Almost atween the tips.

One after one by *the horned Moon*
(Listen, O Stranger! to me)
Each turn'd his face with ghastly pang
And curs'd me with his ee.[63]

And as she walks home, the magical lines are still in her memory, and the moon which she sees is the Mariner's moon. Nothing could be more right and meet than that the first recorded impression of 'The Ancient Mariner' should be a transfer of the phrase which had haunted Coleridge to her own familiar and beloved moon. And nothing could more exquisitely typify that interpenetration of the familiar and the strange in which the very triumph of the poem consists than this March crescent, which is at once itself and yet a denizen of visionary skies.[65]

IV

The hornèd moon with her one presaging star, and the softly ascending moon with her attendant star or two beside, give place to a moon whose satellite stars dance wanly between the flickering banners of a mysteriously lighted sky. And if the familiar skies of Somerset are in *this* picture, their traces are as dim as the dancing stars themselves. And once more we are off along far and circuitous ways.

'By grace of the holy Mother' (so reads the gloss) 'the ancient Mariner is refreshed with rain.' And when he wakes, 'He heareth sounds and seeth strange sights and commotions in the sky and the element.'[66] The stanzas opposite which these last words stand in the margin are these:

And soon I heard a roaring wind:
It did not come anear;
But with its sound it shook the sails,
That were so thin and sere.

The upper air burst into life!
And a hundred fire-flags sheen
To and fro they were hurried about!
And to and fro, and in and out,
The wan stars danced between.

And the coming wind did roar more loud,
And the sails did sigh like sedge;
And the rain poured down from one black cloud;
The Moon was at its edge.

The thick black cloud was cleft, and still
The Moon was at its side:
Like waters shot from some high crag,
The lightning fell with never a jag,
A river steep and wide.[67]

Where had Coleridge, or the whole college of meteorologists at Pekin, ever seen such a concourse of strange sights and commotions in the element as that concatenation of northern lights, stars, moon, and lightning?[68] Let us hold the bewildering juxtaposition in abeyance for a moment, and see what is to be said for the details.

In the first place, a calm at the Line and a thunderstorm involve no inconsistencies. Coleridge found warrant enough in Purchas (to go no farther) for bringing the two together. 'Wee drew towards the Line,' he would read in the account of 'The second Circum-Navigation of the Earth,' 'where wee were becalmed the space of three weekes, but yet subject to divers great Stormes, terrible Lightnings and much Thunder.'[69] And Davis's experience, recorded in the same volume, was identical with Drake's.[70] What, however, of the accuracy of a description of lightning which fell like a river from a chasm in a cloud? Coleridge had pretty certainly never seen the like in Devon or Somerset. But lightning—the lightning of the tropics, 'such . . . as in Europe is altogether unknow,'[71] to quote the observation of a voyager in these same seas—had been so seen, and Coleridge, in those ocular spectra of his which kept pace with his reading, had definitely seen it.

The fifth chapter of Part II of Bartram's *Travels*, it will be remembered, had sown the Note Book broadcast with its delectable flora and fauna. And from the very focal point of Coleridge's interest in it, flanked on the one hand by the alligators and the snake-birds, on the other by the wilderness-plot and the Gordonia lasianthus, came the brief jotting about the roaring of the crocodiles: 'The distant thunder sounds heavily—the crocodiles answer it like an echo.'[72] On the next page of Bartram the threatened tempest breaks.

Now whenever occasion offers (as in Georgia and Florida occasions do not lack) Bartram lets himself go to the top of his bent on the theme of subtropical thunderstorms. At the close, then, of the paragraph describing this particular downpour Coleridge had read: 'the rain came down with such rapidity and fell in such quantities, that every object was totally obscured, excepting the *continuous streams or rivers of lightning* pouring from the clouds.'[73] Revelling later in still another cataract Bartram writes: 'The hurricane *comes in roaring . . . the dark cloud opens over my head, diveloping* [*sic*] *a vast river* of the etherial fire.'[74] And Coleridge had hardly begun the book, when he was plunged into a similar account: 'when instantly the lightning, as it were, *opening a fiery chasm in the black cloud*, darted with inconceivable rapidity on the trunk of a large pine tree.'[75] And when, with Bartram fresh in mind (as was assuredly the case),[76] he came to 'The Ancient Mariner,' he wrote:

> *The thick black cloud was cleft*,[77] and still
> The Moon was at its side:
> *Like waters* shot from some high crag,
> *The lightning fell* with never a jag,
> *A river steep and wide.*[78]

Rogers speaks of lightning which '*fell* as if it had been liquid,'[79] and Bruce of 'sheets of lightning, which ran on the ground *like water.*'[80] But Bartram was obviously the centre of one of those strange confluences of recollections (to come back to Coleridge's own phraseology) which formed 'a sort of nucleus in the reservoir of the soul,' upon which 'cluster points on cluster points' of reminiscences converged.[81] And in this instance a most remarkable cluster point, it would seem, was close at hand.

Bartram begins his account of the tempest which the crocodiles had heralded, as follows:

> How purple and fiery appeared the tumultious [*sic*] clouds! *swiftly ascending or darting from the horizon upwards;* they seemed *to oppose and dash against each other, the skies appeared streaked with blood* or purple flame overhead, the flaming lightning *streaming and darting about in every direction* around, *seems to fill the world with fire;* whilst the heavy thunder keeps the earth in a constant tremor.[82]

Strike out the clouds and the thunder, and that is an uncommonly vivid and typical description of an *aurora.* Since I am, for the time being, fairly well versed myself in eighteenth-century descriptions of auroras,[83] I caught it as such when I read, before its bearing on the bewildering meteorology of these stanzas flashed on my mind. And for Coleridge the confluence of associations was, I think, inevitable. Here are a few phrases from accounts of the aurora which he had not only read but had actually made use of in the 'Destiny of Nations';

> '*Fires* of a thousand Colours . . . *light up the Sky*'; 'bright Light, *with its extremities upon the Horizon, which . . . glides swiftly up the Sky*'; 'the Sky tinged with so lively a red, that . . . Orion *look'd as if it had been dipt in blood*'; '*they look red, and the streams move vehemently*'; '*it is . . . call'd Streaming . . . darting out Rays and Streams every way*'; '*Dart* from the North on pale *electric streams*'; like 'horsemen . . . *encountering and running one against another*.'[84]

'These hands are not more like' than the terms in which the two skies are described—the one streaming with the lightning, the other with the northern lights. What happened, then, when Coleridge read his Bartram?

There is a striking passage in *The Friend* which I think will help us to see. 'The window of my library at Keswick,' wrote Coleridge (that window of the many vigils, when he was a watcher of the skies), 'is opposite to the fire-place, and looks out on a very large garden that occupies the whole slope of the hill on which the house stands. Consequently, the rays of light transmitted through the glass (that is, the rays from the garden, the opposite mountains, and the bridge, river, lake, and vale interjacent), and the rays reflected *from* it (of the fire-place, etc.) enter the eye at the same moment. At the coming on of evening, it was my frequent amusement to watch the image or reflection of the fire, that seemed burning in the bushes or between the trees in different parts of the garden or the fields beyond it, according as there was more or less light; and which still arranged itself among the real objects of vision, with a distance and magnitude proportioned to its greater or lesser faintness.'[85] Now substitute for the trees and bushes* Bartram's narrative of the storm, and for the superimposed image of the fire Coleridge's clustered recollections of the aurora, and we have a fair analogy with the telescoping of the two sets of images as Coleridge read. He carried away, in a word (if our premises are granted), a recollection of Bartram's lightnings which trailed along with it the kindred imagery of the northern lights. And when, with Bartram's lightning, falling like a river, powerfully visualized in his mind's eye, he came to his own equatorial tempest, the auroral streamers already associated with the lightning poured in too. And so,

> The upper air burst into life!
> And a hundred fire-flags sheen,
> To and fro they were hurried about!
> And to and fro, and in and out,
> The wan stars danced between.[86]

And if strange signs indeed stand in conjunction in the element, we have an eminently Coleridgean association of ideas to thank for it.

And once started, the train of associations comes thick and fast. The 'fire-flags' have streamed in from Hearne and Maupertuis. The northern lights, says Hearne, 'make a rustling and crackling noise, *like the waving of a large flag* in a fresh gale of wind.'[87] 'Their Motion,' writes Maupertuis, 'is most commonly *like that of a pair of Colours waved in the Air*.'[88] And it is the aurora which has carried with it into the mystifying picture of the storm the alien moon and stars. The moon—'even the Full-Moon'—shines 'bright,' or 'with great splendor,' together with the aurora, in Ellis, and Maupertuis, and Hearne.[89] But the 'wan stars' had glimmered first in other and surprising skies.

For some reason (I suspect because they proved to be a treasure-house of raw materials for his long-meditated Hymns) the opening canto of the *Botanic Garden* and at least the first part of the second, set, with their Notes, all manner of curious projects stirring in Coleridge's 'shaping and disquisitive mind.'[90] The first two entries in the Note Book were inspired by them,[91] and there is other matter which, just now, is still more pertinent. Coleridge had used in the sonnet to Godwin, as we have seen, the aurora's 'electric streams' of Canto I, 129; and he had copied in the Note Book a part of Darwin's comment ('Central Fires') on Canto I, 139.[92] And between these two lines—129 and 139—which we know he had read with an ingenuously predatory eye, stood this:

Alarm with comet-blaze the sapphire plain,
The wan stars glimmering through its silver train.[93]

On these last two lines Darwin has an 'Additional Note,' which precedes by only a page the passage on 'Central Fires' which Coleridge transcribed.[94] And in this 'Additional Note,' at the head of which the lines on the 'wan stars' are repeated, Coleridge would read the following: 'Dr. Hamilton observes that *the light of small stars are* [*sic*] *seen undiminished through* both *the light* of the tails of comets, and *of the aurora borealis.*'[95] The lines, in a word, about the stars which glimmered through the comet's 'silver train' (shades of Milton's 'horrid hair' that burned in Ophiuchus huge!) had found their lodgement in Coleridge's memory in immediate conjunction with the aurora, and Darwin's note explicitly links the comet's tail with the northern lights. And so, again,

The upper air burst into life!
And a hundred fire-flags sheen,
To and fro they were hurried about!
And to and fro, and in and out,
The wan stars danced between.[96]

The line in which Coleridge saw the aurora, as he later saw the clouds, 'give away [its] motion to the stars'[97]—a line as simple as it is hauntingly suggestive—owes its birth to this grotesque *mélange:*

Alarm with comet-blaze the sapphire plain,
The wan stars glimmering through its silver train;
Gem the bright Zodiac, stud the glowing pole,
Or give the Sun's phlogistic orb to roll.

'Lord,' exclaimed Ophelia, 'we know what we are, but know not what we may be.' And no truer dictum, mad or sane, was ever uttered, touching the stuff of poetry.*

V

There is another passage of curious interest which may perhaps have bearing here. On one of the most wildly incoherent pages of the Note Book Bartram's lightnings apparently stream again. At least if they are not Bartram's lightnings, I have not the remotest notion what they are. The lines which follow belie their looks, for they are (be it promptly said) the lines of the fragmentary excerpt from the Note Book, spaced as Coleridge spaced them, and not a modern impressionistic poem:

a dusky light—a purple *flash*
crystalline splendor—light blue—
  Green lightnings—
in that eternal and delirious [pang]
  wrath fires—
                  inward desolations
  an horror of great darkness

great things—on the ocean
counterfeit infinity—[103]

The lightning-streaked skies in the *Travels* are distant only a paragraph from the sentence about the thunder-echoing roar of the crocodiles, which is entered on an earlier leaf of the Note Book,[104] and the 'purple flash' of the unintelligible jumble now before us is very like the 'purple flame' of Bartram's 'purple and fiery clouds' from which the 'flaming lightning' streamed.[105] And the 'light *blue*' and '*green* lightnings,' in seeming conjunction with the ocean, fantastically suggest the ubiquitous animalcule of our earlier adventures. At all events, the vivid hues of the lightning stood for some image or other which was printed deep on Coleridge's memory, for they took still another remarkable turn—this time in a letter to Sara Coleridge written in May, 1799, during a walking tour in the Hartz. After a visit to some smelting furnaces, Coleridge wrote: 'a scene of terrible beauty is a furnace of boiling metal, *darting, every moment blue, green, and scarlet lightning*, like serpents' tongues!'[106] The visual image of the blue and green lightning which the jotting in the Note Book had struggled vainly to express, imposed itself upon the image of the glowing metal, as the 'spectrum' of the aurora imposed itself upon the thunder-storm. But whatever the enigmatic entry in the Note Book may have meant, as an amorphous particle of poetic protoplasm it is not without significance, and it may have been at least a contributory blur in the nebulous mass which finally took form in the auroral lightnings of the Mariner's sky.

The 'roaring wind' (to return for a moment to the stanzas) is Bartram's 'dreadful . . . roaring . . . every where around [him],' as 'the hurricane comes on roaring';[107] and its 'sound [that] shook the sails' is seemingly transferred from 'the heavy thunder [that] keeps the earth in a constant tremor.'[108] The sails themselves, 'that were *so thin and sere*,' are the transfigured sails of the veritable ship from which the actual albatross was shot: 'Our sails,' wrote Captain Shelvocke, '. . . were now grown *so very thin and rotten*.'[109] And the hint for a line which, for union of sense and sound, has few rivals in poetry—'And the sails did sigh like sedge'—came, I suspect, from a sentence at the heart of another star-cluster of associations. For in the narrative of Barents's last voyage, two pages distant from the 'swounding' by the sea-coal fire, three from 'a weary time,' seven from 'that glorious light' of the reappearing sun, and only ten from the phrase about the 'strange sight in the Element' embodied in the gloss to these very stanzas, we read this: 'Wee fetched *Segges* from the Sea-side, and layd them upon the *Sayle*'[110]—a sentence which sighs like sedges in its untutored prose. And just before, they had buried the ship's carpenter 'under the *sedges*, in the clift of a hill.'[111] It is trifles, as everybody knows from personal experience, which are apt to be most potently suggestive, and associations such as these fly together, through what Coleridge calls the 'polarity' of the imagination,[112] as by some occult affinity. And through such labyrinths of association a line of haunting music may emerge from a storm in an alligator-swamp in Florida.

VI

The moon in 'The Ancient Mariner,' like the sun, is more than a luminary in the sky. Both are merged with the dramatic movement of the poem, and that movement culminates during the long night-watches at the Line. The gloss is explicit, should the poem leave us blind. Under the star-dogged moon, the Mariner's 'shipmates drop down dead.'[113] At the very moment when 'the spell begins to break,' 'in his loneliness and fixedness he yearneth towards the journeying Moon.'[114] 'Beneath the lightning and the Moon'—that wild moon of the meteor-lighted skies—'the bodies of the ship's crew are inspired and the ship moves on.'[115] And when 'the ancient Mariner beholdeth his native country,'[116] the familiar landscape is transfigured by the moon:

> The harbour-bay was clear as glass,
> So smoothly it was strewn!
> And on the bay the moonlight lay,
> And the shadow of the Moon.
>
> The rock shone bright, the kirk no less,
> That stands above the rock:
> The moonlight steeped in silentness

The steady weathercock.

And the bay was white with silent light . . . [117]

No need to go to Milton or to Bartram or to the *Philosophical Transactions* for that! That is the moon which Coleridge saw the month before 'The Ancient Mariner' was finished, when, with Hartley asleep in the cradle beside him, he wrote:[118]

Therefore all seasons shall be sweet to thee,
. . . whether the eave-drops fall
Heard only in the trances of the blast,
Or if the secret ministry of frost
Shall hang them up in silent icicles,
Quietly shining to the quiet Moon.

'When half-gods go, The gods arrive.' There was to have been a 'Hymn to the Moon.' What Coleridge would have done with it I do not know. In the light of the Note Book one can only guess—and shudder. But the stuff of the discarded Hymn was swept, when the creative impulse woke, within the compass of a great plastic design. And the passing of the earlier project, with its enveloping haze of metaphysic moonshine, ushered in the journeying moon itself, which soars, compact of the light of many moons, above enchanted seas.

---

*She was (and the fact gives her half her inalienable charm) 'A

Spirit, yet a *Woman* too!' A few lines earlier in the same entry she had written thus: 'I went through the fields, and sate for an hour afraid to pass a cow. The cow looked at me, and I looked at the cow, and whenever I stirred the cow gave over eating.' And the first recorded words that Coleridge wrote about her were: 'She is a woman indeed!' What further he had to say of her (it was when he brought 'Wordsworth and his exquisite sister' back with him from Racedown to Stowey, on the occasion signalized by 'dear Sara' and the skillet of boiling milk); and what she had already written at Racedown about him; and the curious and unwitting coincidences between the two first-impressions—all this may be seen in the *Biographia Epistolaris*, I, 136, and in the *Letters of the Wordsworth Family*, I, 109, respectively.

†'Was accompanied by Mrs. Nicholson as far as Rydale,' she adds. 'This was very kind, but God be thanked, I want not society by a moonlit lake.'

*If Dorothy was 'sipping beverage divine' from William's and Coleridge's lips, she had more sublunary nectar too. For the next engaging sentence reads: 'I drank a little brandy and water, and was in heaven.'

*he reference (for 'thy' is addressed to Wordsworth) is to the 'little *Boat*, Whose shape is like the crescentmoon' in the Prologue to 'Peter Bell'—'My little vagrant Form of light, My gay and beautiful *Canoe*.'[29] William's adoring sister would not forget that touch!

*It is very strange, this flowing in of memory upon perception. On this evening of September 15, 1801, there streamed in on the setting moon, as we have just seen, the imagery of 'Lewti.' But behind the imagery of 'Lewti,' in turn, lay certain striking passages in Bartram.[37] And when, just a little later, in the spring of 1802, Coleridge saw the old moon in the new moon's arms (that slim, bright crescent embracing the dimly outlined dark) there swam up to memory and merged with his perception Bartram's delineation of the moon in eclipse—the moon which shone for him one night on his Alatamaha, and which then had lent to 'Lewti' the gleam which 'heaved upon Tamaha's stream.' 'At length, *a silver thread* alone *encircles* her temples,' Bartram had written of his moon.[39] And so when Coleridge saw at Keswick, on that eventful night for the three friends, the dark of the moon rimmed with its circumambient brightness, it too was '*circled* by a *silver thread*.' Leaving aside the architectonics and the magic, it is hard to set a limit to the potency of that deep, thronging reservoir of latent memories, prompt at a touch to flow in upon the impulses of immediate impression.

*An astonishingly similar observation was recorded in England some two hundred years before. In Harrison's *Chronologie* occurs the following entry:

1587. A Sterre is sene in the bodie of the mone vpon *the* [blank] of Marche, whereat many me*n* me*r*ureiled, & not wi*th*out cause, for it stode directly betwene *the* pointe*s* of her hornes, *the* mone being chaunged, not passing 5 or 6 daies before.[47]

Coleridge could not possibly have seen the entry, for the *Chronologie* was never published, and the manuscript was lost until 1876. But the record at least demonstrates this: the startling phenomenon, however explained, was not unique. And we shall meet it again in a moment, within hail of 'The Ancient Mariner.'

*'It is a common superstition among sailors, "that something evil is about to happen, whenever a star dogs the Moon." ' That is Coleridge's own manuscript note.[54]

*This paragraph, exactly as it stands, was written December 19, 1919. On November 18, 1920, I read for the first time Sir Arthur Quiller-Couch's suggestion to the same effect, published in 1920, in his Introduction to Sampson's edition of the *Biographia Literaria*.[64] I have allowed my own statement to stand unchanged, happy in the corroboration afforded it by the independent observation of so acute and sympathetic an interpreter of letters and of life.

*I am merely paraphrasing Coleridge's own elucidation of

Luther's apparition of the Devil.

*The ancient Mariner was not the only sailor who had seen dim stars through the auroral lights. Forster, in his story of Cook's voyage, writes: 'The stars were sometimes hid by, and *sometimes faintly to be seen through the substance of these Southern lights.*'[98] Wordsworth, who also was interested in auroras,[99] tried his hand, just after 'The Ancient Mariner' was finished,[100] at depicting the same phenomenon:

> Haste! and above Siberian snows
> We'll sport amid the boreal morning,
> Will mingle with her *lustres gliding*
> *Among the stars, the stars now hiding*
> *And now the stars adorning.*[101]

I imagine that auroras were sometimes talked about at Nether Stowey and Alfoxden; but Wordsworth had read travels too.[102]

CHAPTER XII

'DEAR GUTTER OF STOWEY

'OVER what place does the moon hang to your eye, my dearest Sara?' were the first words Coleridge wrote home from Germany, less than three weeks after 'The Ancient Mariner' left the press. 'To me it hangs over the left bank of the Elbe, and a long trembling road of moonlight reaches from thence up to the stern of our vessel, and there it ends.'[1] Uncounted thousands of us mortals have known at some time what that means—the poignant recollection of the moon of home, when the same moon shines, above ways that are not ours, upon a stranger in a strange land.* I am not indulging in gratuitous sentiment. Coleridge in Germany was undergoing in his own person an experience which in imagination he had already grasped, and which he had woven with rare felicity into the fabric of the Mariner's voyage. The art with which polar ice and equatorial suns and the vicissitudes of the wandering moon are incorporated in the large design is obvious. But even that masterful bending of the elements themselves to the uses of the poem is rivalled in its effectiveness by the Mariner's yearning recognition in almost everything about him—when 'the sky and the sea, and the sea and the sky Lay like a load on [hisl weary eye, And the dead were at [his] feet'—of something which reminds him of the familiar sights and sounds of 'mine own countree.' Nothing in the poem is more imaginatively conceived than that transference to a strange and spectral setting of a profoundly human trait. And as the great pattern grows on the loom, it is things seen and heard by Coleridge at Nether Stowey, or years earlier among the mountains of North Wales, which rise, like a mirage, out of the silence of the Mariner's sea.

I

The thing itself is real enough. 'Sometimes I thought myself in the coombs about Stowey, sometimes between Porlock and Linton,' writes Coleridge again to his Sara from Germany; and as he walks there come back to him in memory 'the great rocky fragments which jut out from the hill . . . at Porlock, and which, alas! we have not at dear Stowey.'[3] 'The sky and colours of the clouds are quite English,' he tells her in a postscript at eleven o'clock one night, 'just as if I were coming out of T. Poole's homeward with you in my arm.'[4] Wordsworth, like Coleridge, spent a homesick winter in Germany, and no poems which he ever wrote are more steeped in the loveliness of England than the few which bear in some form the heading: 'Written in Germany.' And particularly in the loneliness of solitary and alien seas, the visions of the inner eye impose themselves upon the testimony of the senses with enhanced intensity. That, like the flake of cloud invested with the light of visionary moons, is but a special aspect of a fact of general experience.

The books of the voyagers are full of it. In that same Fifth Volume of the *Philosophical Transactions* in which Coleridge found the rainbow in the spray, and the shining fishes in the wakes of ships, and the moon with a star 'within the Horn of it,' he could have read (and probably did) 'An Account of a Calenture.' 'I observ'd,' says the writer, 'he [the seaman] often cry'd out, he would go into the green Fields,' and 'when they are seiz'd with this . . . Disorder,' the account continues, 'they steal privately over-board into the Sea, imagining they are going into the green Fields.'[5] And so sailors in tropical latitudes, like the dying Falstaff, 'babble of green fields,' and in the hallucination of fever the inarticulate longings of parched throats and weary eyes find expression in absolute vision. But the hallucination is only the waking dream intensified. Frézier, in his *Voyage to the South Sea*, tells how, as the endless days wore on, he contrasted 'the Beauty of the Fields adorn'd with Flowers, with the Horror of the Waves that swell'd up like Mountains; the sweet Repose a Man enjoys on a green Turf, with the Agitation and perpetual Shocks of so violent a Rolling.'[6] In that engrossing narrative ('intermixt with vast variety of Adventures and Discoveries'), *The dangerous*

Voyage and bold Attempts of Capt. Bartholomew Sharp and others in the South Sea,[7] written by Basil Ringrose, Gent., the buccaneers are storm-stayed on unknown islands just north of Magellan Straits, after eighteen months at sea. Everything is strange, from the penguins that 'pad on the Water with their Wings very fast,' to 'the Magellan Clouds, so Famous among Mariners in the South Seas,' the least of which 'was about the bigness of a Man's Hat.'[8] And Ringrose writes: 'The Weather now was very warm . . . and the Birds sung as sweetly as those in England. We saw here both Thrushes and Blackbirds, and many other sorts of those that are usually seen in our own Country.'[9] And through the long voyage, object after object reminds the daring adventurers of home: 'We found Cockles like those we have in England'; 'Night being come'—after a day filled with the roaring of sea-lions—'we made our Beds of Fern, whereof there is huge plenty upon this Island; together with great Multitudes of Trees like English Box'; Cape San Francisco, seen off Ecuador, 'looked very like Beachy-head in England,' and as they sailed on south, to windward was 'Woody Land, which causes the Country all over to look like so many enclosures of Ripe Corn Fields.'[10] Captain John Saris, feeling his way through a maze of uncanny islands into the China Sea, saw and seized on as a landmark 'a steepe Rock . . . verye like Cherin [Charing] cross.'[11] 'Some of these Rocks,' wrote Frederick Martens, in that description of the ice-fields of the North which Coleridge read to such good purpose, 'appear[ed] like an old decayed Wall; they smell very sweet, as the green Fields do in our Country in the Spring when it rains.'[12] And this time the simple words are instinct with the feeling of a poet. And doubly affecting through the very incongruity of the suggestion, are Van der Brugge's words (in *The Journal or Day-Book kept by Seven Sailors during their Wintering in Spitzbergen*), when at last, after a winter of bitter cold and darkness, during which 'at night, the Northern light gleamed terribly,' there came in April, 1634, a day of warm sunshine, and 'the blubber in the boats melted in many places, so that we held that it could not be finer weather this day in the home country.'[13] The Sieur Raveneau de Lussan, in the Freebooters' narratives once more, sums it all up in a passage which takes us back to that moving phrase 'at home in our own Countrey' which Coleridge had read in the narrative of Barents's last voyage: 'Thus were we forced to endure such contrary Seasons, as well when we travelled, as when we reposed ourselves . . . but the hopes of getting once more into our Native Country, made us patiently to endure all their Toils, and served as so many Wings to carry us.'[14] 'For this bodily frame,' wrote Coleridge once, 'is an imitative thing, and touched by the imagination gives the hour which is past as faithfully as a repeating watch.'[15] That is truer of no class of men than of the most intrepid mariners, when, in the solitude of distant seas, a fleeting hint of what is native and familiar sends memory flashing home. And over and over again, some access of feeling which touches the springs of the imagination lends to their narratives ineffaceable charm.

Now everything in the poem is seen through the Mariner's eyes. And the Mariner has a poet's vision. So had those mariners who gave to many a round, unvarnished tale in Hakluyt and Purchas an unconscious beauty. So, for that matter, had Frederick Martens, and Herman Melville, and Joseph Conrad, and John Masefield, when they sailed the seas. The sea has nurtured poets, articulate and inarticulate, from the days when first it caught in its strong toil of grace and mystery and terror those who go down to it in ships. And the ancient Mariner is endowed with a vision which is singularly true to type. But Coleridge's collaborator at the inception of the poem did not seem to think so, and the question which he raised confronts us here.

In an amazing dictum, which he actually printed as a note in the second edition of *Lyrical Ballads*,* Wordsworth named as first among the 'four great defects' which 'the Poem of my Friend has indeed,' the fact that 'the principal person *has no distinct character*, either *in his profession of Mariner*, or as a human being who having been long under the control of supernatural impressions might be supposed himself to partake of something supernatural.'[16] Waiving for the moment the second division of the stricture (which has only two great defects: if true, its application is fallacious, and it is not true) one wonders precisely what insignia of his profession Wordsworth wanted the Mariner to bear. In these same *Lyrical Ballads* there is, as it happens, a professional character of Wordsworth's own, Simon Lee, 'The Old Huntsman.' And what he did with his 'Old Huntsman' may be taken, not unfairly, as a criterion of what he felt should have been done with (or to) 'the Old Navigator,' as Coleridge afterwards delighted to call him. And here is enough of the poem for our purpose:

> A long blue livery-coat has he,
> That's fair behind, and fair before;
> Yet, meet him where you will, you see
> At once that he is poor.
> Full five and twenty years he lived
> A running huntsman merry;
> And, though he has but one eye left,
> His cheek is like a cherry . . .
>
> And he is lean, and he is sick,
> His little body's half awry[;]
> His ancles they are swoln and thick;
> His legs are thin and dry.
> When he was young he little knew
> Of husbandry or tillage;
> And now he's forced to work, though weak,
> —The weakest in the village.[18]

If that be 'distinct character . . . in [one's] profession,' let us thank the blessed troop of angelic spirits sent him by his guardian saint that the Mariner had none!

> It is an ancient Mariner,
> And he stoppeth one of three
> '*By thy long grey beard and glittering eye,*
> Now wherefore stopp'st thou me?' . . .
>
> *He holds him with his skinny hand,*
> 'There was a ship,' quoth he.

And the three powerfully suggestive particulars set the imagination winging, while livery fair behind and fair before strips every feather from its pinions.

Nobody has ever pictured more clearly—or with more exquisite tact—the discrepancy between Wordsworth's and Coleridge's genius than Coleridge himself, in the delightful account of their attempt to collaborate in 'The Wanderings of Cain':

> The title and subject were suggested by myself, who likewise drew out the scheme and the contents for each of the three books or cantos, of which the work was to consist, and which, the reader is to be informed, was to have been finished in one night! My partner undertook the first canto: I the second: and which ever had *done first*, was to set about the third. Almost thirty years have passed by; yet at this moment I cannot without something more than a smile moot the question which of the two things

> was the more impracticable, for a mind so eminently original to compose another man's thoughts and fancies, or for a taste so austerely pure and simple to imitate the Death of Abel? Methinks I see his grand and noble countenance as at the moment when having dispatched my own portion of the task at full finger-speed, I hastened to him with my manuscript—that look of humourous despondency fixed on his almost blank sheet of paper, and then its silent mock-piteous admission of failure struggling with the sense of the exceeding ridiculousness of the whole scheme—which broke up in a laugh: and the Ancient Mariner was written instead.[19]

When it came to the writing of 'The Ancient Mariner,' Wordsworth himself again had the grace to see the impossibility of collaboration: 'Our respective manners,' he told Miss Fenwick many years after, 'proved so widely different, that it would have been quite presumptuous in me to do anything but separate from an undertaking upon which I could only have been a clog.'[20] The pity is that the same recognition of a patent fact did not similarly stay his hand when it held the critic's pen.

I have not been indulging in a digression. For Wordsworth's obtuseness merely serves to throw into still clearer relief the penetrating insight into the psychology of loneliness at sea with which the Mariner is conceived, and the beauty—as of sunny fields and quiet orchard closes—in which that singular fidelity to fact has found expression. For the Mariner, in those fleeting images of memory which are the phantasms of his longings, remembers as sailor and poet at once.

> Alas! (thought I, and my heart beat loud)
> How fast she nears and nears!
>
> Are those her sails that glance in the Sun,
> *Like restless gossameres?*
>
> Her beams bemocked the sultry main,
> *Like April hoar-frost spread.*
>
> And the coming wind did roar more loud,
> *And the sails did sigh like sedge.*
>
> *Sometimes a-dropping from the sky*
> *I heard the sky-lark sing;*
> *Sometimes all little birds that are,*
> *How they seemed to fill the sky and air*
> *With their sweet jargoning!*
>
> It ceased; yet still the sails made on
> A pleasant noise till noon,
> *A noise like of a hidden brook*
> *In the leafy month of June,*
> *That to the sleeping woods all night*
> *Singeth a quiet tune.*
>
> But soon there breathed a wind on me,

Nor sound nor motion made:
Its path was not upon the sea,
In ripple or in shade.

It raised my hair, it fanned my cheek
Like a meadow-gale of spring—
It mingled strangely with my fears,
Yet it felt like a welcoming.[21]

Sir John Edwin Sandys, in a study of the infinitely complex interweavings of reminiscences in 'Lycidas,' speaks, apropos of Amaryllis and Neæra, of 'the liquid letters of those radiant names, that have floated down the stream of pastoral song.'[22] Here too is the familiar sylvan loveliness which has likewise floated down the stream of poetry, from Theocritus till now. But its beauty that falls like balm on the sailor, in moments of vision home from sea, has gained from its unwonted background a fresh poignancy; and in that heightening of beauty through the implications of a deeply human trait lies one of the most unerring imaginative perceptions of the poem.[23]

II

'*Sanctum et amabile nomen!*' wrote Coleridge, thirty years after 'The Ancient Mariner,' of Nether Stowey; 'rich by so many associations and recollections.'[24] 'Dear gutter of Stowey!' he had exclaimed, in livelier vein, a year and a half before he went to live there.* 'Were I transported to Italian plains, and lay by the side of the streamlet that murmured through an orange grove, I would think of thee, dear gutter of Stowey, and wish that I were poring on thee!'[25] That is a curious foreshadowing of the mood of the ancient Mariner himself, and it was Nether Stowey—'*amabile nomen*' or 'dear gutter,' as one will—that lent its rich associations and recollections to the Mariner's waking dreams.[26]

The 'restless gossameres' (to follow the traces of those recollections) take us back to one of the many elusive coincidences between Dorothy Wordsworth's *Journals* and the poems on which Coleridge was engaged in the spring of 1798. Under date of February 8th, with the end of 'The Ancient Mariner' just six weeks off, occurs this entry in the Alfoxden *Journal:* 'Went up the Park, and over the tops of the hills, till we came to a new and very delicious pathway, which conducted us to the Coombe. Sat a considerable time upon the heath. Its surface *restless and glittering* with the motion of the scattered piles of withered grass, *and the waving of the spiders' threads.*'[27] And here is 'The Ancient Mariner' again:

> Are those her sails that *glance in the Sun,*
> *Like restless gossameres?*

Was Dorothy seeing once more through the eyes of the poem? Or was Coleridge recalling, as he wrote, the restless surface of the heath as she had made him see it? Or had they, perhaps, sat on the heath together? We can only recognize another of those 'subtle shining secrecies'[29] which will always baffle us in their relations. But the strange accordance in expression deepens our sense of the interpenetration of two kindred spirits, and leaves no doubt that the glancing filaments which the sails of the spectre-bark brought back to the Mariner's memory had glittered for Coleridge in the coombes of Quantock.

Months before, however, something else had been written upon what Coleridge called 'the palimpsest tablet of [his] memory,'[30] and as he wrote, the half obliterated traces seem to have acquired, as if through some impalpable reagent, legibility again. Here is the context of the glancing sails:

> The western wave was all a-flame.
> The day was well nigh done!
> Almost upon the *western wave*
> Rested the broad bright Sun;
> When that strange shape drove suddenly
> Betwixt us and the Sun.

And then:

> Are those her *sails* that *glance in the Sun*,
> Like restless gossameres?[31]

In that mad performance of William Gilbert, *The Hurricane*,[32] are the following lines:

Just where the horizon bends to meet *the wave*,
Within the farthest.reach of human ken,
A SAIL appeared. *The mild ray far beaming*
From the Western Sun glanced on her canvas . . . [33]

Now Gilbert begins his 'Advertisement' to *The Hurricane* as follows:

> A Friend is the occasion of this Advertisement; who, having printed some lines of this Poem in a Miscellany that could not fail to introduce it respectably, in the best sense of the word, has thereby acquired a right to have his feelings attended to, in things that may affect the credit of the Poem.
>
> He once passed to me a very strong opinion against the Metre of some verses—[34]

whereupon Gilbert embarks on an elucidation of his own views. The 'Friend' of the 'Advertisement' was Coleridge,[35] who had printed in *The Watchman*, just before *The Hurricane* was published, a cento of extracts from it.[36] And the cento ends only fifteen lines before the passage I have quoted. Coleridge, it is clear, had been both a critical and a sympathetic reader of the poem. There exist very few verses better attested as known to him than the lines before us. And it is hard to believe that this picture from the pen of the brilliant unfortunate who had so enlisted his interest did not flash out, as he wrote, from the palimpsest tablet, and merge, in the gleam of the sails, with the restless glistening of the cobwebs seen across the Quantock heaths.[37]

In the sails that sighed, and in the moonlight spread like April hoar-frost on the sea, impressions of books seem once more to have blended with the recollections of personal experience. That Coleridge had heard with his own ears the sedges sigh, I have no doubt. But I also suspect that *sails* and sedges first came into conjunction in his memory through the phrase about the sedges fetched from the sea-side and laid upon the sail, in de Veer's great narrative in Purchas[38]—a narrative which he had read (as his unmistakable echoes of its wording show) with a connoisseur's zest in its phraseology. As for the line: 'Like April hoar-frost spread' (which displaced in 1800 the original: 'Like morning frosts yspread'), his own eyes, without a moment's question, were enough. Yet even here the weaving shuttles of association were apparently at work, to call up this image and not another; and it is not impossible, perhaps, to catch glimpses of their operation.

Let us, for a moment, retrace our steps. What do we know to have been stirring in Coleridge's mind when the triad of stanzas to which this frostlike, moonlit sea belongs, was born? We know, for one thing, that the ubiquitous red and blue and green of Captain Cook's protozoa were singularly active. And we know, too, that Father Bourzes's account of his phosphorescent fishes and his rainbow in the spray was there, and that, with the last, Frederick Martens's sea-bow in the shadow of the sail had coalesced. And Martens's account of his sea-bow is a corollary of his description of the needles of the frost. Now let us re-read what Martens writes in the paragraph which immediately precedes the charming picture of the 'pleasant reflexion' in 'the Shadow of the Sail':

> Concerning the Meteors generated in the Air, I observed that the *Rime* fell down in the shape of small Needles of Snow into the Sea, *and covered it as if it was sprinkled all over with Dust*: these small Needles increased more and more, and lay as they fell cross one over the other, and looked very like a Cobweb . . . [*so*] *that the Sea seemed covered by them, as with a Skin, or a tender Ice.*[39]

Hoar-frost spread like dust or cobwebs on the sea, till the sea was covered as with a skin or a tender ice—there is the vivid picture which (I think we may be sure) was one means of blending the frost-covered fields of Coleridge's own memory with the charmèd deep on which the moonbeams lay, 'like April hoarfrost spread.'

That picture, at all events, was an integral part of the teeming cluster of images out of which the trinity of stanzas sprang. But just at this time Coleridge was reading a book which was intimately associated with his old Bristol circle, Amos Cottle's translation of the *Edda of Saemund*, for which Southey had written dedicatory verse.[40] And Coleridge had the book out of the Bristol Library from December II, 1797, to January 24, 1798[41]—six weeks of the very time, that is, while 'The Ancient Mariner' was on the stocks. How the *Edda* and Dante together had added an uncommonly soaring structure to his endless succession of castles in the air, we have already seen in his plan to write, in the manner of Dante, a poem on the wanderings of Thor.[42] However feebly rendered, the *Edda* is a provocative poem. And there is one striking phrase in Cottle's epitome of the northern mythology, in a note to the first Song, which, fresh as it must have been in Coleridge's mind, may well have left its conscious or unconscious mark upon the line: 'Thence [from the rivers called Elivagi] arose a poisonous exhalation which *spread* around *like a hoar frost*.'[43] '*Like* April *hoar-frost spread*'—so Coleridge later wrote. All, however, that I am asking for the moment is tentative recognition of imagery which had slipped, before or during the composition of the poem, into the 'thousand-celled darkness' of Coleridge's unconscious mind.

There was, moreover, still another tentacle of association which at least might have drawn into the picture (whether it did or not) the element of frost. The combination of red and green and blue had with Coleridge, as we have seen, a peculiar aptitude for setting up new clusters of associations.* And these three colours, now present in the stanzas as the 'still and awful red' of the charmèd water, and the 'blue, glossy green' of the water-snakes, possessed already another definite association in his mind. There is in the Note Book a long passage from a 'Description of a Glory, by John Haygarth,' transcribed from the third volume of the *Manchester Memoirs*.[44] And this entry almost immediately precedes the jotting about Father Bourzes's rainbow. Haygarth's last sentence is as follows:

> And the sun shining on a surface of snow covered with a *hoarfrost*, exhibits . . . beautiful brilliant points of various colours, as, *red, green, blue*, etc., reflected and refracted at different angles.[45]

Now although this sentence is not a part of the description of the glory, and although it is three pages distant from the paragraph which is transcribed, Coleridge was sufficiently impressed by it to make a separate note:

> the beautiful colors of the hoar frost on snow in sunshine—red, green, and blue, in various angles.[46]

The three colours, in a word, which dominate these three stanzas had been (not far, apparently, from this same time) explicitly coupled in Coleridge's mind with frost. Whatever we choose to conclude from it, there is the fact.

Into that strange subliminal cluster of associations, accordingly, out of which the stanzas grew, vivid impressions of frost were doubly, perhaps trebly, interwoven. And the exquisite line, it would seem, is Coleridge's conscious fashioning of suggestions which reached him, in a sense automatically, by hidden ways of which he may have been himself unaware. The Spirit of the Well is once more dealing the cards for the shaping Spirit, with unerring art, to play.

And short of the creative act itself, all this, after all, is a matter of general experience. Our trouble, as we strive to comprehend the marvel, lies in the unlucky fact that only through a tortuous labyrinth of inferences can we recover the thronging impressions which underwent transmutation in the poem. Could we but dispense with the indispensable evidence, the facts themselves would be, I think, comparatively unconfusing and unconfused. Perhaps, as one whom Lamb would call a sober citizen who never went astray upon the mountains of Parnassus, I may be allowed to throw myself into the breach to make that clear.

I am looking from my window, as I write, at a rushing brook which sparkles in the sunlight, and a solitary heron, grave and vigilant, upon a rock. When, an hour ago, the gleaming of the water caught my eye, it called up (I suspect because, thanks to Coleridge, my mind was at the moment occupied with images of the sea) the 'myriad laughter'—the ἀνήριθμον γέλασμα—of the sea in the *Prometheus*. And that in turn carried in its train two pictures which before, as it happened, had brought the phrase of Æschylus to mind—the flashing of oars seen from the window of another room in which I write, as a crew swept by upon the Charles, and a laughing, dancing stretch of Lake Lugano in the morning light. And the solitary heron (I suppose because of these sea-reminiscences) rather perversely summoned up Homer's Chryses—**βῆ δ'ἀκέων παρὰ θῖνα πολυφλοίσβοιο θαλάσσης** — and that last phrase brought back Macbeth's 'multitudinous seas.' And instantly, because I had once used the Æschylean and Shakespearean phrases in conjunction, the paragraph which had suggested them flashed up to memory, and with it the glory of the summer morning on a broad Atlantic beach when it was written. I am not a poet, and nothing happened when this troop of associated images awoke from sleep. Had I been a poet, and had I been intent upon a poem, who can tell what subtle metamorphoses its imagery might not have undergone through such a confluence of reminiscences? Be the answer as it may, the throng of associations that underlie the stanza with the luminous imagery of which the April hoar-frost blended are (to compare great things with small) of a piece with yours and mine. The difference lies in that heavenly alchemy, which, in words that Coleridge himself applied (as we have seen) to the imagination,

turns
Bodies to spirit by sublimation strange . . .
And draws a kind of quintessence from things.[48]

The 'hidden brook,' whose quiet tune to the sleeping woods the Mariner heard, as the sails made on a pleasant noise till noon, is the brook that 'runs down from the *Comb*' (as

Wordsworth tells us), 'in which stands the village of Alford, through the grounds of Alfoxden.'[49] It is 'The roaring dell, o'erwooded, narrow, deep, And only speckled by the mid-day sun,' of 'This Lime-Tree Bower my Prison'; it is the 'brook in mossy forest-dell' in 'The Nightingale,' and 'the chattering brook' of 'The Three Graves.'[50] John Thelwall wrote home to his wife from Alfoxden about it: 'a wild, romantic dell in these grounds, through which a foaming, rushing, murmuring torrent of water winds its long artless course.'[51] And above all, it was to have been the theme of another of those phantom *magna opera* which paved in such glittering profusion Coleridge's particular Inferno. 'I sought for a subject,' he tells us in the *Biographia Literaria*,[52]

> I sought for a subject, that should give equal room and freedom for description, incident, and impassioned reflections on men, nature, and society, yet supply in itself a natural connection to the parts, and unity to the whole. Such a subject I conceived myself to have found in a stream, traced from its source in the hills among the yellow-red moss and conical glass-shaped tufts of bent, to the first break or fall, where its drops become audible, and it begins to form a channel; thence to the peat and turf barn, itself built of the same dark squares as it sheltered; to the sheep-fold; to the first cultivated plot of ground; to the lonely cottage and its bleak garden won from the heath; to the hamlet, the villages, the market-town, the

> manufactories, and the sea-port. My walks therefore were almost daily on the top of Quantock, and among its sloping combes. With my pencil and memorandum book in my hand, I was *making studies*, as the artists call them, and often moulding my thoughts into verse, with the objects and imagery immediately before my senses.[53] Many circumstances, evil and good, intervened to prevent the completion of the poem, which was to have been entitled 'THE BROOK.'

Wordsworth, twenty years later, was a little concerned lest in the Duddon sonnets he 'was trespassing upon ground preoccupied, at least so far as intention went, by Mr. Coleridge,' and declared that he would 'gladly believe, that "The Brook" will, ere long, murmur in concert with "The Duddon." '[54] But the Duddon murmurs unaccompanied, and all we have is the studiously elaborated plan, with the one lovely stanza which is its residuary legatee. For 'The Rime of the Ancient Mariner' has fallen heir to the precious hoardings of Coleridge's unborn poems. And for myself, I do most potently and powerfully believe that these flawless stanzas, brief as the instant of vision itself, in which the voice of all brooks that ever were sings quietly, and the moving moon goes softly up the sky, and the charmèd water burns alway its still and awful red, far outweigh the loss of the 'Hymns to the Sun, Moon, and the Elements,' and of 'The Brook' itself. 'Whatever in Lucretius is poetry is not philosophical,' wrote Coleridge to Wordsworth in 1815; 'whatever is philosophical is not poetry.'[55] That, like most epigrams, is too neat to be wholly true; but in Coleridge's case, of one thing at least we may be sure. No 'sublime enumeration of all the charms and Tremendities of Nature' coupled with 'a bold avowal of Berkeley's system' in the 'Hymns,' and no 'impassioned reflections on men, nature, and society' interspersing the long-drawn itinerary of 'The Brook,' could ever have inspired the sheer, transcendent beauty of these moments of exalted perception which now are part and parcel of a moving action, controlling and controlled. For there is really nothing in the poem, I think, more penetratingly imaginative than the agency through which the union is accomplished. At the centre of the action is the ship, and the spirit of the ship is in its sails, and it is through sails—glancing in the sun like restless gossamers, singing like a hidden brook, sighing like sedge—that there falls for a fleeting moment on desperate seas the familiar loveliness of combe and dell.

'The imagery,' said Wordsworth, as he enumerated the four 'great defects' of 'The Ancient Mariner,' 'is somewhat too laboriously accumulated.'[56] Without Wordsworth's deep vision into 'the wonder and bloom of the world,' the world, I know, would be inestimably poorer; but his eyes were holden that he should not see the effortless simplicity and truth of that imagery of field and brook and meadow-gales and bird-notes, which gives point to these lucid interspaces of recollection slipping in between the relentless obsessions of eye and ear during weary vigils on a lonely sea.

But other spots than Stowey lent their personal associations to the poem, and the Mariner's moments of vision were not the only form in which such memories found expression.

III

In the summer of 1794 Coleridge and his friend John Hucks set out from Oxford on a walking tour in North Wales, where they were later joined by two other friends, Berdmore and Brookes.[57] Coleridge, during his visit to Oxford, had met Southey, and the first letters of their long and checkered correspondence were written on the expedition.[58] And these letters to Southey, effervescing with boyish spirits, together with a still more ebullient epistle to Henry Martin,[59] give a racy account of Coleridge's experiences. Hucks, however, did still better. For in 1795 he published a slim volume entitled *A Pedestrian Tour through North Wales in a Series of Letters*, to which 'are subjoined,' the Preface painstakingly informs us, 'the names of the most noted places that they visited in the course of their route, and their distances from each other. Those marked with one or more asterisks imply the number of nights they remained at each.'[60] 'My companion,' Coleridge remarks in his first letter to Southey, 'is a man of cultivated, though not vigorous understanding,'[61] and the naïve little book bears out both statements. Even the quaint idea of the asterisks was not, I fear, original with Hucks, for Coleridge, in his letter to Martin, stars similarly the same halting-places in their itinerary, with the explanation: 'To whatever place I have affixed the mark *, there we slept.'[62] Whether Coleridge too contemplated printing his impressions, I do not know, but at least he had provided for the contingency! 'I have bought a little blank book, and portable ink horn; [and] as I journey onward, I ever and anon pluck the wild flowers of poesy, "inhale their odours awhile," then throw them away and think no more of them. I will not do so! Two lines of mine:

> And o'er the sky's unclouded blue
> The sultry heat suffus'd a brassy hue.'[63]

The fact that the two lines faintly foreshadow the 'hot and copper sky' of 'The Ancient Mariner' may reconcile us to their preservation; but it is not the wild flowers of poesy (including 'Perspiration. A Travelling Eclogue')[64] which the letters contain that reveal the youthful vividness of the impressions which were pouring in.

Now we know from Coleridge himself that at least one reminiscence of the walking tour in Wales got into 'The Ancient Mariner.' The two stanzas which describe the effects of thirst, as the ship lies becalmed and the spectre-bark appears, are these:

> With throats unslaked, with black lips baked,
> We could nor laugh nor wail;

Through utter drought all dumb we stood!
I bit my arm, I sucked the blood,
And cried, A sail! a sail!

With throats unslaked, with black lips baked,
Agape they heard me call:
Gramercy! *they for joy did grin*,
And all at once their breath drew in,
As they were drinking all.[65]

Thirty-two years later, Coleridge declared (as it is recorded in the *Table Talk*): 'I took the thought of "*grinning for joy*," in that poem ['The Ancient Mariner'], from poor Burnett's remark to me, when we had climbed to the top of Plinlimmon, and were nearly dead with thirst. We could not speak from the constriction, till we found a little puddle under a stone. He said to me,—"You grinned like an idiot!" He had done the same.'[66] For 'Burnett' we should certainly read either 'Berdmore' or 'Brookes,' and for 'Plinlimmon,' 'Penmaenmaur,' as the letter to Martin and Hucks's account together make clear.[67] But if Coleridge's memory slipped on the names, it was tenacious enough of the essential facts. 'We rose early,' says Hucks, writing the next day (as the happy conjunction of his asterisks with the letter demonstrates),

> . . . for the purpose of ascending to the top of Paenman Mawr . . . We rashly took the resolution to venture up this stupendous mountain without a guide, and

> therefore unknowingly fixed upon the most difficult part to ascend, and consequently were continually impeded by a vast number of unexpected obstructions. At length we surmounted every danger and difficulty, and safely arrived at the top; but the fatigue we had undergone, and the excessive heat of the day . . . occasioned a tormenting thirst that we were not able to gratify; for water was an article which we searched for in vain. Preparing, in the utmost despondency, to descend, we accidentally turned over a large flat stone that concealed a little spring. . . . The parched-up soldier of Alexander's army could not have felt greater joy in the discovery of his little treasure than we did of ours.[68]

A week later Coleridge makes his only contemporary reference to the incident which has come down to us: 'Brookes, Berdmore, and myself, at the imminent hazard of our lives, scaled the very summit of Penmaenmaur. It was a most dreadful expedition. I will give you the account in some future letter.'[69] But if he did, the letter is lost. It is perfectly clear, however, that when the two stanzas depicting the horrors of thirst were written, Coleridge had vividly in mind his own actual experience of thirst in Wales, and it is no less obvious that his recollection of the state in which he and his companions found themselves, instead of ending with the single phrase which he later mentioned, permeates the entire scene.

It would not be strange, then, if into these same stanzas should have slipped another metamorphosed recollection of the adventures of the little group in Wales. The thing which Coleridge remembered after the lapse of thirty-two years was their inability to speak, from the constriction of thirst, until moisture had touched their lips. And it is that same inability which gives to the two stanzas their dramatic climax. For there is no water on the Mariner's ship, and so—

> I bit my arm, *I sucked the blood*,
> And cried, A sail! a sail!

Was Coleridge still thinking of unslaked throats in Wales, as he wrote that? 'From Llangunnog,' says the second letter to Southey, 'we walked over the mountains to Bala—most sublimely terrible! It was scorchingly hot. *I applied my mouth ever and anon to the side of the rocks and sucked in draughts of water* cold as ice, and clear as infant diamonds in their embryo dew!'[70] This, on the evidence of Hucks's asterisks, was a week before the ascent of Penmaenmaur, and the one day of heat and thirst and mountaineering would scarcely come back to Coleridge's memory without the other. Both the association and its imaginative transfer are natural enough, and I suspect that the road from Llangunnog to Bala, as well as the rocky declivities of Penmaenmaur, contributed its quota to a picture in which phantom sails that glanced like the floating cobwebs on the Quantocks vanished in the swift fall of a night that had descended in Norway and the West Indies and on the Nile, while a star-dogged moon came up whose horns had first hung portentous over Boston.

There was, however, one incident of the expedition which so impressed both Coleridge and Hucks that between them they tell it three times—Coleridge to both Martin and Southey, and Hucks in his book, 'At Denbigh,' wrote Coleridge to Martin, 'is the finest ruined castle in the kingdom; it surpassed everything I could have conceived. I wandered there two hours in a still evening, feeding upon melancholy. Two well dressed young men were roaming there. "I will play my flute here," said the first; "it will have a romantic effect." "Bless thee, man of genius and sensibility," I silently exclaimed. He sate down amid the most awful part of the ruins; the moon just began to make her rays predominant over the lingering daylight; I preattuned my feelings to emotion;—and the romantic youth instantly struck up the sadly pleasing tunes of *Miss Carey—The British Lion is my sign—A roaring trade I drive on*, etc.'[71] The account to Southey[72] is substantially the same, and Hucks might have been looking over Coleridge's shoulder as he wrote! 'The moon,' he says, 'was just rising in the horizon, when I perceived two gentlemen approach.' One proposed to the other '(as he had brought his flute in his pocket), to retire into a remoter part of the castle, and play some *soft airs;* God bless thee for the thought, said I to myself, amidst these solitary ruins, by the faint light of the moon, to listen to the soft cadence of distant musick, stealing its mournful melody, on the deluded ear like "sounds of heavenly harmony," must be altogether a soothing and romantic occupation for the mind.' Whereupon the 'romantic disciple of Orpheus, *struck up* the tender air of *Corporal Casey*.'[73] Did the absurd episode, harmonized in memory with the mood and with the beauty of its setting, come back to Coleridge when he wrote one of the loveliest lines in the poem?

> Around, around, flew each sweet sound,
> Then darted to the Sun;
> Slowly the sounds came back again,
> Now mixed, now one by one . . .
>
> And now 'twas like all instruments,
> *Now like a lonely flute;*
> And now it is an angel's song,
> That makes the heavens be mute.[74]

With his Welsh experiences rising to the surface as he wrote, the notes of the flute in the moonlight at Denbigh[75] may well have been among the wandering sounds that 'slowly . . . came back again' to memory—as just this clustered imagery of flying sounds, and the hidden brook with its quiet tune, and the sky-lark in the sky came flooding back to him when years later he wrote of Stowey:

Eight springs have flown, since last I lay
  On sea-ward Quantock's heathy hills,
  Where quiet sounds from hidden rills
Float here and there, like things astray,
  And high o'er head the sky-lark shrills.[76]

IV

There is one more musical instrument in the poem, the bassoon that played so signal a part in the strategy of the voyage. And that brings us back from. Wales to Nether Stowey. Coleridge's most intimate friend in Stowey was his next-door neighbour, Thomas Poole. And one of Poole's interests was the Nether Stowey church choir. 'We find him writing,' says Mrs. Sand-ford, in *Thomas Poole and his Friends*, 'to Dr. Langford, in December 1797, to report that "our singers are more than commonly active" . . . and if he would now send "the Bassoon and the Music" that he had promised, "I think, sir," says Tom Poole, "that we shall make good use of them." '[77] In December 1797, 'The Rime of the Ancient Mariner' was in full swing. And I think we may safely agree with Mrs. Sandford that the instrument which caused the Wedding-Guest to beat his breast, and which incidentally struck out of the voyage the stretch from the Equator to the Cape, sounded first in the church at Nether Stowey.

The Alfoxden brook appears once more towards the close of the poem, once more in association with the sails which had already murmured with its song:

> 'Strange, by my faith!' the Hermit said—
> 'And they answered not our cheer!
> The planks looked warped! and see those sails,
> How thin they are and sere!
> I never saw aught like to them,
> Unless perchance it were
>
> *Brown skeletons of leaves that lag*
> *My forest-brook along.*'[78]

And the next two lines serve as a picture in little of a typical merging of images:

> When *the ivy-tod is heavy with snow,*
> *And the owlet whoops to the wolf below.*

Now it is not impossible, as Hutchinson suggests,[79] that Coleridge may have recalled a passage from Beaumont and Fletcher's *Bonduca*, which Lamb, in a letter of June 14, 1796, sent him (from 'a little extract book I keep') to add to 'your list of illustrative personifications, into which a fine imagination enters.' The lines, as Lamb quotes them (not quite accurately), read: 'Then did I see these valiant men of Britain, like boding owls creep into tods of ivy, and hoot their fears to one another nightly.'[80] The owl and the ivy-tod, then (I grant), may have been a literary reminiscence *via* Charles Lamb.[81] But Hutchinson (in common, apparently, with all the commentators) has overlooked the fact that 'Like an owl in an ivy-bush' (or 'ivytod') is a proverbial phrase which men of letters have freely made their own, and with which Coleridge must have been familiar. Beaumont and Fletcher use it again: 'Could not you be content to be an owl in such an ivy-bush?' Swift has it in the First Dialogue of the inimitable *Polite Conversation:* ' "Pr'ythee how did the Fool look?" "Look! Egad he look'd for all the World like an Owl in an Ivy Bush." '[82] It gives point to one of the most diverting anecdotes of the eighteenth century: the tale of the trick played by the Rev. Samuel Wesley—author of 'Maggots,' Rector of Epworth, and father of John and Charles—on that worthy but vain man, his parish clerk.[83] Drayton employs it:

> And like an owl, by night to go abroad,
> Roosted all day within an ivy-tod.

And in *Ralph Roister Doister* it appears in a form which has much in common with Coleridge's lines:[84]

> As the *howlet* out of an yvie bushe should *hoope*.*

Through some of the numerous possible channels the proverb, assuredly, was present in Coleridge's memory as he wrote.

But, with no less assurance, things heard and seen at Nether Stowey and Alfoxden had once more played their part. For (like the rainbow off the Cape which acquired the snow of Arctic seas) the ivy-tod is heavy with the snow of the winter of

1797–98 in Somerset—those 'tufts of snow on the bare branch Of mossy apple-tree' in the orchard just outside Coleridge's window as he wrote, that February, 'Frost at Midnight'; while, as he wrote, "The owlet's cry Came loud—and hark, again! loud as before.'[85] Moreover, Coleridge had certainly seen what Dorothy Wordsworth saw, and in January and February, 1798, when the *Journal* is richest in its mysterious correspondences with 'The Ancient Mariner' and 'Christabel,' she writes: "The *ivy* twisting round the oaks like bristled serpents'; 'A deep snow upon the ground . . . The branches of the hollies *pendent with their white burden*. . . . The bare branches of the oaks *thickened by the snow*.'[86] The ivy and the owls of Stowey—those owls whose cry rings bodingly through 'Christabel' (as it hoots through the contemporary 'Idiot Boy')—had recalled the ancient proverb, rich in all manner of lettered associations, and again, as in the images of the hoar-frost and the sedges, things read have blended with things seen.†

Among the sleeping images, then, which moved towards the light at the summons of the shaping plan, were sights and sounds from Somerset and Wales. And as Coleridge's imagination filled out with vividly concrete imagery the great curve of the voyage, not only ocular spectra from the printed page, but recollections of immediate experience were wrought into the design.

V

Meadows white with April hoar-frost, sweet with the winds of Spring, glancing with myriads of filmy threads; pools with their rim of whispering sedges; bird-notes and flute-notes—that is the imagery which gives, as we read, the sense of a known and familiar landscape, touched with the strangeness of some unwonted play of light. There is another group of images which stirs deeper-lying responses, and this time keys our mood to that eerie light itself, which the beauty of sunlit meadows only makes more spectral. And this other imagery, drawn neither from books nor from the eye, but from the shadowy tracts which fringe, like the dusk, our normal experience, is as direct in its appeal as are the fields and brooks in theirs. And in the insensible blending of the two sets of associations lies in part the secret of that subtle merging of the strange and the familiar which Coleridge set out deliberately to achieve.

For what he has done is to awaken, together with the recollections of sleeping woods and meadow gales and frosty fields, memories of those obscure sensations which haunt the borderland of consciousness, where distinctions of real and unreal lose their sharpness and are confused. No one whose returning consciousness after a swoon has struggled up, like a submerged and suffocating swimmer, from abysmal depths, while the sick and wavering sense of personality gropes dizzily to find itself through hideous noises of an unrelated and disembodied world; no one who has gone up a lonesome stairway in the dark with firm, unhurried steps, *knowing* (as we say!) that nothing 'did close behind him tread,' and then has swiftly closed and locked the door on IT; no one who has felt the deathly suction as of a vacuum about his heart, or whose eyeballs have beat time to the pulsations of his blood—no one who has ever gone through these experiences can read, without carrying into the poem something of his own recovered sense of things alien yet intimate, such passages as these:

> The ice was here, the ice was there,
> The ice was all around:
> *It cracked and growled, and roared and howled,*
> *Like noises in a swound!*[89]
>
> *Like one, that on a lonesome road*
> *Doth walk in fear and dread,*
> *And having once turned round walks on,*
> *And turns no more his head;*
> *Because he knows, a frightful fiend*
> *Doth close behind him tread.* *
>
> We listened and looked sideways up!
> *Fear at my heart, as at a cup,*
> *My life-blood seemed to sip!*[90]
>
> I closed my lids, and kept them close,
> *And the balls like pulses beat.*[91]

And that imagery, which again is its own answer to the charge of too laborious accumulation, leads us at once to the second of the great structural elements of the poem. For the voyage, as a voyage, is at last behind us. But the mysterious forces which impel the action are yet to reckon with.

---

*'Monday evening, July 9, 1804, about eight o'clock. The glorious evening star coasted the moon, and at length absolutely crested its upper tip. . . . It was the most singular and at the same time beautiful sight I ever beheld. *Oh, that it could have appeared the same in England at Grasmere!*' So wrote Coleridge in his loneliness at Malta.[2]

*I have given it in full in the Notes.[17] I am sorry that of necessity Wordsworth appears in this volume chiefly in connection with 'The Rime of the Ancient Mariner,' for nothing in his career more clearly showed his limitations (or less became him) than his attitude towards the poem in 1799 and 1800. I say this once for all, lest otherwise, through an unavoidable emphasis, I seem to fail in recognition of Wordsworth's greatness as a poet or of his loftier traits of character.

*The Stowey 'gutter' belies the modern associations of its name. The phrase just quoted reads, as Coleridge actually wrote it (B.M. Add. Mss. 35.343):

'Dear Gutter (i.e. a dear brook) of Stowy' [*sic*]. It was, as Mrs. Sandford describes it in *Thomas Poole and his Friends*, 'a straight gutter bordering the street in Stowey, through which a running stream passes.' And Coleridge gives it first place—naming it even before his 'sweet Orchard' with the gate into Tom Poole's garden—in the buoyant account of his surroundings which he sent to Dr. Estlin just after he came to Stowey: 'Before our door a clear brook runs of very soft water.' The runnel was as distinctive of the village as 'the four huge elms' which marked Alfoxden.[28]

*The singular fascination which the colours blue and green seem to have had for him appears again in a note of (apparently) 1803: 'Bright reflections, in the canal, of the blue and green vitriol bottles in the druggists' shops in London.'[47]

*It is tempting to continue, still throwing chronology to the winds. T. B. [Thomas Brewer] makes apt use of the proverb in that edifying tract *The Life and Death of the Merry Deuill of Edmonton. With the Pleasant Pranks of Smug the Smith, Sir John, and Mine Host of the George, about the Stealing of Venison.* Old Daniel Pell sagely remarks: 'Thet's no small wisdom in the Owl, who hides her head all day long in an Ivy-bush.' In the March Eclogue of 'The Shepheards Calendar' Spenser, with sly humour, substitutes Cupid for the owl:

At length within an yvie todde

(There shrouded was the little god).[87]

Once let the ivy-tod be mentioned, and the owl must follow, as the night the day.

† The wolves, which lend to imagery recalled from the familiar landscape of the Quantocks a touch of the remote and strange, are probably another reminiscence of Bartram's *Travels*. In that part of the book which Coleridge read most intently, only four pages from the Great Sink, a dozen from the Seminoles, and a score from the Savanna crane, Bartram tells of observing 'a company of *wolves . . . under a few trees* . . . sitting on their hinder parts.' 'We then *whooped*,' he adds.[88] And unless all signs fail, the owlet's whoop to the wolf below echoed in Coleridge's memory that whoop to the wolves in Florida.

*That this stanza, which is sheer, inimitable Coleridge, was nevertheless suggested by a bit of Dante at his most Dantesque, I learned, long after this chapter was written, from a pencilled scrawl in Coleridge's own copy of *Sibylline Leaves*. But for the facts I must refer the reader to the Notes.[92]

BOOK III

Me who have sailèd
Leagues across
Foam haunted
By the albatross . . .

WALTER DE LA MARE

Suntne, o Marce, multa dœmonum genera? Multa, inquit, atque diversa . . . adeo ut et aër, qui supra nos est, et qui circa nos, sit plenus dœmonum, plena et terra, mareque, et loca abdita atque profunda.

MICHAEL PSELLUS

CHAPTER XIII

THE BIRD AND THE DÆMON

ACROSS the course of the voyage, just where its great loop swings around the southern termination of the continent, the albatross comes through the fog. And the shooting of the albatross sets the forces of the invisible world in motion. And the action of those forces is in turn bound up with the normal evolution, in experience, of cause and consequence. The albatross, in a word,—'that white phantom [which] sails in all imaginations,' as Herman Melville in an eloquent passage calls it[1]—binds inseparably together the three structural principles of the poem: the voyage, and the supernatural machinery, and the unfolding cycle of the deed's results.

It is the second of the three which we must now take into account. And the supernatural machinery, like the architectonic conception of the voyage, falls into our scheme, not as a series of interesting and often singular details, but as a controlling imaginative design. It determines, in a word, the *action* of the poem, precisely as the ground-plan of the voyage set its course and fixed its background. And like the voyage, the unfolding of the action stirs to life, and sweeps within its compass, and fuses into unity, the latent imagery of those deep-lying tracts which we have called 'the Well'—'that lifeless, twilight, realm of thought,' in Coleridge's phrase, which is, for thoughts, 'the confine, the *intermundium*'[2] between consciousness past and consciousness perhaps to come. We are simply approaching from a fresh angle our old theme—the assimilating and incorporation power of the shaping spirit. And the ingredients with which that spirit this time had to work were these: the figure of the Mariner himself; the shooting of the albatross; the 'spectral persecution'; the skeleton bark; the navigation of the ship by the dead sailors; and the angelic interposition at the end. Those are the constituent elements of the action, and the fortuitous fashion in which, on a dark November evening, they combined, is matter of curious record. And that record we must first be clear about. But more important far than the quaint accessories of their conjunction are the operations of these ethereal chemicals (to paraphrase John Keats) upon the potential stuff of poetry in Coleridge's brain. And upon that interplay of masses of associations falls the emphasis in the three chapters now to come.

I

The day, almost the hour, when fragmentary hints of birds and ships and mariners and spectres flashed back and forth from mind to mind and swiftly wove a shining plan, along a road that went down to the sea—this eventful day is fixed for us by Dorothy Wordsworth, who wrote November 20, 1797:

> We have been on another tour: we set out last Monday evening at half-past four. The evening was dark and cloudy; we went eight miles, William and Coleridge employing themselves in laying the plan of a ballad, to be published with some pieces of William's.[3]

November 20 fell that year on Monday. 'Last Monday,' accordingly, was the 13th. Of the two other members of the party, Coleridge has left one brief comment on the expedition,[4] but Wordsworth reverted to it often in his later years.

In the long prefatory note to 'We are Seven,' dictated to Miss Fenwick in or about 1843, Wordsworth, with the privileged inconsequence of age, broke into his account of the little girl at Goodrich Castle, and of the joke before the 'little tea-meal' about 'dear brother Jem,' to tell a less domestic story. It is ancient history, but every word of it is needed:

> In the autumn of 1797, he [Coleridge], my sister, and myself, started from Alfoxden pretty late in the afternoon, with a view to visit Linton, and the Valley of Stones near to it; and as our united funds were very small, we agreed to defray the expense of the tour by writing a poem . . . Accordingly we set off, and proceeded, along the Quantock Hills, towards Watchet; and in the course of this walk was planned the poem of the 'Ancient

Mariner,' founded on a dream, as Mr.Coleridge said, of his friend Mr. Cruikshank. Much the greatest part of the story was Mr. Coleridge's invention; but certain parts I suggested; for example, some crime was to be committed which should bring upon the Old Navigator, as Coleridge afterwards delighted to call him, the spectral persecution, as a consequence of that crime and his own wanderings. I had been reading in Shelvocke's Voyages, a day or two before, that, while doubling Cape Horn, they frequently saw albatrosses in that latitude, the largest sort of sea-fowl, some extending their wings twelve or thirteen feet. 'Suppose,' said I, 'you represent him as having killed one of these birds on entering the South Sea, and that the tutelary spirits of these regions take upon them to avenge the crime.' The incident was thought fit for the purpose, and adopted accordingly. I also suggested the navigation of the ship by the dead men, but do not recollect that I had anything more to do with the scheme of the poem. . . . We began the composition together, on that to me memorable evening. . . . As we endeavoured to proceed conjointly (I speak of the same evening), our respective manners proved so widely different, that it would have been quite presumptuous in me to do anything but separate from an undertaking upon which I could only have been a clog.[5]

A few years earlier, in a significant connection, Wordsworth had given to the Reverend Alexander Dyce substantially the same account, which was first made public in a note to 'The Ancient Mariner' in the *Poems* of 1852:

> When my truly honoured friend Mr. Wordsworth was last in London, soon after the appearance of De Quincey's papers in 'Tait's Magazine,' he dined with me in Gray's Inn, and made the following statement, which, I am quite sure, I give you correctly: ' "The Ancient Mariner" was founded on a strange dream, which a friend of Coleridge had, who fancied he saw a skeleton ship, with figures in it. . . . I had very little share in the composition of it, for I soon found that the style of Coleridge and myself would not assimilate. . . . The idea of *"shooting an albatross" was mine; for I had been reading Shelvocke's Voyages, which probably Coleridge never saw*. I also suggested the reanimation of the dead bodies, to work the ship.'[6]

The signal importance of Wordsworth's contributions to the scheme of 'The Ancient Mariner' admits no question. He suggested the shooting of the albatross, the 'spectral persecution,' and the navigation of the ship by the dead men. The first two are the main-springs of the action, and the third is an essential stage in its development. Yet Wordsworth was not so generous as just, when he declared that 'much the greatest part of the story was Mr. Coleridge's invention.' The 'skeleton ship, with figures in it,' of Cruikshank's dream, and the 'Old Navigator' himself were clearly in Coleridge's mind from the beginning, and they are presupposed in Wordsworth's suggestion of the crime and of its supernatural avenging. And granting unreservedly that Wordsworth supplied the links which knit the loose materials of narrative into a story, and fanned to flame a smouldering conception, it remains no less true that the magnificent imaginative elaboration of the jointly assembled ingredients of a plot is Coleridge's own, as truly as *Hamlet* and *Lear* and *Anthony and Cleopatra*, on grounds essentially the same, are Shakespeare's. Wordsworth, in fact, had builded far better than he knew. His suggestions stirred to life the throngs of dormant memories which had been gathering for just this fateful hour, and before the evening which saw the poem's birth was ended, he had recognized that the spirits which he had evoked called Coleridge master but not him.[7]

Five of the six determining factors of the action, then, fell into place while talk flew fast in the nipping air, and the tang of the sea grew sharper, as Watchet neared. Two owed their origin to Coleridge, three to Wordsworth, and the part played by angelic intervention may or may not have been an afterthought. Each of the six tapped a brimming reservoir, and the shooting of the albatross comes logically first.

II

The albatross brings us to Shelvocke, and the history of Wordsworth's copy of the *Voyage* suggests an irresistible postscript to the Fenwick Note. There is in the Widener Collection in the Harvard College Library a precious little volume—outwardly a cheap household account-book, suggesting in its general physiognomy that 'butcher-ledger-like book' in which the first jottings of 'In Memoriam' were kept[8]—which has written in ink on the cover: 'Account of the Books lent out of the Library at Rydal Mount.' The entries, with ruled columns for names and dates of withdrawal and return, are in the hands of the various members of the Wordsworth family, and show that from 1824 on, Wordsworth's books were at the service of his friends and neighbors.* On November 8, 1832, 'Shelvockes Voy.' was lent to a 'Mrs. Godwin.' The volume, then, was on Wordsworth's shelves as late as 1832. And it was still in his Library a dozen years later, when the Fenwick note was made, for it was among the books sold at public auction after his death.[9]

Now the passage which Wordsworth had been reading in Captain George Shelvocke's *Voyage round the World by the Way of the Great South Sea* is of interest in more ways than one. Let us turn first to a couple of sentences a dozen pages before the important paragraph:

From the latitude of 40 deg. to the latitude of 52 deg.

> 30 min. we . . . were constantly attended by Pintado birds. . . . These were accompanied by *Albitrosses, the largest sort of sea-fowls, some of them extending their wings 12 or 13 foot.*[10]

Wordsworth's statement to Miss Fenwick is worth looking at again:

> I had been reading in Shelvocke's Voyages, a day or two before, that, while doubling Cape Horn, they frequently saw *albatrosses in that latitude, the largest sort of sea-fowl, some extending their wings twelve or thirteen feet.*

Wordsworth was seventy-three when he dictated these words, and the reading to which he referred lay forty-five years behind him. Had Shelvocke's exact phraseology stuck in his memory for almost half a century? I doubt it. The book was there in the library at Rydal Mount, and I strongly suspect that while the adoring Isabella Fenwick waited, pen in hand, her 'beloved old poet' walked over to the book-case and refreshed his memory!

However that may be, the passage in Shelvocke which set the action of 'The Ancient Mariner' going is this:[14]

> We had continual squals of sleet, snow and rain, and the heavens were perpetually hid from us by gloomy dismal clouds. In short, one would think it impossible that any thing living could subsist in so rigid a climate;

and, indeed, we all observed, that we had not had the sight of one fish of any kind, since we were come to the Southward of the streights of *le Mair*, nor one sea-bird, except a disconsolate black *Albitross*, who accompanied us for several days, hovering about us as if he had lost himself, till *Hatley*, (my second Captain) observing, in one of his melancholy fits, that this bird was always hovering near us, imagin'd, from his colour, that it might be some ill omen. That which, I suppose, induced him the more to encourage his superstition, was the continued series of contrary tempestuous winds, which had oppress'd us ever since we had got into this sea. But be that as it would, he, after some fruitless attempts, at length, shot the *Albitross*, not doubting (perhaps) that we should have a fair wind after it.

That raises at once an interesting question. What was this 'disconsolate black Albitross' which Captain Hatley shot? The albatross which Captain Shelvocke earlier describes, with its wing-spread of twelve or thirteen feet, is clearly the great Wandering Albatross (*Diomedea exulans*) of the Southern Seas, and that is white. It is the bird which Buffon depicts across the page, and which Herman Melville rhapsodizes over in a famous passage in the chapter on 'The Whiteness of the Whale.' For the layman it is the albatross *par excellence*, and we have tacitly assumed that it was Coleridge's albatross. But there is another bird, the so-called 'sooty albatross' (once *Diomedea fuliginosa*, now, in scientific parlance, *Phœbetria palpebrata antarctica*), which haunts the same latitudes; and this albatross, as its name in the vernacular implies, may quite properly be called black.[15] I have never seen it living, but I have seen it dead, and I have little doubt that it was the bird which Captain Hatley shot. Whether or not it was Coleridge's albatross is quite another matter. He may or may not have known that albatrosses are not all alike. But in any case we may, I think, acquit him of one charge.

The size of the albatross, in a word, has long been a stone of stumbling to matter-of-fact souls, who protest that Coleridge has strained verisimilitude to the breaking point through his patent misconception of the albatross's size.* For he has suspended about a sailor's neck a bird the sweep of whose regal wings was twice a tall man's height, and, in the poem as it originally stood, has fed the Brobdingnagian creature 'biscuit worms,' as if it had the tastes and the dimensions of a wren. There is little to choose, such unbending spirits will complain, between Coleridge and that paragon of cheerful faith, the visionary gardener in *Sylvie and Bruno:*

> He thought he saw an Albatross
>   That fluttered round the lamp;
> He looked again, and saw it was
>   A Penny-Postage-Stamp.

One may admit at once the piquant incongruity of the biscuit worms, which were promptly banished from the poem. As for the rest, Coleridge was intent upon poetic truth, not ornithological fact. But even a poet may be presumed to know that size is a matter of species and age, and the sooty albatross, which is much the smaller bird, might readily enough, as I know from experiment, have been carried suspended from a sailor's neck. And in another passage which entered into the very fabric of 'The Ancient Mariner' there is warrant enough for Coleridge's impression. For the three sentences which immediately follow the well-conned account of the luminous protozoa in Captain Cook tell of 'two large birds [which] settled on the water, near the ship.' And one of them, which was little more than half the size of the other, 'seemed to be of the *albatross* kind . . . upon the whole, *not unlike the sea-gull, though larger*.'[16] In the use to which Coleridge puts the albatross in the poem, neither ornithological fact nor poetic truth moults a feather.

All this, however, is beside the main point. The essential matter is that the incident in Shelvocke crystallized the structural design of the poem. The earlier chapters of this book have made it clear that a vast concourse of images was hovering in the background of Coleridge's brain, waiting for the formative conception which should strike through their confusion, and marshal them into clarity and order. And among them, on Wordsworth's evidence, was the person of the Mariner himself. What Wordsworth did was to catch up Coleridge's Old Navigator out of general space, where presumably he was floating unattached, and to set him down definitely, cross-bow in hand, at the entrance to the South Sea, after the doubling of Cape Horn. But that implied the circumnavigation of the continent. And on 'A Correct Map of the World Describing Capt. Shelvocke's Voyage round,' prefixed to the book, runs, in a distinct dotted line from Equator to Equator around the Cape, the great curve of the voyage. I think (for reasons which I have given in the Notes)[18] that Coleridge saw this curve; but whether he did or not, the shooting of the albatross carried in its train the ground plan of the poem. And the thronging images which that released we have already seen.

But Wordsworth's suggestion set free another host. ' "Suppose," said I, "you represent him as having killed one of these birds on entering the South Sea, *and that the tutelary spirits of these regions take upon them to avenge the crime.*" ' Precisely what Wordsworth may have had in mind, I do not know. But what sprang into life in Coleridge's memory is dear enough. For the albatross flies into a supramundane *mise en scène* which had been preparing even longer than the background of the voyage, which Wordsworth's suggestion also stirred to life. The fitness of the setting in Antarctic seas is obvious enough. But I question if ever another fowl, before or since, found itself intermeddled (as Chaucer would say) with Plotinus and

Porphyry, the Platonic Constantinopolitan, Michael Psellus, and Marsilio Ficino of the Florentine Academy. The lucky bird, to be sure, is immortal as they are now; and it is so, largely by virtue of this imaginative merging of its brief career with the visions of centuries, which just then, like the ancient associations of the southern voyage, were once more stirring in men's minds.

III

One of those 'wingy mysteries' which haunt the upper regions of the air, and descend to earth at intervals to captivate the thinking of a period is that elusive changeling left by Plotinus in Plato's house, and nurtured there by Porphyry and Iamblichus and Proclus, and their followers. This is no place for an exposition of Neoplatonism, even were I a competent expositor. To call it the shimmering mist into which the cloud-capped towers and gorgeous palaces of Plato's luminous fabric had dissolved,, would be, I know, to the Greeks foolishness, and anathema to spirits of sternly philosophic mould. But as Sir Thomas Browne has comfortably said, 'where there is an obscurity too deep for our reason, 'tis good to sit down with a description, periphrasis, or adumbration,' and that astute procedure is the better part in dealing with 'airy subtleties . . . which have unhinged the brains of better heads.'[19] Nor for our purpose is rigid definition needful. It is happily not the collective profundities of the system, but a single aspect only of its occult and misty supernaturalism, with which we have to do.

To follow the strand, however, which leads to 'The Ancient Mariner,' we must go back for a moment to the early Christian centuries. For through Plotinus, and Porphyry, and Iamblichus, and Proclus, and their followers, there came about a singular impregnation of Platonic philosophy with the theosophic mysticism of the Orient, and the more esoteric tenets of Judaism and Christianity. With the nebulous and grandiose conceptions which resulted, we have nothing whatever to do. The one thing which does come into our reckoning is the fact that into this metaphysical cloudland there drifted strange waifs and strays from those obscure fastnesses of the supernatural, the rites and mysteries of the ancient cults. The *mélange*, with its soaring visions and its haunted deeps, was as cosmopolitan as the crumbling empire, and in that catholic but utterly uncritical inclusiveness lay, in part, the secret of its fascination for imaginative minds. And on the roll of its adherents is a galaxy of starry names: the Emperor Julian the Apostate, who gave of late to Ibsen a high theme for tragedy; that Hypatia of Alexandria, who shines, snow-white, in Kingsley's pages; her friend Synesius, 'the hyper-platonic Jargonist' (I quote the Note Book),[20] whose recondite Hymns Coleridge translated with his mother's milk (one gathers!) scarce dry upon his lips; Macrobius, whose voluminous commentary on the Dream of Scipio cast a spell upon the Middle Ages; the grave and lofty figure of Boethius, who numbered among his translators a king, a queen, and two illustrioùs poets—Alfred the Great, Jean de Meun, Chaucer, and Elizabeth. Even Michael Psellus, preserved for most of us in Coleridge's gloss, like some glittering but forgotten fly in amber, has come to life again, in 1921, in the *Eudocia* of Eden Philpotts! Dreamers they were, if you will, but assuredly no feeble line of mere visionary spinners of the cobwebs of the brain. And all these rich and varied minds called Plato master.

Then came, in the fulness of time, the stirring of fresh life, through the Renaissance, in the forgotten mysteries. And the Platonic Academy at Florence fell eagerly upon Plato, and no less avidly upon the Neoplatonists. Marsilio Ficino translated into Latin not only the works of the master, but also the mystical teachings of Plotinus and his followers. And as Iamblichus and Proclus had incorporated with the Platonic myths the hoary mysteries of Egypt and Mesopotamia and Tyre, so the most brilliantly gifted of the Florentine Academicians, Pico della Mirandola, sought to blend with Neoplatonic philosophy the vast, bizarre agglomeration of the Jewish Cabbala. And so reinterpreted, Neoplatonism permeated the mystical thought and fitfully glimmered through the poetry of the next two centuries. Then, at the close of the eighteenth century, history repeated itself. And that brings us back to Coleridge, and, in the end, to the immortal albatross.

One of the most pithy and memorable letters that Coleridge ever wrote was addressed to John Thelwall, before the two men met. It is dated from Bristol, November 19, 1796,[21] and I doubt if more of Coleridge were ever packed in briefer compass. It contains an almost matchless *tour de force* of self-description—equalled only, perhaps, by that ineffable portrait of himself which the aged but still gallant Samuel Richardson penned for a lady who had never seen him[22]—and I am reluctant to omit a line of it.[23] But I shall, and here is the part which is pertinent:[24]

> I am, and ever have been, a great reader, and have read almost everything—a library cormorant. I am *deep* in all out of the way books, whether of the monkish times, or of the puritanical era.[25] I have read and digested most of the historical writers; but I do not *like* history. Metaphysics and poetry and 'facts of mind,' that is, accounts of all the strange phantasms that ever possessed 'your philosophy'; dreamers, from Thoth the Egyptian to Taylor the English pagan, are my darling studies. In short, I seldom read except to amuse myself, and I am almost always reading. Of useful knowledge, I am a so-so chemist, and I love chemistry. All else is *blank;* but I *will be* (please God) an horticulturalist and a farmer. [That is *not* pertinent; but as quintessential comedy I leave it in] . . . Such am I. I am just going to read Dupuis' twelve octavos, which I have got from London. I shall read only one octavo a week,

> fori cannot *speak* French at all and I read it slowly.[26]

Then follows a characteristic postscript, which rivals the letter in significance:[27]

> P.S. I have enclosed a five-guinea note. The five shillings over please to lay out for me thus. In White's (of Fleet Street or the Strand, I forget which—O! the Strand I believe, but I don't know which), well, in White's catalogue are the following books:—
>
> 4674. Iamblichus, Proclus, Prophyrius, etc., one shilling and sixpence, one little volume.
>
> 4686. Juliani Opera, three shillings: which two books you will be so kind as to purchase for me, and send down with the twenty-five pamphlets. But if they should unfortunately be sold, in the same catalogue are:—
>
> 2109. Juliani Opera, 12s. 6d.
>
> 676. Iamblichus de Mysteriis, 10s. 6d.
>
> 2681. Sidonius Apollinaris, 6s. And in the catalogue of Robson, the bookseller in New Bond Street, Plotini Opera, a Ficino, £1.1.0, making altogether £2.10.0.
>
> If you can get the two former little books, costing only four and sixpence, I will rest content with them.

'Thelwall,' says E. H. Coleridge, 'executed his commission. The Iamblichus and the Julian were afterwards presented by Coleridge to his son Derwent. They are still in the possession of the family.'[28]

The postscript is a bead-roll of Coleridge's 'dreamers.' 'Thoth the Egyptian' (Milton's 'thrice-great Hermes') is there, concealed beneath the pregnant 'etc.' of the 'one little volume' which heads the memorandum. 'Taylor the English pagan,' otherwise Thomas Taylor the Platonist, credulous, uncritical, and pedestrian in style,[29] but fired with the ardour of a devotee, was doing for England what Marsilio Ficino, three centuries before, had done for Italy, and was at the moment busily translating everybody mentioned in Coleridge's list—Iamblichus, Proclus, Porphyrius, Julian, and Plotinus—with the sole exception of Sidonius Apollinaris.[30] Nor was this commission to Thelwall Coleridge's first or last attempt to possess himself, by hook or crook, of his precious purveyors of strange phantasms. In a batch of memoranda of 1807, which no one who would see how Coleridge browsed, or (better, *grazed*) in bookshops can afford to overlook, he is still proposing to 'hunt for Proclus.'[31] Charles Lamb wrote racily in 1796, and again in 1814, about pressing instructions from Coleridge to pick up Plutarch and Porphyry and Proclus,[32] The famous passage in 'Christ's Hospital Five-and-Thirty Years Ago' is no less in point—that description of 'the young Mirandula . . . unfolding in [his] deep and sweet intonations the mysteries of Iamblichus or Plotinus.' And Iamblichus and Plotinus and their followers down to Pico starred his pages to the end. The errand on which Thelwall was dubiously sent to either Fleet Street or the Strand not only exhibits one of Coleridge's inveterate preoccupations, but also epitomizes one of the strangest tendencies which marked the tumultuous exit of the century. For Neoplatonism was again in the air, and in Coleridge's postscript Bristol and London join hands, through Florence, with Alexandria, Constantinople, Athens, and Rome—the eighteenth century, through the fifteenth, with the Platonizing third, fourth and fifth.

But what of Dupuis's twelve octavos which Coleridge was painfully going through, a volume a week, in French? Well, if Thomas Taylor was the plodding British counterpart of Marsilio Ficino, the eighteenth century had also its flock of inglorious, though anything but mute, Mirandolas, and the voluminous Dupuis was one of them. The title of his work is: *Origine de tous les Cultes, ou Religion universelle*, par Dupuis, Citoyen François. And it was printed 'L'an III. de la République, une et indivisible' (which in years of Our Lord was 1795), and on the title-page below the date stands the legend: 'Liberté, Égalité, Fraternité.' The treatise is, I am compelled to think (for I have sedulously turned some hundreds of its pages), a mad performance, as the flaunted banner of its title-page might lead us to suspect.[33] I doubt whether Coleridge got anything from it beyond those unconsidered trifles which genius has the trick of filching as it goes, for conversion into jewels rich and strange. But explicit in its footnotes and implicit in its text are the ubiquitous Neoplatonists—Plotinus, Porphyry,

Iamblichus, Proclus, Julian, Hermes, and Marsilio Ficino.[34] And mingled with the testimony of the ancient witnesses is an array of observations, reported by voyagers and explorers, touching the rites and customs, the genii and dæmons and angel guardians, of primitive tribes. And excerpts from these same voyages were even then enriching with anthropological data the *Philosophical Transactions*.

Ancient cults, in a word, and primitive religions, Neoplatonic speculations,[35] ethnology and oxygen and electricity were all seething together in men's minds. And with the new wonders of the air which science was disclosing merged the immemorial beliefs in its invisible inhabitants, whether vouched for by Iamblichus, or Hermes Trismegistus, or Captain Cook. Nobody who knows the period can dream of isolating its poetry from the ferment of its thought, or of detaching Samuel Taylor Coleridge from that ferment. And when Wordsworth suggested his 'spectral persecution,' all this accumulated lore, held in solution in Coleridge's brain, was precipitated in the strange vengeance which overtook in haunted seas the slayer of a solitary albatross. What the fortunate bird acquired, in fact, along with immortality, was the efficient, if belated, championship of a fully accredited Neoplatonic dæmon.

IV

For the cloud of witnesses whom we have summoned from here and there along the course of sixteen centuries were unanimous in the recognition they accorded to one powerful order in the hierarchy of being—the order of the *dæmons*.[36] I have no intention of going into the beginnings of Greek and Roman dæmonology. That has been done to repletion in two colossally learned monographs in the *Transactions* of the Berlin and Leipzig Academies respectively,[37] for anyone who cares to track his dæmons from the egg. But I do wish to observe that Coleridge, whatever the obliquities of slipshod editors, spells the word correctly in his gloss. For a *dæmon* and a *demon* are not one and the same thing. And it is dæmon, in its Platonic sense of a being intermediary between gods and men—not demon, with its Judæo-Christian import of an unclean, evil, or malignant spirit—that we must keep in mind. This would once have been superfluous caution, but not, alas! when Coleridge is made to mention, in school editions of the poem, 'The Polar Spirit's *fellow-demons*' (that pair of dæmons of the air who are the Chorus of the poem) as if the 'voice as soft as honey-dew' boasted, as appanages, horns, hoofs, and tail.

The gloss of the first stanza in which the Polar Spirit appears reads thus:

A Spirit had followed them; one of the invisible

> inhabitants of this planet, neither departed souls nor angels; concerning whom the learned Jew, Josephus, and the Platonic Constantinopolitan, Michael Psellus, may be consulted. They are very numerous, and there is no climate or element without one or more.[38]

Let us turn back, now, to that No. 4674, catalogued by White at one and sixpence, which Coleridge wanted, and Thelwall got for him. It contained, in its 543 closely printed, four-and-a-half by three inch pages, Iamblichus *De Mysteriis Ægyptiorum, Chaldæorum, Assyriorum;* Proclus *In Platonicum Alcibiadem de Anima, atque Dæmone;* Porphyrius *De Divinis atque Dæmonibus;* Psellus *De Dæmonibus;* and the *Pimander* and *Asclepius* of Hermes Trismegistus—all edited by Marsilio Ficino.[39] It is a *vade mecum* of Neoplatonic dæmonology, and a most seducing and frequently unintelligible little volume. And quite the most seductive pages in it are those which bear the heading: 'Ex Michaele Psello de Dæmonibus, Interpres Marsilius Ficinus.'[40] For Michael Psellus writes of dæmons, not with the philosophic detachment of Porphyry or Proclus, but with the conviction of one who has himself hobnobbed with them on occasion. Witness, for example, his engaging tale of the dæmon who seems to have carried on a conversation in Armenian,[41] and the nice point raised by Psellus whether dæmons employ the language of the country of which they are (as it were) 'nationals,' so that a Chaldæan dæmon should properly speak Chaldee, a Greek dæmon Greek—and so on for Persian, Syrian, Hebrew, and Egyptian dæmons. It is, accordingly, perfectly good form, dæmonically speaking, that in the poem the Polar Spirit's fellow-dæmons should 'lispeln englisch' in their aërial dialogue. Apropos of Polar Spirits, moreover, one is interested to learn that the bitterest cold is nothing to dæmons (cum enim in locis *habitent profundissimis, ad summum quidem frigidis*),[42] and that the dæmons of the water sometimes take the form of birds (*Aquatiles vero . . . se avibus . . . similes reddunt*).[43] But the point on which Psellus lays most stress, with rich and curious detail, is the distribution of the dæmons among the elements[44]—earth, air, fire, and water—with the subterraneous and light-shunning orders (these last a jocund company, *genus lucifugum, imperscrutabile, ac penitus tenebrosum*)[45] for good measure. The last thing that Coleridge, who knew good dæmonology when he saw it, would be likely to forget would be that panorama of the peopled elements. And when Wordsworth, with Shelvocke's albatross in mind, suggested tutelary spirits to avenge a creature of the sea and sky, the flood-gates of Coleridge's Neoplatonic lore were opened, and the invisible inhabitants of the waters and the middle air, with Michael Psellus as their sponsor, took possession of the poem.

But Coleridge's acquaintance with Psellus was not confined to Marsilio Ficino's little book. He certainly knew the *Chaldœan Oracles*, for he jots down in the Note Book a fragment of one of the most magnificent of them[46] (that **Χρή σε σπεύδειν πρὸς τὸ φάος καὶ πρὸς πατρὸς αὐγάς** , which Meredith might have been translating in his 'Cleave thou thy way with fathering desire Of fire to reach to fire'), and any edition of the *Oracles* which he knew would include the Commentary of Michael Psellus. And in his commentary Psellus once more unfolds his doctrine of the dæmons of the elements. But Coleridge encountered the conception at every turn in the books that he was reading at the time. He took a volume of Apuleius from the Bristol Library in November, 1795—enthusiastically scrawling in the Library record, in lieu of the date, a pæan of victory: '9 Dutch ships taken, with 3000 troops Bravo'[47]—and he speaks with admiration of the *Florida*.[48] And the *De Deo Socratis* of Apuleius contains the most lucid and entertaining and suggestive discourse on elemental dæmons that I know. But it was not only on his Neoplatonists that Coleridge drew. Dupuis's first two volumes are a riot of genii, dæmons, angel guardians, and tutelary spirits of every feather. To the uninitiated it is bewildering balderdash, but, as Charles Lamb says of brawn, ' 'tis nuts to the adept.' And Coleridge was nothing if not that. And now the haunts of the albatross come into the picture. The astrologers, Dupuis tells us, divide the universe into climates and regions ('there is no climate or element,' says the gloss, 'without one or more'), and five planets are assigned to the five zones. The south polar zone (la zône glaciale du pôle austral) falls to Mercury, but not to Mercury alone. For genii or angels are also guardians of the zones (On put en faire autant de Génies ou d'Anges tutélaires des zônes), and among them are included *Polar* Spirits.[49] Maurice, whose bubble of ice and Chinese astronomers caught Coleridge's fancy, tells also, in the same *History of Hindostan*, of 'ancient Indian geographers,' who represent 'the southern hemisphere that is the region immediately under them . . . as a land of darkness and horrors, inhabited by evil dæmons.'[50] The austral seas are still the haunted *mare tenebrosum*. Finally (for even dæmons may wear out their welcome) Taylor the English pagan quotes, in his commentary on the *Phœdrus*, from the Platonic Hermias: 'But there are other dæmons transcending these, *who are the punishers of souls, converting them to a more perfect and elevated life*.'[51] And Taylor was one of Coleridge's 'darling studies,' and that is the function of the polar dæmon in the poem.

Then straight into that huge conglomeration flew an unsuspecting bird! There was really no escape for the albatross. It was doomed to its dæmon from the first.

But what is the learned Jew, Josephus, doing in that galley? With adepts by the score to choose from, why should he, in the field of dæmonology no more than an authority of sorts, be singled out? He was, to be sure, not without standing as a witness to the phenomena of demoniacal possession. In the curious treatise, for example, of Balthazar Bekker, Doctor of Divinity, entitled *The World Bewitched*, he is drawn on for pertinent evidence,[52] and that eminent authority on all matters dæmonological, Johannes Wierus, takes issue with him on a knotty point, when, in his edifying work on the Illusions of Dæmons (*De Præstigiis Dæmonum*), he discusses the treatment of those who are so hapless as to fall victims to the sorceries of lamias.[53] And other names might easily be added. But without special reason, Josephus was indubitably a bird of strange feather to flock with Michael Psellus.

There is, I think, an answer to the question, and it lies in a most interesting association of ideas. There is excellent reason why Josephus was very definitely present in Coleridge's mind at just this period. It will be remembered that in the preface to 'The Wanderings of Cain' Coleridge declared that after he and Wordsworth had made a botch of that particular essay at collaboration, 'the Ancient Mariner was written instead.' And in *Aids to Reflection* he states explicitly that 'The Wanderings of Cain,' 'The Ancient Mariner,' and 'the first Book of Christabel' were written in the same year.[54] Now since nobody has paid any real attention to the Note Book, it is not remarkable that nobody has observed that Coleridge was getting ready to write his 'Cain' by reading Josephus. For in the Note Book stand, in the Greek, two excerpts from the second chapter of Book I of the *Antiquities*, which contains certain uncanonical information about Cain.[55] Cain, and the 'Old Navigator,' and a strange and shadowy third were moving almost simultaneously towards the light, in Coleridge's brain.

And with Cain was associated Josephus. But besides this large and general connection there was a closer link. Just three pages before Psellus 'Concerning Dæmons' in Coleridge's little Neoplatonic Bible, stands, in Porphyry's discourse 'On the Abstinence of the Ancients,' a summary of Josephus's account of the Essenes.[56] And Porphyry's summary, with the name of Josephus in its first line, centres about the doctrine of departed souls—disembodied spirits, who 'possesse the empire of the aire.' Three pages later, in his opening paragraph, Psellus draws a sharp distinction between angels and dæmons, in their respective natures. There, in a word, within three compact pages, are Josephus, and Psellus, and departed souls, and angels, and daemons. Turn, now, once more to Coleridge's description of his dæmon: 'one of the invisible inhabitants of this planet, *neither departed souls nor angels;* concerning whom the *learned Jew, Josephus*, and *the Platonic Constantinopolitan, Michael Psellus*, may be consulted.' Whether Coleridge wrote the gloss at or near the time when the poem was composed, or later, before 1817, makes little difference. To such a reader Josephus and Michael Psellus were grappled together, once for all, by hoops of steel.

V

There is a remarkable passage in Jerome Cardan, physician and philosopher of the sixteenth century, from that richly curious chapter of his work 'On the Variety of Things' (*De*

Rerum Varietate) which treats illuminatingly of 'Dæmons and the Dead' (*Dæmones et Mortui*):

> Do not wonder, Reader, a man is no more able to know about a dæmon than a dog about a man. The dog knows that the man is, that he eats, drinks, walks, sleeps—no more. It knows also his form: so with a man in the case of dæmons. But you say, a man has a mind, a dog has not. But the mind of a dæmon differs far more in its operation from the mind of a man, than the mind of a man from the sense of a dog.[57]

That reads amazingly like a remark of William James which stands, not without pertinence, at the head of the first chapter in Algernon Blackwood's *The Centaur:* 'We may be in the Universe as dogs and cats are in our libraries, seeing the books and hearing the conversation, but having no inkling of the meaning of it all.' Let me quote again:

> Every element has its own living denizens. Can the celestial ocean of ether, whose waves are light, in which the earth herself floats, not have hers, higher by as much as their element is higher, swimming without fins, flying without wings, moving, immense and tranquil, as if by a half-spiritual force through the half-spiritual sea which they inhabit, rejoicing in the exchange of luminous influence with one another, following the slightest pull of one another's attraction, and harboring, each of them,

an inexhaustible inward wealth?

That is not Apuleius on the daemons of the elements (though it might well be!), but an excerpt from an exposition of the philosophy of Gustav Fechner, who died in 1887.[58] And more profoundly eloquent than all is Goethe's confession of faith in the Dæmonic (das Dämonische), near the opening of the last book of *Dichtung und Wahrheit*. Are there still peopled deeps which obscurely call, while the intellect claps its fingers to its ears, to strangely peopled deeps in us?

'I can easily believe,' wrote Thomas Burnet in the lines from the *Archæologia Philosophicæ* which Coleridge in 1817 prefixed as a motto to 'The Ancient Mariner'—'I can easily believe that there are more Invisible than Visible beings in the Universe (Facile credo, plures esse Naturas invisibiles quam visibiles in rerum universitate).'[59] And in a moment, as Burnet goes on, the old familiar faces, passed over by Coleridge as he quotes, reappear: 'The Ethnic Theologians philosophize at large about the invisible World—the World of Souls, of Genii, of Manes, of Dæmons, of Heroes, of Minds, of Powers, of Gods. As one may see in Iamblichus on the Mysteries of the Egyptians, in Psellus and Pletho on the Chaldean Oracles, and everywhere in the Platonic writers.' Yet the stately prologue which ushers us into an invisibly populated world closes on another note: 'But in the mean Time, we must take Care to keep to the Truth, and observe Moderation, that we may distinguish

Certain from Uncertain Things, and Day from Night.' 'Facile credo . . . sed veritati interea invigilandum est': what, after all, *do* we readily believe, and what is the moderation that we keep, as we come under the compelling magic of the poem?

Coleridge announced, in the *Biographia Literaria*, 'the critical essay on the uses of the Supernatural in poetry, and the principles that regulate its introduction: which the reader will find prefixed to the poem of The Ancient Mariner.'[60] The essay—with its counterpart 'on the "Preternatural," ' to be annexed to 'Christabel'[61]—lives only, with other phantasms, as one of the invisible inhabitants of this planet, and neither Josephus or Michael Psellus can this time lend us aid. But one pregnant sentence in the *Biographia* goes far to console us for our loss. Coleridge set out in the *Lyrical Ballads*, he tells us, to deal with 'persons and characters supernatural . . . yet so as to transfer from our inward nature . . . a semblance of truth sufficient to procure for these shadows of imagination that willing suspension of disbelief for the moment, which constitutes poetic faith.'[62] And as for dæmons, the grounds of our willing suspension are clear. They belong, like spectre-barks and eternal wanderers, to that misty midregion of our racial as well as literary inheritance, towards which we harbour, when the imagination moves through haunted chambers, the primal instinctive will to believe. And as the immemorial projections of elemental human questionings and intuitions—shadows of things divined, 'which having been must ever be'—they are the poet's inalienable possession.

VI

Now let us clear our minds of possible confusion. The incommunicable beauty of 'The Ancient Mariner' is probably not enhanced one whit for anybody by a single line which I have written in this chapter. I am neither so ingenuous nor so pedantic as to cherish that particular illusion. The spell of beauty in the poem is sovereign in its exercise, and apt to pour on rashly proffered aid its beautiful disdain, and I have had another aim. For the ways of the spirit which creates the spell challenge the arduous effort to *understand*, by virtue of that very beauty in the thing created which exalts the faculty that gives it birth. And if that faculty be supreme, as we with one accord proclaim it is, then no attempt to fathom its workings is labour wholly lost—unless, indeed, we have recourse, as a last shift, to the miraculous, and relegate the plastic spirit of imagination to the category of the thaumaturgic and occult. If, then, I have made it clear—whether for daemons of the elements, or water-snakes, or sun, or moon—that the rich suggestiveness of a masterpiece of the imagination springs in some measure from the fact that infinitely more than reached expression lay behind it in the shaping brain, so that every detail is saturated and irradiated with the secret influence of those thronged precincts of the unexpressed—if I have made that clear, my purpose is attained, I am not forgetting beauty.

It is because the worth of beauty is transcendent that the subtle ways of the power that achieves it are transcendently worth searching out.

For 'The Rime of the Ancient Mariner' is 'a work of pure imagination,' and Coleridge himself has so referred to it.[63] And this study, far from undermining that declaration, is lending it confirmation at every turn. For a work of pure imagination is not something fabricated by a *tour de force* from nothing, and suspended, without anchorage in fact, in the impalpable ether of a visionary world. No conception could run more sharply counter to the truth. And I question, in the light of all that is now before us, whether any other poem in English is so closely compacted out of fact, or so steeped in the thought and instinct with the action which characterized its time. Keats, in 'La belle Dame sans Merci,' distilled into a single poem the quintessence of mediaeval romance and balladry. And what 'La belle Dame sans Merci' is to the gramarye of the Middle Ages, 'The Rime of the Ancient Mariner' is to the voyaging, Neoplatonizing, naively scientific spirit of the closing eighteenth century. It has swept within its assimilating influence a bewildering diversity of facts in which contemporary interest was active. The facts are forgotten, and the poem stays. But the power that wrought the facts into the fabric of a vision outlasts both. And if we are rifling the urns where the dead bones of fact have long quietly rested, it is because the unquenchable spirit which gives beauty for ashes is there not wholly past finding out.

---

*Sara Coleridge, in a letter to Matilda Betham in 1810, adds a touch of spice to the subject of Wordsworth's books. 'Coleridge,' she writes, 'sends you his best thanks for the elegant little book; I shall not, however, let it be carried over to Grasmere, for *there* it would soon be *soiled*, for the Wordsworths are woeful destroyers of good books, as our poor library will witness.'[11] That, to be sure, is the Sara Coleridge who wrote with cheerful comprehensiveness in a postscript, while Coleridge and Wordsworth were in Germany, 'The Lyrical Ballads are not liked at all by any.'[12] But De Quincey's testimony[13] (including the lamentable incident of Wordsworth, Burke's *Works* and the butter-knife) is to the same effect, and these somewhat unkind contemporary observations have received odd confirmation within recent years through a note in the *Athenæum* for May 30, 1896 (p. 714), on the prospective sale of Wordsworth's library. 'It may be only a coincidence, of course,' writes the correspondent (who signs himself W. R.), 'but it is curious to note that most of the books which contain Wordsworth's signature are in some respects defective, and give one the impression of having been badly cared for.' How far this was due to Wordsworth's generosity in putting his library at the disposal of the neighborhood, and how far to the family's 'woeful' carelessness, is matter for idle but not uninteresting conjecture.

*Even Hawthorne—by no means a matter-of-fact soul!—was disturbed. The museum at Warwick, he wrote in the *English Note Books*,[17] was 'rich in specimens of ornithology, among which was an albatross, huge beyond imagination. I do not think Coleridge could have known the size of the fowl when he caused it to be hung round the neck of his Ancient Mariner.' That is perfectly possible. But it is also possible that Hawthorne may not have known that there were other albatrosses.

CHAPTER XIV

HOW AN OLD NAVIGATOR MET STRANGE COMPANY IN LIMBO

BUT other ghosts were raised, and other shapes than dæmons flitted, along the road that went down through the dark to the sea. If an 'Old Navigator' was present from the beginning in Coleridge's mind, then obviously he was not, before Wordsworth's suggestions equipped him with a setting and a crime, precisely the ancient Mariner whom we know. Something happened to him as a result of that November afternoon. What was it? To answer that, is to tell a curious story.

I

In a play (which will meet us again in a moment) performed at Drury Lane in 1797, the heroine is discovered reading:[1]

> [*Reads.*] 'At this dread moment the whole distorted face of nature, smote with convulsive sympathy, appear'd to share the horrors of the scene.' Oh! how I admire this new glorious German stile of novel-writing! Bleeding Nuns, flirting Friars, caves and daggers, ghosts on

> horseback, and every thing that's delightfully alarming, and sublimely unintelligible! [*Reads*] 'Instantly I heard a heavy step advance, and while my heart beat with terror, I felt a cold hand seize my——'

The interruption need not concern us. Three years earlier, in November, 1794, Coleridge wrote to Southey:[2]

> 'Tis past one o'clock in the morning. I sat down at twelve o'clock to read the 'Robbers' of Schiller. I had read, chill and trembling, when I came to the part where the Moor fixes a pistol over the robbers who are asleep. I could read no more. My God, Southey, who is this Schiller, this convulser of the heart? Did he write his tragedy amid the yelling of fiends? I should not like to be able to describe such characters. I tremble like an aspen leaf. Upon my soul, I write to you because I am frightened. I had better go to bed.

In July, 1796, Lamb wrote to Coleridge about one of the five translations of Bürger's 'Lenore' which were published in England in that single year:[3]

> Have you read the Ballad called 'Leonora,' in the second Number of the 'Monthly Magazine'? If you have!!!!!!!!!!!!!![4]

It is fairly obvious that England was discovering Germany,

and was finding the discovery exciting.[5]

Now Coleridge was making provocative discoveries with the rest. At some time before (or early in) 1797 he had extended his acquaintance with Schiller beyond *The Robbers*. For from March to October, 1797, he was engaged on his tragedy of *Osorio*,[6] and the plot of *Osorio* is drawn freely from the Sicilian's tale in Schiller's *Der Geisterseher*.[7] I do not know whether or not he read the romance in the original. He 'Coleridgeized' (as Lamb would say)[8] a good deal, about this time, with regard to his knowledge of German. In April, 1796, he 'had some thoughts of translating . . . with an Answer' a work of that 'most formidable Infidel' Lessing, 'entitled, in German, *Fragments of an Anonymous Author*,'[9] but refrained, lest the work should be more potent than the answer! In May of the same year he was studying German, and was going to be able in about six weeks 'to read that language with tolerable fluency.' And so he goes on, 'I have some thoughts of making a proposal' (I suppose when the six weeks were up!) 'to Robinson, the great London bookseller, of translating all the works of Schiller, which would make a portly quarto, on condition that he should pay my journey and my wife's to and from Jena, a cheap German University where Schiller resides, and allow me two guineas each quarto sheet, which would maintain me.'[10] That is mild to what follows, but this is not a guide to Coleridge's Cloudcuckoolands. More than a year and a half later, in December, 1797, he was still daily studying German, and translating Wieland's *Oberon:* 'it is a difficult language, and I can translate at least as fast as I can construe.'[11] *Die Räuber* had been translated into English in 1792; *Der Geisterseher* in 1795.[12] The play he had pretty certainly read in English. The romance he could have read in German, but the question is of little consequence, for it was the story only that he used. And in that story, as the element of most absorbing interest, he found the mysterious figure of the Wandering Jew.

But the baffling stranger met him elsewhere. We know that Coleridge owned Percy's *Reliques of Ancient English Poetry*, for in August, 1800, Lamb includes it in the list of Coleridge's books which he was forwarding to Keswick, along with 'three ponderous German dictionaries,' razors and shaving-box and strap, and the 'dressing-gown . . . in which you used to sit and look like a conjuror, when you were translating "Wallenstein" '[13]—not to mention the most engagingly mysterious item of the batch, 'that drama in which Got-fader performs.'* Attended by all that cloud of witnesses, the *Reliques*, I think, may safely be conceded. And in Percy's *Reliques* is the ancient ballad of 'The Wandering Jew.' More than that, Percy prefixes to the ballad a couple of paragraphs about the legend, with references, for inquiring readers, to Matthew Paris, and Calmet's *Dictionary of the Bible*, and *The Turkish Spy*.[14] If Coleridge followed his familiar practice and looked them up, he found, particularly in *The Turkish Spy*, not a little curious and interesting information.

There was, however, a highly sensational treatment of the story close at hand. Matthew Gregory Lewis was at the climax of his career. *The Castle Spectre*, 'having been received' (as the play-bills tell us) 'with unbounded and universal applause' at Drury Lane in December, 1797, was announced for repetition until further notice.[15] It was being performed in Boston in December, 1798, as a 'Magnificent Spectacle' (with 'an elegant View of the Castle of Conway,' 'A Gothic Chamber,' and 'the subterraneous caverns where Reginald has been confined 16 years'), 'more calculated to interest the feelings of an audience, to surprise and astonish, than any dramatic representation ever seen in America.'[16] Wordsworth saw it in Bristol in June, 1798, and said that 'it fitted the taste of the audience like a glove.'[17] And Coleridge had already sent to Wordsworth, in January of the same year, a scathing criticism of the play.[18] It is in the true 'new glorious German stile,' and is not without odd bearing on 'The Ancient Mariner.' But *The Castle Spectre* rode to its brief *éclat* on the wave of a still more notable success. From the time of its publication in 1795, Lewis's *The Monk* had enjoyed that species of notoriety which for prompt results throws fame into the shade. And in *The Monk* the Wandering Jew plays a melodramatic and unforgettable part.

And that part, we now know, was fresh and vivid in Coleridge's memory. There has just been published for the first time, in Professor Greever's *A Wiltshire Parson and his Friends*, a letter from Coleridge to William Bowles which was certainly written before, but not much before, March 25, 1797.[20] And in this letter, after stating that 'the plan I have sketched for my tragedy [i.e., *Osorio*] is too chaotic to be transmitted at present,' and after adding that 'it is "romantic and wild and somewhat terrible," ' Coleridge proceeds: 'But indeed I am almost weary of the terrible, having been an hireling in the Critical Review for these last six or eight months. I have been lately reviewing the Monk, the Italian, Hubert de Sevrac, etc., etc., in all of which dungeons, and old castles, and solitary Houses by the Sea Side, and Caverns, and Woods, and extraordinary characters, and all the tribe of Horror and Mystery, have crowded on me—even to surfeiting.'[21] These reviews Professor Greever has identified,[22] and that of *The Monk* appears in the *Critical Review* for February, 1797. One remark of Coleridge's is pertinent here: 'The tale of the bleeding nun is truly terrific; and we could not easily recollect a bolder or more happy conception than that of the burning cross on the forehead of the wandering Jew (a mysterious character, which, though copied as to its more prominent features from Schiller's incomprehensible Armenian, does, nevertheless, display great vigour of fancy).'[23] The incomprehensible Armenian will meet us significantly in a moment. As for *The Monk*, we now have it from Coleridge himself that the figure of the Wandering Jew, in the year of 'The Ancient Mariner,' had impressed itself, in peculiarly striking fashion, upon his memory.

I more than suspect that Wordsworth also was an accessory before the fact. When Coleridge heard *The Borderers* read at Racedown in June, 1797, he grew almost as rhapsodical as when *The Robbers* swam into his ken, two years and a half before. Indeed *The Robbers* now takes second place. '[Wordsworth's] drama,' he wrote Cottle, 'is absolutely wonderful. . . . There are in the piece those *profound* touches of the human heart which I find three or four times in "The Robbers" of Schiller, and often in Shakespeare, but in Wordsworth there are no *inequalities*. T. Poole's opinion of Wordsworth is that he is the greatest man he ever knew; I coincide.'[24] And in the closing lines of *The Borderers*, Marmaduke becomes, in all essentials, the Wanderer himself.[25] Wordsworth's interest in the subject—though scarcely, alas! his inspiration by it—is attested by his 'Song for the Wandering Jew' composed in 1800, in which the singer points out, in a stanza to each, that mountain-torrents, clouds, the chamois, the sea-horse, the raven, and the ostrich all find rest, but never he. Long before this, Southey had written to a friend from Herefordshire in 1793: 'Like the Wandering Jew, you see I am here, and there, and everywhere.'[26] The tale was plainly a familiar one in Coleridge's circle.

But the enigmatic figure of the Jew was exercising on every hand its fascination upon imaginative minds. Coleridge was once more, as in his travel-lore and dæmonology, responding to influences which were everywhere abroad in his world. Goethe conceived, as early as 1774, the idea of an epic treatment of the theme, and, as he tells us in the poem, sprang out of bed in the middle of the night to begin it.[27] And the manuscript, scrawled diagonally across the page, after his wont when his *Dämon* had him in its grip, bears his assertion out.[28] The poem exists in fragments only, and even these were never printed until 1836. Nothing under Heaven could be more remote from Coleridge, who obviously never saw it. Byron, in the mood of 'The Vision of Judgment,' might have written parts of it, and one highly irreverent passage—'Da kam der Sohn ganz überquer Gestolpert über Sterne her'[29]—oddly anticipates his superb characterization of young Henry Fox as 'a halting angel, who has tripped against a star.'[30] But Byron never saw the poem either.

The German poet Schubart (as we learn from the Memoir by his son)[31] had a grandiose conception of the Jew, seated on a mountain cliff, looking out across the boundless ocean of time through which his course had lain, and depicting, as in a great epic fresco (ein grosses episches Fresco-Gemälde), all the spectacles, and revolutions, and convulsions of which he had been part—the fall of the Roman Coliseum, the birth of empires, 'the giant-apparition of the Papacy,' the meteoric figures of the Reformation and the Renaissance, the thrilling drama of Columbus, the monuments and masterpieces of almost two thousand years. But the sole realization of the vast design pondered long and lovingly over the wine (beim blinkenden Kelchglas), is the brief 'Lyric Rhapsody,' published in 1783, in which Ahasuerus, maddened by endless life, rehearses, in a torrent of rhetoric, his vain attempts to die.[32] Shelley 'picked it up, dirty and torn . . . in Lincoln's Inn Fields' (its author and the title of the work from which it came unknown to him) and translated it as a note to the episode of Ahasuerus, in 'Queen Mab.'[33] But Coleridge probably never saw it. And for us, Schubart's preoccupation with the theme, like Goethe's, serves merely to enhance our recognition of the potent influence which at the close of the century the inscrutable passer-by was exercising on the romantic spirit of the time. But in England the story was achieving a curious popularity of another sort.

In May, 1797, there was performed at the Drury Lane Theatre (for which, at the moment, Coleridge was writing *Osorio*)[34] a farce called *The Wandering Jew, or Love's Masquerade*,[35] by an obscure playwright, Andrew Franklin. It is the play from which I have already quoted the heroine's panegyric on the 'delightfully alarming and the sublimely unintelligible,' and its drift is made sufficiently clear in a couple of sentences from a critique of its first London performance, preserved in Genest's huge collection of theatrical clippings:[36]

> The Farce takes its title from the character of a young adventurer, who, failing in other expedients, assumes the garb of the Wandering Jew, attended by a brother fortune-hunter, dressed in a similar habit. The latter, who is an Irishman, gives some very curious descriptions

> of the exploits in their days of Julius Cæsar, and other remote periods, blended with modern occurrences. This is a very excellent idea, but a part of the audience appeared to misconceive the meaning of the author.

What to Schubart was an epic vision becomes in Franklin's hands the stuff of comedy. The play itself is utterly trivial and unimportant, but it offers enlightening evidence of the degree to which, during the very months when 'The Ancient Mariner' was being written, the legend was attaining currency

The play-bills in the great collection of Mr. Robert Gould Shaw, now, with Genest's clippings, in the Harvard College Library, make it possible to follow its somewhat checkered history. It was announced at Drury Lane on March 14, 1797, for production 'in a few days'; was postponed again and again during March and April; was at last performed on May 15th; and after having been given at least eight times was produced—apparently for the last time in London—on March 15, 1798, as a pendant to *The Castle Spectre*.[37] During the year that followed its first announcement, then, it appears in the play-bills at least a score of times. It crossed to America, and was given in New York, at the New Park Theatre, May 2, 1798, for the 'first time here.'[38] In Boston it appeared at the Hay-Market Theatre, May 27, 1799 ('as performed in London, and . . . New York, with the most unbounded applause'),[39] and again on June 24[40]—this time on the same bill with another Drury Lane production, James Cobb's *Cherokee*, a burlesque called 'Shelty's Travels,' and a topical song (for which I shall refer the interested reader to the Notes),[41] entitled 'Bow, Wow, Wow.' That 'redemption of the British stage . . . from horses, dogs, elephants, and the like zoölogical rarities'[42] which Coleridge declared to have been one aim of Drury Lane was still in Boston a far-off, divine event! The late eighteenth-century stage, as seen in the fierce light of its own exhibition of its wares in the contemporary press, was a motley affair. Finally, the play was advertised for performance in Charleston, South Carolina, December 5 and December 7, 1799.[43] In England and America alike, the Wandering Jew, transmogrified but recognizable, was reaching an audience that knew not Schiller. It was not merely in those bookish circles on which we are apt too rigidly to fix our eyes, that the tale was in the air.*

Now in the Note Book, as one of the ghostly troop of Coleridge's literary projects, stands this entry:

> Wandering Jew, a romance.[44]

Like Goethe, and Schiller, and Schubart, and Lewis, Coleridge too had come under the spell of the theme. And together with Count Benyowski, and Christian the Mutineer, to say nothing of Jonah and Thor, the Wandering Jew haunted the frontiers of consciousness, waiting to be moved towards the light. And of that varied and inviting company of shades, he was the only one to cross the border. For cross it he did, in the person of the ancient Mariner.

The romance, to be sure, was never written, but the summons to the Wanderer nevertheless came. When Wordsworth proposed for the central figure whom Coleridge already had in mind the commission of a crime to be expiated by the offender's wanderings, the deeps were stirred. And as the hint of the agency of tutelary spirits called to life the dæmons of the Neoplatonic universe, so this suggestion created for the Old Navigator of Coleridge's invention precisely that character, 'supernatural, or at least romantic,' required by the conditions of the plan—that much discussed and well considered plan out of which the *Lyrical Ballads* grew. And into the shadowy outline that was soon to be the ancient Mariner, melted, as in a dream, the wraith of the Wandering Jew.

II

Now the Jew was a figure of romance in two quite different ways. In *The Ghostseer* and *The Monk* he enters, as a determining influence upon the action, a romantic tale of which he is not himself the central character. But his own experience, as he wandered changeless through the changing centuries, was itself of the very essence of romance. That is the theme which even the ballad in the *Reliques* dimly foreshadows; it is developed pithily in outline in *The Turkish Spy*, where O. Henry long after found it, and out of it spun a characteristic yarn;[45] Schubart saw in it a mighty panorama; degraded to broad farce, it is still potentially present in Franklin's play; and it is elaborated with tedious and uninspired detail in *Der Ewige Jude, Geschicht- oder Volksroman, wie man will*, in 1785. I have no reason to suppose that Coleridge knew either the *Roman* (which anticipates his very title, as it stands in the Note Book), or the French original on which it drew.[46] But it was obviously this larger theme of the Wanderer's experiences, and of his absorbing tale, which laid hold upon his imagination. And with consummate art he has cast the glamour of it over his own conception.

For the Mariner is *not* the Wandering Jew. Coleridge's art is not so crass as that. The poem is no 'New Adventures of Ahasuerus.' It is a subtle transfer to a figure which is essentially a new creation, of associations that had long been gathering about an accepted and mysterious personality of legend. And through this happy annexation of a tract of the marvellous grown familiar through long credence, the Mariner in his turn is invested with that *sine qua non* of the requisite illusion, 'a human interest and a semblance of truth sufficient to procure for these shadows of imagination that willing suspension of disbelief for the moment which constitutes poetic faith.' The secret of the Mariner's hold on our imagination lies, in large part, precisely in this interpenetration of the Old Navigator and the Eternal Wanderer in Coleridge's visionary world. And that transfusion becomes explicit as the tale draws to its end:

Since then, at an uncertain hour,
That agony returns:
And till my ghastly tale is told,
This heart within me burns.

I pass, like night, from land to land;
I have strange power of speech;
That moment that his face I see,
I know the man that must hear me:
To him my tale I teach.[47]

That haunting utterance of the very substance of the legend (even to the 'strange power of speech')[48] endows at a stroke the ancient Mariner with the unassailable verisimilitude which generations of acceptance had conferred upon his prototype. I am not sure that it is not the supreme touch of genius in the poem.

Wordsworth, to be sure, insisted, as we may recall, that one of the 'great defects' of his Friend's poem was the fact 'that the principal person *has no distinct character*, either in his profession of Mariner, or as a human being who having been long under the control of supernatural impressions *might be supposed himself to partake of something supernatural.*'[49] When I read that, with all my fealty to the Wordsworth of the glorious, winged moments when his pen was dipped in heaven, I can only fall back, for adequate expression, upon the Scriptures: 'And Elisha prayed, and said, Lord, I pray thee, open his eyes that he may see. And the Lord opened the eyes of the young man; and he saw: and, behold, the mountain was full of horses and chariots of fire round about Elisha.' There was nobody about, I fear, when the smug, complacent paragraph was penned, to pray for William Wordsworth.

But did the two figures merge in Coleridge's mind only when the poem was within a dozen stanzas of its close? Or do the great lines in which the Mariner passes with the inevitability of night, reveal, like a sudden finger-post, the direction of a half-guessed road we have been travelling from the first? Let us look for a moment at something often overlooked—the obvious.

Coleridge knew the Sicilian's Tale in *Der Geisterseher* as one knows the thing one has lived with from March until October.[50] For during the month before 'The Ancient Mariner' was begun he had finished turning the plot of the story into a play. Now the Sicilian prefaces his tale with a graphic account of the mysterious personage who is known, in the circles which he enters, only by the name of 'The Unfathomable' (der Unergründliche).[51] And the climax of this story which Coleridge knew by heart, is a wedding feast.

> The guests are met, the feast is set:
> Mays't hear the merry din—

every detail is there. And at the feast the inscrutable stranger—who has earlier appeared as an Armenian and a Russian, and who (as Coleridge in his review of *The Monk* had recognized) *is* the Wandering Jew—stands, in the guise of a Franciscan monk, motionless and silent, and holds the wedding-guests spellbound by his look.[52] Coleridge omitted this part of the Sicilian's story in *Osorio*. But in the month which had elapsed between the completion of the drama and the beginning of the poem he had not forgotten it. For on the very threshold of the 'Rime' we hear the music of a wedding feast, and the ancient Mariner—who like the Stranger does not *come*, but *is*—casts his spell upon a Wedding-Guest through a power of the eye which he shares with his counterpart. Coleridge's unwritten Romance slipped its moorings, and the Wanderer assumed a sailor's guise, at the moment when the poem was begun. And as the narrative unfolds, there subtly develops with it the illusion of an ageless visitant from an indeterminable past.

> We were the first that ever burst
> Into that silent sea.

Before Magellan was, the Mariner sailed.[53] And the Wedding-Guest is not the first who cannot choose but hear, nor for all we know, is this, more than another land, the Mariner's 'own countree,' nor its tongue his native speech. The 'blending and (as it were) fusing' of the two conceptions, 'each into each,' underlies the very genesis of one of the most profoundly imaginative figures of romance. And I hope that to others, as certainly to me, our seemingly dubious absorption in strange currents of the times, 'aloft, in secret veins of air,' and with their confluences and dissipations through forgotten books and plays, has justified itself in an enhanced appreciation of the ways of that power strong in beauty, which (as we say with little thought of what we mean) *creates*.

III

The Mariner's glittering eye, however, demands a postscript. Professor Oliver Elton has interesting things to say (though not in immediate connection with 'The Ancient Mariner') about 'the pair of terrible eyes that [from the end of the eighteenth century] haunt English fiction; they are seen in *Vathek* and *The Monk*, and they descend through Byron's poems to the villains of Bulwer Lytton and Dickens.'[54] And he suggests that 'their original ancestry is perhaps found in the "baleful eyes" of Milton's Satan.' Of that last I do not feel so sure. Literary ancestry is a complicated business, and without gainsaying the remote paternity of Satan, I should hazard the guess that the Armenian in *Der Geisterseher* had, as old Thomas Heywood puts it, either an entire hand or at least a main finger in starting the terrible eyes on their long Romantic and Victorian career. And the Armenian is the Wandering Jew. The Jew of *The Monk*, in turn, is the Armenian melodramatized, and his eyes, 'large, black, and sparkling,' lent 'a something to his look, which . . . inspired . . . with a secret awe, not to say horror.' 'You already,' he declares to Don Raymond, 'feel the influence of the charm, and with every succeeding moment will feel it more.'[55] There can be no question of the immediate ancestry of the Mariner's hypnotic eye. But the conception could scarcely be Coleridge's, were it quite so simple as all that. The power of fascination which the eye of the Wandering Jew exerts, becomes, in the case of the Mariner, irresistible. Such heightening of effect, to be sure, is an obvious device, but there is curious evidence that this time a definite influence was at work.

Just after the lovely stanza in which the sails make on their pleasant noise till noon, there stood, in the *Lyrical Ballads* of 1798, these lines:

> Listen, O listen, thou Wedding-guest!
> 'Marinere! thou hast thy will:
> '*For that, which comes out of thine eye, doth make*
> '*My body and soul to be still.*'[56]

That is a plain case of the old doctrine of magnetic emanation, and as an intruded fragment of unassimilated fact (or pseudo-fact) it snaps the spell. And Coleridge later very properly expunged the stanza. But like the banished biscuit-worms, it gives up, before it goes, its secret—the clue (this time) to another element which merged, in the conception of the Mariner's ocular fascination; with the recollection of the Wanderer's compelling gaze.[57]

Professor Lane Cooper, in an illuminating paper on 'The

Power of the Eye in Coleridge'[58] (to which I am indebted for the information in this paragraph), calls attention to the extraordinary vogue of mesmerists and animal magnetizers in London and Bristol during the eighties—a vogue which was at its height at the very time when Coleridge, trudging to the London Hospital (where his brother Luke walked), 'every Saturday [he] could make or obtain leave,' reading incessantly 'English, Latin, yea, Greek books of medicine . . . became wild to be apprenticed to a surgeon.'[59] And when, at times, upwards of three thousand persons were crowding about a house at Hammersmith, unable to gain admission to the demonstrations of a mesmerist within,[60] it is incredible that Coleridge, who was then in London, steeped in medical lore, should have been unimpressed. Later in life, as we know, he became so engrossed in the subject of animal magnetism that he proposed (as usual!) to write a book on it. Nor (again as usual) was his preoccupation hidden from his friends. 'He will begin,' wrote Southey to his wife in 1817, with a touch of not unnatural asperity, 'as he did when I last saw him, about Animal Magnetism, or some equally congruous subject, and go on from Dan to Beersheba in his endless loquacity.'[61] Carlyle, in his contemptuous and cruel sketch of June 24, 1824,[62] refers to him as 'a kind, good soul, full of religion and affection, and poetry and animal magnetism.' And the Wedding-Guest's reference to magnetic emanation is unmistakable evidence that in 1798, as well, the subject was working in Coleridge's mind—reinforced, as 'Christabel' irresistibly suggests, by who can tell what midnight delvings in occult Latin treatises on fascination.

A characteristically Coleridgean interest in ocular hypnosis, then, is one of the blending elements in the conception of the Mariner. But it is operant only in a subtle heightening of the Wanderer's mysterious power. The Mariner is no more a mesmerist than he is the Wandering Jew. Yet though neither, he partakes, through the alchemy of genius, of the attributes of both. And in the eye that holds spellbound one of three, another of those strange 'facts of mind' which were Coleridge's darling studies, has lent to a denizen of the borderland between two worlds that 'credibilizing effect'[63] which secures for these shadows of imagination our willing suspension of disbelief.

IV

Let us return now for a moment to the road across the Quantock Hills to Watchet. A tentative Navigator in Coleridge's brain is feeling about for a story to fit him. And Wordsworth suggests that the curse of perpetual wandering be brought upon him, with what swift confluence of 'streamy associations' from Coleridge's late engrossing interests, we have seen. But Wordsworth also proposed that the curse should come through the killing of an innocent fellow-creature. And that hint of an inoffensive victim set stirring afresh in Coleridge's memory another very recent concourse of associations, and with the traits of one mysterious and fated Wanderer there was blended a second and no less fateful strain.

Like South Sea voyages, and the daemons of the elements, and the Wandering Jew, the antediluvians were also, at the moment, in the air. The huge, cosmic span of the legendary generations; the crepuscular figures of the fathers of the arts; the giant offspring of sons of God and daughters of men; their primordial violence and lusts, 'vaster than empires, and more slow'; the piquant dash of the abnormal, even of the monstrous, in their histories—all this has always served to whet a half-unlicensed curiosity, and never more than during that strange electrical tension of the late eighteenth century, when the tracking of uncanny correspondences between the patriarchs before the flood and Egyptian and Phoenician deities of none too blessed memory was an accredited diversion. And the older and well-thumbed authorities on the pastime ranged from the scholarly inquiries of the gentle Cumberland and the ponderous disquisitions of Heidegger to the richly-spiced naughtiness of Bayle. For the antediluvians have always kept a reminiscent relish of forbidden fruit.

Now Coleridge jots down in the Note Book, with a faintly discernible touch of zest, the following brief but suggestive memorandum: '*Ham*—lustful rogue—Vide Bayle under the Article *Ham.*'[64] He had, then, been consulting the lively and reprehensible articles in Bayle on the patriarchs—not omitting, we may safely guess, the particularly racy and obnoxious notes on Eve. But why? The entry immediately preceding answers the question. It is one of the two excerpts, in the Greek, from Josephus's account of Cain, the other being separated from it by a single item only. Coleridge was plainly looking up the antediluvian fathers with special reference to his projected 'Wanderings of Cain.'

But now there comes into the stream another (and a captivatingly incongruous) German tributary. In 1760 Salomon Gessner published *The Death of Abel* (*Der Tod Abels*). '[It is] wrote'—I am quoting the felicitous exposition in which, the next year, its first English translator, Mary Collyer, anticipates by a century and a half the modernists—'it is wrote in a kind of loose poetry, unshackled by the tagging of rhymes, or counting of syllables. This method of writing seems perfectly suited to the German language, and is of a middle species between verse and prose: It has the beauties of the first, with the ease of the last.'[65] The 'loose poetry' which 'the ingenious Mrs. Collyer' herself essays, in her zeal to emulate 'the almost inimitable graces of the charming original,' is best passed over in discreet and awe-stricken silence. But the work at once achieved enormous popularity.[66] It is, an anonymous critic of 1766 rhapsodically declares, 'the most finished human copy of primeval nature anywhere extant.' 'It traces'—I am quoting the same amiable enthusiast—'and often gains upon, Milton in his very brightest tracts; and moves on, unclouded by any of the spots in that most glorious luminary.'[67] And the suggestion (on the merits of which I venture no opinion) that Gessner's *Abel* and Klopstock's *Messiah* 'may be read alternately before and after communion' is not wholly unenlightening. The 'delightfully alarming' was finding its complement in the tenderly sentimental. And in 1814 the *Quarterly Review* could state (I imagine with substantial warrant) that 'no book of foreign growth has ever become so popular in England as the *Death of Abel*. . . . It has been repeatedly printed at country presses, with worn types and on coarse paper; and it is found at country fairs, and in the little shops of remote towns almost as certainly as the *Pilgrim's Progress* and *Robinson Crusoe*.'[68] The cheap little coarse-paper edition before me as I write was printed at Newburyport, Massachusetts, in 1794, and between 1792 and 1825 at least seventeen reprints were published in America.[69] Scott, as a child, was allowed to read *The Death of Abel* on Sundays, along with *Pilgrim's Progress*, 'to relieve the gloom of one dull sermon succeeding to another.'[70] Byron read it when he was eight years old, and denied with a little too much emphasis its influence on *Cain*.[71] Wordsworth, in 'The Prelude,' names (together with the Evangelists, Isaiah, Job, Moses, Shakespeare, Dante, and Ossian) '[him] who penned, the other day, the Death of Abel,'[72] as a repository of pulpit eloquence. William Taylor, to be sure, had disrespectful things to say of Gessner's 'trim shrubberies, peopled with cosset lambs and pinioned nightingales.'[73] But 'the elegant and sentimental Turn of Mr. Gessner's Writings,' at which a feminine rival of Mrs. Collyer tried her hand in 1762,[74] was clearly holding its own with 'Bleeding Nuns and flirting Friars' in that other 'new glorious German stile.' The brooks of Eden were mazily murmuring soft strains of Teutonic sentiment. And this exuberant sentiment was lavished upon Cain!

Now Coleridge, with little doubt, owned a copy of *The Death of Abel.* Among those 'some few Epic Poems' which Lamb sent on to Keswick, with the *Reliques* and the razors, the 'one about Cain and Abel, which came from Poole,'[75] can scarcely have been anything else. But the question of ownership is unimportant. That Coleridge had the poem in mind in 'The Wanderings of Cain' is certain, for we have his word for it. It was impracticable, he smilingly recalls, in the account (already quoted) of his futile attempt to collaborate with Wordsworth, 'for a taste so austerely pure and simple [as Wordsworth's] *to imitate the Death of Abel.*'[76] And even did no such acknowledgment exist, the fragment itself affords ample evidence of Gessner's influence.[77] Josephus, and Bayle, and Gessner—'learned Jew,' skeptical Frenchman, and Teutonic sentimentalist—were accordingly collaborating, with rather more success than Wordsworth, in the genesis of a Coleridgean Cain.

But the figure thus evoked is that of Cain the *Wanderer*—the Cain of the primal eldest curse, 'a fugitive and a vagabond in the earth'; that Cain with whom Bolingbroke in *Richard II* bids the king's murderer 'go wander through the shades of night.' Was he, however, while the oddly assorted ingredients were blending in Coleridge's brain, a solitary figure there? The fragment of 'The Wanderings of Cain,' it will be remembered, was drafted or composed, or both, just before 'The Ancient Mariner' was written.[78] And during those same months, as we know, the unfathomable Stranger of *Der Geisterseher* and *The Monk* was hovering in the background of *Osorio*. Cain and the Wandering Jew were tenants of Coleridge's 'shaping and disquisitive mind' together. And the inevitable happened. Here is a bit of what seems to be a rough draft of 'The Wanderings':

> Midnight on the Euphrates. Cedars, palms, pines. Cain discovered sitting on the upper part of a ragged rock . . . The Beasts are out on the ramp. . . . Cain advances, *wishing death*, and the *tigers* rush off. . . . He comes to an immense gulph filled with water, whither they descend followed by *alligators* etc.[79]

And here are the words ('Schiller Lewis-ized,' as Coleridge said of the 'Castle Spectre')[80] of the Wandering Jew in *The Monk:*

> *Fain would I lay down my miserable life*. . . but *death eludes me*, and flies from my embrace. . . . The hungry *tiger* shudders at my approach, and the *alligator* flies from a monster more horrible than itself[81]

There is no need to point the moral. One more indication will suffice. The face of Cain in 'The Wanderings,' like the face of the Wandering Jew, 'told in a strange and terrible language of agonies that had been, and were, and were still to continue to be.'[82] And that is no less the face of the ancient Mariner.

Before the Mariner was conceived, then, in that 'reservoir of the soul' of which Coleridge once wrote, the Wandering Jew and Cain had already undergone a singular osmosis. Then, while this 'chaos of elements' was still in suspension in Coleridge's memory, came the flash that precipitated the solution. Wordsworth, with the melancholy Captain Hatley stirring in *his* memory, made his uncannily apposite suggestion. Let the Old Navigator wantonly kill an inoffensive victim, and let his wanderings then become the expiation of his act.

There was only one thing that could happen. The whole hovering cloud of reminiscences must stream in upon the conception of the Old Navigator, and colour it with memories of Cain. And so imbued, the Old Navigator became the ancient Mariner. Yet the Mariner is not Cain. He is a shadow of imagination in a visionary world. But a suggestion as powerful as his fated passing like the night, lends once more to a visionary world the illusion of reality:

> Instead of the cross, the Albatross
> About my neck was hung.[83]

And that haunting adumbration of the mark of Cain invests the Mariner with the 'credibilizing' associations of still another legend, which was hoary when the Wandering Jew was born.

But there is another strange tie between the legends. The Wandering Jew, as Coleridge knew him, also bore a mark. And that mark was the cross. 'God has set his seal upon me,' says the Jew in *The Monk*, 'and all his creatures respect this fatal mark.' 'I raised [my eyes]'—it is the horror-struck Don Raymond who is speaking—'and beheld *a burning cross* impressed upon his brow.'[84] And the burning cross glows ominous throughout the episode, and was, as we have seen, the feature of the tale which impressed itself most vividly on Coleridge. As for the mark of Cain, there is in Bayle a strange fancy, caught from the flotsam and jetsam of legendary lore, which Coleridge, who seems to have remembered Cain's fierce countenance and eyes of blood from another passage in Bayle's account only a few lines below, could not well have overlooked: 'D'autres veulent que cette marque ait consisté dans. . . *le signe de la croix*.'[85] The mark of the Wandering Jew was also the mark of Cain. But in the case of the Wandering Jew the cross was the sign of the crime.[86] And as a similar emblem the albatross was borne about the ancient Mariner's neck. I wonder (and venture no farther than surmise) if something beyond the obvious crucifix[87] (let alone the still more obvious demands of rhyme) were not latent in Coleridge's mind when, with the three figures merged in the deeps from which they sprang, he wrote the lines:

> *Instead of the cross*, the Albatross
> About my neck was hung.

The interpretation of 'cross' as 'crucifix' is there for him who will. But the act, however taken, is the most profoundly symbolic in the poem. And it may well have been tinged for Coleridge with a deeper symbolism still.

There is, finally, a curious accident worth mention, which falls in with the equally fortuitous conjunction of a just discovered Captain Hatley with the shapes which at the moment were peopling Coleridge's brain. I imagine it would have been hard in any case to keep Cain out of the reckoning. For there was a further chance association which was bound to draw him in. The goal of the November pilgrimage, we know from Wordsworth, was the famous Valley of Stones near Linton.[88] And the Valley of Stones, with its wild and fantastic chaos of rocks—'the very bones and skeleton of the earth,' as Southey calls them, shapeless as 'a palace of the Preadamite kings, [or] a city of the Anakim'[89]—this vale towards which the three were walking, had already furnished the setting for Coleridge's 'Wanderings of Cain.' For just after 'The Ancient Mariner' was finished Coleridge repeated the same excursion, this time in the company of William Hazlitt. And Hazlitt, like Southey, gives a graphic picture of the landscape (with a fleeting glimpse of Coleridge 'running out bare-headed [in a thunder-storm] to enjoy the commotion of the elements in the Valley of Rocks'), and at the end of it adds this remark: 'Coleridge told me that he and Wordsworth were to have made this place the scene of a prose-tale, which was to have been in the manner of, but far superior to, the *Death of Abel*, but they had relinquished the design.'[90] The design of collaboration was relinquished, but the fragment which Coleridge wrote, alone, attests the accuracy of Hazlitt's recollection. For the Valley of Rocks is unmistakable in the setting of 'The Wanderings of Cain':

> The scene around was desolate; as far as the eye could reach it was desolate: the bare rocks faced each other, and left a long and wide interval of thin white sand. . . . The pointed and shattered summits of the ridges of the rocks made a rude mimicry of human concerns, and seemed to prophecy mutely of things that then were not; steeples, and battlements, and ships with naked masts.[91]

And towards that very scene, against which was already etched deep in Coleridge's memory the tragic figure of Cain, the course of the expedition was directed, while talk of the Navigator's person and adventures went more and more eagerly on. Who can doubt that from its old haunt among the 'huge and terrific masses' of the Valley of Stones, the shade of Cain the Wanderer beckoned to one of three?

And here ends the tale of what happened to an Old Navigator in quest of incarnation on an autumn afternoon. And if ever there was an exemplification of the strange union of accident and intent, of subliminal confluence and conscious design in the workings of the shaping spirit, it is found in this true story of how the Wandering Jew and Cain together took possession of the astral body of an ancient Mariner.

---

*Since this sentence was written, the item has ceased to be a mystery, but it has lost thereby none of its engaging quality. See the Notes.[19]

*It is not wholly without pertinence to mention that at the moment when I am writing, to wit, the evening of January 13, 1922, there is being presented at another Boston theatre 'The Wandering Jew—The Most Amazing Drama of All Time.' The deathless stranger passes still, like night, from land to land.

CHAPTER XV

WEFTS AND SPECTRES

DÆMONS and Cain and the Wandering Jew are venerable figments, but they have no inherent associations with the sea. Yet the sea has its own brood of legends. And 'The Ancient Mariner' is a sea-tale *par excellence*. Coleridge, moreover, Devon-born and sometime citizen of Bristol, passed, boy and man, his most impressionable years at the ancient fountain-heads of British nautical tradition. Is it probable that to anyone thus born and bred some current terms and superstitions of the sea should not have come by word of mouth, or that, if the auditor were Samuel Taylor Coleridge, they should not have left both deep and permanent impressions? And if such impressions did, indeed, lie dormant in Coleridge's memory, what was apt to happen when a tale which was the very abstract of the mystery and terror of the sea began to clothe itself in concrete imagery? These are for the moment hypothetical questions only. On the hint, however, which they afford, let us come back from another angle to the poem.

I

There is a line in the first version of 'The Ancient Mariner' which has, I suspect, a curious bearing on our questions. In 1798 the first stanza of Part Two read as follows:

> The Sun came up upon the right,
> Out of the Sea came he;
> *And broad as a weft* upon the left
> Went down into the Sea.[1]

The reviewer in the *British Critic* for October, 1799, declared that 'the author, who is confidently said to be Mr. Coleridge, is not correctly versed in the old language which he undertakes to employ. "Noises of a *swound*" . . . and "broad as a *Weft,*" are both nonsensical.'[2] In the second edition of *Lyrical Ballads* (1800) Coleridge obligingly struck out both phrases. The inspired line 'Like noises in a swound' (with the change from 'of' to 'in') was happily afterwards restored. But 'broad as a weft' disappeared forever, and the close of the stanza has ever since read:

> *Still hid in mist*, and on the left
> Went down into the sea.[3]

Yet the discarded 'weft,' like the rejected biscuit-worms and magnetic emanations, flashes its passing gleam upon the huddle of converging currents that were pouring—as if all the reservoirs of memory were opening at once—into the matrix of the poem.

For 'weft,' as here used, is not a literary word at all. It is a term of battle and distress and pursuit and capture on the sea—a word of glorious associations with that 'meteor flag of England' which yet terrific burns, and later with Leviathan himself, when 'his eyes are like the eyelids of the morning . . . and he maketh the deep to boil like a pot.' It belongs to the Fighting Instructions of the British Navy and to the log-books of the Anglo-Saxon whalers. Every British tar of Coleridge's day would know it—and to every British critic it would be nonsensical. It is, I perceive, a word to grow rhapsodical about, for half the danger and the daring of the sea is latent in it, and therefore it is wise to leave at once the general for the specific.

The term, after the way of words which live chiefly on men's lips, without the stabilizing influence of print to fix them, is found in many forms: 'waffe,' 'weffe,' 'waif,' 'waift,' 'whiff,' 'whift,' 'wheft,' 'wave,' 'waft,' 'weft.' That roll of variants alone would tell the story. Words do not so behave, when the convention of the printed page has set its stamp of uniformity upon them. How a term so rich in stirring associations escaped absorption into literary usage, I do not know. The fact remains that it did escape, and it came to landsmen, if it came at all, almost entirely through direct acquaintance with the sea. So far as I know (and this impression the *Oxford Dictionary* now corroborates), Defoe and Smollett are the only men of letters before Coleridge to employ it. I suspect that it reached Coleridge from the sea, along with other sailors' lore that will concern us in a moment. And so the word becomes a factor of some import in our problem. That amply warrants an attempt to catch its keen-edged flavour—an attempt in which I fear I should indulge in any case, for the sheer human interest of its crowded history.

In the beginning it was not (as Phillips later calls it in his *New World of Words*) a 'Sea-Word' at all. But even from its Scottish cradle it smacks of battle, murder, and sudden death. Its earliest known occurrence in the sense of a signal is in 1530, in the Burgh Records of Aberdeen. I shall give the entry in plain English, leaving its more pungent native Scots to the Notes:

> And, moreover, it is decreed and ordained that there be fetched four persons; that is to say, two to the steeple of the tollbooth, and two to St. Nicholas' steeple, and there to remain every day, so long as daylight lasts; and there to spy what manner of persons on foot or on horse, to what number, or in what gear they come to the town. And the watch that is in St. Nicholas' steeple to have a *waif* or two within the same; and when he sees any man coming to the town riding, if there be but one, give but one knell with the bell, and if there be two, two knells; and if there be more, ay as he can number them, so many men as he judges, to give so many knells. . . . And the watch that

> is in St. Nicholas'steeple, to put on the *waifs* that he has, toward the part of the town he sees them coming to, so that it may be known what gate and quarter of the town they come to.[4]

In 1562, in William Bullein's *Bulwarke of defence against all Sicknes, Sornes, and woundes* we read:[5]

> Then Ariadne rente from her, her womanly apparell, making a *weffe* thereof upon the end of a pole.

In 1600 the word turns up again in the Diary of Robert Birrel, Burgess of Edinburgh, this time in a grimly humorous setting:[6]

> The 2 of April, being the Sabbath day, Robert Achmutie, barber, slew James Wauchope at the combat in St. Leonard's Hill, and, upon the 23, the said Robert put in ward in the tollbooth of Edinburgh: and in the mean time of his being in ward, he hung a cloak without the window of the ironhouse, and another within the window there, and saying that he was sick, and might not see the light: he had aqua fortis continually seething at the iron window, till at the last the iron window was eaten through; so, upon a morning, he caused his prentice boy attend when the town guard should have dissolved, at which time the boy waited on and gave his master a token that the said guard were gone by the show

> or *waiff* of his handkerchief. The said Robert hung out a rope, whereon he thought to have come down; the said guard spied the *waiff* of the handkerchief, and so the said Robert was disappointed of his intention and device; and so, on the 10 day, he was beheaded at the cross upon a scaffold.

In this same year (still in Scottish records) the word is found at sea: 'And when you are about Half a Mile from Shoar, as it were passing by the House, to gar set forth a *Waff*';[7] and at sea, through the rest of its history, it remains.

Thirteen years later it is at home in England. Captain John Saris, in the Journal of his voyage to Japan, printed by Purchas, writes as follows, under date of April 6, 1613:[8]

> Towards evening I standing nearer the shoare then we were willing, but for this occasion, we had sight of a *weft* ashoare; the Skiffe was sent and spake with the Oran Caya, who said the Cloaves were readie.

In 1635 Captain Luke Foxe, in his *North-West Fox; or Fox from the North-west Passage*, is paraphrasing Christopher Hall's account in Hakluyt of Frobisher's first voyage:[9]

> The 19 [he writes] . . . they had sight of 7 Boates which came rowing from the East side to the Hand. Then they returned on shipboard and sent their Boate with 5 men to see which way they tooke, and so with a white Cloth

> *or waffe*, brought one of their Boates with their men in her along the shore.

Hakluyt has only 'and so with a white cloth brought one of their boates,'[10] etc., so that the phrase 'or waffe' is Foxe's interpolation. And it is interesting to observe that as late as 1894 Miller Christy, Esq., the Hakluyt Society's learned editor of *North-West Fox*, has this note on 'waffe': 'This word does not occur in Hakluyt. I cannot explain its origin.' Mr. Christy and the reviewer in the *British Critic* bear common witness, with a century between them, to the curious lack of lettered status of the term.

It is clear from these instances that a weft (or waft) was at first any 'cloth' that could be used to give a signal. And that is its sense in the first nautical dictionary which includes it—Sir Henry Mainwaring's *Sea-Man's Dictionary or Nomenclator Navalis* of 1644:[11]

> Also *wafts* are used for signs to have the boat come aboard (which is a coat, gown, or the like hung up in the shrouds). Also it is a common sign of some extremity when a ship doth hang a *waft* upon the mainstay, either that it hath sprung a leak or is in some distress. Any blanket, gown or the like hung out for a sign is called a *waft*.

And as 'a Coat, or Sea-gown, etc. hanged out in the

Mainshrowds,' it persists in Phillips's *New World of Words* as late as 1720, and so Bailey also retains it down at least to 1782. But more than a century earlier it had acquired another sense. And for that important meaning Falconer's definition, in his *Universal Dictionary of the Marine* of 1769, is sufficient for our purpose: 'a signal displayed from the stern of a ship for some particular purpose, *by hoisting the ensign, furled up together into a long roll*, to the head of its staff.'

Now in this sense the word stands in the Fighting Instructions of the British Fleet from Blake to Rodney—a stretch of a hundred and thirty years. And all the comment in the world is not so potent to call up again its stormy setting of battle-line and shattered sail as half a dozen excerpts from the Signal Books themselves.

> In case any ship shall be distressed or disabled by loss of masts, shot under water, or otherwise so as she is in danger of sinking or taking, he or they are to give a signal thereof . . . and the signal is to be a *weft* of the ensign of the ship so distressed.[12]

That, dated about 1650, is from the 'Instructions for the better ordering and managing the fleet in fighting' during the first Dutch war. In the Sailing Instructions of 1653 by Blake, Deane, and Monck, 'if the chief of the squadron come by the lee and make a *weft* with his jack, that then every ship of his squadron bear under his stern and speak with him';[13] and if strange ships are seen in the daytime, and the distance is too great to use the ensign, 'then you are to lay your head toward the ships or fleet you shall descry . . . and continue . . . making a *weft* with your top-gallant sails (if you have any) until the General doth answer by . . . making a *weft* with his top-gallant sail.'[14] In the Earl of Sandwich's orders to Captain Seymour of the *Pearl* frigate in 1665 we read:[15]

> And if the admiral make a *weft* with his jack-flag upon the flagstaff on the mizen topmast-head and fire a gun, then . . . all the squadrons . . . are presently to clap upon a wind and stand after him in a line.

Prince Rupert's 'Additional Instructions for Fighting,' in 1666, have this:[16]

> When the admiral of the fleet makes a *weft* with his flag, the rest of the flag officers are to do the like, and then all the best sailing ships are to make what way they can to engage the enemy.

And in the Duke of York's Instructions in 1672 the weft is the signal for discovery of a fleet, and for distress.[17]

Those are the instructions; here, in a contemporary news-item, is the translation of one of them into sharp actuality. I am quoting from the *London Gazette* of September 22–25, 1673:[18]

> Edinburgh Sept. 18. An English and Dutch Caper of ten

> Guns apiece having Rencountered on the Coast of this Kingdom, they Engaged, and continued a very smart Fight for several hours. . . . By some unlucky accident, the [English] Ship was blown up by her own Powder and so lost with all her men in her; The Dutch having lost all their Masts and Rigging, and of 80 Men, not left above 7 or 8, lay beating for four days together off at Sea, till at last being driven near the Shore, they made a *waft*, and thereupon a Fisherboat went off with half a dozen Men, and brought the Vessel [in].

The word turns up at intervals in the narratives of the voyagers. Basil Ringrose, in 1681, 'made a *whiff* to a Pinnace';[19] in 1708 Edward Cooke's 'Instructions for keeping Company with her Majesty's Ship the *Hastings*,' on his voyage round the world, give 'a *Waft* with his Jack or Ensign' as a signal of distress; to summon a pilot, he makes a '*Waift*'; and in 'The Dutch Admiral's sailing Orders,' among the 'Signals by Day' is this: 'Losing a Mast, or other Accident, that you cannot keep Company with the Fleet, make a *Waif* with the Ensign . . . and when he is assisted, he is to take in his *Waif*.'[20] In Philips's *Authentic Journal* of Commodore Anson's expedition, the badly disabled *Gloucester* 'made us a Signal by a *waft* of her Ensign.'[21] In Lockman's *Travels of the Jesuits* (translated from the *Lettres édifiantes et curieuses*) we read: 'Immediately we made a *Waft* of our Ensign, which is a Signal for those on Shore to return on Board.'[22] In that absorbing collection of human documents, the *Letters Received by the East India Company from its Servants in the East*, Captain Nicholas Down ton writes in 1612: 'in the morning we saw a small sail unto whom we made a *waft* . . . but he would not come near us.'[23] And as a signal of distress the weft appears and reappears in the Signal Books of the Navy down to Rodney's General Instructions of 1782.[24] Until the close of the eighteenth century, then, when new modes of signalling displaced the old, the word was a living term in the vocabulary of the British Fleet.[25]

Then it was taken over by the whalers. But this no less stirring chapter of its history, which comes to its climax in that titanic and unrivalled epic of the sea, *Moby-Dick*, lies outside our scope.[26]

Here, then, is 'weft'—a 'Sea-Word' if ever there was one; an alien ashore, to land-lubber critics a stumbling-block, and even (to one of them) foolishness. What, now, of Coleridge? For his use of the term leaves no question that the word was a living one to him.

One book at least which he knew thoroughly contained it. He had read *Robinson Crusoe* at six years of age,[27] and in that enthralling scene of the final rescue, where the ship held by the mutineers lies off the island, and Crusoe and the marooned Captain sit watching in suspense, 'we heard the ship fire a gun, and saw her make a *waft* with her ancient, as a signal for the boat to come on board.'[28] In the Second

Part, moreover, after they had sighted 'a great ship on fire in the middle of the sea,' and then had seen through the perspective glasses the lost ship's boats, 'we . . . hung a *waft* out as a signal for them to come on board.'[29] Those are vivid pictures in an incomparably vivid tale, and it is perfectly possible that Coleridge remembered them. It is quite on the cards, moreover, that he knew the word in Smollett. 'You see, brother,' says the irrepressible Captain Crowe in *Sir Launcelot Greaves*, 'how this here Clewline lags astern in the wake of a snivelling b—h; otherwise he would never make a *weft* in his ensign for the loss of a child.'[30] But Defoe's form of the word is not 'weft,' but 'waft,' and nothing in either passage gives an inkling of the specific sense which alone, in the Mariner's line, gives point to the adjective 'broad.' Nor does Smollett's use of the word convey any hint of extension in space. It is entirely possible, again, that Coleridge, with his passion for the voyagers, had run across the term in Basil Ring-rose, or Philips, or Lockman, or Cooke. But in none of these, with their 'whiff' and 'waft' and 'waift,' would he have found the spelling 'weft,' and from none of them could he have learned what his figure shows that he exactly knew—to wit, the form the signal took: 'an ancient,' as Scoresby years afterward graphically described it, 'tied together in such a way as to prevent its being extended up and downwise, but which does not prevent its horizontal extension under a breeze of wind.'[31] So far as I have found in my own reading (which, however,

I hasten to add, has left of necessity many stones unturned) the form 'weft' occurs only in Saris's Journal, in Smollett, and in the official naval documents. And the *Oxford Dictionary*, now at last available for the word, has added nothing more. But in Saris the weft was a mere 'cloth' waved from the shore; in Smollett there is no clue to its shape; and when Coleridge wrote, the Fighting and Sailing Instructions were inaccessible. It is still quite possible, of course, that he owed his knowledge of the term to books. But even 'a library cormorant,' like the rest of us, sometimes learns things by word of mouth. And Coleridge had once been a boy.

'My eldest brother's name was John,' he wrote to Poole. 'He went over to the East Indies in the Company's service; he was a successful officer and a brave one, I have heard. He died . . . there about eight years ago. . . . My third brother, James, has been in the army since the age of sixteen. . . . The ninth child was called Francis. He went out as a midshipman, under Admiral Graves . . . who was a friend of my father's.'[32] These were three brothers, and there were four more—William, Edward, George, and Luke. Of a family of eight boys, two went to sea, and one became a soldier. With the East India Company and the army in the family, and, the British Navy, in the person of a friendly Admiral, waiting at the very door, to what would such a group of 'little Actors' fit their tongues? Surely, if the youngest member of that Devon brood showed himself later curiously at home with unfamiliar nautical terms and the unwritten legends of the sea, it is not a matter to be wondered at. Nor would it be remarkable, either, if sailors' talk in the ancient port of Bristol had also played its part.

At all events, the phrase 'broad as a weft' is evidence enough that Coleridge's knowledge was exact. It is a Mariner who, in the poem, is speaking, and seen through the mist the dim, red sun, cut horizontally at its setting by the line where sea meets sky, calls up to the sailor, who now sees it sinking where it rose before, the image of the horizontally furled ensign, streaming lengthwise, sinister and red. And no one who knew the weft at all, as the familiar signal of distress at sea, could fail to catch in the Mariner's words their ominous suggestion. 'I shot the Albatross' was still sounding in the Wedding-Guest's startled ears, and the bloody sun itself was soon to stand, a portent of disaster, above the mast. No doubt Coleridge, to whom the term may well have been familiar as a household word, forgot his readers' ignorance. But the airy arrogance of the *British Critic* has lost us one of the great imaginative touches of the poem.

But the weft is not the only link between the poem and those traditions of the sea which are not handed down through books. At the heart of the action is the spectre-bark, and the Mariner's own ship is navigated by the bodies of the dead. Both are immemorial legends of the sea. Could Coleridge have learned at first-hand of these, as he seems to have learned of 'weft'?

II

On the 15 th of April, 1819, John Keats let himself go, in a letter to George and Georgiana Keats, as follows:

> Last Sunday I took a walk towards Highgate and in the lane that winds by the side of Lord Mansfield's park I met Mr. Green our Demonstrator at Guy's in conversation with Coleridge—I joined them, after enquiring by a look whether it would be agreeable—I walked with him at his alderman-after-dinner pace for near two miles I suppose. In those two Miles he broached a thousand things—let me see if I can give you a list—Nightingales, Poetry—on Poetical Sensation—Metaphysics—Different genera and species of Dreams—Nightmare—a dream accompanied with a sense of touch—single and double touch—a dream related—First and second consciousness—the difference explained between will and Volition—so many metaphysicians from a want of smoking the second consciousness—Monsters—the Kraken—Mermaids—Southey believes in them—Southey's belief too much diluted[33]—a Ghost story—Good morning—I heard his voice as he came towards me—I heard it as he moved away—I had heard it all the interval—if it may be called so. He was civil enough to ask me to call on him at Highgate. Good night![34]

Why the Coleridgeans have let that priceless document

fust unused it would be hard to say. It is the Note Book in miniature, twenty-odd years after; it is a little precinct of that very chaos which, through fourteen mortal chapters, we have been traversing; it is a fleeting glimpse of the mighty fountain which once flung up enchanted fragments in the symphony and song of 'Kubla Khan'—now jetting automatically in peripatetic prose. Many pages back we saw how bits of Priestley's *Opticks* swam up to memory, like bubbles through still water, in the order of their first impression on Coleridge's mind.[35] Turn, if you will, to the *Anima Poetæ*, and read, from the Notes of 1811–12, the remarks on nightmare, a dream accompanied with a sense of touch, single and double touch[36]—all set down in the very sequence in which, on an April Sunday seven years later, they reappeared. Keats was intent on an entertaining item in a letter; what he further did, unwittingly, but with luminous precision, was to catch and fix indelibly the basic idiosyncrasy of Coleridge's mind. And the meeting in the winding lane had also a strange sequel, long after Keats was dead, which throws yet another ray of light on those same pregnant mental processes. But that comes later in the story,[37] and meantime the letter, in its bearing on our present purpose, is still hanging fire. The Coleridge who talked to Keats, twenty-one years after 'The Ancient Mariner' was written, showed a marked predilection for the supernatural, and especially for the superstitions of the sea—monsters, and Krakens, and Mermaids. And he still had things to say about the proper attitude of mind to cherish towards them. Now let us go back to an earlier conversation.

In 1798, just before Coleridge left for Germany, William Hazlitt paid him a memorable visit at Nether Stowey. At the moment Wordsworth was in Bristol. The day before he returned—wearing the brown fustian jacket and striped pantaloons which, together with his 'northern *burr*, like the crust on wine,' Hazlitt remembered after an interval of twenty years—Coleridge talked to his visitor about him. 'He lamented,' says Hazlitt, 'that Wordsworth was not prone enough to believe in the traditional superstitions of the place, and that there was something corporeal, a *matter-of-fact-ness*, a clinging to the palpable, or often to the petty, in his poetry, in consequence.'[38] Taken in conjunction with what Coleridge said to Keats about Southey twenty-one years later, that is a rather significant statement. Coleridge's insistence on both Wordsworth's and Southey's incomplete suspension of disbelief in popular traditions (which in Wordsworth's case.were specifically 'the traditional superstitions *of the place*') betrays his own attitude. Nobody who held such views was likely to be indifferent to the local traditions of a place in which his own lot was cast. There is ample evidence of Coleridge's profound interest in Obi witchcraft, and Greenland magic, and the medicine-men of the Copper Indians, and of their immediate influence on his poetry.[39] But the palpable implications of his remarks to Keats, and especially to Hazlitt, seem never to have been taken into account.

Now Bristol's traditions had their roots in its maritime history from the great days of the Cabots, and the Armada, and Captain Thomas James, to the period when the city was, as Defoe depicts it, 'the greatest, the richest, and the best Port of Trade in Great Britain, London only excepted.'[40] Samuel Pepys, who enjoyed there in 1668 'plenty of brave wine, and above all Bristol milk' (a beverage which would have warmed the cockles of Falstaff's heart), found the town 'in every respect another London,' and the quay 'a most large and noble place.'[41] Defoe observed that the Bristol merchants, 'being raised by good Fortune, and Prizes taken in the Wars, from Masters of Ships, and blunt Tars, have imbibed the Manners of these rough Gentlemen so strongly, that they transmit it to their Descendents'; and (he adds) 'they say, above 3000 Sail of Ships belong to that Port.'[42] Pope wrote Mrs. Martha Blount[43] that he saw there 'a key along the old wall, with houses on both sides, and, in the middle of the street, as far as you can see, hundreds of ships, their masts as thick as they can stand by one another, which is the oddest and most surprising sight imaginable. This street is fuller of them than the Thames from London Bridge to Deptford.'[44] It was two Bristol ships, the *Duke* and the *Duchess*, which, in their privateering expedition around the world in 1708–11, under Captain Woodes Rogers, rescued from his desert island Alexander Selkirk;[45] and Bristol mariners had their share in a tale as immortal as

'The Ancient Mariner.' Nor was it strange that privateering, eighteenth-century Bristol gave to Stevenson the background for *Robinson Crusoe's* rival, *Treasure Island.* The Bristol of the 1790's had three hundred years of sailors' yarns behind it.

And here is one of them, which, through a happy accident, has lived. George Sandys, in that seventeenth-century translation of Ovid's Metamorphoses which so enriched John Keats, is commenting on the tale of Bacchus and the 'Tyrrhen Pirats,' with remarks on 'the miracles of the ship *sticking* fast in the midst of the deepe' ('Day after day, day after day, We *stuck*, nor breath nor motion'), and on the legends of the Remora. 'But,' he observes in the end, 'these strange effects, which perhaps depend on no naturall causes, may rather proceed from the power of the Divell.' Then he adduces a modern instance, which brings rare grist to our mill:

> I have heard of sea-faring men, and some of that Citty, how a Quarter-master in a Bristol ship, then trading in the Streights, going downe into the Hold, saw a sort of women, his knowne neighbors, making merry together, and taking their cups liberally: who having espied him, and threatning that he should repent their discovery, vanished suddenly out of sight; who thereupon was lame ever after. The ship having made her voyage; now homeward bound, and neere her harbour, *stuck* fast in the deepe Sea . . . before a fresh gaile, to their no small amazement; nor for all they could doe, together with the

> helpe that came from the shoare, could they get her loose, untill one . . . shov'd her off with his shoulder, (perhaps one of those whom they vulgarly call Wise-men, who doe good a bad way, and undoe the inchantments of others) At their arivall the Quarter-master accused these women: who were arraigned, and convicted by their own confessions; for which five and twenty were executed.[46]

There, then, is one of 'the traditional superstitions of the place' in which Coleridge spent the early years of his creative prime. Could such things be, and overcome him like a summer's cloud, without his special wonder? Even during his Cambridge days he had written Mary Evans about a walk on which he and his friend Middleton had got lost at night.

> 'We spy'd something white moving across the common. . . . It proved to be a man with a white bundle . . . The man was as glad of our company as we of his—for, it seemed, the poor fellow was afraid of Jack o'Lanthorns—*the superstition of this county* attributing a kind of fascination to those wandering vapours, so that whoever fixes his eyes on them is forced by some irresistible impulse to follow them. *He entertained us with many a dreadful tale.*'[47]

That was in 1792. As early as 1793 he was interested in the 'superstition [among] the lower orders of the people in

Devonshire' about the Pixies, and in the 'Songs of the Pixies' turned it to account;[48] in 1798, in 'Frost at Midnight,' he gave profoundly imaginative expression to the superstition, current 'in all parts of the kingdom,' which confers on the film that flutters on the grate the name of 'stranger';[49] again in 1798, in 'Recantation,' he made racy use of 'the superstition of the West-Countries' regarding the two ways of fighting with the Devil;[50] and his letters from Germany rehearse traditional superstitions of half a dozen places which he visited—notably the graphic and edifying tale of 'the under petticoat of leather that the devil took from the woman' of Goslar who unluckily mistook midnight for matins.[51] Carlyon, too, in his reminiscences of that carefree Hartzreise of which Coleridge himself has left so vivid an account, tells how Coleridge, in pursuit of a rollicking scheme to astonish the natives, 'after corning over the respective merits of several nonsensical stories which he had in some corner of his brain—such as the tragical ballad of 'Titty mouse brim,' . . . the story of Dr. Daniel Dodds, and his horse Knobs, who drank the wine-dregs at the Dapple Dog, in Doncaster, etc. etc.[52] . . . concluded by giving the preference to *a narrative connected with the traditions of his own native parish.*' And the yarn which he spun for the assembled rustics had to do with a Mistress Moll Row who was reputed to be a witch, and with an old black cat which played the part of her familiar.[53] That was in 1799. And the youth who earlier talked till three o'clock in the morning with a stranger smoking in the chimney-corner of a pot-house;[54] who revelled in the Welsh democrat with the itch at the inn at Bala,[55] and in the lank and greasy tallow-chandler of Birmingham;[56] who talked at Bristol about Indians, and bisons and mosquitoes with the 'most intelligent young man' who had spent five years in America;[57] and who left a manuscript note on 'a common superstition among sailors'[58]—this was not the man to live in a town which was a clearing-house for nautical traditions, and pick up no stories of the sea.* With such likelihood as this implies to lead us, let us come back to the end which justifies this marshalling of particulars—to the ways of the shaping spirit with its incredible materials.

III

The most dramatic of the seven sections of 'The Ancient Mariner' is the third, in which the spectre-bark comes onward without wind or tide, pauses, and shoots away. Now the spectre-bark is the 'skeleton ship, with figures in it,' of Cruikshank's 'strange dream.'[59] So much we know on Wordsworth's testimony. But on the evidence of the poem itself we know far more. For the spectre-bark has evidently been dipped deep in the stuff of other dreams than Cruikshank's. No phantom of that amiable bailiff's sleep, we may be sure, was ever convoyed across enchanted seas by trooping spectra of weary Arctic nights, and of constricting thirst in Wales, and of restless cobwebs on the Quantocks, and of darting stars and gleaming sails that Mary Wollstonecraft and poor mad Gilbert knew, and of sunsets seen by proxy in the West Indies and on the Nile, and of a bewildering moon that once hung over Boston with a star within the horns of it. Yet all these and more flash from the page like the glancing of gossamer sails as the 'plankless spectre' comes and passes. Whatever else about Cruikshank's skeleton ship we do *not* know, one thing at least is obvious: it has been dropped, like Shelvocke's albatross and the germ of the Mariner himself, into what Coleridge would have loved to call, had he had a chance to better Henry James, the 'esem-plastic' waters of the Well.

It merged, without question, in those secret deeps, with unmistakable memories of the legendary apparitions of the sea. I have not the slightest interest in attempting to identify this tale or that as the 'source' of Coleridge's spectre-bark. Any one of a score of them, sleeping in his memory, might have sprung, at the touch of the remembered dream, into the immortality of that amazing realisation of the impalpable in which even spectral shapes, like floating ice or the disk of a vertical sun, assume the sharp-etched clarity of an after-image on the retina. The bark (it is quite enough to know) is more than the strange vessel of the dream; it is, besides, the authentic phantom ship of the traditional superstitions of the sea.[61] The thousand sail of that ghostly fleet may here go uncatalogued; to list them would lead us far afield. But you may know them by an infallible sign—the sign which was patent, for example, to the mariners off Iceland in that 'merie tale' in Hakluyt which Dithmar Blefkins tells: 'namely that a ship of certaine strangers departing from Island, under full saile, a most swift pace . . . met with another ship *sailing against winde and weather*.'[62] Spectre ships, in a word, are not subject to wind or tide. That token Coleridge also knew.

> See! see! (I cried) she tacks no more!
> Hither to work us weal;
> *Without a breeze, without a tide,* *
> She steadies with upright keel![63]

So, in a Cornish tale taken down by Mr. Robert Hunt, the phantom ship was seen 'with all her sails set, *coming in against wind and tide*.'[64] So, in still another story of the Cornish coast, which William Bottrell tells, the spectre bark is 'a black ship scudding away to sea, with all her sails set and *not a breath of wind stirring*.'[65] These are traditions of Coleridge's own west coast. And it was the apparition of an English ship which many saw and vouched for at New Haven, Connecticut, in June, 1647. 'About an Hour before Sun-set,' we read, among the marvels which Cotton Mather sets down in the *Magnalia*, 'a SHIP . . . with her Canvas and Colours abroad (tho' the Wind Northernly) appeared in the Air coming up from our Harbour's Mouth, which lyes Southward from the Town, seemingly with her Sails filled under a fresh Gale; holding her Course North, and continuing under Observation, *Sailing against the Wind* for the space of half an Hour.'[66] Nor is this the only significant detail. It was 'about an Hour before Sun-set' that the phantom ship came up New Haven harbour. 'Dans la plupart de ces récits,' writes that distinguished authority, M. Henri Gaidoz in *Mélusine*, 'le navire fantastique apparaît un peu avant le coucher du soleil.'[67] And in the poem too the spectre is punctual to the traditional hour:

> The western wave was all a-flame.
> The day was well-nigh done!
> Almost upon the western wave
> Rested the broad bright Sun;
> When that strange shape drove suddenly
> Betwixt us and the Sun.[68]

The skeleton ship of the dream, like everything else in the poem, has dissolved, blended with kindred shapes which tenanted the twilight zones of that tenacious memory, and emerged, a recreation. And among those shapes were the traditional phantom ships.

But Cruikshank's dream went voyaging on still stranger seas. Somehow or other it picked up the vivid climax of a Netherlandish yarn, invested it with the pleasing horrors of Mrs. Rad-cliffe and *The Monk*, locked it securely into the basic theme of the Wandering Jew, and then shot over the edge of the world, as a phantom sun's rim dipt. Precisely what the mysterious 'figures' in the lost dream were, it would take a new Astolfo to find out. But the last thing they are likely to have been is what they now are, after a sojourn under the fecundating influence of Coleridge's imaginative processes. If they passed unmodified through that ethereal alembic, they are unique in their intractability. We may safely assume that the figures of the poem represent a coalescence of the figures of the dream with other recollected images. And I think it is possible to be reasonably certain what some of these contributory recollections were.

There is an ancient tale, which belongs to the oral tradition of the Netherlands, of one Falkenberg, who, for murder done, is doomed to wander forever on the sea, accompanied by two spectral forms, one white, one black ('eine weisse . . . und eine schwarze').[69] And in a ship with all sails set, the two forms play at dice for the wanderer's soul.

> Six hundred years has that ship been sailing without either helm or helmsman, and so long have the two been playing for Reginald's soul. Their game will last till the last day. Mariners that sail on the North Sea often meet with the infernal vessel.[70]

A tale, then, of two spectral figures casting dice on a phantom ship for the soul of an eternal wanderer was current on the seas.[71] One thing is clear: somehow (in Devon, perhaps, or Bristol) the story had reached Coleridge, and had merged with Cruikshank's dream. Of the two ghostly forms in the folk-tale the one is black, the other white. The same contrast is heightened, with sinister effect, in the poem as it first appeared:

> And are those two all, all the crew,
> That woman and her fleshless Pheere?
>
> His bones were *black* with many a crack,
> *All black* and bare, I ween;
> *Jet-black* and bare, save where with rust
> Of mouldy damps and charnel crust
> They're patch'd with purple and green.
>
> Her lips are red, her looks are free,
> Her locks are yellow as gold:
> *Her skin is as white as leprosy,*
> And she is far liker Death than he;
> Her flesh makes the still air cold.
>
> The naked Hulk alongside came
> *And the Twain were playing dice.*[72]

Once more, it is open to anyone to insist, without the possibility of contradiction, that the figures in Cruikshank's ship may also have been two, one black, one white, and that these twain were likewise playing dice. But since there is not one of all the multitudinous impressions which we have so far seen swept into the orbit of the voyage that has not undergone incorporation with something else—a fact as significant as any which this study has disclosed—the chances are overwhelming against a reversal of the imaginative procedure here. And I hope I have established Coleridge's open-mindedness to the traditional superstitions of the sea, and charted certain channels through which nautical lore might easily have reached him.*

And once present in his mind, the two spectral forms were predestined, through their associations, to be drawn into the poem. Guilt-haunted wanderers—Cain and the Jew—were the theme which for the moment was magnetic in his brain. And here was a third of that feather, and this third *par excellence* a poster of the sea. Into the vague and tentative concept out of which the poem sprang—that 'Old Navigator' who set out, a bare *nominis umbra*, with Coleridge along the road to Watchet—there entered another plastic element. Wordsworth's pregnant hints, quickened through the concurrent agency of Schiller and Lewis and Gessner and Bayle, had worked their own momentous transformation. And now with the traits of the Jew and Cain there blended the appurtenances of still another fated wanderer—a wanderer for whose soul two unearthly shapes on a spectre-bark played dice. And so Death and Life-in-Death, casting dice on a skeleton ship (a ship made double sure through the coöperant associations of a dream) were added to the *dramatis personæ* of the poem.

But they are precisely what they are, and no longer the black and white lay-figures of the tale, by reason of the confluence of associations into which they have been plunged. The Mariner (it cannot be too insistently repeated) is no more Falk-enberg than he is the Wandering Jew or Cain. But all three figures are indissolubly merged in the conception, and, as was inevitable, considering what Coleridge once called the 'many folds of recollection as they come onward on one's mind,'[73] each has carried with it into the stream the associations of its independent setting. And with the Wandering Jew were bound up, in Coleridge's memory, the uncanny paraphernalia of Gothic romance—'the skeletons, the flesh-and-blood ghosts' that were spawned with the rest of that 'literary brood of the *Castle of Otranto*' which he had already dealt with in the *Critical Review*, and which his merciless scalpel later anatomized in the 'Critique on Bertram.'[74] For when he wrote 'The Mariner,' he was fresh from *The Monk*. And in *The Monk* the Wandering Jew is a *deus ex machina* brought into the tale to lay a most vividly realistic 'flesh-and-blood ghost'—a 'Spectre-woman' κατ' ἐξοχήν—'who thicks man's blood with cold.' At the approach of the Bleeding Nun, 'I felt,' says the narrator, 'a sudden chillness spread itself over my body. . . . My blood was frozen in my veins.' And always, at the fated hour, 'the same cold shivering seized me.'[75] The Wandering Jew and the spectre of Beatrice de los Cisternos could neither of them well be recalled without the other, nor Beatrice without her 'literary brood.' And when the phantom ship of Falkenberg was drawn, through its associations, into the charmed circle of the Eternal Wanderer, its shadowy crew found waiting within that circle precisely the shapes which fit the tale: to wit, a female flesh-and-blood ghost, and skeletons of titillating gruesomeness.[76] It is needless to heap up parallels. Coleridge, like Byron and Shelley and Jane Austen after him, was an adept in the mysteries of the Gothic cult.[77] And every reader of the tales that thrilled our forbears will recognize at once, in the two stanzas I have quoted, the familiar charnel horrors of the genre.

But in this case their mode of entrance is less important than the fact of exit. For in 1817 the superfluous skeleton horrors were ejected, neck and crop, and the powerful suggestion of three startled questions took their place:

> Is that a DEATH? and are there two?
> Is DEATH that woman's mate?

Nothing in the poem, indeed, is more remarkable than the sublimation, as if they had passed through some ethereal alembic, of the crudities which marred the formative elements of Coleridge's unique conception of the supernatural. And his momentary surrender to the unnatural, in the rejected 'Gothic' stanza, throws into sharpest relief the psychological verisimilitude which we have seen and have yet to see displayed in his final delineation of his supernatural universe.

And here is a single instance of the art with which that delineation is achieved. Cruikshank's figures, merged with Falken-berg's spectral escort and then metamorphosed into

Death and Life-in-Death, 'have diced for the ship's crew, and she' (who is Life-in-Death) 'winneth the ancient Mariner.' And now the old tale echoes through the new one like a distant bell. For the Mariner's fate at the fall of the dice is the fate of the Wandering Jew—*the doom of the undying among the dead.* And the infinitely subtle blending of the stories, half deliberate, half through the secret virtue of the Well, is complete.

IV

'I also suggested the navigation of the ship by the dead men,' said Wordsworth to Miss Fenwick in 1843. I'll take Wordsworth's word for a thousand pound, but would that the adoring priestess had made bold to ask her oracle, when the tide of revelation was in full flow: 'But what under Heaven suggested it to *you?*' That priceless note, worth an octavo of 'dear brother Jems,' is lost to us, and we can only guess. But a note that is not lost, appended by Wordsworth to 'The Thorn' in 1800, affords a tenuous basis for conjecture.

The imaginary narrator of 'The Thorn' is (as Mr. Hutchinson dubs him) 'a superannuated skipper,' or, in Wordsworth's less racy phraseology, 'a captain of a small trading vessel . . . who being past the middle age of life, had retired upon an annuity or small independent income to some village or country town. . . . Such men,' Wordsworth adds, 'having little to do, become credulous and talkative from indolence; and from the same cause . . . they are prpne to superstition.'[78] 'The Thorn,' we may grant at once, is the unhappy victim of its author's theories. 'It is not possible,' wrote Coleridge in dismissing it, 'to imitate truly a dull and garrulous discourser, without repeating the effects of dullness and garrulity.'[79] And 'The Thorn,' like 'Simon Lee,' enhances our eternal gratitude that Wordsworth, after his surpassing service in fecundating Coleridge's mind, left him free to work out his own conception of how a mariner should tell a tale. But we may still dally, if we please, with the surmise that some post-middle-aged mariner of England, with a predisposition to the supernatural ('the character,' says Wordsworth, '. . . is sufficiently common'), may in his retirement have held Wordsworth with his superannuated eye, and rehearsed for him one of those legends of the *Todtenschiff* which are current among the grim traditions of the sea.[80] At all events, the lineaments of such a tale are conspicuous in the first version of 'The Ancient Mariner,' and however else such a story may originally have come to Coleridge, we must assume, since Wordsworth claims credit for the notion, that it was he who at least recalled the theme to memory. In the Wordsworthian captain's own heartfelt words, 'More know I not, I wish I did.'*

Of one thing, however, we may be reasonably sure. Wordsworth's suggestions had the trick of awakening and stirring to intense activity Coleridge's sleeping images. Under their influence he was apt to 'kindle'—to use Dorothy Wordsworth's word.[81] Of that we have had abundant evidence.

It is, then, after all, in the 'confus'd Mass of Thoughts tumbling over one another in the Dark' of *Coleridge's*, not Wordsworth's, brain that we must seek our clue to the story as it now appears. And in a curious entry in the Note Book I suspect the clue is found.

But let us first be clear about our facts. 'The navigation of the ship by the dead men' is not an accurate statement of what actually takes place in the poem from the second edition, of 1800, on. Coleridge is now explicit to the point of fourfold repetition. It was *not* the dead men who were the navigators of the ship. When the Mariner tells how

The body of my brother's son
Stood by me, knee to knee:
The body and I pulled at one rope,
But he said nought to me—[82]

the Wedding-Guest with good reason suspects that the Mariner himself is a *revenant:*

'I fear thee, ancient Mariner!'
Be calm, thou Wedding-Guest!
'Twas not those souls that fled in pain,
Which to their corses came again,
But a troop of spirits blest.[84]

That stanza was added in 1800, and the gloss, which is also an addition, is no less unequivocal:

> The bodies of the ship's crew are inspired and the ship moves on; *But not by the souls of the men*, nor by dæmons of earth or middle air, *but by a blessed troop of angelic spirits*, sent down by the invocation of the guardian saint.*

Moreover, even from the first, when the ship drifts into the harbour, white with silent light,

> Each corse lay flat, lifeless and flat,
> And, by the holy rood!
> A man all light, a seraph man,
> On every corse there stood.[85]

And once more the gloss is unambiguous:

> The angelic spirits leave the dead bodies, And appear in their own forms of light.

The ship is navigated by *a troop of angelic spirits*. The bodies of the dead are but their instruments. And that is a radical modification of the original proposal. Whither, then, had Wordsworth's hint this time sent Coleridge's shaping spirit among its myriad recollections?

There stands in the Note Book, between, a memorandum on the Swedenborgian's Reveries and another on the drunkenness of Cato, this singular entry:

> Mem—To remember to examine into the Laws upon Wrecks as at present existing.[86]

Coleridge, then, had at some time been interested in those laws '*as at present existing.*' It is not an unwarranted inference from the phraseology of the note that this interest had been stirred by something which had come to his attention involving *earlier* legal usages with reference to wrecks. That this was something which he had *read* is *a priori* likely, and the probability is heightened by a note which he actually left, in the summer of 1830, in Mr. Gillman's copy of *Robinson Crusoe.* He read in Defoe: 'To think that this was all my own, that I was king and lord of all this country indefeasibly,' etc. And he wrote: 'By the by, *what is the law of England respecting this?* Suppose I had discovered, or been wrecked on an uninhabited island, would it be mine or the kings?'[88] The entry in the Note Book and the query in *Robinson Crusoe* are of a piece. Is it possible to make out what inspired the earlier memorandum?

There is a document which answers all requirements—a document, too, which seventy years ago was adduced as one of the sources of the poem. The powerful confirmatory evidence of the Note Book was then inaccessible. With its support the old conjecture acquires, I think, a new significance.

In 1853 an anonymous writer in *The Gentleman's Magazine* ventured the bold suggestion that in a fourth-century Latin epistle of Paulinus, Bishop of Nola, to Macarius, vice-prefect of Rome, 'will be found the origin of that immortal song ["The Rime of the Ancient Mariner"].'[89] The occasion of the epistle he summarizes with exactness from the information which the document itself affords:

> A vessel laden with corn, the property of one Secundinianus, was driven by stress of weather into harbour on the coast of Lucania: the land adjoining to which belonged to Postumianus—a Christian senator. The factor of Postumianus, *looking on the vessel as a wreck*, had seized upon the cargo, and being summoned before the provincial judge had repelled by force the summoning officers and fled to Rome. The letter of Paulinus entreats the vice-prefect to represent the matter in such a light to Postumianus as would induce him to surrender the cargo without further litigation: the ground for claiming this indulgence being the miraculous preservation of the vessel from the perils of the ocean.[90]

What the skilful epitomizer could not know, however, was the existence of a memorandum of Coleridge's apparently suggested by just such an incident. For the question which this curious problem of the legal status of an ancient wreck would be sure to raise in Coleridge's mind (especially if other matters in the letter had strongly aroused his interest) is precisely the question which is jotted down for further investigation in the Note Book. Were there, then, other particulars of the epistle which Coleridge, with his falcon's eye for the stuff of poetry, would have found uncommonly suggestive?

It will be best to let Paulinus tell the story for himself—with considerate excision of the wealth of pious comment with which the good bishop interlards his narrative. The ship of the tale was overtaken by a storm, and the panic-stricken crew, having taken to the boats, were lost. And now I shall follow the translation of the writer in *The Gentleman's Magazine.*

> One only, an old man who was working at the pump, was left behind. . . . Meanwhile the ship, thus bereft of crew and anchors, drifted out into the open sea. The old man, who knew nothing of what had happened, felt the vessel pitching and rolling, and coming up from the hold found there was *no object within view but the sea and the sky. The feeling of loneliness increased the terror which the perils that surrounded him naturally inspired.* Six whole days and nights he passed without breaking bread . . . *longing only for death to close the dreary scene.* . . . At length our dear Lord . . . deigned to visit the old man in his misery. . . .
>
> Thus tenderly summoned, the mariner would rouse himself, but scarce could he leap forward when he saw that *angelic hands were, busy about his task. No sooner did he touch a rope than the sail ran along the yard, and stood swelling out, the mizzen was set, and the ship made way.* . . . Nothing was left for the mariner to do but to sit admiring *while his labour was forestalled by invisible*

hands. . . . Sometimes indeed it was vouchsafed him to behold an armed band—one may suppose of heavenly soldiers—who kept their watches on the deck and acted in all points as seamen. What crew indeed but a crew of angels was worthy to work that vessel which was steered by the Pilot of the world? . . .

Devious was the course of that vessel, driven by tempests from sea to sea. First it drew near the Imperial City, *where the lighthouse at the harbour caught the wanderer's eye;* next, ran along the coast of Campania; then, seized by a whirlwind, was carried across to the African shore. There another whirlwind caught it and bore it back to the Sicilian coast, where the sea is made rough and boisterous by the numerous islands. Those waters indeed are dangerous even for ships steered by the most able pilots; *yet this vessel, undirected save by the Holy Spirit, avoided every shoal and quicksand*, and kept to the deep water, skilfully choosing each needful turn and winding. At length, after twenty-three days, by God's good grace, it made an end of its perilous course on the Lucanian shore. When now near to land the Eternal Lord did not again neglect to display His enduring mercies. Inspired by Him, *some fishermen put forth from land;* they were in two small boats, and, *seeing the ship in the offing, were in the utmost terror and attempted to fly, for it looked, as they afterwards said, just like a ship of war.* With loud

> and repeated shouts the old man called them back; *they took counsel with each other*, and the Lord inspiring them, they understood they might approach the vessel without fear. *When they came alongside, though the old man assured them there were no soldiers on board, they would not believe him, and at last hardly credited the evidence of their own eyes.* He set before them a breakfast which, at the Lord's bidding, he had prepared long before. . . . The fishermen . . . in requital of the favour towed [the ship] in triumph into the harbour, as if it were returning from a conflict with wind and wave, and had its prow wreathed with the garlands of victory.[91]

That is the tale as Paulinus tells it. And its bearing on the poem warrants respectful consideration.

From the shooting of the albatross to the dramatic climax at the close of the Fourth Part, the impelling agency of the action of 'The Ancient Mariner' is *dæmonic*. From that point to the end the moving forces are *angelic*. The sharpness of the antithesis is blurred for the casual reader by the fact that the polar dæmon still for a time propels the ship; but it does so now, as the gloss explicitly declares, '*in obedience to the angelic troop*.'[92] The course of the action in the last three sections of the poem is determined by angelic intervention. And that shift of driving forces from dæmonic to angelic is an integral element in Coleridge's constructive design. What is more, it is, as it happens, no less his own salvation than the Mariner's. For the close of Part Four left even his fertile invention in a quandary. The Mariner had to be got home, and there was still half the globe to circumnavigate. The great loop of the voyage had superbly played its part, but that was ended, and in the process the wonders and the terrors of the deep had been used up. To throw a second loop around (this time) the Cape of Good Hope was unthinkable. And the loud bassoon could not wisely be pressed into service twice. What happened we know, for the triumphant solution is there before us. But *how* did it happen?

This, at least, is sure. The pious yarn which Paulinus spun, deftly adapted to the situation in which Coleridge now found his Mariner, fitted the exigent requirements of his problem like a glove. And with due allowance for these necessary changes, the story of the Mariner's miraculous homeward voyage *is* essentially the story of the ancient seaman on Secundinianus's ship. Both Mariners are sole survivors. Both ships are navigated by an angelic crew. Both crews appear only on occasion in their proper character. In both narratives the motive power of the vessel is supernatural. Both ships on their return are met from the shore. In both instances the boatmen believe the ship to be manned, and in both they are amazed, as they draw near, at the absence of a crew.[93] The agreement in the central conception of an angelic crew might be coincidence. The correspondence in subsidiary details is difficult to think of as fortuitous.* Add to all this the significant jotting in the Note Book, and the conclusion is well nigh inevitable that the letter of Paulinus gave to Coleridge the happy hint through which, in conjunction with Wordsworth's suggestion, the action of the poem was brought not only to a logical, but also to an expeditious end.[94]

But a greater than Paulinus was also present in Coleridge's memory. For he knew from his boyhood the matchless story of another wanderer's strange return by sea, and, as the poem grew, the *Odyssey* must have hovered in the background of his mind. And Ulysses is brought home to his native country ('Swiftly, swiftly flew the ship') in a trance:

> But now when bending to their work they tossed the water with their oars, upon Odysseus' lids deep slumber fell, sound and most pleasant, very like to death. . . . Safely and steadily [the swift ship] ran; no circling hawk, swiftest of winged things, could keep beside her. Running thus rapidly she cut the ocean waves, bearing a man of godlike wisdom, a man who had before met many griefs of heart . . . yet here slept undisturbed, heedless of all he suffered.[95]

Now read what Coleridge wrote:

> The Mariner hath been cast into a trance; for the angelic power causeth the vessel to drive northward faster than human life could endure.[96]

And as the Mariner, like Ulysses, sleeps,

> The air is cut away before,
> And closes from behind.[98]

Coleridge could not draw Ulysses's bow—but one hears the faint reverberation of Apollo's in the air.[99]

V

But Ulysses, once remembered, was not easily forgotten. And at one point the stories of Paulinus and the Mariner sharply part company. Secundinianus's ship comes safe to shore, as if its prow were wreathed with garlands of victory. But Coleridge knew better far than to take over that banal conclusion. And the supreme art of one of the world's imperishable *dénouements* was, as it happens, still fresh in his memory. He had been reading not long before the tale of the greatest of all wanderers by sea, as the profoundest imagination of the Middle Ages had conceived its ending. For on June 23, 1796, he had taken out of the Bristol Library the first two volumes of the *Divina Commedia*, just translated by the Reverend Henry Boyd.[100] That he was stirred to emulation by Dante's art is clear, for he proposes in the Note Book a 'Poem in three* Books in the manner of Dante on the excursion of Thor.'[101] And Dante's magnificently audacious reversal of Homer's happy ending of Ulysses's wayfaring by sea must have impressed him (as the formidable Boyer's pupil) deeply. Moreover, Ulysses's last voyage, as his restless shade relates it in the *Inferno*,[102] was into the unknown South:

> With measur'd stroke the whit'ning surge they sweep,
> Till ev'ry well-known star beneath the deep
> Declin'd his radiant head; and o'er the sky
> A beamy squadron rose, of name unknown,
> *Antarctic glories deck'd the burning zone*
> *Of night, and southern fires salute the eye.*[103]

So Coleridge read it in Boyd. And when later his own voyager in southern seas was stirring to life the hosts of dormant recollections, the great Dantean climax of the swift, dramatic foundering of a vessel which had safely tempted desperate seas was of their number. And so when the Mariner's bark reached the journey's end, instead of being towed, like Victor's, in triumph to its haven—

> The ship went down like lead.[104]

And with the echo of Dante there blends (as it is meet there should) a clear Virgilian note. As the ship goes down, a mysterious sound rumbles on beneath the waters of the bay. Then—

> Stunned by that loud and dreadful *sound*,
> *Which sky* and ocean *smote*,
> Like one that hath been seven days drowned
> My body lay afloat. . . .

Upon the whirl, where sank the ship,
The boat spun round and round;
And all was still, save that *the hill*
Was telling of the sound.[105]

Back from Christ's Hospital days there had flashed up to memory the great scene of the boat-race in the fifth book of the *Æneid:*

. . . *ferit æthera clamor*
Nauticus . . .
. . . *pulsati colles clamore resultant.*[106]

But what was this loud and dreadful sound beneath the sea? The answer, I think, is clear, and it takes us back, not this time to the *Divine Comedy* or the *Æneid*, but to that eager interest in physical phenomena—phlogiston, and electrometers, and electric light from plants, and haloes, and animal magnetism, and the 'Rumfordizing' of chimneys, and chemical reactions[107]—which led Coleridge to Priestley's *Opticks*, and Maupertuis's *Figure of the Earth*, and the notes to *The Botanic Garden*, and the *Philosophical Transactions*. Eighteenth-century science was still lingering in the stage of wonder—the harbinger of that imaginative interpretation of phenomena out of which eventually leaps discovery. And the *Philosophical Transactions*, as Coleridge read them, were often not unlike the naïf folk who, in the 'Squire's Tale,' are plunged into an orgy of wondering by the horse of brass:

> As sore wondren somme on cause of thonder,
> On ebbe, on flood, on gossomer, and on mist,
> And alle thing, *til that the cause is wist.*[108]

And at the close of Coleridge's century the *Philosophical Transactions*, in their quest for causes, 'wondred sore.' That is in part why they are such fascinating reading—to us, as they obviously were to Coleridge. Strange lights on the dark face of the moon, haloes and mock-suns and auroras, monstrous births, the dimly guessed mysteries of the lightning, phlogiston as the hypothetical principle of fire, tornados and tidal waves, volcanoes and earthquakes—all these and a hundred more are themes that enliven, often with an almost journalistic instinct for the sensational, their yellowing pages, faded leaves shed from the diuturnal tree of knowledge. And nowhere is that instinct exercised more tellingly than in the numerous communications upon earthquakes.

Martyn's *Abridgement* of the *Philosophical Transactions* is one of those works which would go far towards making a desert island tolerable. And the tenth volume of the collection (from 1743 to 1750) contains, under the catholic heading 'Meteorological Observations,' sixty-three consecutive pages about earthquakes.[109] They are, for the most part, records of personal experience, and they are characterized by that peculiar copiousness of realistic detail which the lucky participant in a disaster always revels in. The narrators are Fellows of the Royal Society (including its President and Secretary), and clergymen, and doctors, and lawyers, and gentry innumerable. I mean to quote them pretty fully; they will satisfy, I think, any curiosity we may cherish to know why a poet remembered what he read in the *Transactions*. And among the phenomena of earthquakes which they note, the *sound* stands out preëminent. It is like the noise of thunder,* or of the explosion of a powder magazine, or of cannon, or of a blast of rushing wind, or of the dull fall of a heavy body, or of a heavy vehicle rolling by.[110] But particularly, it is a *rumbling* sound. To Mr. Henry Baker, F.R.S., it was 'like the *rumbling* I have sometimes heard thunder make before a very loud clap.'[112] 'It is, I think, universally agreed,' says the Reverend J. Seddon, 'that an uncommon noise attended the shock, a noise that much resembled distant thunder, or a hollow *rumbling* wind.'[113] To the steward of the Earl of Cardigan, 'the noise that preceded the earthquake was . . . like the *rumbling* of a coach upon a bridge,'[114] and at the home of Sir Francis St. John, Bart., 'a *rumbling* noise was heard.'[115]

And this sound *moves*. 'We were suddenly surprized,' writes the Reverend John Forster, 'with a *rumbling* noise like distant thunder. . . . The noise . . . seemed to come from a distance, and *approached gradually*, in such manner as if a loaded waggon had passed along.'[116] So the Reverend Philip Doddridge of sainted memory declares that 'it is very certain, that all who felt the shock heard a hollow rushing noise which . . . seemed to come in a direction from the S.W. to the N.E.'[117] Moreover, 'a Shepherd belonging to Mr. Secretary Fox at Kensington, the sky being perfectly serene and clear, was much surprized with a very extraordinary noise in the air, rolling over his head, as of cannon close by. . . . This noise passed rushing by him.[118] But Robert Shaw, 'a very sensible Scotchman,' working at the moment in the Inner Temple, waxes emphatic to the limits of typography: 'He was just come into the garden . . . when he heard a GREAT NOISE, LOUDER BY MUCH than the noise of the explosions upon the proof of the *great cannon* at Woolwich, when full charged . . . nay, *louder, he thought, than* ANY *noise he ever heard* . . . the sound in the interim *rolling away* (seemingly from the water-side up towards Temple Bar).'[119]

And as the sound approaches, it *grows louder*. One Thomas Barrat (as the President of the Royal Society reports) 'heard . . . a noise, much like thunder at a distance; which coming from the N.W. continued some small time, *growing louder as it came nearer him*, and gave a crack (so he expressed himself) over his head; and then went off in the same manner it came on.'[120] And this sound is not only said to be 'very strong and awful,'[121] but it is also described in terms little short of startling to a reader of 'The Ancient Mariner.' At Ashley in Northampton divine service was interrupted. 'I really thought,' writes the minister, 'that part of the church betwixt the chancel and the pillar next to it would have sunk into the earth, with *a loud and dreadful noise* from a sort of subterraneous explosion. . . . After that awful noise . . . it *kept rolling on* seemingly from N. to S with an hollow *rumbling*, like thunder at a distance.'[122] And this statement is repeated three pages later in the *Transactions:*[123] the shock was 'attended with *a loud and dreadful noise.** Now let us return to the sinking of the Mariner's ship:

> The boat came closer to the ship,
> But I nor spake nor stirred;
> The boat came close beneath the ship,
> *And straight a sound was heard.*
>
> Under the water it *rumbled on,*
> *Still louder and more dread:*
> It reached the ship, it split the bay;
> The ship went down like lead.
>
> Stunned by *that loud and dreadful sound*
> Which sky and ocean smote,
> Like one that hath been seven days drowned
> My body lay afloat.[124]

It should be added that in three of the accounts on which we have been dwelling the shock was felt beneath a boat;[125] that in Volume Two of Lowthorp's *Abridgement* of the *Transactions*, 'one who was fishing in the channel,' at the time of the Oxford earthquake of 1683, 'heard the Murmur, as of a rising Wind . . . *rumbling* upwards';[126] and that both Narborough and Purchas mention earthquakes felt at sea.[127] There can be no question of the agency through which Coleridge reinforced his reminiscences of Dante and Virgil. With an art, the marvel of which grows upon one as its intimate workings are disclosed, he has retained of the earthquake only its mysterious and dreadful voice, as the herald of a swift and unerringly appropriate catastrophe.

VI

There is one detail which was passed over in its proper place, in order to avoid a break in sequence. But I do not wish to leave it out, for once more Purchas, whose crowded folios were to Coleridge (as to many another of us they have likewise been) enchanted ground, has contributed a phrase. One of the most inviting narratives in that volume of the 1625 edition which contains the heroic saga of Barents and his men, is entitled 'Observations gathered out of the First, Second, Third, and Fourth bookes of Josephus Acosta a learned Jesuite,* touching the naturall historie of the Heavens, Ayre, Water, and Earth at the west Indies.'[128] Its first chapter—'Of the fashion and forme of Heaven, at the new-found World, and of the Ayre and Windes'—is a mine of information touching the meteorology of 'the burning Zone.' It includes a long and illuminating discourse upon 'the Brises,' into which enters an elucidation of the baffling movement of a comet—the only explanation possible, declares Acosta, 'if it be not as we faine, that some Angell or intellectuall Spirit doth walke with the Comet, guiding it.'[129] And at the close of the chapter, with the marginal gloss 'Strange Story,' is an account of what happens in the high deserts of Chile and Peru.

> There runs a small breath, which is not very strong nor violent, but proceeds in such sort, that men fall downe dead, in a manner without feeling . . . [A certain] Captaine reported, that of a good armie which he had conducted by that place, in the former yeares . . . a great part of the men remained dead there, whose bodies he found lying in the Desart, *without any stinke or corruption;* adding thereunto one thing very strange, that they found a yong Boye alive, and being examined . . . saying that he desired nothing more than to dye there with the rest, seeing that hee found not in himselfe any disposition to goe to any other place, nor to take any taste, in any thing.[130]

The learned Jesuit's delightful excursions into meteorology would be among the last things in Purchas that either a dear lover of our early speech[131] or a would-be hymnologist to 'the Heavens, Ayre, Water, and Earth' would skip. And a memory like Coleridge's would not let go the strange story of one living soul that longed for death among the uncorrupted bodies of the dead. And it is not surprising to find on the Mariner's lips the downright phrase 'without any stinke or corruption' reduced to metre without diminution of its bluntness:

> For the sky and the sea, and the sea and the sky
> Lay like a load on my weary eye,
> And the dead were at my feet.
>
> The cold sweat melted from their limbs,
> *Nor rot nor reek did they:*
> The look with which they looked on me
> Had never passed away . . .
>
> Seven days, seven nights, I saw that curse,
> And yet I could not die.[132]

Finally, it is not without interest in its bearing on the association of ideas to observe that this same paragraph in Acosta ends as follows: 'As for the other kinde of ayre *which thunders under the earth, and causeth earthquakes* . . . I will speake thereof in treating the qualities of the Land at the Indies.'

Cruikshank, and Wordsworth, and nameless sailors on forgotten ships, and Monk Lewis and his tribe, and Paulinus, Bishop of Nola, and Dante, and Virgil, and Fellows of the Royal Society, and Purchas and his learned Jesuit—these are a goodly company. But the wonder would be long going from their astonished eyes, could they see themselves together, afloat on a spectre-haunted sea!

Yet sometyme it shal fallen on a day
That falleth nat eft with-inne a thousand yere.

VII

When Coleridge set to work on 'The Rime of the Ancient Mariner,' its plot, not unlike the budding morrow in midnight, lay, *in posse*, beneath a queer jumble of fortuitous suggestions: an old seaman, a skeleton ship with figures in it, a shot bird, a 'spectral persecution,' a ship sailed by dead men, a crew of angelic spirits. The formative design of the voyage, surpassingly adapted as it was to the incorporation of masses of associated impressions, possessed in itself a large simplicity of outline. The supernatural machinery (at the outset a thing of shreds and patches) presented, on the other hand, a problem complex to the last degree. I have tried to make clear in the last three chapters how, in the moulding of the separate fragments that underlie the plot, subliminal associations and conscious imaginative control have again worked hand in hand. And when at last the poem was completed, the plot which Coleridge had wrought from his intractable and heterogeneous elements was a consistent and homogeneous whole.

For the action has a beginning, and a middle, and an end. In the first half of the poem the agency of an avenging dæmon is in the ascendent; in the second, the prevailing power of an angel band. It is an overt act of the Mariner which precipitates the dæmonic vengeance; it is an inner impulse counter to the act which brings to pass the angelic intervention; and in the end it is 'the penance of life' which falls upon the rescued wanderer, a fated wanderer still. Exciting force, rising action, climax, falling action, catastrophe—all are there. And through the transfer to the Mariner of the legendary associations of the Wandering Jew, undying among the dead, Cruikshank's dream—its figures metamorphosed into Death and Life-in-Death—is built into the basic structure of the plot. And under the influence of another ship, sailed by an angelic crew, the suggestion of the navigation of the Mariner's vessel by the bodies of the dead is so transformed as to provide that cardinal antithesis of angelic and dæmonic agencies on which the action of the poem turns. And finally, by a stroke of consummate art, ship and poem alike are brought back in the end to the secure, familiar, happy world from which they had set out. The supernatural machinery is a masterpiece of constructive skill. But only, I think, in the light of the genesis of its component parts can the triumph of the faculty which shaped them into unity be fully understood.

Two of the three architectonic elements of the poem are now before us: the great curve of the voyage, and the mysterious agencies which underlie the plot. And with the third our study of 'The Ancient Mariner' draws towards its end.

---

* Did Coleridge know and avail himself in 'The Ancient

Mariner' of that wild, fantastic creation of folk-etymology and popular superstition, the 'Hand of Glory,' of which effective use has been made by Southey, Scott, Ainsworth, and Barham, and which has been current for at least three centuries? For a tentative answer I must refer the reader to the Notes.[60]

* The sign appears once more, with pregnant implications, in the poem:

> But why drives on that ship so fast,
>
> *Without or wave or wind?*

And this time 'that ship' is the Mariner's—itself now, like the Mariner, a partaker of the supernatural.

* Those who are interested will find other relevant tales and superstitions of the sea in the Notes.

* There is a baffling yarn which drifted to me from off the coast of the Argentine, that includes both the shooting of the albatross, and the ship navigated by the dead. But the albatross is palpably Coleridge's albatross, and the ship as palpably Hauff's *Gespensterschiff*, and the ancient Norwegian mariner who told it to a German ship's boy was clearly doing a bit of Coleridgean blending and fusing of his own. The thing is not without a certain interest, and I have said more about it in the Notes.[83] But I fear it throws no light upon 'The Ancient Mariner.'

* There is, it seems probable, an old book on Vampires mixed up with this gloss. But for that I shall have to refer the interested reader to the Notes.[87]

* For still other parallels, see the Notes.[97]

* In the MS. 'three' is cancelled, and 'one' written in above.

* I cannot forbear quoting the close of the communication of Martin Clare, Esq., F.R.S., who was one of those who heard the sound as 'the noise of a distant thunder': '1 am not certain the building near me moved,' he writes, 'but I fansied it did. My feet I am sure felt great emotion; and a large watering pot, of 9 inches base, that stood near me, was thrown all along, the moment the trembling ceased.

P.S. I have since discovered that my watering-pot was overset by a brick that was thrown off the house by the shock.'[111]

* Compare Lowthorp's Abridgement, II, 403, of the earthquake at Catanea in 1693: 'There was a very great and dreadful Blow, as if all the Artillery in the World had been at once discharged.'

* Did this, I wonder, echo in 'the learned Jew, Josephus' of the gloss?

CHAPTER XVI

THE KNOWN AND FAMILIAR LANDSCAPE

'DURING the first year that Mr. Wordsworth and I were neighbours,' the famous fourteenth chapter of the *Biographia Literaria* begins, 'our conversations turned frequently on the two cardinal points of poetry, the power of exciting the sympathy of the reader by a faithful adherence to the truth of nature, and the power of giving the interest of novelty by the modifying colors of imagination. *The sudden charm, which accidents of light and shade, which moon-light or sun-set diffused over a known and familiar landscape*, appeared to represent the practicability of combining both. . . . In this idea originated the plan of the "Lyrical Ballads"; in which it was agreed, that my endeavours should be directed to persons and characters supernatural, or at least romantic; *yet so as to transfer from our inward nature a human interest and a semblance of truth* sufficient to procure for these shadows of imagination that willing suspension of disbelief for the moment which constitutes poetic faith. . . . With this view I wrote the "Ancient Mariner." '[1]

The far-reaching significance of the paragraphs from which I have just quoted has met with universal recognition. It is, however, their vital bearing on the interpretation of a single basic element of 'The Ancient Mariner' which concerns us now. For if Coleridge's words mean anything, they mean that some interest deeply human, anchored in the familiar frame of things, was fundamental to his plan. What, in a word, *is* the 'known and familiar landscape' which, in the poem, persists unchangeable beneath the accidents of light and shade? Are there truths of 'our inward nature' which do, in fact, uphold and cherish, as we read, our sense of actuality in a phantom universe, peopled with the shadows of a dream?

I

Every mortal who finds himself enmeshed in the inexplicable or the fantastic reaches out instinctively to something rooted deep, in order to retain a steadying hold upon reality. That is the predicament of the reader of 'The Ancient Mariner.' There before him, to be sure, are the tangible facts of a charted course beneath the enduring skies. But the broad bright sun peers through skeleton ribs, and the moon glitters in the stony eyes of the reanimated dead, and the dance of the wan stars is a strange sight in the element. The most ancient heavens themselves have suffered, with the sea, the touch of goblin hands. But Coleridge's sure instinct was not, for all that, at fault. For through the spectral *mise en scène* of 'The Ancient

Mariner,' side by side with the lengthening orbit of the voyage, there runs, like the everlasting hills beneath the shifting play of eerie light, another moving principle, this time profoundly human: one of the immemorial, traditional convictions of the race. And it constitutes the most conspicuous formal element of the poem.

The last stanza of each of the first six parts of 'The Ancient Mariner' marks a step in the evolution of the action. Let us isolate their salient phrases for a moment from their context.

Part I: . . . with my cross-bow
I shot the ALBATROSS.

There is the initial act.

Part II: Instead of the cross, *the Albatross*
About my neck was hung.

And the consequences first attach themselves to the transgressor.

Part III: Four times fifty living men . . .
They dropped down one by one . . .
And every soul, it passed me by,
Like the whizz of my cross-bow!

The consequences pass beyond the doer of the deed, and fall upon his shipmates. And now 'Life-in-Death begins her work on the ancient Mariner,' till at last the turning-point of the action comes:

> O happy living things! no tongue
> Their beauty might declare:
> A spring of love gushed from my heart,
> And I blessed them unaware:
> Sure my kind saint took pity on me,
> And I blessed them unaware.

And then:

> Part IV: The self-same moment I could pray;
> And from my neck so free
> *The Albatross fell off, and sank*
> *Like lead into the sea.*

And so the burden of the transgression falls. But its results march on relentlessly.

> Part V: The other was a softer voice,
> As soft as honey-dew:
> Quoth he, 'The man hath penance
> done,
> *And penance more will do.*'

But the voyage, at least, has a destined end, and with the Hermit's entrance, a new note is heard.

Part VI: He'll shrieve my soul, *he'll wash away*
The Albatross's blood.

But even absolution leaves the doer, now as before, 'the deed's creature.'

Part VII: Since then, at an uncertain hour,
That agony returns:
And till my ghastly tale is told,
This heart within me burns.

I pass, like night, from land to land;
I have strange power of speech;
That moment that his face I see,
I know the man that must hear me:
To him my tale I teach.

The train of cause and consequence knows no end. The Mariner has reached his haven, and his soul is shrieved, and now (in the brief comment of the gloss) '*the penance of life* falls on him.' And with that the action of the poem, though not the poem, ends.

There, thrown into strong relief by the strategic disposition of the stanzas which disclose it, is the ground-plan of 'The Ancient Mariner,' as a master-architect has drawn and executed it. Through it runs the grand structural line of the voyage; and with its movement keep even pace—like those Intellectual Spirits that walk with the comets in their orbits—

the dæmons, and spectral shapes, and angels which are also agents in the action. Each of the three shaping principles has its own independent evolution, and each is interlocked with the unfolding of the other two. The interpenetration and coherence of the fundamental unifying elements of the poem is an achievement of constructive imagination, seconded by finished craftsmanship, such as only the supreme artists have attained. 'I learnt from him,' said Coleridge of his old master, Boyer, 'that Poetry, even that of the loftiest and, seemingly, that of the wildest odes, had a logic of its own, as severe as that of science; and more difficult, because more subtle, more complex, and dependent on more, and more fugitive causes.'[2] And that describes the logic of 'The Ancient Mariner.'

II

But the train of cause and consequence is more than a consolidating factor of the poem. It happens to be life, as every human being knows it. You do a foolish or an evil deed, and its results come home to you. And they are apt to fall on others too. You repent, and a load is lifted from your soul. But you have not thereby escaped your deed. You attain forgiveness, but cause and effect work on unmoved, and life to the end may be the continued reaping of the repented deed's results. That is not a system of ethics; it is the inexorable law of life, than which nothing is surer or more unchanging. There it stands in your experience and mine, 'known and familiar,' if anything on earth is so.

Now art works through illusion—'that poetical and artistic illusion,' as Amiel has it, 'which does not aim at being confounded with reality itself.'[3] But 'the groundwork of the real'[4] must somehow underlie it, or the spell fails to hold. And Coleridge has stated explicitly his aim in 'The Ancient Mariner': it was 'to transfer from our inward nature a human interest and a semblance of truth sufficient to procure for these shadows of imagination that willing suspension of disbelief for the moment which constitutes poetic faith.' As we read the poem, 'we know' (as Dryden says of going to a play) 'we are to be deceived, and we desire to be so.'[5] But we accept illusion only when in some fashion it bears the semblance of truth. And bound in with every living fibre of the poem, bone of its bone and flesh of its flesh, is a truth as old as Cain and as new as yesterday's experience. 'Yes,' we unconsciously say as we read, 'that is true to life—and that—and that'—as one who catches reassuring glimpses of the contours of familiar hills through the fantastic pageantry of cloud or mist. And disbelief, already wavering before the vivid reality of frozen and of tropic seas, is willingly suspended for the poem's fleeting moment—which is all the poet asks.

The sequence, then, which follows from the Mariner's initial act accomplishes two ends: it unifies and (again to borrow Coleridge's coinage) it 'credibilizes' the poem. Has it still another end, to wit, edification? I am well aware of Coleridge's homiletical propensity. Nevertheless, to interpret the drift of 'The Ancient Mariner' as didactic in its intention is to stultify both Coleridge and one's self. For such an interpretation shatters that world of illusion which is the very essence of the poem:

> Du hast sie zerstört,
> Die schöne Welt,
> Mit mächtiger Faust,
> Sie stürzt, sie zerfällt![6]

Coleridge is not intent on teaching (profoundly as he believed the truth) that what a man soweth, that shall he also reap; he is giving coherence and inner congruity to the dream-like fabric of an imagined world. *Given that world*—and were it not given, there would be no poem, and were it otherwise given, this poem would not be—given that world, its inviolate keeping with itself becomes the sole condition of our acceptance, 'for the moment,' of its validity. And that requirement Coleridge, with surpassing skill, has met.

But the fulfilment of the indispensable condition carries with it an equally inevitable corollary. For that inner consistency which creates the illusion of reality is attained at the expense of the integrity of the elements which enter into it. They too, no less than the poet's own nature, are 'subdued to what they work in, like the dyer's hand.' And once wrought into keeping with each other and with the whole, by as far as they have taken on the colours of their visionary world, by so far have they ceased to be, thus coloured, independent entities, with a status of their own. Even poetry cannot transform reality and have it, untransmuted, too. And through the very completeness of their incorporation with the texture of 'The Ancient Mariner,' the truths of experience which run in sequence through it have lost, so far as any inculcation of a moral through the poem is concerned, all didactic value.

For the 'moral' of the poem, *outside the poem*, will not hold water. It is valid only within that magic circle.[7] The great loop of the voyage from Equator to Equator around the Cape runs true to the chart. But dæmons, and spectres, and angels, and *revenants* haunt its course, and the Mariner's voyage, magnificent metamorphosis of fact though it be, can scarcely be regarded as a profitable guide to the fauna of equatorial and arctic seas. The relentless line of cause and consequence runs likewise, unswerving as the voyage, through the poem. But consequence and cause, *in terms of the world of reality*, are ridiculously incommensurable. The shooting of a sea-bird carries in its train the vengeance of an aquatic dæmon, acting in conjunction with a spectre-bark; and an impulse of love for other living creatures of the deep summons a troop of angels to navigate an unmanned ship. Moreover, because the Mariner has shot a bird, four times fifty sailors drop down dead, and the slayer himself is doomed to an endless life. The punishment, measured by the standards of a world of balanced penalties, palpably does not fit the crime. But the sphere of balanced penalties is not the given world in which the poem moves. Within *that* world, where birds have tutelary dæmons and ships are driven by spectral and angelic powers, consequence and antecedent are in keeping—if for the poet's moment we accept the poet's premises. And the function of the ethical background of 'The Ancient Mariner,' as Coleridge employs it, is to give the illusion of inevitable sequence to that superb inconsequence. The imaginative use of familiar moral values, like the imaginative use of the familiar outline of a voyage, is leagues away from the promulgation of edifying doctrine through the vehicle of a fairy-tale.[8]

It would be a work of supererogation thus to labour a point which Coleridge himself might be thought to have rendered fairly obvious, were it not that this rudimentary principle of the poem has been persistently misinterpreted. A distinguished modern critic, for example, after drawing from certain verses of Browning the inference that, in Browning's view, 'to go out and mix one's self up with the landscape is the same as doing one's duty,' proceeds-as follows: 'As a method of salvation this is even easier and more æsthetic than that of the Ancient Mariner, who, it will be remembered, is relieved of the burden of his transgression by admiring the color of water-snakes!'[9] Occurring as it does in a justly severe arraignment of pantheistic revery as 'a painless substitute for genuine spiritual effort,' this statement, despite its touch of piquant raillery, must be taken seriously as an interpretation of what Coleridge is supposed to teach. It is immaterial that the Mariner's admiration of water-snakes is not the means of salvation (to fall in with Professor Babbitt's assumption) which the plain words of the poem state. The value of the criticism lies in its exposition of what happens when one disregards the fundamental premises of a work of art, and interprets it as if it were solely a document in ethics. Carried to its logical conclusion, such an interpretation makes Coleridge precisely to the same degree the serious exponent of the moral fitness of the 'ruthless slaying of the crew because the Mariner had killed a bird'[10]—and that is the *reductio ad absurdum* of everything. Coleridge, in some of those all too frequent moments when he was not a poet, may well have betrayed an addiction to 'pantheistic revery.' But when he wrote 'The Ancient Mariner,' he was constructing on definite principles, with the clearest possible consciousness of what he was about, a work of pure imagination. And the fallacy of such criticism as I have quoted lies in its failure to reckon with the very *donnée* of the poem—'that poetical and artistic illusion which does not aim at being confounded with reality itself.'[11]

Coleridge expressed himself on the subject too. Fifteen years after the definitive statement in the *Biographia Literaria*, and thirty-two years after the writing of the poem, he came back to 'The Ancient Mariner' in conversation:

Mrs. Barbauld once told me that she admired the

> Ancient Mariner very much, but that there were two faults in it, it was improbable, and had no moral.* As for the probability, I owned that that might admit some question; but as to the want of a moral, I told her that in my own judgment the poem had too much; and that the only, or chief fault, if I might say so, was the obtrusion of the moral sentiment so openly on the reader as a principle or cause of action in a work of such pure imagination. It ought to have had no more moral than the Arabian Nights' tale of the merchant's sitting down to eat dates by the side of a well, and throwing the shells aside, and lo! a genie starts up, and says he *must* kill the aforesaid merchant, *because* one of the date shells had, it seems, put out the eye of the genie's son.[12]

There is no mistaking the point of that. Coleridge may (he felt) have carried his premises too far for safety in a world of Mrs. Barbaulds who yearn for a moral with their poetry, as they hanker after bread and butter with their tea. With the moral sentiment so patent in the poem they would be bound to put in their thumb and exultantly pull out their plum—as indeed they have. '*The obtrusion of the moral sentiment so openly on the reader* as a principle or cause of action in a poem of such pure imagination'—that was what gave Coleridge pause. 'The only, or chief fault' of the poem, as he saw it, was a fault of technique. Instead of procuring a momentary suspension of disbelief, he ran the risk of implanting firmly a belief! Of the historic Mrs. Barbauld he need on that score have had no fear. For her, even in the Mariner's valedictory piety, which does, I fear, warrant Coleridge's (and our own) regret†, the moral sentiment was not obtruded openly enough. Had the mariner shot a shipmate instead of an albatross, she would have understood—and there would have been no 'Ancient Mariner.'

For the very triviality of the act which precipitates its astounding train of consequences is the *sine qua non* of the impression which the poem was intended to convey. The discrepancy is essential to the design. And I really know no better short-cut to the comprehension of the poem's unique art than to imagine (as I lightly suggested a moment ago) the substitution of a human being, as the victim, for a bird. A tale the inalienable charm of which (as Coleridge himself perceived) lies in its kinship with the immortal fictions of the *Arabian Nights*, becomes, so motivated, a grotesque and unintelligible caricature of tragedy. Springing from the fall of a feather, it becomes a dome in air, built with music, yet with the shadows of supporting arch and pillar floating midway in the wave. For its world is, in essence, the world of a dream. Its inconsequence is the dream's irrelevance, and by a miracle of art we are possessed, as we read, with that sense of an intimate logic, consecutive and irresistible and more real than reality, which is the dream's supreme illusion. 'The events having no necessary consequence do not produce each other,'[16] Wordsworth complained in his deplorable strictures on the poem. The events in a dream do not produce each other, but they *seem* to. And that is the sole requirement of the action of the poem.

'Draw me, [and] we will run after thee,' cried the damsel, 'nigra, sed formosa,' of the *Song of Songs*. The proof of illusion is the acceptance of it. 'For me,' wrote Charles Lamb to Wordsworth, 'I was never so affected with any human Tale. After first reading it, I was totally possessed with it for many days—I dislike all the miraculous part of it, but the feelings of the man under the operation of such scenery dragged me along like Tom Piper's magic whistle.'[17] There, and not in the verdict of our critical inquisitions, is the touchstone of the poem. And Lamb's attestation, which anticipates the experience of thousands since, may serve as the last word on the illusion—and the 'moral'!—of 'The Ancient Mariner.'

III

It is the ways of the imagination that we are seeking to understand. And now, as the three great strands of the warp of the poem lie clear before us, let us pause for a moment and take our bearings. What firm footing is there in the bewildering region which our long adventure is traversing, where the paradox of conscious and unconscious, fortuitous and designed, confronts us at every turn? Is a poem like 'The

Ancient Mariner' merely the upshot of the subliminal stirrings and convergences of countless dormant images? Or is it solely the product of an unremittingly deliberate constructive energy, recollecting of its own volition whatever is necessary to its ends, consciously willing every subtle blending of its myriad remembered images? Or is the seeming discord susceptible of resolution?

Behind 'The Rime of the Ancient Mariner' lie crowding masses of impressions, incredible in their richness and variety. That admits no doubt. But the poem is not the sum of the impressions, as a heap of diamond dust is the sum of its shining particles; nor is the poet merely a sensitized medium for their reception and transmission. Beneath the poem lie also innumerable blendings and fusings of impressions, brought about below the level of conscious mental processes. That too is no longer open to question. But the poem is not the confluence of unconsciously merging images, as a pool of water forms from the coalescence of scattered drops; nor is the poet a somnambulist in a subliminal world. Neither the conscious impressions nor their unconscious interpenetrations constitute the poem. They are inseparable from it, but it is an entity which they do not create. On the contrary, every impression, every new creature rising from the potent waters of the Well, is what it now is through its participation in a *whole*, foreseen as a whole in each integral part—a whole which is the working out of a controlling imaginative design.

The incommunicable, unique essence of the poem is its *form*.

And that form is the handiwork of choice, and a directing intelligence, and the sweat of a forging brain.* The design of 'The Ancient Mariner' did not lie, like a landscape in a crystal, pellucid and complete in Coleridge's mind from the beginning. It was there potentially, together with a hundred hovering alternatives, in a *mélange* of disparate and fortuitous suggestions. To drive through that farrago, 'straightforward as a Roman road,'[21] the structural lines of the charted voyage, and the balanced opposition of dæmonic and angelic agencies, and the unfolding consequences of the initial act—that involves more than the spontaneous welling up of images from secret depths. Beyond a doubt, that ceaseless play of swift associations which flashed, like flying shuttles, through Coleridge's shaping brain, was present and coöperating from the first. I am not suggesting that Coleridge, on or about the 13th of November, 1797, withdrew from the rest of himself into the dry light of a 'cool cranium' to excogitate his plan, and then and only then threw open the doors to his other faculties, and summoned the sleeping images from their slumber. All his powers, conscious and unconscious, at the inception of the poem no less than while it 'grew and grew,' moved together when they moved at all. And there are few pages of this study which have not disclosed, directly or indirectly, traces of creative forces operating without reference to the bidding of the will. The last thing I have in mind is to minimize that obscure but powerful influence. But the energy which made the poem a poem, rather than an assemblage of radiant images, was the capacity of the human brain to think through chaos, and by sheer force of the driving will behind it to impose upon confusion the clarity of an ordered whole. And over the throng of luminous impressions and their subliminal confluences 'broods like the Day, a Master o'er a Slave,' the compelling power of the design. Whatever their origin, the component images have been wrought into conformity with a setting determined by the conception which constructs the poem. Through that amazing confluence of associations out of which sprang the shining creatures of the calm, strikes the huge shadow of the ship, lending the picture the symmetry which is the secret of its balanced beauty, and at the same time locking it into the basic structure of the poem. The breathless moment when the sun's rim dips, and the stars rush out, and the dark comes at one stride—that magnificent cluster-point in the chaos of elements has its *raison d'être*, not in itself, but in the incredible swiftness which the downward leap of night imparts to the disappearance of the spectre-bark. The bloody sun stands right up above the mast in a hot and copper sky, not for its own sake as a lucidly exact delineation of a galaxy of images, but as a great sea-mark in the controlling outline of the voyage. The images which sow the poem as with stars owe their meaning and their beauty to a form which is theirs by virtue of the evolution of a plan. Coleridge has, in Arnold's pregnant words, 'subordinated expression to that which it is designed to express.' And that is the eternal principle of form.

But Coleridge, it will be pointed out, has put himself on record against himself. For when the poem reappeared, revised, in 1800, he appended a sub-title: 'A Poet's Reverie.' I have no case to make, for the case is clear; but that incident has a history. For when one recalls that in this same volume was printed Wordsworth's meticulously numbered catalogue of the poem's 'great defects,' Coleridge's motive is not far to seek. If even Wordsworth (let alone Southey) was blind as a bat to the art of the poem, what of the innumerable company of Mrs. Barbaulds in the offing, fatuous and secure in their belief that the end of poetry is to *instruct* (*videlicet*, that 'a horse is an animal, and Billy is better than a horse'), and waiting serenely with their verdict of 'improbable'? Call the offending performance 'A Reverie,' and the wind is out of their sails! The inserted subtitle, read in the light of Coleridge's wounded sensibilities, was an exasperated sop to Cerberus. And in *Sibylline Leaves* it was struck out. But Coleridge had printed it, and it periodically returns to plague him.

Charles Lamb, who was neither blind nor fatuous, detected at once the fatal implications of the phrase. For in the letter which he wrote to Wordsworth, 'hurt and vexed' at his censorious reflections on the poem, he has this to say about the new sub-title:

> I am sorry that Coleridge has christened his Ancient Marinere 'a poet's Reverie'—it is as bad as Bottom the Weaver's declaration that he is not a Lion but only the scenical representation of a Lion. What new idea is gained by this Title, but one subversive of all credit, which the tale should force upon us, of its truth?[22]

Coleridge had leaped out of the frying-pan into the fire. For if Wordsworth and Southey and Mrs. Barbauld were impervious to a work of pure imagination, Lamb and his tribe were not. And in reckoning with 'the Barbauld crew,' Coleridge had reckoned without *them*.

But he had also reckoned without the facts. For if there is anything on earth which 'The Ancient Mariner' is *not*, it is a reverie. 'When Ideas,' says Locke, 'float in our Mind, without any reflection or regard of the Understanding, it is that which the French call *Resvery;* our Language has scarce a name for it.'[23] It has now, by the simple expedient of borrowing; but the thing and not the name concerns us, and Locke's description is exact. 'Floating ideas' there were—

> As thick and numberless
>   As the gay motes that people the sunbeams,
> Or likest hovering dreams—

in Coleridge's mind before the poem was, and at every moment of its long slow evolution.[24] *But in the poem they no longer float*. For through that wavering, inconstant flow has moved a controlling, conscious energy, accepting, rejecting, moulding them into keeping with each other and with a lucidly conceived design. Coleridge once spoke, apropos of Raphael's 'Galatea,' of 'the balance, the perfect reconciliation, affected between [the] two conflicting principles of the FREE LIFE and of the confining FORM.'[25] And in the resolution of the transitory freedom of the floating images of reverie (their radiance undiminished) into the permanence of union with the integrity of form, lies the supreme beauty of the poem.

---

* There is a gloriously volcanic outburst of Charles Lamb's which sufficiently elucidates both Mrs. Barbauld and her criticism. Lamb is writing to Coleridge in October, 1802: 'I am glad the snuff and Pi-pos's [Derwent Coleridge's][13] Books please. "Goody Two Shoes" is almost out of print. Mrs. Barbauld's stuff has banished all the old classics of the nursery. . . . Knowledge insignificant and vapid as Mrs. B's books convey, it seems, must come to a child in the *shape* of *knowledge*, and his empty noddle must be turned with conceit of his own powers when he has learnt that a Horse is an animal, and Billy is better than a Horse, and such like; instead of that beautiful Interest in wild tales which made the child a man, while all the time he suspected himself to be no bigger than a child. . . . Damn them!—I mean the cursed

Barbauld Crew, those Blights and Blasts of all that is Human in man and child.'[14]

† I fell back again with joy on Charles Lamb, this time remonstrating with Robert Southey: 'A moral should be wrought into the body and soul, the matter and tendency, of a poem, not tagged to the end, like a "God send the good ship into harbour," at the conclusion of our bills of lading.'[15]

* 'Every line has been produced by me with labor-pangs,' Coleridge wrote of 'Christabel' in a letter of 1800.[18] 'I turn faint and sick,' he wrote again, in a note preserved in the copy of the 1817 *Lay Sermon* which he inscribed to Southey, 'when I reflect on the labor I have expended on the mere endeavor to avoid or remedy imperfections, which not one in ten thousand would have noticed.'[19] 'When he [Coleridge] was intent on a new experiment in metre,' said Wordsworth to Mr. Justice Coleridge, 'the time and labour he bestowed were inconceivable.'[20] The poem, to be sure, is an even better witness than the poet. But no testimony is superfluous which helps drive home conviction of the part which labour-pangs, no less than the flash of vision, play in the framing of a work of pure imagination.

CHAPTER XVII

A SEA-CHANGE

THE host of floating images, then, each luminous one of them still seen as a several star, now shine in 'The Ancient Mariner' as a constellation. And that constellated beauty is no happy accident of genius. It is inherent in the very evolution of the poem, as through the endless, flashing play of these same images in Coleridge's mind there ran the pervading influence of an immanent design. But the imaginative synthesis thus achieved involves another element. Images do not stream up to consciousness in utter nakedness. They clothe themselves as they come—now neatly and precisely, now with the precipitate sketchiness of belated schoolboys tumbling out of bed—they clothe themselves, as they waken to consciousness, with *words*. For sleeping words share with the sleeping images 'that shadowy half-being' (it is once more Coleridge whom I am quoting), 'that state of nascent existence in the twilight of imagination and just on the vestibule of consciousness,'[1] which we have called the Well. And from Coleridge's vast and incredibly varied reading not images only but words no less sank by uncounted thousands into the spacious reservoir of his memory. There they lay, words and impressions in their mysterious interdependence, at the summons alike of chance or choice. And here in the world of accomplished fact is the rare verbal beauty of 'The Ancient Mariner.' What imaginative operations intervened?

Now I am well aware that the analogy between what I have just ventured to call the 'sleeping words' and what Dryden termed the 'sleeping images' may not be pressed too far. Words do not merge, in the sense in which images coalesce; their identity stubbornly persists. But, all metaphysical subtleties aside, they carry with them, as they sink out of immediate consciousness, the colour, the light, the atmosphere of each several whole of which they have been part, and they are vibrant in their intervital sleep to innumerable associations. 'Lamb every now and then *irradiates*,' wrote Coleridge once, 'and the beam, though single and fine as a hair, yet is rich with colours, and I both see and feel it.[2] With some such potentiality of swift irradiation words lie latent over the rim of consciousness, ready at the touch of this or that glancing filament of association to flash back to memory. There is 'a happiness,' says Polonius of Hamlet's replies, 'that often madness hits on, which reason and sanity could not so prosperously be deliver'd of.' And among the immortal things of verse and prose are verbal felicities which have leaped spontaneously into being with a patness and an infallibility which is often the despair of conscious art.

But an occasional unpremeditated felicity of phrase is one thing; the phraseology whose exquisite weave remains of a piece throughout a poem is quite another. And the diction of 'The Ancient Mariner' leaves, as we read, the impression of a *keeping* almost flawless in its integrity—a pervasive simplicity and clarity, as if through all the thousand secret blendings of words and images there had run one 'long level rule of streaming light.' Was that sustained consistency as effortless as some sky-lark's song, 'a-dropping from the sky'? Or was imaginative energy once more deliberately at work? The road to our answer lies for the moment, I think, outside 'The Ancient Mariner.' Coleridge was not forever writing poems, but he was eternally using words. And the ways of his mind in its extra-poetical dealings with words lead us straight to the heart of our problem.

I

Everybody who writes about Coleridge quotes that masterpiece of descriptive art, Carlyle's account of his talk.[3] But Coleridge's own candid and acute analysis of his conversational excesses is less widely known and more to our purpose, and I wish there were space for it all. It occurs in a note book kept at Malta in 1804:[4]

> The second sort [of talkative fellows] is of those who use five hundred more ideas, images, reasons, etc., than

> there is any need of to arrive at their object, till the only object arrived at is that the mind's eye of the bystander is dazzled with colors succeeding so rapidly as to leave one vague impression that there has been a great blaze of colors all about something. Now this is my case, and a grievous fault it is. . . . [I] go on from circle to circle till I break against the shore of my hearers' patience, or have my concentricals dashed to nothing by a snore. That is my ordinary mishap.*

On the soporific effect of the Coleridgean eloquence we need not linger.[5] It is the vivid delineation of a coruscating, dazzling exuberance of ideas and images which for us gives point to the paragraph. And with that polychromatic redundance of concepts and impressions which welled up from the nether deeps there flowed, *pari passu*, the 'tide of ingenious vocables, spreading out boundless as if to submerge the world.'

But there is another passage in this same note which is even more searching in its self-analysis:

> My illustrations swallow up my thesis. I feel too intensely the omnipresence of all in each, platonically speaking; or, psychologically, my brain-fibres, or the spiritual light which abides in the brain-marrow, as visible light appears to do in sundry rotten mackerel and other *smashy* matters, is of too general an affinity with all things, and though it perceives the *difference* of things, *yet is eternally*

> *pursuing the likenesses, or, rather, that which is common [between them].*[6]

That is like a two-edged sword, piercing even to the dividing asunder of the joints and marrow. For that is Coleridge—a spirit eternally pursuing the likenesses of things, led on by 'the streamy nature of the associative faculty,' until we are reminded (as *he* was by his own 'speculations on the esemplastic power') 'of Bishop Berkeley's Siris, announced as an Essay on Tar-water, which beginning with Tar ends with the Trinity, the *omne scibile* forming the interspace.'[7] There is good earnest beneath the jest, and we need not travel far afield for the thrill of confirmation. It is not every mind that can proceed, in the space of three lines and without lapse of logic, from the Platonic omnipresence of all in each to rotten mackerel! And since words and ideas subsist in inseparable conjunction, excursions from Tar to the Trinity by way of the *omne scibile* are apt to involve as their accessories phantasmagorias of words.

For that swift and tirelessly ranging play of association which we have watched drawing heaven and earth, the sea, and all that in them is within its compass, flashed incessantly through the cognate world of words. Sheer play, to be sure, its doings often were, but even the sportive operations of the faculty betray its bent. 'When the pure system of pantisocracy,' wrote Coleridge to Southey in one of those effervescent letters dispatched during the Welsh tour of 1794—'when the pure system of pantisocracy shall have *aspheterized*—from á, non, and σφέτερος, proprius (we really *wanted* such a word), instead of travelling along the circuitous, dusty, beaten highroad of diction, you thus cut across the soft, green, pathless field of novelty! Similes forever! Hurrah!'[8] Two years later, writing, as he remarks, 'with ease and *spirits* . . . under the immediate inspiration of laudanum,' he asks Tom Poole: 'Will you try to look out for a fit servant for us—simple of heart, physiognomically handsome, and scientific in *vaccimulgence?* That last word is a new one, but soft in sound and full of expression. Vaccimulgence! I am pleased with the word.'[9] I like it too; it is what Titania would call a 'sleek, smooth' word. 'What do you think of that case I translated for you from the German?' he wrote Sir Humphry Davy in 1800. 'That I was a well-meaning *sutor* who had *ultra-crepidated* with more zeal than wisdom!! I give myself credit for that word "ultra-crepidated," it started up in my brain like a creation.'[10] There we have it! Creations, verbal and otherwise, were perpetually starting up in Coleridge's brain, as irrepressible as the cockney's eels in *Lear;* you might knap 'em o' the coxcombs with a stick, and cry 'Down, wantons, down'—but still they coiled and swam. 'I envy dear Southey's power of saying one thing at a time, in short and close sentences,' wrote Coleridge once, 'whereas my thoughts bustle along like a Surinam toad, with little toads sprouting out of back, side, and belly, vegetating while it crawls.'[11] And sometimes (to shift back to his other figure) we are vouchsafed dizzying glimpses into those circles upon circles of association which used to break against the shore of his auditors' patience when Coleridge would talk—'talk,' as Carlyle heard him, 'with eager musical energy, two stricken hours, his face radiant and moist, and communicate no meaning whatsoever to any individual of his hearers.'[12]

Here, for example, is a fragment from a note-book of 1810.[13] I do not know to whom it refers. The preceding note in the *Anima Poetæ* is on Jean Paul, and it was probably he who this time set the concentricals revolving:[14]

> His imagination, if it must be so called, is at all events of the pettiest kind—it is an *imaginunculation*. How excellently the German *Einbildungskraft* expresses this prime and loftiest faculty, the power of co-adunation, the faculty that forms the many into one—*ineins-bildung!* Eisenoplasy, or esenoplastic power is contradistinguished from fantasy, or the mirrorment, either catoptric or metoptric—repeating simply, or by transposition—and, again, involuntary as in dreams, or by an act of the will.*

That (God save the mark!) is the faculty the ways of which we have been pursuing through ice and oils and animalculæ and earthquakes and their multitudinous likes. But where in the diction of 'The Ancient Mariner' is the kaleidoscopic play of prismatic vocables which might so easily have matched that infinite variety of images? What, in a word, held in check, through the vortex of impressions out of which the poem grew, those eddying streams of words which the 'giddy voluminous whirl'[15] of association was apt to fling up at any moment? There can be, in the light of the facts, little question of the answer. It was once more a selective exercise of the imagination, this time converting to its ends the *diction* of those very narratives of wayfaring and adventure the pages of which poured into the poem their store of *images*. Diction and images alike are modified, but 'The Ancient Mariner' owes its 'key of words' in large measure to the voyagers. How that is so we shall see more clearly if we first turn for a moment to the narratives themselves.

II

I have tried more than once—as who that has read them has not?—to capture the secret of the charm which the old travellers by land and sea somehow communicated to their style. Does it not lie, after all (we ask ourselves), in those engaging idiosyncracies of speech, with their pungently individual flavour, which strew the pages of the travel-books, as Martens's captivating 'Rose-like-shaped Slime-fish' strewed the sea, 'numerous as Atomes in the Air'? We read, and lay the book aside, and go about our business, and it is ten to one that the relish of some artlessly piquant turn of phrase lingers happily on our palate. The sharp tang of the style has the freshness of the salt smell of the sea.*

But that racy individuality of phrase and diction is not the whole secret of the fascination which the language of the voyagers exerts. If one seek farther, one will come in the end, I suspect, to a trait which almost all the earlier travellers have in common. And this common feature of their language is inseparable from the nature of their undertaking. It is, in a word, the way they have of clothing the very stuff and substance of romance in the homely, direct, and everyday terms of plain matter of fact. There was really little else that they could do. They sailed into regions of the fantastically new, and had words, for the most part, for accustomed things alone. And so the strange assumed perforce the guise of the familiar, and familiar terms took on enchanting connotations through their involuntary commerce with the strange. And all this is simply an old friend with a new face—a fresh aspect of that process of incorporating the unknown with the known, through which (as we have seen before) the adventuring human spirit constructs the never completed, always augmenting fabric of its world. And the language of the adventurers owes a large share of its peculiar savour to the workings of that vast enterprise of assimilation in which the great era of discovery was eagerly engaged.

Nobody ever put the romance of discovery more magnificently into words than Wordsworth, in a poem shot through with reminiscences of William Bartram's glowing delineations of strange beauty:[19]

> Before me shone a glorious world—
> Fresh as a banner bright, unfurled
> To music suddenly.

And again and again in the voyagers that sense of a new and wondrous world finds captivatingly spontaneous and naïve expression. Here is a rhapsody—the length of which will prove, I think, to stand in need of no apology—on one of the products of the western Indies:[20]

> But to proceed further, you Majestie shall understand, that in the place of the stone or coornell [of the coconut], there is in the middest of the said carnositie a void place, which neverthelesse is full of a most cleere and excellent water, in such quantitie as may fill a great Egge shell, or more, or lesse, according to the bignesse of the Cocos, the which water surely, is the most substantiall, excellent and precious to bee drunke, that may be found in the World: insomuch that in the moment when it passeth the palate of the mouth, and beginneth to goe downe the throate, it seemeth that from the sole of the foot, to the crowne of the head, there is no part of the bodie but that feeleth great comfort thereby: as it is doubtlesse one of the most excellent things that may bee tasted upon the earth, and such as I am not able by writing or tongue

> to expresse. And to proceed yet further, I say that when the meate of this fruit is taken from the Vessell thereof, the vessell remayneth as faire and neate as though it were polished, and is without of colour inclining toward black, and shineth or glistereth very faire, and is within of no lesse delicatenesse.*

The glory is departed from the coconut, and a prosaic world has relinquished one delight. But the 'Tree called *Coco*' shares honours on the same page in Purchas with the nightingale:[21]

> There are also many Nightingales, and other Birds which sing marvellously with great melodie and difference in singing: these Birds are of marvellous divers colours the one from the other, some are altogether yellow, and some other of so excellent, delectable, and high a colour, as it were a Rubie . . . being all so faire and beautifull, that in brightnesse and shining they excell all that are in Spaine, or Italie, or other Provinces of Europe.

The old mariners had, as Professor Kittredge says of Chaucer, 'such stupendous luck in always meeting nonpareils!'[22] Frederick Martens tells us of the mackerel: 'All the colours of this Fish shine like to a Silver or Golden Ground, done over with thin, transparent or illuminating colours. . . . It is the beautifulest Fish of all that ever I saw.'[23] He sees a mass of ice, 'curiously workt and carved, as it were, by the Sea, like a Church with arched Windows and Pillars. . . . On the inside thereof,' he goes on, 'I saw the delicatest blew that can be imagined.'[24] Thevet's fish 'like Samons' is 'coloured lyke fine Azure, in such sorte that it is impossible to excogitate or thinke a more fayrer colour.'[25] Basil Ringrose, at the island of Cayboa, after a sad experience with a 'Manzanilla Tree,' makes this note: 'Here I eat very large Oysters, the biggest that ever I eat in my Life.'[26] 'Under the Æquinoctial' they 'spied another Sail creeping close under our Lee. This Vessel looked mighty big. . . . In this Vessell I saw the beautifullest Woman that ever I saw in the South Sea.'[27] Captain James's ship's surgeon 'was diligent, and a sweet-conditioned man as ever I saw.'[28] Sir Walter Raleigh in Guiana was told of 'the Mountain of Christall': 'There falleth over it a mighty river which . . . rusheth over the toppe of it, and falleth to the ground with so terrible a noyse and clamor, as if a thousand great bels were knockt one against another. I thinke there is not in the world so strange an over-fall, nor so wonderfull to behold.'[29] Captain Pedro Fernandez de Quiros, in a petition to the King of Spain 'touching the Discoverie of the fourth part of the World, called Terra Australis incognita,' writes of 'the Haven called The True Crosse': 'Touching the Port, besides the commodities which I have alreadie discoursed of, there is one of marvellous pleasure and contentation. And that is, that at the dawning of the day you shall heare from a Wood which is neere at hand, a sweet and various harmonie of a thousand

Birds of all sorts, among which we could distinguish the Nightingales, Black-birds, Quailes, Gold-finches, Swallowes almost without number . . . and creatures of sundry other kinds, even downe to Grashoppers, and Field-crickets. Every Morning and Evening we received a most oderiferous sweet smell, sent unto our nostrels from the infinite diversitie of Flowers and Herbes.'[30] Commodore Anson saw on the island of Juan Fernandez 'a most charmingly beautiful little red Bird . . . the Colours in its Head so gloriously mix'd and glowing like Gold against the Sun, that it surpasses all Description, Imitation, or even Imagination.'[31] 'O, wonder!' exclaims Miranda—and *The Tempest* itself is bathed in the very atmosphere of the voyages, suffused in its turn with imaginative splendour—

O, wonder!
How many goodly creatures are there here!
How beauteous mankind is! O brave new world,
That has such people in't!

And Miranda's cry is but the echo of the wonder which lends its frequent charm to the old narratives.

But the charm is heightened by a constantly recurring paradox. For into almost every report of new-found marvels there is, as it were, projected, like the shaft of cool freshness which a mountain stream thrusts into the sea, some reminder of wonted and familiar things. And the homely and comfortable presence of cheese, and wheaten flour, and marmalade, and brood-hens in marvellous worlds of fiery worms, and Hottentots, and ambergris, and penguins is a source of unalloyed delectation. The engaging juxtapositions the unexpectedness of which delights us, symbolize the task at which the imagination is everlastingly engaged, and the mariners were often poets without knowing it. They carried (I suppose like most of us) their known and familiar landscape with them, and they had the trick of catching glimpses of it through the strangest lights. That I am speaking of the men who wrote the travel-books, and might be speaking of the ancient Mariner himself is a fact of which the implications need no comment. But the records themselves are more eloquent than all the generalizations in the world. It makes little difference what page we turn, but there is always luck (as Coleridge knew) in Purchas.

Oviedo tells, in his *General History of the Indies*, of certain little birds: 'This Bird, beside her littlenesse, is of such velositie and swiftnesse in flying, that who so seeth her flying in the aire, cannot see her flap or beate her wings after any other sort then doe the Dorres, or humble Bees, or Beetels. . . . And doubtlesse, when I consider the finenesse of the clawes and feete of these Birds, I know not whereunto I may better liken them, then to *the little birds which the lymners of bookes are accustomed to paint on the margent of Church Bookes, and other Bookes of Divine Service.*'[32] And *I* know not which of the two is the more charming—Oviedo's dainty Spanish humming birds, or Narborough's sturdy Saxon penguins: 'they are short legged like a Goose, *and stand upright like little Children in white Aprons, in companies together.*'[33] And the pictures are as typical as they are charming. Home-thoughts of Spain* and England—illuminated missals and prim little scholars—have slipped into alien tracts of new experience, and annexed them once for all to old possessions. And that happy interpenetration of old and new goes on unendingly. The Vicugnes of Peru, which 'are greater then Goates, and lesse then Calves' have hair, Acosta tells us,[34] which 'is *of the colour of dried Roses.*'† Monsieur du Montel's Sea-Unicorn was covered with 'a small soft hair; short as plush, and *of the colour of a wither'd leaf.*'[35] The 'great exhalation or whirlewinde of smoake' from a Mexican volcano 'ascends directly up *like to the shot of a Crosse-bow*';[36] the Sea-Crows on the coast of Panama 'hovering on the Sea . . . seeme to cover the same with *a blacke carpet of cloth or velvet*, going and comming with the Sea';[37] the amazing worms which harbour in the flesh of negroes on the 'golden Coast' of Africa are '*as thicke as great Lute-strings*';[40] venomous serpents of the Congo 'carrie upon the tippe of their tayle, *a certaine little roundell like a Bell*, which ringeth as they goe';[41] the natives of South Africa, in speaking, 'clocke with the Tongue *like a brood Hen*, which clocking and the word are both pronounced together, verie strangely.'[42] In 'a certaine little Iland, to the Southwards of

Celebes,' where Sir Francis Drake touched to grave his ships, there are trees 'amongst [which] night by night, through the whole Land, did shew themselves an infinite swarme of fierie Wormes flying in the Ayre, whose bodies being *no bigger then our common English Flyes*, make such a shew and light, *as if every Twigge or Tree had beene a burning Candle.* In this place breedeth also wonderfull store of Bats, *as bigge as large Hennes.*'[43]

Coleridge left in Mr. Gillman's copy of *Robinson Crusoe* some uncommonly penetrating notes. Defoe, he said in one of them, 'was a first-rate master of periodic style; but with sound judgment, and the fine tact of genius, he has avoided it as adverse to, nay, incompatible with, *the every-day matter of fact realness, which forms the charm and the character of all his romances.* The Robinson Crusoe is like the vision of a happy night-mair[44]. . . . Our imagination is kept in full play, excited to the highest; yet all the while we are touching, or touched by, common flesh and blood.'[45] Well, the travel-books are just such a happy nightmare, in which objects and occurrences the most fantastic are invested with the 'matter of fact realness' of the barnyard of an English farm. When the Hottentots who clucked like hens attacked, under cover of bartering for their cattle, the Zelanders on the second voyage to the Dutch East Indies, 'the Flemmings,' says John Davis, their chief pilot, 'fled before them like Mice before Cats. . . . There was neither courage nor discretion. For we stayed by our Tents being belegred with

Canibales and Cowes; we were in Muster Giants, with great armed bodies, but in action Babes, with Wrens hearts. . . . We went all aboord, only leaving our great Mastive Dogge behind us, who by no meanes would come to us. For I thinke he was ashamed of our Companie.'[46] That homespun narrative, remember, is written of the passing strange, mysterious world of 'antres vast and deserts idle. . . . And of the Cannibals that each other eat, The Anthropophagi'! And the charm and the character of a hundred narratives, with their bewitching criss-cross of incongruous associations, find succinct abridgement in that inimitable 'Canibales and Cowes.'

It is worth while, I think, to make double sure that persistent association of strange with familiar things which is one of the voyagers' most alluring traits, for, like *Robinson Crusoe*, 'The Ancient Mariner' betrays its influence. There, for example, is 'old Dampier, a rough sailor' (as Coleridge called him) 'but a man of exquisite mind.'[47] And Dampier, who declared himself to be 'exactly and strictly careful to give only True Relations and Descriptions of Things,'[48] was master also of a 'dry conciseness' (to borrow Gray's pithy phrase for Aristotle's style)[49] which matched his scrupulous exactitude. Ambergris is 'of a dusky colour, towards black, and about *the hardness of mellow Cheese*';[50] the fruit of the Central American Cabbage-tree 'is *as white as Milk, and as sweet as a Nut*';[51] in the Philippines the Plantain's 'Shell, Rind or Cod, is soft, and of a yellow colour when ripe. *It resembles in shape a Hogs-gut*

Pudding. The inclosed Fruit is *no harder than Butter in Winter*, and is much of the colour of the purest yellow Butter. It is of a delicate taste, *and melts in ones Mouth like Marmalet*'[52]—a phrase as luscious on the tongue as the unctuous fruit itself! There is also Hoc Shu: 'It looks like Mum, and tastes much like it, and is very pleasant and hearty. Our Seamen love it mightily, and will lick their Lips with it: for scarce a Ship goes to China, but the Men come home fat with soaking this Liquor, and bring store of Jars of it home with them.' And the jars, with their 'pretty full belly' and 'small thick mouth' are as pleasant and hearty as the seductive beverage they hold.[53] In Yucatan are 'a sort of Spiders of a prodigious Size, some near as big as a Man's Fist . . . they have two Teeth, or rather Horns . . . which are *black as Jett, smooth as Glass*, and their small End *sharp as a Thorn* . . . the Backs of these Spiders are covered with a . . . Down, *as soft as Velvet*.'[54] Dampier has dealt as tersely with his spiders as Purchas with Mahomet's Paradise, where under the Mountain of Hell, not far from the Land Aliolen and the Sea Alkasem, and other lands and seas, is 'the Land Agiba, *white as Milke, sweet as Muske, soft as Saffron, bright as the Moone*.'[55] But Dampier must yield the palm to Frederick Martens.

Martens, the imaginative beauty of whose style we have more than once had occasion to observe, sailed to Spitzbergen in the good ship *Jonas in the Whale*, and brought to the fauna of Arctic seas a mind teeming with the simple, vivid imagery of everyday experience. The Dolphin's tail is 'crooked . . . *like a Sickle*'; the tail of the Hay is '*like a Leaf of a Lilly*'; a Sea-crawfish 'that I saw in my Voyage to Spain, made with its Head and Tail *just the shape of a Lute*.'[56] The whale's upper lip fits into a cavity beneath it '*as a Knife into a Sheath*'; the whale-bone 'is somewhat bended *like unto a Cimeter*'; the spout-holes 'are bended on each side like an S, or *as the hole that is cut on a Violin*'; the breasts of the female whale are sometimes 'speckled . . . *like a Lapwing's Egg*'; the sperm '*smells like Wheaten-flower*.'[57] The 'Whale's Louse' (which 'hath no resemblance at all to our Lice') becomes, when Martens is done with him, a very compendium of familiar trades and occupations. 'They have a head like a Louse, with 4 Horns; the two short Horns that stand out before have two knobs, *like Kettledrum-sticks*. . . . Its Head hath *almost the shape of an Acorn*. . . . It hath six Plates on the Back; the foremost of them is shaped *like a Weaver's Shutle*. The Tail might be *compared unto a Shield*. . . . On the foremost Plate it hath Feet shaped *like a Sythe;* they are round before, and bent, *like the first Quarter of the Moon;* but on the inside they are *toothed like a Saw*. . . . On each side of the second and third Plait grow out four Legs that are his *Oars . . . they put them upwards together, as the Vaulters do when they jump over Swords*.'[58] No instantaneous photograph of legs flung up in a flying leap could beat that flash of the eye which for a second merges louse and man! And for sheer visualizing quality it is rivalled by this exquisite bit of *genre:* the body of the Star-fish 'hath ten corners, and it hath a Star above with as many Rays; each of these one may compare unto *a Sail of the Windmills that the Children run against the Wind withal.*'[59] Or the reminiscence is winningly commonplace: the saw-fish's tail 'is *like unto a piece of Board, whereon the Dyers widen or stretch their Stockins.*'[60] Martens can on occasion be as fresh and unhackneyed and direct in his comparisons as Dante. And precisely as glimpses of Florence meeting us at every turn make us feel pleasantly at home in Hell, so Martens's quaint touches of homely German life convert Greenland's icy waters into a friendly and almost *gemüthlich* spot.

Now I have torn my illustrations out of their context, and so blotted out the atmosphere which gives them half their charm. And they have been, into the bargain, selected to exemplify a single point. Yet nobody, I think, can read these scattered and fragmentary excerpts from a dozen various documents without feeling that they are, in spite of superficial differences, at bottom astonishingly of a piece. And that keeping is due in large measure to two causes, of which one regards substance, the other, form. If anything was ever written with the eye on the object, it was these old narratives, which are so seldom out of hail of concrete fact that even their liveliest flights wear a beguiling air of authenticity. And one thing which they have in common is that stamp of actuality which a pervading sense of fact imprints upon their style. But they have another common quality. In happy conjunction with that steady influx of new facts clamouring for communication there stood at command a vehicle of expression which was splendidly supple and copious and unjaded. The old mariners and their translators or amanuenses were among the fortunate of earth. For English speech, as they knew it, was still in the hey-day of its blood—fresh, and flexible, and unfaded, and as daringly adventurous as the adventurers themselves. The great era of exploration was a period of incomparable zest in life and of quickened responsiveness to whatever stimuli it had to offer, and its language reflects with singular fidelity both the gusto with which they embarked on fresh experience, and the spirit which left unexploited no resource. And these qualities belonged alike to lettered and unlettered speech, and the voyagers, however untutored in literary art, breathed none the less the spacious air of a day when vocabularies richer, and racier, and fuller flavoured than before or since were (to pilfer an apt phrase) 'in widest commonalty spread.' The diction of Oviedo's description of the coconut, by whomsoever translated, is as succulent as the thing itself, and over and over again a spendthrift profusion of simple, wholesome, instantly intelligible terms imparts to the recitals an inimitable relish. The ant-hills of the western Indies, where there are '*innumerable and infinite* little Ants,' have 'certaine small rifts, *as little and subtill* as the edge of a Knife';[61] bow-strings on the Congo 'are of little woodden twigs like reeds, not hollow within, but *sound and pliable, and very daintie*';[62] the female of certain shell-fishes of Loanda is greatly esteemed for her colour, which is 'very *neat, bright and pleasant to the sight*';[63] the churchia of Central America is '*tawnie, sharpe-snowted, dog-toothed, long-tayled and eared like a Rat.*'[64] In the kingdom of the Congo, says Hartwell in his translation of Pigafetta, 'the raine falleth so greatly, and the drops of it are so big, as it is a wonder to see. *These waters doe marvellously supple the ground.*'[65]

'It is a naturall, simple, and unaffected speech that I love,' wrote Montaigne—and Florio's rendering exemplifies all I have been saying—'so written as it is spoken, and such upon the paper, as it is in the mouth, *a pithie, sinnowie, full, strong, compendious and materiall speech* . . . free, loose and bold, that every member of it seeme to make a bodie; not Pedanticall, nor Frier-like, nor Lawyer-like, but rather downe right, Souldier-like.'[66] Substitute 'Sailor-like,' and you have in a nut-shell the speech of the voyagers, which is, in its essential qualities, the speech of their times. 'They have rain there very seldom, howbeit a gentle wind commonly that bloweth in a little silver dew, which moistneth the earth so finely, that it maketh it fertile and lusty'; the winds coming from the main 'disperse themselves into a wonderful large air and great sea,' and 'so bloweth a jolly cool wind, which refresheth the barbarous people and beasts all the day long.'[67] But that is not Hartwell in Purchas on the climate of the Congo; it is Sir Thomas North, translating Plutarch. And North and his fellows 'pursued their craft in the spirit of bold adventure which animated Drake and Hawkins,' and their translations, again in Charles Whibley's happy phrase, 'call up a vision of space and courage and the open air.'[68] So, precisely, do the narratives of the older voyagers, and for identically the same reason: their speech (to fall into its like for the moment) is the form and pressure of the very age and body of the time. It is the utterance of a period, to repeat what I hope is now reasonably clear, when the substance of romance found its characteristic clothing in the unequivocal, immediate phraseology of fact. And there between the covers of the travel-books it lies—fact saturated in the imagery which memory brought to it; always simple, always sensuous, sometimes (in the word's old import) even passionate; the very stuff of poetry, awaiting only the touch of the shaping spirit to transmute it into poetry itself.

Here, then, was the store of words—fresh, lively, artless, and direct—of the men who sailed the seas. And here was a creative intelligence, profoundly susceptible, as they were not, to the subtler values of words. And here, too, was taking form an imaginative conception into which was being wrought, as its very substance, imagery in part embodied in these very words. Two things were sure to happen. Words of the mariners would be woven into the poem; but they would both give and take colours which the mariners never knew. And now at last we may come back to 'The Ancient Mariner.'

III

For running through the poem, like 'the dominant's persistence [which] must be answered to,' are the *ipsissima verba* of the voyagers themselves.

> And now there came both *mist and snow,*
> And it grew *wondrous cold:*
> And ice, *mast-high, came floating by,*
> *As green as emerald.*[69]

There, as we have seen, simple, lucid, and direct, are the very words of Martens, and Harris, and James. In its graphic fidelity to fact, and in its telling investiture of the far and strange with the imagery of familiar observation, the diction of the stanza might serve as an epitome of the essential qualities which mark the diction of the navigators. And in phrase upon phrase which we have already met with, there stand similarly imbedded the trenchantly concrete terms of the travel-books, with their trick of incorporating unwonted with everyday experience. 'It *cracked* and growled, and *roared* and *howled,* Like noises *in a swound*'; 'Blue, glossy green, and *velvet black,* They *coiled* and *swam;* and every *track* Was a *flash* of golden *fire*'; 'The lightning *fell* with never a jag, A *river* steep and wide'; '*the snowy clifts*'; '*the good South wind*'; '*The breezes* blew'; 'The bloody *Sun, at noon, Right up above* the mast did stand'; 'The water . . . *burnt*'; 'There passed *a weary time*'; 'The Sun's rim *dips*'; '*the shadow of the* ship'; 'a hundred *fire-flags* sheen.' Even lines which exhale the quintessential charm of the interwoven imagery and music of the poem may owe their magic to a phrase which comes straight from a mariner's pen. 'Wee *sayled softly* West North-west.' So wrote, in Purchas, William Cornelison Schouten, who, like the ancient Mariner, 'found and discovered a new passage through the great South-Sea.'[70] And nothing in the poem is more suffused with the unique enchantment of its style than these two lines:

> Swiftly, swiftly flew the ship,
> Yet she *sailed softly* too.[71]

That is woven like a seamless robe of light—and one of its strands is drawn intact from Purchas.

Even with the diction of the gloss—that felicitous conception which has made the poem a great concerted, almost orchestral piece—is interwoven the wording of the travel-books. 'And when the Sunne was about South South-east, *wee saw a strange sight in the Element*.'[72] So Gerrit de Veer, as we have seen, wrote in his unforgettable narrative. And in the gloss, the Mariner 'heareth sounds and *seeth strange sights* and commotions *in* the sky and *the element*.'[73] And again: 'The ancient Mariner beholdeth a sign *in the element* afar off'[74]—as in *Northwest Fox* 'the night before was full of strange Harbours, as they call them, which is a streame *in the Element*, like the flame that commeth forth the mouth of a hot oven.'[75] Nor is it any wonder that we find what we find. For despite the saturation of the gloss in the lore of other and more esoteric folios, it was from the travel-books, without much question, that the inspiration came.

The Moone setteth not nor the Sunne in the Polar Regions. The windes which at other times refresh them, are then by Nature imprisoned in their homes.	Patricius numbreth the linkes of this chaine. . . . The interpretation of this mysticall Philosophie, yee may borrow of him selfe in his Panaug. Panarc. Pamsyc. Pancos, more agreeing with Zoroaster Hermes and some Platonicks.

Those are excerpts from the marginal gloss to *Purchas his Pilgrimage.*[76] And here are fragments of the gloss to Barents's third voyage in the *Pilgrimes:*[77]

Icie thunder.	They see the Sun no more.
Earth on the top of Azure Ice.	Moone continually seene in the Sunnes absence.

How God in our extremest need, when we were forced to lie all the Winter upon the Land, sent us Wood to make us a house, and to serve us to burne in the cold Winter.	Darknesse. Cold relenteth. Strange Birds breeding in strong cold.
Sun riseth South South-east, and goeth downe South South-west, not full above the Earth. Foxes succeed Beares.	Their Scute and Boat layd up for a Monument: how much more worthily then the old worlds Argo.

The gloss, like the poem, is in the very spirit of the voyagers, and, like the poem, it shares their phraseology.

There is, then, incorporated in the verbal texture of 'The Ancient Mariner' an element which has an independent status of its own. Its character is fixed, not by Coleridge, but by antecedent use. And that element is the simple, concrete, yet imaginative phraseology of the voyagers. It is present in the poem, in varying measures of integrity, to a degree which has never been fully recognized. Yet there is another fact which is equally unmistakable. 'The Rime of the Ancient Mariner' possesses a textural *harmony* of diction which vies with its structural unity of line. The lovely half-stanza which I have just quoted is, in its exquisite keeping, an epitome of the poem. Nobody but Coleridge could have written it, yet words that are his and a phrase that is pure Purchas are absolutely of a piece. What conclusion are we to draw?

One thing, at least, is clear. This 'pure, perspicuous, and musical' diction, inevitable in its directness, and redolent of concrete things, was new to Coleridge's verse. It was not without reference to his poetry that I dwelt in the beginning on that 'tide of ingenious vocables,' and that 'great blaze of colours all about something,' which were the normal concomitants of his talk. And I am going remorselessly to quote again those magniloquent lines about the Protoplast and the Profound which have already served another end. Nor will it do any harm, as we moil through the welter of words, to let 'Swiftly, swiftly flew the ship, Yet she sailed softly too' go on singing its quiet tune in some adjacent corner of our brain.

'Maid beloved of Heaven!
(To her the tutelary Power exclaimed)
Of Chaos the adventurous progeny
Thou seest; foul missionaries of foul sire,
Fierce to regain the losses of that hour
When Love rose glittering, and his gorgeous wings
Over the abyss fluttered with such glad noise,
As what time after long and pestful calms,

With slimy shapes and miscreated life
Poisoning the vast Pacific, the fresh breeze
Wakens the merchant-sail uprising. Night
An heavy unimaginable moan
Sent forth, when she the Protoplast beheld
Stand beauteous on Confusion's charmèd wave.
Moaning she fled, and entered the Profound
That leads with downward windings to the Cave
Of Darkness palpable, Desert of Death
Sunk deep beneath Gehenna's massy roots.[78]

That is the Coleridge who said in 1794 to Southey: 'I cannot write without a *body* of *thought*. Hence my poetry is crowded and sweats beneath a heavy burden of ideas and imagery! It has seldom ease.'[79] It is the Coleridge of 'English Bards and Scotch Reviewers,' 'To turgid ode and tumid stanza dear.' It is the Coleridge who sadly admitted to Cottle that his 'Ode to the Departing Year' was thought by the majority of its readers to be 'a rant of turgid obscurity,' and who could protest only the second member of the allegation: 'It is not obscure. My "Religious Musings" I know are, but not this "Ode." '[80] It is, in a word, the Coleridge of the interminable monologues, whose preternaturally agile associative faculty habitually summoned up not only dizzying concentricals of images, but also bewildering galaxies of words. And these were the bents which he brought to the inception of 'The Ancient Mariner.'

They had been, and they were later to be again, disastrous to his achievement as a poet; yet had either now been wanting—that swift facility of association or that unstinted prodigality of words[81]—'The Rime of the Ancient Mariner' had not been. Great art is more often than not the product of tendencies which are art's undoing when uncontrolled. And 'The Mariner' is a case in point.

What intervened to curb and rudder 'the streamy nature of *association*' we have already seen. The chaotic throng of images which, at this or that suggestion, came flocking up to consciousness were moulded into unity through the great imaginative conception of the voyage. But something else which happened is now no less clear. In strikingly similar fashion those fresh and downright pages of the voyagers, in which the strangest, most romantic matter found expression in the simplest, most familiar words, exercised upon that amazing *vocabulary* which was so tickle o' the sere an influence which both restrained its irrepressible exuberance, and set once for all a 'key of words' to be sustained. 'Poetry,' Coleridge once declared, in a note on its diction as compared with that of prose—'*poetry demands a severe keeping.*'[82] And for 'The Ancient Mariner' that keeping was determined by the words and phrases taken over from the travel-books.

And in that limitation imposed upon unbridled freedom lay, in large part, the secret of a diction which has remained (as Coleridge himself divined it would) inimitable. For the qualities demanded, if that 'severe keeping' were to be maintained, were, in the nature of the case, the qualities which marked the speech of the voyagers, as that speech was actually taken up into the poem. And those characteristics were, as it happened, among the crowning attributes of poetry. Only words, that is, which were themselves simple, and sensuous, and imbued with feeling could possibly coexist in harmony with the familiar, concrete, very human phraseology which set the key. 'One omnipresent Mind, Omnific';[83] 'And ice, mast-high, came floating by'—words of those two breeds, like Chaucer's love and lordship, 'wol nought, his thankes, have no felaweshipe.' And the diction of the poem owes its lucid simplicity in large degree to a concord imposed on it by the transparent directness of its incorporated element.

But there is also a simplicity of diction which is merely the reflection of a meagre stock. One need only turn the pages of *Lyrical Ballads* a little beyond 'The Ancient Mariner' itself to find poems enough which attain their bare matter-of-factness through emulation of a rustic's relatively barren speech. But now the opulence of Coleridge's huge vocabulary falls into due place in the scheme of things. The words of the mariners found their like, but they found it in the copious stores of a reservoir where both they and their like were steeped in the associations of a reading vaster far than ever came within the most accomplished navigator's ken. And precisely as the thronging images which tenanted the shadowy tracts below the verge of consciousness suffused and coloured (as we once saw) whatever emerged from their precincts to be taken up into the poem, so the unreckoned wealth of words at Coleridge's command lent its manifold possibilities of atmosphere and colour to that strange sense of verbal congruity which, in an artist's brain, hovers, almost like a sentient thing, above the chaos of potential terms. And so in 'The Ancient Mariner' there was worked one of those miracles which have been the despair of poets ever since: the inviolate keeping of a diction as rich as it is simple; luminously clear, and yet innumerable of stains and splendid dyes undreamed of even in the mariners' vivid speech. Is that hyperbole?

> The moving Moon went up the sky,
> And nowhere did abide:
> Softly she was going up,
> And a star or two beside—
>
> Her beams bemocked the sultry main,
> Like April hoar-frost spread;
> But where the ship's huge shadow lay,
> The charmèd water burnt alway
> A still and awful red.[84]

I do not think I have been guilty of extravagance.

And this winnowing and blending of words, so that each takes colour from the other, until out of the confluence of their impalpable and elusive associations there is born a beauty which no other assemblage of words in the world could give—all this is not one whit less the work of the imagination than its corresponding operations in the world of images. Take for a moment three of the lines which I have just set down:

> But where the ship's huge shadow lay,
> The charmèd water burnt alway
> A still and awful red.

Images caught from the pages of Martens and Cook—the shadow of a sail, and a phosphorescent sea, and glowing animalculæ—flashed together, as we discovered long ago, and coalesced in a single magical impression. The scattered elements of the picture are present, unmistakable, in the travel-books. But the picture itself is bathed in an atmosphere of which there is no slightest trace in Martens or in Cook—an enchantment shed, with the light of the moving moon, from that plastic conception of ominously haunted seas which was unfolding with the evolution of the design. And that enchantment, which is sheer imaginative creation, is Coleridge's alone. But it is conveyed through *words*. And again the scattered elements are present, unmistakable, in the travel-books: 'The *Shadow* of the Sail'; 'the Sea shines vehemently . . . and *burns*'; 'a ruby, or opaline *redness* [that] glows.' And elsewhere stands 'the *charmèd* wave.'[85] There is no question of the influence which set the key. But that blended clarity and mystery, in which terms as pellucid as crystal are pervaded with the sense of something sombre and inscrutable—that triumphant merging of irreconcilables, 'Où l'Indécis au Précis se joint'[86]—is not found in the diction of the voyagers. It is once more the transmuted affluence of Coleridge's own chaos—that 'great blaze of colours all about something' which coruscated dazzlingly when words ran free, now subdued to a harmony like that of the brooding, mysterious hues of the shadowed sea itself. We sometimes forget that the creative energy *creates*.

Other words, too, than those which leaped back to memory from Cook and Martens in conjunction with the images which so amazingly combined, have carried with them into the weaving play of associations the aroma of some ancient mariner's very speech. 'Huge' is a word which the old voyagers dearly loved—as when, in Hakluyt, Burroughs sailed 'so farre, that hee came at last to the place where hee found no night at all, but a continuall light and brightnesse of the Sunne shining clearely upon the *huge* and mightie Sea.'[87] But nowhere in the narratives is it impregnated, as its context has imbued it here, with a haunting sense of something fearsome and unnatural. 'Awful' is perfectly at home in the vocabulary of the voyagers; 'an ancient man of an *aweful* presence with a flag upon a staff' meets us, for instance, in 'The Discovery of the West Indies by Christopher Columbus.'[88] But no mariner ever born could have put into words the lurking, ominous suggestion of the charmèd water's '*still and awful* red,' 'where the ship's *huge* shadow lay.' And whether they be reminiscences or not, both 'huge' and 'awful' are penetrated, like the rest, with a potency of suggestion which they never exercised in Hakluyt or in Churchill. Even Milton's (and Coleridge's) 'charmèd *wave*' has yielded to the assimilating energy which pulses through the lines. Every word has been permeated, as every image has been transmuted, through the imaginative intensity of one compelling creative act. 'Consider it well,' says Abt Vogler of the musician's analogous miracle:

> Consider it well: each tone of our scale in itself is nought:
> It is everywhere in the world—loud, soft, and all is said:
> Give it to me to use! I mix it with two in my thought:
> And, there! Ye have heard and seen: consider and bow the head!

Give Coleridge one vivid word from an old narrative; let him mix it with two in his thought; and then (translating terms of music into terms of words) 'out of three sounds he [will] frame, not a fourth sound, but a star.'

IV

And now we are confronted with a curious paradox. There was another notable influence upon the diction of 'The Ancient Mariner.' And in this influence has commonly been found the key to that very simplicity on which we have so long been dwelling. Coleridge, as we know, was deeply interested in the English and Scottish popular ballads. Nothing in 'The Mariner' is more remarkable than his transmutation of their rude measures, as he knew them, into a music the like of which had never been heard before.[89] And there can be, I think, no question that the vigorous directness of their plain and homespun phraseology likewise left, in some degree, its mark upon the poem. But the immediate effect of Coleridge's preoccupation with the ballads (and herein lies the paradox) was to mar for the moment the exquisite harmony of diction which he had almost achieved.

It is not very difficult to reconstruct, at least in part, what happened. In January, 1798, when 'The Ancient Mariner' was almost exactly 'nel mezzo del cammin,' Coleridge wrote to Wordsworth his unexpurgated opinion of *The Castle Spectre.*[90] One thing alone he found to praise: to wit, 'the pretty little ballad-song introduced, and,' he adds, 'Lewis, I think has great and peculiar excellence in these compositions. The simplicity and naturalness is his own, and not imitated; for it is made to subsist in congruity with a language perfectly modern, the language of his own times, *in the same way that the language of the writer of "Sir Cauline" was the language of his times.'* Now 'The Ancient Mariner,' on which Coleridge was then engaged, was meant to belong, as a ballad, to what he thought of as 'Sir Cauline's' times. And in 'Sir Cauline,' as he read it in his copy of Percy's *Reliques*, he found phrases such as these: 'To be theyr wedded *feere*'; 'I never.can be youre *fere*'; 'I will have none other *fere*'; 'For mee thy faithfulle *feere*'; 'Upon *Eldridge* hill'; 'the *Eldridge* knighte'; 'the *Eldridge* hilles'; 'the *Eldridge* sworde'; 'Will examine you *beforne*'; *I weene* but thou mun dye'; 'The teares *sterte* from his *ee*'; 'Up then *sterte* the stranger knight'; 'Fro manye *a farre countrye*.'[91] In view of the letter to Wordsworth, then, it is not surprising that 'The Ancient Mariner,' as it stands in *Lyrical Ballads* (1798), contains these lines: 'That woman and her fleshless *Pheere*'; 'I look'd upon the *eldritch* deck'; 'As silent as *beforne*'; 'All black and bare, *I ween*'; 'A gust of wind *sterte* up behind'; 'I could not draw *my een* from theirs'; 'And I could move my *een*': 'mine own *countrée*'; 'That come from *a far contrée*.'[92] We have, it is clear, another moulding influence to reckon with in the diction of the poem.

But Coleridge did not confine his reading in Percy to 'Sir Cauline.' A stanza recalled from Percy's version of 'the grand old ballad of Sir Patrick Spence' is prefixed to 'Dejection: An Ode,' and the memorable reference to it which I have just quoted is embodied in the poem. It is highly probable, moreover, that he knew other ballad-collections beside the *Reliques*. The number in print by 1797 was fairly large, and Coleridge was an omnivorous reader. But the *Reliques* we know that he knew, and for our purpose we need go no farther. In Percy's text of 'The Ancient Ballad of Chevy Chase,' for example, occurs the phrase: '*Withouten* any fayle'; in 'The Battle of Otterbourne,' are found the phrases: '*withowghten* stryffe,' '*withowtten* drede,' '*withowghten* naye.'[94] In *Lyrical Ballads* (1798), line 161 of the poem reads: '*Withouten* wind, *withouten* tide'; and line 428: '*Withouten* wave or wind.' The first stanza of 'Edom o' Gordon' in the *Reliques* (to take another instance) begins:

> It fell about the Martinmas
> Quhen the wind blew shril and *cauld*.[95]

And this is the form in which a familiar stanza of 'The Ancient Mariner' stood in 1798:

> Listen, Stranger! Mist and Snow,
> And it grew wond'rous *cauld:*
> And Ice mast-high came floating by
> As green as *Emerauld*.[96]

The spelling 'cauld' might have come from any one of half a dozen Scottish ballads accessible at the time; but whether the *Reliques*, or the *Orpheus Caledonius*, or the *Scottish Tragic Ballads*, or what not, fathered it, the essential point is that its use betrays ballad influence—an influence which carries over to 'Emerauld.'[97] And again the tinge of archaism imparted by the ballads to the diction of the poem is obvious.

But most of the forms which Coleridge found in 'Sir Cauline' and in other ballads were even more familiar to him in Chaucer and Spenser.[98] 'Fere,' in the sense of 'companion' or 'mate,' he would note again and again in both. In both he would also find, as a matter of course, 'beforne,' 'I ween,' the equivalents of 'ee' and 'een,' 'contree,' 'withouten.' And he could not read long in Chaucer without running across 'sterte.' Barring 'eldritch' and 'cauld,' accordingly, that comprises our entire ballad list. And if, as seems probable, 'Sir Cauline' set in the beginning this particular key of words, it is not difficult to guess the direction which Coleridge's actively associative memory would take.

We are prepared, then, to discover in 'The Ancient Mariner' *Chaucerian* words (which were frequently Spenser's too) that had not found a place in the ballad stock—so far, at least, as it was known to Coleridge. And our expectation is amply justified. I shall quote the pertinent lines from the version of 1798.

Ne dim *ne* red, like God's own head,
The glorious Sun *uprist.*

A certain shape, *I wist.*

A speck, a mist, a shape, *I wist!*

Like morning frosts *yspread.*

To Mary-queen the praise be *yeven.*

The Marineres all '*gan* work the ropes.

The Marineres all '*gan* pull the ropes,
But look at me they *n'old.*

Eftsones I heard the dash of oars.

What manner man art thou?[99]

And the use of 'ne,' exemplified in the first quotation, confronts us at every turn: '*Ne* shapes of men *ne* beasts we ken'; '*Ne* any day'; '*ne* breath *ne* motion'; '*Ne* any drop to drink'; *Ne* could we laugh, *ne* wail'; '*Ne* rot, *ne* reek did they'; '*Ne* spake, *ne* mov'd their eyes'; '*Ne* turn them up to pray'; '*Ne* sound *ne* motion made'; 'But I *ne* spake *ne* stirr'd.'[100]

In two instances, however, the Chaucerian influence has far more than verbal interest. In the famous fragment of 'The Romaunt of the Rose' (which, when Coleridge wrote, was accepted implicitly as Chaucer's) is a description of the garden of Sir Mirth. And in the account of its birds occur these lines, which I shall quote from the text which Coleridge probably used:

There mightin men se many flockes
Of Turtels and of *Laverockes*. . .
Thei *song ther song*, as faire and wel
As angels doen espirituell . . .
Layis of love full wel souning
Thei songin in ther *jargoning*.[101]

And here are Coleridge's lovely lines as they stood in 1798:

Sometimes a dropping from the sky
I heard, the *Lavrock* sing;

Sometimes all little birds that are
How they seem'd to fill the sea and air
With their sweet *jargoning*.

And now 'twas like all instruments,
Now like a lonely flute;
And now it is *an angel's song*
That makes the heavens be mute.[102]

No imaginative transmutation of a bare hint, among all the many metamorphoses which the poem has to offer, is more wonderful than that. And 'jargoning' is not so much an archaism as the one inevitable word in the world.

Moreover, Coleridge seems to have read the 'Squire's Tale' with uncommon relish. And neither he nor anybody could forget how (as the lines stood in his text) the king sat

Herking his minstralles hir thinges pley,
Beforne him at his bord deliciously;

or how later

Beforne him goth the loude minstralcie.[103]

And with a visualizing increment which even Dante or Shakespeare might have envied, the minstrels play their things deliciously as the Mariner begins his tale:

The Bride hath pac'd into the Hall,
Red as a rose is she;

> *Nodding their heads* before her goes
> The merry Minstralsy.[104]

But we are like to forget our archaisms, and for the moment the archaisms are the thing. For there is still another consideration which must be taken into account.

It is this. Chaucer and Spenser, as everybody knows, were lending aid and comfort to all the eighteenth-century poets who had what nowadays we call 'romantic' leanings. And Coleridge, as it does not seem in this connection to have been remembered, was keenly interested in the works of his immediate predecessors. And nine out of ten of the archaisms which went into the earliest version of 'The Ancient Mariner' had already imparted a would-be romantic flavour to the pages of Chatterton, and Shenstone, and Thomson, and of such smaller fry as Mickle, and Wilkie, and William Thompson, and Moses Mendez, and Gilbert West. The edition of the Rowley Poems published at Cambridge in 1794 contains Coleridge's 'Monody on the Death of Chatterton,' and in July, 1797, writing to Southey about a proposed new edition, he promised to contribute a preliminary essay to the poems.[105] And among the words which at first lent a spurious 'ancientness' (as Coleridge called it) to 'The Ancient Mariner' itself, 'upryste,' and 'ne,' and 'yeve,' and 'eftsoones,' and 'pheere'[106] are found in Chatterton. But that is only a single item. The romantic 'ancientness' is everywhere.

'Eftsoons' and 'ne' (or 'ne . . . ne') occur, for example, in Shenstone, Thomson, Mickle, West, and William Thompson; 'I wist,' in Shenstone and (as 'iwist') in William Thompson; 'I ween,' in Shenstone, Thomson, Mickle, Mendez, Wilkie, West, William Thompson, and others too numerous to name; 'atween' (which hails from Spenser) in Thomson and Mickle; 'gan' in Mickle and West; while forms in y-, legitimate and bastard, run rampant through the effusions of them all.[107] Starting with the poetical essays 'In the Ancient English Style,' or 'In Imitation of the Ancient Scots Manner,' or 'In Imitation of Spenser' or what not, there had developed by the close of the century a highly artificial and conventional archaic diction, which was one of the most conspicuous earmarks of the new tendencies in verse.

It finds striking exemplification in William Taylor's translation of Bürger's 'Lenore,'[108] and that famous rendering of a famous original (*O matre pulchra filia pulchior*, Wordsworth, as we know, would have exclaimed!)[109] undoubtedly rained its influence in more ways than one upon 'The Ancient Mariner.'[110] But it will scarcely do, I think, for reasons which are discussed in the Notes, to say with Professor Emerson that 'the archaic spelling of the first form of the *Ancient Mariner* is probably directly due to Taylor's similar use.'[111] Of the archaisms common to 'The Ancient Mariner' and 'Sir Cauline,' for example, only two—'I weene' and 'eyne'—are common to 'The Ancient Mariner' and 'Lenora.' And with Chatterton and Chaucer and the *Reliques* and the ballads at his hand, it is hazardous to assume one fountain-head for Coleridge's archaic spelling, or for his archaic words. I should not be surprised to find (were such finding possible) that 'Lenora' gave 'bemocke' to a glorious stanza. And there may well be other verbal reminiscences.[112] The thing to be remembered is the fact that Taylor was but one of a host of devotees of the archaic, and that the archaizer of the first draft of 'The Ancient Mariner' was equally familiar with many of the rest.

Coleridge, in a word, was following a literary fashion. With the fixing of that fashion the ballads undoubtedly had much to do. But the influence of the ballads on the diction of 'The Ancient Mariner' is merged and lost in a full stream of many tributaries, and the one fact of consequence is Coleridge's paradoxical response to a clearly defined contemporary tendency.

For it *is* paradoxical, and therein lies the consideration which saves (I hope) all this pother about a score or so of antiquated terms from utter triviality. For vastly the larger part of 'The Ancient Mariner' comes down unchanged from the poem as it first saw the light. The great passages of supreme imaginative beauty, whatever throes may have accompanied their composition, have in the main been untouched by the reviser's pen. With rare exceptions, the transformation of the elements that blended in them was from the first complete. And in that very fact lies the clue to the meaning of the curious discrepancy which we have been observing. The diction of the voyagers, impregnated with Coleridge's own rich associations, had definitively set the key. But there was present from the first a powerful counter influence. For the poem itself was cast in the ballad mould, and set in motion through that influence (which, paradoxically again, made at the same time for directness and simplicity) another very special set of words streamed up to memory—words long ago familiar, but now romantically remote. And Coleridge essayed through them to lend the poem that touch of strangeness which often constitutes, indeed, the most alluring quality of beauty. But for once his contriving intellect parted company with his creative faculty. And because they were contrived and not created, the archaisms remained, for the most part, untransmuted and unassimilated entities. For their strangeness was an obvious and at times obtrusive strangeness, whereas the secret of the poem's spell lay in the subtle art through which, apart from them, the strange took on the guise of the familiar. Yet, after all, we cannot but be grateful for the error. For nothing, I think, could throw into stronger light the profoundly imaginative element in that concord of its diction which now adds lustre to the poem, than this momentary aberration.

For the singular lapse of judgment which had marred an exquisitely woven fabric was rectified with a thoroughness and expedition which leave no doubt of Coleridge's belated but acute perception of its gravity.[113] When the second edition of *Lyrical Ballads* appeared in 1800, the spellings 'cauld' and 'Emerauld,' the nineteen 'ne's, 'withouten,' 'Pheere,' 'atween,' 'eldritch,' 'yspread,' 'yeven,' 'Lavrock,'[114] 'beforne,' 'n'old,' and 'een,' had all disappeared. 'Eftsones' had been dropped, to return as 'eftsoons' in *Sibylline Leaves*.[115] 'I ween,' 'sterte,' and 'what manner man' went out in 1817.[116] Only 'I wist,' ' 'gan,' and 'countree' were finally retained unchanged. The language of the poem, through unobtrusive turns of speech and words which dimly stir old memories, still calls up the past; but the past evoked is of no dated period. The flavour which the diction keeps, of an age that is not quite our own and yet essentially is one with it, is the friendly flavour of the English of the voyagers. We read: 'The ice *did* split with a thunder-fit'; 'The bloody Sun, at noon, Right up above the mast *did* stand'; 'The very deep *did* rot'; 'The moving Moon went up the sky, And no where *did* abide'; 'And the coming wind *did* roar more loud.'[117] And as we read, we catch again the very savour of countless phrases in Hakluyt, and Purchas, and James: 'The Ice withall *did* drive against her, and gave her many fearfull blowes'; 'The Ice *did* open something'; 'The Sunne *did* shine very cleere'; 'This *did* comfort us very much'; 'It was very darke, and it *did* blow hard'; 'The Ship *did* labour most terribly'; 'It *did* snow and freeze most extremely'; 'The seventh day was so extremely cold that our noses, cheekes, and hands *did* freeze as white as paper.'[118] The tinge of archaism which remains takes its colour from the travel-books. There is one stanza which sums up the whole story I have been telling—a stanza which, in the severe keeping of its direct and simple words has few rivals in the poem:

> I looked upon the rotting sea,
> And drew my eyes away;
> I looked upon the rotting deck,
> And there the dead men lay.[119]

For the third line, Coleridge first wrote:

> I look'd upon the *eldritch* deck.[120]

And in the substitution, in the very spirit of the seamen's narratives, of the plain and downright 'rotting' for the obscure associations of an uncanny ballad word,* is epitomized the resolution of a discord which came perilously near impairing the integrity of a diction which has now few equals in its rigorous consistency.

V

There is a remarkable passage in that quintessentially mid-Coleridgean omnium gatherum, *The Friend.* It parallels in substance a weighty paragraph of the criticism, in the *Biographia Literaria*, of Wordsworth's theory of poetic diction,[121] and it is there directly applied to poetry. Here are the essentials of the statement in *The Friend:*

> What is that which first strikes us, and strikes us at once,

> in a man of education, and which, among educated men, so instantly distinguishes the man of superior mind, that (as was observed with eminent propriety of the late Edmund Burke) 'we can not stand under the same archway during a shower of rain, without finding him out?' Not the weight or novelty of his remarks; not any unusual interest of facts communicated by him. . . . Still less will it arise from any peculiarity in his words and phrases. . . . There remains but one other point of distinction possible. . . . It is the unpremeditated and evidently habitual arrangement of his words, grounded on *the habit of foreseeing, in each integral part, or* (*more plainly*) *in every sentence, the whole that he then intends to communicate.*[123]

There, in another guise, is once more the reconciliation of 'the FREE LIFE, and of the confining FORM.'[124] It was that overruling sense of a whole, implicit in every part, which, with a larger scope than a hypothetical archway offered, brought, in 'The Ancient Mariner,' order and congruity out of a chaos of *impressions*. And through that same 'prospectiveness of mind, that surview,'[125] as Coleridge called it—which is the power of seeing each particular, as every artist sees it, in the light of a whole, conceived as a whole, and as a whole present at every step—through that same power as operant in the chaos of *words* there was preëstablished and maintained another harmony:

the accord of the diction with the unity of impression which the whole was intended to produce. The words are inseparable from the images, and the images from the words, and both, in their indissoluble union, from the design. It is more than the diction which is all of a piece. It is the *poem*. 'Nothing of it that doth fade'—the sliminess of Arctic and the oiliness of southern seas, noises of ice and earthquakes and sedges and flutes, shadows of sails, and colours that flash and are gone, the glancing of cobwebs, snatches of speech caught from sailors and scientists and mystics, pondered design and subliminal suggestion—

> Nothing of it that doth fade
> But doth suffer a sea-change
> Into something rich and strange.

Τὰ ἀρχᾶια παρῆλθεν, ἰδοὺ γέγονεν καινά: the old things are passed away; behold, they are become new.

Here ends our long preoccupation with the ways of the shaping spirit as they come to light in 'The Ancient Mariner.' And now we have yet stranger paths to trace.

---

* Would that Coleridge could have seen, in Max Beerbohm's ineffable caricature, his own tirelessly discoursing figure, and that ponderous, pyramidal snore!

* That (to borrow a choice Coleridgean phrase) is 'involved

in an almost Lycophrontic tenebricosity'![16] But it is child's play to the labyrinthic convolutions of ideas and expression which strew Coleridge's way through what he called 'the holy jungle of transcendental metaphysics.'[17] There is one amazing page of his essay 'On the Prometheus of Æschylus,' read before the Royal Society of Literature in 1825,[18] the verbal feats of which must have made the members of even that augustly learned body (if an exposition of sleep had not already come upon them) stare and gasp. And that page is but a Brobdingnag among its peers.

* Since this is a chapter on diction, it is incumbent upon me, in view of this sentence, to say a word for 'tang.' In a sorely needed and characteristically delightful article in the *Atlantic Monthly* (August, 1924), Miss Repplier thus stigmatizes 'tang': 'a bit of educated slang worse than the slang of the gutters' (p. 185). That is a scathing indictment, and it is not without warrant. But (and this I am bound to insist) the fact that a word is mercilessly abused may not be permitted to debar its proper use—else we must face, in these slack days, an intolerable impoverishment of our inherited vocabulary. Few Englishmen have written more pure, perspicuous, racy, and idiomatic English than Thomas Gray, and when I read, for example, in his letters: 'The language has a tang of Shakespeare,' I decline to let the slang of the day dispossess me of my inheritance. When 'tang,' or any other great (or

little) injured word, says precisely what we mean to say, it is still indefeasibly ours to use. I need scarcely add that I am defending a principle, and not a particular case which has no slightest interest to anybody but myself.

'Colourful,' by the way, which Miss Repplier pillories with 'tang,' is in a totally different category, and has no leg to stand on in any court. Spawned in a London magazine in 1890, it is an upstart pure and simple, 'without father, without mother, without descent.'

* 'Such as have accustomed to drinke in these Vessells,' Oviedo proceeds, with a dexterous shift of view (and of vocabulary!) from beauty to utility, 'and have beene troubled with the Disease called the fretting of the guts, say that they have by experience found it a marvellous remedie against that Disease.

* Don Garcia Silva Figueroa saw in Persepolis the ancient monuments: 'Yee may see in these Tables some men sitting, with great majestie, in certayne loftier chayres, *such as use to bee with us in the Quires and Chapter-houses of Cathedrall Churches.*'[38]

†Sir John Narborough, who found, 'dead and whole,' what he thought was one of, them, and opened its paunch to look for the bezoar-stone, saw its coat (I suspect) through the

learned Jesuit's eyes; 'All his Back had pretty long Wooll *of the colour of dried Rose-leaves*.'[39]

* 'This, I think,' he goes on, 'a rare merit: at least, I find, *I* cannot attain this innocent nakedness, except by *assumption*. I resemble the Duchess of Kingston, who masqueraded in the character of 'Eve before the Fall,' in flesh-coloured Silk.' That *had* been so, and was to be again. But when, in January, 1798, he made that penetrating observation on his earlier style, he was writing verse of which a later critic was justly to say: 'Coleridge's words have the unashamed nakedness of Scripture, of the Eden of diction ere the voluble serpent had entered it.'[93]

* Coleridge had the advantage, as his readers had not, of Percy's Glossary:[122] 'Eldridge, (*Scoticè*), Elriche, Eltritch, Elrische; *wild, hideous, ghostly. Item, lonesome, uninhabited, except by spectres, etc.*'—a definition supplemented by examples from Allan Ramsey, Gawin Douglas, etc. The change in 1800 from 'eldritch' to 'ghastly' was scarcely felicitous. The one right word did not come in until *Sibylline Leaves*.

BOOK IV

If a man could pass through Paradise in a dream, and have a flower presented to him as a pledge that his soul had really been there, and if he found that flower in his hand when he awoke—Ay! and what then?

COLERIDGE, *Anima Poetæ*

Cotal son io, chè quasi tutta cessa
mia visione, ed ancor mi distilla
nel cor lo dolce che nacque da
essa.

DANTE, *Paradiso*

CHAPTER XVIII

THE HOOKED ATOMS

SUPPOSE a subliminal reservoir thronged, as Coleridge's was thronged, with images which had flashed on the inner eye from the pages of innumerable books. Suppose these images to be fitted, as it were, with links which render possible indefinite combination. Suppose some powerful suggestion in the field of consciousness strikes down into this mass of images thus capable of all manner of conjunctions. And suppose that this time, when in response to the summons the sleeping images flock up, with their potential associations, from the deeps—*suppose that this time all conscious imaginative control is for some reason in abeyance.* What, if all this were so, would happen?

That hypothetical question fairly covers, I think, the case of 'Kubla Khan.' The fragment is a thing of unique and imperishable beauty, and if I thought that an essay at the elucidation of its genesis would dull its brightness, I should be tempted to let the facts, however remarkable, rest undisturbed.[1] But that triumphant beauty is secure. And Coleridge himself has told enough to raise a host of questions which he has left unanswered, and which, from then till now, have piqued legitimate curiosity.* For those to whom the mystery of the poem's birth is dear, that mystery will remain when I have done. I have no desire to explain away the unexplainable, and behind the discoverable processes through which beauty is created, whether in 'The Ancient Mariner' or 'Christabel' or 'Kubla Khan,' is and will always be something inscrutable, which no analysis can reach—or harm.

I propose, then, first of all to consider very briefly, but more explicitly than we have hitherto considered them, Coleridge's associations of ideas. 'Représentons-nous,' says Henri Poincaré in that weighty account of his own unconscious processes which I have already quoted—'représentons-nous les éléments futurs de nos combinaisons comme quelque chose de semblable aux atomes crochus d'Épicure.'[3] How did Coleridge's 'hooked atoms'—those impressions and images equipped, in his own phrase, with 'hooks and eyes of the memory'[4]—behave? That is the first question which demands an answer.

I

Let us begin with one or two cases of association in which no merging of 'the images of memory'[5] into a *tertium quid* has taken place. At intervals during the year 1797 Coleridge wrote to Thomas Poole a series of letters of superlative interest, rehearsing graphically his recollections of his boyhood. And one incident which he relates had a curious sequel. There had been a childish quarrel between Coleridge and his brother Frank, and Coleridge, who expected a flogging, ran away, as he says, 'to a hill, at the bottom of which the Otter flows, about one mile from Ottery':

> I distinctly remember my feelings when I saw a Mr. Vaughan pass over the bridge, at about a furlong's distance, *and how I watched the calves in the fields beyond the river*. It grew dark and I fell asleep. It was towards the latter end of October, and it proved a dreadfully stormy night. I *felt the cold in my sleep*, and dreamt that I was pulling the blanket over me, and actually pulled over me a dry thorn bush which lay on the hill. In my sleep I had rolled from the top of the hill to within three yards of *the river, which flowed by the unfenced edge at the bottom.* I awoke several times, and *finding myself wet and stiff and cold*, closed my eyes again that I might forget it.[6]

Some six years after the writing of the letter, on 'Tuesday night, July 19, 1803,' Coleridge made this note:

> Intensely hot day; left off a waistcoat and for yarn wore silk stockings. Before nine o'clock, had unpleasant chillness; heard a noise which I thought Derwent's in sleep, listened, and found it was a calf bellowing. Instantly came on my mind that night I slept out at Ottery, and the calf in the field across the river whose lowing so deeply impressed me. Chill + child and calf-

lowing, probably the rivers Greta and Otter.[7]

We have, in a word, Coleridge's own analysis (jotted down, characteristically, while the incident was still vividly present in his mind), of the links of association which had called up instantly an experience that lay twenty-three years behind the moment of recollection. Out of a fortuitous conjunction of impressions a flash of memory leaped. That is enough for the present to remember.

There is another instance of association, of which Coleridge made no note, but which has an unusual interest of its own. It is connected with that casual meeting between Coleridge and Keats on an April Sunday morning in 1819, upon which Keats set down his breezy but singularly penetrating observations. On August 13, 1832, Coleridge, on receiving the news of the death of his young friend and disciple, Adam Steinmetz, wrote to John Kennard a quintessentially Coleridgean letter. And in it occurs this sentence:

> Not once or twice only, after he had shaken hands with me on leaving us, I have turned round with the tear on my cheek, and whispered to Mrs. Gillman, 'Alas! there is *Death* in that dear hand.'[8]

That was written on August 13. The next day, August 14, Coleridge, in a conversation recorded in the *Table Talk*, reverted to the meeting thirteen years before:

> A loose, slack, not well-dressed youth met Mr.——and myself in a lane near Highgate.——knew him, and spoke. It was Keats. He was introduced to me, and stayed a minute or so. After he had left us a little way, he came back, and said: 'Let me carry away the memory, Coleridge, of having pressed your hand!'—'There is death in that hand,' I said to——, when Keats was gone; yet this was, I believe, before the consumption showed itself distinctly.[9]

The writing of the phrase last quoted from the letter had, it is clear, recalled to memory the earlier incident, and to that association of ideas we owe at least a famous literary anecdote.

But such flashes of association are matters of general experience, and I have rehearsed these two examples simply for the light they throw on others more significant. For ideas thus called up and juxtaposed have a curious trick of *blending*. A phrase of Boccaccio's (to revert to an illustration which I have already used)[10] recalls to Chaucer a corresponding phrase in Dante. As a result, the two passages which contain the common phrase are present simultaneously in his mind. And in the stanza which he is at the moment translating from Boccaccio appears a list of names made up of *all* the names in *both* the passages. Juxtaposition of ideas equipped with 'hooks and eyes' often passes into actual combination.

II

There is a singular instance of such amalgamation which has apparently gone unobserved. One of Coleridge's favourite notions was that of a correspondence between fancy and imagination on the one hand, and delirium and mania on the other. It first turns up, so far as I know, in a conversation recorded by Crabb Robinson in his *Diary* on November 15, 1810:

> He [Coleridge] made an elaborate distinction between fancy and imagination. The excess of fancy is delirium, of imagination mania. Fancy is the arbitrarily bringing together of things that lie remote, and forming them into a unity. The materials lie ready for the fancy, which acts by a sort of juxtaposition. On the other hand, the imagination under excitement generates and produces a form of its own. The 'seas of milk and ships of amber' he quoted as fanciful delirium. He related, as a sort of disease of imagination, what occurred to himself. He had been watching intently the motions of a kite among the mountains of Westmoreland, when on a sudden he saw two kites in an opposite direction. This delusion lasted some time. At last he discovered that the two kites were the fluttering branches of a tree beyond a wall.[11]

In that portion of the *Biographia Literaria* which was written at some time during 1815, the distinction reappears, again illustrated, in the case of fancy, by the 'seas of milk and ships of amber':

> Milton had a highly *imaginative*, Cowley a very *fanciful* mind. If therefore I should succeed in establishing the actual existences of two faculties generally different, the nomenclature would be at once determined. To the faculty by which I had characterized Milton, we should confine the term *imagination;* while the other would be contradistinguished as *fancy*. Now were it once fully ascertained, that this division is no less grounded in nature, than that of delirium from mania, or Otway's
>
> 'Lutes, lobsters, seas of milk, and ships of amber,'
>
> from Shakespear's
>
> 'What! have his daughters brought him to this pass?' . . .
>
> the theory of the fine arts, and of poetry in particular, could not, I thought, but derive some additional and important light.[12]

Now Otway's line is taken from *Venice Preserved, or A Plot Discovered*,[13] a play the sub-title of which, with its veiled reference to the contemporary 'Popish Plot,' had given Coleridge as early as 1795 the title for his own political pamphlet, *The Plot Discovered.* There is no question of his long familiarity with the play. But the line as he quotes it is wrong. Otway wrote:

Lutes, *laurels*, seas of milk, and ships of amber.

The line as Coleridge recalled it is

Lutes, *lobsters*, seas of milk, and ships of amber.

How did the lobsters get into the list?

Coleridge had another illustration which he employed to exemplify fancy. It appears in the *Table Talk* under date of June 23, 1834:

> You may conceive the difference in kind between the Fancy and the Imagination in this way, that if the check of the senses and the reason were withdrawn, the first would become delirium, and the last mania. The Fancy brings together images which have no connection natural or moral, but are yoked together by the poet by means of some accidental coincidence; as in the well-known passage in Hudibras:—
>
> 'The sun had long since in the lap
> Of Thetis taken out his nap,
> And *like a lobster boyl'd*, the morn
> From black to red began to turn.'[14]

Coleridge, in a word, seems to have used indifferently illustrations of his theory of fancy drawn respectively from *Venice Preserved* and *Hudibras*. The recurrence of his pet analogy between fancy and delirium[15] would, accordingly, be apt to call up the two passages together. And on this occasion, as a result of that association, Butler's lobster has ousted Otway's laurels (not without help, perhaps, from the contiguous 'seas'), and thereby most engagingly enhanced the aptness of the illustration.

It may, however, be urged that we have no evidence of Coleridge's use of the lines from *Hudibras* before 1834, whereas the lobsters slipped into Otway's line nineteen years earlier. I grant, of course, that such a position is perfectly tenable. But nobody (experto crede) can long read Samuel Taylor Coleridge without acutely realising that age could not wither nor custom stale (for him!) the stock themes of what Southey once unkindly called 'his endless loquacity.'[16] Such trifles as dates—1810, 1815, 1834—in the timeless flow of these recurrent topics of discourse melt placidly into one another; 'their years,' in Wordsworth's phrase, 'make up one peaceful family.' The incident of the two kites which Coleridge employed as an illustration on November 15, 1810, he had jotted down in his note-book in November, 1803,[17] and the use of Otway's line itself in 1815 was a repetition of its use in 1810. The identical sequence of ideas ('Nightmare—a dream accompanied by a sense of touch—single and double touch') in which Keats heard him discourse on April 15, 1819, appears in a notebook of 1811–12.[18] John Sterling remarks, in his notes of his first conversation with Coleridge in the winter of 1827–28, that he 'went into a long exposition of the evils of commerce and manufactures; the argument of which, I think, is to be found in one of the Lay Sermons.'[19] And the *Lay Sermons* had been printed ten years earlier. One remembers, too, that Hazlitt, in view of the repeated advertisements of the first *Lay Sermon* before it was published, had somewhat cruelly observed: 'We can give just as good a guess at the design of this Lay Sermon, which is not published, as of *the Friend . . . the Watchman, the Conciones ad Populum*, or any of the other courtly or popular publications of the same author.'[20] Coleridge's habit of repeating himself (which, be it noted, was itself in large measure due to his exceptional tenacity of association) was notorious.[21] And if the conjunction of Butler's lines with delirium and mania in 1834 was their first appearance in this connection, then in 1834 the leopard changed its spots.

If, however, one prefer that assumption, there is another curious link which may well have played its part in any case. That Coleridge read Frederick Martens before 1798 we have now abundant evidence. And in Martens occurs this characteristic observation: '[The Sea Crawfish] of Spitzbergen hath a Head *like a Lobster*, but the male of them that I saw in my Voyage to Spain, made with its Head and Tail *just the shape of a Lute*.'[22] If the route by way of Butler, then, be regarded as suspect, the extraordinary conjunction of a lobster and a lute in Martens was quite enough to establish an association which unconsciously called up 'lobsters,' when Coleridge wrote (or uttered) 'lutes.' 'Seeing a mackerel' he had once said—and it is his own illustration of 'contemporaneity as the *condition* of *all* association'[23] that I am again quoting—'seeing a mackerel, it may happen, that I immediately think of gooseberries, because I at the same time ate mackerel with gooseberries as the sauce. The first syllable of the latter word, being that which had coexisted with the image of the bird so called, I may then think of a goose.'[24] I am not deeply concerned to decide whether Butler or Martens provided the channel through which the lobsters floated into seas of milk. In either case (or both), through the association of obviously linked ideas, a new combination was effected. In itself it could scarcely be more trivial. As an index of processes through which new shapes of beauty may be created, its significance is not easy to exaggerate.

III

But similar combinations are already familiar to us from our study of 'The Ancient Mariner.' And two of these I shall recall, in order to refresh our memory. For the point involved is fundamental to our understanding of the genesis of 'Kubla Khan'—so fundamental, indeed, that the obvious course of referring back to the earlier pages will scarcely serve our ends. For I wish this time to eliminate all implications of the facts but one.

Coleridge, then, read in Frederick Martens this:

> We see in these falling Needles a Bow like a Rain-bow of *two colours*, white and a pale *yellow*, like *the Sun*, reflected by the dark Shadows of the Clouds.
>
> After this I proceed to the Description of an other Bow, which I call *a Sea-bow*. This is seen *when the Sun shines* clear and bright, not in *the great Waves, but in the Atmosphere of the Sea-water, which the Wind blows up, and which looks like a Fog.*[25]

But that is not quite the whole picture. For the 'falling Needles' referred to have been specifically called, two sentences earlier, *snow:* 'This [Rime] is small Snow.' On the preceding page, moreover, the rime is said to fall 'in the shape of small Needles of Snow.' And the remainder of the chapter is given over to a charmingly detailed account, embellished with six illustrations of snow crystals, of the various sorts of 'needly' and 'starry' snow.[26] The setting of the picture, then, is falling *snow*. And the waves are specifically called '*great*.'

Now Coleridge, following a clue which he had found in Priestley, read in the *Philosophical Transactions* these lines of Father Bourzes:

> I shall add one Observation more concerning *Marine Rain-bows*, which I observed after a great Tempest off the Cape of Good Hope. The Sea was then very much tossed, and *the Wind carrying off the Tops of the Waves made a kind of Rain*, in which *the Rays of the Sun* painted

> the Colours of a Rain-Bow. . . . We could distinguish only *two Colours, viz.* a dark *Yellow* on that side next the *Sun*, and a pale Green on the opposite side.[27]

And this time Coleridge (just when it is impossible to say) made a memorandum of the passage in his Note Book:

> Sun paints rainbows on the *vast* waves
> *during snow storms* in the Cape.[28]

But in the narrative which inspired the note nothing whatever is said of the size of the waves, nor is there a word which even hints at snow-storms. The increments have somehow slipped, like the lobsters in Otway's line, into a *milieu* where they did not originally belong. How did they get there?

One thing is plain. If ever there were 'hooked atoms' in the world they are here in these two pictures of sea-rainbows. The strikingly similar descriptions of the spindrift; the identical phrase 'two colours'; the recurrence of 'yellow,' in each case associated with 'the sun'—with such 'hooks and eyes' between them, the one picture could not but flash for an instant into conjunction with its counterpart. But in that counterpart there was a bow not in the spindrift only, but *in the snow*, and the waves from which the spindrift flew were '*great* Waves'—'as bigg' (a few pages earlier) 'as Mountains.' And when Coleridge jotted down his note, whether he was conscious of what was happening or not, the visual imagery called up by the words of Father Bourzes and the imagery which Martens's page had earlier stamped on his memory, had telescoped into a single picture. That is identical with the well-known phenomena of dreams, but it is far from uncommon in waking moments too. And this time the resulting entity was neither Father Bourzes nor Frederick Martens, but a *tertium quid* into which had entered elements of each.

The jotting, then, embodies a confluence of images through the agency of definite associative links—links quite as definite as chill + child + calf + river, or mackerel + gooseberries + goose. The memorandum, which is not a finished performance, is of negligible æsthetic value. No more, however, in the case of the snow-storms than in the instance of the lobsters am I at this juncture interested in the intrinsic worth of the result. The one thing which concerns us is the fact that the 'atomes crochus' combine, when something brings them, as it were, within each other's field of influence, and that the resulting combination is a new whole which is distinct from either. Nor need the elements which come together have been, in their original setting, contiguous in space. Ocular spectra derived by way of the printed page from impressions of regions as remote from one another as Spitzbergen and the Cape of Good Hope have in this case merged in a perfectly consistent unity. And that is typical. Provided they are furnished with effective links, images inherently the most incongruous may undergo complete amalgamation.* And this too we shall have occasion to remember.

I have thus far drawn intentionally for my illustrations upon confluences of ideas which have no inherent interest, as combinations, beyond the points which they illustrate. But identically the same processes may give, not a fragmentary note, but a great imaginative unity. And so before threading the labyrinth ahead of us, I mean to recall, for light on our way later, the links which drew together a chaos of elements into shapes of sheer beauty. How images from half a dozen books flashed, as ocular spectra, on Coleridge's retina, then dropped below the level of conscious recollection and blended in the stanzas through which move those shining creatures of the calm, the water-snakes—all this it is needless to repeat. But the 'hooks and eyes' with which the subliminal cluster of impressions was equipped have immediate bearing on the strange facts which are to come, and, stripped of their context, I shall briefly recapitulate them here. Father Bourzes's playing fishes 'made a *kind of artificial Fire* in the Water'; Captain Cook's animalculæ 'had *a faint appearance of glowing fire*.' Father Bourzes's fishes were '*playing in the Sea*'; Leemius's dolphins, '*in mari ludens*.' Cook's protozoa were *blue, red, and green*, 'with a *burnished* gloss'; Bartram's bream had scales powdered with *blue, red, and green*, and the fish itself was the colour of '*burnished* brass.' Leemius's dolphin moves '*in . . . gyros et spiras*'; Falconer's dolphins wanton '*in curling wreaths*.' Father Bourzes's fishes 'leave behind 'em *a luminous Track*'; the '*tracks*' of Falconer's dolphins '*burn in silver streams.*' The water in Father Bourzes is '*fat and glutinous*'; in Captain Cook it is 'covered with *a kind of slime*'; in Sir Richard Hawkins it could not be drawn 'cleare of *some corruption* withall.'[30] Those are the amazing copulas of the 'atomes crochus.' What couplings they made, and what imagery they carried with them into the complex, and what radiant shapes of light emerged—all that we have long ago seen. But I have recalled it for a very definite end. For it is of the utmost moment that we come to 'Kubla Khan' with one thing clear in mind. In the weaving of the most ethereal fabric of imagination an almost magical potency is exercised by the associative links. And therein lies, I think, the clue to the mystery upon which we must now enter. But before we enter, a mistake must be corrected, and a preliminary statement made.

IV

The mistake is a curious slip on the part of the most rigorously accurate of Coleridgean scholars, Mr. James Dykes Campbell, whose scrupulous exactness is proverbial. Yet in a matter which has important bearing on the history of 'Kubla Khan' he has fallen into an error which has carried with it unfortunate implications.

In a note on 'Kubla Khan' in his edition of Coleridge's poems, Mr. Campbell makes the following statement:[31]

I believe no manuscript of *Kubla Khan* exists, but some

> changes must have been made in the draft before it was printed, for in her lines 'To S. T. Coleridge, Esq.' Mrs. Robinson ('Perdita,' who died Dec. 28, 1800) writes:—
>
> 'I'll mark thy "sunny dome," and view
> Thy "caves of ice," thy *"fields of dew."* '
>
> the phrase italicised not being found in the published text.

On the strength of this, apparently, Ernest Hartley Coleridge, in his edition of the poems, writes as follows:[32]

> In her 'Lines to S. T. Coleridge, Esq.,' Mrs. Robinson (Perdita) writes:—
>
> 'I'll mark thy "sunny domes" and view
> Thy "caves of ice," and "fields of dew." '
>
> It is possible that she had seen a MS. copy of *Kubla Khan* containing these variants from the text.

From the editors the inference has passed to the critics. Havelock Ellis, for example, in *The World of Dreams*, closes a somewhat skeptical account of the genesis of 'Kubla Khan' with these words: 'Moreover, there is reason to believe that the first draft of "Kubla Khan" was not the poem as we now know it.'[33] And he cites Campbell's note as his authority. Charles D. Stewart, the author of an elaborate disquisition upon 'Kubla Khan,' waxes very bold, and on the hint of Perdita's 'fields of dew' sees Coleridge tinkering at the poem for eighteen years.[34]

Now the text of 'Kubla Khan' may have undergone changes at Coleridge's hand before the poem was printed. No one, in the absence of proof to the contrary, can positively say that it did not, and anyone who chooses is at liberty to guess that some revision may have taken place. The sole point which I wish to make is this. The only evidence which has been adduced to prove that the first draft *was* changed (namely, Perdita Robinson's quotation marks) turns out not to exist. For the quotation marks about 'fields of dew,' on which the whole argument hinges, are not in Mrs. Robinson's text at all. And E. H. Coleridge has further confused the issue by misreading Perdita's 'dome' as 'domes' (not to mention 'and' for 'thy' in the second line, and an omitted comma in the first), and by thereupon assuming *two* variants instead of one. It would be difficult to find more blunders within the compass of two lines than actually underlie this luckless argument.

For in point of fact there are no variants whatever. The lines entitled 'Mrs. Robinson to the Poet Colridge' [*sic*][35] were first printed in 1801 in the fourth volume of *Memoirs of the Late Mrs. Robinson, Written by Herself. With some Posthumous Pieces*. In the second volume the poem (there entitled 'Ode to S. T. Coleridge, Esq.') is included in a 'List of Poetical Pieces, Written between Dec. 1799 and Dec. 1800. By Mrs. Robinson.'[36] And the poem itself, signed 'Sappho,' is dated

'Oct. 1800.' The lines which Campbell quotes are actually printed thus:

> I'll mark thy "sunny dome," and view
> Thy "caves of ice," thy fields of dew![37]

Twice later in the poem the phrases 'sunny dome' and 'caves of ice' appear, marked each time as quotations. But the fields of dew are not again referred to.

In 1806 *The Poetical Works of the Late Mrs. Mary Robinson* appeared in three volumes, and the lines 'To the Poet Coleridge' were reprinted with the rest. But the phrases which, in 1801, had been included within quotation marks, are in 1806 printed in italics wherever they occur, and the lines in which we are particularly interested now stand thus:

> I'll mark thy *sunny dome*, and view
> Thy *Caves of Ice*, thy fields of dew![38]

The fields of dew are once more set off sharply from Mrs. Robinson's actual recollections of the poem.*

Should it, however, be felt that the fields of dew as they stand still constitute evidence of a lost draft of 'Kubla Khan' which Mrs. Robinson had seen, I can only remark that this draft, on this modified assumption, must have been an astonishing performance. For the *context* of the two misquoted lines has now precisely the same value, in the absence of quotation marks, as the fields of dew themselves. And here that context is:

Now by the source, which lab'ring heaves
The mystic fountain, bubbling, panting,
While gossamer its net-work weaves,
Adown the blue lawn, slanting!
I'll mark thy "sunny dome," and view
Thy "caves of ice," thy fields of dew!
Thy ever-blooming mead, whose flow'r
Waves to the cold breath of the moon-light hour!
Or when the day-star, peering bright
On the grey wing of parting night;
While more than vegetating pow'r
Throbs, grateful to the burning hour,
As Summer's whisper'd sighs unfold
Her *million—million** buds of gold![39]

And by the same token the 'stately pleasure-dome' must have been in the original a startlingly different edifice:

Or, when the glassy stream,
That through the deep dell flows,
Flashes the noon's hot beam,
The noon's hot beam, that midway shows
Thy flaming temple, studded o'er
With all Peruvia's lus'trous store![40]

'She overloads everything,' wrote Coleridge (whose

admiration for Mrs. Robinson was deep and sincere) of a poem of 'Perdita's,' in January of the year in which she died.[41] And overloading, not recollection, gives to the fields of dew their sole significance. There is not in the passage a shadow of evidence of changes, made before printing, in the draft of 'Kubla Khan.'[42]

Finally, there can no longer be any doubt that 'Kubla Khan' was composed under the influence of opium. But the implications of that fact may best be considered later. And now we are ready for the dream.

---

* Coleridge declared that he published the fragment of 'Kubla Khan' 'rather as a psychological curiosity, than on the ground of any supposed *poetic* merits.'[2] The poem is infinitely more than 'a psychological curiosity,' but the psychological problem which it presents is unescapable. For the psychologist, however, the value of what follows (as of what precedes) lies not in my conclusions, but in the facts—facts which, in my judgment, are indispensable to any adequate understanding of the nature of the processes involved.

* To quote Coleridge himself, rolling off with gusto the clangorous polysyllables, 'we may best apply Sir Thomas Browne's remark, that many things coagulate on commixture, the separate natures of which promise no concretion.'[29]

* Rhyme, *et præterea nihil*, accounts for their innocent presence. What else, given 'view,' could Perdita have said?

* 'Perdita' is recalling, as in 'gossamer,' 'The Ancient Mariner' too—in the version of 1798. The italics this time are mine.

CHAPTER XIX

THE SLEEPING IMAGES

COLERIDGE'S own account of the genesis of 'Kubla Khan' is as follows. It was first published in 1816, with the poem.*

> In the summer of 1797, the Author, then in ill health, had retired to a lonely farm-house between Porlock and Linton, on the Exmoor confines of Somerset and Devonshire. In consequence of a slight indisposition, an anodyne had been prescribed, from the effects of which he fell asleep in his chair at the moment that he was reading the following sentence, or words of the same substance, in 'Purchas's Pilgrimage': 'Here the Khan Kubla commanded a palace to be built, and a stately garden thereunto. And thus ten miles of fertile ground were inclosed with a wall.' The Author continued for about three hours in a profound sleep, at least of the external senses, during which time he has the most vivid confidence, that he could not have composed less than from two to three hundred lines; if that indeed can be called composition in which all the images rose

> up before him as *things*, with a parallel production of the correspondent expressions, without any sensation or consciousness of effort. On awaking he appeared to himself to have a distinct recollection of the whole, and taking his pen, ink, and paper, instantly and eagerly wrote down the lines that are here preserved. At this moment he was unfortunately called out by a person on business from Porlock, and detained by him above an hour, and on his return to his room, found, to his no small surprise and mortification, that though he still retained some vague and dim recollection of the general purport of the vision, yet, with the exception of some eight or ten scattered lines and images, all the rest had passed away like the images on the surface of a stream into which a stone has been cast, but, alas! without the after restoration of the latter![1]

That is all we know. The year 1797, as Ernest Hartley Coleridge has clearly shown, is wrong.[2] The one thing which Coleridge seems to have been constitutionally incapable of remembering correctly was a date that concerned himself.[3] The visit to the farm-house between Porlock and Linton took place in the early summer of *1798* and 'Kubla Khan,' instead of preceding 'The Ancient Mariner,' closely followed it. That is important, as we shall see.

For 'the images [which] rose up before him as *things*,' rose up from somewhere. And our study of 'The Ancient Mariner' has revealed the fact that Coleridge's memory was tenanted by throngs of visual images derived from books. If, then, we can reconstruct, for the moment when Coleridge fell asleep over *Purchas His Pilgrimage*, the elements, even in part, of that subliminal chaos, we shall have taken a long step towards the clarification of our problem. Those elements, on Coleridge's own testimony, were images with the objective distinctness of *things*—the 'ocular spectra,' in a word, of his favourite terminology. But they had, in the first instance (to employ that terminology once more), 'flashed' from *words*. And it is only through those words that we, in our turn, can arrive at them. Our sole hope, accordingly, of reconstituting any portion of the sleeping imagery which at the moment of the dream was susceptible of movement towards the light, lies again in an examination of the books which Coleridge had been reading. And as in the case of 'The Ancient Mariner' that avenue is open. But before we enter on it, I wish to guard against a misunderstanding which may easily arise—the assumption, namely, that the passages which I shall quote are, in themselves and as they stand, the constituents, or even (in the stock sense of the term) the 'sources' of 'Kubla Khan.' They are not that. Their very words, undoubtedly, were now and then remembered. But that is incidental. What they did for Coleridge was to people the twilight realms of consciousness with *images*. And the thing they enable *us* to do is to gain some inkling of what those subliminal 'atomes crochus' were—those mysterious elements out of whose confluences and coalescences suddenly emerged the poem. If, then, in this chapter the poem itself should seem far away, it is because we must, as Drayton has it, 'adventure upon desperate untrodden ways'—must pass, indeed, in very truth

From the presence of the sun,
Following darkness like a dream.

I

Most fortunately we know, from Coleridge himself, what it was that struck down into the dark and waked the sleeping images to an intense activity. For he tells us what was before his eyes at the instant when he fell asleep, and the poem begins with the actual words on which his eyes had closed. It would be hard to come closer than that to the point at which waking slips over the verge into sleep. The last conscious impressions had been communicated by these lines:[5]

> *In Xamdu did Cublai Can* build *a stately* Palace, encompassing sixteene *miles of* plaine *ground with a wall*, wherein are *fertile* Meddowes, pleasant springs, delightfull Streames, and all sorts of beasts of chase and game, and in the middest thereof a sumptuous house of *pleasure*, which may be removed from place to place.*

The images which first rose up 'as *things*' had taken on this correspondent form:

In Xanadu did Kubla Khan
A stately pleasure-dome decree:
Where Alph, the sacred river, ran
Through caverns measureless to man
        Down to a sunless sea.
So twice five *miles of fertile ground*
With walls and towers were girdled round:
And there were gardens bright with sinuous rills,
Where blossomed many an incense-bearing tree;
And here were forests ancient as the hills,
Enfolding sunny spots of greenery.

And there, for the moment, we may pause.

Into those thronged precincts, then, 'just on the vestibule of consciousness,' where the sleeping images maintain their 'shadowy half-being,' there had sunk, at the very instant when conscious control had been suspended, a new and richly suggestive concourse of impressions. That, at least, is clear. But so is something else. Once granted that conjunction, it was inevitable that flashes of association should dart in all directions, and that images endowed with the potentiality of merging should stream together and coalesce.* I know that these are 'goings-on' (to use Coleridge's phrase)[7] which 'matter-moulded forms of speech' are hard put to it to express. But something not wholly remote from what they adumbrate certainly took place.

For even in the few lines of 'Kubla Khan' which I have quoted are details which by no farthest stretch of fancy can be thought of as implicit in the sentence from the *Pilgrimage*.

> Where Alph, the sacred river, ran
> Through caverns measureless to man
> Down to a sunless sea.

The images, for instance, which underlie that startling metamorphosis of Purchas's 'delightful streames' had obviously flashed from other pages than the one which Coleridge was reading when he fell asleep. So, with no less certainty, had most of the vividly distinct and concrete imagery of the remainder of the poem. What the impressions from Purchas had done, in a word, was to summon up other images, and set swift trains of association interweaving. And the enterprise before us now is the attempt to reconstruct in part those evanescent operations, which yet builded of their fleetingness a fabric beside which

> . . . rocks impregnable are not so stout,
> Nor gates of steel so strong.

No mortal can hope to call back all that insubstantial pageant which once moved through a long-vanished dream. Most of it faded on the instant, and left not a rack behind. But some of the elements which streamed together are yet traceable, nor is it impossible even to gather, sometimes, how and why they merged. The sequence, however, in which their coalescences occurred is something which I am not so reckless as to attempt to guess.[8] And so the order which we shall follow in the sequel is simply the order which clarity in setting forth the facts demands.

II

Let us return to the sentence in Purchas which Coleridge was reading. Obviously something else—perhaps even before unconsciousness descended—had flashed back to his memory. For Coleridge knew well not merely *Purchas His Pilgrimage*, but *Purchas His Pilgrimes* too. It was in the third volume of the *Pilgrimes* that he had read of William Barents and of the icefields of the North. And in this same volume was another and more detailed account of Kubla Khan. Whether this parallel account had come back to his memory before or after consciousness lapsed is immaterial; in some form or other it was there. For it betrays its presence. I do not know what edition of the *Pilgrimage* Coleridge was reading. If by any chance he had taken Wordsworth's copy with him to his retreat, he had before him the edition of 1617.[9] In that event the name of Kubla's city as it would meet his eye had the cacophanous form 'Xamdu'—as was also the case if his edition were that of either 1614 or 1626. If, on the other hand, it was the first, of 1613, the form he saw was 'Xaindu.' But the name which lends its euphony to the poem's opening line is neither; it is '*Xanadu*'. And that is the form which he knew in the

Pilgrimes, 'Xandu'—now 'unfurled to music suddenly.'

At or after the moment, then, when Coleridge fell asleep, recollections of the *Pilgrimes* had been stirred to life by the reading of the *Pilgrimage*. Anything else, indeed, when (as here) the two narratives ran parallel, would have been, even disregarding 'Xanadu,' well nigh incredible. Let us see what that involves. In the account of Xamdu (or Xaindu) which Coleridge was reading in the *Pilgrimage* was a '*house of pleasure*,' in the midst of 'fertile Meddowes, pleasant springs, delightfull Streames.' But in the *Pilgrimes*, in the marginal gloss to the parallel account of Kubla's palace, was a 'house of pleasure' too. And just eight pages before this remembered account of Xandu in the *Pilgrimes* is one of the most unforgettable passages in the book. And in it also are '*houses of pleasure*,' in the midst of 'a goodly Garden, furnished with the best trees and fruits.' There was, then, between the two narratives a palpable associative link. What happened?

The passage in the *Pilgrimes* is the famous account of the Old Man of the Mountain.* I shall first quote a couple of sentences from the beginning of it:

> His name was Aloadine, and was a Mahumetan. Hee had in a goodly Valley betwixt two Mountaynes very high, made *a goodly Garden, furnished with the best trees* and fruits he could find, adorned with divers Palaces and *houses of pleasure*, beautified with gold Workes, Pictures, and Furnitures of silke.[10]

That the sentence which Coleridge read in the *Pilgrimage* brought back this definitely linked passage in the *Pilgrimes*, and that the images which rose up from the two of them blended in the dream, it is difficult to doubt. The 'fertile Meddowes, pleasant springs, delightfull Streames' and the 'goodly Garden, furnished with the best trees' have slipped together, like Martens's snow and Father Bourzes's rainbow in the spray, into an exquisitely lucid whole compact of both—and, as we shall see, of something else:

> And there were *gardens bright with sinuous rills*,
> Where blossomed *many an* incense-bearing *tree*.

But the spell of the Old Man of the Mountain was more potent far than that. And its presence now becomes unmistakable.

For now I shall take up again the account of Aloadine's house of pleasure at the exact point where I broke it off, and shall then set down at once the wonderful last paragraph of 'Kubla Khan.' What gave Coleridge the two vivid figures—the damsel with a dulcimer and the youth with flashing eyes and floating hair—who appear in the poem out of nothing, with a dream-like suddenness and a dream's serene oblivion of their inconsequence? Here, at all events, are the inmates of Aloadine's Paradise:

> There by divers Pipes answering divers parts of those Palaces were seene to runne Wine, *Milke, Honey*, and cleere Water. In them hee had placed goodly *Damosels*

skilfull in Songs and Instruments of Musicke and Dancing, and to make Sports and Delights unto men whatsoever they could imagine. They were also fairely attyred in Gold and Silke, and were seene togoe continually sporting in the Garden and Palaces. He made this Palace, *because Mahomet had promised such a sensuall Paradise to his devout followers . . .*

Aloadine had *certaine Youthes* from twelve to twentie yeares of age, such as seemed of a bold and undoubted disposition, *whom hee instructed daily touching Mahomets Paradise*, and how hee could bring men thither. And when he thought good, *he caused a certaine Drinke to bee given unto* ten or twelve of *them*, which cast them in a dead sleepe: and then hee caused them to be carryed into divers Chambers of the said Palaces, *where they saw the things aforesaid* as soone as they awaked: *each of them having those Damosels to minister Meates and excellent Drinkes*, and all varieties of pleasures to them; *insomuch that the Fooles thought themselves in Paradise indeed.* When they had enjoyed those pleasures foure or five dayes, they were againe cast in a sleepe, and carryed forth againe. After which, hee . . . questioned where they had beene, which answered, by your Grace, *in Paradise*. . . . Then the old man answered, This is the commandement of our Prophet, that *whosoever defends his Lord, he make him enter Paradise:* and if thou wilt bee obedient to mee, thou shalt have this grace. And having thus animated them, *hee was thought happie whom the old man would command, though it cost him his life: so that other Lords and his Enemies were slaine by these his Assasines, which exposed themselves to all dangers, and contemned their lives.*[12]

Now let us return to the poem:

A damsel with a dulcimer
In a vision once I saw:
It was an Abyssinian maid,
And on her dulcimer she played,
Singing of Mount Abora.
Could I revive within me
Her symphony and song,
To such a deep delight 'twould win me,
That with music loud and long,
I would build that dome in air,
That sunny dome! those caves of ice!
And all who heard should see them there,
And all should cry, Beware! Beware!
His flashing eyes, his floating hair!
Weave a circle round him thrice,
And close your eyes with holy dread,
For he on honey-dew hath fed,
And drunk the milk of Paradise.

There can be little question of what has happened. Behind the strange and haunting beauty of the dream's imagery recollected fragments of the striking picture of the pleasure-houses flash and fade and cross and interweave: 'goodly Damosels' with 'Songs and Instruments of Musicke,' seen between sleep and sleep; the milk and honey of Paradise, drunk and eaten at the singing, playing damsels' hands; the desire on waking out of sleep to live again the lost delights ('Could I revive within me Her symphony and song'); the duped inmates of the palace, fired, that so they may regain a Paradise once tasted and now withdrawn, with a fanatic zeal to kill:

> And all who heard should see them there,
> *And all should cry, Beware! Beware!*
> His flashing eyes, his floating hair! . . .
> For he on honey-dew hath fed,
> And drunk the milk of Paradise.

They are at once the same and not the same, as you and I have known their like to be a hundred times in dreams. Nobody in his waking senses could have fabricated those amazing eighteen lines. For if anything ever bore the infallible marks of authenticity it is that dissolving panorama in which fugitive hints of Aloadine's Paradise succeed each other with the vivid incoherence, and the illusion of natural and expected sequence, and the sense of an identity that yet is not identity, which are the distinctive attributes of dreams. Coleridge's statement of his experience has more than once been called in question. These lines alone, in their relation to the passage which suggested them, should banish doubt.[13]

Whence, however, slipped into the dream—like journeying stars which enter unannounced—Abyssinia, and Mount Abora, and the dome in air, and the caves of ice, and Alph the sacred river with its caverns and its sunless sea? They are all, I think, distinctly traceable. But to reach them we must first meander with a mazy motion through regions already traversed in our earlier quest.

III

Is it possible to repeople with its vanished images another corner of Coleridge's unconscious mind into which may have flashed those associations which are the stuff of dreams? With the aid of the Note Book I believe it is.

In April, 1798, Coleridge, who had been suffering from an infected tooth, wrote as follows, in a letter to his brother George:

> Laudanam gave me repose, not sleep; but you, I believe, know how divine that repose is, *what a spot of enchantment, a green spot of fountain and flowers and trees* in the very heart of a waste of sands![14]

Now when Coleridge wrote that, he was recalling and echoing, consciously or unconsciously, something else. For in the Note Book (which, as we know, belongs to this same period) appears this memorandum:

> —*some wilderness-plot, green andfountainous* and unviolated by Man.[15]

Is it possible to discover what lies behind this note?

The entry is sandwiched in, together with Hartley's tumble and his tears which glittered in the moonlight, between the two parts of the long note on Bartram's crocodiles. That note, in turn, is transcribed from pages 127–30 of Bartram's *Travels*. The next entry in the Note Book is from Bartram's 140th page; the next from pages 161–62; the next from pages 132–33. And on page 157, flanked on one side by our old friends the crocodiles and snake-birds, and on the other by the Gordonia lasianthus, stands the following:

> I was however induced to . . . touch at the inchanting little Isle of Palms. This delightful spot, planted by nature, is almost an entire grove of Palms, with a few pyramidal Magnolias, Live Oaks, golden Orange, and the animating Zanthoxilon; what a beautiful retreat is here! *blessed unviolated spot of earth!* rising from the limpid waters of the lake; its fragrant groves and blooming lawns invested and protected by encircling ranks of the Yucca gloriosa; a fascinating atmosphere surrounds this blissful garden; the balmy Lantana, ambrosial Citra, perfumed Crinum, perspiring their mingled odours, wafted through Zanthoxilon groves. I at last broke away from *the enchanting spot* . . . then traversing a capacious semi-

> circular cove of the lake, verged by low, extensive grassy meadows, I at length by dusk made a safe harbour.

And two pages earlier 'the dew-drops twinkle and play . . . on the tips of the lucid, green savanna, sparkling' beside a 'serpentine rivulet, meandering over the meadows.'[16]

Those lines from Bartram, then, are in the very thick of the pages which Coleridge was ardently transcribing in his Note Book, and the picture which they painted made a profound impression on his mind. For he twice came back to it. It inspired the memorandum in the Note Book, for the 'wilderness-plot,[17] green and fountainous and *unviolated* by Man' is unmistakably the 'blessed *unviolated* spot of earth' on which Bartram lavished such a wealth of words. It no less clearly underlies the passage in the letter, whose '*spot of enchantment*' is Bartram's '*enchanting spot*,' and whose 'green spot of fountain' is the 'plot, green and fountainous' of the Note Book. And in the letter it becomes the symbol of the 'divine repose' induced by opium, and the letter was written not more than a month or two before 'Kubla Khan.' Of one thing, then, we may be certain: impressions of Bartram's 'inchanting little Isle of Palms' were among the sleeping images in Coleridge's unconscious memory at the time when 'Kubla Khan' emerged from it.

But a thousand other impressions coexisted with them there. Did this particular cluster constitute what we have called an *atome crochu?* Had it, in other words, hooks and eyes which might draw it into the extraordinary complex which was taking form? If it *were* so equipped, its attraction within the circle was almost inevitable. For it lay, so to speak, just over the threshold of consciousness. Twice already its imagery had recurred to memory and clothed itself with words. And recurrence to memory soon becomes a habit. Conspicuous, now, among its details were 'grassy meadows,' a 'blissful garden,' 'fragrant groves,' and multitudes of trees. And at the moment of the dream, by way of Purchas, impressions of 'fertile Meddowes,' conjoined with a 'goodly Garden' furnished with trees, were stirring actively in Coleridge's brain. Clearly, then, there were sufficient links between the images from Purchas which were sinking into the Well, and the images from Bartram which were already there.

And they *did* coalesce. Here are the lovely lines of the fragment once again:

> And there were *gardens bright with sinuous rills,*
> Where *blossomed* many an *incense-bearing* tree;
> *And here were forests* ancient as the hills,
> *Enfolding sunny spots of greenery.*

'As I bent my head,' wrote Coleridge to Godwin in words which I have quoted once before, 'there came a distinct, vivid spectrum upon my eyes; it was one little picture—a rock, with birches and ferns on it, a cottage backed by it, and a small stream. Were I a painter I would give an outward existence to this, *but it will always live in my memory.*'[18] Even so into the dream had come remembered ocular spectra from Bartram—images which rose up before the dreamer 'as *things*.' There were Bartram's '*balmy* Lantana, *ambrosial* Citra, *perfumed* Crinum, *perspiring their mingled odours*.' But the dreamer was Coleridge, not Bartram, and so the mass of particulars melted into a single line, redolent of the odours of all spicy shores: 'Where blossomed *many an incense-bearing tree*.' Into the dream, moreover, had slipped the image of an image of an image—that luminous visualization in the letter (still only a few weeks old) of the same scene as it came up through the Note Book from Bartram: 'a spot of enchantment, *a green spot* of fountain and flowers and trees.' And so in the dream there are 'forests ancient as the hills, Enfolding sunny *spots of greenery*.' And the '*serpentine rivulet*' meandering through 'the *lucid, green savanna*' sparkling with sunlit dew—that too, merged with another recollection, rose up in the dream as 'one little picture,' to which were fitted, 'without consciousness of effort,' perfect words: 'And there were gardens *bright with sinuous rills*' Even 'enfolding' is a transmuted flash of memory. For in Bartram's 'enchanting spot' are 'blooming lawns *invested . . . by encircling* ranks' of towering flora. And these 'blooming' forest-glades are seen in the blossoming of the incense-bearing trees. Every detail in the four lines which recollections of Purchas leave wanting or incomplete, reminiscences of Bartram have supplied. But neither *Travels*, nor *Pilgrimage*, nor *Pilgrimes*, nor all of them combined, supplied the resultant beauty.

IV

We have by no means finished, however, with the Isle of Palms. For the images which rose from Bartram were furnished with still other powerful links. It will be remembered that in the Note Book Bartram's 'blessed unviolated spot of earth' appeared as a 'wilderness-plot, green and *fountainous*,' and that in the letter it reappeared as 'a green spot of *fountain* and flowers and trees.' But there were no fountains in Bartram's Isle of Palms. Yet even before the dream fountains had somehow become fixed in Coleridge's mental picture. How had they entered it?

The account of the Isle of Palms is on Bartram's 157th page. The Gordonia lasianthus is on pages 161–62. Coleridge, then, was still intently reading on. And the entry in the Note Book touching the 'Siminoles,' which draws on pages 212–13, and the footnote to 'This Lime-Tree Bower my Prison,' which quotes verbatim a sentence from page 221,[19] afford ample evidence that he had read still farther. Now on page 165, just three pages beyond the Gordonia lasianthus, is this:

> I seated myself upon *a swelling green knoll*, at the head of the chrystal bason. Near me, on the left, was a point or projection of an entire grove of the aromatic Illisium Floridanum; on my right and all around behind me,

> was a fruitful *Orange grove*, with *Palms* and *Magnolias* interspersed; in front, just under my feet was the *inchanting and amazing chrystal fountain.*

The fountain and the Isle of Palms are separated by eight pages only, and a passage entered in the Note Book lies between. They may easily have been read at the same sitting, and the associative links between the two—green knoll, aromatic groves, oranges, palms, magnolias—are patent at a glance. At all events, the Note Book and the letter are evidence that before the dream was dreamed the two green and fragrant spots of trees and flowers had coalesced in Coleridge's memory. And into the picture which was later to haunt the dream had been carried the imagery suggested by 'the inchanting . . . chrystal fountain.'

Now let us see a little more of this amazing fountain. The account of it proceeds:

> Just under my feet was the inchanting and amazing chrystal fountain, *which incessantly threw up, from dark, rocky caverns below, tons of water every minute, forming* a bason, capacious enough for large shallops to ride in, and *a creek* of four or *five* feet depth of water, and near twenty yards over, *which meanders six miles through green meadows*, pouring its limpid waters into the great Lake George. . . . About twenty yards from the upper edge of the bason . . . is a *continual and amazing ebullition, where*

> *the waters are thrown up in such abundance and amazing force*, as to jet and swell up two or three feet above the common surface: *white sand and small particles of shells are thrown up with the waters . . . when they . . . subside* with the expanding flood, and gently *sink again.*[20]

That, then, before the dream, Coleridge had seen in his mind's eye. What did he see in the dream?

> And from this chasm, *with ceaseless turmoil seething,*
> As if this earth in fast thick pants were breathing,
> *A mighty fountain momently was forced:*
> Amid whose swift half-intermitted burst
> Huge *fragments vaulted* like rebounding hail,
> Or chaffy grain beneath the thresher's flail:
> And 'mid these dancing rocks at once and ever
> *It flung up momently the sacred river.*
> *Five miles meandering* with a mazy motion
> *Through wood and dale* the sacred river ran,
> *Then reached the caverns* measureless to man,
> *And sank* in tumult to a lifeless ocean.

The images which rose up in the dream, in conjunction with 'sunny spots of greenery,' were images which had risen up before, in similar conjunction, when Coleridge, with that preternatural visualizing faculty of his, was eagerly devouring Bartram. They are that beyond the shadow of a doubt. But they are also, as so often happens in a dream, simultaneously something else. That something else must wait its turn, however, since we have still to do with Bartram.

For Bartram was inordinately fond of letting himself go on the subject of ebullient fountains—which were, indeed, in all conscience, remarkable enough.[21] And certain striking details from one or two of these other lively descriptions had fixed themselves in Coleridge's memory. Ernest Hartley Coleridge, who saw so much that has enriched us, missed the 'inchanting and amazing chrystal fountain' which reappears in such startling fashion in the dream.[22] But he calls attention, in a footnote to the lines of 'Kubla Khan' before us, and more fully in a paper read before the Royal Society of Literature in 1906, to 'William Bartram's description of the "Alligator Hole." '[23] Now that description is only seventeen pages beyond the account of the savanna crane, of which Coleridge quotes half a dozen lines,[24] and we may be certain that he read it. And what he read included the story, as told by an eye-witness, of the last eruption from the vast orifice. Here is enough of it to serve our purpose:

> On a sudden, he was astonished by an inexpressible rushing noise, like a mighty hurricane or thunder storm, and looking around, he saw the earth overflowed by torrents of water. . . *attended with a terrific* noise and *tremor of the earth*. . . . He immediately resolved to proceed for the place from whence the noise seemed to come,

> and soon came in sight of *the incomparable fountain*, and saw, with amazement, *the floods rushing upwards many feet high*, and the expanding waters . . . spreading themselves far and near. . . . It continued to *jet* and flow in this manner for several days, *forming a large . . . river*, descending and following the various. . . . *windings* of the valley, for the distance of seven or eight miles, emptying itself into a vast savanna, where there was a. . . *sink which received . . . its waters*. . . . At places, where ridges or a swelling bank . . . opposed its course and fury, are *vast heaps of fragments of rocks*, white chalk, stones and pebbles, *which were . . . thrown* into the lateral vallies.[25]

The two descriptions could not but recall each other, and in the dream their images coalesced. The sense of a tremendous force is heightened: the 'white sand and small particles of shells . . . thrown up' by 'the inchanting fountain' give place to 'fragments of rocks . . . thrown' in vast heaps into the vallies; the 'terrific tremor of the earth' now pulsates through the dream, 'As if this earth in fast thick pants were breathing.' But the concourse of the hooked atoms is not yet complete.

Just eight pages earlier Coleridge had read of still another 'grand fountain,' 'the admirable Manate Spring':

> The ebullition is astonishing, and continual, *though its greatest force or fury intermits*, regularly, *for the space of thirty seconds of time*. . . . the ebullition is perpendicular upwards, from *a vast ragged orifice through a bed of*

> *rocks . . . throwing up small particles or pieces of white shells*, which subside with the waters, at the moment of *intermission*. . . yet, before the surface becomes quite even, the fountain vomits up the waters again, and *so on perpetually*.[26]

And so there is added, with fresh emphasis on the '*ceaseless* turmoil,' the suggestion of the '*swift half-intermitted* burst.' The imagery of the 'mighty fountain' in the vision is an amazing confluence of images from these separate yet closely linked reports of actual fountains which Coleridge had read.[27] Yet in another sense the confluence is not 'amazing'; it is the normal mechanism of a dream.[28]

V

And now among the elements which blended in the panorama appears a train of imagery stranger and more startling than any which has gone before. For through the dream, mysteriously flooding and subsiding, flows 'the sacred river.'

One of the books most widely read at the close of the century was James Bruce's *Travels to Discover the Source of the Nile*. And Coleridge knew it well. He made use of it (as we have seen) in his 'Religious Musings,' dated 'on the Christmas Eve of 1794,' and in a footnote to the poem he quotes Bruce's graphic description of the Simoom.[29] In 1801 he makes a memorandum of his intention to use, in a comparison after the manner of Jeremy Taylor, the idea of 'seeking the fountains of the Nile.'[30] And in 1807 he recommends the last edition of the *Travels* to Lady Beaumont as 'a book that [she] ought by all means to have.'[31] It was no wonder that he did so. Bruce, in Richard Garnett's words, 'will always remain the poet, and his work the epic, of African travel.'[32] And as the tale of an attempt to penetrate the mystery which had veiled for centuries the sources of the most venerable of all historic streams, the narrative was and is one to stir imagination. Nor should we expect a superb contemporary chapter in the romance of discovery to leave Coleridge's tenacious memory bare of images.

Certainly no one who ever read it would forget the dramatic climax of the story. Bruce, baffled and annoyed by the shifts and evasions of his native guide, lost his temper:

> Come, come, said I . . . no more words; it is now late, lose no more time, but carry me to Geesh, and the head of the Nile directly, without preamble, and shew me the hill that separates me from it. He then carried me round to the south side of the church, out of the grove of trees that surrounded it. 'This is the hill, says he, looking archly, that . . . was between you and *the fountains of the Nile;* there is no other; look at *that hillock of green sod* in the middle of that watery spot, it is in that the two *fountains of the Nile* are to be found: Geesh is on the face of the rock where *yon green trees* are: if you go the length

> of the fountains pull off your shoes . . . for these people are all Pagans . . . and they believe in nothing that you believe, but only in this river, *to which they pray every day as if it were God.*' . . . Half undressed as I was by loss of my sash, and throwing my shoes off, I ran down the hill towards *the little island of green sods*; . . . the whole side of the hill was *thick grown over with flowers*, the large bulbous roots of which appearing above the surface of the ground, and their skins coming off on treading upon them, occasioned two very severe falls before I reached the brink of the marsh; I after this came to *the island of green turf*, which was in form of an altar, apparently the work of art, *and I stood in rapture over the principal fountain which rises in the middle of it.*
>
> It is easier to guess than to describe the situation of my mind at that moment—standing in that spot which had baffled the genius, industry, and inquiry of both ancients and moderns, for the course of near three thousand years.[33]

We need not pursue Bruce's meditation farther; but in that thrilling moment the 'little island of green sods' held, both for him and for his readers, the answer to a question older than the riddle of the sphinx. And for two long chapters this other 'wilderness-plot, green and fountainous,' is in the foreground of the narrative.

Now Bruce, in his attempt to prove himself the first European to reach the sources of the Nile, discusses at great length the narrative of Father Peter Paez, who claimed to have discovered the two fountains on April 21, 1618. And he quotes, on the authority of Athanasius Kircher, Paez's description of the fountains, in which, after declaring that he 'saw, with the greatest delight [summaque animi mei voluptate], what neither Cyrus king of the Persians, nor Cambyses, nor Alexander the Great, nor the famous Julius Cæsar, could ever discover,' he mentions certain striking details which have for us peculiar interest:

> The second fountain lies about a stone-cast west from the first: the inhabitants say that *this whole mountain is full of water*, and add, that the whole plain about the fountain is floating and unsteady, a certain mark that there is water concealed under it; for which reason, the water does not overflow at the fountain, but *forces itself with great violence out* at the foot of the mountain. The inhabitants . . . maintain that that year it trembled little on account of the drought, but other years, that *it trembled and overflowed so as that it could scarce be approached without danger.*[34]

It would be hard to imagine 'hooks and eyes of the memory' more effective than those which link the description of that fountain with the accounts of its congeners in Florida.

The 'hillock of green sod,' like the 'swelling green knoll' by the 'inchanting fountain'; the hillside 'thick grown over with flowers'; the plain about the fountain that 'trembled'; the water that 'forced itself out with great violence': every detail recalls some parallel in Bartram. But there is a further correspondence so close as to verge on the uncanny. The Nile, just after it has left the fountain, 'makes so many sharp, unnatural *windings*, that it differs,' says Bruce, 'from any other river I ever saw, making above twenty sharp angular peninsulas *in the course of five miles*.'[35] The stream thrown up by Bartram's 'amazing chrystal fountain' '*meanders six miles* through green meadows.'[36] Coleridge being Coleridge, with that prehensile associative faculty of his, it was really the inevitable which happened. '*Five miles meandering* with a mazy motion'—so ran the sacred river which the mighty fountain in the dream flung up. And that is Bartram and Bruce in one. The vivid images of fountains in Florida and Abyssinia, with their powerfully ejected streams, have coalesced in the deep Well and risen up together, at once both and neither, in the dream. And by virtue of that incomprehensible juggling with identities which is the most familiar trick of dreams, 'the sacred river' *is* the Nile—while at the same time it is *not*. Only in a dream, I once more venture to believe, could the phantasmagoria which now for the first time it is possible to estimate, have risen up.

VI

And now certain other mysterious features of the dream fall into place. Why was the damsel with a dulcimer 'an Abyssinian maid'? The answer is not far to seek. The fountains of the sacred river are in Abyssinia; almost from beginning to end the scene of Bruce's narrative is laid in Abyssinia; and Abyssinia hovered in the background of the vision, to become suddenly explicit in this seemingly unaccountable detail. And for still another instant Abyssinia held the foreground of the dream:

> It was an Abyssinian maid,
> And on her dulcimer she played,
> *Singing of Mount Abora.*

What was Mount Abora, unknown to any map, I think, since time began?

The account which I have quoted of Bruce's rapturous plunge down the flowery hillside to the fountains of the Nile is on pages 596–97 of his third volume. Between pages 580 and 588 occurs fifteen times—six times on page 587 alone—a name which has not appeared before. It is that of the river, or valley, or plain of *Abola*. 'The river Abola'—a tributary of the Nile—'comes out of the valley between [the] two ridges of mountains of Litchambara and Aformasha,' which Bruce at once identifies with 'the Mountains of the Moon, or the *Montes Lunæ* of antiquity, at the foot of which the Nile was said to rise.'[37] No reader of Bruce could reach the story of the fountains of the Nile without 'Abola' ringing in his ears. And 'Abola' was itself amply sufficient to suggest the dream-word 'Abora,' as 'Xamdu' or 'Xaindu' suggested 'Xanadu.'[38] But there was another name in Bruce which with little doubt blended in Coleridge's memory with 'Abola,' to bring about the metamorphosis.

Only eight pages beyond Bruce's account of his thrilling discovery is a description of the island of Meroë: 'That island . . . having a twilight of short duration' (a remark peculiarly adapted to catch Coleridge's eye) 'was placed between the Nile and *Astaboras*.'[39] In the next chapter (still the 'Description of the Sources of the Nile') the name turns up repeatedly again. 'It seems very clear that the *Atbara* is the *Astaboras* of the ancients'; 'Meroë . . . was inclosed between the *Astaboras* and the Nile'; 'Pliny says, Meroë . . . is called *Astaboras*. . . . "Asta-bores lævo alveo dictus." '[40] Moreover, the first appearance of the Astaboras in the narrative is not without suggestion: 'this prodigious body of water. . . *tearing up rocks* and large trees in its course, and *forcing down their broken fragments* scattered on its stream, with a noise like thunder echoed from a hundred hills . . . is very rightly called the "terrible." '[41] 'Astaboras,' then, can scarcely have failed to print itself on Coleridge's memory, and the accented element of the name is '*abora*.' And the obvious relation between the modern 'Atbara' and the ancient 'Astaboras' would serve to fix attention on this central element. Between '*Abola*' and

'*Astaboras*,' accordingly, Coleridge's 'Abora' seems to have slipped into the dream.[42]

But why should hints from the names of two *rivers* have contributed a *mountain* to the dream? Whatever the suggestion, it doubtless flashed for an instant and was gone, 'impalpable as the wind, fleeting as the wings of sleep'—*par levibus ventis volucrique simillima somno*. Yet to recapture it (if recapture it we can) we must traverse with heavy feet the labyrinth through which it fled like light. But we have long been doing that.

Some years ago, Professor Lane Cooper suggested, in an article on 'The Abyssinian Paradise in Coleridge and Milton,'[43] that Coleridge's 'Mount Abora' was really Milton's 'Mount Amara.' In the sense In which 'the sacred river' at the same time is and is not the Nile, I think he is right; and in the light of the facts already presented in this chapter his suggestion takes on new significance. Mount Amara closes the bead-roll of those enticing earthly Paradises which Milton, in the fourth book of *Paradise Lost*, sets over against his glowing account of the true Paradise of Eden:

> Not that fair field
> Of Enna, where Proserpin gathering flowers,
> Herself a fairer flower, by gloomy Dis
> Was gathered—which cost Ceres all that pain
> To seek her through the world—nor that sweet grove
> Of Daphne, by Orontes and the inspired

Castalian spring, might with this Paradise
Of Eden strive . . .
Nor, *where Abassin kings their issue guard*,
Mount Amara (though this by some supposed
True Paradise) under the Ethiop line
By Nilus' head, enclosed with shining rock,
A whole day's journey high.[44]

No one will doubt that Coleridge, who knew his Milton through and through, and who believed that 'in the description of Paradise itself. . . [Milton's] descriptive powers are exercised to the utmost,'[45] was thoroughly conversant with the lines on Amara, in their passingly lovely context. Had they, however, associations which might blend some fugitive recollection of them with the dream?[46]

The links are there, not single spies, but in battalions. The setting of Mount Abora in the dream is a flashing stream of reminiscences of that Paradise of the Old Man of the Mountain wherein 'Fooles thought themselves in Paradise indeed'; Milton's Mount Amara is such another pseudo-Paradise, like Aloadine's, 'by some supposed True Paradise.' Through the imagery of the dream ebbs and flows the sacred river, and the sacred river, as we now know, is the Nile; Mount Amara is 'under the Ethiop line By Nilus' head'—those fountains which by way of Bruce flung up the sacred river in the dream. And by way of Bruce Mount Amara itself might have found, together with the fountains, ready entrance. For Bruce writes of Amhara too, as one of the geographical divisions of Abyssinia:

> It is a very mountainous country, full of nobility; the men are reckoned the handsomest in Abyssinia, as well as the bravest. . . . What, besides, added to the dignity of this province, was the high mountain of Geshen, or the grassy mountain, *whereon the king's sons were formerly imprisoned.*[47]

'Nor, *where Abassin kings their issue guard*, Mount Amara'! It would be hard for Coleridge to read the first without a flash of recollection, on the very threshold of the sacred river, to the second. Into the dream, moreover, had poured the imagery of that enchanting spot in Bartram, where balmy trees 'perspir[ed] their mingled odours'; 'Groves whose rich trees wept odorous gums and balm' precede by only thirty lines the Miltonic Amara. And in the '*fertile ground*' of Eden, and its 'many a *rill*' that rolled 'with *mazy* error,' and its river which 'through the shaggy hill *Passed underneath ingulfed*,' are correspondences which compel belief that Milton's Paradise, and with it his Mount Amara, lent fleeting touches to the panorama of the dream.[48] And in that phantasmagoria 'Amara' (well worthy of commemoration in an Abyssinian damsel's symphony and song) has passed, under the spell of sounds more closely associated with the sacred river, through 'Abola' and 'Astaboras,' into 'Abora.'*

All this is enhanced by the further fact (to which Professor Cooper also calls attention)[49] that Purchas has an entire chapter in his *Pilgrimage* entitled 'Of the Hill Amara,'[50] and it was this chapter which inspired Milton's lines. It is one of the most memorable purple patches of the book, and nobody who knew the *Pilgrimage* would be likely to forget it. Coleridge, certainly, in that quest of materials for his 'Hymns to the Sun, Moon, and the Elements' which led him to Maurice and Quintus Curtius, could not well have overlooked it, for on the hill 'there are two Temples, built before the Raigne of the Queene of Saba, one in honour of the Sunne, the other of the Moone, the most magnificent in all Ethiopia.'[51] And its links with the dream are as obvious as Milton's.[52] It is difficult to believe that Coleridge did not know it; and through it, or through both (I think we may be sure), Mount Amara—its name merged with the name of the river that flowed by the Mountains of the Moon—was drawn into that concourse of impressions which, as Coleridge sat sleeping over Purchas, was slipping through the ivory gate.

VII

I am aware that to some of my readers all this ado about a name will be regarded as the veriest trifling. But I beg such readers to remember that nothing is trivial which contributes to our understanding, on the one hand, of the strange workings of the mind in dreams, and on the other, of the waking operations of the creative faculty. There is not, in my judgment, among all existing records of the human mind, an opportunity of studying the two together which is comparable to that afforded by 'The Ancient Mariner' and 'Kubla Khan.' We shall see, I hope, when the materials which it is the formidable business of this chapter to elucidate are all before us, that the workings of the dream throw welcome light upon the waking processes. If that be so, no clue is too slight to follow where it leads. And there are more for us to follow.

For still other reminiscences of Bruce seem to have blended with the dream—recollections which

> Stream'd onward, lost their edges, and did creep
> Roll'd on each other, rounded, smooth'd, and brought
> Into the gulfs of sleep.

Let me set down in Bruce's words a few glimpses of the Abyssinian landscape caught as the little caravan approached the fountains of the Nile:

> The [whole mountain] was covered with thick wood, which often occupied the very edge of the precipices on which we stood. . . . Just above this almost impenetrable wood, in a very *romantic* situation, stands St. Michael, in a hollow space like a nitch between two hills. . . . The

> Nile here is not four yards over. . . [The whole company] were sitting in the shade of *a grove of magnificent cedars*. . . . The banks [of the Nile]' . . . are covered with black, dark, and thick groves . . . a very rude and awful face of nature, *a cover* from which our fancy suggested a lion should issue, or some animal or monster yet more *savage* and ferocious. . . . 'Strates,' said I, 'be in no such haste; remember the water is *inchanted*.'. . . In the middle of this cliff [at Geesh], in a direction straight north towards the fountains, is *a prodigious cave*. . . . From the edge of the cliff of Geesh . . . *the ground slopes* with a very easy descent due north. . . . On the east *the ground descends* likewise with a very easy . . . slope. . . . From [the] west side of it . . . the ascent is very easy and gradual . . . all the way covered with good earth, *producing fine grass*.[53]

And here is the landscape of the dream:

> But oh! that deep *romantic chasm* which *slanted*
> *Down the green hill* athwart a *cedarn cover!*
> *A savage place!* as holy and *enchanted*
> As e'er beneath a waning moon was haunted
> By woman wailing for her demon-lover!

Other, impressions, to be sure, after the fashion of the sleeping images, have merged in the dream with the ocular spectra which had flashed from Bruce's panoramic pages. But allowing for the wizardry of sleep, the 'deep romantic chasm' of 'the sacred river' is essentially the setting of the fountains of the Nile.

One other picture seems to owe its startling vividness to Bruce. Few images in the dream can have risen up more thrillingly as *things* than that apparition from the 'bewitched enclosure' of Aloadine's Paradise:

> And all should cry, Beware! Beware!
> *His flashing eyes, his floating hair!*

And as one of Aloadine's Tartar damsels becomes, thanks to Bruce, an Abyssinian maid, so, through the same influence, one of Aloadine's fanatic devotees is visualized (it would seem) as an Abyssinian king.

One of the most dramatic scenes in Bruce occurs a few pages after the fountains of the Nile are left behind. Bruce has joined the king of Abyssinia, Tecla Haimanout, who is fighting for his throne. And now the following extraordinary incident takes place:

> [The king] had desired me to ride before him, and shew him the horse I had got from Fasil. . . . It happened that, crossing the deep bed of a brook, a plant of the kantuffa hung across it. I had upon my shoulders a white goat-skin, of which it did not take hold; but the king, who was dressed in the habit of peace, *his long hairfloating all around his face*, wrapt up in his mantle, or thin cotton cloak, *so that nothing but his eyes* could be seen, was

paying more attention to the horse than to the branch of kantuffa beside him; it took first hold of his hair, and the fold of the cloak that covered his head . . . in such a manner that . . . no remedy remained but he must throw off the upper garment, and appear . . . with his head and face bare before all the spectators.

This is accounted great disgrace to a king, who always appears covered in public. However, he did not seem to be ruffled . . . but with great composure, and in rather a low voice, he called twice, Who is the Shum of this district? Unhappily he was not far off. A thin old man of sixty, and his son about thirty, came trotting, as their custom is, naked to their girdle, and stood before the king. . . . The king asked if he was Shum of that place? he answered in the affirmative, and added . . . that the other was his son.

There is always near the king, when he marches, an officer called Kanitz Kitzera, the executioner of the camp; he has upon the tore of his saddle a quantity of thongs made of bull's hide . . . this is called the *tarade*. The king made a sign with his head, and another with his hand, without speaking, and two loops of the tarade were instantly thrown round the Shum and his son's neck, and they were both hoisted upon the same tree, the tarade cut, and the end made fast to a branch. They were both left hanging. . . . [54]

That is not the sort of tale which one forgets. And with images of Tartary and Abyssinia already freely telescoping in the dream, it seems highly probable that some leap of association from Aloadine's assassins called up that sharp-etched picture of the ruthless Abyssinian king whose floating hair precipitated such a tragedy.

And now, with the kaleidoscopic swiftness of a dream, the scene shifts from Abyssinia to Cashmere. But even that surprising shift is not fortuitous. For Abyssinia and Cashmere were linked, for Coleridge, through a circumstance which we have now to see.

VIII

I said 'for Coleridge,' since Coleridge's associations of ideas are all that count in Coleridge's dream. And among the sleeping images below the threshold of his consciousness there was one of Cashmere which was definitely associated with the Nile. That will be clear, if we turn back to the reading on which Coleridge was intent at the time when he was jotting down matters of interest in Bartram.

In the Note Book, it will be remembered, a few pages after the excerpts from Bartram, appears the following entry:

> Hymns Moon
>
> In a cave in the mountains of Cashmere an Image of Ice, which makes it's appearance thus—two days before the new *moon* there appears a bubble of Ice which increases

> in size every day till the 15th day, at which it is an ell or more in height: then as the moon decreases, the Image does also till it vanishes.
>
> Read the whole 107th page of Maurice's Indostan.[55]

Coleridge, that is, was collecting materials for his projected 'Hymns to the Sun, the Moon, and the Elements—six hymns,' and was reading Maurice with an eye alert for imagery which he could turn to account in the great work which was never to be.[56] The five mathematicians on the lofty tower in Pekin, who were somehow to enliven the Hymn to Air, he made note of from Maurice,[57] and Maurice, as we shall see in a moment, gave him a hint for the Hymn to the Sun. Lore associated with the Sun, Moon, or the Elements, accordingly, was unlikely at this juncture to escape a treasure-seeker's vigilant eye.

The passage which he first made note of reads, in its context, as follows:

> I have already noticed the remarkable circumstance of 360 *fountains . . . sacred to the moon*, at Kehrah, a town in Cashmere; Cashmere, probably the most early residence of the Brahmins, and the theatre of the purest rites of their theology.
>
> In a cave of the same mountainous subah a very singular phænomenon is said, in the Ayeen Akbery, at certain periods to make its appearance. . . . In this cave, says Abul Fazil, is sometimes to be seen an image

> of ice, called AMERNAUT, which is holden in great veneration. The image makes its appearance after the following manner—[58]

and the rest is substantially as Coleridge sets it down.[59]

Now the image of ice is on pages 106–07. Keeping in mind the suggestive reference to *fountains*, let us pass to the next entry in the Note Book:

> Sun
> Hymns——Remember to look at Quintius [*sic*] Curtius—lib. 3. Cap. 3 and 4.[60]

But why? On the page in Maurice (105) immediately preceding the cave with its bubble of ice are these two footnotes:

> See Quinti Curtii, lib. 3. cap. 3.
> Ibid. lib. 3. cap. 4.

It was Maurice, then, who was sending Coleridge to Quintus Curtius, and it is easy to see why Coleridge was anxious not to forget to look him up. For Maurice had just given, on the authority of these two passages, two highly picturesque details which were a godsend to a poet with a Hymn to the Sun obstinately hanging fire:

> He [Quintus Curtius] declares it to have been an immemorial custom among the Persians, for the army never to march before the rising of the sun; that a trumpet, sounding from the king's pavilion, proclaimed the first

> appearance of its beam, and that a golden image of its orb, inclosed in a circle of crystal, was then displayed in the front of that pavilion, which diffused so wide a splendour that it was seen through the whole camp. . . .
>
> The grooms appointed to train and conduct these horses [one of which was called THE HORSE OF THE SUN] . . . bore in their hands golden rods, or wands, pointed at the end in imitation of the solar ray.[61]

Coleridge's mind, it is plain, was picking up like a magnet imagery associated with the sun and moon. But (since we are for the moment working backwards) he had just been reading, a couple of pages earlier, a striking account of honours paid to the sun and moon in *Egypt*. And his eye—as quick to take notice as those of any five Chinese astronomers!—would assuredly catch this:

> The whole of the annual magnificent festival of Osiris and Isis was in the most pointed manner allusive to the influence of the SUN and MOON upon the earth. . . . To the MOON,* or Isis, they were by no means ungrateful for affording, by night, her kindly ray to conduct the mariner . . . over the boundless ocean, and the benighted traveller over deserts of sands . . . as well as her immediate utility in swelling the waters of *that sacred river*, whose annual inundations were the perpetual and abundant source of plenty.[62]

And for another page the mutations of the Nile are Maurice's theme.

This, then, is clear. The Nile and Cashmere were definitely connected, through the moon, in Maurice. The Image of Ice, accordingly, in the cave in the mountains of Cashmere, sank below the threshold as an *atome crochu*. And its particular 'hook of the memory'—that potentiality of junction which it carried with it—was the sacred river. And through their association with the sacred river the caves of ice were drawn into the dream:

> Through wood and dale *the sacred river* ran,
> Then reached the caverns measureless to man . . .
> Where was heard the mingled measure
> From the fountain and the caves.
> It was a miracle of rare device,
> A sunny pleasure-dome with *caves of ice!*

That is no fortuitous concourse of atoms. The elements of the dream are knit together through linkages like filaments of steel.[63]

And now it is possible to take another step. In Maurice's Preliminary Chapter occurs the following sentence:

> I have immediately directed my own and my reader's attention to the intelligent Memoir, and very accurate map of Hindostan, presented to the world by *Major Rennell*, whose unwearied efforts to elucidate her

> intricate geography, must secure him the applause of all those who are either interested in the commerce, or attached to the literature, of the East.[64]

That is the sort of thing on reading which Coleridge was apt to find his heart moved more than with a trumpet, and the next entry in the Note Book is brief but pregnant:

> Major Rennell.[65]

We know Coleridge's habit of verifying references, and the memorandum is conclusive evidence of his intentions in the present case. And since at the moment he was on a hot scent of promising materials for his galaxy of Hymns, there is special reason for assuming that his purpose was carried out.*

Now the work to which Maurice had referred, the *Memoir of a Map of Hindoostan* (1793), contains an uncommonly inviting description of the landscape of Cashmere. And in it are certain significant details:

> The valley or country of Cashmere, is celebrated throughout upper Asia for its *romantic* beauties, [and] for *the fertility of its soil*. . . . It is . . . surrounded by steep mountains, that tower above the regions of snow; and . . . its soil is composed of the mud deposited by *a capital river*, which originally formed its waters into a lake . . . until it *opened itself a passage through the mountains*. . . . The author of the Ayin Acbaree dwells

> with rapture on the beauties of Cashmere. . . . Only light showers fall there: these, however, are in abundance enough to feed some thousands of cascades, which are precipitated into the valley, from every part of *the stupendous and romantic bulwark that encircles it*. . . . In a word, the whole scenery is beautifully picturesque; and a part of the *romantic* circle of mountains, makes up a portion of every landscape. The pardonable superstition of the sequestered inhabitants, has multiplied the places of worship of Mahadeo [whose image it was that appeared in the cave], of Bishen, and of Brama. *All Cashmere is holy land; and miraculous fountains abound*. . . . To sum up the account of Cashmere, in the words of [Abul Fazil], '*It is a garden in perpetual spring*.'[66]

Now let us reread a few lines of the poem:

> But oh! that *deep romantic chasm* which slanted
> Down the green hill athwart a cedarn cover!
> A savage place! As *holy* and enchanted
> As e'er beneath a waning moon was haunted . . .

There are links in plenty to catch up Major Rennell's picture into that stream of images which were rising before the sleeping Coleridge as *things*—the miraculous fountains, and the fertile ground, and the river that opened a passage through the mountains, and the sunny garden spot. And the landscape of the deep romantic vale of Cashmere and the landscape of the valley of the upper Nile seem to have melted into one another in the dream, and the enchanted territory of the poem becomes '*holy* land.'

IX

Purchas and Bartram and Bruce and Maurice we know beyond peradventure that Coleridge had read. Major Rennell we know that he meant to read, and probably did. Up to this point, whatever may be said of our conclusions, the facts on which they rest admit no question. Coleridge had read these things; and the images which we have just been calling back had sunk into those secret tracts where all that is forgotten waits, keyed to associations at the lightest touch of which the sleeping past may flash up again—like a Venetian thoroughfare—to recollection. For

> Zwar ist's mit der [Traum]-Fabrik
> Wie mit einem Weber-Meisterstück,
> Wo Ein Tritt tausend Fäden regt,
> Die Schifflein herüber hinüber schiessen,
> Die Fäden ungesehen fliessen,
> *Ein Schlag tausend Verbindungen schlägt.*[67]

But there are two or three other books which I cannot definitely prove that Coleridge had read, yet which, for the strongest reasons, we may be reasonably certain that he had. It is their probable contribution to the dream which I shall now present. And the first is directly connected with the *Memoir of a Map of Hindoostan.*

At the beginning of his notice of Cashmere, Major Rennell refers as follows to a famous narrative: 'The reader may collect from Bernier (*the most instructive of all Indian travellers*), in what mode the emperors travelled to Cashmere; as he has written a full account of his journey, when he travelled thither in the suite of Aurungzebe, in the year 1664.'[68] Just two pages beyond the account of the image of ice, moreover, Maurice in his turn, having already whetted his reader's interest in Bernier's journey to Cashmere,[69] devotes more than a page to an incident in his travels, 'so curious and interesting, that,' as he says, 'I cannot use the reader so ill as to pass it over.'[70] And *Mr. F. Bernier's Voyage to Surat*, which had given Dryden the materials for *Aurenge-Zebe*, was easily accessible.[71] The normal chances that Coleridge would look it up were heightened, moreover, by the peculiar circumstances of the moment. For (once more) it must not be forgotten that Coleridge was just then avowedly collecting data for his six Hymns; that the scope of the Hymns was appalling, with 'a sublime enumeration of all the charms and Tremendities of Nature' as a single item; that their hopeful projector was striking out, as the Note Book shows, from one book to another in directions which seemed to promise contributions; and that from both Maurice and Rennell the guide-posts pointed straight and enticingly to Bernier.

Now Bernier, who is as entertaining as he is instructive,

and whose account of his experiences en route to Cashmere is diverting to the last degree, gives in his Ninth Letter 'An exact description of the kingdom of Kachemire . . . together with an answer to five considerable questions of a friend.'[72] It is worth pausing to note that the fifth of the friend's demands is this: 'That I would at length decide unto you the old controversy touching *the causes of the increase of the Nile*.'[73] And in his answer Bernier tells, on the authority of 'two ambassadors of Ethiopia' whom he met at Delhi, how the Nile 'issueth out of the earth at two big bubbling springs,' and how, as 'a pretty river . . . it runs bending' thence.[74] If Coleridge did read Bernier, there was curiously enough a second hook to draw Cashmere and the fountains of the Nile together in the dream.

But he would also find a lively account of Cashmere itself, set down with a wealth of picturesque detail—an account which is extraordinarily rich in its links with that other reading which we know to have poured its imagery into the dream. It is out of the question to give all the parallels. Like Aloadine's Paradise and Kubla Khan's demesnes the vale is a spot of goodly gardens, houses of pleasure, pleasant springs, delightful streams:

> Out of all these mountains do issue *innumerable sources and rivulets*. . . . All these rivulets, descending from the mountains, make the plain and all those

> hillocks so fair and fruitful, that one would take this whole kingdom for *some evergreen garden*. . . . The lake hath this peculiar, that 'tis full of little isles, which are as many *gardens of pleasure*, that appear all green in the midst of the water. . . . Beyond the lake, upon the side of the hills, there is nothing but *houses and gardens of pleasure . . . full of springs and rivulets*.[75]

Like Bartram's Florida, the vale abounds in ebullient fountains:

> Thence I went to find out a fountain, which hath something that's rare enough in it; bubling up gently, and rising with some little impetuosity, and making small bubbles of air, and carrying with it, to the top, some small sand that is very fine, which goeth away again as it came, the water becoming still, a moment after it, without ebullition, and without bringing up sand; and soon after beginning afresh as before, and so continuing its motion by intervals, which are not regular.[76]

That might have come straight out of Bartram. There is, moreover, a cave of ice ('a grotto of odd congelation'), which is clearly identical with the cave of the bubble of ice in Maurice; and there is a subterranean cavern; and 'the wall of the world' slopes down green hills to the plain; and not far away in the story are the fountains of the Nile.[77] There are other correspondences, but these must serve. If Coleridge had ever read the *Voyage to Surat*, its marvels could not but have linked themselves in the dream with the like 'charms and Tremendities of Nature' in Purchas and Bartram and Bruce and Maurice.

All this, however, might have found its way into the dream had Coleridge never laid eyes on Bernier. But there is one group of pictures in the *Voyage* which it is well nigh impossible to believe that he had not seen. The structure which Kubla Khan decreed in Xanadu was 'a stately pleasure-*dome*,' and it stood, in the dream, in close proximity to the fountain which flung up the river:

> *The shadow of the dome of pleasure*
> *Floated midway on the waves;*
> Where was heard the mingled measure
> From the fountain and the caves.

There is no hint of all that in Purchas or Bartram or Bruce or Maurice. But among Bernier's pleasant little vignette sketches are these:

> Returning from Send-brary I turn'd a little aside from the road to go and lie at Achiavel, which is *an house of pleasure* of the ancient kings of Kachemire, and at present of the great Mogol. That which most adorns it is *a fountain. . . . It breaks out of the earth, as if by some violence it ascended up from the bottom of a well, and that with such an abundance as might make it to be called a*

> *river* rather than a fountain. . . . The garden itself is very fine, there being curious walks in it, and *store of fruit-bearing trees.*[78]

> The most admirable of all these gardens is that of the king, which is called Chah-limar. From the lake, one enters into it by a great canal, border'd with great green turfs. . . . It leadeth to a great cabinet in the midst of the garden, where begins another canal far more magnificent . . . and in the midst of it there is a long row of jets of water. . . . And this canal ends at another great cabinet.
>
> These cabinets, which are in a manner *made like domes,* [are] *situate in the middle of the canal, and encompassed with water.*[79]

> I left my way again, to approach to a great lake, which I saw afar off, through the middle whereof passeth the river that runs to Baramoulay. . . . In the midst of this lake there is an eremitage with its little garden, which, as they say, *doth miraculously float upon the water.*[80]

There, without question—together with that '*great and vast dome* of white marble' which Bernier saw with delight surmounting Shah Jehan's Taj-Mahal at Agra[81]—are elements which might have risen up, blended and transfigured, in the lovely image of the dream. And in their light the probability that Coleridge had looked up Bernier approaches certainty.

And in the darting play of associations which called up the picture of the floating image of the dome upon the wave, Bartram's fountains (which were, merged with the Abyssinian springs, the very fountain of the dream) may well have had a part. For in the bason of his 'inchanting and amazing chrystal fountain' Bartram saw 'the pendant golden Orange dancing on the surface of the pellucid waters'; and the waters of the Manate Spring 'appear of a lucid sea green colour . . . owing to the reflection of the leaves above.'[82] A shadow that floated on the wave was printed on the very image of the wave itself as it arose. Admit Bernier's magic touch to set the simulacrum of the *dome* beside the wave, and the images were foreordained to blend. Dreams do behave in just that fashion, and the suggestion that this dream was no exception at least strains no probabilities.

X

Our exploration of the crowded antechambers of the vision is almost at an end. There remain but two or three cluster-points of imagery the confluence of which in Coleridge's memory we shall attempt to trace. And they are (if I am right) among the most remarkable.

They carry us back from the vale of Cashmere to the idiosyncrasies of the sacred river:

Where *Alph*, the sacred river, ran
Through caverns measureless to man
Down to *a sunless sea . . .*
Through wood and dale the sacred river ran,
Then reached *the caverns measureless to man*,
And sank in tumult to *a lifeless ocean*.

Whence came the 'caverns measureless to man,' and the 'lifeless ocean,' and the 'sunless sea'? Above all, what lost suggestion underlies that most mysterious of appellations, 'Alph'? Let us take up the riddles in their order.

From the day of the Fathers down to Coleridge's own century (and since) one of those still-vex'd questions which have stretched the *pia mater* of many a subtle brain has been the identity of two of the four rivers—Pison, Gihon, Hiddekel, and Phrath—which, on the authority of *Genesis*, went out of Eden. That the last two represent the Tigris and Euphrates has always been matter of common consent. As for the other pair, in the dispute which waxed and waned through centuries, Pison was now the Indus, now the Danube, now the Nile, but far more frequently the Ganges; whereas Gihon, in spite of scattering voices raised in favour of the Orontes, or the Araxes, or the Oxus, was almost universally believed to be the *Nile*. But between Mesopotamia (which, barring a few fantastic guesses, was the accepted site of Paradise) between Mesopotamia and the regions where admittedly the Nile, as mortal eyes behold it, takes its rise, lay the deserts of

Arabia and the Red Sea. How, on the venerable and orthodox assumption, did the now doubly sacred river make its way?

There could, of course, be but one answer. It must flow under ground and under sea. And that myth of the subterranean-submarine passage of the Nile from Asia through to Africa Coleridge certainly knew. It is needless to conjecture how often, in 'the wide, wild wilderness' of his early reading, he had met it. He could scarcely have escaped it in Pausanias and the Life of Apollonius of Tyana,[83] but the book entitled 'Of the Primæval Earth, and Paradise' in that *Sacred Theory* of Thomas Burnet which he twice proposed to turn into blank verse, and later bracketed with Plato—not to mention that other work of Burnet's which gave the motto to 'The Ancient Mariner'—these two afford evidence enough. The ancients, says Burnet, 'supposed generally, that paradise was in the other hemisphere . . . and yet they believed that Tygris, Euphrates, Nile, and Ganges, were the rivers of paradise, or came out of it; and these two opinions they could not reconcile . . . but by supposing that these four rivers had their fountain-heads in the other hemisphere, and by some wonderful trajection broke out again here.'[84] 'To this sense also,' he remarks again, 'Moses Bar Cepha often expresseth himself; as also Epiphanius, Procopius Gazseus, and Severianus in Catena. Which notion amongst the ancients, concerning the trajection or passage of the paradisiacal rivers under ground, or under sea, from one continent into another, is to me, I confess, unintelligible.'[85] It is Moses bar Cepha, however, who is most explicit, and Moses bar Cepha Coleridge probably knew, if not at first-hand, at least through the learned pages of another then celebrated work.

Bruce's paragraph about the ebullience of the second fountain of the Nile,[86] which so strikingly parallels Bartram, is quoted from his translation of pages 57 and 59 of the first volume of Athanasius Kircher's *Œdipus Ægyptiacus.* I must regretfully forego the opportunity thus afforded of dwelling on the astonishing Athanasius and his still more dumbfounding works.[87] It is enough to say that the *Œdipus Ægyptiacus* is prefaced by dedicatory verses to its patron in Latin, Greek, Italian, Spanish, French, Portuguese, English, German, Hungarian, Bohemian, Illyrian, Old Slavonic, Serbian, Turkish, Hebrew, Syriac, Arabic, Chaldean, Armenian, Persian, Samaritan, Coptic, Ethiopic, the Brahman alphabet, Chinese, and Egyptian Hieroglyphics. It is a book after Coleridge's own heart; his old friend Dupuis has copious references to it; Bruce's long extract would be enough to send him to it, if he had not already gone. And I have no doubt (though this I cannot prove) that he read the fascinating farrago on the subject of the Nile which fills the half-dozen pages just before the account which Bruce excerpts. And Moses bar Cepha heads the list of Kircher's, as of Burnet's, authorities.

And what Moses bar Cepha states is picturesque enough:

The name of the second river is Gihon (*which is also*

> *called the Nile*): it flows through all the land of Chus. For no sooner has it come out of Paradise than it vanishes beneath the depths of the sea and the streams of Ocean, whence, through secret passages of the earth, it emerges again in the mountains of Ethiopia. . . . But [says bar Cepha] someone will ask, how is it possible that these rivers, when once they have passed out of Paradise, should be precipitated beneath the streams of Ocean and the heart of the sea, and should then at length emerge in this our land?

The obvious answer follows: With men this is impossible, but with God all things are possible. Whereupon Moses bar Cepha takes up his parable again:

> This also we assert, that Paradise lies in a much higher region than this land, and so it happens that the rivers, impelled by so mighty a force, descend thence through *huge chasms* and subterranean channels, and, thus confined, are hurried away beneath the bottom of the sea, and *boil up* in this our orb.*

This is immediately followed in Kircher by an extract from the *Geographia Arabica Medicca*, in which the plain of the Nile is said to be full of *cedars* (plena Cedris), and the whole land cavernous within—a region of mighty abysses (est enim tota hæc terra intus cava, et abyssos habens ingentes).[88] The Arabic geography now disposed of, Kircher cites as a further witness

Odoardus Lopez Lusitanus, who declares that the inhabitants of these quarters affirm with one accord that the Nile, plunging headlong through certain horrible and impenetrable valleys, through *chasms inaccessible to man* (per præcipitia hominibus inaccessa) and pathless deserts, is swallowed up in valleys so exceedingly deep that it is, as it were, received within the very bowels of the earth, and absorbed by its abysses. After which it reappears, and, passing the cataracts, flows with many meanders (multiplici gyro) into the sea.[89] Moreover, to add the crowning touch, between the accounts of Moses bar Cepha and the Arabic geographer, Kircher inserts a 'True and Genuine Topography of the Fountains of the Nile [*Vera et genuina fontium Nili topographia*], made by P. Peter Pais on the 21st of April in the year 1618 in the presence of the Emperor,' in which the two fountains are depicted on the summit of a craggy hill, encompassed with a prim circle of (one hopefully conjectures) incense-bearing trees, whence the Nile, meandering with a conspicuously mazy motion, forms the boundary of a plainly labelled kingdom of Amara (Amhara Regnum). And on the maps of Odoardus and the Arabic geographer engraved on the same plate, the river's maziness rivals that of the Dædalian labyrinth.[90] The traditional association of the Nile with mighty caverns (to say nothing of meanderings and chasms) was still plentifully current in Coleridge's day.

And once more the link with Bartram is singularly close.

For again and again Bartram might almost be paraphrasing Kircher's Latin. One passage, just before the account of the Manate Spring, will serve to bring out the curious correspondence:

> These waters . . . augment and form . . . subterraneous rivers, which wander in darkness beneath the surface of the earth, by innumerable doublings, windings and secret labyrinths; no doubt in some places forming vast reservoirs and subterranean lakes . . . and possibly . . . meeting irresistable obstructions in their course, they suddenly break through these perforated fluted rocks, in high, perpendicular jets. . . . Thus by means of those subterranean courses . . . they emerge . . . in those surprising vast fountains.[92]

Bartram's subterranean caverns and the mythical abysses of the Nile are two of a kind. It would be next to impossible for Coleridge to read of either without some reminiscence of the other. And the two were probably associated in his memory long before the moment of the dream.

As for caverns '*measureless to man*,' Paez states that he twice tried the depth of the second fountain and could find no bottom—'fundum nullum invenimus . . . denuo rem tentavimus, sed nec sic fundum tenere potuimus';[93] and Kircher, in his remarks upon Paez's account, refers to the depth of the fountain as 'inexplorabilis.'[94] Lobo asserts[95] that 'we could find no Bottom, and were assured by the Inhabitants, that none ever had been found.' Whatever Coleridge knew or did not know about these accounts, he knew and had long known his Herodotus.[96] And Herodotus has a most interesting tale. He found, he says, no one who professed any knowledge of the source of the Nile, except a single person, a scribe in the city of Saïs. And the scribe's story was this:[97]

> Between Syêné. . . and Elephantiné, there are two hills with sharp conical tops; the name of the one is Crophi, of the other, Mophi. Midway between them are the fountains of the Nile, *fountains which it is impossible to fathom*. . . . The fountains were known to be unfathomable, he declared, because Psammetichus . . . had made trial of them. He had caused a rope to be made, many thousand fathoms in length, and had sounded the fountain with it, *but could find no bottom*.*

'Caverns measureless to man' had been for twenty-three centuries associated with the legend of the Nile. It is little wonder, given what we now know about 'the sacred river,' that they turned up in the dream.

The image of the sacred river, then, which rose up before Coleridge as a *thing*, was a dream-picture, foreshortened and reversed as if it lay in an enchanted crystal, of the tremendous Odyssey of the legendary Nile. Visualized under the spell of Bartram's springing fountains, the river in the vision bursts from immeasurable depths, traverses mazily, its cosmic sweep diminished to a *coup d'œil*, five miles of wood and dale—then sinks in tumult to immeasurable depths again. 'From the great deep to the great deep it goes'—to the 'lifeless ocean' and the 'sunless sea' beneath the upper lands and waters of the world.

And I suspect that with the imagery of these nether seas of ancient story there was merged a conception vaster still, which had long been hovering in Coleridge's restless head. Between the two memoranda in the Note Book in which he dallied with the project of turning the *Telluris Theoria Sacra* into verse, stand, as we have seen,[98] certain entries which show beyond question that he had read, with kindled imagination, the whole of Burnet's 'grand Miltonic romance.' Now Burnet's daring cosmogony is built about the central waters and the central fires. Beneath the hollow shell of the earth lay, from the beginning, the waters of the great abyss. At the deluge the fountains of the deep were broken up, and the shattered frame of the earth sank beneath the rush of the ascending floods. Subterranean rivers still pursue their way 'through the dark pipes of the earth,' and beneath us still are gathered up, in subterranean lakes and seas, the cataracts of the abyss. And at the end, when the earth shall melt with fervent heat, the waters that are under the earth, pent up and turned to steam, will lend their shattering aid again, to bring about the last catastrophe. Had Coleridge ever carried out his chimerical scheme of versifying Burnet's gorgeous prose, a Hymn to Water of epic grandeur would have made his own superfluous. But while the project was stirring in his brain, the Deluge and the Conflagration were storing the cells of memory with images. And Burnet's titanic conception of a dark, illimitable ocean, lurking beneath the unmeasured gulfs and chasms of the world, was present (I think we may safely assume) somewhere in the background of the dream.

XI

There was another storied river which sank beneath the earth, and flowed under the sea, and rose again in a famous fountain. As was inevitable, it was constantly associated with the legendary Nile. And Coleridge, like every schoolboy, knew it:

> . . . *Alpheum* fama est hue Elidis amnem
> occultas egisse vias subter mare; qui nunc
> ore, Arethusa, tuo Siculis corifunditur undis.[99]

But his sources of information were by no means limited to Virgil.

Burnet has a delightful note about Alpheus,[100] but for us the ancients are more to the point. No one who has followed Coleridge's reading will doubt, I think, his acquaintance with Pausanias. Were there no other reason, Thomas Taylor had translated *The Description of Greece* in 1794, professing to 'have unfolded,' in his highly neo-Platonic notes, 'a theory which seems for many ages to have been entirely unknown.'[101]

And 'Taylor the English pagan' was among Coleridge's 'darling studies.'[102] Here, then, are two excerpts from Taylor's translation of Pausanias:

> But the Alpheus appears to possess something different from other rivers; for it often hides itself in the earth, and again rises out of it. Thus it . . . merges itself in the Tegeatic land. Ascending from hence in Asæa, and mingling itself with the water of Eurotas, it falls a second time into the earth, emerges from hence, in that place which the Arcadians call the fountains, and running through the Pisæan and Olympian plains, pours itself into the sea. . . . Nor can the agitation of the Adriatic sea restrain its course; for running through this mighty and violent sea, it mingles itself with the water of Arethusa in Ortygia . . . retaining its ancient name Alpheus.[103]

> From the water of Alpheus, therefore, mingling itself with that of Arethusa, I am persuaded the fable respecting the love of *Alpheus* originated. Such indeed of the Greeks or Ægyptians as have travelled to Æthiopia . . . relate that *the Nile* entering into a certain marsh, and gliding through this no otherwise than if it was a continent, flows afterward through lower Æthiopia into Egypt, till it arrives at Pharos and the sea which it contains.[104]

The Nile and the Alpheus, then, are immediately associated in Pausanias.

How early Coleridge knew Strabo I do not know. There is every reason to believe that the youngster who translated Synesius at the age of fifteen, and who expounded Plotinus and recited Homer and Pindar in their Greek at Christ's Hospital, had read the *Geography* during his school days. He certainly was much at home in it later, for he quotes from the Greek text in a notebook of 1806–07, and again in *Omniana*, in both of which he recognizes Strabo's hand in a noble sentence of Ben Jonson's dedication to *The Fox*.[105] At all events, here are a few remarks of Strabo, who discusses the Alpheus at great length:

> People tell the mythical story that the river Arethusa is the Alpheius, which latter, they say, rises in the Peloponnesus, flows underground through the sea as far as Arethusa, and then empties thence once more into the sea.[106]. . . Marvellous tales of this sort are stretched still further by those who make the Inopus cross over from *the Nile* to Delos. And Zoïlus the rhetorician says . . . that *the Alpheius* rises in Tenedos.[107]

Again, in a context of ebullient fountains and subterranean rivers disappearing in a chasm, Strabo continues:

> The territory of the Palici has craters that spout up water in a dome-like jet and receive it back again into the same recess. The cavern near Mataurus contains an immense gallery through which a river flows invisible for

> a considerable distance, and then emerges to the surface, as is the case with the Orontes in Syria, which sinks into the chasm [χάσμα] . . . rises again forty stadia away.
>
> Similar, too, are the cases both of the Tigris in Mesopotamia and of *the Nile* in Libya . . . and again, the water near the Arcadian Asea is first forced below the surface and then, much later, emerges as both the Eurotas and *the Alpheius.*[108]

Once more, the Nile and the Alpheus are linked together as kindred streams.

That Coleridge, with his tastes, and classical training, and cormorant habits, had read Seneca's *Quæstiones Naturales* before 1798, is a reasonable assumption. It must not be forgotten that he wrote Thelwall in 1796: 'I have read almost everything'[109]—a statement which few who know their Coleridge will seriously doubt! His later knowledge of Seneca has ample attestation.[110] And Seneca, whose *Quæstiones Naturales* are a veritable mine of lore about the elements, has in that remarkable treatise matter of no small interest touching the Alpheus. In the twenty-sixth chapter of Book Three—a chapter which begins with mention of the Nile—Seneca quotes a passage from Ovid's *Metamorphoses* about Lycus, swallowed up by the yawning earth, and then proceeds:

> In the East as well as the West this happens. The Tigris is absorbed by the earth and after long absence

reappears at a point far removed, but undoubtedly the same river. . . . Thence [from the behavior of the fountain Arethusa] comes the belief that the Alpheus makes its way right from Achaia to Sicily, stealing under sea by secret sluice, and reappearing only when it reaches the coast of Syracuse.[111]

But the most significant passage is in the Sixth Book:

I do not, indeed, suppose that you will long hesitate to believe that there are underground rivers and *a hidden sea*. From what other cause could the rivers burst out and come to the surface?. . . And what are you to say when you see the *Alpheus* . . . sink in Achaia and, having crossed beneath the sea, pour forth in Sicily the pleasant fountain Arethuse? And don't you know that among the explanations given of the occurence of the inundation of *the Nile* in summer, one is that it bursts forth from the ground?[112]

Whereupon follows the story which Seneca heard himself from the lips of two non-commissioned officers sent by Nero to investigate the sources of the Nile.

But that is not all. For the preceding chapter contains a vivid picture of the 'lifeless ocean' and the 'sunless sea' out of which such rivers as the Nile and the Alpheus rise, and to which they return:

Now surely a man trusts too much to the sight of the

> eyes and cannot launch out his imagination beyond, if he does not believe that *the depths of earth contain a vast sea* with winding shores. I see nothing to prevent or oppose the existence of a beach down there *in the obscurity*, or a sea finding its way through the hidden entrances to its appointed place. There, too, . . . the hidden regions being desert *without inhabitant* give freer scope to the waves of the nether ocean.[113]

Moreover, that Bernardinus Ramazzinus from whom Burnet quotes *in extenso* the Abyssinian account of the deluge, links the Nile and the Alpheus on the same page.[114] And finally, in the *Argonauticon* of Valerius Flaccus, the two rivers share a single line:

> Ceu refluens Padus aut septem proiectus in amnes
> *Nilus* et Hesperium veniens *Alpheos* in orbem.[115]

The traditional links between the Nile and the Alpheus are like hoops of steel.

Now some, if not all, of these passages Coleridge without doubt had read. And just as ocular spectra which 'flashed' from Bartram's fountains and from the fountains of the Nile had telescoped in the dream, so there seem to have merged linked reminiscences of the Alpheus and the Nile. And by one of those puckish freaks of the dream intelligence which are often so preternaturally apt, 'Alpheus' has been docked of its syllabic excess, and dream-fashioned, as 'Alph,' into a quasi-equivalence with 'Nile.' The *artifex verborum of* the dream—witness 'Xanadu' and 'Abora'—was no less adept than the waking Coleridge in the metamorphosis of words.* And none of us who has ever dreamed can doubt how exquisitely right and meet and natural 'Alph' must in the dream have seemed—a name which sprang like a fountain from the inmost nature of the thing, rising up, like the dream-music, a 'mingled measure' from the Alpheus and the Nile.

XII

The last sentence Coleridge had read before his eyes rested on the words 'In Xamdu did Cublai Can build a stately Palace,' was a remarkable expression of the belief among the Tartars of the survival of the dead.[116] And he had turned the page but once since he had read another statement of that belief more striking still:

> When he is dead, if he be a chiefe man, hee is buried in the field where pleaseth him. And hee is buried with his Tent, sitting in the middest thereof, with a Table set before him, and a platter full of meate, and a Cup of Mares-milke. There is also buried with him a Mare and Colt, a Horse with bridle and saddle: and they eate another Horse . . . stuffing his hide with straw, setting it aloft on two or foure poles, that hee may have in the other world a Tabernacle and other things fitting for his use.[117]

And between the two passages, within less than a page of the words that slipped bodily into the dream, stands this:

> Their Priests were diviners: they were many, but had one Captaine or chiefe Bishop, who alwayes placed his house or Tent before that of the Great Can, about a stones cast distant . . . When an Eclipse happens they sound their Organs and Timbrels, and make a great noyse. . . . They foretell holy dayes, and those which are unluckie for enterprises. *No warres are begunne or made without their word.*[118]

Of this at least, then, we are sure: when Coleridge fell asleep, the last impressions which he received included images of dead warriors surviving in the other world, in their habit as they lived; of things foretold, heard through 'a great noyse'; and of wars undertaken only at the diviners' word. And among the images which rose up before him in the dream was this:

> And *'mid this tumult* Kubla heard from far
> *Ancestral voices prophesying war!*

Between the sinking into Coleridge's mind of that confluence of suggestions and the rising of the magnificently phrased conception of the dream lay, it would seem, a period measured by minutes. And meantime hosts of other images had been thronging up.

For I suspect that we are once more in the presence of a

cluster-point of the 'hooked atoms.' Recollections of Bruce, as we know, were actively astir. Now by far the most vivid personality in Bruce's narrative, except Bruce himself, is Ozoro Esther, the young wife of the old vizier of that king of Abyssinia whose floating hair, on the expedition against the rebels, got him into Absalom's predicament. And in his account of this expedition, Bruce gives a dramatic rehearsal of a talk he had with Ozoro Esther:

> 'But, pray' [says Bruce], 'what is the meaning of the Ras's speech to me about both armies wishing to fight at Serbraxos? Where is this Serbraxos?'—'Why, says she, here, on a hill just by; *the Begemder people have a prophecy, that one of their governors is to fight a king at Serbraxos*, to defeat him, and slay him there: in his place is to succeed another king, whose name is Theodorus, and in whose reign all Abyssinia is to be free from war . . . and the empire of Abyssinia to be extended as far as Jerusalem.'—'All this destruction and conquest without war! That will be curious indeed. I think I could wish to see this Theodorus,' said I, laughing—'See him you will, replied Ozoro Esther; peace, happiness, and plenty will last all his reign, and a thousand years afterwards. Enoch and Elias will rise again, and will fight and destroy Gog and Magog, and all this without any war.' 'On which I again said . . . And now, why does Ras Michael choose to fight

> at Serbraxos?'. . . 'Why, says she, *all the hermits and holy men on our side, that can prophesy, have assured him he is to beat the rebels this month at Serbraxos:* and a very holy man, a hermit from Wal-dubba, came to him at Gondar, and obliged him to march out against his will, *by telling him this prophecy, which he knows to be true*, as the man is not like common prophets. . . . Such a man as this, you know, Yagoube, cannot lie.'[119]

Like the incident of the floating hair, that is told in a fashion which stamps it on the memory, and which may quite possibly have brought about another fusion of Tartary and Abyssinia in the dream. Both passages, at all events, had certainly slipped, with their fleeting impressions, below the threshold of Coleridge's consciousness, and of such buried treasure is the stuff of dreams.

I wish I could say, with the complete assurance which is based on evidence, that Coleridge had read *Vathek*. As it is, I have neither doubt nor proof. Henley's translation, which preceded the French original by a year, had been twelve years in circulation—since Coleridge, that is, was a school-boy of fourteen. If he did read it, he could no more than the rest of us forget it. And its earlier pages are conceived in the very spirit of the dream. There were the Palaces of the Five Senses—'pleasure-houses' *par excellence;* there was a Paradise, with cedars and incense-bearing trees; there were four fountains, like the 'four sacred rivers' which watered Eden; and at the foot of the hill of the Four Fountains there was 'an immense gulph' or 'chasm.'[120] And as Vathek, after the Giaour had disappeared in the abyss, looked over the edge,

> One while, he fancied to himself *voices arising from the depth of the gulph:* at another, he seemed to distinguish the accents of the Indian; but, all was no more than *the hollow murmur of waters, and the din of the cataracts that rushed from steep to steeps* down the sides of the mountain.[121]

The tumult, as in the dream, is the tumult of the waters, and it rises with the voices, as in the dream, from the abyss. That a reminiscence of it flashed through the interweaving fancies of the vision is well within the bounds of possibility.

XIII

One other detail, this time a phrase, slipped into the dream from the limbo of sleeping *words*, at the touch of a determinate association. Coleridge had planned an edition of Collins and Gray, which twice appears among his projects in the Note Book.[122] There need be, then, no question of his familiarity with Collins's exquisite though slender sheaf of verse, even had we not his outburst of ardent admiration in a letter to Thelwall of December, 1796:

> Collins's 'Ode on the Poetical Character,'—that part of it, I should say, beginning with 'The band (as

> faery legends say) Was wove on that creating day,'—has inspired and whirled *me* along with greater agitations of enthusiasm than any the most *impassioned* scene in Schiller or Shakespeare.[123]

Now in 'The Passions' occur these charming lines on Melancholy, who,

> In notes by distance made more sweet,
> Pour'd thro' the mellow horn her pensive soul:
> And, dashing soft from rocks around
> Bubbling runnels join'd the sound;
> Thro' glades and glooms *the mingled measure* stole;
> Or o'er some *haunted* stream, with fond delay
> Round an *holy* calm diffusing,
> Love of peace and lonely musing,
> In hollow murmurs died away.[124]

And in the dream, just after the tumult of the river's fall,

> . . . was heard *the mingled measure*
> From the fountain and the caves.

The ceaseless tumult of the sacred river recalled the mellower tumult of the bubbling runnels dashing soft from rocks around, as Coleridge's 'Through wood and dale,' but eight lines earlier, had echoed Collins's 'Thro' glades and glooms.' And 'haunted' and 'holy,' still in successive lines, had already stolen into the measures of the dream:

A savage place! as *holy* and enchanted
As e'er beneath a waning moon was
haunted . . . [125]

'Kubla Khan' is the fabric of a vision, but every image that rose up in its weaving had passed that way before. And it would seem that there is nothing haphazard or fortuitous in their return.

XIV

There are other elements of the dream which refuse to divulge their secrets, and which 'sweetly torment us' (as Emerson, quoted by William James, felicitously puts it) 'with invitations to their inaccessible homes.'[126] How could it possibly be otherwise? About some of these teasing phantoms of association I confess, of course, to cherishing more or less colourable conjectures.[127] But if this chapter possess any worth, that value lies, not in its conjectures, but in its evidence—the evidence which it offers of the amazing power of association in the dream. Beyond that evidence, which can at least be weighed and tested, I do not for the present care to go.*

But I do wish, before leaving this huge phantasmagoria, to direct attention to an implication of material importance. I have emphasized, throughout the discussion of 'The Ancient Mariner,' the profoundly significant part played in imaginative creation by the associations of ideas—whether those associations wrought their synthesis before the impressions so combined sank into the subliminal reservoir, or during their submergence there, or at the instant of their flashing back to consciousness. And I have offered no little evidence of their activity. But in 'The Ancient Mariner' a determining will was constructively at work, consciously manipulating and adjusting and refashioning the associated images of memory into conformity with a design. And through that conscious imaginative moulding the links of association, as was inevitable, were often obliterated, or at least obscured. Yet sufficient traces of them still remain, as our scrutiny of Coleridge's reading soon disclosed, to establish their enormous influence. Do the facts before us contribute any further light?

I think they do. For in 'Kubla Khan' the complicating factor—the will as a consciously constructive agency—was in abeyance. 'All the images rose up before him as *things*, with a parallel production of the correspondent expressions, without any sensation or consciousness of effort.' The dream, it is evident, was the unchecked subliminal flow of blending images, and the dreamer merely the detached and unsolicitous spectator. And so the sole factor that determined the form and sequence which the dissolving phantasmagoria assumed, was the subtle potency of the associative links. There was this time no intervention of a waking intelligence intent upon a plan, to obliterate or blur them. And it is largely that absence of deliberate manipulation which has made it possible to disengage, to a degree unattainable in our study of

'The Ancient Mariner,' the bewildering hooks and eyes of the memory which were the irresponsible artificers of the dream.

But the facts thus established carry with them, as I have said, an important consequence. For we have only to recall those passages in 'The Ancient Mariner' in which the formative associations have been traceable, to recognize that their operations are essentially the same. The mass of evidence now before us corroborates with singular cogency our earlier conclusions. The subliminal blendings and fusings from which springs the insubstantial architecture of the dream are also latent beneath the complex workings of design. And that is no less essential to our understanding of the creative process than the further fact that in the one case the 'streamy' associations are unruddered, whereas in the other they are masterfully curbed.

The linked images, then, which are now before us are, with little question, constituent elements of the dream. But the dream itself is another matter. And it is high time that we pass from the crowded vestibule of consciousness to the winged wonder which emerged into the light.

---

*Coleridge later dreamed another poem—this time a quatrain. For his account of it see the Notes.[4]

*There is a singular coincidence to which Henri Cordier has called attention in his edition of Yule's *Cathay and the*

Way Thither. In a thirteenth century Arabic account of Xandu (Shang-tu), which was not translated into any Occidental language until years after Coleridge had dreamed his dream, occurs this statement: 'On the eastern side of that city a *karsi* or palace was built called Langtin, *after a plan which the Kaan had seen in a dream and retained in his memory*.'[6] In ancient tradition the stately pleasure-dome of Kubla Khan itself came into being, like the poem, as the embodiment of a remembered vision in a dream.

*All that, in one form or another, is common experience. I heard footsteps crunching in the snow beneath my open window as I lay in bed last night, and instantly I was back in a room in the Hotel Vapore in Venice, where, all through a hot midsummer night twelve years ago, disembodied, furtive footsteps padded and slunk and shambled at intervals, like uncanny spawnings of the night, along the Merceria just beneath another open window. I had heard ten thousand footsteps in the interim, without the remotest echo of that haunted thoroughfare. But some obscure, inexplicable quality in these eminently sober steps struck deep down—somewhere!—and without an instant's warning the familiar, even hackneyed sounds of a midwinter night in Cambridge had coalesced with the goblin noises of a midsummer night in Venice. That gives a hint of what happened, I think, when a page of Purchas, instead of a footstep, likewise struck deep down—where things forgotten are eternally remembered.

*Of which, indeed, as a further link, Coleridge may have just been reading a briefer version only forty pages earlier in the *Pilgrimage*.[11]

*Mr. Fausset, in his *Samuel Taylor Coleridge* (1926), pp. 183–84, following, I take it, Professor Cooper (he merely says: 'as a critic has recently pointed out'), enumerates some of these same details.

*The capitals are in Maurice—as are those in the preceding quotations.

*'I seldom read except to amuse myself, and I am almost always reading. . . . I compose very little, and I absolutely hate composition' (*Letters*, I, 181). When Coleridge meant to *read a book*, he usually read it. When he meant to *write a poem*, he generally did not.

*The Latin text is appended in the Notes.[91]

*Herodotus learned also that 'the river wind[s] greatly, like the Mæander.'

*There is abundant evidence of the invention of new words in dreams—see, for example, Havelock Ellis's *selvdrolla* and *jaleisa* (*The World of Dreams*, pp. 43–44, 49). Kraeplin's monograph 'Ueber Sprachstörungen im Traume' (*Psychologische Arbeiten*, Bd. v, 1906, pp. 1–104), to which Havelock Ellis refers, will satisfy anybody who runs over its classified lists of dream-fabricated vocables that 'Xanadu,' and 'Abora,' and 'Alph' are perfectly normal formations, when judged by the semasiology of dreams.

*I wish to state with emphasis that I am dealing in this study with what psychoanalysts call the material content of the dream, and with that alone. With its so-called latent content—its possible symbolism of wish-fulfilment or conflict or what not—I have nothing whatever to do. Even granting one or another of the conflicting assumptions of modern dream psychology, I do not believe that after the lapse of one hundred and twenty-seven years the intimate, deep-lying, personal facts on which alone such an analysis must rest are longer discoverable, and I doubt whether any trained psychoanalyst would venture an interpretation. 'I believe,' wrote one of the most brilliant and withal most sane of recent investigators in this field, the late Dr. W. H. R. Rivers, 'I believe that a really satisfactory analysis of a dream is only possible to the dreamer himself or to one who knows the conflicts and experiences of the dreamer in a most unusual way' (*Conflict and Dream*, p. 149). An essay at such an analysis of 'Kubla Khan,' regarded as a dream, has just been made, however, by Mr. Robert Graves, and, since it is illuminating in its method, I have examined it briefly in the Notes.[128] Incidentally, it may be worth while to suggest, without prejudice, that the facts which this investigation has disclosed, with reference to both 'The Ancient Mariner' and 'Kubla Khan,' counsel caution in the prevalent pursuit of so-called Freudian complexes in everything.

CHAPTER XX

THE VISION IN A DREAM

THE linked images bring us to the threshold of the dream—but the dream is fled. Only a fragment of rare beauty, which has translated a few snatches of it into words, is left. And that fragment is but the shadow of the dream—'a garden barred, a spring shut up, a fountain sealed.' Nor are the pictures of old and far-off things which we have just retrieved, as such, its substance. *Davus sum, non Œdipus.* And it is a far cry from identifying lost images of ebullient fountains and subterranean rivers and enchanted Paradises to calling back the magical vision they evoked. Yet we are nearer it, I think, than it has ever been possible to come before. And having come so far, we have no alternative but to venture a little farther.

I

Coleridge himself, in a note which has already served us well, has crystallized our problem in a sentence of two dozen words. Whatever the initial impulse which sets the shuttles of association weaving in a dream—be it a page of Purchas, or interrupted circulation, or a sudden sound—'The imagination . . . the true inward creatrix, instantly out of the chaos of elements or shattered fragments of memory, *puts together some form to fit it.*'[1] This form, in which the shattered fragments suffer miraculous redintegration, *is* the dream. We may, if we can, reproduce it in words, but the words are not it. And so the first question which our portentous array of links and scattered recollections thrusts upon us, is this. Is it possible in any way to gain some inkling of that fabric of visual imagery which, on a vanished summer day, out of the chaos of impressions now before us the inward creatrix actually put together—that vision which hung for an instant against the curtains of the eyes, before it faded forever into words?

For Coleridge *saw* the thing which simultaneously took on verbal form; it was (in words which mean precisely what they say) '*A Vision in* a Dream.' And we must somehow bring ourselves to realize both that it was a pageant *seen*, and that, as seen, the elements which entered into it—those images of Tartary, and Florida, and Abyssinia, and Egypt, and Cashmere—had certainly become (in Coleridge's own words) 'as difficult to separate [as] two dew-drops blended together on the bosom of a new-blown Rose'[2]—'indistinct,' in the words of a greater than Coleridge, 'As water is in water.' Behind the poem as a poem stands the dream as a dream. And perhaps an actual dream picture, which I venture to give because I can vouch for its fidelity, may aid us to conjure up some semblance of that irretrievable vision which was neither the several images that flashed up from oblivion to frame it, nor yet the imperishably lovely words which veil it, as they reveal it, to our eyes.

Five years ago, while I was giving the substance of this book as lectures and so had the matter of it much in mind, I came home from New York, after one of the talks, with a feverish cold, and passed a wild night of fantastic dreams. After I had spent some time in taking 'Kubla Khan' out of a clothes basket in successive layers like stiff and freshly laundered shirts, the dream abruptly shifted from its impish travesty of my waking efforts to a vision so lucidly clear that after the lapse of five years, as I write, it is as fresh as when I actually saw it.* It was, I knew (as one knows in a dream), the stately pleasure dome of Kubla Khan. But it hung like a mirage, on the remote horizon of an endless plain. And there, far and distinct as if seen through the reverse lens of a field-glass, on the crest of a high white cliff rose a shimmering golden dome, with tall, feathery palms, delicate as a spider's tracery, on either side of it. And down the cliff fell, slim and stationary in the distance, a cataract of foam which sent up. a luminous golden mist that bathed the whole landscape in unfathomable amber light. And over it all one felt what one could not see—the profound stillness of a summer noon. To me, as the spectator of the dream, it was, as I say, the sunny dome in Xanadu, and the deep romantic chasm, and the sacred river, and the incense-bearing trees. Yet not the faintest hint of what I saw had ever entered into any conscious visualization of the setting of the poem.

But when the picture, which was curiously ineffaceable, was scrutinized with open eyes, there came out, as in a palimpsest, shadowy vestiges of past experience: the Roman campagna, dilated and etherealized, as one looks down upon it from the Villa d'Este; Saint Peter's, rising spectrally across the everlasting wash of air; Beachy Head, beyond the wide plain of the Channel; the Lauterbrunnen, latent for two score years in memory—all (and I know not what more) melted into a unity so incredibly aërial that the water-colours of Turner which I had been looking at but a few days before, and which had unmistakably imposed their pattern on the plastic substance of the dream, were dim and faded things beside its clarity. But not one single detail retained the setting or configuration which it had when the original impression was recorded by the memory. The picture of the dream was a fabric of *transmuted* images of memory, juxtaposed as they had never been juxtaposed before. And the agency which called the picture into being was an intense and recent preoccupation with the elements of the poem.

Now that, I take it (*sic parvis componere magna*), dimly represents the form in which the spectra of memory rose up before Coleridge in his sleep. Bartram's fountains, and Aloadine's Paradise, and the subterranean caverns of the Nile, together with their linked associates, were there, as the

Campagna, and Saint Peter's, and the Lauterbrunnen were formatively present in my dream. But as these dissolved, and rose like an exhalation, in shape and very essence incredibly transmuted, so those, beyond shadow of doubt, melted similarly into new and magical integrity. That Coleridge was conscious of constituent elements in the entrancing spectacle that rose before him, any more than I was conscious of constituents in mine, I do not for a moment believe. The network of links had done its business well. The clusters of images so caught together had coalesced like light, and neither the links which we have been at such pains to discover, nor the several images which we have sedulously disengaged were present as such (we may be sure) to consciousness at all. Yet apart from them the dream had never been—the dream which was and is the miracle of their swift and secret flowering.

II

All the king's horses and all the king's men, accordingly, cannot put together again the scattered fragments into the enthralling pictures which Coleridge actually saw. But at least we can reassemble what we can never retransmute. And the vision (or what is left of it) is a panorama in four scenes: the stately pleasure-dome in the midst of its bright purlieus; the deep romantic chasm flinging up its sacred river; the shadow of the dome of pleasure floating in the stream; and then the damsel with a dulcimer and the youth with floating hair.

The first three are detached yet contiguous sections of one comprehensive view. The fourth stands curiously by itself.

They constitute a series of fleeting vistas into strange depths of time and space. The unfathomable caverns of the mighty river which went out of Paradise lie underneath a garden bright with the sinuous rills and fragrant with the incense-bearing trees of Eden—an Eden which, as seen through Milton's eyes, has melted into Aloadine's enchanted Paradise, and both together into the 'spot of enchantment' which Bartram saw in Florida, that 'green spot of fountain and flowers and trees' which for weeks had haunted Coleridge's brain as a symbol of divine repose. And rising from its sunny spot of greenery beside the disappearing waters, which are mingled of the Alpheus and the Nile, is the pleasure-dome of Kubla Khan. All these, distilled in the alembic of the dream, rose as shining shapes against the dark. And that is the first scene.

And now Alph the sacred river, which dominates with its metempsychoses the shifting panorama, flows for an instant, freighted with all the legendary associations of the Nile, into regions bathed in sheer romance. Its huge chasms inaccessible to man dissolve into the deep romantic valley, where the green hill and the cedarn cover which Bruce saw in Abyssinia are holy and enchanted as the green and fountainous valley of Cashmere—a vale now lit by a waning moon, and haunted (as if all at once the picture had merged with the realm of wizardry from which 'Christabel' arose) 'By woman wailing for her demon lover.' And then, swift as a shuttle, the kaleidoscope shifts again.

There is a singularly suggestive note of Coleridge's which at this juncture is oddly to the point:[3]

> It is eleven o'clock at night. See that conical volcano of coal, half-an-inch high, ejaculating its inverted cone of smoke—the smoke in what a furious mood—this way, that way, and what a noise!
>
> The poet's eye in his tipsy hour
> Hath a magnifying power,
> Or rather emancipates his eyes
> Of the accidents of size.
> In unctuous cone of kindling coal,
> Or smoke from his pipe's bole,
> His eye can see
> Phantoms of sublimity.*

Something akin to that (not without the prevenient aid, I suspect, of the euphemistic 'anodyne') apparently took place in the dream. Like the ebullient cone of kindling coal, Bruce's 'hillock of green sod' in Abyssinia, with its ebullient fountain which was the infant Nile, was emancipated of the accidents of size, and then, through strange transubstantiation into that 'amazing and inchanting chrystal fountain' which flung up its stream in Florida, rose as a 'phantom of sublimity.' But only for a moment, for without premonition the sacred river which for this moment is at once Bartram's creek in Florida and Bruce's Nile, contracts, and peacefully meanders five miles through wood and dale. And then, with the perfect equanimity of 'the fantastic universe of dreams,' it once more monstrously dilates, and once more is neither the historic Nile nor a stream in the green savannahs of America, but the huge primordial river of the antediluvian world, sinking in tumult to the caverns measureless to man, to the sound of divining voices once heard, as Coleridge read, in Tartary. And that is the phantasmagoria of the second scene.

Then the kaleidoscope turns again, and the tumultuous abysses of the eternally wayfaring Nile pass into a picture of serene, pellucid beauty—the shadow of the dome of pleasure floating, to strange music, on the waves,[5] after the fashion of those domes which Bernier saw reflected in still waters in Cashmere. And the cave in Cashmere with its image of ice, in some manner which even in the dream is felt to be a marvel, multiplies, and all at once is paradoxically part and parcel of a *sunny* dome. And with that fleeting glimpse of what is certainly 'a miracle of rare device,' the third scene begins and ends.

And now without an instant's warning the whole setting of the vision abruptly shifts. Up to this point the dreamer is out of the picture; in the fourth scene he is definitely there—so strangely, indeed, that the lines themselves must be again before us, if we are to follow the mazy footing of this new stage of the dream:

> A damsel with a dulcimer
> In a vision once I saw:
> It was an Abyssinian maid,
> And on her dulcimer she played,
> Singing of Mount Abora.
> Could I revive within me
> Her symphony and song,
> To such a deep delight 'twould win me,
> That with music loud and long,
> I would build that dome in air,
> That sunny dome! those caves of ice!
> And all who heard should see them there,
> And all should cry, Beware! Beware!
> His flashing eyes, his floating hair!
> Weave a circle round him thrice,
> And close your eyes with holy dread
> For he on honey-dew hath fed,
> And drunk the milk of Paradise.

Abyssinia and the enchanted Paradise of the Old Man of the Mountain are indissolubly interfused, as we have seen, but that is of a piece with all the rest. It is something else which this time constitutes the riddle. The river has vanished from the picture, and the dome with its circumambient landscape has dissolved, to rise again for an instant, built with music, as a vision within the vision of the dreamer, who now suddenly is present in the dream. And with utter inconsequence, as the caves of ice glance and are gone, the Abyssinian damsel with a dulcimer is there, a tantalizing phantom of a dream-remembered dream, unlocalized, without the slightest sense of unreality, in space; while the Tartar youth with flashing eyes is projected against the background of that twice phantasmal dome in air, dream-built within the dream. It is a bafflingly complex involution—dreams within dreams, like a nest of Oriental ivories, 'sphere in sphere.'[6]

I wonder which (if either) of two things happened. Coleridge once characterized the state of dreaming as 'the shifting current in the shoreless chaos of the fancy in which the *streaming* continuum of passive association is broken into *zig-zag* by sensations from within or from without.'[7] Did some such interruption, from within or from without, infringe upon the 'continuum of passive association' which streams, with the sacred river, through the first three scenes, and break it up into the 'zig-zag' of the fourth? Or did the fateful knock of the person on business from Porlock break in upon the actual transcription of those last bewildering lines? And was the phantom world, thus rudely touched, already vanishing, and Coleridge struggling to recapture recollections already growing, as he put it, 'vague and dim'—'as a dream when one awaketh'?

A damsel with a dulcimer
In a vision once I saw . . .
Could I revive within me
Her symphony and song . . .
I would build that dome in air . . .

Whether all that be the troubled surface of the recollection or the troubled surface of the dream, it is impossible to know. In either case, with a picture of unimpaired and thrilling vividness, the fragment ends. And with it ends, for all save Coleridge, the dream.

'The earth hath bubbles as the water has, and this is of them.' For 'Kubla Khan' is as near enchantment, I suppose, as we are like to come in this dull world. And over it is cast the glamour, enhanced beyond all reckoning in the dream, of the remote in time and space—that visionary presence of a vague and gorgeous and mysterious Past which brooded, as Coleridge read, above the inscrutable Nile, and domed pavilions in Cashmere, and the vanished stateliness of Xanadu. For none of the things which we have seen—dome, river, chasm, fountain, caves of ice, or floating hair—nor any combination of them holds the secret key to that sense of an incommunicable witchery which pervades the poem. That is something more impalpable by far, into which entered who can tell what traceless, shadowy recollections—memories whose footsteps in the dream were 'like those of a wind over the sea, which the coming calm erases.'[8] The poem is steeped in the wonder of all Coleridge's enchanted voyagings.

III

They rose like a fountain, then, these endlessly dissolving, coalescing images, each for its instant luminous and distinct (like that magical foreshortening of the Nile) as a landscape mirrored in some untroubled pool. But now, as a result of our interrogation of Coleridge's reading, we know something which has never come into the reckoning before. For the subliminal tract which quickened to consciousness in the dream was the tract which the creative impulse in 'The Ancient Mariner' had also stirred to life. Coleridge's mind in sleep was wandering through part of the very regions which, for months not long before, it had traversed awake, in the working out of a complex design. And those regions were the familiar territory of the travel-books. Purchas and Bartram and Bruce were common ground, and the rest were kindred soil. 'Kubla Khan' and 'The Ancient Mariner' are built of essentially the same materials.

The two poems, then, have a highly significant common factor: each draws, for the elements which compose it, upon sources which are virtually the same. It was brave narratives of travel and adventure which poured their multifarious imagery into the balanced framework of 'The Ancient Mariner'; it was a fleeting, shining stream of blending images—'Bright shootes of everlastingnesse'—from books of travel and discovery which rose up in the visionary pageantry of 'Kubla Khan.' And the presence of that common factor throws into sharp relief a radical divergence between the two, which brings us definitely back once more to the ways of the shaping spirit. In the light of all we now know, it will not take many words, I think, to make the difference clear.

For one glorious moment, in the dream, those vivid simulacra which arose when words 'flashed images' as Coleridge read, had unfettered scope. All checks were off, and the hooked atoms, once set in motion, streamed up spontaneously, combining as they came. And caught though the vision is, and struck forever into immobility, it is none the less clearly a *stream* of blending images with which we have to do. For even now, as line follows line, one picture melts imperceptibly into another picture, each with something of the pristine freshness of creation still upon it, and even yet it is possible, if once we sink ourselves into the poem, to feel the swift, bright flowing of the dream. But precisely this it is which tells the story. For despite their vividness and beauty, the pictures are, in Coleridge's penetrating phrase, a 'streaming continuum of *passive* association.' Volition for the moment was asleep; it was the sleeping images that were awake and in motion. And with only the radiating streams of spontaneous association to determine their combining, they followed one another in that strange self-evolving succession which replaces ordered sequence in the world of dreams.

Beneath the making of 'The Ancient Mariner' also moved the streaming procession of linked images. We have watched their multitudinous evolutions through more pages than I care to contemplate. But in 'The Ancient Mariner' that self-evolving flow became the plastic stuff for the creative exercise of choice, and a disposing will, and the shaping spirit of imagination. And without the loss of one whit of the pellucid loveliness or instantaneous picturing power of the random imagery in 'Kubla Khan,' the imagery in 'The Ancient Mariner' took on besides the transcendent beauty of design. That is the case in a nutshell; but a single one of many pictures, chosen because by now we know it through and through, will help to make it clear.

It is the poised and luminous unity of those three constellated stanzas in which the ship's huge shadow lies across the still and awful waters of a charmèd sea. Into it poured, as we know, a throng of mingling reminiscences as bewildering in their variety as any of the confluences of the dream. So far as it is possible to see, in both the stanzas and the dream the swift coalescence of the linked impressions was identical. The images which streamed together in the two had flashed from the absorbing pages of essentially the same books. And for utter clarity of visualization the picture of the stanzas is unsurpassed, if not unmatched, by anything in 'Kubla Khan.' But there the likeness ends.

For out of the kaleidoscopic play of images from Father Bourzes and Captain Cook and Leemius and Bartram and Purchas and Dampier and Falconer—a medley as fantastic in its elements as the whimsical conjunction of Tartary, Florida, Abyssinia, Mesopotamia, Cashmere, and Greece in the dream[9]—out of this segment of chaos there was framed a shape of balanced symmetry, a lucid equipoise of part with part which as a form foreseen had been imposed upon the flux of interpenetrating images of memory. And then, thus perfected in its own inner harmony, this complex structure, deliberately built out of the stream, was locked, in all its radiant succinctness, into the crescent arch of the design. Not even in the magical four and fifty lines of 'Kubla Khan' is sheer visualizing energy so intensely exercised as in 'The Ancient Mariner.' But every crystal-clear picture there, is an integral part of a preconceived and consciously elaborated whole.

The conclusion of the whole matter, then, is this. In 'Kubla Khan' the linked and interweaving images irresponsibly and gloriously stream, like the pulsing, fluctuating banners of the North. And their pageant is as aimless as it is magnificent. But through the merging flow of reminiscences from all the seven seas and the four corners of the earth moves, in 'The Ancient Mariner,' a conscious will intent upon the execution of a complex structural design. And the streaming continuum of association is as clay in the potter's hand. The stuff of dreams has become the organ of the shaping spirit. And the key to the difference lies in that other pregnant phrase of Coleridge himself: '*the streamy nature of association*, which *thinking curbs and rudders*.'[10] To the making of both poems went the ceaseless, vivid flow of the linked images. But in 'The Ancient Mariner,' 'thinking' was imperially present; in 'Kubla Khan' it had abdicated its control.*

There is, then (for of invidious comparisons there is happily no question), one glory of 'Kubla Khan' and another glory of 'The Ancient Mariner,' as one star differeth from another star in glory. But the differences between the two starry metamorphoses of a huddle of impressions essentially the same illuminate, as nothing else perhaps can do, the ways of the shaping spirit which, through its diversity of operations, created both.

And there I should leave the mystery of 'Kubla Khan,' were it not that from its admittedly abnormal element there have been drawn conclusions which, in view of the evidence now before us, may not be left unchallenged.

---

*I should add, however, that the dream was set down at once. I am not relying on later memory.

*These lines (from a note book dated August 28, 1800) appear 'in a more decorous version' (as E. H. Coleridge remarks) in 'The Historie and Gests of Maxilian.' I append them as a mournful example of an appeal from Philip drunk to Philip sober:

The poet in his lone yet genial hour
  Gives to his eye a magnifying power:
  Or rather he emancipates his eyes
  From the black shapeless accidents of size—
  In unctuous cones of kindling coal,
  Or smoke upwreathing from the pipe's trim bowl,
  His gifted ken can see
  Phantoms of sublimity.[4]

*What is one to say of the paradox of a seemingly conscious control of sheer metrical technique displayed in the marvellous rhythms of 'Kubla Khan'? I have hazarded a tentative answer in the Notes.[11]

CHAPTER XXI

'NOT POPPY NOR MANDRAGORA'

'WHAT then does the name of Coleridge finally represent for us in literature? Principally, we must say, a handful of poetry with a singular charm; *an abnormal product of an abnormal nature under abnormal conditions*.'[1] So wrote Mr. John Mackinnon Robertson in 1893, at the close of a well-known essay. And phenomena of infinite complexity were never more adroitly simplified, or formulated with more neatness and dispatch. The trouble is, the telling formula is far too simple to be true.

In the last analysis, Mr. Robertson's ten words which I have set off by italics turn out to be reducible to one—namely, *opium*. The thesis of his brilliant but (as I believe) misleading essay may best be stated by himself:

> It may seem an extravagant thing to say, but I cannot doubt that the special quality of this felicitous work is to be attributed to its being *all* conceived and composed under the influence of opium in the first stages of the indulgence—the stages, that is, in which he himself felt

> as if new-born, before the new appetite itself proved to be a disease.[2]

I have italicized 'all,' since that is the corner stone of the whole structure. For 'all' coördinates 'The Rime of the Ancient Mariner' and the first part of 'Christabel,' in both their conception and their composition, with 'Kubla Khan.' That view I believe to be erroneous, and I am briefly reopening the question because the facts before us constitute fresh evidence which must be reckoned with.

I

I shall begin by stating Mr. Robertson's case more strongly than it was possible for him to state it for himself. For he was unaware, when he wrote, of any recourse to opium on Coleridge's part before 1796.[3] We now know that Coleridge had used the drug before 1791. For in an unpublished letter to his brother George, dated November 21, 1791, he writes: 'Opium never used to have any disagreeable effects on me.'[4] When that was written, Coleridge was just nineteen, and there is every reason to believe, with Ernest Hartley Coleridge, that laudanum had been prescribed for him at school (which he had left but two months before), when he was suffering from rheumatic fever.[5] At all events we hear no more of opium until 1796, in which year the letters show that he resorted to it at least twice—once (apparently) to relieve insomnia, and once to allay pain.

There is, in the first place, a letter in the Library of Trinity College, Cambridge, dated 'Saturday, 12 March, 1795,' in which occur the following sentences:

> Since I last wrote you, I have been tottering on the edge of madness—my mind overbalanced on the e contra side of Happiness—the repeated blunders of the printer, the forgetfulness and blunders of my associate etc. etc. abroad, and at home Mrs. Coleridge dangerously ill, and expected hourly to miscarry. Such has been my situation for the last fortnight—I have been obliged to take laudanum almost every night.[6]

The date of the letter, however, is wrong; the year should be 1796.* On November 5, 1796, moreover, 'under the immediate inspiration of laudanum' (actually 'twenty-five drops . . . every five hours' to allay pain which drove him 'nearly frantic'),[7] there was written to Poole the long and vivid and 'flighty' letter† which is one of the most memorable documents in the case, and which should be read in full.[8] A third reference has been wrongly taken as evidence of a third indulgence. On December 17, 1796, Coleridge wrote Thelwall: 'A nervous affection from my right temple to the extremity of my right shoulder almost distracted me, and made the frequent use of laudanum absolutely necessary.'[9] But that refers back unmistakably to the occasion of the preceding letter.

Finally, in April, 1798, in a letter to his brother George

occurs the sentence (referring to his sufferings from an ulcerated tooth) which I have already quoted more than once: 'Laudanum gave me repose, not sleep; but you, I believe, know how divine that repose is, what a spot of enchantment, a green spot of fountain and flowers and trees in the very heart of a waste of sands!'[10] For the period which alone concerns us, this constitutes the accessible first-hand evidence.*

Now several things are clear from these passages in the letters. In the first place, it is necessary to disregard entirely Coleridge's later statements, so far as they purport to give the time at which his use of laudanum began.[11] His memory for dates, always treacherous, was no longer to be relied on, and he apparently left out of account as unimportant his occasional resort to the drug as an anodyne before the fatal *habit* had been formed. The letters before us, written without the slightest effort at concealment, offer conclusive evidence of Coleridge's use of opium before and during the Nether Stowey period. But in the second place, they make equally clear the fact that this earlier recourse to the drug had as its object the relief of pain or sleeplessness, and it is a fair inference from the letters that this employment was infrequent. We have actual record of but three occasions (excluding the case of 'Kubla Khan') during a period of seven years—from 1791 to 1798. It would be rash to assume, despite the entire freedom with which Coleridge spoke of his experience, that these occasions were the only ones. But it is no less rash to conclude that at this period Coleridge had become *addicted* to the drug. The first hint of the deadly peril lurking in the remedy appears (so far as published evidence makes it possible to judge) in the letter of April, 1798, written just after the completion of 'The Ancient Mariner,' and just before the birth of 'Kubla Khan.' For in the reference to the divine repose of opium and to the spot of enchantment which it creates a new and ominous note is heard—a note, moreover, which one can but feel to be distinctly reminiscent. It is hard to believe, after reading Coleridge's words, that in that richly dowered 'month before the month of May' the enchantment attendant on the remedy had been experienced for the first time. That Charles Lloyd, moreover, in spite of his denials, had Coleridge in mind in certain passages which describe the hero of *Edmund Oliver* (published in Bristol, 1798), there can be, I think, no doubt.[12] And however little weight may be attached to the figments of a brain which even then was wavering from balance, and however out of drawing the details which gave just offence to Coleridge obviously are, the references to Edmund Oliver's use of opium have probably some foundation in the known facts which we have just considered.[13] The question is a baffling one. But if we dispassionately weigh the scant contemporary evidence, we must conclude, I think, that during the fall of 1797 and the spring of 1798 the use of opium had not yet become habitual, but had with little doubt begun to exercise its spell.[14] On that point Mr. Robertson's contention is borne out by the facts.

All this, however, concerns us solely in its bearing on the conception and execution of the poems. And on that score we need not linger over 'Kubla Khan.' For regarding that the case is clear. An unpublished manuscript note of Coleridge, dated November 10, 1810, and discovered in 1893 by Ernest Hartley Coleridge, leaves no question of the nature of the ambiguous 'anodyne.'[15] For the memorandum connects Coleridge's retirement to the lonely farmhouse between Porlock and Linton with a recourse to opium to relieve his mental distress over the bitter quarrel with Charles Lloyd. The fact that in 1810 this resort to the drug was referred to by Coleridge as his 'first' is for our purpose immaterial. The dream was plainly an opium-dream, and the poem, if one choose to call it so, 'an abnormal product,' conceived and composed 'under abnormal conditions.' Barring the large assumption of 'an abnormal nature,' there is little cause to quarrel with Mr. Robertson's formula so far as it applies to 'Kubla Khan.' Nor is that admitted abnormality of the conditions inconsistent with the facts thus far disclosed about the poem. An opium-dream, like any other dream, draws for its elements upon past experience. 'If a man, "whose talk is of oxen," ' observes De Quincey, 'should become an opium-eater, the probability is, that (if he is not too dull to dream at all)—he will dream about oxen.'[16] And granting that the immediate influence of opium enhanced the vividness and susceptibility to combination of the imagery which rose up before Coleridge in sleep, the fact remains that the sources of that imagery were independent of the drug. But all this, however necessary to consider, is beside the crucial point.

II

For Mr. Robertson's main contention is that *all* the work of Coleridge's poetic prime was 'conceived and composed under the influence of opium in the first stages of the indulgence.' And since this view, in some form or other, has obtained wide currency, an examination of its validity becomes imperative.

Mr. Robertson's argument turns on a fact of which every reader of Coleridge is well aware—the sharp discrepancy between 'The Ancient Mariner,' the First Part of 'Christabel,' and 'Kubla Khan' on the one hand, and Coleridge's previous achievement on the other.

> They ['The Ancient Mariner' and 'Kubla Khan'] are both abnormal to his whole previous technique, which ran to rhetoric and involution, turning thought and feeling to abstraction, whereas the uniqueness of the new work consists in the extreme concrete simplicity given to visions far aloof from experience. . . . Coleridge's poetic bent hitherto had been almost wholly didactic or reflective; and though his early fancifulness or 'shaping spirit of imagination' implied the gift on which the drug worked, *it is only as a result of abnormal brain-states that*

> *the new and great performance becomes intelligible.* So that what men regard as his mere bane, the drug to which he resorted as a relief from suffering . . . is rather, by reason of its first magical effects, *the special source of his literary immortality.*[17]

Over against the words which I have printed in italics I should be willing to set at once the facts which constitute the substance of this book, and rest my case on them without a word of argument. But something of permanent value will be gained, I think, by following a less summary procedure.

'The extreme concrete simplicity' of 'The Ancient Mariner' and 'Kubla Khan' demands, then, 'abnormal brain-states' to account for it. That proposition need scarcely be carried to its logical conclusion. It is the usual outcome of an attempt to simplify by leaving out of consideration all but one set of facts. In the omitted passage indicated by the asterisks,[18] to be sure, Mr. Robertson considers the influence of Wordsworth and his sister 'Dora' as a possible contributory factor of significance. But he dismisses it, on the ground that the effect of 'the mere influence of Wordsworth' is represented in the 'depths of bathos' and the 'imbecilities' of 'The Three Graves.'[19] And since 'The Ancient Mariner' is 'quite un-Wordsworthian,' we are thrown back upon opium and abnormal brain-states to explain this freedom from ineptitude.

Now there is no question of the gulf between Coleridge's

'new and great performance' and his 'previous technique.' Its saliency has time and again been dwelt on in this study. But there were ample causes to account for it, had poppies never yielded up their magic juice. And Wordsworth and his sister were such a cause. One sometimes fails to realize how tremendously fructifying to each was the association of Coleridge and Wordsworth at Nether Stowey and Alfoxden. Before that auspicious conjunction each had been palpably derivative in his poetry; each now struck out adventurously along new paths. We forget so easily that they were *young*—and when we are young (as Hazlitt wrote in that priceless story of his visit to the two at Nether Stowey) 'we . . . have indistinct but glorious glimpses of strange shapes, and there is always something to come better than what we see.'[20] And it was glorious glimpses that they saw, of a new poetry to come. Wordsworth was not concocting fiction when he wrote to Coleridge of 'the buoyant spirits That were our daily portion when we first Together wantoned in wild Poesy.'[21] And as we read between the lines of Dorothy's *Journal* we catch some inkling of how, indoors and out, they met incessantly, and talked, and read. For the first time in his life Coleridge lived (and I am quoting Arnold's words from a pregnant context) 'in a current of ideas in the highest degree animating and nourishing to the creative power.'[22] And Wordsworth, who stirred him to enthusiastic admiration,* was a fecundating influence the potency of which it is not easy to exaggerate.

He did for Coleridge what the great Italians (not opium!) did for Chaucer: he 'awoke him to consciousness of power that was his own.'[23] 'The Ancient Mariner' itself, as we have seen, owed its birth to the impregnation of Coleridge's latent stores and dormant energies by Wordsworth's faculty of provocative suggestion.† And the quickening influence of Dorothy Wordsworth's exquisite mind and eye I have already tried to show. Yet all that sane and wholesome and buoyant intercourse of three eager, youthful intellects the theory of 'abnormal brain-states' disregards.

It overlooks another thing. The free play of creative energy is, without question, as Mr. Robertson implies, subtly responsive to favouring conditions, and there was one condition to which Coleridge's 'genial spirits' were peculiarly susceptible—'that equipoise of the intellectual and emotional faculties, which he christened "joy." '[24] There are few more exceeding bitter cries than his lament for it after it was irrecoverably gone, in the lines which, first addressed to Wordsworth, are now familiar as the 'Ode to Dejection':

> Joy, William, is the spirit and the power
> That wedding Nature to us gives in dower,
> A new Earth and new Heaven . . .
> And thence comes all that charms or ear or sight,
> All melodies an echo of that voice!
> All colours a suffusion from that light![25]

And the loss of it

> Suspends what nature gave me at my birth,
> My shaping spirit of Imagination.[27]

I am not arguing what should be; I am simply stating the thing that was.

Now during his life at Nether Stowey Coleridge, with inevitable lapses, was *happy*, as he had never been before,[28] and was, alas! never to be again. We have Wordsworth's testimony, in the memorable lines addressed to Coleridge in 'The Prelude,' recalling

> That summer, under whose indulgent skies,
> Upon smooth Quantock's airy ridge we roved
> Unchecked, or loitered 'mid her sylvan combs,
> Thou in bewitching words, *with happy heart*,
> Didst chaunt the vision of that Ancient Man,
> The bright-eyed Mariner, and rueful woes
> Didst utter of the Lady Christabel.[29]

And Hazlitt's story of his visit bears Wordsworth out, and so (in spite of our feeling that the Coleridge family was, for the occasion, engagingly on its good behavior) does Richard Reynell's delightful account of his.[30] And Cottle's diverting yarn of 'a bottle of brandy, a noble loat, and a stout piece of cheese,' on the day when Wordsworth and Coleridge essayed to unharness a horse,[31] and his rhapsody on the idyllic feast in the 'Jasmine harbor,' when 'there must have been some downright witchery in the provisions,' and 'when Mr. C. took peculiar delight in assuring me . . . how happy he was,'[32] give glimpses of care-free merriment which pleasantly round out the picture.

Even Coleridge's passionate yearning for the last thing on earth the Lord had made him for attained fruition. '*I will* be (please God),' he had written Thelwall from Bristol in November, 1796. 'an horticulturalist and a farmer.'[33] And three months later he writes him again from Stowey:[34] 'I raise potatoes and all manner of vegetables, have an orchard, and shall raise corn with the spade, enough for my family. We have two pigs, and ducks and geese.'* And the preceding paragraph tells a tale of equipoise attained:

> I never go to Bristol. From seven till half past eight I work in my garden; from breakfast till twelve I read and compose, then read again, feed the pigs, poultry, etc., till two o'clock; after dinner work again till tea; from tea till supper, *review*. So jogs the day, and I am happy. I have society—*my friend* T. Poole, and as many acquaintances as I can dispense with. There are a number of very pretty young women in Stowey, all musical, and I am an immense favourite: for I pun, conundrumize, *listen*, and dance. The last is a recent acquirement. We are very happy, and my little David Hartley grows a sweet boy and has high health; he laughs at us till he makes us weep

for very fondness.[35]

'*So jogs the day, and I am happy*'—there could be no more normal conditions for creative work. A month earlier he had written to Cottle, underlining the last four words; 'from all this you will conclude *that we are happy*.'[36] And Dorothy Wordsworth's Alfoxden *Journal* bears besides on almost every page its tacit witness to the joys of companionship between the 'three people, but one soul.'[37] Yet all that the theory of 'abnormal conditions' completely disregards.

Above all, for the first time in his life Coleridge had hit upon a theme which fired his imagination, and set him voyaging again through all the wonder-haunted regions of all his best-loved books. 'This is the thing,' he might have said with Samuel Daniel, 'that I was born to do.' Of course the result was 'abnormal to his whole previous technique'—whatever precisely that may mean. You do not write about the splendid terrors of the polar ice and the portent of a bloody sun above a mast and the huge shadow of a ship upon a moonlit sea as you write (to let Coleridge pour his own scorn upon his 'previous technique') of 'such shadowy nobodies as cherub-winged *Death*, Trees of *Hope*, bare-bosomed *Affection* and simpering *Peace*.'[38] Nor need we invoke the fumes of poppy as the source (*mirabile dictu!*) of an 'extreme concrete simplicity' which owed its inspiration to the vivid, matter-of-fact directness of the travel-books. And the 'visions far aloof from experience' we now know to be experience itself, alive in the pages which Coleridge had read, and endowed with a life beyond life through his intense vicarious participation in their actuality. The change of technique on which Mr. Robertson founds his argument—a change which amounts to a metamorphosis—is the last thing I should be willing to deny. It is the inevitable consequence of the passage of a great creative artist from tentative fumblings with abstractions to the supreme endeavour to transmute concrete realities into the enduring fabric of a vision. And unless all the facts behind us in this book are wrong, it was upon concrete realities that Coleridge built the visionary structure of his masterpiece.*

Finally (so far as this aspect of the matter is concerned), to argue backwards from 'Kubla Khan' to 'The Ancient Mariner' is both bad logic and bad psychology. That 'Kubla Khan' is an 'abnormal product' everybody from Coleridge on admits. But to assume that, because 'Kubla Khan' is an opium-vision, the powers exhibited in 'The Ancient Mariner' are therefore 'abnormal brain-states' induced by a resort to the same drug, is to overlook the logical alternative that normal powers already present in 'The Ancient Mariner' operated in 'Kubla Khan' under abnormal conditions with abnormal intensity. Mr. Robertson's assumption puts the cart before the horse. I shall not argue the point. The chapters behind us afford the evidence in the light of which the two alternatives may be dispassionately weighed.

III

We have been considering thus far just one thing—the contention that only on the assumption of the determining influence of opium can the radical change in Coleridge's *modus operandi* as exhibited in 'The Ancient Mariner,' as well as in 'Kubla Khan,' be accounted for. That contention, so far as it touches 'The Ancient Mariner,' falls to the ground. It disregards too many other influences which were powerfully at work. But there is more than negative evidence to rest on. The assumption that 'The Ancient Mariner' is the product of 'abnormal brain-states' induced by a resort to opium is contradicted by 'The Ancient Mariner' itself. We need blink no facts. There is no doubt that Coleridge had taken opium as a remedy before November, 1797. It is clear from the letter of April, 1798, that he had already felt its enchantment. It is perfectly possible that such apparently infrequent experiences may have left traces in 'The Ancient Mariner.' But if so—and this is fundamental—they were plainly of a piece with the other thronging recollections: materials for the shaping spirit of imagination to work with, and never an influence which suspended its control. For superb, unwavering imaginative control is the very essence of the poem. And that is not the gift of opium.

What is this gift? De Quincey (whose gorgeous rhetoric and whose petty rancours we may discount as we will) knew, if any mortal did, the ways of opium. And he has set them down in a compendious and illuminating summary: 'Opium gives and takes away. It defeats the *steady* habit of exertion; but it creates spasms of irregular exertion. It ruins the natural power of life; but it developes preternatural paroxysms of intermitting power.'[41] That, I take it, is undisputed testimony, and the facts are plain. The very quality which opium defeats is the quality which 'The Ancient Mariner' signally displays; and of the spasmodic and paroxysmal effort which the drug creates,[42] the poem's evolution, as we have traced it, shows no hint. The fact which stands out, salient as a mast against the sky, is this. The qualities demanded for the conception and execution of a design like that which underlies 'The Ancient Mariner,' and the qualities of an abnormal product of abnormal brain-states induced by opium, are diametrically opposed. Mr. Robertson's assumption is negatived by the facts.

That assumption I wish in closing to state again, in another of its succinct and telling formulations. For a catching phrase may do more execution than an argument. 'The chance brain-blooms of a season of physiological ecstasy':[43] so in his concluding paragraph Mr. Robertson styles the group of works of which 'The Ancient Mariner' is one. That states the issue in a nutshell, and there is little need to beat about the bush. If a complex design wrought out through the exquisite adjustment of innumerable details be the result of chance, and if steady adherence to that design through a distracting profusion of associations be the ear-mark of physiological ecstasy, then without more ado we may accept 'The Ancient Mariner' as a fortuitous 'brain-bloom,' and credit its close-knit coherence to the flighty spell of opium. Once more it is simply a question of fact. Either 'The Ancient Mariner' is the deliberate, consecutive working out of a controlling imaginative design, or it is not. And I shall not restate the evidence—for that were to repeat the book.

I am entirely ready to grant, to any one who will have it so (for evidence there is none), the possibility that this or that image in the poem may previously have flashed before Coleridge's inner eye at some time when the enchantment of the drug was on him, and may owe in consequence some measure of its singular vividness to that. Sleeping images from books, that is, which rose up at some moment of 'divine repose' may conceivably have sunk again into the Well with the magic of the dream still on them, and, when they were once more called up, may have come still touched with the enchanted brightness. That without doubt, in view of the indulgences of which we positively know, is possible. Yet even though we grant that possibility,* we are as far from Mr. Robertson's contention as before. For nothing in the poem shows more deliberate art, as we have seen, than the consummate skill with which these same ocular spectra are built into the structure of a developing design. In the conscious operations of the shaping spirit which underlie the composition of the poem, 'The Rime of the Ancient Mariner' is as normal as the *Odyssey*.

*It could not have been 1795. Coleridge was not married until October of that year; on March 30, 1796, he wrote in almost identically the same terms: 'Since last you saw me I have been well nigh distracted. The repeated and most injurious blunders of my printer out-of-doors, and Mrs. Coleridge's increasing danger at home,' etc. (*Letters*, I, 156; B. E., I, 65); Hartley Coleridge was born September 19, 1796 (*Letters*, I, 169); and March 12 fell on a Saturday in 1796, but not in 1795. Since Coleridge's notorious inability to get dates right has often made it necessary to correct him, it is well for once to catch him definitely in the act.

†It recalls, in a certain irresponsible exuberance, the delectable epistle which Thackeray wrote Tennyson in an 'ardour of claret and gratitude' ('the landlord gave *two* bottles of his claret and I think I drank the most') about the 'Idylls of the King' (*Memoir*, I, 444–46).

*Mr. Fausset makes the categorical statement in his *Samuel Taylor Coleridge* (1926, p. 128), that 'three years before [the letter of 12 March, 1796, quoted above], in a letter to Mary Evans, he had confessed to taking "rather a strong dose of opium"; now . . . he was obliged to take laudanum almost every night.' The 'confession' to Mary Evans would be important additional evidence, had it ever been made. But it was not. Mr.

Fausset is quoting the phrase 'rather a strong dose of opium' (though, in accordance with his uniform practice, he gives no reference) from a letter of February 7, 1793 (*Letters*, I, 47–52). Coleridge has just written out (p. 51) for Mary Evans his 'Complaint of Ninathóma,' and immediately continues: 'Are you asleep, my dear Mary? *I have administered rather a strong dose of opium;* however, if in the course of your nap you should chance to dream,' etc. (the italics are mine). Precisely so, a year earlier (*Letters*, I, 35), after copying his 'Ode in the Manner of Anacreon,' he had proceeded: 'Are you quite asleep, dear Mary? Sleep on,' etc. The 'opium' of Mr. Fausset's (undesignedly) misleading statement was a supposedly soporific poem, and, such as it was, it was administered, not taken! The remark is simply an instance of what Mr. Fausset himself elsewhere calls (p. 62) 'dear "Brother Coly's" facetiousness.'

*For the overwhelming evidence of this statement see the Notes.[26]

† However grievously Wordsworth lapsed within two years, that fact remains impregnable. Nor is it strange. For once more we keep forgetting that the Wordsworth of those days was not the prosy septuagenarian who dictated the Fenwick note about the poem, but the youth who just five years earlier had come back from his passionate experiences in France—when 'Bliss was it in that dawn to be alive, But to be young was very Heaven!' And the Vision of Youth had not

yet, in 1797, died away.

*In the spring of 1798, with 'The Ancient Mariner' and 'Christabel' and for aught I know 'Kubla Khan' still in his head, Coleridge took out of the Bristol Library Volumes X and XI of the *Transactions of the Society for the Encouragement of Arts, Manufactures, and Commerce.*[39] And their copious and judicious expositions of the most approved methods of raising turnips and potatoes mingled happily, we may suppose, with Bartram's fountains, and the Grand Observatory at Pekin, and Father Bourzes's rainbow in the spray, and Priestley's fishes.

*'The quality which in Coleridge had to serve for strength of character,' Mr. Robertson writes again, 'namely intellectual zeal, here [in 'The Rime'] attains to a success of sincerity which is perhaps only possible in virtue of *a weak relation to actuality*. The mariner's visionary tale is told with a conviction that would be notable in fiction of the most natural kind; and it is the sincere and simple expression of the unreal tale *in terms of the most vivid of real perceptions* that gives it its irresistible impressiveness. The psychological method is much the same as that of Poe, *that other abnormal neurotic type*.'[40] The italics are mine. In the light of all we now have seen, the assumption of 'a weak relation to actuality' in 'The Ancient Mariner' runs counter to the facts, and 'the most vivid of real perceptions' owe their vividness, not to abnormal neurosis in Samuel Taylor Coleridge, but to the fact that Captain James

Cook, and the men who wrote in Purchas, and a score or so of other voyagers and travellers and scientists had eyes.

*When I recall, however, the child who before he was six years old, after reading the *Arabian Nights*, 'was haunted by spectres, whenever [he] was in the dark'; who, at the same period, 'acted over what [he] had been reading or fancying, . . . with a stick cutting down weeds and nettles, as one of the seven champions of Christendom'; and who, a little later, 'going down the Strand, in one of his day-dreams, fanci[ed] himself swimming across the Hellespont' (with remarkable results)[44]—when I recall all this and more, I feel no urgent need of invoking opium to account for ocular images of whatever intensity and vividness.

CHAPTER XXII

IMAGINATION CREATRIX

WE set out, long ago, through a glimmering chaos across which lingered, faintly luminous, like the tracks of shining creatures in the sea, the trace of the adventuring imagination. And by strange and devious ways that glimmering track has led us into the trodden highway of the creative energy. And for a moment only, since the inexorable bounds of time and space have long since warningly displayed their flaming sword, we may follow it beyond the tract we have traversed. For in linking 'The Rime of the Ancient Mariner' with the *Odyssey*, through the ways of the imagination which underlie them both, I have had far more than a passing argument in mind. We are not, to put it in a word, drawing general conclusions from a special case. And a theme which only another volume could develop must be compacted into a dozen paragraphs.

I

Every great imaginative conception is a vortex into which everything under the sun may be swept. 'All other men's worlds,' wrote Coleridge once, 'are the poet's chaos.'[1] In that regard 'The Ancient Mariner' is one with the noble army of imaginative masterpieces of all time. Oral traditions—homely, fantastic, barbaric, disconnected—which had ebbed and flowed across the planet in its unlettered days, were gathered up into that marvel of constructive genius, the plot of the *Odyssey*, and out of 'a tissue of old *märchen*' was fashioned a unity palpable as flesh and blood and universal as the sea itself. Well nigh all the encyclopedic erudition of the Middle Ages was forged and welded, in the white heat of an indomitable will, into the steel-knit structure of the *Divine Comedy* There are not in the world, I suppose, more appalling masses of raw fact than would stare us in the face could we once, through some supersubtle chemistry, resolve that superb, organic unity into its primal elements. It so happens that for the last twenty-odd years I have been more or less occupied with Chaucer. I have tracked him, as I have trailed Coleridge, into almost every section of eight floors of a great library. It is a perpetual adventure among uncharted Ophirs and Golcondas to read after him—or Coleridge. And every conceivable sort of thing which Chaucer knew went into his alembic. It went in *x*—a waif of travel-lore from the mysterious Orient, a curious bit of primitive psychiatry, a racy morsel from Jerome against Jovinian, alchemy, astrology, medicine, geomancy, physiognomy, Heaven only knows what not, all vivid with the relish of the reading—it went in stark fact, 'nude and crude,'[2] and it came out pure Chaucer. The results are as different from

'The Ancient Mariner' as an English post-road from spectre-haunted seas. But the basic operations which produced them (and on this point I may venture to speak from first-hand knowledge) are essentially the same.

As for the years of 'industrious and select reading, steady observation, insight into all seemly and generous arts and affairs'[3] which were distilled into the magnificent romance of the thunder-scarred yet dauntless Rebel, voyaging through Chaos and old Night to shatter Cosmos, pendent from the battlements of living sapphire like a star—as for those serried hosts of facts caught up into the cosmic sweep of Milton's grandly poised design, it were bootless to attempt to sum up in a sentence here the opulence which countless tomes of learned comment have been unable to exhaust. And what (in apostolic phrase) shall I more say? For the time would fail me to tell of the *Æneid*, and the *Orlando Furioso*, and the *Faërie Queene*, and *Don Juan*, and even *Endymion*,* let alone the cloud of other witnesses. The notion that the creative imagination, especially in its highest exercise, has little or nothing to do with facts is one of the *pseudodoxia epidemica* which die hard.

For the imagination never operates in a vacuum. Its stuff is always fact of some order, somehow experienced; its product is that fact transmuted. I am not forgetting that facts may swamp imagination, and remain unassimilated and untransformed. And I know, too, that this sometimes happens even with the masters. For some of the greatest poets, partly by virtue of their very greatness, have had, like Faust, two natures struggling within them. They have possessed at once the instincts of the scholar and the instincts of the artist, and it is precisely with regard to facts that these instincts perilously clash. Even Dante and Milton and Goethe sometimes clog their powerful streams with the accumulations of the scholar who shared bed and board with the poet in their mortal frames. 'The Professor still lurks in your anatomy'—'Dir steckt der Doktor noch im Leib'—says Mephistopheles to Faust.[4] But when, as in 'The Ancient Mariner,' the stuff that Professors and Doctors are made on has been distilled into quintessential poetry, then the passing miracle of creation has been performed.

II

But 'creation,' like 'creative', is one of those hypnotic words which are prone to cast a spell upon the understanding and dissolve our thinking into haze. And out of this nebulous state of the intellect springs a strange but widely prevalent idea. The shaping spirit of imagination sits aloof, like God as he is commonly conceived, creating in some thaumaturgic fashion out of nothing its visionary world. That and that only is deemed to be 'originality'—that, and not the imperial moulding of old matter into imperishably new forms. The ways of creation are wrapt in mystery; we may only marvel, and bow the head.

Now it is true beyond possible gainsaying that the operations which we call creative leave us in the end confronting mystery. But that is the fated terminus of all our quests. And it is chiefly through a deep-rooted reluctance to retrace, so far as they are legible, the footsteps of the creative faculty that the power is often thought of as abnormal, or at best a splendid aberration. I know full well that this reluctance springs, with most of us, from the staunch conviction that to follow the evolution of a thing of beauty is to shatter its integrity and irretrievably to mar its charm. But there are those of us who cherish the invincible belief that the glory of poetry will gain, not lose, through a recognition of the fact that the imagination works its wonders through the exercise, in the main, of normal and intelligible powers. To establish that, without blinking the ultimate mystery of genius, is to bring the workings of the shaping spirit in the sphere of art within the circle of the great moulding forces through which, in science and affairs and poetry alike, there emerges from chaotic multiplicity a unified and ordered world.

For the operations which we have been tracing are, in essentials, the stuff of general experience. We live, every one of us—the mutest and most inglorious with the rest—at the centre of a world of images. And they behave with us, and you and I behave with them, in such fashion that were only the ineffable increment of genius present, 'Ancient Mariners' might hang on every bush. No one could with more unchallenged fitness represent the mute majority than I, and here, fresh-picked, is a commonplace case in point. I received an hour ago (as I now write) a letter from an English friend. I had last seen him at an international conference of scholars, and instantly, as I read the letter, pictures connected with that gathering began to rise and stream. And before I knew it, as I sat for a moment thinking (if what was going on may properly be labelled 'thought') associated images from far and near were crowding on each other's heels. They flashed, by way of a distinguished mediævalist who, as one of a hundred services, had edited 'The Pearl,' to the river and cliff at Durham, which I long had thought of as oddly suggestive of the etherealized landscape of that baffling poem. And with what seemed utter inconsequence I instantly saw, sharp as if etched, a dark alley debouching on a river, and a policeman holding with one hand (his pistol in the other) a kicking, struggling ruffian, while a pair of sinister figures intent on rescue manœuvred for position in the background. Yet that, like the cliff at Durham, crowned with its mighty pile, was paradoxically called up by that most otherworldly of performances, 'The Pearl.' For the scene was an incident of the last midnight walk I had taken with a friend (now dead) who years ago had speculated brilliantly about the problem of the poem—and had been answered by the writer of my letter! Then (although in reality the strands of recollection were simultaneously interweaving like a nest of startled snakes) with another leap of association I was on an island in the Thames, where, of a Sunday afternoon, there used to recline against a tree, like a glorious old British river-god with white and curling beard, the Chaucerian whom Chaucer would have most dearly loved. And in a twinkling the island in its turn dissolved, and the river-god became the *genius loci* of the tea-shop in New Oxford Street where, in a flowing tie of unforgettable flamboyancy, he still lives in a thousand memories. And at once there slipped into the picture, displacing that glorified establishment, a dingy A. B. C. eating-house in Aldgate Street, where thirty years ago delectable little lamb-pies were to be had. And off in every direction all the while were shooting other associations, recalling and linking other fleeting glimpses of yesterday, and long ago, and far away. And then the telephone incontinently cut the panorama off.

There is an instance, normal enough, of 'the streamy nature of association.' And two or three perfectly obvious facts are pertinent enough to call to mind. I am not, for example, perpetually haunted by the pictures of this morning's casual raree-show. At the moment when I tore my letter open they had, for the 'I' of that moment, absolutely no existence. Collectively and severally they were not. Where, indeed, at any given instant, *are* all the countless facts we know, and all the million scenes we have experienced? Wherever that shadowy limbo may be, these were. The Well is only a convenient symbol for a mystery. And there they had lain, 'absorbed by some unknown gulf into some unknown abyss,'[5] to all intents and purposes in utter non-existence—asleep, some for weeks, some for months, and some for a period of years. Then, all at once, they awoke.

And they awoke at the summons of a definite suggestion. Had that particular letter not arrived, they might have slept on for yet more months and years, or even never have waked at all. But once called, they came pell-mell, as if the fountains of the deep were broken up. Moreover, to my certain knowledge, most of them had never come into conjunction in the field of consciousness before. 'The Pearl' in the course of five hundred years had never consorted with quite this queer gallimaufry. Dr. Furnivall on his beloved island in the Thames and a policeman with a pistol on the banks of the Cantabrigian Charles achieved propinquity, I can affirm with confidence, for the first time. Yet there they were—like the marine fauna of Spitzbergen and the phosphorescence of tropical seas. A definite impetus had struck down into the Well and set the sleeping images in motion. And when they emerged, they were linked in new and sometimes astonishing combinations. Nor, be it noted, am I now discussing the inception of a poem.

But there is more. The panorama was set in motion and unrolled without my will. For the moment I simply allowed the images to stream. Then I deliberately assumed control. For when, an hour later, I came back to write, I saw that here, like manna from heaven, was grist for my mill. The sentence about the world of images at the centre of which we live stood already on the page, and the skeleton of a plan was in my head. And with the play of free associations fresh in mind, a new agency was interposed. For I have now consciously selected and rejected among the crowding elements of the phantasmagoria, and the elements accepted have been fitted into my design. The streamy nature of association has been curbed and ruddered—and the result is as innocent of poetry as a paradigm.

Now all that, trivial though it be, is a perfectly normal and typical proceeding. The thronged yet sleeping subliminal chambers; the summons which unlocks their secret doors; the pouring up of images linked in new conjunctions provocative of unexpected *aperçus*; the conscious seizing and directing to an end of suggestions which the unconscious operations have supplied—not one stage of the process, nor even the transaction as a whole, is the monopoly of poetry. It is the stuff of which life weaves patterns on its loom; and poetry, which is life enhanced and glorified, employs it too in fashioning more rarely beautiful designs. Intensified and sublimated and controlled though they be, the ways of the creative faculty are the universal ways of that streaming yet consciously directed something which we know (or think we know) as life.

Creative genius, in plainer terms, works through processes which are common to our kind, but these processes are superlatively enhanced. The subliminal agencies are endowed with an extraordinary potency; the faculty which conceives and executes operates with sovereign power; and the two blend in untrammelled interplay. There is always in genius, I imagine, the element which Goethe, who knew whereof he spoke, was wont to designate as 'the Dæmonic.'[6] But in genius of the highest order that sudden, incalculable, and puissant energy which pours up from the hidden depths is controlled by a will which serves a vision—the vision which sees in chaos the potentiality of Form.

III

Out of the vast, diffused, and amorphous nebula, then, with which we started, and through which we have slowly forged our way, there emerged, framed of its substance, a structure of exquisitely balanced and coördinated unity—a work of pure imaginative vision. 'The imagination,' said Coleridge once, recalling a noble phrase from Jeremy Taylor's *Via Pacis*, '. . . *sees all things in one*.'[7] It sees the Free Life—the endless flux of the unfathomed sea of facts and images—but it sees also the controlling Form. And when it acts on what it sees, through the long patience of the will the flux itself is transformed and fixed in the clarity of a realized design. For there enter into imaginative creation three factors which reciprocally interplay: the Well, and the Vision, and the Will. Without the Vision, the chaos of elements remains a chaos, and the Form sleeps forever in the vast chambers of unborn designs. Yet in *that* chaos only could creative Vision ever see *this* Form. Nor without the cooperant Will, obedient to the Vision, may the pattern perceived in the huddle attain objective reality. Yet manifold though the ways of the creative faculty may be, the upshot is one: from the empire of chaos a new tract of cosmos has been retrieved; a nebula has been compacted—it may be!—into a star.

Yet no more than the lesser are these larger factors of the creative process—the storing of the Well, the Vision, and the concurrent operation of the Will—the monopoly of poetry. Through their conjunction the imagination in the field of science, for example, is slowly drawing the immense confusion of phenomena within the unfolding conception of an ordered universe. And its operations are essentially the same. For years, through intense and unremitting observation, Darwin had been accumulating masses of facts which pointed to a momentous conclusion. But they pointed through a maze of baffling inconsistencies. Then all at once the flash of vision came. 'I can remember,' he tells us in that precious fragment of an autobiography—'I can remember the very spot in the road, whilst in my carriage, when to my joy the solution occurred to me.'[8] And then, and only then, with the infinite toil of exposition, was slowly framed from the obdurate facts the great statement of the theory of evolution.* The leap of the imagination, in a garden at Woolsthorpe on a day in 1665, from the fall of an apple to an architectonic conception cosmic in its scope and grandeur is one of the dramatic moments in the history of human thought. But in that pregnant moment there flashed together the profound and daring observations and conjectures of a long period of years; and upon the instant of illumination followed other years of rigorous and protracted labour, before the *Principia* appeared. Once more there was the long, slow storing of the Well; once more the flash of amazing vision through a fortuitous suggestion; once more the exacting task of translating the vision into actuality. And those are essentially the stages which Poincaré observed and graphically recorded in his 'Mathematical Discovery.' And that chapter reads, as we saw long ago, like an exposition of the creative processes through which 'The Ancient Mariner' came to be. With the inevitable and obvious differences we are not here concerned. But it is of the utmost moment to more than poetry that instead of regarding the imagination as a bright but ineffectual faculty with which in some esoteric fashion poets and their kind are specially endowed, we recognize the essential oneness of its function and its ways with all the creative endeavours through which human brains, with dogged persistence, strive to discover and realize order in a chaotic world.

For the Road to Xanadu, as we have traced it, is the road of the human spirit, and the imagination voyaging through chaos and reducing it to clarity and order is the symbol of all the quests which lend glory to our dust. And the goal of the shaping spirit which hovers in the *poet's* brain is the clarity and order of pure beauty. Nothing is alien to its transforming touch. 'Far or forgot to [it] is near; Shadow and sunlight are the same.' Things fantastic as the dicing of spectres on skeleton-barks, and ugly as the slimy spawn of rotting seas, and strange as a star astray within the moon's bright tip, blend in its vision into patterns of new-created beauty, 'herrlich, wie am ersten Tag.' Yet the pieces that compose the pattern are not new. In the world of the shaping spirit, save for its patterns, there is nothing new that was not old. For the work of the creators is the mastery and transmutation and reordering into shapes of beauty of the given universe within us and without us. The shapes thus wrought are not that universe; they are 'carved with figures strange and sweet, All made out of the carver's brain.' Yet in that brain the elements and shattered fragments of the figures already lie, and what the carver-creator sees, implicit in the fragments, is the unique and lovely Form.

I have said that this book was not to be about Coleridge himself. So in my ignorance I thought when I began to write. But now I know that the figure of Coleridge has been a living presence all the way—an eager and divinely gifted spirit with piteously trailing wings, 'forever Voyaging through strange seas of Thought, alone'; the Artificer, for a few bright moments, out of the rare and curious spoils of his wide wayfaring, of shapes touched with something as near magic as we mortals reach, and wrought into inimitable beauty.

---

*I found a few months ago, while on the trail of Coleridge, that Keats had blended in the Indian maiden's song quite unsuspected scraps of Diodorus Siculus and Rabelais with the well-known fragments of Sandys's Ovid, and reminiscences of a glowing masterpiece of Titian, and phrases touched with the magic of 'The Ancient Mariner' itself. And into the four books of *Endymion*, after dipping out of every fountain-head to which he came, Keats emptied helter-skelter all his brim-filled bowls.

**Mutatis mutandis*, that was Goethe's experience over again, as he tells it in his story of the genesis of *Werther*.

A LIST OF ABBREVIATIONS USED FOR THE WORKS MOST FREQUENTLY REFERRED TO IN THE FOLLOWING NOTES

The date given in each case is that of the edition to which reference is made.*

A. M.	The Rime of the Ancient Mariner.
A. P.	See under Coleridge.
Abernethy.	The Rime of the Ancient Mariner, Christabel and other Poems, ed. Julian W. Abernethy. New York, [1907.]
Archiv.	Herrig's Archiv für das studium der neueren sprachen und literaturen, XCVII (1896). See under Note Book.
Archiv, CXVIII.	*Ibid.*, Vol. CXVIII (1907).

B.E.	See under Coleridge.
B.L.	See under Coleridge.
B.L.	See under Coleridge.
B.L.(1847).	See under Coleridge.
B.L(sampson).	See under Coleridge.
Bartram.	William Bartram, Travels through North and South Carolina, Georgia, East and West Florida, etc. Philadelphia, 1791.
Bayle.	Dictionnaire historique et critique (troisième édition). Rotterdam, 1720.

Belden.	The Ancient Mariner and Select Poems, ed. Henry Marvin Belden. New York, [1908.]
Benyowski.	Memoirs and Travels of Mauritius Augustus Count de Benyowski. London, 1790.
Bersch.	Georg Bersch, S. T. Coleridge's Naturschilderungen in seinen Gedichten (Marburg dissertation, 1909).
Benvan and Phillott.	W. L. Bevan and H. W. Phillott, Mediæval Geography. An essay in illustration of the Hereford Mappa Mundi. London and Hereford, 1873.

Botanic Garden. Erasmus Darwin, The Botanic Garden; A Poem, in Two Parts. Parti. Containing The Economy of Vegetation. Part II. The Loves of the Plants. With Philosophical Notes. London, 1791.

Brandl(1886). Alois Brandl, Samuel Taylor Coleridge und die englische Romantik. Strassburg, 1886.

Brandl (1887). Alois Brandl, Samuel Taylor Coleridge and the English Romantic School. English edition by Lady Eastlake. (Assisted by the Author.) London, 1887.

Bruce. James Bruce, Travels to Discover the Source of the Nile, in the Years 1768, 1769, 1770, 1771, 1772, and 1773. In five volumes. Edinburgh, 1790.

Bucaniers. The History of the Bucaniers of America . . . now Collected into one Volume. The third edition. London, 1704.

Burnet, S. T. [Thomas Burnet,] The Sacred Theory of the Earth . . . In Four Books. I. Concerning the Deluge. II. Concerning Paradise. III. The Burning of the World. IV. The New Heavens and New Earth. Glasgow, 1753.

—— T. T.	[Thomas Burnet,] Telluris Theoria Sacra . . . Libri duo priores de Diluyio et Paradiso, London, 1681; Libri duo posteriores de Conflagratione Mundi, et de Futuro Rerum Statu, London, 1689.
Callander.	John Callander, Terra australis cognita, etc. [Translated from Comte de Brossas.] In three volumes. London, 1766–68.
Campbell, Narrative.	James Dykes Campbell, Samuel Taylor Coleridge. A Narrative of the Events of his Life London, 1894.

—— Poems.	The Poetical Works of Samuel Taylor Coleridge. Edited with a Biographical Introduction by James Dykes Campbell. London, 1893.
Carlyon.	Clement Carlyon, Early Years and Late Reflections. In four volumes. London, 1858.
Carver.	Jonathan Carver, Travels through the Interior Parts of North-America, in the Years 1766, 1767, and 1768. London, 1778.
Christabel (E. H. C).	See under Coleridge.

Churchill. A Collection of Voyages and Travels . . . In six volumes. To which is prefixed, An Introductory Discourse (supposed to be written by the Celebrated Mr. Locke . . .). The third edition. London: Printed by assignment from Messrs. Churchill, 1744–46.

——. The same, Volumes VII–VIII. London: Printed for and sold by Thomas Osborne, 1747.

Coleorton. See under Coleridge.

Coleridge, A. P. Anima Poetæ. From the Unpublished Note-Books of Samuel Taylor Coleridge. Edited by Ernest Hartley Coleridge. Boston and New York, 1895.

—— Aids. Aids to Reflection in the Formation of a Manly Character . . . By S. T. Coleridge. London, 1825.

Coleridge, B. E. Biographia Epistolaris. Being the Biographical Supplement of Coleridge's Biographia Literaria. Edited by A. Turnbull, London, 1911.

—— B.L.	Biographia Literaria. By S. T. Coleridge. Edited with his Æsthetical Essays by J. Shaw-cross. Oxford, 1907.
—— B. L. (1847).	Biographia Literaria or Biographical Sketches of my Literary Life and Opinions, by Samuel Taylor Coleridge. Second edition, prepared for publication in part by the late Henry Nelson Coleridge. Completed and published by his widow [Sara Coleridge]. London, 1847.

—— B. L. (Sampson).	Coleridge, Biographia Literaria, Chapters I–IV, XIV–XXII. Wordsworth, Prefaces and Essays on Poetry, 1800–15. Edited by George Sampson with an Introductory Essay by Sir Arthur Quiller-Couch, Cambridge, 1920.
—— Christabel (E. H. C.).	Christabel, by Samuel Taylor Coleridge, illustrated by a Facsimile of the Manuscript . . . by Ernest Hartley Coleridge. London, 1907. Published under the direction of the Royal Society of Literature.

—— Coleorton.	Memorials of Coleorton, Being Letters from Coleridge, Wordsworth and his Sister, Southey, and Sir Walter Scott to Sir George and Lady Beaumont of Coleorton, Leicestershire, 1803 to 1834. Edited . . . by William Knight. Boston and New York, 1887.
—— Conciones.	Conciones ad Populum, or Addresses to the People. By S. T. Coleridge, 1795. Preface dated Clevedon, Nov. 16, 1795.
—— D. N.	The Destiny of Nations.

—— Estlin Letters. Unpublished Letters from Samuel Taylor Coleridge to the Rev. John Prior Estlin. Communicated by Henry A. Bright. [Philobiblon Society, 1884.]

—— The Friend.	The Friend; A Literary, Moral, and Political Weekly Paper, excluding Personal and Party Politics and the Events of the Day. Conducted by S. T. Coleridge, of Grasmere, Westmoreland. No. 1. Thursday, June 1, 1809—No. 27, Thursday, March 15, 1810 (with an unnumbered part, dated Thursday, January 11, 1810, between Nos. 20 and 21). Penrith: Printed and Published by J. Brown.
—— ——	Works (see below), Vol. II.

—— L. B. 1798.	Lyrical Ballads, with a Few Other Poems. London: Printed for S. and A. Arch . . . 1798.
—— L. B. 1800.	Lyrical Ballads, with Other Poems. In Two Volumes. By W. Wordsworth. London, 1800.
—— L. B. (Hutchison).	Lyrical Ballads by William Wordsworth and
Coleridge.	S. T. Coleridge, 1798. Edited with Certain Poems of 1798 and an Introduction and Notes by Thomas Hutchinson. London, second edition, 1907.
—— Lectures and Notes.	Lectures and Notes on Shakspere, and other English Poets, ed. T. Ashe. London, 1893.

—— Letters.	Letters of Samuel Taylor Coleridge, edited by Ernest Hartley Coleridge. In two volumes. London, 1895.
—— Literary Remains.	The Literary Remains of Samuel Taylor Coleridge. Collected and edited by Henry Nelson Coleridge. London, 1836–39.
—— Miscellanies.	Miscellanies, Æsthetic and Literary: to which is added The Theory of Life. By Samuel Taylor Coleridge. Collected and arranged by T. Ashe. London, 1885.

—— Notes.	Notes, Theological, Political, and Miscellaneous. By Samuel Taylor Coleridge. Edited by the Rev. Derwent Coleridge. London, 1853.
—— Omniana.	Included, for purposes of reference, under 'Notes' above.
—— Poems.	The Complete Poetical Works of Samuel Taylor Coleridge, including Poems and Versions of Poems now published for the first time. Edited with textual and bibliographical notes by Ernest Hartley Coleridge. In two volumes: Vol. I: Poems; Vol. II: Dramatic Works and Appendices. Oxford, 1912.

—— ——	See also under Campbell, above.
—— S. L.	Sibylline Leaves: A Collection of Poems. By S. T. Coleridge, Esq. London, 1817.
—— Table Talk (T. T.).	The Table Talk and Omniana of Samuel Taylor Coleridge, arranged and edited by T. Ashe, London, 1923.
—— Watchman.	The Watchman. No. I. Tuesday, March 1, 1796. [No. X. Friday, May 13, 1796.] Published by the Author, S. T. Coleridge, Bristol.

—— Works.	The Complete Works of Samuel Taylor Coleridge. With an Introductory Essay . . . Edited by Professor Shedd. In seven volumes. New York, 1854.
Cook, Journal.	[James Cook,] A Journal of a Voyage round the World, in His Majesty's Ship Endeavour, in the Years 1768, 1769, 1770, and 1771. London, 1771.

—— Voyage towards the South Pole.	A Voyage towards the South Pole and round the World. Performed in His Majesty's Ships the Resolution and Adventure, in the Years 1772, 1773, 1774, and 1775. By James Cook, Commander of the Resolution. In two volumes. Third edition, London, 1779.

Cook, Voyage to the Pacific Ocean.	A Voyage to the Pacific Ocean. Undertaken by the Command of His Majesty for making Discoveries in the Northern Hemisphere . . . In his Majesty's Ships the Resolution and Discovery, in the Years 1776, 1777, 1778, 1779, and 1780. In three volumes. Vol. I and II written by Captain James Cook . . . Vol. Ill by Captain James King. London, 1784.

Cooke, Edward. Captain Edward Cooke, A Voyage to the South Sea, and round the World, Perform'd in the Years 1708, 1709, 1710, and 1711. [Vol. I, unnumbered.] A Voyage, etc. Containing A Journal of all memorable Transactions during the said Voyage . . . London, 1712. 'Vol. II. and last.' A Voyage . . . 1711, by the Ships Duke and Dutchess of Bristol. Being a Continuation of the Voyage from California, through India, and North about into England . . . London, 1712.

Cottle, Recollections.	Joseph Cottle, Early Recollections; Chiefly relating to the late Samuel Taylor Coleridge, during his long residence in Bristol. In two volumes. London, 1837.
—— Reminiscences.	Joseph Cottle, Reminiscences of Samuel Taylor Coleridge and Robert Southey. New York, 1847.
Crantz.	David Crantz [Cranz], The History of Greenland: Containing a Description of the Country and its Inhabitants Translated from the High-Dutch. In two volumes. London, 1767.

D. N.	The Destiny of Nations.
D. N. B.	The Diotionary of National Biography.
D. W. Journals.	Journals of Dorothy Wordsworth. Edited by William Knight. Two volumes. London, 1897.
Dalrymple.	A Collection of Voyages Chiefly in the Southern Atlantick Ocean. Published from Original MSS. By Alexander Dalrymple. London, 1775.
Dampier.	Dampier's Voyages . . . By Captain William Dampier. Edited by John Masefield. In two volumes. London, 1906.

Davis.	The Voyages and Works of John Davis the Navigator. Edited by Albert Hastings Markham. Hakluyt Society, 1880.
De Quincey, Works.	The Collected writings of Thomas De Quincey. New and enlarged edition by David Masson. In fourteen volumes. Edinburgh, 1889–90.
Dupuis.	Origine de tous les cultes; ou Religion Universelle. Par [Charles François] Dupuis, Citoyen François. A Paris, L'an III. de la République, [1795,] une et indivisible. Seven volumes in twelve.

Eden. The Decades of the newe worlde or west India. . . . Wrytten in the Latine tounge by Peter Martyr of Angleria, and translated into Englysshe by Rycharde Eden. London, 1555.

—— (ed. Arber). Reprinted in Edward Arber, The First Three English Books on America. Birmingham, 1885 (pp. 43–200).

Eden and Willes.	The History of Trauayle in the West and East Indies, and other countreys lying eyther way, towardes the fruitfull and ryche Moluccaes . . . Gathered in parte, and done into Englyshe by Richarde Eden. Newly set in order, augmented, and finished by Richard Willes. London, 1577.
Edgar.	The Ancient Mariner and other Poems by Samuel Taylor Coleridge. Edited by Pelham Edgar, New York, 1910.
Edwards.	Bryan Edwards, The History, Civil and Commercial, of the British Colonies in the West Indies. In two volumes. London, 1793.

Egede.	Hans Egede, A Description of Greenland. Translated from the Danish. London, 1745.
Eichler.	Albert Eichler, Samuel Taylor Coleridge, The Ancient Mariner und Christabel, mit liter-arhisorischer Einleitung und Kommentar (Wiener Beiträge, Bd. XXVI, 1907).
Ellis.	Henry Ellis, A Voyage to Hudson's-Bay, by the Dobbs Galley and California, in the years 1746 and 1747. London, 1748.
Elton.	Oliver Elton, A Survey of English Literature, 1780–1880. In four volumes. New York, 1920.

Emerson.	See p. 578, n. 108, below.
Estlin Letters.	See under Coleridge.
Facsimile Reproduction.	See under White.
Forster.	George Forster, A Voyage round the World, in His Britannic Majesty's Sloop, Resolution, commanded by Capt. James Cook, during the Years 1772, 3, 4, and 5. In two volumes. London, 1777.
Foxe.	The Voyages of Captain Luke Foxe of Hull, and Captain Thomas James of Bristol, in Search of a North-west Passage, in 1631–32. Edited by Miller Christy. In two volumes. Hakluyt Society, 1894.

Frézier. Amédée François Frézier, A Voyage to the South-Sea, and along the Coasts of Chili and Peru, in the Years 1712, 1713, 1714. London, 1717.

Friend, The. See under Coleridge.

Garnett. The Poetry of Samuel Taylor Coleridge. Edited by Richard Garnett (The Muses Library). London, 1898.

Gillman. James Gillman, The Life of Samuel Taylor Coleridge, Vol. I (no more published). London, 1838.

God's Power and Providence.	Edward Pellham, God's Power and Providence; Shewed, In the Miraculous Preservation and Deliverance of Eight Englishmen, etc. London, 1631. (In A Collection of Documents on Spitzbergen and Greenland, ed. Adam White, Hakluyt Society, 1855).
Hakluyt.	Richard Hakluyt, The Principal Navigations Voyages Traffiques and Discoveries of the English Nation. Glasgow, 1903–05. In twelve volumes. (Hakluyt Society, Extra Series.)

Haney. John Louis Haney, A Bibliography of Samuel Taylor Coleridge. Philadelphia: Printed for private circulation, 1903.

Harper. George McLean Harper, William Wordsworth. His Life, Works, and Influence. New York, 1916.

Harris. John Harris, Navigantium atque Itinerantium Bibliotheca. Or, A Complete Collection of Voyages and Travels. . . . Now carefully Revised, with Large Additions. Two volumes in folio. London, 1744.

Hawkesworth. John Hawkesworth, An Account of the Voyages Undertaken by the Order of His Present Majesty for Making Discoveries in the Southern Hemisphere. . . . In three volumes. London, 1773.

Hazlitt, Works. The Collected Works of William Hazlitt, edited by A. R. Waller and Arnold Glover. In twelve volumes and an Index. London, 1902–04.

Hearne. Samuel Hearne, A Journey from Prince of Wales's Fort in Hudson's Bay, to the Northern Ocean. London, 1795.

Herbert. Sir Thomas Herbert, Some Yeares Travels into Africa and Asia the Great. London, 1677.

Hermit, The. See p. 458, n. 59, below.

House of Letters. A House of Letters. Being Excerpts from the Correspondence of Miss Charlotte Jerningham . . . Lady Jerningham, Coleridge, Lamb, Southey . . . and others, with Matilda Betham. Edited by Ernest Betham. A new edition. London, n. d. [1919.]

Hucks. J. Hucks, A Pedestrian Tour through North Wales, in a Series of Letters. London, 1795.

Iamblichus. Iamblichus de Mysteriis Ægyptiorum, Chaldæorum, Assyriorum. Proclus in Platonicum Alcibiadem de Anima, atque Dæmone . . . Porphyrius de divinis atque dæmonibus.

James. Psellus de Dæmonibus. Mercurii Trismegisti Pimander. Eiusdem Asclepius. Lugduni, 1570. The Voyages of Captain Luke Foxe of Hull, and Captain Thomas James of Bristol, in Search of a North-west Passage, in 1631–32. Edited by Miller Christy. In two volumes. Hakluyt Society, 1894.

James, Ivor.	The Source of 'The Ancient Mariner.' By Ivor James. Cardiff, 1890.
Keats, Works.	The Complete Works of John Keats. Edited by H. Buxton Forman. In five volumes. Glasgow, 1900–01.
L. B.	See under Coleridge.
Lamb, Works.	The Works of Charles and Mary Lamb. Edited by E. V. Lucas. In seven volumes. London, 1903–[1905.] (Letters, Vols. VI–VII.)
—— Letters.	The Works of Charles Lamb. Edited by William Macdonald. In twelve volumes. London, 1903. (Letters, Vols. XI–XII, also numbered Letters, I–II.)

—— —— The Life and Works of Charles Lamb. In twelve volumes. With Introduction and Notes by Alfred Ainger. London, 1899–1900. (Letters, Vols. IX–XII.)

—— —— Letters of Chas. Lamb. In five volumes. The Bibliophile Society. Boston, 1905.

—— —— (ed. Hazlitt.) Letters of Charles Lamb. With Some Account of the Writer, his Friends and Correspondents, and Explanatory Notes by the late Sir Thomas Noon Talfourd. An entirely new edition carefully revised and greatly enlarged by W. Carew Hazlitt. In two volumes. London (Bohn's Standard Library), 1886.

Lawson. John Lawson, The History of Carolina; Containing the Exact Description and Natural History of that Country. . . . . London, 1718.

——	Also in [John Stevens,] A New Collection of Voyages and Travels, Vol. I (1711).
Lectures and Notes.	See under Coleridge.
Leemius.	Knud Leems . . . Beskrivelse over Finmarkens Lapper . . . (Canuti Leemii . . . De Lapponibus Finmarchise). Copenhagen, 1767.
Letters.	See under Coleridge.
Letters from the Lake Poets.	Letters from the Lake Poets, Samuel Taylor Coleridge, William Wordsworth, Robert Southey, to Daniel Stuart. London, 1889.

Linschoten.	John Huighen van Linschoten. His Discours of Voyages into y[e] Easte and West Indies. London, [1598.]
—— (ed. Hakluyt Society.)	The Voyage of John Huyghen van Linschoten to the East Indies. From the old English translation of 1598. In two volumes. London, Hakluyt Society, 1885.
Literary Remains.	See under Coleridge.

Lockman. Travels of the Jesuits, into Various Parts of the World: Particularly China and the East-Indies. . . . Translated from the celebrated Lettres édifiantes et curieuses . . . By Mr. [John] Lockman. Second edition, corrected. London, 1762.

Long. [Edward Long,] A History of Jamaica. . . . In three volumes. London, 1774.

M. L. N. Modern Language Notes.

Manchester Memoirs. Memoirs of the Literary and Philosophical Society of Manchester. Warrington and Manchester. Vol. I, 1785; Vol. II, 1785; Vol. III, 1790; Vol. IV, 1793; V, i. V, 1798.

Martens. Frederick Marten[s]. The Voyage into Spitzbergen and Greenland, in An Account of Several Late Voyages and Discoveries to the South and North. . . . By Sir John Narborough, Captain Jasmen Tasman, Captain John Wood, and Frederick Marten of Hamburgh. London, 1694.

—— (Hakluyt.) A Collection of Documents on Spitzbergen and Greenland, Comprising a translation from F. Martens' Voyage to Spitzbergen. . . . Edited by Adam White. Hakluyt Society, 1855.

Maupertuis. The Figure of the Earth, Determined from Observations Made by Order of the French King, at the Polar Circle. . . . Translated from the French of M. [Pierre Louis Moreau] de Maupertuis. London, 1738.

Maurice.	[Thomas Maurice,] The History of Hindostan. . . . By the author of Indian Antiquities. London, Vol. I, 1795; Vol. II, 1798 [1799].
Mavor.	Historical Account of the most celebrated Voyages, Travels, and Discoveries. . . . By William Mavor. In twenty volumes. London, 1796–97.
Miscellanies.	See under Coleridge.
Mod. Philol.	Modern Philology.
Monk, The.	[Matthew Gregory Lewis,] The Monk: A Romance. In three volumes. London, 1796.

N. E. D.	A New English Dictionary on Historical Principles. Oxford, 1888–
Narborough.	An Account of Several Late Voyages and Discoveries to the South and North. . . . By Sir John Narborough, Captain Jasmen Tasman, Captain John Wood, and Frederick Marten of Hamburgh. . . . London, 1694.
Note Book.	The so-called 'Gutch Memorandum Book,' printed as 'S. T. Coleridges Notizbuch aus den Jahren 1795–1798' in Herrig's Archiv für das studium der neureren sprachen und litteraturen, XCV1I (1896), 333–72.

Notes.	See under Coleridge.
P. M. L. A.	Publications of the Modern Language Association of America.
Parkinson, Journal.	Sydney Parkinson, A Journal of a Voyage to the South Seas, in His Majesty's Ship, The Endeavour. London, 1773.
Paul, Wm. Godwin.	William Godwin: His Friends and Contemporaries. By C. Kegan Paul. London, 1876.
Phil. Trans.	Philosophical Transactions of the Royal Society of London.

Phipps, Journal.	The Journal of a Voyage . . . For making Discoveries towards the North Pole. By the Hon. Commodore Phipps. London, 1774.
—— Voyage.	A Voyage towards the North Pole undertaken by His Majesty's Command, 1773. By Constantine John Phipps. London, 1774.
Pitman.	The Rime of the Ancient Mariner. By Samuel Taylor Coleridge. Edited by Norman Hinsdale Pitman. Richmond, n. d.
Poems.	See under Coleridge.

Pound. — Coleridge's The Rime of the Ancient Mariner and Other Poems. With Introduction, Notes and an Appendix by Louise Pound. Philadelphia and London, n. d.

Prelude (Selincourt). — The Prelude or Growth of a Poet's Mind, by William Wordsworth. Edited from the Manuscripts with Introduction, Textual and Critical Notes, by Ernest de Selincourt. Oxford, 1926.

Priestley, Opticks. — The History and Present State of Discoveries Relating to Vision, Light, and Colours. By Joseph Priestley. London, 1772.

Purchas.	Hakluytus Posthumus or Purchas His Pilgrimes. In twenty volumes. Glasgow, 1905–07.
Purchas (1617).	Purchas his Pilgrimage, or Relations of the World and the Religions observed in all Ages and Places discovered, from the Creation unto this Present. . . . By Samuel Purchas. London, 1617.
—— (1625).	Hakluytus Posthumus or Purchas His Pilgrimes. . . . By Samuel Purchas. London, 1625.
Quarll.	See p. 458, n. 59, below.

Rainaud. Armand Rainaud, Le continent austral. Hypothèses et découvertes. Paris, 1893.

Robberds. A Memoir of the Life and Writings of the late William Taylor of Norwich. By J. W. Robberds. In two volumes. London, 1843.

Robertson. New Essays towards a Critical Method. By John Mackinnon Robertson. London and New York, 1897.

Robinson, Crabb. Diary, Reminiscences, and Correspondence of Henry Crabb Robinson. Selected and edited by Thomas Sadler. In three volumes. London, 1869.

—— ed. Morley.	Blake, Coleridge, Wordsworth, Lamb, etc., being Selections from the Remains of Henry Crabb Robinson. Edited by Edith J. Morley. Manchester and London, 1922.
Rogers.	A Cruising Voyage round the World. . . . Begun in 1708, and finished in 1711. Containing . . . An Account of Alexander Selkirk's living alone four Years and four Months in an Island. . . . By Captain Woodes Rogers. London, 1712.
S. L.	See under Coleridge.
Sandford.	See under T. P.

Santarem, Histoire. — Le Vicomte de Santarem, Essai sur l'histoire de la cosmographie et de la cartographie pendant de moyen-âge. . . . I—III. Paris, 1849–52.

—— Recherches. — Recherches sur la priorité de la découverte des pays situés sur la côte occidentale d'Afrique . . . et sur les progrès de la science géographique . . . au XVe siècle. Paris, 1842.

Shelvocke. — A Voyage round the World by the Way of the Great South Sea, Performed in the Years 1719, 20, 21, 22, in the Speedwell of London. . . . By Capt. George Shelvocke. London, 1726.

Southey, Life and Correspondence.	The Life and Correspondence of Robert Southey. Edited by his son, the Rev. Charles Cuthbert Southey. Second edition. In six volumes. London, 1849–50.
Studies in Honor of J. M. Hart.	Studies in Language and Literature in Celebration of the Seventieth Birthday of James Morgan Hart. . . . New York, 1910.
Sykes.	Select Poems of Coleridge, Wordsworth, Campbell, Longfellow. Edited by Frederick Henry Sykes. Toronto, 1895.

T. P. Thomas Poole and his Friends. In two volumes. By Mrs. Henry Sandford. London, 1888.

Table Talk (T. T.). See under Coleridge.

Tom Wedgwood. Tom Wedgwood the First Photographer. An Account of his Life, his Discovery, and his Friendship with Samuel Taylor Coleridge, including the Letters of Coleridge to the Wedgwoods. By R. B. Litchfield. London, 1903.

Ulloa.	A Voyage to South America. . . . By Don George Juan and Don Antonio de Ulloa. In two volumes. The second edition, revised and corrected. London, 1760.
Wafer.	A New Voyage and Description of the Isthmus of America. By Lionel Wafer. Reprinted from the original edition of 1699. Edited by George Parker Winship. Cleveland, 1903.
Watchman.	See under Coleridge.
Wedgwood.	See Tom Wedgwood.

West Indies.	A Short Journey in the West Indies, in which are Interspersed Curious Anecdotes and Characters. In two volumes. London, 1790.
White, Facsimile Reproduction.	Coleridge's Poems. A Facsimile Reproduction of the Proofs and MSS. of Some of the Poems. Edited by the late James Dykes Campbell. With Preface and Notes by W. Hale White. Westminster, 1899.
Wise.	A Bibliography of the Writings in Prose and Verse of Samuel Taylor Coleridge. By Thomas J. Wise. London: Printed for the Bibliographical Society, 1913.

——	Coleridgeiana. Being a Supplement to the Bibliography of Coleridge. By Thomas J. Wise. London: Printed for the Bibliographical Society, 1919.
Wollstonecraft, Letters.	Letters Written during a Short Residence in Sweden, Norway, and Denmark. By Mary Wollstonecraft. London, 1796.
Wordsworth, Dorothy.	See D. W. Journals.
—— Social Life.	Social Life at the English Universities in the Eighteenth Century. Compiled by Christopher Wordsworth. Cambridge, 1874.

—— Letters of the Wordsworth Family.	Letters of the Wordsworth Family from 1787 to 1855. Collected and edited by William Knight. In three volumes. Boston and London, 1907.
Memoirs.	Memoirs of William Wordsworth, Poet-Laureate, D. C. L. By Christopher Wordsworth. In two volumes. London, 1851.

---

*This is in no sense a bibliography of the subject. The numerous books which are referred to only once or twice are not included. The purpose of the list is simply to save the large expenditure of space otherwise required for the constant repetition of long titles in the Notes.

NOTES

Motto, Book I. The motto is the first line of 'World's Secret,' in *The Lyrical Poems of Hugo von Hofmannsthal*, translated by Charles Wharton Stork (1918). The original line is: 'Der tiefe Brunnen weiss es wohl' ('Weltgeheimnis,' *Die Gedichte und kleinen Dramen von Hugo von Hofmannsthal*, Leipzig, 1922). I am indebted to Mrs. Beatrice Ravenel for calling my attention to the phrase.

CHAPTER I

1 It is *Add. MSS.* 27901. It belonged at one time to Coleridge's old school fellow, John Mathew Gutch, and was purchased by the Trustees of the British Museum in 1868 (*Poems*, II, 988, n.).

2 These dates are based on an independent study of the document, but my conclusions agree with Brandl's (Herrig's *Archiv*, XCVII, 334–35). I shall go into the evidence fully in the edition of the Note Book mentioned above. Meantime it need only be said here that the *terminus a quo* seems to be given by an entry on fol. 5[a] (*Archiv*, p. 342): 'People starved into

War—over an enlisting place in Bristol a quarter of Lamb and piece of Beef hung up.' That is plainly a note for the address 'On the Present War,' delivered in Bristol, February, 1795, in which occurs the following sentence: 'Over a recruiting place in this city I have seen pieces of Beef hung up to attract the half-famished Mechanic' (*Conciones ad Populum*, 1795, p. 60; cf. Preface, p. 3). See Brandl, *Archiv*, pp. 334–35, 342, n. 9. That the Note Book was freely used during the spring of 1798 there is abundant evidence. See, for example, p. 513, n. 76, below.

3 *Archiv*, XCVII (1896), pp. 333–72 (*S. T. Coleridge's Notizbuch aus den Jahren 1795–1798*). There is a reprint of the article which I have not been able to see. It is that, apparently, to which E. H. Coleridge refers (see note below). Professor Brandl's first copy of the manuscript was made in 1882, and corrected on later visits to London (*Archiv*, p. 334).

4 *Poems*, II, 988, n.: 'The notebook as a whole was published by Professor A. Brandl in 1896 (*S. T. Coleridge's Notizbuch aus den Jahren 1795–1798*).' That is all; there is nothing to indicate where it is to be found. Fragments from the Note Book are printed by E. H. Coleridge (*Poems*, II, 988–95); and by Campbell (*Poems*, pp. 453–58). Some of them are also printed in Coleridge's *Literary Remains* (1836), I, 277–81, and in the earlier pages of *Anima Poetæ*.

5 See *A Common-Place Book of John Milton*, Reproduced by the Autotype Process from the Original Manuscript . . . under the direction of the Royal Society of Literature, 1876.

6 *Note Books of Percy Bysshe Shelley*, from the Originals in the Library of W. K. Bixby. Deciphered, transcribed, and edited, with a full commentary, by H. Buxton Forman. In three volumes. Privately printed for W. K. Bixby, 1911.

7 For an account of these note books, see E. H. Coleridge's Preface to *Anima Poetæ*.

8 *Note Book*, fols. 31[a]–37[a] inclusive; *Archiv*, pp. 358–61.

9 Printed in *Poems*, II, 992 (No. 34); Campbell, *Poems*, p. 456 (No. 34).

10 Fol. 31[a]; *Archiv*, p. 358. Under the first quotation is written 'Shak. Sonnets'; under the second, 'Id.'

11 Fol. 31[a]; *Archiv*, p. 358. See 'Christabel,' ll. 16–19, and especially the notes in *Christabel* (ed. E. H. C.), pp. 62–63. But on p. 63 for 'Feb. 27' read 'Jan. 27,' and cancel 'Jan. 27' after the quotation from Wordsworth. The manuscript of the 'Gutch Memorandum Book' (our 'Note Book') is now numbered by leaves, not by pages; but even so, E. H. C.'s reference to 'p. 39' is wrong. It should be, in the earlier numbering, 'p. 59' (the present fol. 31[a]).

12 Printed in *Poems*, II, 993 (No. 36); Campbell, *Poems*, p. 456 (No. 36): 'The subtle snow in every breeze rose curling from the grove, like pillars of cottage smoke.' Cottage smoke seems to have had a peculiar charm for Coleridge. In the story, in 'My First Acquaintance with Poets,' of the famous walk to Linton and the Valley of Rocks, Hazlitt has this to say: 'We returned on the third morning, and Coleridge remarked the silent cottage-smoke curling up the valleys where, a few evenings before, we had seen the lights gleaming through the dark' (*Works*, XII, 274). And in *Osorio* (Act II, l. 156) the shadow of the 'puny cararact' is 'For ever curling, like a wreath of smoke.' In one of the letters from Germany Coleridge writes of a 'dale of pines, up which the little mists crept like smoke from cottage chimneys' (*Archiv*, CXVIII, 65). In a note of 1803, 'the pillar of smoke from the chimney rises up in the mist' (A. P., p. 28). And in 'The Picture' (*Poems*, I, 373, ll. 149–50) 'The smoke from cottage-chimneys, tinged with light, Rises in columns.' So (*Aids to Reflection*, Conclusion, p. 390), 'As the column of blue smoke from a cottage chimney in the breathless Summer Noon,' etc.

13 Fols. 31^b–33^a; *Archiv*, p. 359.

14 Copied, freely, from Bartram (see Note 22, below), p. 129.

15 Coleridge is following the English reprint (1792) of

the first edition (Philadelphia, 1791). See Note 22, below. The American original has: 'Just *like* a hen does her brood of chickens.'

16 Bartram, pp. 127–28.

17 *Ibid.*, p. 128.

18 Printed in Campbell, *Poems*, p. 456 (No. 37).

19 Bartram, p. 157. The MS. reads, by a slip of the pen, 'my Man' for 'by Man.' For the significant bearings of this entry, see above, pp. 364 ff.

20 *Ibid.*, pp. 129–30. Coleridge has written 'continue to' for 'continue the.'

21 *Ibid.*, p. 140.

22 The full title is *Travels through North and South Carolina, Georgia, East and West Florida, the Cherokee Country, the Extensive Territories of the Muscogulges, or Creek Confederacy, and the Country of the Chactaws; containing an Account of the Soil and Natural Productions of those Regions, together with Observations on the Manners of the Indians.* I shall refer throughout to the first edition, Philadelphia, 1791. The crocodile passages are on pp. 127–30, 140. But they also turn up elsewhere. On March 28, 1796, Coleridge

drew from the Bristol Library the *Anthologia Hibernica*, which he kept until April 25 (*Mod. Philol.*, XXI, 319). And in the first volume of the *Anthologia*, pp. 259–60, is an item of a page and a half entitled 'Crocodiles and their Nests. From *Bartram's Travels*, lately published.' The pages in the Note Book, however (as a comparison shows beyond doubt), were not copied from the *Anthologia*. There is also in *The Wonderful Magazine*, IV (1793–94), 358, a 'Surprising Account of American Crocodiles,' which is also drawn from Bartram—a piece of information for which I am indebted to Professor A. E. Longueil. Alligators were obviously good copy at the close of the eighteenth century. And I should like to seize this opportunity to say at once that those critics who treat the Romantic movement as if it were the brilliant aberration of a group of *literats* would do well to read, mark, and inwardly digest the late eighteenth-century periodicals. For there one gets surprising glimpses of the subterranean streams from which the fountains sprang.

Brandl, in his edition of the Note Book, is silent regarding Coleridge's authority for his alligators; in his life of Coleridge he unluckily is not: 'The notebook of this date contains long paragraphs upon the alligators, boas, and crocodiles of antediluvian times' (*Samuel Taylor Coleridge*, 1887, p. 202; 'in vorsündflutlichen Lagunen,' *S. T. C.*, 1886, p. 214). Apart from the fact that there are no boas in the Note Book (nor, as distinct from alligators, any crocodiles: 'I have made use of the terms alligator and crocodile indiscriminately for this animal,' says Bartram, p. 90, n., alligator being the country name'), one wonders which of the antediluvian patriarchs was supposed to be eye-witness of the scene in the lagoon. A young German scholar shyly corrects in his doctoral dissertation the master's error (Bersch, pp. 75, 101; see below, p. 587, n. 22), and Ernest Hartley Coleridge had already communicated the facts to the Royal Society of Literature (*Transactions*, Second Series, XXVII, 1906, pp. 69–92). As I plunged into the Note Book without waiting (as Carlyle would say) to 'accumulate vehiculatory gear,' I was lucky enough to have the pleasant thrill of discovering for myself the passages in Bartram, before I knew that E. H. Coleridge and Bersch had been ahead of me. The 'green and fountainous wilderness plot' was all that, between them, they had left me. But that turned out to be the richest find of all.

There is another description of alligators in the Carolinas, which Coleridge may or may not have known, in John Lawson's *History of Carolina* (London, 1718), pp. 126–28. They are there included, together with Rattle-Snakes, under the heading: 'Insects of Carolina.' Lawson's book is extremely interesting reading, particularly as a companion-piece to Bartram, though its purpose is somewhat less disinterested. For as Thomas Cooper (see below, p. 554, n. 57) wrote his book with a view to enticing settlers to the banks of the Susquehanna, so Lawson (see especially pp. 163–67) is urging on prospective colonists the charms of Carolina. And when one reads his chapter 'Of the Vegetables of Carolina' (pp. 89–115)—including 'that noble Vegetable the Vine'—and then goes on to the accounts of game and fish, one wonders that anybody was left in England.

For the date at which Coleridge first read Bartram, see below, p. 513, n. 76. Long after, in 1818, he purchased a copy for himself (*Poems*, I, 460, n. and especially *Trans. Royal Soc. of Lit.*, Second Series, XXVII, 89–90). The edition is that of 1794, and the volume (which I have seen) is in the possession of the Rev. G. H. B. Coleridge. In the *Biographia Literaria* (II, 128–29; cf. 294) he transcribed freely a few lines from the *Travels* (pp. 36–37), with faulty recollection of the name of a tree on pp. 29–30 ('magnolia magni-floria' = magnolia grandiflora). And in T. T., March 12, 1827 he remarks: 'The latest book of travels I know, written in the spirit of the old travellers, is Bartram's account of his tour in the Floridas.' Wordsworth probably had the volume with him in Germany, for 'Ruth' ('Written in Germany') is saturated with Bartram (see Note 28, below) in such a way as to suggest that the book was a companion of that long and lonely winter. And Bartram was again in Wordsworth's mind when, in 1804, he wrote 'She was a phantom of delight' (compare lines 21–22 of the poem with *Travels*, p. 179, third paragraph).

23 See the amazing medley of the abandoned draft of 'The Wanderings of Cain' (*Poems*, I, 285, n.–286, n.; cf. Hutchinson, L. B., pp. 259–60) in which the alligators, drawn this time from Bartram's 'Great Sink' (Bartram, pp. 203–07), appear at 'Midnight on the Euphrates' among the 'cedars, palms, pines' of Florida, in conjunction with tigers on the ramp; a fiery shape (now a luminous orb, now a form with the lineaments of a man) which dances from rock to rock down interminable precipices; a dæmon with the countenance of Abel; and the archangel Michael sailing slowly down the air! E. H. Coleridge refers the alligators to Bartram (see reference to *Poems* above), but does not identify the passage. For the connection of all this with 'Kubla Khan,' see below, p. 587, n. 28.

24 *Poems*, I, 266–67, ll. 98–105:

. . . And once, when he awoke

In most distressful mood (some inward pain

Had made up that strange thing, an infant's dream—)

I hurried with him to our orchard-plot,

And he beheld the moon, and, hushed at once,

Suspends his sobs, and laughs most silently,

While his fair eyes, that swam with undropped tears,

Did glitter in the yellow moon-beam!

One could wish that the direct and vivid transcript of fact had been less smothered in conventional poetic phraseology. Campbell (*Poems*, pp. 611–12) compares 'Christabel,' ll. 315–18, which without much question recall the same incident.

How Hartley saw the moon from his father's arms another time, and what he said, together with his 'theologico-astronomical hypothesis' about the stars, may be learned from the *Letters*, I, 342–43, 323. Indeed, half an hour could hardly be more divertingly spent than in following Hartley (and his father!) with the aid of the index, through the letters and the *Anima Poetæ*. 'My David Hartley laughs, cries, and sucks with all imaginable vivacity' (*Estlin Letters*, p. 28); 'David Hartley is well, saving that he is sometimes inspired by the god Æolus, and like Isaiah, "his bowels sound like an harp" ' (*Letters*, I, 176); 'little Hartley, who uses the air of the breezes as skipping ropes' (*Letters*, I, 359); 'he is the darling of the sun and of the breeze' (Paul, *Wm. Godwin*, II, 10); 'That child is a poet, spite of the forehead, "villainously low," which his mother smuggled into his face' (*Letters*, I, 395); 'Hartley and little

Derwent running in the green where the gusts blow most madly, both with their hair floating and tossing, a miniature of the agitated trees' (*Letters*, I, 408; cf. A. P., p. 3); 'Hartley is a spirit that dances on an aspen leaf' (B. E., I, 201); 'Southey says wickedly that "all Hartley's guts are in his brains, and all Derwent's brains are in his guts" ' (*Letters*, I, 443); 'Derwent is a cube of fat' (*Coleorton*, I, 25; for Derwent's 'system of Derwentogony' see Southey, *Life and Correspondence*, II, 232). And what would we not give for the whole of that nursery-song which Sara Coleridge tells us (B. L., 1847, Vol. I, Pt. II, p. 355; and see Lamb, *Works*, VI, 73–74) that her father composed, and which began: 'Did a very little babby make a very great noise?' All this may serve as a healthy corrective to the proposed poems (sketched in one of the note books) on an infant 'asleep with the polyanthus held fast in its hand, its bells dropping over the rosy face,' or 'seen asleep by the light of glow-worms' (A. P., p. 3), and to the Wordsworthian infant, 'That, deaf and silent, read[s] the eternal deep, Haunted forever by the eternal mind.'

25 See above, pp. 364 ff.

26 Fols. 33^{b}–34^{b}; *Archiv*, pp. 359–60. Taken from Bartram, pp. 161–62. See Campbell, *Poems*, p. 456 (No. 38).

27 *Poems*, I, 257, l. 6.

28 See 'Ruth,' stanza 10:

He spake of plants that hourly change
Their blossoms, through a boundless range
Of intermingling hues;
With budding, fading, faded flowers
They stand the wonder of the bowers
From morn to evening dews.

The towering magnolia of the next stanza immediately precedes the Gordonia lasianthus in Bartram (pp. 160–61); the cypress (see especially pp. 90–91 for its 'flat, horizontal top') has borrowed its 'spire' from the 'sharp cone' of the magnolia on p. 161; the 'flowers that with one scarlet gleam Cover a hundred leagues, and seem To set the hills on fire' are the 'fiery Azalea, flaming on the ascending hills,' of which 'the blossoms cover the shrubs in such incredible profusion on the hill sides, that . . . we are alarmed with the apprehension of the hills being set on fire' (Bartram, pp. 322–23); the savannas and the lakes of stanza 12 are everywhere (with reflections in the water on p. 160); and the strawberry gatherers of the ninth stanza are from pp. 355–58. See also E. H. Coleridge, *Trans. Royal Soc. of Lit.*, Second Series, XXVII, 85–89; Dowden,

Poems of William Wordsworth (Athenæum Press Series), pp. 378–79.

'She was a phantom of delight,' line 22, is a reminiscence of Bartram, p. 179. See Dowden as above, p. 435.

29 Fols. 34[b]–35[a]; *Archiv*, p. 260. From Bartram, pp. 132–33. Italics Coleridge's.

30 Bartram, p. 133.

31 Fol. 35[a]; *Archiv*, p. 360.

32 *Notes*, p. 317. So again, in *Aids to Reflection*, Moral and Religious Aphorisms, XLI (p. 116): '. . . as the smell of a dead dog at a distance is said to change into that of Musk.'

33 *Archiv*, p. 360.

34 Quoted in Campbell, *Narrative*, p. 261, from Froude, *T. Carlyle*, I, 292. I have borrowed Campbell's 'full flavoured'—which is the inevitable word.

35 That the tale of our dozen pages may be complete, I set down the omitted entries (fols. 35[a]–36[a]; *Archiv*, p. 360) here:

> Plagiarists *suspicious* of being pilfer'd—as pickpockets are observed commonly to walk with their hands in their breeches-pockets.

> An abrupt beginning followed by an even and majestic greatness compared to the Launching of a Ship, which after sails on in a steady breeze. The Infant playing with its mother's Shadow—
>
> Rocking its little sister's cradle and singing to her with inarticulate voice.—
>
> The flat pink-colour'd stone painted over in jagged circles and strange parallelograms with the greenish black-spotted lichens.—

36 Fol. 36[a]; *Archiv*, pp. 360–61. Adapted from a charming passage in Bartram, p. 212; cf. p. 213, foot. Coleridge's interest in the North American Indians (see also below, p. 514) began early and in unexpected fashion, as we learn from a letter of Lamb to him, Oct. 23, 1802: 'There will come with it [a parcel of books] the *Holy Commonwealth*, and the identical North American Bible which you helped to dog-ear at Christ's' (*Letters*, ed. Macdonald, I, 230). A week or so later (Nov. 4) Lamb wrote him again: 'Observe, there comes to you, by the Kendal waggon tomorrow . . . a box, containing the Miltons, the strange American Bible, with White's brief note to which you will attend; Baxter's Holy Commonwealth,' etc. (*Works*, VI, 255). That this was a Bible in the Indian language is plain from a letter of Southey to Coleridge, dated June 11, 1804: 'I have ventured to lend Turner your German Romances . . . I

also sent him the Indian Bible, because I found him at the Indian grammar, for he is led into etymological researches' (*Life and Correspondence*, II, 293). There can be little doubt that the book was one of John Eliot's Indian Bibles, though which it is probably impossible to tell. Copies of the various editions in considerable numbers are known to have been owned in England, as the exhaustive study of Dr. Wilberforce Eames makes clear. His invaluable monograph, in which all known extant copies are traced, is published in J. C. Pilling, *Bibliography of the Algonquian Languages* (Smithsonian Institution, Bureau of Ethnology, 1891), pp. 127–84. See further, for the various editions, Evans, *American Bibliography* (Privately printed, Chicago, 1903–1925), Nos. 64–65, 72–75, 85, and Sabin, *A Dictionary of Books relating to America*, VI (1873), 137–39. Dr. Eames kindly writes me: 'I find nothing to connect the "Indian Bible" [once owned by S. T. Coleridge] with any of the copies described in my monograph on the subject.'

37 *Notes*, p. 362:

Ἐν τῷ φρονεῖν μηδὲν ἥδιστος βίος. *Soph.*

His life was playful from infancy to death, like the snow which in a calm day falls, but scarce seems to fall, and plays and dances in and out till the very moment that it gently reaches the earth.

The next item, headed 'The Universe,' is also excerpted from the Note Book (fol. 15[a]; *Archiv*, p. 348).

38 Fol. 36[a]; *Archiv*, p. 361. Printed in *Poems*, II, 993 (No. 37); Campbell, *Poems*, p. 456 (No. 39).

39 Fol. 36[b]; *Archiv*, p. 361. Italics Coleridge's. Used by Coleridge in the first draft of 'Love.' See *Poems*, I, 333, n., II, 993 (No. 38), 1056; and especially Campbell, *Poems*, pp. 456, 613 and note. Compare what Hazlitt says of Coleridge's method of composition: 'Coleridge has told me that he himself liked to compose in walking over uneven ground, or breaking through the straggling branches of a copse-wood' (*Works*, XII, 271). The rest of the sentence contrasts with this Wordsworth's method.

40 Fol. 36[b]; *Archiv*, p. 361. See *Poems*, I, 265, II. 43–49; cf. Campbell, *Poems*, p. 456 (No. 42).

41 D. W., *Journals*, I, 18.

42 Fol. 37[a]; *Archiv*, p. 361. Italics Coleridge's.

43 See James Jennings, *Observations on Some of the Dialects in the West of England, particularly Somersetshire* (1825), p. 70: 'To Smoor. *v.a.* To smooth, to pat.' Repeated in the second and revised edition, 1869. See also Wright's *English Dialect Dictionary, s.v.* 'smoor.' For another Somersetshire word in

Coleridge, see *Poems*, I, 276, note on 1. 225.

44 The first five entries are on fol. 2[a]; the last two on fol. 2[b]. See *Archiv*, p. 340.

45 Printed in *Poems*, I, 292; Campbell, *Poems*, p. 64 (see his note, No. 91, on p. 581).

46 Printed in Campbell, *Poems*, p. 453 (No. 1), with note.

47 Fol. 3[b]; *Archiv*, pp. 341–42. The next line in the Note Book is: 'an involuntary Burlesque.' Brandl reads a comma after 'Whale,' and regards the three lines as one entry. That is both tempting and possible, but I doubt it. The phrase is Young's ('On Lyric Poetry'), and is probably a separate entry.

48 Vol. LXXVII (1787), Pt. II, pp. 371–450: 'Observations on the Structure and Œconomy of Whales,' by John Hunter, Esq., F. R. S.

49 *Letters*, I, 93.

50 Fol. 4[a]; *Archiv*, p. 342. The last three words of the entry are almost illegible. Brandl transcribes them as 'on Whitmon [day],' which is certainly wrong. I do not feel sure, after repeated scrutiny of the manuscript, that the reading which I have given is correct. At least it does no violence to the

scrawl.

51 Fol. 4[b]; *Archiv*, p. 342. Used by Coleridge in 'Verses addressed to J. Home Tooke,' etc. (*Poems*, I, 151, 1. 47). See also *Estlin Letters*, p. 24.

52 Fol. 4[b]; *Archiv*, p. 342.

53 This graceless tale might have reached Coleridge through any one of a number of channels, the most familiar of which (and therefore in his case the most unlikely!) is *The Faërie Queene*, II, x, 7–9. But Spenser has nothing to say of the 'ship unmann'd,' with its faint suggestion of the spectre bark and the Mariner's ship itself. That detail does occur (at least by implication) in most of the elder chroniclers of Britain who tell the story, but the correspondences between the entry in the Note Book and Milton's account are verbal, and there can be no question of Coleridge's immediate source. The story is also told in the *Eulogium Historiarum* (Rolls Series, II, 216–18; the ship is 'absque remis, vehiculis, gubernatoribus'); *The Chronicle of John Hardyng* (London, 1812), chaps, i–vi; Rous (or Rows, or Ross), *Joannis Rossi Historia Regum Angliœ* (ed. Hearne, Oxford, 1745), pp. 10–18 (an uncommonly graphic tale; the ship is 'sine remigio'); Holinshed, *Chronicles* (London, 1807), I, 434–36 ('without maister, mate or mariner'); *The Brut, or the Chronicles of England* (E.E.T.S., Pt. I, pp. 1–4); Grafton, *Chronicle at Large* (1569), p. 33;

Fabyan, *Concordance of Histories* (1559), p. 7; etc. See also Ward, *Catalogue of Romances in the Dept. of MSS. in the British Museum*, I, 198–203; Carrie A. Harper, *The Sources of the British Chronicle History in Spenser's Faërie Queene* (Bryn Mawr dissertation, 1910), pp. 44 ff.

54 Fol. 4^b; *Archiv*, p. 342. The term, common in the theological literature of the day (e.g., Burnet, T. T., I, 221, 229, 266, etc.), is not uncommon in Coleridge. See D. N., l. 290 (*Poems*, I, 140); A. P., p. 81; *Works*, II, 446–47.

55 Fol. 5^b; *Archiv*, p. 343.

56 On Tuesday, March 25, 1794, while Coleridge was still in the King's Regiment of Light Dragoons, the Cambridge group to which he belonged met 'to consult for the first time on a projected periodical publication' (Diary of Christopher Wordsworth, printed in Christopher Wordsworth, *Social Life at the English Universities in the Eighteenth Century*, Cambridge, 1874, pp. 592–93). 'It is intended,' the Diary goes on, 'to begin publishing it early next October.' It did not appear, however, until January, 1795. The numbers for January and February, 1795, are preserved in the Cambridge University Library, and with them is bound up the following advertisement:

STOLEN or STRAYED, this day, between *Magdalen*

Bridge and the *Petty Cury*, on its road to the PRESS,

THE
UNIVERSITY MAGAZINE

Had on when it disappeared a *Strait Waistcoat.*

Whoever will give information thereof to its distressed owners shall receive a reward of *Eighteen Pence*, or 3000 copies printed on very soft paper.

N.B. Messrs. *Wit, Common Sense*, and *Grammar*, are totally unsuspected of knowing any thing about it. *Sydney College*, March 1st, 1795.

The Cambridge University Library has also a pamphlet, dated 1795, entitled *A Strait Waistcoat for Lunatics*, made up of criticisms upon the articles in the *University Magazine*. The facts which I have given are found in Canon Wordsworth's book, but I have myself seen all the documents.

There can be little doubt, I think, that the jotting in the Note Book refers to this escapade (the next entry is a reference to the *British Critic* for May, 1795). Coleridge had left Cambridge at the close of 1794, but he had not lost touch with the magazine. It contains his 'Monody on the Death of Chatterton,' and it announces that 'Mr. Coleridge of Jesus College, will shortly publish some Sonnets.' He would certainly know of its fortunes, and the entry suggests that he may even have had a hand in the practical joke.

57 Fol. 6[a]; *Archiv*, p. 343. Printed in *Poems*, II, 988 (No. 1); Campbell, *Poems*, p. 453 (No. 2). The lines were later incorporated in 'The Eolian Harp' (*Poems*, I, 101, II. 20–25; cf. II, 1022, ll. 20–27), with changes well worth the attention of the student of Coleridge's technique. Just when the birds of Paradise became 'footless' it would be interesting to know. On March 28, 1796, Coleridge took from the Bristol Library the *Anthologia Hibernica*, keeping it until April 25 (*Mod. Philol.*, XXI, 319; see Note 110, below). In Vol. I of the *Anthologia*, pp. 407–13, is an entertaining article 'On the Birds of Paradise and the Phœnix,' from 'Dr. R. Forster's *Essay on India*,' in which are recounted (p. 409) the 'idle fables . . . that they have no feet, are always on the wing, pass their lives in the air, and feed on this element.' The volume in which 'The Eolian Harp' appeared was published April 16, 1796 (*Poems*, II, 1135, n. 2), and Coleridge refers to it as 'finished' on March 30 (B. E., I, 66). The article in the *Anthologia* is so striking that one is tempted to guess that Coleridge may have changed the lines in proof. But he could have learned the tradition elsewhere—e.g., Purchas (1617), pp. 642, 688, cf. 842; Cook, *Voyage to the Pacific Ocean*, II, 207–08. The footless bird is pictured in Caroli Clusii Atribatis [Charles de L'Écluse], *Exoticorum libri decern* [Antwerp], 1605, p. 360. On the drunkenness of birds

of Paradise, see Callander, III, 199.

58 Fol. 7[a]; *Archiv*, p. 344.

59 The book, according to the *Cambridge History of English Literature* (XI, 489), seems to have been first published in 1727. The earliest edition which I have seen is that of 1786, in *The Novelist's Magazine*, Vol. XXI, London, 1786. There the title reads: *The English Hermit; or, Unparalleled Sufferings, and Surprizing Adventures, of Mr. Philip Quarll, who was lately discovered on an uninhabited Island in the South-sea; where he had lived above fifty years, without any human assistance.* The narrative is signed 'Ed. Dorrington,' and there is an interesting Preface, signed 'P. L.,' which refers to the vogue of *Robinson Crusoe, Moll Flanders, and Colonel Jack*. It also gives an account of 'Mr. Edward Dorrington [who] is descended from a very ancient and honourable family in Staffordshire.' There is a sketch of the family, and it is stated that Edward's father died in 1708. P. L. vouches for the author's veracity, and avers that 'the *first* Book herein was wholly written by himself, and the *second* and *third* Books were faithfully transcribed from Mr. Quarll's parchment roll' The Preface is undated.

There is a chapter on *The English Hermit* in W. Alfred Jones, *Characters and Criticisms* (N.Y., 1857), pp. 82–95, in which it is stated that ' "The Adventures of the English Hermit" were first published, in chapters, in a weekly newspaper, called the

Public Intelligencer, shortly after the appearance of Robinson Crusoe' (p. 83). This statement is repeated on the Library of Congress card for the book (*s. v.* Dorrington, Edward, *pseud.*? 1786). But the *Public Intelligencer* ran only from Oct. 1–8, 1655 to May 28–June 4, 1660; Robinson Crusoe was published in 1719; and there are no signs of the story in the *Public Intelligencer*, which was the last sheet imaginable to print fiction. (Incidentally, the closing sentence of the book, in the edition of 1786, is: 'This was the conclusion of his adventures in 1724.'). Mr. Jones also suggests (p. 87) that Defoe himself was the author. That is scarcely a tenable hypothesis, though one may grant Defoe's influence. Edward Dorrington is pretty certainly a pseudonym; the dictionaries of pseudonyms, anonyms, and initials give no clue; and the author remains unknown. 'I do not know who wrote Quarll,' declared Lamb (*Works*, VII, 600). 'I never thought of Quarll as having an author. It is a poor imitation; the monkey is the best in it, and his pretty dishes made of shells.'

I thought I caught now and then, as I read *The English Hermit*, a strong reminiscent flavour of Dampier. Then I recognized a passage which was unmistakable. And if the reader cares to compare the following pages, he will find as pretty a bit of bare-faced lifting as he is often privileged to see. My references are to the first American from the sixth London edition (1795) of *The Hermit*, and to Masefield's edition

(1906) of Dampier: *The Hermit*, pp. 46–47 = Dampier, I, 409–10, 123–24; *The Hermit*, p. 51 = Dampier, I, 99, 101–03; *The Hermit*, pp. 52–53 = Dampier, II, 354–56. There is more, I dare say, but that is all it seemed worth while, even for amusement, to run down. For other references to *The Hermit*, see note below, and pp. 478, 484.

60 The three references to the *Arabian Nights' Entertainments* are in *The Friend* (*Works*, II, 137–38, n.); in one of the priceless autobiographical letters to Poole (*Letters*, I, 12, cf. 16; B. E., I, 12); and in one of the lectures of 1811 (*Letters*, I, 11, n.). The last quotation in the paragraph is from Gillman, p. 20 (cf. B. E., I, 28). Wordsworth's testimony ('The Prelude,' V, 460–76) to the spell of the *Arabian Nights* is scarcely less interesting—that account of his 'precious treasure [he] had long possessed, *A little yellow, canvas-covered book*, A slender abstract of the Arabian tales;' of how he learned 'that there were *four large volumes*, laden all With kindred matter'; of how he and his friend made a covenant to hoard up their joint savings till they could buy the whole book; and of how the savings of months were not enough, 'Nor were we ever masters of our wish.' In the rest of their boyhood reading, too, Coleridge and Wordsworth strikingly agree. 'I read through all the gilt-cover little books that could be had at that time, and likewise all *the uncovered tales* of Tom Hickathrift, Jack the Giant Killer, etc. etc. etc. etc. . . . At six years old I remember to have read

Belisarius, Robinson Crusoe, and Philip Quarles [Quarll]; and then 1 found the Arabian Nights' Entertainments' (*Letters*, I, 11–12; cf. B. E., I, 12); and the vivid reference to the *Seven Champions of Christendom* is in Gillman, p. 10; cf. B. E., I, 15. So Coleridge. Wordsworth's list ends likewise with the '*Seven Champions*' ('Prelude,' V, 341–44):

> Oh! give us once again the wishing-cap
>
> Of Fortunatus, and the invisible coat
>
> Of Jack the Giant-Killer, Robin Hood,
>
> And Sabra in the forest with St. Georgel

Crabbe's roster is startlingly similar—'Hermit Quarll . . . in island rare,' and then ('*Unbound* and heap'd,' by 'the pedlar's pack supplied'), the Wandering Jew, 'Thumb the Great,' 'Hickathrift the strong,' and 'Jack, by whose arm the giant-brood were quelled' ('Parish Register,' Introduction, in *Life and Poems*, II, 146–47). Later, in 'Silford Hall; or, The Happy Day' (*Life and Poems*, VIII, 8–9), Crabbe tells of '*Romances in sheets, and poetry unbound*' (including 'Jane Shore and Rosamond the Fair'), and how his hero read of Robin Hood, Jack the Giant-Killer, 'mighty Hickerthrift,' and Robinson Crusoe. And among his 'real books . . . *Bound, or part bound*, were 'Arabian Nights, and Persian Tales . . . *One volume each*, and both the worse for wear'—not to rehearse the fascinating catalogue which follows. Samuel Bamford's early reading (he was born in 1788) was almost identical: 'Every farthing I could scrape together was now spent in purchasing histories of "Jack the Giant Killer," "Saint George and the Dragon," "Tom Hickathrift," "Jack and the Beanstalk," "The Seven Champions of Christendom," tale of "Fair Rosamond" . . . and such like romances' (*Passages in the Life of a Radical*, ed. Dunckley, I, 87; cf. pp. 51 and 91 for a graphic account of the effect of *Pilgrim's Progress* and *Robinson Crusoe*). I am indebted for this reference, and for the reminder of Crabbe, to Elton, *Survey of English Literature, 1780–1880*, I, 425. For the banishment of the old classics of the nursery by the 'stuff' of 'the cursed Barbauld crew,' see Lamb's gloriously impolite letter quoted above (p. 302, note), and Coleridge in 'The Gestes of Maxilian' (*Miscellanies*, p. 268), and a lecture of 1808 (Crabb Robinson, *Selections*, ed. Morley, p. 107); adding Wordsworth's vigorous but less vehement witness to the same effect in 'The Prelude,' V, 293–346, together with William Godwin's list of antidotes to Mrs. Barbauld's stories (Paul, *William Godwin*, II, 118–20), and Coleridge's pronouncement in favour of permitting children 'to read romances, and relations of giants and magicians and genii,' in *Letters*, I, 16 (cf. B. E., I, 17). And what he there says of the formative influences of his own 'early reading of fairy tales and genii, etc. etc.,' is a document in the case—though to attempt to trace the prints of the *Arabian Nights*, and the *Seven Champions, and The Hermit,* and 'Tom Hickathrift' in 'The Rime of the Ancient Mariner,' and 'Christabel,' and 'Kubla Khan' were like seeking the sun and the rain of vanished yesterdays in the limbs and foliage of the oak. But the rain and the sun are there.

There are two puzzles connected with Coleridge's list. In a criticism in the *Biographia Literaria* (B. L., II, 52–53) of Wordsworth's 'discussion on the powers of metre,' Coleridge returns to 'Tom Hickathrift,' 'Jack the Giant-Killer,' 'Goody Two-shoes' (which had set Lamb off!), and 'Little Red Ridinghood.' And he closes with this remark (italics and capitals Coleridge's):

> . . . among the **Θαύματα θαυμαστότατα** even of the present age, I do not recollect a more astonishing image than that of the '*whole rookery, that flew out of the giant's beard*,' scared by the tremendous voice, with which this monster answered the challenge of the heroic TOM HICKATHRIFT!

Now I have gone through all the versions of 'Tom Hickathrift' in the collection of chap-books in the Harvard College Library without finding in any of them this indubitably 'astonishing' detail. Is there a version, printed or oral, in which it actually occurs? Or has Coleridge's imagination unconsciously heightened the tale? If anyone knows of a version in which the birds fly out of the giant's beard, I shall welcome word of it.

The second riddle concerns the *Arabian Nights*. Wordsworth and Crabbe agree in referring explicitly to an edition in *one volume* (which in Wordsworth's case is sharply distinguished from the well-known edition in four volumes), and Coleridge also speaks of 'one volume of these tales' (*Works*, II, 137). Neither the catalogue of the British Museum, nor Graesse, nor Brunet, nor Lowndes, nor Burton, nor Chauvin (in his exhaustive *Bibliographie arabe*) records a one-volume edition (or an 'abstract') published in English in the eighteenth century. From Kirby's note in Burton (ed. Kamashastra Soc., X, 467–68) it seems clear that from 1713 on the six (or four) volumes of the English translation of Galland were often reprinted independently of each other, and this may account for Coleridge's, and perhaps for Crabbe's, 'one volume.' And in 1772 the English translation was issued in farthing numbers, 4 to, thrice a week, and Wordsworth may possibly (though I doubt it) have referred to one of these. The problem is one for the bibliographers, but it has a wider interest too.

The proportion of *chap-books* in the lists which I have quoted is significant to the last degree. Even the physical distinction between bound or 'gilt-cover,' and unbound or uncovered tales is employed in almost every list. This is not the place to dwell on the wider implications of the subject, but a book of surpassing interest could (and should) be written on the neglected influence of these enormously popular books of the folk — 'The coats in tatters, and the cuts in wood'—which, from Autolycus on, 'the pedlar's pack supplied.'

61 Fol. 7[a]; *Archiv*, p. 344. The entry is in pencil. The reference is to Thomas Burnet's *Telluris Theoria Sacra* (*Libri duo priores de Diluvio et Paradise*, London, 1681; *Libri duo posteriores de Conflagratione Mundi et de Futuro Rerum Statu*, London, 1689). Coleridge's copy, now in the possession of the Rev. G. H. B. Coleridge, has the inscription, in Coleridge's hand: 'Presented to S. T. Coleridge by Charles Danvers, **ἄνδρα ἐμοὶ φίλτατον**, quem qui non amat, ilium omnes Virtutes odire!' An English version of the first two books (by Burnet himself) appeared in 1684, and of all four in 1689, under the title, *The Sacrea Theory of the Earth*. 'This English edition,' says Burnet in his Preface, 'is the same in substance with the Latin, though, I confess, it is not so properly a translation, as a new composition upon the same ground.' It may well have been Burnet's own eloquent rendering of his Latin work which suggested to Coleridge the idea of turning the *Telluris Theoria Sacra* into English verse. See further pp. 159, above, 502–03, below.

62 *Notes*, p. 188.

63 B. L., II, II: 'The writings of Plato, and Bishop Taylor, and the "Theoria Sacra" of Burnet, furnish undeniable proofs that poetry of the highest kind may exist without metre.' Cf.

II, 268. Carlyon (I, 95) tells us that Coleridge spoke with approbation of Burnet's 'Theory of the Earth' in Germany.

64 Fol. 24[b] (No. 7); *Archiv*, p. 353. The chapter 'De Montibus' is the ninth of the First Book in the Latin (T. T., I, 82 ff.), and the eleventh in the English (S. T., I, 135 ff.). There is, however, a magnificent passage on the mountains at the close of the twelfth chapter of the Third Book, 'De Conflagratione Mundi' (T. T., II, 121–22), which Coleridge may also have had in mind. I am not sure that in this instance Burnet's English (S. T., II, 121—22) is not more majestic than his Latin. Addison quoted the passage, in conjunction with Plato's report of Socrates's last words, in No. 146 of *The Spectator*, and I shall repeat a part of it here, since it makes Coleridge's enthusiasm comprehensible. After an eloquent *Ubi sunt*—'Where are now the great empires of the world, and their great imperial cities? Their pillars, trophies, and monuments of glory? Shew me where they stood'—follows the great dirge for the mountains:

> Here stood the Alps, a prodigious range of stone, the load of the earth, that . . . reached their arms from the Ocean to the Black Sea; this huge mass of stone is softened and dissolved, as a tender cloud, into rain. Here stood the African mountains, and Atlas with his top above the clouds. There was frozen Caucasus, and Taurus, and Imaus, and the mountains of Asia. And

> yonder, towards the north, stood the Riphaean hills, clothed in ice and snow. All these are vanished, dropt away as the snow upon their heads, and swallowed up in a red sea of fire (II, 122).

But for the full effect the Latin original should be read too. A much longer extract from Burnet, ending with the lines I have quoted, may be found in B. L. (Sampson), pp. 293–94.

65 *Notes*, p. 188.

66 Fol. 7^b; *Archiv*, p. 344.

67 'Little Tommy' is quite certainly 'that Thomas Ward who was a youth, living with Tom Poole as his articled apprentice, at the time when S. T. Coleridge was in Stowey' (T. P., I, 82 and especially 159–60; on p. 84 he is called 'the boy Ward'; see also *Letters*, I, 170). Poole writes, in a letter of January, 1798: 'I . . . sent off *little Tommy* to the post-office' (T. P., I, 259). And in the wildly 'flighty' letter which Coleridge wrote to Poole, Nov. 5, 1796, 'under the immediate inspiration of laudanum' (*Letters*, I, 176), the postscript ends: 'Love to Ward. *Little Tommy*, I often think of thee.' 'Cerberus' seems also to have something to do with Poole. On April 11, 1796, Coleridge wrote in a copy of his poems which he gave to Poole: 'I love to shut my eyes, and bring up before my imagination that Arbour, in which I have repeated so many

of these compositions to you. Dear Arbour! An Elysium to which I have often passed by your Cerberus and Tartarean tan-pits!' (T. P., I, 202). That, as Mrs. Sandford points out, is the 'Jasmine *H*arbour' immortalised by Cottle in his dithyrambic account of the banquet on 'bread and cheese, surmounted by a brown mug of true Taunton ale' (*Reminiscences*, pp. 113–14)—the arbour, I may add, in which 'This Lime-tree Bower my Prison' was written (*Letters*, I, 224–25), and in which Hazlitt and Coleridge sat day after day 'listening to the bees humming round us, while we quaffed our *flip*' (Hazlitt, *Works*, XII, 272)—and the topography of the tan-yard and the garden and Coleridge's cottage is made clear in a letter to Estlin of 1797 (*Letters*, I, 213–14; *Estlin Letters*, pp. 29–31; cf. T. P., I, 200–201). Probably Cerberus in this instance was Tom Poole's dog (on Poole's fondness for animals, especially one of his dogs, see T. P., II, 319–20). As for the dumb-waiter, we may best visualise that through a sentence from Lockhart's *Scott;* 'a tier of tables, rising above each other like the shelves of a dumb-waiter' (letter of 14 April, 1824). See too N. E. D. And when the 'little Tommy' letter of Nov. 5, 1796, was written, Coleridge was ill (and presumably most of the time in bed), and that letter also contains an allusion to 'Cerberus' (*Letters*, I, 173–74).

I suspect that in the cryptic note we have a memorandum for a lost 'Work.' Four days before his assurance to 'little

Tommy' that he often thought of him, Coleridge had written Poole (B. E., I, 96) in a context of gloom and '*day*-main dreams': 'I have no doubt that I should have written to you within the period of my promise, *if I had not pledged myself for a certain gift of my Muse to poor Tommy:* and alas! she has been too "sunk on the ground in dimmest heaviness" *to permit me to trifle.*' Coleridge, then, was going to write for little Tommy 'something childish'—see *Poems*, I, 313, and especially the sentence which precedes the lines in *Letters*, I, 294—and in a letter which shows that Cerberus was in his mind, he sends word that he has not forgotten. And here is a line about a boy, and a dog, and (it would seem) a day in bed, and perhaps another dog called (like Southey's) Dapper (Southey, *Life and Correspondence*, II, 249, 273, 297). Who can say? I have no doubt it is all utterly unimportant—unless, indeed, Terence, with his *nihil humanum*, was after all right! And so I add that Coleridge *did* send a piece of admirable fooling to 'little Tommy' (then not so little) later on; see T. P., I, 303–05.

For those who may (quite inconsequently) be interested in duppies—and duppies are very interesting indeed—I append the following references: Edward Long, *The History of Jamaica* (London, 1774), II, 416; Jekyll, *Jamaican Song and Story (Publications of the Folk Lore Society*, LV [1904]), pp. xxxi, n., xxxv, 174–76; *Folk Lore*, XV (1904), 87–89, 90–92, 94, 206–09, 452; XVI (1905), 68, 70–71; M. G. Lewis, *Journal of a*

West India Proprietor (London, 1834), pp. 98–100, 290–96, 307, 344, 386; H. J. Bell, *Obeah Witchcraft in the West Indies* (1893), pp. 121 ff.; Lady Brassey, *In the Trades, the Tropics, and the Roaring Forties* (1885), p. 215.

68 *Letters*, I, 175.

69 Fol. 8[a]; *Archiv*, p. 344. I am not sure about 'Encyclo.

70 Fol. 10[a]; *Archiv*, p. 346.

71 I am indebted to Professor Alice D. Snyder of Vassar College—who has interpreted with acumen Coleridge's philosophy—for the identification of these lines. I had sent her (apropos of her use of the entry, in an article in *Studies in Philology*, XXI, 616 ff., with the statement that 'the proper name is uncertain') my reading of the last three words as 'Mr. Gunston—Watts,' and the consequent discovery of the passage is her contribution. The lines will be found in Isaac Watts, *Works* (London, 1753), IV, 441. Coleridge was evi dently quoting from memory, and has substituted 'mighty' for 'nightly,' and a second 'round' for 'watch.'

72 Fol. 17[b]; *Archiv*, p. 349.

73 Fol. 17[b]; *Archiv*, p. 350.

74 Fol. 18[a]; *Archiv*, p. 350. Used in the lines 'On a Late

Connubial Rup ture' (*Poems*, I, 152), II. 19–20. In the first draft (July 4, 1796, *Estlin Letters*, p. 21) the lines read (italics mine):

'Then bid your Souls inseparably blend,

Like two bright Dew-drops *bosom'd* in a flower!'

75 Fol. 18[a]; *Archiv*, p. 350. The monumental belly is of no importance to our study whatsoever. But the touch of nature which has endeared Sir John Falstaff and Mr. Pickwick to their kind invites the identification none the less. During the memorable tour in quest of subscribers for *The Watchman*, Coleridge took coach for Worcester. Under date of January, 1796, he wrote to his friend Wade as follows: 'The moment I entered the coach, I stumbled on a huge projection, which might be called a belly with the same propriety that you might name Mount Atlas a mole-hill. Heavens! that a man should be unconscionable enough to enter a stage coach, who would want elbow room if he were walking on Salisbury Plain' (B. E., I, 55). It is at least a good guess that this was the majestic rotundity which slipped into the Note Book, as the Spirit of Comedy decreed, between the dew-drops on the bosom of a new-blown rose, and some unknown beauty's sparkling eyes.

The passage has after all, I find, a curious bearing on our study. For more than eight years later (the letter is dated

April 6, 1804) Coleridge had another fellow-passenger of vast proportions. This time it was on the 'Speedwell,' *en route* for Malta. And the recurrence of the circumstance called up to memory the phraseology used eight years before: 'an unconscientiously fat woman, *who would have wanted elbow-room on Salisbury Plain*,' etc. (*Coleorton*, I, 61; italics mine). She is described with lavish detail in a letter to Southey, written ten days later (*Letters*, II, 472).

76 Fol. 18[a]; *Archiv*, p. 350.

77 Fol. 19[a]; *Archiv*, p. 350.

78 Erasmus Darwin took over the article, hide and hair, in the *Botanic Garden*. In 'The Loves of the Plants' (Litchfield, 1789) he refers to it on p. 106 (note to Canto III, I. 238), and reproduces it *in toto* on pp. 167–73, on the authority of the *London Magazine*. In the *Botanic Garden* (London, 1791) the reference is repeated ('The Loves of the Plants,' pp. 110–11), and likewise the entire article (pp. 183–89), still on the authority of N. P. Foersch and the *London Magazine*. In the fourth edition of 'The Loves of the Plants' (London, 1794), pp. 191–93, it is supplemented by 'Another Account of the Boa Upas, or Poison-tree of Macasser, from an inaugural Dissertation published by Christ. Æjmelæus, and approved by Professor Thunberg, at Upsal.' One or both of these stories Coleridge certainly saw, since he lifted bodily (see Note 80) the

rest of the page in Darwin on which Foersch's tale begins.

79 See the *London Magazine*, N. S., Vol. I, pp. 511–17 (December, 1783). The highly circumstantial yarn purports to come from 'Mr. Foersch, who, we are informed, is at present abroad, in the capacity of surgeon on board an Engitsh vessel' (p. 512), and its translator is a Mr. Heydinger, 'formerly a German bookseller near Temple-Bar.' At the beginning of the article the elusive Mr. Foersch's initials are N. P.; at the end, J. N.; and the editors declare in a note: 'We shall be happy to communicate any authentic [!] papers of Mr. Foersch to the public, through the channel of the London Magazine' (p. 517). *In Sketches, Civil and Military, of the Island of Java . . . comprising . . . Authentic Particulars of the Celebrated Poison Tree*, edited by J. J. Stockdale (2d ed., London, 1812), pp. 311 ff., the whole narrative is repeated (with scathing comment by the editor) from 'The Monthly Repertory' [?]: 'The writer is an Englishman, and only signs his initials C. H.' (Stockdale, p. 311; cf. p. 330). I have made no attempt to follow the alphabet farther.

80 It is a long note (*Poems*, I, 99–100) on lines 91–93 of 'Lines written at Shurton Bars . . . September, 1795,' and it has to 'a whit very curious phenomenon,' apparently electric, observed in Sweden on certain flowers 'by M. Haggern, lecturer in natural history.' It has never been identified, and I wasted many good hours in the attempt to run down the

works of the seemingly not very famous M. Haggern. Then I found the whole note, verbatim, in Erasmus Darwin ('The Loves of the Plants,' 1789, II, 183–84; *The Botanic Garden*, London, 1791, Pt. II, pp. 182–83). He, in turn, had taken it from Rozier's *Observations sur la Physique*, XXXIII, 111. Coleridge first printed it in *the Poems* of 1796, and he had his troubles with the printer. 'Good heavens! what a Gap!'—'Good heavens! what a Gap!'—'Good heavens! what a Gap!'—are his manuscript notes, in the proof-sheets, on the printer's unhappy attempt to space correctly M. Haggern's observations (*Facsimile Reproduction*, pp. [80]–[82]). The notes in the *Botanic Garden* which immediately follow the account of Haggern's experiments are the accounts of the upas tree referred to above (Note 78).

81 *Botanic Garden* (ed. 1791), Pt. II, p. 186.

82 Fol. 4^{a}; *Archiv*, 342.

83 Fol. 20^{b}; *Archiv*, p. 351.

84 It is barely possible that he had been sketchily tracing, and then cancelling, Greek letters. The last three symbols dimly resemble **φτς**— which might either stand for their English equivalent (see p. 467, n. 118, below), or else constitute part of a cipher (see pp. 25–26, above).

85 Italics Coleridge's.

86 Fol. 21[a]; *Archiv*, pp. 351–52.

87 *Letters*, I, 65, 67

88 *Ibid*, I, 67, n. I.

89 *Ibid*., I, 92.

90 *Ibid*., I, 122.

91 *Ibid*., I, 137.

92 *Ibid*., I, 424; A. P., p. 237. For Coleridge's (I trust and believe) jocose etymologizing of the phrase, see Crabb Robinson, *Selections* (ed. Morley), p. 135.

93 Lamb, *Works*, VI, 91. The suggestions which follow repay the reading.

94 *Lettrs*, I, 70. The stage-direction after l. 10 of *Osorio*, III, i, is as follows: 'Here a strain of music is heard from behind the scenes, from an instrument of glass or steel—the harmonica or Celestina stop, or Clagget's metallic organ'(*Poem*, II, 551). See also E. H. Coleridge's note (*Letters*, I, 70), and D. N. B. under Clagget.

95 *Letters*, I, 91.

96 *Ibid*., I, 103.

97 *Life and Correspondence*, II, 190. See also Cottle, *Recollections*, I, 148–49 (repeated in *Reminiscences*, p. 55; cf. 347, n.). To draw up a list of Coleridge's projects—that succession of brilliant and iridescent bubbles which dilated, soared for a moment, touched each other, and were not—would be to write his spiritual biography. But some conception of 'the bubbles that boiled in his idea-pot'—to shift the figure to Coleridge's own (*Letters*, I, 210)—may be gained by the simple expedient of opening the *Biographia Epistolaris*, and turning to the following pages (among others): I, 254, 272, 279; II, 44, 46, 48–49, 68–69, 70, 142, 160, 187, 188, 193, 202, 203, 208–11, 230, 288; *Letters*, II, 530, 583, 772–73. And those are but a drop in the bucket. Compare, too, *Letters from the Lake Poets*, pp. 227, 242, 245, 260, 318; *Coleorton*, I, 10, 45–48, 50; Crabb Robinson, *Selections* (ed. Morley), pp. 69–70, 98; A. A. Watts, *Life of Alaric Watts*, I, 245; etc. etc.—and, very especially, Lamb's delightful sallies in *Works*, VI, 392, 481. But see, too, *Letters*, II, 632, n.

98 Fols. 21^b–22^a; *Archiv*, p. 352. Italics Coleridge's. Coleridge was still interested in brewing when he went to Germany. See *Archiv*, CXVIII, 42.

99 *Letters*, II, 637.

100 Coleridge's facetious remark establishes a definite *terminus a quo* for at least this entry in the Note Book. For the

Habeas Corpus Suspension Act was in effect from May 16, 1794 to the end of 1801. See Sir Thomas Erskine May, *The Constitutional History of England*, Vol. II (1912), pp. 131–33. Coleridge inveighed against the Suspension Act, in February, 1795, in the address 'On the Present War' (*Conciones*, p. 50).

101 Fol. 22[a]; *Archiv*, p. 352.

102 *Letters*, I, 10–11.

103 *Ibid.*, I, 134.

104 *Ibid.*, I, 220.

105 *Ibid.*, I, 229. In the following sentences Coleridge quotes his adaptation of the idea in *Osorio* (see *Poems*, II, 584; cf. 577, n.). He also employed the figure in 'The Triumph of Loyalty' of about 1800; see *Poems*, II, 1071, cf. I, 422.

106 *Letters*, I, 224. See interesting note on the poem (*Poems*, I, 178), with its discreet allusions to the catastrophe, and also the somewhat more specific reference—'Lam'd by the scathe of fire, lonely and faint'—in line two of the draft of the poem sent to Southey (*Letters*, I, 225; *Poems*, I, 178, n.).

107 Fol. 20[b]; *Archiv*, p. 351. Printed in *Poems*, II, 990 (No. 18); Campbell, *Poems*, p. 454 (No. 19).

108 Fols. 22[b]–23[a]; *Archiv*, p. 352.

109 Fol. 23[b]; *Archiv*, p. 353.

110 *Icelandic Poetry, or The Edda of Sæmund Translated into English Verse*, by A. S. Cottle, of Magdalen College, Cambridge (Bristol, 1797). From 1794 to 1798 the Eddas and Dante were both more or less in the air in Coleridge's circle. Southey himself, in 1795, twice took out the 'Edda Sæmundina' from the Bristol Library (July 13–16, Oct. 14–Nov. 12), at a time when he and Coleridge were signing interchangeably for books. And in 1794 he had had out the first volume of Boyd's Dante (Sept. 25–26), and (Sept. 26–Oct. 24) the second. Coleridge had from the library the first two volumes of Boyd's Dante from June 23 to July 4, 1796 (cf. pp. 287, above, 567, n. 100, below), and the 'Sæmunda Edda' (obviously Cottle's translation) from December 11, 1797 to Jan. 24, 1798. Wordsworth wrote Joseph Cottle, December 13, 1797: 'I received by the hands of Coleridge sometime since a volume of Icelandic poetry translated by your brother' (*Letters of the Wordsworth Family*, I, 112). Southey made some interesting remarks about the translation to William Taylor in 1799 (Robberds, I, 246). And Coleridge's and Lamb's friend George Dyer twice (pp. lxxix, n., 295, n.) refers to Cottle's translation in his *Poems* (1801).

For the facts about Coleridge's and Southey's use of the Bristol Library, see *Mod. Philol.*, XXI, 317–20 (Paul Kaufman, 'The Reading of Southey and Coleridge: The Record of their Borrowings from the Bristol Library, 1793–98'). This invaluable list, compiled from the original registers, supersedes the summary published by James Baker in *Chambers Journal*, Feb. I, 1890, pp. 75–76, and reprinted in his *Literary and Biographical Studies* (1908), pp. 211–18.

Coleridge remained a subscriber to the Bristol Library during his residence at Nether Stowey. See the amusing and characteristic letter of May, 1797, to the Librarian, George Catcott, printed in B. E., I, 128–29. In February of the same year Coleridge wrote Thelwall: 'I send and receive to and from Bristol every week' (*Letters*, I, 220). Two years later, to be sure, he wrote from Germany to Poole: '[Wordsworth's] chief objection to Stowey is the want of books. The Bristol Library is a hum, and will do us little service' (*Letters*, I, 270). But that damnatory colloquialism need not be taken too seriously. The Bristol Library had simply suffered the fate of the circulating library in King Street, Cheapside: the *helluo librorum* (*sc.* 'library cormorant') had by that time devoured it.

111 Fol. 23^{b}; *Archiv*, p. 353.

112 *Ibid.*

113 'I am anxious that my children should be bred up from earliest infancy in the simplicity of peasants . . . I never shall, and I never will, have any fortune to leave them . . . I am

peculiarly delighted with the 21st verse of the 4th chapter of Tobit, "And fear not, my son! that we are made poor: for thou hast much wealth, if thou fear God, and depart from all sin and do that which is pleasing in His sight" ' (B. E., I, 106). Brandl reads Ωσταλ, transliterating (I suppose) the obsolete character representing *στ* (which Coleridge constantly uses when he is writing Greek), and inadvertently omitting the following *ρ*.

114 *Letters*, II, 597, n.

115 'My Sara' occurs frequently in the letters of this period. See for example, *Letters*, I, 145, 186, 205, 214; B. E., I, 227; *Estlin Letters*, p. 31; etc.

116 Fol. 24[a]; *Archiv*, p. 353.

117 Fols. 24[b]–25[b]; *Archiv*, pp. 353–54. In the manuscript the entries follow one another as usual down the page. They are printed across it here to save space:

> 1. An Essay on Tobit. 2. On the art of prolonging Life—by getting up in a morning. 3. On Marriage—in opposition to French Principles. 4. Jacob Behmen. 5. Life of John Henderson. 6. Ode to a Looking Glass. 7. Burnet de montibus in English Blank Verse. 8. Escapes from Misery—a Poem—Halo round the Candle—Sigh visible. 9. Cavern-candle. [10] Life of David—a Sermon.

11. Wild Poem on Maniac—στ. 12. Ode on St. Withold. 13. Crotchets, by S. T. Coleridge. 14. Edition of Akenside. 15. Of Collins and Gray. 16. Hymns to the Sun, the Moon, and the Elements—six hymns. . . . 17. Letter, to Godwin. 18. Randolph consecrating D. of York's banners—19. Ode to Southey. 20. Egomist, a metaphysical Rhapsody. 21. Berk[e]ley's Maxims—Vol. II, 345. [No number] Ode to a Moth—against accumulation. 22. Adventures of CHRISTIAN, the mutineer. 23. Military anecdotes—N.B. promised to be serjeants. 24. History of Phrases—ex. gr. The King must have men. 25. Hymn to Dr. Darwin—in the manner of the Orphics. 26. Address to the Clergy against the two Bills. 27. Satire addressed to a young Man who intended to study medicine at Edinburgh.

118 Fol. 24[b]; *Archiv*, p. 353. There is another transliteration (**Ευνυχ**)in the Note Book (fol. 76[b]; *Archiv*, p. 368), and at the close of a letter from Ramsgate to Gillman in 1819 Coleridge adds (his companions presumably being innocent of Greek): 'Do come down to me—to us, I suppose I ought to say. We are all as should be **Βυτ μονστρουσλι φορμαλ**(*Letters*, II, 701). The phrase is followed by asterisks, so that I fear we have been deprived of some still more engaging indiscretion. Cf. *Notes*, p. 67: 'it looks very like 'TMBTT.'

119 Like the Elizabethans the early Romanticists were

much addicted to lunatics. But we are apt to forget, when we shrug a dubious shoulder at the recurrence of the theme, that in the eighteenth century, by roadside and in almshouse, the phenomena of mental alienation were constantly in evidence. The 'wanderer in Somersetshire' who inspired Wordsworth's 'Ruth,' and 'the poor creature' whom a lady in Bristol saw, and who suggested 'The Mad Mother' ('Her eyes are wild'), and Samuel Bamford's account (*Passages in the Life of a Radical*, ed. Dunckley, pp. 72–75) of the harmless lunatics with whom in the yards of the workhouse at Manchester the boys of the town played, are cases enough in point.

120 See Bardsley, *Dictionary of English and Welsh Surnames* (1901); Harrison, *Surnames of the United Kingdom* (1912); Lower, *Patronymica Britannica* (1860). See also *Somerset and Dorset Notes and Queries*, III, 51; *Herts Genealogist and Antiquary*, III, 104; etc.

121 Fol. 24^{b}; *Archiv*, p. 353.

122 *Letters*, I, 110–11. His 'Complaint of Ninathóma' (*Poems*, I, 39), sent in a letter from Jesus College to Mary Evans, Feb. 7, 1793 (*Letters*, I, 50–51) was to be set by Charles Hague 'to wild music.' And he was still thinking of 'wild' poems ten or fifteen years after our entries. In a note book of 1808–09 he writes: 'If I have leisure, I may, perhaps, write a wild rhyme on the *Bell*, from the mine to the belfry,'

etc. (A. P., p. 178). 'Wild' sprinkles plentifully the pages of his early poems. See, for example, *Poems*, 1, 3, 5, 10, 16, 17, 43, 50, etc.

123 *Letters*, I, 110–11.

124 Fol. 25^b; *Archiv*, p. 354.

125 For Lieutenant Bligh's narrative, see his *Narrative of the Mutiny, on board His Majesty's Ship Bounty, and the subsequent Voyage of part of the Crew, in the Ship's Boat*, etc., 1790 (*ibid.*, with additional particulars, 1853); *An Account of the Mutinous Seizure of the Bounty, and the succeeding Hardships of the Crew*, etc. (London, 1792); and his *Voyage To the South Sea* (London, 1792), pp. 154 ff. For other accounts, see John Martin, M.D., *An Account of the Natives of the Tonga Islands, compiled and arranged from the extensive communications of Mr. William Mariner* (1817); Sir John Barrow, *The Eventful History of the Mutiny and Piratical Seizure of H.M.S. Bounty* (London, 1831); Walter Brodie, *Pitcairn's Island and the Islanders, in 1850* (London, 1851); Thomas Boyles Murray, *Pitcairn: The Island, the People, etc.* (London, [1858]); Lady [Diana] Belcher, *The Mutineers of the Bounty* (London, 1870); Rosalind Amelia Young, *Mutiny of the Bounty and Story of Pitcairn Island, 1790–1804* (Oakland, Cal., 1895). For Byron's use of the story, see *Works of Lord Byron* (ed. E. H. Coleridge), *Poetry*, Vol. V, pp. 581–84.

126 Coleridge was still labouring under the same misapprehension as late as 1817, for in a note to the eighteenth chapter of the *Biographia Literaria* (II, 55, n.) he observes, after a reference to the 'Night-Mair' in his own *Remorse:* 'N.B. Though Shakespeare has, for his own *all-justifying* purposes, introduced the Night-*Mare* with her own foals, yet Mair means a Sister, or perhaps a Hag' (italics Coleridge's). Southey, in a letter of July 17, 1796 (*Life and Correspondence*, I, 285), remarks (perhaps recalling Coleridge's earlier letter to him): 'The exploit of Mr. Burnett is far beyond that of St. Withold—though, by the by, he met the nine foals into the bargain.' The reading 'nine foals' occurs, so far as I know, in no text of 'King Lear.' It probably goes back to a remark of Tyrwhitt's on 'ninefold': 'Put, for the sake of rhyme, instead of *nine foals*.'

127 Bligh, *Voyage to the South Sea*, p. 161.

128 Fol. 25[a], cf. 25[b]; *Archiv*, p. 354.

129 See above, pp. 75 ff., 208, etc.

130 Fol. 30[a]; *Archiv*, pp. 357–58.

131 A. P., p. 50.

132 Wordsworth *Memoirs*, I, 192–200; D. W., *Journals*, I, 127.

133 On August 13, 1800, Dorothy Wordsworth (who had 'walked with Coleridge in the Windy Brow woods' the week before) wrote in her *Journal* (I, 46): 'Made the Windy Brow seat.' On October 21, 1800, Coleridge printed in the *Morning Post* an 'Inscription for a Seat by the Road Side half-way up a Steep Hill facing South' (*Poems*, I, 349), which he signed 'Ventifrons'—'dog-Latin,' as E. H. Coleridge remarks, 'for Windy Brow.' And in the poem he refers to the seat as 'this seat of *sods*' (I.24). The 'sopha of sods' of the note of 1803 is clearly 'the Windy Brow seat' which he and Dorothy had made on Latrigg in 1800. And it turns up again in another note of 1803: 'The tree or seaweed like appearance of the side of the mountain, all white with snow, made by little bits of snow loosened. Introduce this and the stones leaping rabbitlike down on my sopha of sods' (A. P., p. 25). 'Lack-wit' (superseding the original 'ideot' of the Note Book) falls in with a discussion of the relative poetic values of 'idiot' and 'lack-wit' in Wordsworth's impassioned vindication of his own 'Idiot Boy' in the letter to North: 'It is probable that the principal cause of your dislike to this particular poem lies in the *word* Idiot. If there had been any such word in our language, *to which we had attached passion*, as lack-wit, half-wit, witless, etc., I should have certainly employed it in preference; but there is no such word' (*Memoirs*, I, 198; italics Wordsworth's). And Coleridge, who at this period was constantly at Grasmere (D. W., *Journals*, I, 120–34), could not but have been an

interested party to the argument. Incidentally, he uses the word himself in a letter of 1810 (*Letters*, II, 564). There is a cave and a waterfall in Wordsworth's 'Idiot Boy' (L. B. 1798, ll. 238, 241, 357, 370, etc.; compare 'The Prelude,' Bk. XIV, ll. 404–06), but 'the *Yorkshire* cave, where the waterfall is' of Coleridge's note is 'Hardrane' waterfall, which Wordsworth and his sister visited on their walking tour from Sockburn to Grasmere in December, 1799, and which Wordsworth vividly described in a letter to Coleridge written a few days later (*Memoirs*, I, 149–54, esp. 152–54; *Letters of the Wordsworth Family*, III, 369–74, esp. 372–74). 'Hardrane,' however, is a ghost-word. Christopher Wordsworth remarks in a footnote (p. 149): 'The original of this letter is very difficult to decypher, and I cannot, therefore, vouch for exact accuracy in the transcript.' The word which he read 'Hardrane' is 'Hardraw,' and the reference is to Hardraw Force. Knight (IX, 202, 205) and Grosart (III, 240) have followed Canon Wordsworth in the error, without consulting a map. Mr. Gordon Wordsworth has corrected it in *Letters of the Wordsworth Family*, III, 445, n. The connection of lack-wit and the clock with the sopha of sods, and the reason for the transfer of the idiot's goal from the open field of the Note Book to the Yorkshire cave and waterfall we can only guess. But on Oct. 4–6, 1802, Dorothy Wordsworth had accompanied William and Mary on their brief wedding trip over this same Yorkshire road (D. W., *Journals*, I, 148–54), and the earlier tour was constantly in her mind as she went. Coleridge's note may well have been suggested by some reminiscence of this twice-travelled road which later that year or (more probably) in 1803 Dorothy Wordsworth imparted to him as they sat together on the Windy Brow seat.

Finally, E. H. Coleridge (A. P., p. 50) thought that 'lack-wit and the clock' referred to *Wordsworth's* 'Idiot Boy.' But he had obviously forgotten that the *clock* belonged only to Coleridge's idiot. And therein lies the justification of our curiosity. For the singular note on the 'sopha of sods' turns out to be a tissue of reminiscences—of Coleridge's own project of five or six years before, and of the lively discussion the previous year, and of Wordsworth's five-year-old poem, and of halcyon hours on Windy Brow, and of the twice-told tale of happy wanderings. And such confluences of recollections are, as we shall see, of no small consequence.

There is a rather terrible incident of 'a poor ideot boy, who exactly answered my description' in a letter to Poole of 1801 (T. P., II, 68).

134 Coleridge made use of this passage from the *Republic* in D. N., ll. 20–23 (*Poems*, I, 132). The lines are among those originally included in *Joan of Arc*. Garnett (p. 305) calls attention to the parallel, without reference to the passage in the Note Book.

135 See fols. 28[b]–29[a]; *Archiv*, pp. 356–57.

136 Fol. 45[b]; *Archiv*, p. 363. Italics Coleridge's. This entry and the next are from Thomas Maurice, *The History of Hindostan; its Arts and its Sciences*, etc., London, I (1795), 106–07, 277–78. For Maurice's text, see pp. 380, above, 591, n. 59, below, and the next note.

137 Fol 49[a]; *Archiv*, p. 363, The passage of which Coleridge made memorandum is in Maurice, I, 277–78:

> They [the Chaldean observations] were probably made after the same manner in which the Chinese astronomers of the ancient academy, notwithstanding they have now the use of European instruments in the new grand observatory of Pekin, continue to make them. 'Five mathematicians,' says Le Compte, 'spend every night in the tower, vigilantly observing what passes over head; one directs his eye towards the zenith; a second towards the east; a third towards the west quarters of the heaven; the south falls under the notice of a fourth; and the north of a fifth astronomer; so that nothing of what happen [*sic*] either in the meridian, or in the four corners of the world, can escape their diligent observation. They take notice of the winds, the rain, the air; of unusual phænomena, such as eclipses, the conjunction or opposition of planets, fiery meteors, and of whatever, during the night, is worthy of

remark.'

Maurice is quoting Le Comte, *Memoirs and Observations . . . made in a late Journey through the Empire of China* (1699), pp. 69–70. The description of the observatory comprises pp. 63–71. Maurice's quotation is not exact, and Coleridge's note agrees in phraseology with Maurice, where Maurice diverges from Le Comte. In the original (*Nouveaux Mémoires sur l'état present de la Chine*, 1696, I, 138 ff.) there are beautifully engraved illustrations of the astronomical instruments. Another account of the observatory is found in *Histoire générale des voyages* (1748), VI, 272 (with plate), and in Dupuis, I^1, 214–15. See also Purchas, XII, 424.

138 Fols. 73^b–74^a; *Archiv*, p. 367. The exact title of 'Manchester Trans.' (which Brandl glosses as 'Transactions, eine Zeitung') is *Memoirs of the Literary and Philosophical Society of Manchester*. Volume III is dated 1790, and the page-reference in the Note Book is correct. Coleridge borrowed Volume II of the *Memoirs* from the Bristol Library, Apr. 20–May 22, 1798 (*Mod. Philol.*, XXI, 320). The note in full is as follows:

> On the thirteenth of February, 1780, as I was returning to Chester, and ascending, at Rhealt, the mountain which forms the eastern boundary of the Vale of Clwyd,—in the road above me, I was struck with the

> peculiar appearance of a very white shining cloud, that lay remarkably close to the ground. The Sun was nearly setting but shone extremely bright. I walked up to the cloud, and my shadow was projected into it; the head of my shadow was surrounded at some distance by a circle of various colours whose centre appeared to be near the situation of the eye, and whose circumference extended to the shoulders. The circle was complete except where the shadow of my body intercepted it—it exhibited the most vivid colors, red being outermost—all the colors appeared in the same order and proportion that the rainbow presents to our view.

In an undated poem which bears the marks of a later period ('Constancy to an Ideal Object,' *Poems*, I, 455–56), Coleridge makes striking use of this passage, in lines 25–32. And he appends the following note: 'This phenomenon . . . of which the reader may find a description in one of the earlier volumes of the *Manchester Philosophical Transactions*, is applied figuratively to the following passage in *Aids to Reflection*' (1825, p. 220)—a passage easily accessible in the note. See also the vivid picture of a glory around the sun in 'The Three Graves,' ll. 505–13 (*Poems*, I, 284).

Since this note was written there has come to the Harvard College Library in the Norton Perkins Collection an annotated copy of *Aids to Reflection* (1825) in which Coleridge has commented as follows on the passage just referred to (p. 220, Aphorisms on Spiritual Religion, VIII, Comment, II, note):

> This refers to a curious phenomenon which occurs occasionally when the air is filled with fine particles of frozen Snow, constituting an almost invisibly subtle Snow mist, and a person is walking with y[e] Sun behind his back. His shadow is projected, and he sees a figure moving before him with a glory round his head. I have myself seen it twice, and it is described in the 1st or 2d vol. of y[e] Manchester Phil[l]. Transact[ns].

Compare the note referred to on p. 482, n. 14, below.

139 Fol. 74[a]; *Archiv*, p. 367. This is also from the third volume of the *Manchester Memoirs*, but from the *close* of the article (pp. 466–67). The text is quoted above, p. 205.

140 These three entries, all in pencil, are on fol. 76[a]; *Archiv*, p. 368.

141 Fol. 77[b]; *Archiv*, p. 369. Italics Coleridge's.

142 Fol. 80[b]; *Archiv*, p. 370. Brandl reads, in the jotting about Ham, 'lustful rogues.' But he has mistaken, I think, a characteristic twist of the final *e* for *s*.

143 Fol. 86[a] (pencil); *Archiv*, p. 371.

144 *Ibid.* (ink).

145 Fol. 87^b (written vertically along the righthand edge of the page); *Archiv*, p. 371. In a long note on 'Human Life' (p. 269) in Mr. H. T. Butler's copy of *Sibylline Leaves* (p. 504, n. 54, below), Coleridge quotes, as he says, 'some lines I wrote at Stowey, in a poetic epistle to my Friend T. Poole, describing our pursuits and conversations.' The first lines are these:

> Or while in too perverse a scorn I hold
>
> The lengthy poets who, like Gower of old,
>
> Make drossy lead as ductile as pure gold.

The lines immediately following, on Donne, are printed, with several variants, in *Poems*, I, 433. I am indebted to Mr. Butler's kindness for a transcript of the poem.

146 That a document as catholic in its inclusiveness as the great sheet knit at the four corners and let down to earth, wherein were all manner of four-footed beasts and wild beasts and creeping things and fowls of the air—that such a document should be teeming with the germs of poetry, it is not, at first blush, easy to believe. Yet to poetry, as to Peter on the housetop, nothing is common or unclean. What would have been in Shakespeare's note book—had Shakespeare ever kept a note book—during the years which led up to *Macbeth?*

It takes no Œdipus to guess. Cats and toads as familiars of witches, rats without tails that gnaw holes in the bottom of ships, mariners spell-bound for nine times nine weeks, the vaporous drop on the tip of the moon, plants the roots of which deprive of reason, air-drawn daggers with gouts of blood, maddened horses that devour each other, charms of all sorts, from the sweltered venom of the toad to grease from a murderer's gibbet, the strange phenomena of somnambulism, ghost-lore, the habits of the rhinoceros, the behavior of owls. And that is nothing to the farrago of the note book which might have preceded *Lear*. The mysteries of Hecate, parents that eat their offspring, dragons, disasters of sun, moon, and stars, cuckoos and candles, serpent's teeth, crabs, oysters, snails and wagtails, beggars who stick pins, nails, and sprigs of rosemary into their arms, bears, monkeys, eels, vultures, and halcyons, fen-sucked fogs, foul fiends and star-blasting, pelicans, hogs, foxes, lions, wolves, frogs, toads, tadpoles and water-newts, cow-dung, rats, mice, crows, choughs, beetles, nightmares and witches, Nero and the lake of darkness, Hobbididance, prince of dumbness, Mahu and Modo and Flibbertigibbet, and fiends with a thousand noses. I have deliberately broken down in each case, to be sure, a supremely organic entity into certain of its primordial elements. But the elements of *Macbeth* and *Lear*, no less than Coleridge's strange and fragmentary jottings, existed as dispersed impressions before they were marshalled by the imagination into unity. And however wild and whirling the welter of the Note Book, it is potentially as apt material for the exercise of the creative energy. The implied comparison between Coleridge and Shakespeare will not, I know, bear putting on all fours. 'Shakespeare,' as Mr. Compton Mackenzie tersely has it, 'didn't sit all day in the reading-room of the British Museum.' But in essentials the analogy holds good.

CHAPTER II

1 Fol. 45[b]; *Archiv*, p. 363. See above, p. 29.

2 Brandl's statement (*Archiv*, p. 363, n. 3) that this page 'handelt über die Entstehung des Schachspiels' is wrong. He has inadvertently turned to p. 111 instead of 107.

3 See above, pp. 379 ff.

4 Fol. 47[a]; *Archiv*, p. 363.

5 See also Maurice, I, 105.

6 Fol. 47[a]; *Archiv*, p. 363.

7 'That consummate Geographer, and most accurate investigator, Major James Rennell,' as Mathias calls him ('Shade of Alexander Pope,' note on l. 278, which refers to

'Rennell's keen decisive labours'). For his career, see D. N. B.

8 Maurice, I, 12–13: 'Instead of guiding myself by the uncertain and obsolete maps of those travellers, I have immediately directed my own and my reader's attention to the intelligent Memoir, and very accurate map of Hindostan, presented to the world by Major Rennell, whose unwearied efforts to elucidate her intricate geography, must secure him the applause of all those who are either interested in the commerce, or attached to the literature, of the East. To this map . . . I must constantly refer the inquisitive reader, as to an unerring guide.' Compare p. 19. In the Note Book Major Rennell's name seems to have been written first, near the top of the page, and then the reference to Quintus Curtius inserted above it.

9 See above, pp. 382 ff.

10 Maurice, I, 277. See above, p. 29.

11 Fol. 2[a]; *Archiv*, p. 340.

12 Lamb, in that letter of February, 1797 (VI, 91–92) in which he suggested the Origin of Evil as the subject for a poem, continued: 'Or the description (from a Vision or Dream, suppose) of an Utopia in one of the planets (the Moon, for instance).' And Coleridge knew from his admired Burnet that it was the 'notion or opinion amongst the ancients

concerning *paradise*, that it was seated as high as the sphere of the moon' (S. T., I, 266). Compare also Burnet's reference (S. T., I, 249–50) to Paradise as 'in the moon, or in Jupiter, or hung above like a cloud or a meteor.' And some such conceit may have been in the back of Coleridge's head when he came on the passage in Darwin.

13 Coleridge knew Erasmus Darwin early; see B. L., I, 11–12, referring to his 'first Cambridge vacation.' And Darwin was the subject of eager discussion in Coleridge's circle at Cambridge in 1793 (Christopher Wordsworth's diary for Oct. 17, 24, Nov. 5; see Wordsworth, *Social Life*, etc., pp. 588–89). Compare *The Friend* (*Works*, II, 427), dating his knowledge of the *Phytologia* from its first appearance in 1800. Pertinent references in the letters for the period which concerns us may be found in *Letters*, I, 152–53 (Jan., 1796, Coleridge's meeting with Darwin); 161 (May, 1796), 164 (May, 1796): 'I absolutely nauseate Darwin's poems'; 211 (Dec., 1796), 215 (February, 1797): 'On the whole, I think, he is the first *literary* character in Europe, and the most original-minded man' (italics Coleridge's); and compare Carlyon, I, 88. See also the Note Book (fols. 16^b, 25^b; *Archiv*, pp. 349, 354), and compare *Lectures*, p. 48. Darwin's note on M. Haggern and his electric plants (p. 464, n. 80, above) is quoted in the volume of 1796, explaining a reference in a poem written in September, 1795 (see *Poems*, I, 99–100). Coleridge's later opinion of

Darwin need not be considered here. It is worth recalling that Wordsworth's 'Goody Blake and Harry Gill,' written at Alfoxden in 1798, was drawn from the *Zoönomia* (II, 359). There is an interesting note on Darwin, with specimens of what may be called the 'general texture of his work,' in B. L. (Sampson), pp. 271–73.

14 *Botanic Garden* (1791), Part I, p. 66 (note on Canto II, l. 82: 'And roll'd round Earth her airless realms of frost').

15 Fol. 2[a]; *Archiv*, p. 340.

16 *Botanic Garden* (1791), Pt. I, Contents of the Notes, p. 212.

17 *Botanic Garden* (1791), Pt. I, pp. 41–42 (Canto I, II. 427–30).

18 *Ibid.*, p. 42, and Additional Notes, pp. 79–93 (No. XXXIII).

19 See Hazlitt's account, in 'My First Acquaintance with Poets,' of his visit with Coleridge, in 1798, to the Valley of Rocks: 'In the morning of the second day, we breakfasted luxuriously in an old-fashioned parlour, on tea, toast, eggs, and honey, in the very sight of the bee-hives from which it had been taken, and a garden full of thyme and wild flowers that had produced it. . . . It was in this room that we found

a little worn-out copy of the *Seasons*, lying in a window-seat, on which Coleridge exclaimed, "*That* is true fame!" ' (*Works*, XII, 273; cf. 346).

20 'Winter,' ll. 843 ff. For Lapland, see above, pp. 94 ff.

21 *Ibid.*, l. 875.

22 See p. 445, above, under 'Maupertuis.' A diluted résumé of Maupertuis's descriptive passages is given in Rev. John Adams's *The Flowers of Modern Travels . . . Intended chiefly for Young People of both Sexes* (3d ed., 1792), II, 270 ff. But it had nothing to offer Samuel Taylor Coleridge. A much fuller abstract (largely in the words of the translation) of the non-technical parts of *The Figure of the Earth* is found in Mavor, XII, 277 ff. Mavor's collection (wanting volumes III, VI, and VII) was in Wordsworth's library (*Trans. Wordsworth Soc.*, VI, 212, No. 139), and Coleridge may have gone to that. But Maupertuis's volume itself does not seem to have been inaccessible.

23 See pp. 101–02, above.

24 See pp. 96 ff., 189, above.

25 What Coleridge says of Watt, apropos of his '*armed eye*,' is applicable to himself: 'the genial spirit, that *saw* what it had been *seeking*, and saw *because* it sought' (*Miscellanies*, pp.

251–52, italics Coleridge's).

26 For other evidence of this practice, see pp. 38–42, 495, n. 31.

CHAPTER III

1 *Poems*, I, 123. See also the sonnet to Priestley (*Poems*, I, 81; *Letters*, I, 116), especially the last three lines; B. E., I, 36, 42; and Charles Lamb's letters to Coleridge in *Works*, VI, 10, 78, 83, 84. Coleridge drew 'Priestley's Corruption' (presumably *An History of the Corruptions of Christianity*, 1782) from the Bristol Library (signing Southey's name), March 27, 1795 (*Mod. Philol.*, XXI, 319). Later references to Priestley do not concern us.

2 Optics is included among the subjects in which Coleridge, in 1796, proposed to instruct Charles Lloyd (B. E., I, 109). And that he was reading Sir Isaac Newton's *Optics* at this same time—and reading with an intensely active mind—we know from the long note to l. 34 of Book II of *Joan of Arc* (reprinted in *Poems*, II, 1112–13; Cottle, *Recollections*, pp. 242–44), as well as from two entries, fols. 11[a] and 15[a] (*Archiv*, pp. 346, 348), of the Note Book. See also *Letters*, I, 352.

3 Priestley, p. 572.

4 Line 274.

5 Eight hundred and seven of text. The remaining five comprise a list of technical terms.

6 Priestley, p. 807.

7 Fol. 2[a]; *Archiv*, p. 340.

8 I am indebted for the following note to Professor James Devadasan, of the Theological Seminary, Bareilly, India:

> Among the so-called Syrian Christians of South India, who trace their Christianity to the ministry of St. Thomas, the following custom is observed in connection with their marriage ceremony: The bride and the groom, returning from the church to the home of the former, are stopped in front of the door by two girls, each holding in her hand a lighted candle. The bride takes one candle and the bridegroom takes the other, and they put them both together so as to make them burn in one combined flame for some time, or until the candles have been burned away.

I suspect that we have to do with a singular coincidence; but it is not impossible that Coleridge ran across an account of this striking custom in some travel-book. If so, I have failed to find it.

9 The entry in the Note Book (fol. 2[b]; *Archiv*, p. 340) is quoted above, PP. 13–14.

10 Candles suggested two more subjects in the Note Book (fol. 24[b]; *Archiv*, P.353): 'Halo round the Candle—Sigh Visible' (on which the best commentary is *Osorio*, IV, 24–26), and 'Cavern-candle.' There is not space (as I wish there were) to quote, but any one who cares to reincarnate the dry bones of the references which follow will be amply rewarded by a curiously interesting set of variations on a single theme: A. P., pp. 22 (top); 46 (Dec. 28), 47 (Dec. 30), 64 ('A Simile'), 86 ('Verbum sapientibus'), 146 (second note), 151 (top; see *Miscellanies*, p. 275), 203 (last note); *Letters*, I, 307 (second letter); B. E., I, 229; *The Friend, Works*, II, 368; *Lectures*, p. 389 ('the candle-flame cone of an epigram').

11 Priestley, p. 573.

12 The reference is to the *Philosophical Transactions*, abridged by Henry Jones, Vol. V, Pt. II, pp. 213–15. The same account, *without the marine rainbow* (see above, pp. 67, 350), is in Motte's abridgment, II, Pt. III, pp. 113 ff. The original paper is in No. 337 (Vol. XXVIII, for the year 1713), pp. 230–35.

13 *Lettres édifiantes et curieuses*, IX (1730), 359–75; ed. Aimé-Martin, II (1843), 389–92. The letter is also printed in

Lockman's *Travels of the Jesuits* (translated from the *Lettres*), II (1762), 317–23.

14 *Phil. Trans.* (as above), V, 214.

15 Ll. 280–81.

16 *Phil. Trans.*, V, 215.

17 Fol. 76[a]; *Archiv*, p. 368. This entry is in pencil, and is somewhat blurred in the manuscript. But it is as I have given it, and not (as Brandl has it) 'Sun paints with rainbows,' etc.

18 *Phil. Trans.*, Vol. V, Pt. II, pp. 161–62. The Abridgment is drawing on No. 339 (Vol. XXIX, for 1714–16), pp. 62–71. The reference to the moon and the star in Vol. XXIX is on pp. 65–66.

19 Ll. 209–11. For the textual history of these lines, which reached their present form in *Sibylline Leaves* (1817), see below, p. 508, n. 45.

A word is necessary at this point regarding the text of 'The Ancient Mariner. The first version of the poem appeared in *Lyrical Ballads* in 1798. This text is easily accessible in *Poems*, II, 1030–1048 (in the one-volume edition, pp. 528–46); in Campbell, *Poems*, pp. 512–20; in Hutchinson, *Lyrical Ballads* (Centenary Reprint, London, 1898), pp. 1–27; and elsewhere (see *Poems*, II, 1030, n. 1). The poem reappeared in the second edition of L. B. (1800), having undergone considerable revision. The changes can be made out, with some difficulty, from the textual notes in *Poems*, I, 186–209, and from Campbell's notes to the text of 1798 (Campbell, *Poems*, pp. 512–20). It was reprinted without material change in L. B., 1802 and 1805, and not again until 1817, when it appeared in *Sibylline Leaves*, accompanied for the first time by the gloss, and revised in some important particulars, for which E. H. Coleridge's textual notes to the poem may be consulted. After 1817 no changes of importance were made. The text followed by E. H. Coleridge in his edition of the *Poems* is 'that of the last edition of the *Poetical Works* published in the author's life-time—the three-volume edition issued by Pickering in the spring and summer of 1834' (*Poems*, I, iii). Campbell follows the edition of the *Poetical Works* 'published in 1829, as being the last upon which [Coleridge] was able to bestow personal care and attention' (Campbell, *Poems*, p. vii). But the variations between the two texts (E. H. Coleridge's and Campbell's) of 'The Ancient Mariner' are very few in number, and are wholly confined to punctuation and the use of capitals and italics. See lines 41, 78, 82, 121, 131–32, 183, 185, 188–89, 190, 193, 210, 270, 336, 343, 432, 480, 600, and the gloss to lines 240 and 582.

In my own quotations from the poem I have used, as

a rule, the final version of the text. Every divergence from that practice is recorded in the Notes. And whenever the text which is followed differs in any significant way from the earlier versions, the variants are likewise given in the Notes. It is immaterial for my purpose at what stage in the composition of the poem the reminiscences which we are tracing came to the surface—except so far as the possible lapse of time between the reading and the recollection may constitute a factor in the problem.

For there is one important consideration which, so far as I know, has been overlooked. There is no reason, in a word, to suppose that the changes which first appeared, together with the gloss, in *Sibylline Leaves* in 1817 were made at, or even near, the time at which, in 1815, that volume was put together (for the date, see B. L., I, xc–xcii; Campbell, *Narrative*, pp. 212–15, and compare Sampson's appendix, 'Stages in the Growth of *Biographia Literaria*,' in his edition of B. L., pp. 248–60). The last reprinting of 'The Ancient Mariner' had been ten years before, and the last printing with changes, five years before that. Alterations made as early as 1801, in other words, would have had to wait until 1815 (in point of fact, till 1817) to see the light. The date of publication affords no evidence whatever of the date of composition. A single analogous instance will suffice to make this clear. The one change which we know to have been actually made in 1817 (see above, pp. 164 ff.)

remained unpublished, for precisely similar reasons, until the next printing of 'The Ancient Mariner' in 1828—a period of eleven years. The changes first *printed* in 1817 may have similarly lain in manuscript at least as long, or even longer. And there is reason to suspect that they did.

For from the close of 1802 through the year in which the poems collected in *Sibylline Leaves* were brought together, Coleridge's creative faculty was in eclipse. One need ohly look at the list of poems assigned by E. H. Coleridge to the years between 1802 and 1815 (remembering that most even of these, as the notes make clear, are of doubtful date) for concrete evidence, materially strengthened if one actually reads the poems, of what the known facts of these years would lead one to expect. It is possible (one may grant at once) that superb poetry such, for example, as lines 199–208 of 'The Ancient Mariner,' flawless in their keeping with the rest of the poem, may have been the birth of some hour of inspiration even in that distressed and distressing year, 1815, the pitiful tale of which Campbell tells with such restraint (*Narrative*, pp. 210–16). But it is needless to subject probability to such a strain. It is far more likely that these and other changes which first appeared in *Sibylline Leaves* had been made in more auspicious days, and now for the first time found release from manuscript through a reprinting of the poem.

And there was such a propitious interval in 1802, just

two years after the poem's first revision. It was the period of Coleridge's magnificently imaginative lament, in 'Dejection,' for the loss of his imagination—a lament which parallels in its imaginative sweep his tremendous outburst to Godwin a little earlier (B. E., I, 228–29) on the death of his imaginative power. His creative energy was dying, but it was still glorious in its throes. It was a period of renewed association with the Wordsworths (D. W., *Journals*, I, 97 ff., esp. 111–37); of the stimulating correspondence with William Sotheby and Robert Southey (*Letters*, I, 369–410); and of the visit—'three full weeks'—from Charles and Mary Lamb (Lamb, *Works*, VI, 243–44). All the incentives, in a word, which were lacking in 1815 were now present, together with the power to respond. And the undated correction referred to above (*Poems*, I, 195, n.,—beginning 'With never a whisper') is very much in point. It is all, to be sure, a matter of probability. But everything points to a date far earlier than the period when *Sibylline Leaves* was in the press for the final revision of the poem. And I suspect that most of the changes in the poem were made within a very few years from its date of composition.

20 *Phil. Trans.*, V, Pt. II, 159, 161. A copy of the letter which the *Transactions* epitomize is to be found in the Gay transcript of Cotton Mather's letters, made from the Letter-Book of the Royal Society, and now in the Library of the Massachusetts Historical Society in Boston; see G. L. Kittredge, 'Cotton

Mather's Scientific Communications to the Royal Society' (*Proceedings of the American Antiquarian Society*, April, 1916), pp. 18–57. The pertinent passage is as follows (Gay MS., fols. 92–93): 'You will but bestow a smile upon it, if I tell you that we have a Tradition among us, and you have it particularly asserted in a Book published *by* a Gentleman in the year 1674, with a Dedication to the *Royal Society;* That in the Month of *November*, 1668, there appeared a *Star* below ye Body of y^e^ *Moon*, and within the Horns of it.' What was the book? To attempt to identify a volume of which both the title and the author's name are wanting is a little like hunting a black cat in the dark. But thanks to the *Term Catalogues*, it was possible to get at the books printed in 1674, and examine them, and the passage turned up at last in Josselyn's *An Account of Two Voyages to New-England* (London, 1675), p. 53; reprint of 1865, p. 45: 'In November following [1668] appeared a Star between the horns of the Moon in the midst.'

21 See above, pp. 180 ff.

22 Ll. 267–81. Save for the second line of the first stanza quoted (see above, p. 203), and a comma or two, the text of this passage as first printed in 1798 underwent no change.

23 *Letters*, I, 63–64.

24 *Gentleman's Magazine*, Dec., 1834, p. 606. Quoted, in

part, in B. E., I, 31, and in B. L. (1847), II, 335–36. For Le Grice, see further Lamb, *Works*, VI, 8, 11; *Letters* (ed. Hazlitt), I, 94–95, and notes.

25 See my articles on 'Chaucer and Dante' (*Mod. Philol.*, XIV, 705–35), and on 'Chaucer and Dante's Convivio' (*ibid.*, XIII, 19–33), and the references in Hammond, *Chaucer: A Bibliographical Manual*, pp. 81–83.

26 See the full evidence in *Mod. Philol.*, XIV, 706–08.

27 *Works*, II, 31; B. E., II, 53, 59; with the last reference compare *Fraser's Magazine*, XII (1835), 627.

28 *Phil. Trans.*, V, Pt. II, 213–14.

29 *Essays and Tales*, by John Sterling, ed. Julius Charles Hare (London, 1848), I, xx. Cf. D. W., *Journals*, I, 195.

30 Cook, *Voyage to the Pacific Ocean*, II, 257. This passage is quoted in the valuable school edition of 'The Ancient Mariner' by Professor Pelham Edgar (New York, 1900), p. 103. It had been used earlier by Sykes (p. 192).

31 The adjectives which Coleridge uses ('*shining* white,' '*glossy* green'), together with the patent connection of his passage with the stanza depicting the water that 'burnt green, and blue and white' (see above, pp. 81 ff.), render the immediate

suggestion of the colours unmistakable. Without question Coleridge had read in the voyagers accounts of varicoloured fishes, such as the dorado—described, for example, in Thevet, *Les singulartez de la France Antarctique*, 1558, fol. 37vo (English translation, *The New found worlde, or Antarctike*, 1568, fol. 32): 'As I sayd before, that there is fish found of al colours, red, as those who*m* they named Bonnites, the others Azure, and like golde, shining brighter than fine Azure, as those named Dorades, others greene, gray, blacke.' So Davies, *History of the Carriby-Islands* (translated from Rochefort), London, 1666, p. 99 (and compare the rainbow-coloured marine creatures on pp. 119–27): 'It is called Dorado, because in the water the head of it seems to be of a green gilt, and the rest of the body as yellow as gold, and azur'd, as a clear sky.' Frézier, too, describes them (*A Voyage to the South Sea*, 1717, p. 8): 'On their Scales appears the brightest Lustre of Gold intermix'd with Shadowings of Azure, Green and Purple, than which nothing more beautiful can be imagin'd.' And there is a striking passage earlier (I, 217) in Cook's narrative. Barring the last, I have no evidence that Coleridge read any of these books. But he may have done so, and the contributory presence of such associations is of course perfectly possible. The essential point, however, is that the connection between the poem and the passage in Cook is demonstrable; the evidence, as we shall see, is cumulative.

Whether he remembered it or not, it is at least worth mentioning that as a child Coleridge had read this in Philip Quarll (*The Hermit*, p. 34):

> At length being come to the pond, I was surprised at the clearness of the water, at the bottom of which seemed to be large rubies, emeralds, jacinths, and other coloured stones; till, being come to the brink of it, those which I took for precious stones, proved to be fishes by their swimming about, which, to my thinking, looked like stars shooting from place to place in the sky.

32 According to Frederick Martens (p. 136), 'some [whales] are as black as Velvet.' In Josephus Acosta the foxes are 'blacker then blacke velvet' (Purchas, XV, 219).

33 Purchas, II, 135, gloss.

34 *Travels*, pp. 153, 158.

35 Purchas, *Pilgrimage* (1617), p. 1086. This is Purchas's retelling, with slight condensation, of Sir Richard Hawkins's own account, which may be read in the *Pilgrimes* (XVII, 76), or (if the 1622 edition of Hawkins is not available) in *The Observations of Sir Richard Hawkins, K^{nt}, in his Voyage into the South Sea in the Year 1593* (Hakluyt Soc., 1847), p. 58

I am indebted to Mr. James H. Pitman of New Haven

for calling my attention to the fact that Goldsmith quotes this passage in the *History of The Earth and Animated Nature*, chap. XV (2d. ed., 1779, vol. I, p. 239). If Coleridge read (as he may have done) Goldsmith's compendium, we have another string to our bow. Long after this chapter was written I found that a writer in the New York *Nation* for April 2, 1914 (p. 360) had also connected Hawkins's observations off the Azores with Coleridge's water snakes.

36 The 'gellies' constitute a further link with the 'gelatinous' protozoa of Captain Cook (see p. 46, above).

37 A. P., pp. 175–76. The stanzas, original and revised; Wordsworth's note; and Lamb's defense (*Works*, VI, 456) of 'the good honest tub' are conveniently brought together in B. L. (Sampson), pp. 315–17. See also *Letters of the Wordsworth Family*, III, 414. For Wordsworth's further use of Dampier, see *Prelude* (Selincourt), pp. 604–05. The contrast with Coleridge's *modus operandi* is illuminating. There is a little known addendum to the story of this luckless stanza. In her edition of the *Biographia Literaria* Sara Coleridge comments on Wordsworth's lines, as her father quotes them in his twenty-second chapter (see *Works*, III, 465). In her own copy of B. L. (1847) is a manuscript note (II, 135–36) in which she tries her hand at a substitute for Wordsworth's original couplet. Here, alas! it is:

A tub of common form and size,

Such as each rustic home supplies.

'This,' she says, 'I ventured to suggest to the venerable author at Bath, March, 1847. He did not reject the notion altogether. S. C.' (*North British Review*, XL, 88).

38 T. T., Sept. 4 1833.

39 *Ibid.*, March 17, 1832.

40 A. P., p. 175. See also for Coleridge's opinions of Dampier, *Miscellanies*, p. 160; *The Friend, Works*, II, 486.

41 Egerton 2800, f. 105. I have not identified all the references, but some of the jottings are from passages to be found in Dampier, ed. Masefield (1906), II, 165, 172.

42 Dampier, II, 435, 461, 522. Dampier tells also of 'Water Serpents' (II, 429), and of 'Sea-snakes' (II, 432, 463). The 'Water-snake' of II, 398, is the anaconda. There are also 'sea snakes' in Cook, *Voyage to the Pacific Ocean*, I, 334.

43 *Bucaniers of America*, II, 1 ff.

44 *Ibid.*, II, 50, 130. They are variegated also in Edward Cooke's *Voyage to the South Sea, and round the World in 1708–11* (London, 1712): 'Saw . . . abundance of Water-

Snakes . . . Some are Yellow, spotted with Black, and of several Colours, Sorts, and Sizes' ([I], 317, with a picture of one of them in the preceding Plate II); 'Saw many Water-Snakes of great Variety of Colours' ([I], 324). So in *An Authentic Journal of the late Expedition under the Command of Commodore Anson*, by John Philips (London, 1744), we read: 'This Day we saw a prodigious Number of Water Snakes, with black Backs and yellow Bellies' (p. 104). Coleridge may, of course, have read either or both of these; as in the case of Basil Ringrose I have no evidence. If he did, his '*velvet* black' represents the heightening, under the influence of Bartram, of a general impression that water-snakes were sometimes black.

Water-snakes are referred to, without description, in Benyowski's *Memoirs and Travels*, II, 71, 74; Cook, *Voyage to the Pacific Ocean*, I, 334 ('sea-snakes'); Bligh, *Voyage to the South Sea* (London, 1792), p. 224; Herbert, p. 41; Churchill, II, 287. Water-snakes in *fresh* water turn up in Carver, *Travels through the Interior Parts of North-America* (London, 1778), p. 167, and in John Lawson, *A New Account of Carolina*, in [John Stevens], *A New Collection of Voyages and Travels* (1711), I, 130–31, cf. 122. And in *Letters from an American Farmer*, by J. Hector St. John [Michel Guillaume St. Jean de Crèvecœur] (London, 1782), pp. 243–46, there is a tale of an epic conflict between a black-snake and a water-snake.

The earliest account of water-snakes of which I

know belongs to the first century A.D. It is in the **ΑΝΩΝΥΜΟΥ ΠΕΡΙΠΛΟΥΣ ΤΗΣ ΕΡΥΘΡΑΣ ΘΑΛΑΣΣΗΣ** , and I shall quote it from *The Periplus of the Erythræan Sea: Travel and Trade in the Indian Ocean by a Merchant of the First Century*, translated and annotated by Wilfred H. Schoff (1912), § 55 (p. 44): 'As a sign to those approaching these places from the sea there are serpents [**ὄφεις**] coming forth to meet you, black in color, but shorter, like snakes in the head, and with blood-red eyes'. **[μέλανες μὲν καὶ αὐτοὶ τὴν χρόαν, βραχύτεροι δὲ καὶ δρακοντοειδεῖς τὴν κεφαλὴν καὶ τοῖς ὄμμασιν αἱματώδεις].** Linschoten (1598) speaks of 'divers Snakes like Eales and bigger, driving in the sea' (p. 312); and Thomas Pennant, in *The View of Hindoostan* (1798), I, 59–60, writes at some length of 'sea-snakes' off the coast of India.

45 Leemius, *De Lapponibus Finmarchia* (Knud Leems . . . *Beskrivelse Finmarkens Lapper*), Copenhagen, 1767, p. 307.

46 *Ibid.*, p. 332. The Latin note to D. N., l. 74 is taken (freely) from Leemius, pp. 173 and 172; Balda Zhiok (l. 71) is from Leemius, p. 433; Lieule-Oaive (l. 64) from p. 437 ('Lieule-Oaive's vapoury head' is 'Lieule Oaaive *caput vaporis*); the long Latin note on Solfar-kapper (l. 72) is from the same page of Leemius; Vuokho (l. 94), from p. 423; Jaibme Aibmo (note to l. 96), from pp. 416–19.

47 He sent a copy of 'The Shipwreck,' accompanied by a poetical epistle on the poem, to 'Miss K,' at some time before 1818, when the verses were published (*Poems*, I, 424). No one, however, will question Coleridge's acquaintance with Falconer before 1797–98.

48 'The Shipwreck,' Canto II, ll. 63–70, 213–18.

49 Ll. 272–81.

50 B. L., II, 120.

51 *Letters*, I, 377.

52 B. E., II, 482.

53 A. P., p. 206.

54 Henry James, *Works* ('New York Edition'), II, vii: 'I . . . dropped it [my idea] for the time into the deep well of unconscious cerebration: not without the hope, doubtless, that it might eventually emerge from that reservoir, as one had already known the buried treasure to come to light, with a firm iridescent surface and a notable increase of weight.' Francis Thompson makes a strikingly similar remark about Shelley: 'Suspended in the dripping well of his imagination the commonest object becomes encrusted with imagery' (*Shelley*, Introduction by Rt. Hon. George Wyndham, London, 1909,

p. 50). I am indebted for this last reference to one of my students whom I wish I could thank by name.

55 *The Autocrat of the Breakfast Table*, Chap. VI (Riverside Edition, 1891), p. 134. Coleridge has said in other words essentially the same thing (A. P., p. 26):

> For a thing at the moment is but a thing of the moment; it must be taken up into the mind, diffuse itself through the whole multitude of shapes and thoughts, not one of which it leaves untinged, between not one of which and it some new thought is not engendered.

56 *Autocrat*, Chap. V, pp 111–12: 'Did you never, in walking in the fields, come across a large flat stone, which had lain, nobody knows how long, just where you found it? . . . What an odd revelation . . . produced by your turning the old stone over! Blades of grass flattened down, colorless, matted together, as if they had been bleached and ironed; hideous crawling creatures . . . motionless, slug-like creatures, young larvæ, perhaps more horrible in their pulpy stillness than even in the infernal wriggle of maturity!'

57 B. L., II, 12, ll. 12–15; cf. *ibid.*, p. 123, l. 24.

58 *Science et Méthode*, Paris, 1908. I am quoting from the translation of Francis Maitland: *Science and Method*, London, n.d.

59 *Science and Method*, p. 56.

60 *Ibid.*, p. 58.

61 *Ibid.*, p. 61. This passage will meet us again more than once, and it is well to have it as Poincaré wrote it (*Science et Méthode*, p. 60):

> Peut-être faut-il chercher l'explication dans cette période de travail conscient préliminaire qui précède toujours tout travail inconscient fructueux. Qu'on me permette une comparaison grossière. Représentons-nous les éléments futurs de nos combinaisons comme quelque chose de semblable aux atomes crochus d'Épicure. Pendant le repos complet de l'esprit, ces atomes sont immobiles, ils sont, pour ainsi dire, accrochés au mur; ce repos complet peut donc se prolonger indéfiniment sans que ces atomes se rencontrent, et, par conséquent, sans qu'aucune combinaison puisse se produire entre eux.
>
> Au contraire, pendant une période de repos apparent et de travail inconscient, quelques-uns d'entre eux sont détachés du mur et mis en mouvement. Ils sillonnent dans tous les sens l'espace, j'allais dire la pièce où ils sont enfermés, comme pourrait le faire, par exemple, une nuée de moucherons ou, si l'on préfère, une comparaison plus savante, comme le font les molécules gazeuses dans la

théorique cinétique des gaz. Leurs chocs mutuels peuvent alors produire des combinaisons nouvelles.

62 *Science and Method*, pp. 62–63.

63 *Works*, ed. Scott-Saintsbury, II, 129–30.

CHAPTER IV

1 Ll. 267–71.

2 Ll. 272–81.

3 Spenser, 'Ruines of Rome,' st. III.

4 *Aids to Reflection*, Introductory Aphorisms, XXVI (p. 19).

5 Campbell, *Narrative*, p. 93. Only then did Coleridge experience for himself the phosphorescent sea. See *Poems*, I, 408; B. L., II, 141.

6 *Letters*, I, 341, 427; B. E., I, 249. In the letter to Southey Coleridge has just indulged in a rather far-fetched metaphor, and after the sentence which I have quoted adds: 'You remember how incessantly in that room I used to be compounding these half-verbal, half-visual metaphors.' The whole passage is illuminating. See also B. E., I, 217 (foot).

These 'spectra' seem to have been most active during periods of inflammation of the eyes (see the references above in full). But the abundant allusions to words that 'flash images' (see p. 502, n. 23, below), and the exceeding vividness of Coleridge's actual recollections of things seen make it clear that abnormal conditions merely enhanced a normal state. Compare, for example, another letter to Sir Humphry Davy, apropos of the words, in the 'Morning Post Gazeteer,' '*Mr. Davy's Galvanic habitudes of Charcoal*': 'Upon my soul I believe there is not a letter in those words round which a world of imagery does not circumvolve; your room, the garden, the cold bath, the moonlight rocks, Barristed, Moore, and simple-looking Frere, and dreams of wonderful things attached to your name,—and Skiddaw, and Glaramara, and Eagle Crag, and you, and Wordsworth, and me, on the top of them!' (*Letters*, I, 336).

For observations (many of them of the utmost interest) on kindred phenomena, see A. P., pp. 39 (compare Crabb Robinson, ed. Sadler, Macmillan, 1869, I, 306; ed. Morley, pp. 31–32), 45, 122–24, 235; *Miscellanies*, pp. 163 ff.; T. T., Jan. 3, 1823, May 1, 1823; *Works*, II, 127–37 (*The Friend*, First Landing Place, Essays II and III); etc.

7 *Notes of Ben Jonson's Conversations with William Drummond of Haw-thornden, January, 1619*, ed. Laing (Shakespeare Soc., 1842), p. 22; *ibid.*, Bodley Head Quartos, ed. Harrison, 1923, p. 14.

8 A. E. [George William Russell], *The Candle of Vision*, London, 1919, p. 98.

9 Fol. 76[a]; *Archiv*, p. 368. Italics mine. See above, p. 30.

10 *Phil. Trans.* (Jones's Abridgment), V, Pt. II, 215.

11 The evidence in this instance is internal rather than external, but it is very strong. The volume which includes Martens's *Voyage* was in Wordsworth's library (*Transactions of the Wordsworth Society*, VI, 215, No. 171). The edition was that of 1694, from which I am quoting. Coleridge, moreover, had known at least *about* Martens from the days of 'The Destiny of Nations,' for he would find frequent and inviting reference to him in Crantz (I, 26, 49, 87, 107, 127, etc.), who draws on him freely, sometimes with and sometimes without acknowledgment. For the striking parallels with 'The Ancient Mariner,' many of them verbal, see above, pp. 88, 140, 143–46. Martens's work (or rather the English translation of it) is included, under the title *The Voyage into Spitzbergen and Greenland*, in *An Account of Several Late Voyages and Discoveries To the South and North* . . . By Sir John Narborough, Captain Jasmen Tasman, Captain John Wood, and Frederick Marten of Hamburgh (London, 1694). In this volume Martens's name appears incorrectly as 'Marten.' The German original is *Friderich Martens vom Hamburg Spitzbergische oder Groenlandische Reise-Beschreibung gethan*

im Jahr 1671 (Hamburg, 1675). The English translation is reprinted, with interesting remarks in the Preface (pp. i–vi), in *A Collection of Documents on Spitzbergen and Greenland*, edited by Adam White, Esq. (Hakluyt Soc., 1855). The translation is (as Walton says of Marlowe's lyric) 'old fashioned but choicely good,' and it has a flavour wholly its own.

For Martens himself, see *Allgemeine Deutsche Biographie*, XX, 461; Schroder und Klöse, *Lexikon Hamb. Schriftsteller*, V. The last reference I have been unable to verify.

12 Martens, p. 49.

13 See above, pp. 43–44.

14 Martens, pp. 48–49. Coleridge later saw these *spicula* himself, and recorded his observation in one of his notes in *White's Natural History of Selborne* (ed. Grant Allen, p. 500).

15 *Poems*, II, 565 (Act IV, ll. 35–36).

16 Martens, pp. 51–53.

17 *Ibid.*, pp. 29–30.

18 A. P., pp. 33–34. Compare also *Works*, II, 132–33 for a striking (hypothetical) parallel.

19 Martens, p. 49.

20 Eckermann, *Gespräche mit Goethe*, II March, 1828 (ed. Reclame's Universal-Bibliothek, III, 166).

21 *Ibid.*, 24 Feb., 1824 (I, 89).

22 *Ibid.*, 18 March, 1831 (II, 217–18).

23 *Discourses*, Bk. II, chap. V.

24 A. P., p. 46.

25 *Ibid.*, p. 55.

CHAPTER V

1 B, L., II, 12–13. Quoted, with substantial accuracy, from Sir John Davies, 'Of the Soule of Man,' stanzas 90–91. See p. 522, n. 48, below.

2 Fols. 25^{a-b}; 45^{b}, 47^{a}, 49^{a} (*Archiv*, pp. 354, 363).

3 Lamb, *Works*, VI, 27.

4 *Ibid.*, p. 53.

5 *Ibid.*, p. 92.

6 Note Book, fols. 25^{a}'25^{b}; *Archiv*, p. 354. In a letter of January 27, 1796, Coleridge uses the phrase: 'outcastsof a

blind idiot called Nature' (*Letters*, I, 153; B.E., I, 57).

7 *Letters*, I, 385 (July 29, 1802): 'This is no mere dream, like my "Hymns to the Elements." '

8 Letter to Coleridge, February 5, 1797 (*Works*, VI, 91). Lamb is quoting (or misquoting) l. 411 of Coleridge's 'Religious Musings': 'I discipline my young noviciate thought' (text of 1796; *Poems*, I, 124). For the moment Lamb's critical faculty was in eclipse. In the same letter he remarks: 'Sincerely I think it ['Religious Musings'] the noblest poem in the language, next after the Paradise lost, and even that was not made the vehicle of such grand truths' (VI, 90).

9 B. E., II, 211. In this letter of January, 1821, the Hymns are 'entitled *Spirit, Sun, Earth, Air, Water, Fire*, and *Man*' (italics Coleridge's)—seven Hymns. The list from the nineties in the Note Book is 'Hymns to the Sun, the Moon, and the Elements—six Hymns.' 'Spirit' and 'Man' meant more than 'Moon' to Coleridge in 1821, and the plan, I dare say, was always in a state of flux. It is a mournful fact that after all this 'mighty fret' the only one of the six which, even in title, ever took form—the 'Hymn to the Earth' (*Poems*, I, 327)—is a free translation, unacknowledged, of Stolberg's 'Hymne an die Erde.' The German text is easily accessible in Campbell, *Poems*, p. 615. The best that can be said in the premises has been said by Campbell, apropos of another flagrant instance

and in the light of Sara (Mrs. H. N.) Coleridge's defence: 'Coleridge omitted acknowledgement in at least ten similar instances. Mere carelessness, no doubt, accounts for some; pardonable light-hearted vanity for a few more, perhaps; but there is a residue' (*Poems*, p. 617; see B. L., 1847, I, xxxiv–xxxvi, xl–xliv, n.)See, too, *Englische Studien*, LVIII (1924), pp. 374–89.

10 Fol. 49[a]; *Archiv*, pp. 363–64.

11 'Oft like a winged spider, I am entangled in a new-spun web.' So he wrote Dr. Estlin (*Estlin Letters*, p. 81)—adding: 'By the bye, there is no such creature'—and the parable is apt.

12 For the complicated history of 'The Destiny of Nations,' see *Poems*, I, 131; Campbell, *Poems*, pp. 584–86. 'Joan of Arc' was published in 1796, and Coleridge's revision of his part in it belongs to the same year. Lamb's references to the Hymns are dated June and October, 1796, and early February, 1797 (*Works*, VI, 27, 53, 91–92), and in the letter of June 13, 1796, apropos of 'Joan of Arc,' he writes: 'I conjecture it [your own image of melancholy] is "disbranched" from one of your embryo "hymns." '

13 *Poems*, I, 133, ll. 36–52.

14 *Joan of Arc*, Bk. II, ll. 38–52. For Coleridge's note on

these lines in a copy of *Sibylline Leaves* formerly belonging to Sir Montagu Stuart Samuel, (now to Mr. H. T. Butler), see Garnett, pp. 304–05.

15 *Letters*, I, 378.

16 Campbell, *Poems*, p. 585. The unpublished letter from which Campbell quotes is now in the Norton Perkins Collection in the Harvard College Library. The phrases before the italicized quotation in 2. should read: 'but *so* lovely!—and in love, moreover!'—not, 'in love, more dear,' as it is printed. The quarto referred to by Campbell is (as he says) amusingly described in the *North British Review*, XL (1864), 79–84, where Coleridge's racy and caustic comments on Southey's style still make excellent reading. For another note in (apparently) this same quarto, see B. L. (1847), II, 31; *Works*, III, 386–87.

17 *Poems*, I, 140, ll. 278–93.

18 Campbell, *Poems*, p. 585; *Poems*, I, 140, n.

19 Ll. 123–30.

20 Hazlitt, *Works*, XII, 261. 'He sends well-feathered thoughts straight forward to the mark with a twang of the bow-string'; so Coleridge wrote in his turn of Hazlitt, in the consummate portrait of 1803 (B. E., I, 283).

21 A. P., p. 46; cf. pp. 66–67, above.

22 Ll. 129–30.

23 Cook, *Voyage to the Pacific Ocean*, II, 257. See above, p. 46.

24 Let us pause for a moment, and take our bearings. Few human beings, I take it, have ever pondered more deeply than Coleridge the mysterious 'goings-on' of their own minds, and few who so pondered ever had, perhaps, such complex workings to explore, or such lynx-like intellect with which to track them. And had he been writing expressly about the hints from colour and motion which gave being to these lines, he could scarcely have spoken more directly to the point than in three passages, every one dealing with 'ocular spectra,' which I shall quote. The first is from the acute diagnosis in *The Friend* of the psychology of Luther's famous adventure with the devil and the inkstand. 'It would appear incredible,' Coleridge says, 'to persons not accustomed to these subtle notices of self-observation, what small and remote resemblances, *what mere hints of likeness from some real external object, especially if the shape be aided by colour*, will suffice to make a vivid thought consubstantiate with the real object, and derive from it an outward perceptibility' (*Works*, II, 136). In its essentials, that might have been written of 'The Ancient Mariner.' So might this: 'Influence of mere colour, influence of shape—

wonderful coalescence of scattered colours at distances, and, then, all going to some one shape, and the modification!' But that is the upshot of his minute analysis, jotted down in a note book with scientific accuracy at the moment, of a vivid ocular illusion of his own (A. P., p. 124; cf. pp. 45–46, and *Works*, II, 130–31). And if the amazing faculty which the brightly coloured, moving animalculæ exhibit, of attracting and annexing other images, should still strain even poetic faith to the breaking point, let us hear Coleridge again: 'It is a well known fact,' he wrote in the *Biographia Literaria, 'that bright colours in motion* both make and leave the strongest impressions on the eye. *Nothing is more likely too, than that a vivid image or visual spectrum, thus originated, may become the link of association in recalling the feelings and images that had accompanied the original impression*' (B. L., II, 109–10). Coleridge is generalizing from his own imaginative experience; we are resolving that same experience into its elements. And the analysis and the generalizations agree.

25 *Opticks*, p. 572. See above, pp. 38–42.

26 *Phil. Trans.* (Jones's Abridgment), V, Pt. II, 215. See above, pp. 40–41.

27 *Ibid.*, p. 214; *Opticks*, p. 572.

28 *Phil Trans.* (Jones's Abridgment), V, Pt. II, 201–13.

29 *Poems*, I, 168, l. 142.

30 *Phil. Trans.* (as above), p. 206.

31 Philip Quarll's hermit saw in a dream 'the clouds pouring down vast streams of liquid fire, and the raging ocean all in flames'; 'the sea . . . he imagined was *like a caldron of oil in a blaze*'; and 'he saw a horrid frightful monster . . . rush from the boiling flames' (*The Hermit*, p. 118). That flaming ocean must have left a lurid mark upon a sensitive, six-year-old mind, and it is not impossible that the later picture may owe a dash of its vividness to the unconscious persistence of a childish impression.

32 *Opticks*, p. 575.

33 A. P., p. 88 (italics Coleridge's). See also *Works*, III, 712. Coleridge was not the only member of his circle whose fancy had been caught by the experiments in the phenomena of phosphorescence. John Thelwall, in a letter dated 15 Feb., 1797 (now in the Norton Perkins collection in the Harvard College Library), uses the phrase: 'as superior . . . as the noontide sun to the twinkling of a stinking mackerel in the dark.'

34 *Opticks*, p. 576.

35 Martens, p. 32.

36 Purchas, II, 349.

37 Πέλαγος, p. 277.

38 *Macbeth*, I, iii, 32–34.

39 *Ibid.*, I, iii, 18–25.

40 He had met with it very early indeed. For there is a pleasant description of it in Philip Quarll: 'But the wind and rain abating, we observed, to our great joy, a corpus sanct at the top of our spindle: these corpus sancts are good signs wnen seen aloft; but bad omens and denote a great storm, when seen on the decks. It is a small glimmering light, like a star, when aloft; but when on deck, it appears like a glow worm' (*The Hermit*, p. 46). But as Daniel Pell, 'Preacher of the Word,' observes in his Πέλαγος (London, 1659): 'what it is, or from whence it comes, or whither it goes, none can well tell' (p. 271). Among other accounts (some of them delightfully naïve) which Coleridge might have seen are these: Churchill, *Collection of Voyages*, I, 293; II, I, 526; Linschoten (Hakluyt Soc., 1888), II, 238–39; Pigafetta, *The Vyage rounde about the Worlde* (Arber, *The first Three English books on America*, p. 250): 'leapynge from one [cable] to an other with a certeyne flutterynge noyse lyke byrdes'; Cardanus, *De Subtilitate*, Bk. II (*Opera*, 1663, III, 377); Hakluyt, *Principal Navigations* IX, 345–46; Purchas, II, 86, 351; Sir Thomas Herbert, *Some*

Yeares Travels into Africa and Asia the Great (3d edition, 1677), p. 11; Dampier (ed. Masefield), I, 410; A. F. Frézier, *A Voyage to the South Sea* (1717), pp. 37, 39; M. Adanson, *A Voyage to Senegal* (1759), p. 102; Ulloa, *Voyage to South America* (2d edition, 1760), II, 350. But almost all the ancient Mariners made note of the dancing fires. Coleridge had also, doubtless, read what Burton has to say about these apparitions in the *Anatomy* (Part. I, Sect. II, Memb. I, Subsect. II). But he could not read, as we can, the chapter on 'The Candles' (CXIX) in *Moby-Dick*.

Many examples from other narratives (especially French) are quoted, with notes on the curious lore connected with the apparition, in *Mélusine*, II, 112–17, 255, 382; IV, 116, 381; VIII, 214–15. See also Sébillot, *Légendes, Croyances et Superstitions de la Mer* (1886), II, 87–109; Bassett, *Legends and Superstitions of the Sea and of Sailors* (1885), pp. 302–20.

For a picture of the dancing fires, see the frontispiece of this book, and its accompanying pages (569–74) in Erasmus Francisci, *Der Wunder-reiche Ueber-zug unserer Nider-Welt. Oder Erd-umgebende Lufft-Kreys*, Nürnberg, 1680.

41 Purchas, XIX, ll. Compare *Tempest*, I, ii, 196–201:

. . . now on the beak,

Now in the waist, the deck, in every cabin,

I flam'd amazement. Sometime I'd divide,

And burn in many places. On the topmast,

The yards and bowsprit, would I flame distinctly,

Then meet and join.

See also Charles Mills Gayley, *Shakespeare and the Founders of Liberty in America* (1917), pp. 56–58.

42 Churchill, II, 388.

43 'Ode to the Departing Year' (written December 24–26, 1796), ll. 58–59 (*Poems*, I, 163; cf. 160, n.).

44 *Opticks*, p. 575.

45 *Ibid.*, p. 576.

46 *Ibid.*, pp. 579–80.

47 *Ibid*,., p. 580.

48 *Ibid.*, pp. 583–84.

49 'The death-fires danced' is obviously reminiscent of his own 'danced, like death-fires' in the 'Ode to the Departing Year' (see n. 43, above). And William Taylor's. translation of

Bürger's 'Lenore' (see above, pp. 335–36), may also have lent a moulding touch to the lines:

> *Look, look up*, an airy crcwe
>
> *In roundel daunces reele.*

50 B. L., I, 78–79.

51 *Ibid.*, p. 79.

52 'Whenever we feel several objects at the same time, the *impressions* that are left . . . are linked together. Whenever therefore any one of the movements, which constitute a complex impression, is renewed through the senses, the others succeed mechanically' (B. L., I, 69; italics Coleridge's). Far more to the point is such an actual occurrence as I have recorded on pp. 269–70, above.

53 Ll. 123–26.

54 *Phil. Trans.* (Jones's Abridgment), V, Pt. II, 214; *Opticks*, p. 576.

55 See above, pp. 48–49.

56 *Voyage to the Pacific Ocean*, II, 257.

57 Martens, *Voyage*, pp. 168–75 (chap. XII).

58 *Ibid.*, p. 170.

59 *Ibid.*, p. 171.

60 *Ibid.*, pp. 171–72.

61 *Ibid.*, p. 173.

62 *Ibid.*, pp. 174–75.

63 *Ibid.*, p. 170.

64 L. 238 ('And a *thousand thousand* slimy things') reads, in L. B. 1798, 1800: 'And a *million million* slimy things.' I ran across the phrase 'million million' in one of the voyagers; lost my note; and have been unable to find the passage again in the 'wide, wild wilderness' of the travel-books. Coleridge used it once more (this time too in connection with the ocean) in a striking note (A. P., p. 84) written at Malta in 1804.

If Coleridge cancelled his 'million million' in L. B. 1798 (l. 230) through fear of exaggeration, his scruples were unfounded. Adam White, in his note on Martens's 'Slime Fish like a Fountain' (*A Collection of Documents on Spitzbergen and Greenland*, ed. Hakluyt Soc., pp. 169 ff.), quotes from Scoresby's account (*Arctic Regions*, I, 179) of the medusæ in the seas about Spitzbergen: "The number of medusæ . . . was found to be immense. . . . In this proportion, a cubic inch of water must contain 64; a cubic foot, 110,592; a cubic fathom 23,887,882; and a cubical mile about 23,888,000,000,000,000!'

For notes on the 'Snail Slime-Fish,' the 'Rose-like-shaped Slime-fish,' the 'Slime Fish like a Cap,' and the 'Slime-fish like a Fountain,' see *A Collection*, etc., pp. 134–39 (footnotes), 166, 169.

65 Martens, p. 119. There is a more matter-of-fact description of these same creatures, of 'a fatty, trainy, oily Substance'—some, as in Martens, 'of the Shape of a Spider'—in [Henry Elking], *A View of the Greenland Trade* (1722), p. 24; reprinted in Lord Overstone's *Select Collection of Scarce and Valuable Economical Tracts*, Last Series, 75–76.

66 Purchas, II, 208.

67 B. L., II, 12.

68 Cook, *Voyage to the Pacific Ocean*, II, 257.

69 Ll. 267–71. The second line in L. B. 1798 reads: 'Like morning frosts yspread.' See above, pp. 203–04. The sea (it is at least worth mentioning) is twice 'red as blood' in *The Hermit*—once in a calm near the Line (p. 45), and once in a violent storm (p. 46). And Dorothy Wordsworth notes in her Alfoxden *Journal*, January 23, 1798 (I, 4), that the sea was 'of a gloomy red,' as Coleridge himself may well a dozen

times have seen it. But the immediate conjunction of the stanza with the colours of the water-snakes, together with the whole linked complex of associations, fixes the *determining* suggestion of this particular 'red.' And no one, I think, will accuse me of assuming that any one of Coleridge's impressions was an unblended entity.

70 B. L., I, 86.

71 A. P., p. 206.

72 B. L., II, 120.

73 A. P., p. 55.

74 Baudelaire, *Œuvres posthumes*, Crépet, p. 301. Quoted in Albert Cassagne, *La Théorie de l'Art pour l'Art en France* (Paris, 1906), p. 419, n.

CHAPTER VI

1 See, for *Joan of Arc, Poems*, I, 131, 136, n.; *Letters*, I, 149; cf. 192, 206; Southey, *Life and Correspondence*, I, 184, 197, 214, 243–45; Cottle, *Recollections*, I, 228–30; *Reminiscences*, pp. 97–98; Haller, *The Early Life of Southey* (1917), pp. 96–97. For *Robespierre*, see *Poems*, II, 495; Southey, *Life and Correspondence*, I, 217.

2 *Letters*, I, 117 (italics Coleridge's); *Poems*, I, 86.

3 *Poems*, II, 518; B. E., I, 140, 157; T. P., I, 229–31.

4 *Poems*, I, 133–35.

5 See above, pp. 13, 34–36.

6 See above, p. 36.

7 Crantz, I, 28. Goldsmith quotes the passage—'with a very few alterations,' which amount to a rewriting!—in *Animated Nature* (2d ed., 1779, I, 246–47). But we know from the notes to the 'Destiny of Nations' that Coleridge was drawing directly on Crantz. See also above, p. 101.

8 *Poems*, I, 136, n.

9 *Poems*, II, 551 (Act III, ll. 31–35).

10 *Joan of Arc*, Bk. II, l. 98; cf. 'Destiny of Nations,' l. 98 (*Poems*, I, 135).

11 *Poems*, I, 133–34, ll. 60–80.

12 Lamb, *Works*, VI, 14.

13 Lamb, *Works*, VI, 61, 273. Other Salutation reminiscences may be found in *Works*, VI, 16, 29–30, 74, 88, 103, 107; cf. *Letters*, ed. Hazlitt, II, 148. For a pleasant picture of Coleridge 'over [his] fourth or fifth jorum, chirping about

old school occurrences,' see Lamb, *Works*, VI, 162.

14 *Poems*, I, 86.

15 See above, p. 479, n. 46.

16 Like less opulent mortals, Coleridge not infrequently made a phrase do double duty. See, for example, 'Mother of wildly-working visions' (*Poems*, I, 5, 43); 'wildering fires' (*Letters*, I, 118, 126); 'hunger-bitten baby' (*ibid.*, I, 191, 207); 'faint and rayless hope' (*ibid.*, I, 92, 123); 'laborious polish' (B. E., I, 112, 130); etc.

17 Crantz, I, 202. Compare Hearne, p. 346, n.: 'The idea which the Southern Indians have of this meteor [the aurora] is equally romantic . . . as they believe it to be the spirits of their departed friends dancing in the clouds; and when the *Aurora Borealis* is remarkably bright . . . they say, their deceased friends are very merry'; Egede, pp. 161–62: 'Thus (they'll tell you) the Deceased play at Foot-ball in Heaven, with the Head of a Morse, when it lightens, or the North-light (*Aurora Borealis*) appears, which they fancy to be the Souls of the Deceased.'

18 Maupertuis, p. 88. Brandl reads the first word as 'Nurture.'

19 Fol. 16[a]; *Archiv*, p. 349.

20 See especially Burnet, T. T., II, 47–48; S. T., II, 56 ff., on the sun and the central fires as the two sources of the earth's heat. See below, pp. 502–03.

21 The phrase is Coleridge's. See *Miscellanies*, pp. 251–52.

22 Darwin, *Botanic Garden* (1791), Pt. I, Additional Notes, p. 11 (Note VI).

23 Fol. 17[a]; *Archiv*, p. 349. See detailed note, p. 502, n. 28, below.

24 *Botanic Garden* (1791), Pt. I, note I, Additional Notes, p. 3. Cf. pp. 4–5, in which Darwin discusses Franklin's theory that the aurora is an *electrical* phenomenon.

25 *Ibid.*, Canto I, l. 178.

26 See pp. 34–36, above.

27 See p. 464, n. 80, above.

28 See pp. 189–90, above.

29 Fol. 16[b]; *Archiv*, p. 349. Brandl misreads 'succession' as 'specifier.'

30 B. E., II, 211.

31 Fol. 25[b]; *Archiv*, p. 354.

32 *Letters*, I, 164; see p. 473, n. 13, above.

33 See p. 159 (and notes) above.

34 Maupertuis, p. 78.

35 *Ibid.*, p. 88.

36 L. 63.

37 See *Poems*, I, 143, n. (on ll. 339–40); cf. *Joan of Arc*, Bk. II, l. 149.

38 Maupertuis, p. 102.

39 See above, p. 95.

40 *Poems*, II, 496 (ll. 30–31).

41 *Ibid.*, I, 133, ll. 65–66.

42 *Poems*, I, 133, l. 70.

43 A. P., p. 3.

44 Maupertuis, pp. 55–57; Thomson, 'Winter,' notes on ll. 875–76.

45 Bersch (p. 76, n. 5; cf. p. 75, n. 3), mentions the fact

that Niemi lake is in Maupertuis and Thomson, but has not gone on to investigate Maupertuis, on the chance that Coleridge had read him.

46 Purchas, XIII, 35–162.

47 *Poems*, I, 148, ll. 470–74.

48 Coleridge, B. L., I, 202. Compare *Lectures*, p. 220.

49 Wordsworth, Preface to *Poems*, ed. 1815, I, xxxiii.

50 My heresy now finds aid and comfort (some years after the paragraph above was written) in the 'Note on Fancy and Imagination' in Lascelles Abercrombie, *The Idea of Great Poetry* (London, 1925), pp. 52–58. Professor Abercrombie approaches the problem by another path, but the conclusion which he arrives at (p. 58), is the same:

> Now, the faculty of fancy does not exist: it is one of Coleridge's chimeras, of which he kept a whole stable. Fancy is nothing but a degree of imagination: and the degree of it concerns, not the quality of the imagery, but the quality and force of the emotion symbolized by the imagery.

And compare Professor H. W. Garrod's reference (*Wordsworth:*

Lectures and Essays, Oxford, 1923, p. 145, n.), to 'the famous, but useless, distinction . . . between the imagination and the fancy.'

51 B. L., I, 115–19.

52 *Ibid.*, I, 119–20. 'The Essay on Fasting I am ashamed of,' wrote Coleridge twice (B. E., I, 66, 72).

53 *Letters*, I, 176. The unexpurgated passage is quoted above, p. 454, n. 24. 'Look you, master poet,' wrote Lamb to Coleridge in February, 1797 (*Works*, VI, 92), 'I have remorse as well as another man, and my bowels can sound upon occasion.'

54 See Coleridge's letter to Thelwall of Dec. 17, 1796 (*Letters*, I, 206, cf. 192), and Lamb's letters of Feb. 5 and Feb. 13, 1797 (*Works*, VI, 89 ff., 95 ff.). Compare Cottle, *Recollections*, I, 228–32; II, 241–62, and see also Coleridge, *Poems*, I, 131, where these references are given.

55 See *Poems*, II, 559. Voltaire's lines are written in the margin of MS. II, 'a contemporary transcript sent by Coleridge to a friend' (*Poems*, II, 518), now in the Norton Perkins Collection in the Harvard College library. The quotation consists of lines 96–99 and 104–07 of the *Désastre*, and is not quite correct. 'Souffert' in the third line should be 'soufferts,' and 'Sous' in the eighth line should be 'Tous.'

56 Southey protested vehemently that he had never been guilty of reading *La Pucelle*. 'So you abuse Anna St. Ives,' he writes Bedford, July 17, 1796, 'and commend the Pucelle of the detestable Voltaire. Now, Grosvenor, it was not I who said, "I *have not* read that book";—*I* said—God be thanked that I did say it, and plague take the boobies who mutilated it in my absence,—I said, "I have *never been guilty* of reading the Pucelle of Voltaire" ' (*Life and Correspondence*, I, 283; italics Southey's). There is more, but that is enough.

57 See Cottle, *Recollections*, I, 230.

58 Lamb, *Works*, VI, 89.

59 Cottle, *Recollections*, I, 230.

60 *Poems*, I, 137, ll. 148–53.

61 *Ibid.*, I, 138, ll. 195–217.

62 Lamb, *Works*, VI, 96. The italics are Lamb's.

63 *The Watchman*, p. 200.

64 *Ibid.*, p. 200.

65 Lamb, *Works*, VI, 90.

66 *The Watchman*, pp. 201–02.

67 *Ibid.*, p. 202. Professor Legouis (*La Jeunesse de William Wordsworth*, Paris, 1896, p. 354; *The Early Life of William Wordsworth*, London and N.Y., 1921, p. 342) was not aware of these facts when he suggested that this passage in the 'Destiny of Nations' was 'inspirée par le précédent passage de *Crime et Chagrin*' ('Guilt and Sorrow,' stanzas lxi–lxiii).

68 See above, p. 223.

69 *Letters*, I, 181.

Mottoes, Book II. **Πέλαγος** *Nec inter Vivos, nec inter Mortuos, Neither Amongst the living, nor amongst the Dead. Or, an Improvement of the Sea* . . . By Daniel Pell, Preacher of the Word (London, printed for Livewell Chapman, 1659) is an excessively rare and (as its title would lead one to guess) an almost unbelievably quaint and delectable little book. The lines I have quoted are on p. 189.

The passage from *Moby-Dick* will be found in chap. CXI.

CHAPTER VII

1 'It is a false and feverous state for the Centre to *live* in the Circumference,' wrote Coleridge once (B. E., II, 260). The italics are mine, but with or without them the remark (waiving mathematical misgivings) is profoundly true. That, however,

is a very different matter from the point we are considering.

2 Sir Arthur Quiller-Couch, *Studies in Literature* (First Series, Cambridge, 1919), p. 17, n. 1.

3 Furness, *Variorum, The Tempest* (1892), pp. 308–15; C. M. Gayley, *Shakespeare and the Founders of Liberty in America* (New York, 1917), pp. 40–76; etc.

4 In the heart of Asia lies the huge and sinister desert of Lop or Gobi. It had been traversed from even Chinese time immemorial by one of the mysterious ancient trade-routes stretching dimly into Central Asia, the long lost and recently rediscovered Kan-Suh imperial highway between the Orient and the West. Six hundred years ago Marco Polo crossed, on the road to Cathay, the phantom-haunted sands of Gobi by this very highway. And Marco Polo's travels found a place in *Purchas His Pilgrimes*. And Milton, like Coleridge, was a diligent reader of Purchas, as his Commonplace Book attests. One thing which Milton read of the Desert of Lop was this: 'They say that there dwell many spirits which cause great and mervailous Illusions to Travellers to make them perish. For if any stay behind that he cannot see his company, he shall be called by name, and so going out of the way is lost . . . Consorts of Musicall Instruments are sometimes heard in the Ayre' (Purchas, XI, 216). And it was those goblin voices from the uncanny borders of the Mongol world which were transmuted

into quintessential poetry, as the Lady in 'Comus' speaks, lost and alone in the wood at night:

> A thousand fantasies
>
> Begin to throng into my memory,
>
> Of calling shapes, and beckoning shadows dire,
>
> And airy tongues that syllable men's names
>
> On sands and shores and desert wildernesses.

But the Desert of Lop has a longer poetical history. Two and a half centuries before Milton's day vagrant rumours of its terrible sand-waves flowing like the sea and of a black lake, the Kara-nor, beside it, had drifted back to England along the trade-routes, and Chaucer pointed a telling climax to his rehearsal of a lady's dealings with her lovers by a reference to the remote and perilous sea, which was yet no veritable sea, off at the outposts of *his* world. John Keats, too, read or heard somewhere (I wish I knew just where) about the Desert of Gobi, flanked by a mountain with 'a fan-shap'd burst of blood-red, arrowy fire.' And he weaves it into that startling anticipation of modern aërial navigation, the flight through the air of Crafticant and the Princess in 'Cap and Bells.' The Desert of Lop would seem on the whole to be a somewhat intractable morsel for the imagination to assimilate. Yet at the hands of three great poets—Chaucer, Milton, and Keats—it has undergone, in varying degrees, incorporation with the stuff of poetry. And I have given it a moment here as a striking comment on the theme of this chapter and of the book. References for many of the statements made above will be found in my article on 'The Dry Sea and the Carrenare,' *Modern Philology*, III, 1–46. See also Todd's notes on 'Comus,' ll. 205–09.

5 Rainaud, *Le Continent Austral* (Paris, 1893), p. 201.

6 *Ibid.*, pp. 29, 200.

7 *Ibid.*, p. 29. There is an account of the 'alveus Oceani' in Burnet, T. T., I, 76. See too the graphic description in the English rendering, S. T., I, 124 ff.

8 Santarem, *Recherches*, p. xxxvi, n. 2.

9 Rainaud, p. 140; Santarem, *Histoire*, II, 174, 181, 195, etc.

10 Santarem, *Histoire*, II, 195. So in a mappemonde in a 10th century MS. of Priscian in the British Museum (Santarem, *Atlas*, Paris, 1842–53, sheet 2): 'ut . . . in circuitu orbis mare currat quod calore vel frigore est intransmeabilis.'

11 Santarem, *Histoire*, II, 195.

12 Santarem, *Histoire*, II, 201; Rainaud, p. 161. In Burnet's *Telluris Theoria Sacra*, I, 221–23 (cf. *Sacred Theory*, I, 250–54), there is discussed the view of some of the ancient fathers that this *Zona torrida*, 'inhabitabilis et impermeabilis' (T. T., I, 214), is the flaming sword which barred access to Paradise—a Paradise situated in the austral world (I, 217). Compare also p. 472, n. 12, above.

13 Nordenskiöld, *Periplus* (Stockholm, 1897), p. 61. From a map of Johannes Leardus, 1448. Compare Santarem, *Histoire*, III, 429; II, 121; Rainaud, p. 199, n. 2.

14 Santarem, *Atlas*, sheet 6, no. 3. Compare Santarem, *Histoire*, II, 196.

15 Rainaud, p. 133; Santarem, *Histoire*, I, 27. In the account of the Antichthones (Burnet, T. T., I, 213–17) to which reference has already been made (see Note 12, above), this saying is ascribed to St. Clement on the authority of Origen: '. . . eorum quos' **Αντιχθονας** Græci nominant, atque illius parties Orbis terræ ad quam neque nostrorum quisquam accedere potest, neque ex illis qui ibi sunt quisquam transire ad nos' (T. T., I, 216).

16 Santarem, *Histoire*, I, 80–81. On the whole subject of the Antichthones, see Rainaud's masterly discussion, *Le Continent Austral*, pp. 135–67.

17 Santarem, *Atlas*, sheet 5, no. 5 (Dijon, 11th cent.).

18 Zürich, 1560.

19 Ordo XII (De Cetis), pp. 165–82.

20 See Bevan and Phillott, pp. 40–43 (Note 24, below).

21 F. Q., Bk. II, canto xii, stanzas 23–24.

22 For a fascinating paragraph (with references) on the haunted seas, see Rainaud, p. 165. On the *mer betée*, see *Mod. Philol.*, III, 43–44) esp. 43, n 5.

23 It is described, with full detail, in Santarem, *Histoire*, III, 1–60.

24 For a full description see Santarem, *Histoire*, II, 288–434; and especially Bevan and Phillott, *Mediæval Geography, An Essay in illustration of the Hereford Mappa Mundi* (London and Hereford, 1873). The last is designed as a guide to the great lithographed facsimile of the Hereford map, and is an enormously interesting little book. I know of nothing (short of the maps themselves) which will more quickly disclose the secret of the fascination exerted by mediæval cartography.

25 Santarem, *Histoire*, III, 41.

26 *Ibid.*; see also Bevan and Phillott, pp. 93, 103–04.

27 Santarem, *Histoire*, III, 41.

28 *Ibid.* See also Bevan and Phillott, pp. 102, 37–38. Harris observes in a passage which, for its stout incredulity, I wish I could quote at length: 'No Traveller can make us believe, that, under the Torrid Zone, there are a Nation, every Man of which has one large flat Foot, with which, lying upon his Back, he covers himself from the Sun' (l, 336). 'Maister *Mendax*' in William Bullein's *Dialogue* (pp. 98–99; see Note 39, below) had no such doubts.

29 Santarem, *Histoire*, III, 42; see also Bevan and Phillott, p. 104.

30 Santarem, *Histoire*, III, 42.

31 *Ibid.*; Bevan and Phillott, p. 103.

32 Santarem, *Histoire*, III, 43.

33 *Ibid.*; see Bevan and Phillott, p. 101.

34 Santarem, *Histoire*, III, 43–44; Bevan and Phillott, p. 102. Few of the old cartographers whose maps are so often the repository of the illustrated fiction of their day, take one more engagingly into their confidence than John Speed, 'Mercatorum Scissorum frater, Terrarum nostrarum . . . elegantissimus delineator.' And Speed, like Harris (see Note 28, above), had

moments when his faith was dry. For on his map of Tartary, in the larger 1631 edition, near the head of the river Ob, appears the breathless legend: 'Pliny placeth the Perosites here whom hee saith to be so narrow mouthed that they live only by the Smel of rost meat beleeve it not.' I have cribbed this note from an article of my own, *Mod. Philol.*, III, 16, n. 3.

35 Santarem, *Histoire*, I, 42–43.

36 *Ibid.*, III, 58–59; Bevan and Phillott, pp. 106–08.

37 Bevan and Phillott, p. 108.

38 I have barely touched on the wealth of Santarcm's and Rainaud's volumes. Perhaps, however, the little which was all my purpose warranted is enough to give some hint of their absorbing interest.

39 The mermaids were among the last to go. Columbus saw them. For his son relates (Churchill, II, 485) that 'in his book of his first voyage, he says, "He saw some mermaids on the coast of Menegueta, but that they are not so like ladies, as they are painted" '—a remark as pregnant as it is diverting. Then there was the mermaid—who might still have sat for the portrait of a lady—whom two of Henry Hudson's men saw beyond the North Cape in 1608 (Purchas, XIII, 318): 'This morning, one of our companie looking over boord saw a Mermaid, and calling up some of the companie to see her,

one more came up, and by that time shee was come close to the ships side, looking earnestly on the men: a little after, a Sea came and overturned her: from the Navill upward, her backe and breasts were like a womans, (as they say that saw her) her body as big as one of us; her skin very white; and long haire hanging downe behind, of colour blacke: in her going downe they saw her tayle, which was like the tayle of a Porposse, and speckled like a Macrell. Their names that saw her were Thomas Hilles and Robert Rayner'—and what more can we ask? There was also the earnest-eyed Merman who rose from the waters of the Rappahannock in Virginia as Mr. Thomas Glover, 'an ingenious Chirurgion,' sat at the stern of his sloop reading a small book which he took out of his pocket—a book which, were it not for the 'small,' one might surmise to have been Purchas! 'His skin,' says the ingenious Mr. Glover, 'was tawny, much like that of an *Indian;* the figure of his head was pyramidal, and slick, without hair; his eyes large and black, and so were his eye-brows; his mouth very wide, with a broad, black streak on the upper lip, which turned upwards at each end like mustachoes; his countenance was grim and terrible . . . he seemed to stand with his eyes fixed on me for some time, and afterward dived downe'—and his exit was like that of Hudson's mermaid. All this is soberly recorded in the *Philosophical Transactions*, XI (1676), 625, and repeated in part in Lowthorpe's *Abridgment*, III, 567. It is not at all in the same category as (for example) the testimony of that beguiling 'maister *Mendax*' in William Bullein's *Dialogue against the Feuer Pestilence* (1564; ed. Bullen, 1888, from the edition of 1578, E. E. T. S., Pt. I, p. 98, cf. pp. 94 ff.), who 'telleth newes from Terra Florida' and 'semeth a pretie scholer,' and who avers that 'In the isle called Rue . . . I did see Marmaides and Satyres with other fishes by night, came fower miles from the sea, and climed into trees, and did eat dates and nutmegges.'

Time would fail to tell of the merman and the mermaid who wept for each other when separated by the tide on the coast of Africa (Thevet, p. 28), or of the mermaid whom Father Jerom Merolla da Sorrento saw, in 1682, in the River Zaire in the Congo (Churchill, I, 540)—where Captain Nathaniel Uring, in *A History of* [*his*] *Voyages and Travels* (p. 65), also tells of them as late as 1726—or of that described among other monsters in Egede, p. 86. And if this be regarded as a digression (which I fear it partly is), I can only point out that the water-snakes fall into a long, long line of strange creatures seen by mariners over the side of a ship.

40 The *résumé* which follows is drawn from a good many sources. A fuller summary, with ample references, may be found in Rainaud, pp. 185–474.

CHAPTER VIII

1 Ll. 79–82.

2 He had already used the device in *Osorio*. See Act I, ll. 139–40, and stage direction (*Poems*, II, 524–25).

3 Ll. 25–32.

4 This detail too, of course, is true to the typical voyage around the Horn. Shelvocke writes, on the page before Captain Hatley's albatross appears: 'The winds reigning thus tempestuously, without intermission, in the Western board, we were driven into the Latitude of 61 deg. 30 min. of South Latitude' (p. 71), But Coleridge met with the common experience in many another book. Anson (*Voyage round the World*, 1748, p. 125) uses the Mariner's word, with reference to currents of air 'which sweep with an impetuous and irregular *blast* round Cape Horn.'

5 Ll. 83–86. The second line reads in L. B. 1798: 'And broad as a weft upon the left.' See above, pp. 261 ff.

6 *Poems*, I, 269. The Preface to 'The Three Graves' (except the opening paragraph) was first printed in *The Friend*, Sept. 21, 1809 (see *Poems*, I, 267, n. 1; Hutchinson, L. B., p. 257; cf. Campbell, *Poems*, pp. 589–91), and refers back to a period

'somewhat more than twelve years ago.' Coleridge had the second volume of Edwards (the account of the Obi witchcraft is in II, 88–99) out of the Bristol Library July 14–Aug. 7, 1795 (*Mod. Philol.*, XXI, 319). It has not been observed, so far as I know, that he made definite use of this volume in Book II of *Joan of Arc*, which was published in 1796. The passage in point (with its note) was taken over unchanged into 'The Destiny of Nations,' ll. 442–47, and is readily accessible there (*Poems*, I, 146):

As when the mad Tornado bellows through
The guilty islands of the western main,
Eboe, or Koromantyn's plain of palms,
The infuriate spirits of the murdered make
Fierce merriment, and vengeance ask of Heaven.

Coleridge found Eboe and Koromantyn in Edwards, II, 51–52, 63–76, 85–87 (the account of the Obi witchcraft begins on p. 88), etc. And he twice used, almost *verbatim*, Edwards's phrases. 'Koromantyn's plain of palms' (1. 445), is from a youthful poem of Edwards ('Ode on Seeing a Negro-Funeral'), quoted on pp. 86–87: 'On Koromantyn's palmy soil.' And the phrase in the footnote (which is Note Ninth in *Joan of Arc*): 'The Slaves in the West-India Islands consider Death as a passport to their native country,' is Edwards's: 'the Negroes consider death . . . as a passport to the place of their nativity' (p. 85). Coleridge continues: 'The Sentiment is thus expressed in the Introduction to a Greek Prize Ode on the Slave-Trade,' and the pertinent lines of the Ode (which is printed in full in Campbell, *Poems*, pp. 476–77; cf. also pp. 653–54, and *Letters*, I, 43) then follow. The Ode gained the Browne Gold Medal in 1792, and Edwards's work was not published until 1793. Coleridge must, accordingly, have got his information elsewhere in 1792. Long (whose work was published in 1774) has an extensive account of the 'Coromantyns' (II, 445–75), but I find no mention of their belief in death as a passport to their native land. Coleridge could, however, have found it in Vice-Admiral Vernon's *A New History of Jamaica* (London, 1740), pp. 307–08.

7 On the passages in Edwards and Hearne, see further below, p. 553, n. 39. Coleridge owned a copy of Hearne's *Journey* (the Dublin edition of 1796) which is now in the possession of Dr. James B. Clemens. It contains in Coleridge's hand a long note on pp. 343–45, which gives evidence of the care with which he had read the volume. He seems to have recalled this note in *Aids to Reflection*, Aphorisms on Spiritual Religion, XXIII, Comment (p. 346, note).

8 Edwards, I, 107.

9 Coleridge, of course, knew his Herodotus (see p. 592, n. 96), and might have recalled the passage independently. But here it is, in italics, with its application pointed out, in a book which we know him to have read. The parallel with Herodotus (but not by way of Edwards) has been noted by Sykes (p. 189). See also Eden (ed. Arber), p. 348.

10 Ll. 103–04.

11 Purchas, XV, 16–17.

12 *Ibid.*, XV, 22.

13 *Ibid.*, XIV, 433–34.

14 Compare Purchas, XIV, 435: 'the coast of Terra firme, where the Brises are almost perpetuall.' See, in general, Purchas, XIV, 433–38; XV, 12–23; XVII, 67, 150, 152 ('the Brese'); Hakluyt, X, 46, 291, 429; *Phil. Trans.* (Lowthorp's Abridgement), II, 129: 'It is generally known that there are continual Eastern Winds under the Line, which they call Breezes'; etc.

See, too, *The Naturall and Experimentall History of Winds* ('Written in Latine by the Right Honorable Francis Lo: Verulam, Viscount St. Alban, Translated into English by R. G. Gent.,' London, 1653), under 'Generall Windes. To the second Article,' p. 25: 'It is certain, that to those who saile betweene the Tropicks, in a free and open sea, there blowes a constant and setled winde (which the seamen call a *Breeze*) from East to West.' Compare p. 28: 'That the *Breeze* blowes plentifully between the Tropicks, is most certain.' And see further pp. 29–30. The *Historia Naturalis et Experimentalis de Ventis* (Amsterdam, 1662), under 'Venti Generales, Ad Artic. 2,' has (p. 14): '*Brizam* vocant Nautæ'; (p. 16): 'Quod *Briza* illa,'etc.; and (p. 17) *passim*.

15 This is the reading of L. B., 1798, 1800. For the change in the second line, and Coleridge's own note on it, see *Poems*, I, 190; Campbell, *Poems*, p. 598. For the bearing of the passage on truth of appearance versus truth of fact, see my *Convention and Revolt in Poetry*, pp. 17–18.

16 *Anatomy of Melancholy*, Part II, Sect. II, Mem. III.

17 Ll. 103–06.

18 Narborough, p. vi. Even in Coleridge's day the same proud assertion was possible: 'We are the first Europeans, and I believe I may add, the first human beings, who have reached this point [in the Southern Seas], where it is probable none will come after us' (Forster, I, 527).

19 Purchas, II, 90.

20 *Works*, ed. Buxton Forman (Glasgow, 1901), IV, 187,

48.

21 B. E., II, 153–54. The whole passage, which I have had to condense, is of uncommon interest.

22 *Letters*, I, 11–12 (italics Coleridge's); cf. B. E., I, 12.

23 The passage which Keats remembered (confusing Balboa with Cortez) is in Robertson, *History of America* (1777), I, 203–04; *Works* (1812), VIII, 286–88. Robertson's *History* was in the school library at Enfield (Charles and Mary Cowden Clarke, *Recollections of Writers*, London, 1878, p. 124).

24 L. 107. 'Not a breath was stirring, *our canvas hung straight down* (*West Indies*, I, 13; see above, p. 162); compare, 'the boats were all towing a-head, and *the sails asleep*' (Hawkesworth, I, 174).

25 Ll. 414–25.

26 James (Hakluyt Soc.), II, 588; Campbell, *Poems*, p. 599. But see also pp. 283 ff., above.

27 See further p. 496, n. 21, below.

28 *Letters*, I, 43.

29 *Ibid.*, I, 360–61. See also T. P., II, 65; Campbell, *Narrative*, 126–27.

30 See Christopher Wordsworth's diary under April 1, 1794 (Wordsworth, *Social Life*, etc., p. 593). For another contemporary expedition into Abyssinia which stirred the keen interest of the group, see *ibid.*, p. 587.

31 *Poems*, I, 119, n.; cf. 108. The same paragraph from Bruce (*Travels*, IV, 557) occurs in a note in the *Botanic Garden* ('Economy of Vegetation,' Canto IV, l. 65). In view of Coleridge's predilection for Darwin's notes, it would be quite reasonable to conjecture that he took Bruce's account of the simoom from the *Botanic Garden*. But a comparison of the two passages shows that Darwin's transcript is loose and inaccurate, whereas Coleridge's is exact. He drew, then, for his quotation directly upon Bruce. But he had, with little question, gone to Bruce (led by his ruling passion) in order to verify Darwin's reference. For his own lines on the simoom are unmistakably reminiscent of the *Botanic Garden*. Darwin's simoom 'rides the *tainted* air' (l. 67); in 'Religious Musings'; 'through the *tainted* noon The Simoom sails' (ll. 268–69). There is much Coleridge in this little incident.

32 *Coleorton*, I, 221. Italics Coleridge's. For Coleridge's parallels with Bruce, see above, pp. 162, 370–74, 397–98.

CHAPTER IX

1 Tait's *Edinburgh Magazine*, Vol. I (1834), p. 511; De Quincey, *Works*, II, 145.

2 *Letters*, I, 236.

3 *Mod. Philol.*, XXI, 320. He had it out again May 31'July 13, 1798 (*ibid.*).

4 See Benyowski's detailed account of the ice in *Memoirs and Travels*, I, 302, 318–27.

5 At the Federal Street Theatre, 28 Oct., 1799. See the clipping in the Robert Gould Shaw Collection (Harvard College Library), volume for 1797–1802, p. 5vo.

6 A. P., p. 37; see below, p. 507, n. 36; above, p. 177.

7 B. E., I, 163–64 (italics Coleridge's). This is the text as Coleridge printed it in *The Friend* (*Works*, II, 336–37). The original (and more graphic) version is in *Letters*, I, 275–76.

8 The following sentence from the letter has a curious interest:

> . . . the *melancholy* undulating *sound* from the skate, *not* without variety; and, when very many are skating

together, the sounds give an impulse to the *icy trees*, and the woods all round the lake *tinkle*.

Compare:

> The leafless *trees* and every *icy* crag
>
> *Tinkled* like iron; while far-distant hills
>
> Into the tumult sent an alien *sound*
>
> Of *melancholy, not* unnoticed . . .

The italics are all mine, except '*tinkle*' in the first passage, which is Coleridge's.

The first is from the skating scene in Coleridge's letter, as it was written at Ratzeburg, Jan. 14, 1799 (*Letters*, I, 276; cf. B. E., I, 164; *Works*, II, 337); the second is from the skating scene at the close of Wordsworth's 'Influence of Natural Objects,' etc., which, as the sub-title states, was 'Written in Germany' (see also Wordsworth *Memoirs*, l, 136–37). Ernest de Selincourt states (*Prelude*, p. 507, note on ll. 468–69) that Coleridge wrote the sentence in the letter 'soon after receiving from D. W. a letter containing this passage.' Recollection was again flowing in upon the impulses of immediate perception.

9 Purchas, XIII, 62. For an account of strange *sounds* 'in the element,' which reminds one startlingly of Caliban's lines in

The Tempest (III, ii, 144–47), and which, indeed, Shakespeare may have read, see Eden and Willes, *The History of Trauayle* (1577), p. 350.

10 If Coleridge read of Barents in the edition of 1609, he saw a counterfeit presentment of the 'strange sight in the Element.' It is reproduced in *The Three Voyages of William Barents* (Hakluyt Soc., 1876), after p. 76, and in this volume opposite p. 138, above. See also p. 156, n., above.

11 Purchas, XIII, 63.

12 Wordsworth, *Memoirs*, I, 108.

13 *Ibid.*, I, 106; see above, p. 222.

14 D. W., *Journal*, I, 14.

15 *Coleorton*, I, 10. Lowell misquotes it (as 'a garment of light') in the passage quoted (in part) on p. 139, above.

16 Purchas, XI, 399.

17 Lowell, *Works* (Standard Library Edition), VI, 75. Quoted by Pelham Edgar in his edition of 'The Ancient Mariner' (New York, 1900), p. 100.

18 Martens, pp. 5–6.

19 *Ibid.*, p. 12. Compare 'But when *the Ice comes floating* on too hard' (*ibid.*, p. 18).

20 Ll. 51–54. The text is that of L. B. 1798.

21 *The Strange and Dangerous Voyage of Captaine Thomas James, in his intended Discovery of the Northwest Passage into the South Sea*, etc., London, 1633, pp. 7, 8, 106, 13. The corresponding pages in the edition of the Hakluyt Society (*Voyages of Foxe and James to the Northwest*, ed. Christy, London, 1894) are Vol. II, pp. 463, 464, 587, 470. The copy of the edition of 1633 now in the Bristol Library was not there in Coleridge's day (*Athenæum*, No. 3254, March 8, 1890, p. 306, col. 3; cf. Ivor James, *The Source of 'The Ancient Mariner*,' Cardiff, 1890, pp. 14–16). But the *Voyage* is included in Harris (II, 406 ff.) and Churchill (II, 407 ff.), and both Harris and Churchill were in the Bristol Library when Coleridge was a subscriber (*Athenæum*, as above). Churchill's *Collection* was also in Wordsworth's library (*Transactions of the Wordsworth Society*, VI, 215, No. 172), and Coleridge refers explicitly to Harris (Paul, *Wm. Godwin*, II, 16). Moreover, the *Strange and Dangerous Voyage* was constantly referred to in books widely read in Coleridge's time. It is quoted frequently, for illustrative purposes, in Robert Boyle, 'The Experimental History of Cold' (*Works*, II, 1744, pp. 262–328); and notice is taken of it in J. R. Forster, *History of the Voyages and Discoveries made in the North* (1786), pp. 367 ff.; in Ellis, pp. 62 ff.; in

Narborough, pp. xxii, xxv; in [Drage], *An Account of a Voyage for the Discovery of a North-west Passage* (1749), II, 27, 161 ff.; etc.

The little book (now very rare) of Mr. Ivor James referred to above is an attempt to show that Captain James's *Voyage* is the chief (indeed almost the only) source of 'The Ancient Mariner.' It is an extremely interesting performance, but fails completely to make its case—as, indeed, any simple explanation of highly complex phenomena is doomed to do. That was recognized at once by the reviewer in the *Athenœum* (No. 3255, March 15, 1890), and in the letter in the preceding number, to which reference has been made. But Mr. James has shown conclusively that Coleridge drew certain details from his ancient townsman's narrative, and some of the passages which I have just quoted in the text are among them. See also Campbell, *Poems*, pp. 595–96, 597–98, 599; Hutchinson, L. B., pp. 211, 216.

Forster in the Antarctic seas passed a mass of ice 'at least as high again as our main-top-gallant-mast head' (*A Voyage round the World*, I, 93); and in Crantz the ice-masses 'often overtop the ship' (I, 33).

22 'The highest colour is delicate blew,' says Martens, 'of the same colour with the blewest Vitriol, somewhat more transparent, yet not so clear as that in our Country' (p. 38);

'You see the Ice under water as deep as you can see. It is all of a blew colour, but the deeper you look the purer blew you see' (*ibid.*, p. 41); 'the fairest blew that can be, is seen in the cracks of these Ice-hills . . . I once saw one of these pieces that was curiously workt and carved, as it were, by the Sea, like a Church with arched Windows and Pillars, the Doors and Windows hung full of Icikles, in the inside thereof I saw the delicatest blew that can be imagined' (*ibid.*, p. 43). 'In some places we saw,' writes Capt. Wood in the same volume, 'high hillocks of blue colour, but all the rest of the Ice very white' (Wood in Narborough, p. 162); 'It was not like other Ice,' writes Gerrit de Veer, 'for it was of a perfect Azure colour like to the Skies' (*Purchas*, XIII, 78); 'The ice is . . . often tinged . . . with a most beautiful sapphirine or rather berylline blue,' says Forster (I, 101); 'of a pale green colour, and some pieces sky-blue,' declares Crantz (I, 26).

23 Halley in Dalrymple, p. 35.

24 Crantz, I, 32. Martens (p. 38) speaks of it as 'of the same colour with the *blewest* Vitriol.'

25 Purchas, XIII, 64.

26 Martens, p. 35.

27 Harris, II, 381. Coleridge refers to a passage in Harris, giving volume and page, in a letter to Godwin of 1800 (Paul,

William Godwin, II, 16).

28 *Voyages of Foxe and James*, II, 556.

29 Purchas, XIV, 322.

30 Dalrymple, p. 35.

31 This phrase (quoted at second hand) sums up the weighty passage in *The Varieties of Religious Experience* (1902), pp. 18–20.

32 Crantz, I, 5.

33 Cook, *Voyage to the Pacific Ocean*, II, 455. See also Foxe, II, 387–88: 'the land lying hid in snow, doth cause a white reflexe in the Ayre all night, as though it were dawning or twi-light.' So [Drage], *An Account of a Voyage for the Discovery of a North-west Passage*, etc. (London, 1748), I, 16: 'an extraordinary bright Whiteness in some Parts of the Sky . . . an Indication of Ice beneath.' See also Forster, I, 101, 108; Phipps, *Voyage*, p. 71; Mallet, *The Excursion* (London, 1798), p. 28.

34 Martens, pp. 17–18.

35 *Ibid.*, p. 20.

36 *Ibid.*, p. 37.

37 Purchas, XIII, 81.

38 *Ibid.*, p. 86.

39 *Ibid.*, p. 93.

40 *Ibid.*, p. 147. Compare Anson, *A True and Impartial Journal*, etc. (London, 1745), p. 95: 'white Clifts, which look like Snow.'

41 There are three beautiful examples of *clift* = *cleft* in Philip Quarll: 'a *clift* in the rock, through which he saw a light' (p. 6; four lines below, it becomes 'the *cleft*'): 'he . . . thought probably it might lie in that *clift* of the rock, into which he was thrown' (p. 126); 'fishes in the *clifts* and holes of the rocks' (p. 207). Capt. Cook (*Voyage to the Pacific Ocean*, I, 87), on the other hand, once 'saw [an albatross] sitting in the *cliff* of a rock.' And the 'ignipotent or salamandrine spirits' of Greenland 'inhabit the *clefts* of the rocks by the sea-side,' which clefts, five lines below, become '*cliffs*' (Crantz, I, 208).

42 Martens, p. 19.

43 *Ibid.*, p. 24.

44 *Ibid.*, p. 20

45 Narborough, p. 189.

46 *Ibid.*, p. 194.

47 Ll. 55–56.

48 See above, p. 136.

49 Benyowski, I, 318–30.

50 Crantz, I, 36.

51 Purchas, XIV, 309, 323, 324, 336; *God's Power and Providence*, etc., pp. 259, 272; Phipps, *Journal*, p. 39 ('the driffs of ice'); Cook, *Voyage to the Pacific Ocean*, II, 456, 464; III, 191, 247; etc.

52 Ll. 57–58. For 'Nor . . . nor' L. B. 1798 has 'Ne. . . . ne.'

53 Purchas, XIII, 129.

54 Shelvocke, p. 72. See below, p. 530, n. 18.

55 Purchas, XIV, 310.

56 Hakluyt, IV, 124.

57 Crantz, I, 20.

58 *The Voyages and Works of John Davis* (Hakluyt Society, 1880), pp. 3–4; cf. Phipps, *Journal*, etc. (London, 1774), p.

108.

59 Hakluyt, IV, 124.

60 Purchas, XIII, 506.

61 *Ibid.*, XIV, 313.

62 *Ibid.*, XIII, 80.

63 Phipps, *Journal*, etc., p. 82. Haydon one day related to Keats some of the experiences of 'young Hoppner, who went with Captain Ross on a voyage of discovery to the Poles' (Keats, *Works*, IV, 192–93). And it is interesting to note how many of the points which Keats recalled from the story to pass on to his brother and sister in his journal letter are the phenomena of the Arctic voyages which had stamped themselves on Coleridge's memory. The passing of the ship through a mass of ice which splits asunder is one of them. See, too, Keats's brief account (*Works*, V, 48) of 'the Panorama of the Ship at the north Pole,' in which he took much pleasure.

64 Purchas, XIII, 99–101. Hutchinson (L. B., pp. 211–12) declares that Coleridge took 'swound' from 'Sir Cauline' in Percy's *Reliques*. Coleridge undoubtedly knew it there (see above, pp. 244, 321); but its conjunction with the noises of polar ice in another book which he also knew, establishes the immediate suggestion.

65 Ll. 59–62, 69–70.

66 *Dichtung und Wahrheit*, Bk. XIII (Weimar ed., Abt. I, bd. 28, p. 221).

67 I suppose I am offering a counsel of perfection, but if there is no other way, I am not at all sure that it is not well worth while to be knocked senseless (within reasonable limits), for the sake of the unique experience of coming to. At all events, nobody who has not come up through those bizarre and sinjster noises is quite competent to catch the powerful suggestion of the simile. As Lamb once wrote of a less advisable experiment: 'Dream not Coleridge, of having tasted all the grandeur and wildness of Fancy, till you have gone mad' (*Works*, VI, 17).

68 Crantz, I, 49; cf. I, 43; II, 258.

69 Martens, p. 24.

70 *Ibid.*, p. 50. See further Egede, p. 57: 'In the Winter Season they are . . . plagued with the Vapour called Frost-Smoak, which when the Cold is excessive, rises out of the Sea as the Smoak out of a Chimney.' This is quoted in Harris, II, 381, and in Goldsmith, *Hist, of the Earth* (1779), I, 386. 'Frost Smoak' is referred to in Ellis, pp. 287, 302; cf. Crantz, I, 43. Coleridge uses the compound 'fog-smoke' again in 'The Destiny of Nations,' l. 185 (*Poems*, I, 138).

71 Martens, p. 3.

72 Purchas, XIII, 144. The good south wind is the turning-point of William Cornelison Schouten's voyage (the sixth circumnavigation of the globe), as it is of the ancient Mariner's, and Coleridge probably read Schouten in his Purchas. Up to, and through, the Straits of Magellan 'for the most part,' writes Schouten, 'we had [like the ancient Mariner] . . . continuall . . . mists, moist and thicke weather, with much haile and snow: whereby wee endured much trouble, miserie and disease.' They passed the Straits, and then 'we hoysed all our sayles, because we entered into a peaceable Sea . . . with . . . a South, and South Southeast wind'; and a little later, 'we set our course North-west . . . *with a good South gale of wind*' (Purchas, II, 246, 248).

73 Ll. 71–78.

74 L. 65 (L. B. 1798).

75 See E. H. Coleridge, *Christabel* (Royal Society of Literature), pp. 61–62.

76 Purchas, II, 88–89, 90–91; Arber, *First Three Books on America*, p. 252. There is another striking passage which it is possible that Coleridge read. It is in *The History of the Life and Actions of Adm. Christopher Columbus*, by his son, chap. xciv (Churchill, II, 587): 'having been now above eight months

at sea . . . what with the heat and moisture of the sea, the bisket was so full of maggots, that, as God shall help me, I saw many that stajed till night to eat the pottage or brewice made of it, that they might not see the maggots.' The rest is interesting too! There is a reference in Forster, *A Voyage Round the World* (1777), I, 542–43, to 'rotten and stinking' biscuit, and in Candish's [Cavendish's] *Second Voyage to the South Sea*, in Hakluyt, XI, 415, we are told how the dried penguins bred 'a most lothsome and ugly worme,' which mightily increased till 'there was nothing that they did not devoure, only yron excepted.'

CHAPTER X

1 Purchas, XIII, 122; *Voyages of Foxe and James*, II, 464; Narborough, p. 194.

2 Isaiah, 43, 5–6.

3 See the remarkable passage in A. E. [George William Russell], *The Candle of Vision*, p. 86.

4 *Tamburlaine*, Part I, Act V, sc. ii, ll. 1952–54 (ed. Wagner).

5 Ll. 97–98. L. B. 1798 reads 'Ne . . . ne' for 'Nor . . . nor.'

In L. B. 1800 'like an Angel's head' replaced 'like God's own head,' which, in *Sibylline Leaves*, was restored. The reviewer in the *British Critic* for October, 1799, remarked on 'the very unwarrantable comparison of the Sun to that which no man can conceive:—"like God's own head," a simile which makes a reader shudder; not with poetic feeling, but with religious disapprobation.' Hutchinson, L. B., p. 211, also quotes the *British Critic*, but not quite accurately.

6 Crantz has a note (I, 33) which might well have sent Coleridge hotfoot to Barents's voyages, if he were not already familiar with the narrative. It begins: 'There are very few accounts of these kinds of difficulties, dangers, and wonderful deliverances, to be read with such a shuddering amusement as William Barents.' But no reader of Purchas could escape the tale.

7 Purchas, XIII, 88.

8 Purchas, XIII, 103; ed. 1625, III, iii, 497. For the convenience of the reader, all my references to the *Pilgrimes* are to the easily accessible modern reprint (see above, p. 446). But whenever (as here) the relative position of two passages is involved, a reference to the original edition is added.

9 Ll. 143–48. These lines in their present form first appeared in *Sibylline Leaves*, 1817. In L. B. 1798 Pt. Ill began:

'I saw a something in the Sky No bigger than my fist,' and the rest of the stanza is identical with the present second stanza (ll. 149–52). In L. B. 1800 the stanza began: 'So past a weary time, each throat Was parch'd and glaz'd each eye, When, looking westward,' etc. The 'weary time,' accordingly, entered the poem between 1798 and 1800.

As for the 'something in the sky *No bigger than my fist*' of L. B. 1798, one thinks of the 'little cloud out of the sea, like a man's hand,' in one of the most dramatic stories in the Bible (1 Kings, 18, 44). But there is a closer parallel in Linschoten's great narrative (p. 168): 'In that place likewise [while passing 'the land of Christmasse'] with a cleare and fayre weather there commeth a certayne cloude, which in the W seemeth *no bigger then a mans fist*'; and when that cloud is seen all sails are struck, for like Elijah's 'sign in the Element,' it is followed at once by a 'heaven . . . black with clouds and wind.' I cannot be sure that Coleridge read the *Discours of Voyaging into the . . . Indies*. If he did (as is probable), de Veer and Linschoten and the Bible may have melted together in his memory.

10 Purchas, XIII, 109–10; ed. 1625, III, iii, 499. The italics are in the edition of 1625, but not in the reprint.

11 Ed. Grant White, p. 500.

12 Ll. 464–67, 570–71. 'Firm land,' it must be remembered,

is a term constantly employed by the early voyagers (and others) in the general sense of 'mainland'—or (to use the equally common equivalent term) '*Terra firme*.' 'Indies of the West, are all the Ilands and *firme Land* comprehended within the markes of the Crown of Castile and of Lyon' (Purchas, XIV, 552); 'Of the manners and customes of the Indians of the *Firme Land*' (*ibid*., XV, 209); 'Besides the Tigre and other beasts before mentioned, in the *firme Land* are the Beori' (*ibid*., XV, 219); 'Sancta Maria Antiqua, the fyrst habitation of the spaniardes in the *fyrme lande*' (Eden, ed. Arber, p. 163, gloss); 'betweene Bardes and the *Firm land* there is but a little ryver' (Linschoten, Hakluyt Soc., II, 165; cf. *ibid*., I, 52); and see the account of the province of '*Terra firma*, or *Firm Land*' in Richard Rolt, *A New and Accurate History of South-America* (London, 1756), pp. 428 ff., esp. 429. Coleridge had seen it a hundred times, and it carries with it into the poem the aroma of the voyagers' living speech.

13 Purchas, XIII, 110; ed. 1625, III, iii, 499–500. For the astronomical problem involved in this unexpected reappearance of the sun, see the *Three Voyages of William Barents* (Hakluyt Soc.), pp. cxliv-clvi.

14 Purchas, XIII, 113–14; ed. 1625, III, iii, 501.

15 'With a true Relation,' the title-page goes on, 'of all their miseries, their shifts and hardship they were put to, their food,

etc., such as neither Heathen nor Christian men eVer before endured.' And on the title-page are quoted the 23rd and 24th verses of the 107th Psalm. The book was printed in 1631, and it is reprinted in Churchill's *Collection*, IV, 808 ff., and in *A Collection of Documents on Spitzbergen and Greenland* (which includes also the translation of Frederick Martens's *Voyage*), edited by Adam White for the Hakluyt Society (1855).

16 Wordsworth owned a set of Churchill, though Vol. IV was missing when his library was sold (*Trans. Wordsworth Soc.*, VI, 215, No. 172.) In any case, the work was easily accessible and widely read.

17 Compare (as one of the links between the two narratives) the reference to the aurora in Purchas's gloss to de Veer (see above, p. 155). And see (for its interest) Foxe, II, 395.

18 *God's Power and Providence* (ed. Hakluyt Soc.), pp. 276, 278. Did Edward Pellham know his Shakespeare?

> Aurora, with her *golden face*, smiled . . . for now the *glorious*
>
> Sunne . . . began to *guild* the highest *tops* of the loftie *mountains*.

ADDENDA AND CORRIGENDA

Page 25. Ω[στ]ραλ still remains inscrutable. Three of my correspondents have independently suggested that it stands for *Austral.* I wish I could think so. But the necessity involved of substituting Αυ for an unmistakable Ω seems to me to put this solution out of court. Bertram Davis, Esq., of Bristol, adds the alluring suggestion that Austral, which he proposes, stands for *Southey.* But apart from the difficulty of equating Ω and Αυ, the entry falls pretty certainly late in 1796, when Coleridge and Southey were still estranged (see, for example, *Letters*, I, 210–11). In view, however, of the fate of Erastus Galer (see next note) I have no desire to dogmatize.

I have cancelled in proof a page or so of happy suggestions which led nowhere. After a dispassionate reading of them in cold type, I could only echo Chaucer's bewildered disciple of Plato, when 'the privy stoon' was explained to him: 'This is *ignotum per ignotius.*' And so I leave the riddle—at dulcarnon!

Page 26. '*Wild Poem on Maniac*—Ερα[στου] Γαληρος. ἀτ. .' The riddle of *this* entry is at last solved, and the solution comes, as it should, from a citizen of Bristol. My own guess was clearly wrong—wrong chiefly because I discarded too quickly, in favour of the temptingly obvious 'Erastus Galer,' a possible reading since suggested by half a dozen of my correspondents. The Latin *galerus*, of course, means a cap or hat. The transliteration of the English 'hat' (ἀτ), accordingly, would be, on this assumption, an explanatory equivalent of the transliterated Latin 'galērus' (Γαληρος). Ερα[στου], taken at its face value, is the genitive of ἐραστής:, a lover. The phrase, then, with its mixture of good Greek, transliterated Latin, and transliterated English, should mean '*the lover's hat*.' And the entry as a whole would then read: 'Wild Poem on [a] Maniac—the Lover's Hat.' That was admittedly possible, but as compared with 'Erastus Galer' it seemed to me improbable. And so the matter stood until Bertram R. Davis, Esq., of Bristol, to whom all Robert Southey is an open book, happened to read the paragraph on page 26 above.

For what he recalled at once was an extant 'wild poem on a maniac,' in which *a lover's hat* is actually the instrument of the catastrophe—only it was Southey, not Coleridge, who wrote it. That will concern us in a moment. Meantime, Southey's ballad of 'Mary, the Maid of the Inn' begins, in the text of 1797 (p. 163), as follows:

> Who is she, the poor Maniac, whose wildly-fix'd eyes
> Seem a heart overcharged to express?

The maniac is Mary, whose lover is the 'idle and worthless' Richard, and the poem relates the strange occurrence which unhinged her mind. Two guests at the inn, late on a stormy night, lay a wager that Mary will not dare to go through night and storm, and enter the ruined Abbey. She accepts the challenge fearlessly, but once within the ruin she hears footsteps, and as the moon shines out above a cloud she sees two ruffians carrying between them the body of a murdered man.

> Then Mary could feel her heart-blood curdle cold!
>   Again the rough wind hurried by,—
> It blew off *the hat* of the one, and behold
> Even close to the feet of poor Mary it roll'd,—
>   She felt, and expected to die.
>
> 'Curse *the hat*'! he exclaims, 'nay come on and first hide
>   'The dead body,' his comrade replies.
> She beheld them in safety pass on by her side,
> She seizes *the hat*, fear her courage supplied,
>   And fast thro' the Abbey she flies.

In terror she reaches the inn, and then:

> Ere yet her pale lips could the story impart,
>   For a moment *the hat* met her view;—
> Her eyes from that object convulsively start,
> For—oh God what cold horror then thrill'd thro' her heart,

When the name of her Richard she knew!

Her lover, convicted by the hat which she herself unwittingly had placed in evidence, is hanged, and Mary's reason is dethroned.

That, beyond question, is the tale to which Coleridge's jotting refers. And it takes us back with assurance to those halcyon days of 1795 in Bristol, when Coleridge, Southey, and Burnett lodged together at 48, College street, and when Southey could write to Bedford (February 8, 1795): 'Coleridge is writing at the same table; our names are written in the book of destiny, on the same page' (*Life and Correspondence of Robert Southey*, I, 231). Ideas kept flying, during those eager months, incessantly back and forth between them, and it was clearly Southey who, whether he knew it or not, contributed to the book of destiny the lover's hat. For the tale was his. 'The story of the . . . ballad was related to me, when a schoolboy,' he later wrote in a note in the *Poems* of 1797, 'as a fact which had really happened in the North of England.' And the date of Coleridge's entry, at which we can make a fairly close guess, fits the time. For in the list of subjects in which it is No. 11 (see p. 467, *n*. 117, above), No. 18 ('Randolp[h] consecrating D. of York's banners') refers to an incident reported in *Felix Farley's Bristol Journal* for Nov. 8, 1795—the same number which contained the belated announcement of Southey's marriage. **Ερα[στου] Γαληρος. ἀτ.** belongs to the period of close association with Southey. And the fact is not without its irony that of the twenty-eight subjects in Coleridge's list, the only one (so far as we know) which ever got beyond the Note Book, did so in a poem of Southey's.

The date at which the poem was written is not wholly clear. It is included, as 'Mary,' in the volume of 1797, but it was originally printed in *The Oracle* in February of that year (see *Life and Correspondence of Robert Southey*, I, 304). Southey himself long afterwards assigned it to 1796, but I agree with Mr. Davis that it was probably included in that mysterious 'volume of poems' which, on August 22, 1795, as Southey writes to Bedford, was to 'go to the press to-morrow,' and in which 'his [Coleridge's] poems and mine will appear together; two volumes elegant as to type and hot-pressed paper' (*Life and Correspondence of R. S.*, I, 246). 'This is an office' [that of 'corrector plenipotent'] he remarks, 'Coleridge and I *mutually* assume, and we *both* of us have sense enough, and taste enough, to be glad of *mutual* correction' [italics mine]. In August as in February close collaboration between Coleridge and Southey was still going on; almost at once thereafter came the break; and the volume (to which we have only this tantalizing reference) never appeared. But it is a fair assumption, in view of Southey's statement, that Coleridge had at least a critic's hand in the poem. In later editions of his poems Southey states that the original story is in Robert Plot's *Natural History of Stafford-shire* (Oxford, 1686), p. 291. As told in that most instructive treatise, however, the tale is innocent of either hat or maniac, and agrees with the ballad only in the incident of a nocturnal visit, on an ale-house wager, to a terrifying spot—in this instance 'the black Meer of Morridg.' Coleridge could not have derived his entry from Plot's tale. Incidentally, he refers to 'Mary the Maid of the Inn' in a letter to Southey dated July, 1797 (*Letters*, I, 223).

Page 56. '*The deep Well.*' I am indebted to Professor F. L. Powicke for reminding me of the analogy between the conception of 'the deep Well,' taken over from Henry James, and Ruskin's remarkable statement, apropos of Turner's imaginative processes, in *Modern Painters*, Part V, chapter ii, esp. § 17:

> Imagine all that any of these men [Dante, Scott, Turner, Tintoretto] had seen or heard in the whole course of their lives, laid up accurately in their memories as in vast storehouses, extending, with the poets, even to the slightest intonations of syllables heard in the beginning of their lives, and, with the painters, down to minute folds of drapery, and shapes of leaves or stones; and over all this unindexed and immeasurable mass of treasure, the imagination brooding and wandering, but dream-gifted, so as to summon at any moment exactly such groups of ideas as shall justly fit each other: this I conceive to be the real nature of the imaginative mind.

This passage is marked, I now find, in the edition of *Modern Painters* which I eagerly read thirty years or so ago. It was not consciously recollected while I was busy about this book, but it had indubitably at one time impressed me strongly, and I should like to think that, though seemingly forgotten, it nevertheless played its part. Much more to the point, however, is the fact that Turner's procedure offers an illuminating parallel with Coleridge's—a parallel which opens up for some one a richly rewarding study.

Page 127 (line 3 from foot). 'The singular circumstance which had so impressed *Herodotus*' should read, to be quite accurate, 'which had so impressed *Bryan Edwards*.' For Bryan Edwards mistranslated Herodotus, and Coleridge followed the mistranslation. Herodotus wrote (IV. 42): **ὡς περιπλώοντες τὴν Λιβύην τὸν ἥλιον ἔσχον ἐς τὰ δεξιά.** —'that in sailing round Libya they *had the sun* on their right hand.' It was Edwards who wrote: 'the sun *rose* on the right hand.' That Herodotus does not say. See, for other instances of the misconception, R. W. Macan, *Herodotus: The Fourth, Fifth, and Sixth Books* (London, 1895), I, 28–29. I am indebted to two of my correspondents, Mr. F. L. Lucas and Mr. Laurance Riggs, Jr., for calling attention to my telescoped statement. The fact which so impressed *Herodotus* was, of course, 'the tell-tale shift of the sun to the right' (p. 128, above). Coleridge was unmistakably following Herodotus by way of Bryan Edwards.

Pages 147–48 (cf. pp. 261, 498, *n*. 64). Coleridge came back to 'swound' thirty years or so after 'The Ancient Mariner' was written, and made an interesting remark. It is a marginal note in a richly annotated copy of Charles Tennyson Turner's *Sonnets and Fugitive Pieces* (Cambridge, 1830), now in the collection of my friend Frank B. Bemis, Esq., to whom I am indebted for permission to quote it. In Sonnet XIX occur the lines:

> The things that own most motion and most sound
> Are tranc'd and silent in a golden *swound*.

On the word 'swound' Coleridge has made this comment:

> *Swound?* od's wounds!—Such Gypsey jargon suits my 'ancient Mariner,' but surely not this highly polished and classical Diction.—

Neither the characteristic pun in 'od's wounds' nor the phrase 'Gypsey jargon' is particularly happy. But the old emphasis on verbal 'keeping' (see p. 327, above, and Chap. XVII, *passim*) has lost none of its weight—a conviction borne out by the comment on 'scene' in the penultimate line ('Sink deeply in my thought, surpassing *scene*!') of the sonnet:

> Suffer me, dear young Poet to conjure you, never to use this Cov. Gard. Drury Lane Word, unless some distinct allusion or reference be made to a Theatre. This 'Scene

and Scenery' I think is in the villainous slang-fineries of the last century—

Coleridge had used 'gipsie-jargon,' in a letter to the Wedgwoods of Jan. 5, 1798 (B.M., Add. Mss. 35, 343, f. 160^{Vo}), of the language of party politics.

Page 166, ll. 11–14. Professor J. S. P. Tatlock suggests that Coleridge may have recalled the Prayer Book version of the phrase from the nineteenth Psalm: 'the sun which . . . rejoiceth as a giant to run his *course*.'

Page 180. It is clear from the evidence on pp. 180–81 and 509–10 above, that the idea of a star seen within the horns of the moon, or within its dark body, was more widely accepted, as within the bounds of possibility, than we commonly suppose. And now I owe to Commander (Retired) I. V. Gillis of Peking, who has put me greatly in his debt in many ways, a bit of evidence which throws the curious belief more than a thousand years farther back. It is in a rare manuscript work on the subject of prognostications and portents from observation of the heavens—the *Kuan Hsiang Wan Chan*—written by Li Shun-fêng in the seventh century A.D. And in a section headed 'Portents from Eclipses of the Moon' is a sentence which Commander Gillis translates: 'When during an eclipse a star is observed in the middle [of the moon], it signifies that the high ministers are plotting rebellion.' A photostat of the passage was sent by Commander Gillis to

Dr. John C. Ferguson for his reading of the crucial phrase, and Dr. Ferguson writes: 'In my opinion the phrase [quoted by him in the Chinese characters] means "when the moon is in eclipse and therein is a star." This is a literal translation, but a clearer translation in which there is no departure from the essential meaning is "when a star is seen in the moon at the time of eclipse." ' Like the sixteenth-century entry in Harrison's *Chronologie*, the Chinese observation is of value as showing that the Mariner's strange sight in the element, however explained, was not unique. And one could wish that Coleridge, whose interest was stirred by the five astronomers on the tower of the Grand Observatory in Peking, might have known of the *Kuan Hsiang Wan Chan*.

Page 198. For Professor Lane Cooper's interesting strictures on the implications of this page, see P.M.L.A., XLIII, June, 1928, pp. 584–85, and *passim*; and compare his article in Herrig's *Archiv*, 125 (1910), 89–92.

Since humanity, which Coleridge once divided into Aristotelians and Platonists, has been less happily parcelled out, by implication, into Words-worthians and Coleridgeans, it needs no knack at divination to discover in which category, by exclusion from the other, Mr. Cooper places me. I have no intention of restating my position, such as it is, or of traversing his. When he writes (p. 583): 'Mr. Lowes assumes that *The Rime of the Ancient Mariner* is a very fine poem . . . But Wordsworth on the whole thought otherwise,' I grant both charges with equanimity. When I have observed (p. 314, above) that 'nobody ever put the romance of discovery more magnificently into words than Wordsworth' in three lines of 'Ruth':

> Before me shone a glorious world—
> Fresh as a banner bright, unfurled
> To music suddenly;

and when Mr. Cooper (p. 589) comments on my statement thus: 'The passage from *Ruth* is not to be commended until it is read as the utterance of a dubious character who, in Wordsworth's view, exaggerates'—then I recognize, without presuming to pass judgment, that in certain matters we speak different languages. Just such discrepancies, however, lend spice to life—and incidentally (and happily for the reader) preclude argument. I have, in a few of the addenda which follow, acknowledgments to make to Mr. Cooper, and in one of them an exception must be taken. Beyond that, discussion of a most interesting (and suggestive) article is irrelevant to the purpose of these notes.

Page 201, *n.** '*Before our door* a clear brook runs of very soft water.' So Coleridge refers, in the letter to Dr. Estlin, to the 'dear Gutter (i.e. a dear brook) of Stowy.' And the statement seems to run flatly counter to the facts. For the Coleridge cottage fronts on Lime Street, and the gutter enters Lime Street at the junction with Castle Street, a hundred yards or so away. It could never have flowed past Coleridge's house along Lime Street, for to do so it would have had to run uphill. And since Coleridge's statement has greatly puzzled some of his readers, it may be well to clear the matter up.

Coleridge's description is perfectly accurate. One is apt (especially if one is an American) to think of the phrase 'before our door,' when used without qualification, as referring to the *street* door of a house. But 'our door' meant to Coleridge the door which opened, not on the street, but on what a Scotchman would call the 'policies'—on the 'very pretty garden,' and the 'sweet orchard,' and the gate which led into Tom Poole's garden and orchard, and to the 'Jasmine Harbour,' later to become immortal (see p. 462, *n*. 67, above). And all this lay to the *rear* of the house—precisely as (for example) the lovely, tranquil garden through which the little Nadder likewise flows 'before the door' of George Herbert's house at Bemerton, is invisible and undreamed of from the street.

It was, then, through Tom Poole's garden that the 'clear brook' ran. It still runs where the garden was (and is, alas! no longer), but now it passes, like the Nile, under ground. It comes down, a rapid little stream, from the Quantocks through Over Stowey; runs to the west of 'The Mount'; then along Mill Lane; then east across the fields and through a conduit to Castle Street, at a point about eighty paces above Tom Poole's house. Thence it is carried, through a channel partly open, partly covered, down Castle Street and along Lime Street to Court Farm, where it feeds the duck-pond; out of which it flows into the near-by fish-ponds of Stowey Manor, and thence into the Yarrow, thence into the Parret, thence into the sea.

Page 235, foot. The date which I gave for the withdrawal of Apuleius from the Bristol Library is wrong. It should be *1796*, not 1795. Since I had not then been able to consult at first hand the Bristol Library registers, I followed Professor Kaufman's recent list (p. 537, *n.* 47, above). When I later examined the registers for myself, I found that Mr. Kaufman had confused the years, and that the date given in James Baker's earlier list (see p. 466, *n.* 110, above) was correct.

The exact day of the month is easy to get at. The entries of withdrawals immediately preceding and immediately following are each dated November 4. And on that Friday the news of the naval victory which had just come down from London was evidently running like wildfire through the Bristol streets. The three Bristol newspapers published the next day (Saturday, Nov. 5) print the details, based on Admiral Elphinstone's dispatches from the Cape of Good Hope. Felix Farley's *Bristol Journal* enumerates ten ships, and reports (somewhat ambiguously) the capture of 2000 troops. Bonner and Middleton's *Journal* gives nine ships, and 4000 troops; Sarah Farley's *Journal*, nine ships. The official dispatches in *The London Chronicle*, Nov. 3–5, 1796, pp. 437–39 (see No. 6, p.

439) give nine ships and 1972 men. Coleridge had evidently got his information by word of mouth, and the faded entry calls up a vivid picture of his triumphal progress through the humming streets to the Library desk.

Pages 242–60 (Chap. XIV). Eino Railo's *The Haunted Castle* (London, 1927) was published after this book appeared. His accounts of the Wandering Jew (pp. 191 ff., esp. 191–98 and Notes 211–16) and of Cain (*ibid.*, p. 193 and Note 213) constitute an independent study, and, based as they are upon many of the same documents, interestingly, parallel, at several points, the accounts given in this chapter. Railo, however, does not connect either Cain or the Wandering Jew (except incidentally on p. 256) with 'The Ancient Mariner.' See also his remarks on p. 255 about the Wedding Guest—a happy surmise which is confirmed by the evidence of Coleridge's intimate acquaintance with *Der Geisterseher* (see p. 251 above), of which Railo was apparently not aware. His suggestion (p. 147) that 'in the final setting of *The Ancient Mariner* . . . we find the traditional hermitage with its inhabitant, who is a characteristic property of the "Gothic" school,' links the poem at another point with the romantic tradition which gives the title to his book. See also Lane Cooper, 'The "Forest Hermit" in Coleridge and Wordsworth,' M.L.N., XXIV, 33–36.

Page 259. In reading the reprint of *The Diary of Henry Teonge, Chaplain on Board H.M.'s Ships Assistance, Bristol, and Royal Oak, 1675–1679* (London, 1927), I was struck by the entry for June 24, 1675 (p. 39):

> This day two seamen that had stolen a piece or two of beef were thus shamed: they had their hands tied behind them, and themselves tied to the mainmast, each of them a piece of raw beef tied about their necks in a cord, and the beef bobbing before them like the knot of a cravat; and the rest of the seamen came one by one, and rubbed them over the mouth with the raw beef; and in this posture they stood two hours.

That curiously resembles in principle the Ancient Mariner's punishment, in that in each case the object through which the offence has come is hung about the offender's neck. Was the Mariner's penalty suggested by a disciplinary practice at sea, which perhaps reached Coleridge by word of mouth (cf. p. 562, ll. 2–6, and pp. 268–69 above)? For other examples of naval punishments by hanging some object about the culprit's neck, see Commander Charles N. Robinson, R.N., *The British Tar in Fact and Fiction* (London, 1909), pp; 54–91.

There is, too, another parallel, which is at once closer and more remote. Hunter Eaton, Esq., who besides writing fiction trains police-dogs, reminds me of the ancient and wide-spread practice, among trainers, of punishing a chicken-killing dog by hanging the victim for two or three days securely about its neck. The punishment seems to be old enough and common enough to have been known to Coleridge, who was familiar with semi-rural life, and it is not impossible that some fleeting recollection, possibly from boyhood days, may have played its part in suggesting the hanging about the Mariner's neck of the dead bird which he had shot.

Pages 333–34. A substitute has been proposed by Professor Cooper (P.M.L.A., June, 1928, pp. 589–90) for the lines which I cited from 'The Romaunt of the Rose,' as offering in part the suggestion for Coleridge's 'Lavrock' stanza. It is a passage from Gower's *Confessio Amantis* (V, 4097–4105). I have included in brackets the lines which Mr. Cooper omits, and have used by preference Macaulay's text. The reference is to the antics of Medea:

> [Bot tho sche ran so up and doun,]
> Sche made many a wonder soun,
> Sometime lich unto the cock,
> Sometime unto the *Laverock*,
> [Sometime kacleth as a Hen
> Sometime spekth as don the men:]
> And riht so as hir *jargoun* strangeth,
> In sondri wise hir forme changeth,
> [Sche semeth faie and no womman;]

Coleridge knew both Chaucer and Gower. But words for him as they recurred to memory, 'flashed images.' And if the reader will turn back to the lines from the 'Romaunt' on p. 334, and, with Gower's lines still in mind, will visualize (after Coleridge's fashion) the two passages, a comparison of the respective pictures with Coleridge's own lines will leave, I think, little question of the probabilities. And, as it happens, we now know definitely, on Coleridge's own testimony (see the next note), that Chaucer had already stirred him to emulation earlier in the poem.

The fragment, on the other hand, which Mr. Cooper quotes from Bartram (*Travels*, London, 1794, p. 284; Philadelphia, 1791, p. 288), about the '*small birds* of passage' which in the spring 'appear very suddenly in Pennsylvania, is quite another matter: 'At once the woods, the groves, and meads, are *filled with their melody*, as if they *dropped down from the skies*.' And here (with *Lavrock* and *jargoning* also set off by italics) are Coleridge's lines:

Sometimes *a dropping from the sky*
  I heard the *Lavrock* sing;
Sometimes all *little birds* that are
How they seem'd *to fill the* sea and air
  With their sweet *jargoning*.

I doubt whether Coleridge was himself aware of the exquisite dovetailing in the stanza of words and imagery which had slipped back to memory, perhaps unconsciously, from his reading of Bartram and the 'Romaunt.'

Page 334. Nodding their heads before her goes
  The merry Minstralsy.

That Coleridge had 'The Squire's Tale' in mind when he wrote these lines (as is suggested in the text) there can now be no doubt. For in a copy of *Sibylline Leaves* in the collection of Owen D. Young, Esq., Coleridge has marked the margin opposite these two lines, and has written at the foot of the page:

Chaucer. Squire's Tale—v. 260. Beforne him *goth* the loude minstralsie.

> Till he come to his chamber of paraments,
> Ther as they *sounden* divers instruments.

The italics are Coleridge's. I am indebted to Mr. Young for permission to print this welcome bit of evidence.

Page 354, ¶ 2: 'For in point of fact there are no variants whatever.'—'This,' says Professor Lane Cooper (P.M.L.A., XLIII, 590), 'is not strictly true. "There" in line 8 has a variant reading "here." "Enfolding," line 8 [read 'line 11'], appeared in 1816 as "And folding" [and, he might have added, 'drunk,' in line 54, appeared in 1816 as 'drank']; and perhaps we may add Charles Lamb's [Qy. Leigh Hunt's?] "ordain" for "decree" in line 2.' It is unfortunate that Mr. Cooper, before calling the truth of a statement in question, did not take the precaution of reading its context. For 'variants,' in that statement, has nothing whatever to do with the variant readings which Mr. Cooper adduces. It harks back directly to 'variants' three lines earlier, and that in turn to the last line of E. H. Coleridge's note (p. 353, above). The sole point under discussion, in other words, is the existence or nonexistence of variants *before the poem was printed*—of certain specific variants, that is, explicitly cited, which had been incautiously assumed by Tames Dykes Campbell and E. H. Coleridge on the basis of a misreading of one of 'Perdita' Robinson's poems. Variants in the *published text* of 'Kubla Khan' are not even remotely in question.—This rehearsal of the obvious would have been gladly forborne, had not an array of irrelevant facts beclouded a point of some importance.

'Ordain' for 'decree'in line 2 of 'Kubla Khan,' however, although not pertinent as cited above, belongs in a different category. I am indebted to one of my former students, Dr. George Dumas Stout, for calling my belated attention to a passage which does raise, in provokingly inconclusive fashion, the question of possible changes made in the text of 'Kubla Khan' before its publication. It is in Leigh Hunt's *Imagination and Fancy* (London, 1883, p. 261), and is Hunt's comment on the opening lines of the poem:

I think I recollect a variation of this stanza, as follows:

In Xanadu did Kubla Khan
  A stately *pleasure-house ordain*,
Where Alph, the sacred river, ran,
Through caverns measureless to man,

> Down to a sunless *main.*
>
> The nice-eared poet probably thought there were too many *n*'s in these rhymes; and *man* and *main* are certainly not the best neighbors: yet there is such an open-sounding and stately intonation in the words *pleasure-house ordain*, and it is so superior to *pleasure-dome decree*, that I am not sure I would not give up the correctness of the other terminations to retain it.

One's pulse does not quicken at such evidence. *Imagination and Fancy* was published in 1844, forty-six years after the poem was composed, twenty-eight after its publication, and ten after Coleridge's death; and Leigh Hunt '*thinks*' he recollects. On the other hand, Mrs. Robinson, who had certainly either seen the poem in manuscript or heard it read before October, 1800 (see p. 354 above), remembered and quoted the phrase 'sunny *dome*' ('Kubla Khan,' l. 47) forty-four years before Hunt thought that he remembered 'pleasure-*house*.' And 'sunny dome' in line 47 (which repeats 'that dome in air' of the preceding line) carries with it 'sunny pleasure-*dome*' in line 36, '*dome* of pleasure' in line 31, and 'pleasure-*dome*' in the second line. It seems clear that in 1800 Hunt's dubiously recollected reading was not in the poem. If, then, Hunt's ghost of a recollection rests on anything else than somebody's misquotation of the lines, it must involve the initial act of composition, and in that case its source, direct or indirect, must be Coleridge himself, who alone could impart the information. And Coleridge then becomes a witness against himself. Our choice, in other words, lies between Hunt's 'I think I recollect,' and Coleridge's explicit avowal: 'On awaking he . . . instantly and eagerly wrote down *the lines that are here preserved*' (Preface to 'Kubla Khan'; see p. 356, above). Coleridge's memory in 1816 may have been at fault. No one can securely deny that possibility. But the weight of evidence is still against it.

Page 376, *n*. The critic to whom Mr. Fausset refers is obviously Mr. I. A. Richards. See his *Principles of Literary Criticism* (London, 1925), pp. 30–31. My regret that I was unable to read Mr. Richards's book before my own was published, is lessened by the fact that the parallels with Milton which we both point out have gained thereby the value of independent observation.

Pages 415–17. There is a piece of evidence bearing on Coleridge's earlier use of opium, which has never been published, and which has apparently remained unknown. It is in the collection of Owen D. Young, Esq., to whom I am indebted for bringing it to my attention, as well as for allowing me to print it.

It is a scrap of paper on which Coleridge has hastily written a note to Cottle. It is undated, but internal evidence fixes, within two or three days, the time at which it was written. It reads as follows:

MY DEAR COTTLE

I feel pain in being disappointed—and still greater pain in the idea of disappointing—but I am seriously ill. The complaint, my medical attendant says, is nervous—and originates in mental causes. I have a Blister under my right ear—and I take Laudanum every four hours, 25 drops each dose.—God be praised for all things! A faith in goodness *makes* all nature good.

Yours affectionately
S. T. COLERIDGE

S.T.C.
Oh that ~~he~~ had never taken more than 25 drops each dose.

In the letter to Poole of Nov. 5, 1796 (*Letters*, I, 172–76; see p. 415 above), Coleridge had written:

> I am very unwell . . . My medical attendant decides it to be altogether nervous, and that it originates either in severe application, or excessive anxiety . . . I have a blister under my right ear, and I take twenty-five drops of laudanum every five hours.

In spite of the discrepancy between the intervals of the doses, the two letters unmistakably refer to the same occasion.

It is, of course, the postscript to the scrawl which is significant.

And its. importance lies in the mournful corroboration which it gives to my statement on p. 417 above, that '*on that point* Mr. Robertson's contention is borne out by the facts.' I have italicized 'on that point,' because I still take issue with Mr. Robertson's inferences from the facts.

Page 453, ¶ 2. I add with pleasure a third name to the list of those whose priority in discovering Coleridge's use of Bartram is acknowledged on p. 453. Professor Cooper points out (P.M.L.A., XLIII, 591, *n.*) that not only E. H. Coleridge (1906) and Bersch (1909), but he too had been 'ahead of [me] in comparing Wordsworth [*sic*] with Bartram's *Travels*.' It was, to be sure, *Coleridge*, not Wordsworth, about whom at the moment I happened to be writing, the theme of the paragraph (p. 453) being Coleridge's transcripts from Bartram in the Note Book. That, however, is incidental; and I confess at once that I *had* overlooked an article on '*Wordsworth* Sources' in the London *Athenæum* (Apr. 22, 1905, pp. 498 ff.), in which Mr. Cooper states that it was 'while running through Bartram's romantic descriptions in order to fix their responsibility for some of the images in Coleridge's "Kubla Khan,"' that he found the parallels with Wordsworth. And he gives, in a parenthesis, a reference to pp. 165 ff. (ed. 1791) of the *Travels*. And these (if one look the reference up) are the pages which contain the account of 'the inchanting and amazing chrystal fountain' (seep. 368, above). Later in the article is a passing, but none the less significant, allusion to 'the tumultuous imagery that passes from Bartram into "Kubla Khan." ' All this gives Mr. Cooper; accordingly, undisputed priority of publication, so far at least as the 'chrystal fountain' is concerned, over both E. H. Coleridge and Bersch; and I am proud, in the words of Pandarus, to 'hoppe behind' three instead of two.

Page 458, *n.* 59. For an account of the two issues of the first (1727) edition of *The Hermit*, see the paper by Arundell Esdaile ('Author and Publisher in 1727: "The English Hermit" ') in *The Library*, Fourth Series, Vol. II, Dec. 1921, pp. 185–92. The story of the issue which Esdaile calls 'II' is both curious and interesting, but is too long for rehearsal here. The title omits all mention of Edward Dorrington; and 'P. L.,' who now lays claim to the authorship and denounces Dorrington as an impostor, is an otherwise unknown Peter Longueville. If he is to be trusted in his statement that he has employed some of his time 'these six Years, in Writing the following History,' the inception of the story, as Esdaile points out, is thrown back to 1721, or two years after *Robinson Crusoe*. Both issues are in the British Museum, and Esdaile's I is now in the Norton Perkins collection in the Harvard College Library.

There is another chapter in the history of *The English Hermit*, which, so far as I know, has escaped notice. In the Robert Gould Shaw Collection in the Harvard College Library are two play-bills of Sadler's Wells, for June 20th and July 11th, 1803 respectively, in each of which is announced 'the favourite Serio Comic Pantomime called PHILIP QUARLL.' The *dramatis personæ* are Philip Quarll, Beaufidelle (*His Monkey*), Pirate Captain, Black Chief, English Lieutenant, Pirate Boatswain, Black Leaders of Tribes, And the Lady. The cast included the then stars of the pantomime stage. The part of Philip Quarll was taken by Grimaldi, that of the Black Chief by Signor Belzoni, Bologna was Pirate Captain and Leader of Tribes, and Madame St. Amand the Lady. The pantomime played a part in the checkered career of Giovanni Baptista Belzoni (who had made his first appearance at Sadler's Wells on April 11, 1803, as the Patagonian Sampson), and it is further bound up, through Belzoni, with the history of a baffling and fascinating manuscript satire which falls in Belzoni's later period. But that is another story.

Page 487, *n.* 13. For a much earlier, if not the earliest reference to 'The Salutation and Cat,' see the note to 'Page 554, *n.* 57' (p. 604*s* below).

Page 493, *n.* 4. The '*Storm-blast*' *stanza*. In their editions of Wordsworth's poems both Dowden, 1892 (II, 261), and Knight, 1896 (II, 170), call attention to the correspondence between 1. 15 of Wordsworth's 'The Waterfall and the Eglantine' ('The Flood was *tyrannous and strong*') and l. 42 of 'The Ancient Mariner' ('And now the STORM-BLAST came, and he Was *tyrannous and strong*). Wordsworth's poem was composed and published in 1800; lines 41–44 of 'The Ancient Mariner' first appeared in their present form in *Sibylline Leaves*. Coleridge could certainly have known 'The Waterfall and the

Eglantine' in or after 1800, though the evidence adduced for 1802 rests chiefly on an inference of Knight's; see D. W., *Journals* (I, 111–12), April 23, 1802 (misread by Dowden, followed by Lane Cooper *infra*, as 'August' 23). It has been assumed, accordingly, that in *Sibylline Leaves* Coleridge recalled Wordsworth's line. In *The Athenæum*, Sept. 5, 1903, p. 328, Professor Lane Cooper suggests that *Cymbeline*, I.3.36 ('And, like the *tyrannous breathing of the north* Shakes all our buds from growing') may have been the associative link between the waterfall and the blast. That the phrase might have stuck in Coleridge's memory nobody, I suppose, would question.

But all this guesswork leaves out of account a rather important consideration. For it seems to have quite overlooked the fact that Coleridge himself had used the phrase 'tyrannous and strong' not later than 1806, and more probably in 1800. The first two lines of the poem (*Poems*, I, 347) entitled 'A Thought suggested by a View of Saddleback in Cumberland' (or, in *Friendship's Offerings*, 1834, p. 168, 'A Versified Reflection') are these:

On stern Blencartha's [*F.O.*, Blencarthur's] perilous height
The winds are [*F.O.*, wind is] *tyrannous and strong.*

And the phrase, as in 'The Ancient Mariner,' is applied to wind, and not, as in Wordsworth's poem, to a waterfall. The 'Reflection' appears in a Malta notebook, with the comment:

'Olevano [Tuscany], March 8, 1806' (Campbell, *Poems*, p. 634: cf. *Poems*, I, 347). In *Friendship's Offering* the lines are accompanied by a note: 'The following stanza . . . or versified reflection, was composed while the author was gazing on three parallel *Forces*, on a moonlight night, at the foot of the Saddleback Fell.—S.T.C.' One may settle as one will the seeming discrepancy between the notebook and *Friendship's Offering*. Coleridge's statement in *F.O.* is categorical, and the lines in the notebook may well have been set down from recollection. In any case the weight of evidence points to 1800 as the date of actual composition of the stanza.

For the first two lines of the 'Reflection' are adapted from the first two lines of a poem by Isaac Ritson, 'addressed to Mr. Head, an ingenious painter,' and published in William Hutchinson's *History of the County of Cumberland* (1794), I, 336:

> The winds upon *Blenkarthur's* head,
> Are often loud and strong.

And Coleridge read Hutchinson's *History* in 1800, while he was engaged on the Second Part of 'Christabel,' and drew upon it for that poem (see E. H. Coleridge, *Christabel*, pp. 20–27, and with 'Christabel,' Pt. II, ll. 407, 493–97, compare Hutchinson, I, 99–102—text and notes—for Roland de Vaux of Tryermain, Irthing flood, Halegarth Wood, and Knorren Moor). Moreover, in the autumn of 1800, Coleridge again, in a letter to Davy of Oct. 18, applied 'tyrannous' to wind: 'At the bottom of the Carrock Man I seated myself for shelter, but the wind became so fearful and *tyrannous*, that I was apprehensive some of the stones might topple down upon me' (*Letters*, I, 339; B.E., I, 211). Compare, too, the letter of Nov. 1 to Josiah Wedgwood (B.E., I, 213): 'The wind from the Skiddaw and Borrowdale was often as loud as wind need be.' In 1800 Coleridge, new to the Lakes, was revelling in the mountains (see his letters of the period, *passim*). There is no reason to suppose that when, in 1817, he revised his two lines as they had stood since 1800 ('strong,' since 1798).

But now the Northwind came more fierce,
There came a Tempest strong—

he was recalling anybody's phrase but his own.

It is a matter of small consequence whether, in this instance, Coleridge recalled Wordsworth, Wordsworth Coleridge (which is equally possible), or neither the other. But since the question has several times been raised, it has seemed worth while to set down briefly certain considerations which in any case must come into the reckoning. It should, perhaps, be added by way of caution, that the statements in the collected editions of Coleridge's poems about the date of publication of the 'Reflection' are a tissue of curious errors. But this is not the place to go into that.

Page 503, *n.* 28, l. 18 from foot ('Compare the line: "Or

like an isle forced up by nether fires" '). Add the variants of this line in Coleridge's handwriting in Mr. Drinkwater's copy of 'Zapolya' (John Drinkwater, *A Book for Bookmen*, London, 1926, p. 99): 'A sea-born Isle forced up by nether fires—'; 'Like to some island Mass from Ocean's Bed Unloosed, and shoulder'd up by nether fires'; 'By nether fires unloos'd, and struggling upward.'

Page 504, *n*. 51. Through an oversight I omitted to insert at this point the note of James Dykes Campbell (*Poems*, p. 598) on another borrowing from *Osorio*, in lines 414–17:

> 'Still as a slave before his lord,
> The ocean hath no blast;
> His great bright eye most silently
> Up to the Moon is cast—'

Campbell's note reads:

> Borrowed half from Coleridge's own *Osorio*—
>
> 'Oh woman!
> I have stood silent like a slave before thee'
> (*Dying speech of Osorio*)

and half from Sir John Davies:—

'For lo the *sea* that fleets about the land,
  And like a girdle clips her solid waist,
Music and measure both doth understand:
  For his great chrystal eye is always cast
  Up to the moon, and on her fixed fast.'

Orchestra; or, A Poem on Dancing. St. xlix. ed. 1773, p. 155.

For an earlier reference to the borrowing from Davies, see Mary A. (Mrs. Humphrey) Ward, in Ward's *English Poets*, I (1880), 550—a reference for which I am indebted to Professor Cooper.

Page 505, *n*. 58 (and p. 166). See T. J. Wise, *Two Lake Poets* (1927), p. 79, with photographic reproduction opposite, for an identical inscription to 'W. Hood, Esqre,' in the first volume of *Biographia Literaria* (1817).

Pages 507–08, *n*. 36. I *did* overlook the needle in the haystack, but Professor Alice D. Snyder found it. Wolff's phrase is in *Psychologia rationalis* (1734), p. 20, § 24: 'imaginatio quoque in actum apperceptionis influit.' Coleridge evidently quoted it from memory.

Page 525, *n*. 92, ¶2. Seth B. Watson cannot have been 'a member,' in 1822–23, of the Thursday evening group at Highgate, since he was 'aged 18' when he matriculated at St.

John's College, Oxford, in June, 1829 (see Professor Alice D. Snyder's demonstration of this fact, from the *Alumni Oxonienses*, in the *London Times Literary Supplement*, Aug. 25, 1927, p. 576). The Mr. Watson of B.E., II, 248–49, 251, 267–68, and of *Letters*, II, 726, seems to have been (and again we are indebted to Miss Snyder, *London Times Literary Supplement*, Sept. 30, 1926, p. 654) that *John* Watson who, on Oct. 11 (or 17; the second numeral may be either 1 or 7), 1823, inscribed a copy of Milton's *Poems upon Several Occasions* (ed. Thomas Warton, London, 1791) to 'S. T. Coleridge Esqre with the love, regard & esteem of his obliged and grateful friend J. Watson.' The volume is now in the Norton Perkins collection in the Harvard College Library. For a later inscription in the same volume referring to John Watson, see John Drinkwater, *A Book for Bookmen* (London, 1926), p. 69; and compare Mrs. Lucy E. Watson (née Gillman), *Coleridge at Highgate* (London, 1925), p. 152. Finally, on the first (loose) cover of the manuscript commonplace book described on p. 604*p* below, Coleridge has written, with two other addresses, 'J. Watson, Dalston, Carlisle.'

Seth B. Watson, confused (it would seem) with John Watson by James Dykes Campbell, A. Turnbull, Colonel Prideaux, and the present writer, was obviously a *later* member of the Highgate circle, but was in the direct line of its tradition.

Page 526. *Coleridge's possible knowledge of Dante.* Professor Albert R. Chandler suggests in a letter certain parallels between the approach of the spectre-bark and the coming of the 'vasello snelletto e leggiero' in the second canto of the *Purgatorio*. In Dante the coming light of the boat is compared to that of Mars seen 'per li grossi *vapor*' (l. 14); the spectre-bark 'seemed *a mist*' before it took a certain shape. Dante saw on each side of the light '*un non sapeva* che bianco' (l. 23); the spectre-bark is first seen as '*a something* in the sky.' In each case the ship, when its mission is accomplished, departs with startling swiftness; in the one, 'ed ei sen gì, come venne, veloce (l. 51; cf, ll. 17–18: . . . 'venir sì ratto, che il mover suo nessun volar pareggia'); in the other, 'Off shot the spectre-bark.' It might be added that the angelic vessel, like the spectre-bark, takes definite shape by clearly defined degrees (*Purg*., II, ll. 19–27; A.M., ll. 149–152); and that Dante's comparison of the first sight of the boat with Mars seen through the mists, 'giù *nel ponente sopra il suol marino*' (l. 15), could have suggested Coleridge's 'when *looking westward*, I beheld A something *in the sky*.' It is hard to resist the feeling that through the one account one catches echoes of the other.

Mr. Chandler also suggests that details from the story of Ugolino (*Inferno*, XXXIII) are woven into Part III of 'The Ancient Mariner.' There is, to be sure, a verbal parallel between '*cascar* li tre *ad uno ad uno*' (l. 71) and 'They *dropped down one by one* (l. 219, cf. l. 212); but that is conventional phraseology. As for the rest, the difference in situation (I feel) outweighs the scattered resemblances in detail.

Page 528. The reference (in the last line but one of Note 92) to the *London Times Literary Supplement*, No. 1252, p. 28 (the date is Jan. 14, 1926), had to be inserted in page-proof, when only a half-line was available. I take this opportunity to reprint the note, by H. O. White, Esq., The University, Sheffield, on a curious parallel to Coleridge's 'lonesome road' stanza.

> It [the parallel] occurs in a poem on the Battle of Culloden addressed to the Duke of Cumberland by G. Masters, 1747:—
>
> 'As when a swain belated on his way
> Sees as he fancies through the close of day
> A ghostly spectre—struck with pale affright
> He measures back the ground in hasty flight,
> Whilst his own shadow by reflection clear
> Of silver Luna seen, augments his fear.
> At every breeze, each rustling of the wind.
> Startled he stops, yet dreads to look behind;
> Still he believes the phantom at his heels
> And his cold touch imaginary feels.'
>
> Coleridge was an omnivorous reader, and his appetite often led him to unlikelier places than Masters's now-forgotten poem. It may well be that some memory of this

passage lurked in his mind when he wrote:

'Like one that on a lonesome road
Doth walk in fear and dread,
And having once turned round, walks on,
And turns no more his head;
Because he knows a frightful fiend
Doth close behind him tread.'

It is quite possible that Coleridge knew Masters's poem. Whether he did or not, however, it is worth noting that the *raison d'être* of the Preface of 1800 to *Lyrical Ballads* is latent in the almost startling contrast between these two treatments, fifty years apart, of a common theme.

Finally, with reference to my statement (p. 526) that 'nobody, so far as I know, seems ever to have suspected Dante's influence on [this same 'lonesome road' stanza],' it must now be added that Mr. Cooper (P.M.L.A., XLIII, p. 591, *n*) protests that 'it *has* [italics his] been suspected before; I caught it twenty years ago while following up Charles Lamb in *Witches and other Night-fears*.' That fact, had I known it, I should gladly have recorded; but unluckily, like Chaucer in one sole respect, 'I nam no divinistre.'

Page 533, *n*. 30. For facsimiles of the corrections printed in this note see T. J. Wise, *Two Lake Poets* (1927), pp. 63–64.

Page 537, *n*. 40. *The 'one little volume' and Shakespeare*. I am indebted to Professor John D. Rea for an offprint of a note ('Jacques on the Microcosm,' *Philological Quarterly*, IV, 345–47, October, 1925) in which, before my suggestion was printed, attention was called to still another possible use by Shakespeare (in the famous speech in *As You Like It* on the seven ages, and in Sonnet XV) of a passage in Marsilio Ficino's volume (ed. 1577, p. 231; ed. 1570, pp. 233–34).

Page 542, *n.* 19. This note must now be rewritten. 'Die ungeleichen Kinder Eve, wie sie Gott, der Herr, anredt,' remains beyond question the play to which Coleridge referred in talk with Carlyon in Germany and later in the lectures of 1808 and 1818. That identification still holds. But it is now no less clear that 'that drama in which Got-fader performs' (p. 244 above), which Lamb sent in the brown-paper parcel to Keswick, was another and a more extraordinary play. For since the note on pp. 542–44 was written, a manuscript which had long disappeared from view has come to light again.

In a valuable article entitled 'Books borrowed by Coleridge from the Library of the University of Göttingen, 1799' (*Mod. Philol.*, XXV, Feb., 1928, pp. 377–80) Professor Alice D. Snyder called attention in a note (p. 379) to a 'Manuscript Volume in Quarto,' containing notes and transcripts in Coleridge's hand. It appeared in the catalogue of the library of J. H. Green, sold by Sotheby, Wilkinson, and Hodge, July, 1880, and it was later described in Scribner and Welford's *Catalogue of Scarce and Valuable Books*, issued in April,

1884. Beyond that point Miss Snyder was unable to trace it. The manuscript as described contained, among other things, a transcript, 'with the musical notes to the songs,' of *Adams und Evens Erschaffung und ihr Sündenfall, ein geistlich Fastnachtspiel mit Sang und Klang*, with the note: 'Transcribed June 17, 1799, S. T. Coleridge.' And Miss Snyder expressed the belief that this was 'the play he [S. T. C.] copied from the Helmstedt manuscript.' That I am sure it is not; but it *is*, beyond reasonable question, the play to which Lamb refers. For Miss Snyder's note has made it possible to identify and trace the elusive manuscript itself. And the success in that search I owe to the expert aid of my friend Edgar Huidekoper Wells, Esq., of New York. The 'Manuscript Volume in Quarto' is now in the Henry E. Huntington Library, San Marino, California, and I am indebted to Dr. Max Farrand, Director of Research, for permission to make use of it, and to Captain R. B. Haselden, Curator of Manuscripts, for a description of the document, and for photostatic copies of certain parts of it.

The book is a manuscript on paper of 754 consecutively numbered pages, 334 of which are blank. 'The paper was made by Pieter de Vries, with a watermark of an allegorical female figure bearing a hat of liberty on a spear with the words "Pro Patria" above, and seated within a ring fence in which the Dutch line also appears. This mark is similar to that used by the great Dutch makers Villedary and Van Gerrevink.' It is obvious that Coleridge provided himself with the book while in Germany, though he used it as late as 1823. Since he seems to have opened it quite as often upside down as right side up, the paging of several items runs backwards, with the numerals upside down at the foot (which the head has now become) of the page. And the drama, which is the only portion of the manuscript that concerns us, runs for this reason from p. 750 to p. 652. Its title-page, as Coleridge has copied it on p. 750, is as follows: Adams und Evens/Erschaffung/und ihr/Sündenfall/Ein/geistlich Fastnachtspiel/mit/Sang und Klang/aus/dem Schwabischen [*sic*], in's Oesterreichische/versezt. Below this is roughly sketched the outline of a cut, in the two spaces of which are scrawled the words 'Adam' and 'Eve.' On the odd-numbered pages which follow is transcribed the Swabian text of the play, with the music; on the even-numbered pages, the corresponding Austrian text. The hand in each is unmistakably Coleridge's own. The music, on the contrary, is copied with a practical skill and fluency which it is difficult to believe that Coleridge possessed, and I suspect that the musical score was transcribed for him. And 'Gottvater' stares one in the face on almost every page, whereas in 'Die ungeleichen Kinder Eve' God is always 'der Herr.' There can be no doubt that this is the play which Lamb sent to Coleridge in August, 1800, with the German dictionaries, and Percy's *Reliques*, and Cain and Abel, and the razors.

I am indebted to my colleague, Professor Taylor Starck,

for its prompt identification as the dialect masterpiece of Sebastian Sailer (1714–1777), stories of whose vivid and versatile personality were still current in Germany in Coleridge's day. For the mass of literature which has grown up about him it is enough to refer to Karl Goedeke, *Grundriss zur Geschichte der deutschen Dichtung* (Dresden, 1900), VII Bd., 7 Buch, 2. Abt., pp. 547–48. There are editions of Sailer's works, including *Adams und Evens Erschaffung*, by Sixt Bachmann (1819), K. D. Hassler (1843), and Dr. Owlglass (1914). Others will be found in Goedeke. But the volume of chief interest here is the extremely rare edition of the play published, without indication of place, in 1783. For it was without question the text and the music of this volume which Coleridge transcribed. I have not been able to see a copy of it, but I have seen a photostat, and its musical score is reprinted (pp. 149–54) in the invaluable monograph of Dr. Robert Lach on 'Sebastian Sailers "Schöpfung" in der Musik' (*Denkschriften*, 60 Bd., 1 Abh., *Kaiserliche Akademie der Wissenschaften in Wien, Philosophisch-historische Klasse*, pp. 1–174, Vienna, 1917). A comparison of the manuscript with Dr. Lach's reprint establishes their identity. The accompanying facsimile of two opposite pages of the manuscript—on the left the Swabian original with the music, on the right the Austrian translation—makes clear the disposition of the manuscript.

It is little wonder that Coleridge was fascinated by the play. There are, I suspect, of its sort few livelier and more divertingly indecorous performances, and few which are conceived and executed with more irresistible buoyancy and verve. And the racy vigour of its dialect adds to its effectiveness. There has long been evidence of Coleridge's attention, while in Germany, to the earlier literature in the Swabian dialect (see *Mod. Philol.* as above, p. 378, *n.* 1)—evidence now strikingly corroborated by the list of books which he drew from the University Library at Göttingen (*ibid.*, p. 378, Register I, esp. Nos. 1 and 2). But his interest in the current colloquial dialect—an interest sufficiently attested by the laborious transcriptions of ninety-eight exacting pages—is another matter, and, thanks to the play, we now know something more about Coleridge's preoccupations while at Göttingen.

Finally, this cannot be the play which he transcribed at *Helmstedt* (see p. 543, above). The signed note on the last page of his manuscript copy reads: 'Transcribed June 17th, 1799.' The records of the University Library at Göttingen show that on June 16 he drew from the Library Christian Gottfried Schutz's *Ueber Lessings Genie und Schriften* (*Mod. Philol*, XXV, 380). He was, then, still in Göttingen on June 16. That he could have reached Helmstedt and copied ninety-eight pages of difficult German within the next twenty-four hours is manifestly impossible. It took the diligence which carried the Wordsworths just twelve hours to reach *Goslar* from Brunswick, and Goslar was but half way on the road to Göttingen. 'You can have no idea,' wrote Dorothy Wordsworth, 'of the badness of the roads' (*Letters of the Wordsworth Family*, I, 119). And see, for more striking evidence, *Letters of S. T. C.*, I, 278–79.

Moreover, the play which he says he transcribed at Helmstedt *was not this play*. His statement about that drama leaves no question:

> I have myself a piece of this kind, which I transcribed a few years ago at Helmstadt, in Germany, on the education of Eve's children, in which, after the fall and repentance of Adam, the offended Maker . . . condescends to visit them, and to catechize the children . . . The good children say the ten Commandments, the Belief, and the Lord's Prayer; but Cain and his rout, after he had received a box on the ear for not taking off his hat, and afterwards offering his left hand, is prompted by the devil so to blunder in the Lord's Prayer as to reverse the petitions and say it backward! (*Lectures and Notes*, p. 198).

And that is Hans Sachs's 'Die ungeleichen Kinder Eve.'

'It seems strange,' Miss Snyder observes (p. 379), 'that [Coleridge] should have transcribed that play from a Helmstedt manuscript when it was already in print in Vol. I of the edition of Sachs that he used at Göttingen'—namely, Georg Weller's edition of 1558–79 in five volumes, four of which he drew from the Library on May 25 (*Mod. Philol.*, XXV, 379: cf. B.L. I, 140). It *does* seem strange, and some confusion of

Coleridge's later memory is far from impossible. But until we know more than we do of Coleridge's movements in Germany, it is hazardous to assume too confidently, in spite of the probabilities suggested on pp. 543–44 above, that Coleridge's visit to Helmstedt occurred after, rather than before, his stay in Göttingen. 'Die ungeleichen Kinder Eve' may have been copied first. And even if Helmstedt followed Göttingen, it is still not impossible that Coleridge made good in the University Library there a purpose which procrastination (or what not) had kept him from carrying out while at Göttingen. But that is guesswork.

It is worth noting, incidentally, that on June 15 (see *Mod. Philol.*, XXV, 380), two days before he finished transcribing 'Adams und Evens Erschaffung,' Coleridge drew from the University Library 'Klotz Leben von Hausen'—i.e., C. R. Hausen, *Leben und Charakter Herrn. Chr. A. Klotzens* (1772). And on pages 649–48 of the Huntington Library manuscript, separated by only two blank pages from the play, is a biographical memorandum upon Christian Adolph Klotz. Like Milton (but with a difference) Coleridge might have added: *Caelum non animum muto dum trans mare curro*.

After these notes were in type there turned up, in an uncommonly interesting document, Coleridge's own confirmation of the date on which he left Göttingen (see p. 543, foot, above). Carlyon (*Early Years*, etc., I, 170) states: '. . . we left the U-niversity [he had just quoted the famous song from *The Rovers*, in *The Anti-Jacobin*] at noon, on Midsummer-day, 1799.' There has now come to the Harvard College Library the manuscript of *Wallensteins Tod* which Coleridge used, prepared for translation by Schiller himself, and containing his autograph attestation, together with corrections in his hand (for an account of the MS. see Hans Roscher, *Die Wallensteinübersetzung von Samuel T. Coleridge und ihr deutsches original*, Borna-Leipzig, 1905). The manuscript, which is bound, contains the book plate of James Gillman, and on the inside back cover is pasted a farewell note to Coleridge signed 'Ihr Blumenbach.' It is clear, from its reference to the Harz, that it is from Georg Heinrich Wilhelm Blumenbach, the son of Professor Joh. Friedrich Blumenbach, Coleridge's favorite preceptor at Göttingen (see *Letters*, I, 279, 298–99; B.L., I, 138; B.E., I, 196–97; Carlyon, I, 45, 187–91; etc.). The younger Blumenbach had accompanied Coleridge, Carlyon and their party, on the Harzreise of May 11–18, 1799 (see Coleridge's list of the party in *Archiv*, CXVIII, 41, and cf, 44, 56; Carlyon, I, 32, and cf. 35, 46, 126, 136), and there had been 'a most entertaining take-leave evening . . . at Professor Blumenbach's' on the eve of Coleridge's departure, at which young Blumenbach's fellow tourists on the Harzreise were the guests (Carlyon, I, 161). The letter, which Coleridge so carefully preserved, is as follows:

> Wenn Sie, bester Freund, auch in Ihrer Heimat die Natur bewundern, wie wir beydes es auf dem Harze

gethan haben, so errinern Sie sich des Harzes, und ich darf dann hoffen, dass Sie auch mich nicht vergessen werden.

Leben Sie wohl, und reisen glücklich!— Ihr Blumenbach

Beneath the signature, in Coleridge's hand, is the memorandum: 'Written Midsummer day, 1799.'

Below that, in turn, is scrawled, still in Coleridge's hand, but obviously at another time: 'Hübscher Wein—Man sieht hie sehr weit in die Welt—.' One would like to think that this auspicious jotting on the margin of his recent letter was made the next day on the Brocken (see Carlyon, I, 170–72), but a remark of Carlyon's (I, 172, *n.*)—contrasting Mrs. Trollope's later luck in wine at the Brocken inn with Coleridge's—rules, I fear, that interpretation out: 'An admirable bottle of Steinberger on the summit of the Brocken! Spirit of Coleridge, think of this!' Coleridge's note, however, was probably penned somewhere between Göttingen and Brunswick.

Below this, again (still in the margin of the letter), is another scrawl: 'May 2nd—very ill in the evening—,' followed by three tantalizingly illegible words. This cannot have been written before 1800. Coleridge ended a visit to the Wordsworths at Grasmere on May 4, 1800 (B.E., I, 193), but of that there is no further record. The memorandum best fits the black May of 1801 (see esp. the letters to Davy of May 4 and May

20, 1801, in *Fragmentary Remains . . . of Sir Humphry Davy*, London, 1858, pp. 89–91; T.P., II, 42–49; and cf. *Letters* I, 354). Nor would it have been out of place on May 2nd of several later years.

—And now, just as these sheets go to press, the letter has been detached, disclosing on the verso a full page of Coleridge's pencilled notes, written June 24 at Hardenberg Castle, *en route* to the Brocken.

Page 551, *n.* 26 (*weft*). Two particularly interesting examples of the survival of 'weft' in contemporary usage have reached me since the note above was written. In the first the word has clearly come down from the New England whalers, and I am indebted for it to a letter from Laurance Riggs, Jr., dated May 12, 1928:

> A friend of mine at Woods Hole [Massachusetts] reports that the net mender, himself somewhat of an ancient mariner, had invited her to accompany him on his rounds some day, and had suggested that she *wave him a weft*, when he was passing in his boat. She had just been reading the chapter of your book on wefts, and asked him what kind of a weft. To which he replied, 'Oh one of your dish-towels, *or any piece of cloth*.'

That last is the sense in which Captain Luke Foxe used the word in 1635 (see p. 264, above).

It is to Commander (Retired) I. V. Gillis of the United

States Navy, that I owe information which brings the *nautical* use of the term down to the present day. Commander Gillis writes: 'when the last International Signal Code was adopted in 1901, it was arranged that the answering pennant be tied with a *weft* and a black ball hoisted above it during the year, to differentiate between the use of the old code and the new.' The latest English edition of the *International Code of Signals* (Printed and Published by His Majesty's Stationery Office) is that of 1926. On p. 529, under 'Distant Signals,' 'three different methods of making Distant Signals are explained,' of which (*b*) is 'By Balls, Square Flags, Pennants, and *Whefts*.' Among 'the Shapes used as symbols (6),' is (*b*): 'A Pennant with the fly tied to the halyards, or a *Wheft* for the drum. (A *wheft* is any flag tied in the centre.)' See the rest of the paragraph; 7.4 on the same page; and p. 531. In the last American edition (1929) of the *International Code*, see pp. 523 foot, 524, 528, top.

Page 554, *n*, 57. The letter about the 'intelligent young man' from America is now printed in full, and for the first time accurately, by Mr. Wise, *Two Lake Poets* (1927), pp. 54–56. It discloses the interesting fact that the conversation took place 'at an Ale-house, by courtesy called a "Coffee-House."—"The Salutation and Cat" in Newgate Street' (see above, p. 487, *n*. 13). See also pp. 16, 97, above.

Page 555, *n*. 57. In the Note Book, f. 7^b (*Archiv*, p. 344) is an entry which Brandl printed as 'Coope Materialism:

Arguments in favor of a soul—' But the word which he read as 'Coope' is really 'Cooper,' as a closer examination of the manuscript has made clear. The reference is to *Tracts, Ethical, Theological and Political:* By Thomas Cooper, Esq., Vol. I [no other published], Warrington, 1789. The volume contains a 'Sketch of the Controversy on the Subject of Materialism,' with the running title: 'On Materialism.' And one section is entitled: 'Of the Impossibility of the Existence of an Immaterial Indiscerptible, Immortal Soul.' Coleridge, then, set down a reminder to excogitate counter arguments. The next entry but two in the Note Book, hopelessly misread in *Archiv*, can be dated with certainty, rightly read, between April 5 and April 11, 1796 (see my forthcoming edition of the Note Book). Coleridge, then, who had read *Some Information respecting America* a year and a half before, had come back to Cooper a second time. And for a second time nothing came of it!

Page 583, *n.* 35. The spelling of Coleridge's name seems to have particularly baffled Bristol and Nether Stowey. In the certificate of marriage in the parish register at St. Mary Redcliffe, it is spelled 'Colridge'—Coleridge's own signature, of course, being correct. In the announcements of the marriage in Felix Farley's *Bristol Journal*, Oct. 17, 1795 (to 'Miss Sally Fricker, daughter of Mrs. Fricker, Schoolmistress on Redcliffe-hill'), Bonner and Middleton's *Journal*, Oct. 10, and the *Bristol Gazette and Public Advertiser*, Oct. 15, it is uniformly spelled 'Coldridge.' The registers of the Bristol Library contribute further vagaries. Volumes taken from the building had to be signed for, and during the Nether Stowey period it is evident from the registers that Coleridge sent up for books by some of his fellow Stoweyites (compare p. 422, above, first line). For his name is signed, from time to time, in various hands and with sundry spellings: 'Mr. Sam Colridge' (Dec. 11, 1797); 'Mr. Sam Coloridge' (Jan. 8, 1798); 'Mr. Sam Colredge' (Apr. 20, 1798); etc. But, if we except 'Coloridge,' the weight of evidence is in favor of the disyllabic pronunciation. And Leigh Hunt's remark, in the *Autobiography* (ed. Ingpen, London, 1903, I, 82), suggests that the trisyllabic form was the exception: 'The master [Boyer], inspired by his subject with an eloquence beyond himself, once called him, "that sensible fool, Colērĭdge," pronouncing the word like a dactyl.'

Page 584, *n*. 3. For an interesting note by Coleridge himself, in the margin of his copy of *Reliquiae Baxterianae*, on his own confusion about the date of his birth, see Wise, *Two Lake Poets* (1927), p. 119.

Page 585, *n*. 6: *The site of Xanadu*. See, for information supplementing Laurence Impey's article in *The Geographical Review* on 'Shangtu, the Summer Capital of Kublai Khan' (p. 586, above), a series of four articles entitled 'In the Footsteps of Kubla Khan,' which Mr. Impey contributed to the London *Daily Telegraph*, Apr. 4, 5, 10, and 11, 1928. I am indebted to Frederick Lauriston Bullard, Esq., for sending me the series.

Commander I. V. Gillis of Peking has referred me to a brief

account by Frederick McCormick (*Journal of the North China Branch of the Royal Asiatic Society*, . . . XLIII, 1912, p. 133) of the ruins at Tung-king, which present startling resemblances to the site described in the poem:

> In 1908 two American travelers, Mr. Straight and Commander Gillis, described ruins in the neighborhood of the old Manchurian capital of Tung-king, Kirin province, which they found to correspond to the image of Coleridge's poem. A mazy river flowed through matchless scenes and disappeared; there were wells in which ice could be seen although it was July; the foundations of a summer house on an islet that at one time cast its shadow over the Water, were reached by a ruined bridge; there was a waterfall and rustics about told a legend of a hapless maiden princess, buried beneath. There was also in the neighborhood a legend concerning a venerable tortoise which lived under the waters surrounding the islet. In fact the coincidences of the features of the poet's city with the site of this ancient Manchurian capital were so striking as to have part convinced the travelers that Coleridge had reproduced a description of a place which he had erroneously assigned to Shangtu.

This paragraph has been reprinted in Herbert Croly, *Willard Straight* (New York, 1924), pp. 264–65.

Commander Gillis refers me to the 'Liu Pieu Chi Lüeh,'

and to the Chronicles of the Liao Dynasty; but writes me that he 'doubts very much whether any Chinese books describing Tung Ching Ch'êng and the vicinity had been translated into any European language at the time that Coleridge wrote "Kubla Khan." '

CPSIA information can be obtained at www.ICGtesting.com
Printed in the USA
LVOW12s0141170714

394727LV00001B/136/P

9 781408 630426